Macroeconomics

Student:

To help you make the most of your study time and improve your grades, we have developed the following supplement designed to accompany Ekelund/Tollison *Macroeconomics,* 3/e:

- Study Guide by John Keith Watson
  0-673-52100-1

You can order a copy at your local bookstore or call HarperCollins Publishers directly at 1–800–638–3030.

Macroeconomics

Third Edition

Robert B. Ekelund, Jr.
Auburn University

Robert D. Tollison
George Mason University

HarperCollins*Publishers*

Sponsoring Editor: Bruce Kaplan
Development Editor: Kathy Richmond
Project Coordination, Four-Color Text Design, and Cover Design: Proof Positive/
    Farrowlyne Associates, Inc.
Text Design: Russell Schneck Design
Photo Research: Kelly Mountain
Production: Michael Weinstein
Compositor: Omegatype Typography, Inc.
Printer and Binder: R. R. Donnelley & Sons Company
Cover Printer: New England Book Components

Macroeconomics, Third Edition

Library of Congress Cataloging-in-Publication Data

Ekelund, Robert B. (Robert Burton), 1940–
    Macroeconomics / Robert B. Ekelund, Jr., Robert D. Tollison.—
3rd. ed.
        p.   cm.
    Includes index.
    1. Macroeconomics.   I. Tollison, Robert D.   II. Title.
HB172.5.E42   1990   90-48463
339—dc20   CIP

ISBN 0-673-52097-8 (student edition)
ISBN 0-673-49951-0 (teacher edition)

90 91 92 93 9 8 7 6 5 4 3 2 1

For my mother and for faithful friends, who are the medicine of life
RBE

For Anna, April, Mark, and my parents
RDT

BRIEF CONTENTS

CONTENTS

PREFACE

Ask students what first comes to mind when they think of the term *economics,* and the majority will answer "money." Some students may think of economics as a set of dry, analytical concepts or tools used in financial matters. But economics is much more than this. The third edition of *Macroeconomics* was written to stress that economics is a way of thinking. It is not concerned primarily with money. It is not dry and boring. It is a vibrant, exciting way of weighing the costs and benefits of actions and policies in every facet of life. It is true that the economic way of thinking can be used to analyze the function of money and prices. But it can also be used to understand how roommates are selected or what factors affect a job search. The versatility and depth of an economic way of thinking is shown in a broad array of examples drawn from daily life and history, as well as contemporary policy issues that one finds in the newspapers and that one traditionally classifies as economics.

Macroeconomics is packed with applications. These are not opportunities for the authors to display how much they know of the technical apparatus of the discipline or to overwhelm students with impenetrable terminology. Rather, we think that only by appealing to student intuition and common sense in these applications can we show the usefulness and power of an economic way of thinking. This is why we include important elements of college life such as roommate selection and tuition costs, as well as more traditional market and global applications. This helps shun the more arcane applications often found in other principles of economics texts.

This third edition of *Macroeconomics* is thoroughly modern in its scope. We firmly believe that the economic way of thinking comes alive in the immediacy of current issues, events, and policies. Sprinkled throughout are such current global concerns as the 1992 integration of the European Community, the opening of Eastern Europe to a different kind of economic structure, debt repayment, the U.S. savings and loan crisis, and Iraq's 1990 invasion of Kuwait. But "modern" means more than this. We discuss the direction that modern economic research is taking. In this way, we hope to give students a sense of the excitement that is generated when the economic way of thinking is used at the frontiers of knowledge, revising or discarding old concepts and approaches and creating new ones.

NEW TO THE THIRD EDITION

The third edition of *Macroeconomics* expands the application of principles into new areas and presents streamlined coverage. New full-color sections reinforce key economic ideas. New graphical interpretations of data show students important trends in macroeconomics. These sections again demonstrate how economics fits into the student's daily life. New features and textual material on the global economy help students understand modern economic theory and contemporary policy. For example, problems of trade and protection are investigated immediately following the discussion of specialization and trade in Chapter 2. The importance of economic institutions is illustrated with an essay in Chapter 3 on North and South Korea. An application from the world cashmere market demonstrates supply and demand principles in Chapter 4. Japanese unemployment problems are considered in Chapter 6. The possibilities for European inflation under a common currency agreement in 1992 are developed in Chapter 17, and the economic problems facing a vastly changed Eastern Europe and Soviet Union—and their relation to U.S. macroeconomic growth—are considered in Chapter 23.

In addition to incorporating recent international developments into this third edition, we have reorganized material appearing in previous editions. These structural improvements are most apparent in Parts Two and Three of *Macroeconomics*. An entire chapter, Chapter 8, is now devoted to classical macroeconomics. This chapter provides the contrasting counterpoint to two reorganized chapters on Keynesian economics (Chapters 9 and 10). Taken together, these three chapters provide the basis for a complete and solid understanding of aggregate demand and aggregate supply analysis (covered in Chapter 11), fiscal and supply-side policies (Chapter 12), and the macroeconomic issues of taxation and debt (Chapter 13).

Once again, Part Three is devoted to monetary theory and policy; we have made an effort in this edition to more fully integrate monetary control and inflation into the discussion. Chapters 14, 15, and 16 cover money, the role of banking, and the social regulation of money in the United States. This prepares the way for the thorough discussion of monetary policy and inflation in a newly organized Chapter 17. The organizational changes made in Part Three—and throughout the third edition—represent much more than a shuffling of preexisting elements; our aim was a more logical presentation of macroeconomics. To that end we have also eliminated numerous unnecessary, potentially confusing details.

Three policy chapters make up Part Four. Chapter 18 examines contemporary schools and views of macroeconomic policy. Our discussion of unemployment and its attendant problems is now combined with the principles and problems related to business cycles in Chapter 19. We treat matters relating to economic growth and labor productivity in Chapter 20.

The connection made in Chapter 20 between economic growth and trade leads naturally to the material in Part Five, which deals with international trade and economic development. Comparative advantage and the benefits of trade are related to quota and tariff restrictions in Chapter 21, with an emphasis on nontariff barriers. New material relating trade deficits and budget deficits to the overall competitiveness of the U.S. economy has been added to

Chapter 22, along with an analysis of debtor nations in the 1990s. In Chapter 23, we highlight the struggles of the Soviet Union and Eastern Europe to restructure their political and economic systems, keeping in mind the lingering effects of a decades-long reliance on central planning.

We lack space here to mention all of the changes made in this third edition. All the changes, however, further our original goal for *Macroeconomics*—the formulation of a clear introduction to basic theory with relevant and interesting applications to economic and social problems.

SPECIAL FEATURES

Each chapter opens with an overview of the topics covered and a bulleted list of chapter objectives. Many other pedagogical elements appear in the text.

1. Key concepts and key trends in macroeconomics are shown in special full-color sections. These two sections summarize important macroeconomic principles and demonstrate current data trends to enhance text discussion.
2. Key terms are **boldfaced** at the first text mention, and definitions appear in the margin.
3. Graphs are drawn simply, with background grids where appropriate to help students understand the relationships in the graph. Standard notation is used in graphs and equations. Many of the graphs are color-coded: demand curves in black, supply curves in color. Throughout, shifts in curves move from darker to lighter shades.
4. "Focus" boxes in each chapter give interesting perspectives on theory and institutions. Titles include "Price Changes from Truman to Bush", "The Low Saving Rate in the United States," "The Future of Cash," "The Macroeconomic Consequences of Peace," "1992: Dawn of the European Community," and "Debtor Nations in the 1990s."
5. "Economics in Action" sections, which end most chapters, provide applications of chapter topics. Topics in "Economics in Action" sections range from things students likely have always wondered about—Why is money used as a medium of exchange?—to things most students have never thought to consider—Do GNP rates affect the quantity of leisure time we have? How do the decaying infrastructures of our cities relate to the nation's growth potential?
6. Chapters conclude with a summary, a list of key terms, questions for review and discussion, and, where appropriate, problems to work.
7. Each part of *Macroeconomics* concludes with a historical Point-Counterpoint. This feature gives short biographies of two important economic thinkers and compares or contrasts their theories. For example, Part Five, "International Trade and Economic Development," ends with a Point-Counterpoint on P. T. Bauer and Gunnar Myrdal—two economists with very different views on development in the Third World.
8. Special appendixes to selected chapters give instructors the option of more extensive coverage. The appendix to Chapter 9, for example, is beyond the scope of the chapter (An Introduction to Keynesian Economics) but will prove useful to many students.
9. A glossary of terms with text page references and a thorough index at the back of the book provide useful tools for study.

ORGANIZATION

Macroeconomics is divided into five parts: "The Power of Economic Thinking," "Private-Sector and Public-Sector Macroeconomics," "Money: Its Creation and Management," "Monetary and Macroeconomic Problems and Policy," and "International Trade and Economic Development."

The Power of Economic Thinking

Part One introduces the basic tools of economic analysis, including opportunity cost, marginal analysis, specialization, trade, comparative advantage, supply and demand, market equilibrium, and elasticity. We have packed these chapters with lively, interesting issues and applications. In Chapter 2, for example, the concept of specialization and trade via comparative advantage is illustrated with an example of marriage and roommate selection. Chapter 4 discusses how rent controls affect the allocation of apartments in a college town, then gives an example of international price controls. The importance of time and other transaction costs, mentioned initially in Chapter 1, is stressed in the discussion of full price in Chapter 4. With more than a dozen applications, Chapter 5 brings home to students the important concept of elasticity; students come to understand how the prices of products as diverse as jogging shoes and salt are affected by elasticity of demand and supply.

Private-Sector and Public-Sector Macroeconomics

Part Two opens with two chapters on the basic tools of macroeconomics—concepts such as real and nominal GNP, two-flow models of national income, and price indexes. A simple, intuitive explanation of aggregate demand and aggregate supply is given. Chapter 8 analyzes the classical view of the long-run, self-regulating economy and discusses how classical theory and policy are related. Formal Keynesian models as reactions to classical thought are fully developed in Chapters 9 and 10. Chapters 11 and 12 build upon classical and Keynesian theories to develop a modern approach to macroeconomics—the theory of aggregate demand and aggregate supply. Chapter 12 makes the theory more concrete by discussing fiscal and supply-side policies and the influence of politics within the aggregate demand–aggregate supply framework. Chapter 13 completes our integration of theory and policy with a discussion of taxation, deficits, and debt, including an analysis of crowding out.

Money: Its Creation and Management

Part Three is a complete introduction to money, monetary institutions, monetary policy, and monetary theory—with particular attention paid to the enormous changes in money use and financial institutions. For example, a "Focus" in Chapter 15 contemplates the future of cash in society, and the "Economics in Action" for Chapter 16 discusses Federal Reserve policy and the savings and loan crisis. In addition to a full discussion of inflation in Chapter 17, the role of money is analyzed according to classical, Keynesian, and modern views.

Monetary and Macroeconomic Problems and Policy

Part Four extends macroeconomic theory into current policy debates. Chapter 18 shows how new Keynesians and new classical writers—those leaning toward monetarist or rational expectationist theories—view fiscal and monetary policy. Chapter 19 links the problem of unemployment to business cycles and shows how macroeconomic policy varies with business conditions and politics. Finally, Chapter 20 deals with some key features of U.S. economic growth, past and present.

International Trade and Economic Development

The three chapters of Part Five cover international trade and finance, comparative economic systems, and economic development. Chapter 21 extends the theory of comparative advantage—first covered in Chapter 2—into the areas of international specialization and trade, touching on such things as tariffs and quotas. Chapter 22 details pressing international finance problems, including debt repayment by developing countries. The last chapter reviews changing economic systems worldwide, focusing on Eastern Europe and the Soviet Union; we emphasize the potential for substantial economic gains following such restructuring, but we do not neglect the potential costs.

THE COMPLETE *MACROECONOMICS* PACKAGE

Printed Supplements

- The *Study Guide* to accompany the third edition of *Macroeconomics,* by John Keith Watson, University of Southwestern Louisiana, helps students learn and review key concepts. Each chapter includes a summary, learning objectives, study tips, and fill-in reviews. Students can use the true-false, multiple-choice, and short essay questions to test mastery of concepts; then they can check their answers to discover where more study is needed. Timely articles from newspapers and magazines guide students in using an economic way of thinking about real-world situations. Every question in the study guide is answered, and answers to the questions in the "Economics in Action" sections in the text are provided.
- The *Instructor's Manual* to accompany the third edition of *Economics,* also by John Keith Watson, contains chapter outlines, lecture suggestions, and answers to all text questions and problems. Additional readings and problems are included for many chapters.
- The *Test Bank* to accompany *Economics,* prepared by Neal Davis, has doubled in size from the previous edition. It now includes more than six thousand multiple-choice items—an average of 150 questions per chapter. Questions closely follow topic coverage; each is keyed to the corresponding text page. Test items are coded to indicate different forms of the same question, and they are divided into four categories: recall, inference, calculation, and graph/table interpretation. Instructors can use the categories

and codes to tailor each exam. All test items are available on microcomputer software.

• Over 100 two-color overhead *Transparencies* of important figures and tables from the text are provided.

Software Supplements for Students

An economics software package is available. EconSim, by Robert Brooks, University of Alabama, and David Swanger and Chuck Warlick, Auburn University, contains simulations that stimulate student interest in major economic concepts. It is available on floppy disk for the IBM PC.

Software Supplements for Instructors

TestMaster operates on IBM PC and compatible microcomputers to provide the printed *Test Bank* questions in a computerized format. In addition to allowing you to develop, maintain, and revise the *Test Bank,* TestMaster enables you to add your own questions or even create your own test bank. This test generator has been designed for easy use.

ACKNOWLEDGMENTS

The extensive scope of this revision would have been impossible without the help and advice of scores of friends and critics. We gratefully acknowledge the following colleagues and students, who selflessly gave their advice and time: John Allen, Andy Barnett, Raymond Battalio, Randy Beard, Don Boudreaux, Katherine Boudreaux, Bill Breit, Butch Browning, Steve Caudill, Roy Cordato, Pat Culbertson, Elynor Davis, Charles DeLorme, David Gay, Kathy Gilbert, Dan Gropper, Bob Hebert, Randy Holcombe, John Jackson, Ethel Jones, Dave Kaserman, Roger Koppel, Dwight Lee, Jim Long, Charles Maurice, François Melese, Margaret O'Donnell, Karen Palasek, Chris Paul, Phil Porter, Ed Price, Jennie Raymond, Richard Saba, David Saurman, Tom Saving, Henry Thompson, and David Whitten. For special help and assistance we thank Gary Anderson, Richard Beil, Bill Shughart, and, especially, Mark Thornton. We are also grateful to Debra Beil for her expert proofreading and advice and to Rand Ressler for able help in data gathering and checking. Neal Davis has done yeoman's work on our *Test Bank.* To our good friend Keith Watson, who wrote the *Study Guide* and *Instructor's Manual* and who provided expert assistance throughout the entire project, we owe a special thanks.

No one other than the authors is more responsible for the direction and quality of *Macroeconomics* than Richard Ault, Auburn University. His firm and intuitive control of traditional and modern principles of economics helped us immeasurably.

We thank graduate assistants Manisha Perrera, Bharat Vijayan, Brian Goff, Ladd Jones, Dan Berry, Doug Bunn, Yvan Kelly, Paul Gentle, Kendall Somppi, Jim Tillery, Deborah Walker, and Biff Woodruff for help with all three editions of *Macroeconomics.* Secretaries Cathy Kruse and Kim Johns were of very able help.

We also wish to thank our developmental editor Kathy Richmond, who went beyond all job expectations, and Bruce Kaplan, our economics editor, for solid support of this third edition. Will Sanford of Proof Positive/Farrowlyne Associates, Inc., saved us from many errors.

Official reviewers and contributors for the third edition are Douglas K. Agbetsiafa, Indiana University at South Bend; Ralph E. Ancil, Southwestern Missouri State University; Robert A. Baade, Lake Forest College; Robert Carbaugh, Central Washington University; George Shih-Fan Chu, University of Nevada at Reno; Barbara Craig, Oberlin College; Robert D. Crofts, Salem State College; Steve Cunningham, University of Connecticut; William W. Davis, Western Kentucky University; David Denslow, University of Florida; Andrew W. Foshee, McNeese State University; Jack Goddard, Northeastern State University; William B. Green, Sam Houston State University; Jan M. Hansen, University of Wisconsin–Eau Claire; Steven C. Hine, State University of New York at Binghamton; Arthur E. Kartman, San Diego State University; Philip King, San Francisco State University; Gary F. Langer, Roosevelt University; Stephen E. Lile, Western Kentucky University; Lawrence W. Martin, Michigan State University; Mary Ann Meiners, Middle Tennessee State University; Khan A. Mohabbat, Northern Illinois University; Edd Noell, Westmont College; Donald Owen, Ottawa University; Gerald Pelovsky, College of the Sequoias; Steven C. Pitts, Houston Community College; J. M. Pogodzinski, San Jose State University; Doralia Reynolds, Seward County Community College; Carlos E. Santiago, State University of New York at Albany; John Wakeman-Linn, Williams College; Harold Warren, East Tennessee State University; and Walter J. Wessells, North Carolina State University.

Thanks also go to reviewers of the second edition: Lori Alden, California State University–Sacramento; Gary M. Anderson, California State University–Northridge; Richard K. Anderson, Texas A&M University; Ian Bain, University of Wisconsin–Milwaukee; Samiran Banerjee, University of Minnesota–Minneapolis; Peter Barger, Eastern Illinois University; Robert Barry, College of William and Mary; Anthony D. Becker, Northeastern University; Benjamin Bental, Technion Israel Institute of Technology; W. Carl Biven, Georgia Institute of Technology; Howard Bloch, George Mason University; George Blyn, Rutgers University at Camden; Thomas W. Bonsor, Eastern Washington University; Don Boudreaux, George Mason University; Ronald C. Brandolini, Valencia Community College; Pamela J. Brown, California State University–Northridge; the late Jacqueline M. Browning, Texas A&M University; Donald M. Bumpass, Texas Tech University; Shirley Cassing, University of Pittsburgh; Adhip Chaudhuri, Georgetown University; Bobby N. Corcoran, Middle Tennessee State University; Judith Cox, University of Washington; Larry G. Cox, Southwest Missouri State University; Al Culver, California State University–Chico; Larry Daellenbach, University of Wisconsin–La Crosse; Albert L. Danielsen, University of Georgia; Neal Davis, Auburn University; Arthur Diamond, University of Nebraska–Omaha; Harold W. Elder, University of Alabama; Donald Ellickson, University of Wisconsin–Eau Claire; Michael G. Erickson, Eastern Illinois University; Keith D. Evans, California State University–Northridge; Susan Feiner, Virginia Commonwealth University; Trey Fleisher, George Mason University; Pauline Fox, Southeast Missouri State University; Peter Frevert, University of Kansas; Richard M. Friedman, California State University–Northridge; David E. R. Gay, University of Arkansas; Kathie Gilbert, Mississippi State University; Otis

Gilley, University of Texas–Austin; Brian Goff, Western Kentucky University; William T. Harris, University of Delaware; William R. Hart, Miami University (Oxford); George E. Hoffer, Virginia Commonwealth University; Elmer Holt, George Mason University; Jonathan Hughes, Northwestern University; William J. Hunter, Marquette University; Eric D. Jacobson, University of Delaware; J. Paul Jewell, Kansas City Community College (Kansas); Walter L. Johnson, University of Missouri; John Kane, State University of New York–Oswego; Ki Hoon Kim, Central Connecticut State University; Peter Kressler, Glassboro State College; David Kreutzer, James Madison University; Dwight Lee, University of Georgia; Eva Marikova Leeds, Villanova University; Patrick M. Lenihan, Eastern Illinois University; William J. Leonard, Saint Joseph's University; James F. McCarley, Albion College; Richard McIntyre, University of Rhode Island; Jim McKinsey, Northeastern University; Erwin S. Mayer, Western Washington University; François Melese, Naval Postgraduate School; Yale Meltzer, College of Staten Island; Herbert Milikien, American River College; H. Lynn Miller, Central Florida Community College; Janet Mitchell, University of Southern California; Mike Montgomery, University of Houston; Daniel A. Myers, Western Kentucky University; Jamal Nahavandi, University of New Hampshire; Timothy G. Nash, Northwood Institute; Norman Obst, Michigan State University; Margaret O'Donnell, University of Southwestern Louisiana; Ted Oleson, University of Nevada–Reno; Anthony L. Ostrosky, Illinois State University; Samuel Parigi, Lamar University; James H. Peoples, Jr., Rutgers University–Newark; Glenn Perrone, Pace University; Bruce Peterson, Northwestern University; John Pisciotta, Baylor University; L. Wayne Plumly, Jr., Valdosta State College; Martin T. Pond, Purdue University; Phil Porter, University of South Florida; E. O. Price III, Oklahoma State University; John Price, San Francisco State University; Robert Pulsinelli, Western Kentucky University; Robert F. Rooney, California State University–Long Beach; Gregory S. Rose, California State University–Sacramento; Mark Rush, University of Florida; Raymond D. Sauer, University of New Mexico; Terri A. Sexton, University of California–Davis; Nat Simons, Ohio State University; David E. Sisk, San Francisco State University; Menahem Speigal, University of Connecticut; John Paul Stein, St. Thomas College; Don Street, Auburn University; Osman Suliman, Eastern Illinois University; Donald Tailby, University of New Mexico; Allan J. Taub, Cleveland State University; Chris Thomas, University of South Florida; Abdul M. Turay, Mississippi State University; Karen S. Vorst, University of Missouri–Kansas City; Robert Waller, U.S. Air Force Academy; Michael Watts, Purdue University; Donald A. Wells, University of Arizona; Arthur L. Welsh, Penn State University; Walter J. Wessels, North Carolina State University; Everett E. White, Loyola University; Donald R. Williams, Kent State University; Paula R. Worthington, Northwestern University; Thomas L. Wyrick, Southwest Missouri State University; William Zahka, Widener University; George Zodrow, Rice University; and Armand J. Zottola, Central Connecticut State University.

RBE and RDT

Macroeconomics

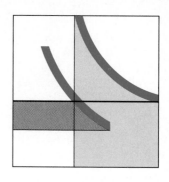

PART ONE

The
Power of
Economic
Thinking

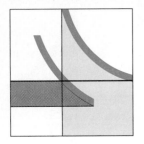

Economics in Perspective

Does economics matter? More to the point, why should you spend precious time and money learning economics when there are so many other activities, products, and services—not to mention other college courses—competing for your attention? The answer: Economics touches all facets of our lives from the trivial to the fundamental as consumers of gasoline and home computers, as voters for political candidates, and as workers and employers. Economics analyzes why we are poor or rich as individuals and extends its scope to government policies about inflation, unemployment, economic growth, and international trade. Economics not only deals with large issues, but with personal decisions as well—how much time to spend cleaning the apartment or studying, how to decide whether more education is called for, how to select a mate. Close study of economics gives us a new perspective on a wide variety of human activities and institutions. When you finish Chapter 1 you should understand

- how individuals, societies, and nations solve the basic economic problem caused by scarce resources and unlimited wants.
- the functions of prices and how they act as signals to producers, consumers, and governments in any economy.
- the basis on which all individuals actually make economic decisions.
- how economics gives insight into human behavior and social problems.

WHAT ECONOMICS IS (AND WHAT IT ISN'T)

Goods:
All tangible things that satisfy people's wants and desires.

Services:
All forms of intangible but useful activities that are valued by people.

Most people would say that economics deals with the stock market or with how to make money by buying and selling gold, land, or some other commodity. This common view contains a grain of truth but does not touch on the richness, depth, and breadth of the matter. Economics is a social science—the oldest and best developed of the social sciences. As such, it studies human behavior in relation to three basic questions about an economy: What **goods** and **services** are produced? How are goods and services produced? For whom are goods and services produced?

All societies and all individuals have faced these three questions. Since goods and the means to produce them have never existed in limitless amounts, the insistent questions—How? What? and For whom?—must be asked; for at least two hundred years, economists have tried to analyze how individuals and societies answer them. Consider some famous economists' definitions of economics:

Adam Smith (1776): Economics or political economy is "an inquiry into the nature and causes of the wealth of nations."[1]

Nassau William Senior (1836): Political economy is the "science that treats the nature, the production, and the distribution of wealth."[2]

Alfred Marshall (1890): "Political Economy or Economics is a study of mankind in the ordinary business of life . . . it is on the one side a study of wealth; and on the other, and more important side, a part of the study of man."[3]

Lionel Robbins (1935): "Economics is the science which studies human behavior as a relationship between ends and scarce means which have alternative uses."[4]

Milton Friedman (1962): "Economics is the science of how a particular society solves its economic problems."[5]

Paul Samuelson (1980): "Economics is the study of how people and society end up *choosing,* with or without the use of money, to employ *scarce* productive resources that could have alternative uses—to *produce* various commodities and *distribute* them for consumption, now or in the future, among various persons and groups in society. Economics analyzes the costs and the benefits of improving patterns of resource use."[6]

Economics: A Working Definition

There is merit in each of the preceding definitions. Economics *is* the study of how nations produce and increase wealth. Economics also studies the activities of people in producing, distributing, and consuming wealth. It analyzes how people and societies choose among competing goals or alternatives.

A common thread runs through all definitions of economics. Each definition emphasizes the inescapable fact that **resources**—the wherewithal to produce goods and services—are not available in limitless quantities and that people and societies, with unlimited desires for goods and services, must make some hard choices about what to do with the resources that are available. Our working definition of economics may be expressed as follows:

Resources:
Those things used to produce goods and services. These include land, machines, energy, and human labor and ingenuity. Resources are also called factors of production.

---

[1]Adam Smith, *An Inquiry into the Nature and Causes of the Wealth of Nations,* ed. Edwin Cannan (1776; reprint, New York: Modern Library, 1937).

[2]N. W. Senior, *An Outline of the Science of Political Economy* (1836; reprint, New York: A. M. Kelley, 1938).

[3]Alfred Marshall, *Principles of Economics* (London: Macmillan, 1920), p. 1.

[4]Lionel Robbins, *The Nature and Significance of Economic Science,* 2nd ed. (London: Macmillan, 1935), p. 16.

[5]Milton Friedman, *Price Theory* (Chicago: Aldine, 1962), p. 1.

[6]Paul A. Samuelson, *Economics* (New York: McGraw-Hill, Inc., 1980), p. 2.

Economics is the study of how individuals and societies, experiencing virtually limitless wants, choose to allocate scarce resources to satisfy their wants.

Unlimited wants, scarcity, and the choices they force on us are thus the key elements in understanding economics and the economic problem. Consider the nature of scarcity.

The Economic Condition: Scarcity

Scarcity:
The condition whereby the resources, goods, and services available to individuals and society are limited relative to the wants and desires for them.

What, exactly, is **scarcity**? More to the point, what are scarce resources? Dorothy Parker, an American humorist, once said, "If you can't get what you want, you'd better damn well settle for what you can get." The entire study of economics amplifies and expands on Parker's proposition. As individuals and as a society, we cannot get all of what we want because the amount of available resources is limited. The role of the economist and of economics in general is to explain how we can make the most of this problem of scarcity—in Parker's terms, how to get as much as we can of what we want.

The most important problem in economics is that while the wants of individuals and societies must be satisfied by limited resources, the wants themselves are not limited; rather, they are endless. We are never satisfied with what we have. Individuals are forever lured by more tempting foods, more cleverly engineered computers, more up-to-date fashions. Societies continually desire safer highways, more national security, greater Social Security benefits, or more cancer research. Problems of scarcity and unlimited wants—economics itself—apply to all nations regardless of political, social, and religious orientation. Moslems, Jews, and Christians all face the eternal problem of satisfying limitless wants with limited means. Methods of dealing with scarcity will, of course, differ from society to society depending on cultural differences and on particular endowments of resources within political boundaries, but the fundamental problem is the same everywhere.

Scarcity is relative to time and fortune. Our generation has many more services and goods to choose from than our parents and grandparents did. The quantity and quality of goods and services may have grown from primitive to modern times, but the supply of resources needed to produce them is limited, and human wants are not.

Economic goods and services:
Goods and services that are scarce.

Costs:
An implication of scarcity; the necessary sacrifices associated with making any choice.

All scarce goods—from television to chlorinated water—are called **economic goods.** Their scarcity leads to **costs.** While it is customary to associate cost with the money price of goods, economists define *cost* as the value of the good or activity given up in place of the good or activity actually chosen. Since all unlimited wants cannot be met with scarce resources, individuals have to make choices—between, for instance, more steaks and more computer games. Societies may have to choose between safer highways and more accurate missiles. Cost is, therefore, the direct result of the scarcity of resources. Scarcity of resources means that both individuals and societies must endure the costs of acquiring more of any good or service. That cost is the value of the good or activity given up in place of the good chosen. Think for a moment about that scarce resource, time. Being absolutely limited in supply for each of us, time—or, rather, the use of time—bears a definite cost. No college student, certainly, has escaped being confronted with economic decisions arising from the need to allocate this costly resource. (See Focus, "Scarcity, Economizing, and the College Student's Time.")

FOCUS   Scarcity, Economizing, and the College Student's Time

College students know the principle of scarcity all too well. Indeed, a successful student needs an ability to make sound and efficient economic decisions, not only in the more obvious case of scarce monetary resources but in the allocation of scarce time resources as well. Time is a valuable resource to all human beings, but it exists in finite quantities of 24 hours a day, 168 hours a week, and (approximately) 720 hours a month.

Every student knows that he or she cannot have and do everything and that *economic* decisions, whether they are recognized as such or not, must be made every day. Most familiar is the weekly or monthly monetary budget derived from savings, family support, or private or government loans. Too grand a splurge on meals, clothes, or entertainment in the first weeks of the month demands a Spartan existence (peanut butter and TV) in that last week. (Poverty is a hard taskmaster!) Likewise, summer school attendance will produce a degree sooner, but at the expense of income from a summer job or other alternatives.

A student's time often must be allocated over a day or a week. A weekend trip to an out-of-town football game must be "paid for" not only in monetary terms but also in less time to work on the English paper due on Wednesday. The end of a term always necessitates economizing: Given the limited time available, should an additional two hours be directed to chemistry or art history? Actual choices will depend on perceived net gain or potential net gain from the array of alternatives. Ordinarily, most activities or goods and services selected, if they are divisible, will be combined by the choice-maker to maximize satisfaction (for example, one hour spent on chemistry and one hour spent on art history).

College students are not alone, of course. For anyone, the choice may be between listening to a rock band or attending a Bach organ recital. We may have chosen a career in acting or dance instead of law or computer programming. A retiree may choose to return to the classroom rather than to spend time fishing or playing bridge. Economizing—maximizing the value of monetary or time resources under conditions of scarcity—forms the foundation of human behavior. Students, workers, politicians, philanthropists, business executives—all must make choices, and an analysis of these choices forms the basis of the social science of economics.

You may feel that some things are not scarce and that some things—such as love, sunshine, and water—are free. In economic terms, **free goods** are goods that are available in sufficient amounts to satisfy all possible demands. But are many things truly free? Surface water is usually unfit for drinking except in areas far from human habitation. Water suitable for drinking must be raised to the surface from deep wells or piped from reservoirs and treatment plants, operations involving resources that are scarce even when water itself is not. Scarcity of winter sun in the North results in costly winter vacations in the snowbird states. And if you think love is free. . . .

Scarce Resources and Economic Problems

There are basically two categories of scarce resources: human resources and nonhuman resources (see Table 1). **Human resources** encompass all types of labor, including specialized forms of labor such as management or entrepreneurship. **Nonhuman resources** include the rest of the bounty: land, natural resources such as minerals and water, and capital.

Examples of human resources abound. By definition, all human resources apply talent and energy to produce goods and services. The cook at the Chicken Shack, the hairstylist at the Mad Hacker, the chief executive of a computer firm, and the assembly-line worker at a General Motors plant all represent human resources. Obviously, labor includes a huge variety of skills, both general and precise. Knowledge, or know-how, is also part of human resources. Economists are interested not only in the scarcity of labor but in its quality. The quality of human resources can be enhanced through investments in education and training.

Economists view *entrepreneurship* as a special form of labor. An entrepreneur is a person who perceives profitable opportunities and who combines resources to produce salable goods or services. Entrepreneurs attempt to move resources from lower- to higher-valued uses in the economy and take the risk that they can make profits by doing so. Lemonade-stand entrepreneurs, for example, see an opportunity to make a profit by combining lemons, ice, and cups and by selling the resulting beverage product. *Management,* a second special form of labor, guides and oversees the process by which separate resources are turned into goods or services. The successful lemonade entrepreneur could hire a manager to oversee the opening of new stands around the neighborhood.

Human resources utilize nonhuman resources such as land, minerals, and natural resources to produce goods and services. A plot in Manhattan, an

Free goods and services: Things that are available in sufficient amounts and provide all that people want at zero cost.

Human resources: All forms of labor and skill used to produce goods and services.

Nonhuman resources: All resources other than human resources, such as machines and land.

TABLE 1

Economic Resources

Economic resources include all human and nonhuman resources that are scarce in supply.

Human Resources	Nonhuman and Other Resources
Labor, including entrepreneurship and management	Land
	Natural resources, including minerals and water
	Capital

acre in Iowa, a coal deposit in Pennsylvania, a uranium mine in South Dakota, and a timber stand in Oregon are all scarce nonhuman resources. New deposits of minerals can be discovered, forests can be replanted, and agricultural land can be reclaimed from swamps. But at any one time, the available supply of nonhuman resources is limited.

Capital, another category of nonhuman resources, comprises all machines, implements, and buildings used to produce goods and services either directly or indirectly. A surgeon's scalpel, a factory, an electric generator, and an artist's brush are all used to produce goods and services and, thus, are considered capital.

Many different forms of capital may be needed to produce a single economic good. With a wheat harvesting machine, a South Dakota farmer can reap a huge crop. But the wheat must also be milled into flour and transported from South Dakota to bakeries in California. Once the wheat has arrived, bakeries must utilize brick or convection ovens to produce bread. The harvesting and milling machines, the railroad, and the baker's ovens are all capital goods, created to increase the amount of final production.

Capital—and the resources used to produce it—is scarce. To create capital, we must sacrifice consumer goods and services because the production of capital takes time away from the production of goods that can be consumed in the present. Societies and individuals must therefore choose between immediate consumption and future consumption. That choice is crucial to growth and ultimate economic well-being. We return to this important issue in Chapter 2.

Other Factors Affecting Resources and Growth

Quantities of human and nonhuman resources are only one prerequisite for economic growth and well-being in an economy. The institutional framework of an economy, such as the nature of its legal system and its form of government, is also critical for economic growth and development, as are other factors such as technology and information. Consider, first, the nature of technology and information.

Technology:
Knowledge of production methods associated with producing a particular good.

Technology and information assist resource utilization in a modern, functioning economy. **Technology,** in general, is composed of know-how, inventions, and innovations that help us get more from scarce resources. An improvement in technology implies that we can produce more. Existing technology is the outcome of many inventions, some of which were the invention of new resources—such as aluminum and hybrid plants. All inventions that increase the productivity of labor and capital can be considered improvements in technology. Innovation is the application of technology to the production of goods and services. Technology, then, helps make other resources less scarce.

Information:
A scarce and important element in the process of economic exchange and growth.

Information is a scarce and costly ingredient in the economic process. The acquisition of information for economic decision making has never been free. In the nineteenth and early twentieth centuries, businesses hired armies of bookkeepers to provide sufficient information for managers to make decisions. The development of the digital computer in the mid-twentieth century made the storage and retrieval of information less costly (while having little effect on the scarcity of the information itself). Technology has progressed so rapidly that the quantity of information that could be stored in a warehouse-sized computer in 1950 can now be placed on a chip the size of a fingernail! Advertising is a form of information that can help us economize on the use of scarce time. With price, quality, and other information provided through advertising, we can spend less time searching for goods and services. Information, then, helps us economize on the use of scarce resources.

Resources, both human and nonhuman, never operate in a vacuum; they always exist in some real-world setting that includes government, a legal system, and a structure of property rights. **Property rights** are those rules that establish and govern the ownership and control of resources. Property rights are established by laws developed within a society's traditions and social relations. **Institutions** are the sum total of the traditions, mores, laws, and governmental structures of an economy. Institutions in the United States include the Constitution and the laws of the fifty states. Some of these institutions restrict and define the rights to own and use resources. Others enhance the flow of resources between individuals and states. The U.S. Constitution, for example, guarantees the free movement of resources from state to state.

We live in a world filled with many governments representing many different institutional structures. Some countries are blessed with huge quantities of land and natural resources but still do not manage to achieve economic growth and development beyond the barest minimum. Prior to the 1980s, China's communist government directed almost all human and nonhuman resources from the highest levels of bureaucracy. Despite China's huge resource base, these institutions reduced the country's ability to produce economic development. More recently, and in spite of periodic political repression, the Chinese government has tentatively embraced a Western-style free market system in which some areas of the economy, such as agriculture, are given over to self-interested production, distribution, and exchange. However slowly, Western institutions and technology *are* being adopted in China because they have encouraged a more efficient use of human and nonhuman resources in producing goods and services.

When property rights are not assigned to scarce resources, the resources tend to be wasted. The old adage "What is owned by all, is cared for by none" means the failure to legally assign property rights to specific resources will ensure that the resources will not be utilized in the most efficient fashion. Most Western economists believe that private rights over property—combined with free and unregulated private markets for human and nonhuman resources—are essential to growth in any nation. The success stories of relatively free and unrestricted economies such as Hong Kong, Taiwan, and Singapore—each endowed with very modest quantities of resources—are often presented as proof that noninterventionist institutions contribute greatly to economic development. The shift in New Zealand's economy from more to less regulation of resources has produced heightened growth there, while the coexistence of private property and extensive controls on resource use in the Indian economy has produced stagnation. The lesson to be learned from these cases is that institutions—especially the form of government and the nature of controls over resources and resource utilization—are keys to productivity and economic growth in any society.

Scarcity of resources *and* scarcity of imagination in designing institutions to facilitate resource use are at the heart of all economic problems. Resources can be augmented over time; indeed, we are much better off materially than our grandparents, and our grandparents were better off than their

Property rights:
Any legal and/or enforceable rights to the use of resources of any kind.

Institutions:
The sum total of the traditions, mores, laws, and governmental structures of an economy.

grandparents. At any one time, however, individuals and societies cannot get all of what they want. Given scarcity, individuals and societies must make choices, and a primary role of economists is to analyze scarcity and the process of choosing. With their analyses they make predictions and recommendations regarding productivity and economic growth.

THE POWER OF ECONOMIC THINKING

All economists of all political stripes have common fundamental ways of thinking. These perspectives, at the core of the science of economics, appear many times throughout this book. When properly and consistently used, they brand a person as adept in the economic way of thinking. A look at these economic perspectives in simple, commonsense language should convince you that economics and economic reasoning are closely related to decisions you make every day. Indeed, economics may be usefully characterized as a way of thinking about both familiar and unfamiliar events.

Resources Cost More Than You Think

What does it cost you to take a skiing weekend in the mountains or to make a trip to the beach during spring break? Your instant reply might include the costs of gasoline, auto depreciation, airfare, lift tickets, food, drink, entertainment, and a motel room. These money expenditures are called **accounting costs,** or explicit money costs.

Accounting costs:
Actual money expenditures associated with any activity; out-of-pocket costs.

Explicit costs:
Accounting costs.

Implicit costs:
Nonpecuniary costs associated with the consumption of a good or service.

Opportunity costs:
The highest-valued alternative forgone in making any choice.

Economists define *costs* more broadly than accountants do. In addition to the **explicit** (money) **costs** considered by accountants, economists consider additional **implicit costs** associated with an action. In the case of a ski trip, an economist would recognize that an additional implicit cost of a ski weekend is the forgone opportunity of using the time in its next most valuable use when all viable alternatives are considered. For example, if the student who goes skiing would otherwise have spent the weekend watching TV or working at a part-time job, an implicit cost of skiing is the income that would otherwise have been earned, if working is the highest-valued alternative. Therefore, the full economic cost of the ski weekend—the **opportunity cost**—equals the explicit money costs (that money does have an alternative use) plus the implicit costs of the forgone income. (See Focus, "Opportunity Cost: The Case of Professional Line-Standers.") Opportunity costs always include all accounting costs.

Greg is a self-employed lawyer who charges $125 per hour for his services. A next-door neighbor owns four large cats who howl at night, disturbing Greg's sleep. Unable to convince his neighbor to quiet the cats, Greg spends 10 work hours preparing a lawsuit to demand satisfaction. Greg bears an opportunity cost, although he paid no lawyer to handle his case. If Greg's next best alternative was to work for a client (and we assume that it is), he could have earned $1250. An economist would say that his opportunity cost of the lawsuit against his neighbor was $1250, for that is what his choice to prepare the lawsuit cost him in terms of forgone legal billings. Therefore, bringing the suit is costly to the lawyer even though no explicit costs (accounting costs) are incurred.

Such opportunity costs also exist for society. Use of government lands in Wyoming and Montana as recreation areas or national forests entails a cost. Through lease or purchase, these lands could be used as a source of oil, minerals, and timber. Such use would contribute to society's well-being, but park land serves the recreational needs of society as well. Whatever choice society makes for the use of the land will imply a cost in economic terms. An opportunity must be forgone when the land is used in either manner.

A favorite saying of economists is "There is no such thing as a free lunch." The first fundamental principle of economics is that most things in life come at the opportunity cost of something forgone. They are never free. For many activities, accounting, or out-of-pocket, costs understate opportunity cost. In economics, opportunity cost is the true, total measure of the costs of anything.

Economic Behavior Is Rational

The second fundamental principle of economics is that people behave according to **rational self-interest.** Economists selected from a number of alternative views of human behavior and settled on a very simple one—that of *Homo economicus* (economic man or woman). Rather than viewing humans as inconsistent, incompetent, selfish, or altruistic, economists argue that human behavior is predictably based on a person's weighing the costs and benefits of decisions. This choice making is influenced by constraints such as the availability of options, personal tastes, values, and social philosophy. A student will choose to eat lunch at the local health food restaurant rather than the fast-food cafeteria on campus if the personal benefits of doing so, say eating nutritious food in a pleasant atmosphere, outweigh the costs, such as longer lines and greater distance to be walked.

When costs or benefits change, behavior will change. Consider Jack, a poor but honest man. When he finds $100 cash in a phone booth, he turns it in to authorities. Had Jack found $1000, he might have acted similarly, but discovery of $100,000 might have caused Jack to pause. It may be more costly to be honest under some circumstances.

The view of the individual espoused by economists has always been subject to misinterpretation. When economists say that humans are self-interested, they do not mean that other views of human behavior and motivation are unimportant or irrelevant. Altruistic or charitable behavior, for example, is perfectly compatible with *Homo economicus.* If a person values altruism, then an act that benefits others will carry emotional benefits and will therefore be in that person's rational self-interest. Economists simply maintain that people calculate the costs and benefits of their decisions in acting in their own self-interest.

If the IRS were to quadruple the income tax deduction for charitable contributions, economists would predict an increase in charity. No economist would deny that love, charity, and justice are important aspects of human behavior. Indeed, an economist has argued that "that scarce resource Love" is in fact "the most precious thing in the world" and that humans are therefore compelled to conserve it in ordering the affairs of the world.[7] Economists

[7]D. M. Robertson, "What Does the Economist Economize?" in *Economic Commentaries* (London: Staples, 1956), p. 154.

FOCUS   Opportunity Cost: The Case of Professional Line-Standers

Matters of opportunity cost fill our lives, although we seldom stop to think of the mechanics of this central principle of economics. Our time, for example, may be thought of as a resource of 24 hours a day. Consider the plight of a Washington, D.C. doctor who was faced with the opportunity cost of an unpleasant task. According to the *Washington Post*, " . . . last month, Dr. Howard Hoffman took a morning off from work to try to register his son's 1983 Honda Prelude. He got to the District's Department of Motor Vehicles [DMV] at 'what I thought was the crack of dawn, and it seemed like there were 300 people in there,' Hoffman said. 'I was overwhelmed by this sense of futility when I saw this line of people armed with newspapers and sandwiches. I would have had to spend my whole morning in there.' "[a] The opportunity cost of standing in line was high to Dr. Hoffman. His opportunity cost of standing in line was the highest-valued alternative, for example, working, sleeping later, or playing tennis. (Note that the highest-valued alternative does not have to be lost income from missed work time.)

Dr. Hoffman, however, did not stand in line. Robert Long came to his rescue. Long is a professional line-stander—he stands in line for pay. Hoffman filled out the automobile registration forms, gave them to Long, who, for $25, handled the DMV transaction on the same day. Hoffman concludes: "I was really very tickled by the whole thing. It was well worth whatever I paid."

Robert Long is not alone. Two brothers in the Washington, D.C. area have started a business handling DMV trans-actions for customers. They drop by professional offices, pick up the completed forms, take them to the DMV office, and return with car registrations for their customers. As one of the brothers, Nicholas Montgomery, observes: "These are really people who don't have time to do these things. . . . Some of them are a bit wary about handing over their cars, but then, the people who use the service tend to have pretty expensive cars."

The economics of the professional line-stander illustrates that individuals have different opportunity costs of time. The brisk business in expensive car registration reflects the fact that high-earning, high-income individuals, whose opportunity costs are high, are using the service. When opportunity costs of any given activity (e.g., waiting in line) become large compared to the benefit derived from the activity, individuals will seek alternatives to their advantage. In all such cases, it can be profitable for people to part with their money instead of their time.

The emergence of professional line-standers also illustrates the concept of entrepreneurship. The entrepreneur is someone alert to new opportunities to provide valuable goods and services. The professional line-stander is an entrepreneur who makes himself or herself and those who are willing to pay to avoid standing in line better off economically.

[a]*Washington Post,* July 28, 1986, p. A5.

have merely advanced the simple but powerful proposition that, given personal tastes, values, and social philosophy, rational self-interest is a better guide to predicting behavior than any other assumption about why people act as they do.

The economists' view of the rational self-interested individual applies not only to economic behavior but also to other realms of behavior. Animals other than humans, such as birds or rats, can be shown to be self-interested in that they act to maximize their own well-being given their constraints. Politicians maximize their self-interest by wooing voters to elect and reelect them. Since politicians face periodic elections, political behavior such as garnering support from particular voters can be predicted using the economic self-interest assumption. Even activities such as dating, marriage, and divorce have been analyzed using the self-interest assumption! After more than two hundred years of economic theorizing, rational self-interest remains a most powerful predictor of behavior.

Choices Are Made at the Margin

Margin:
The difference between costs or benefits in an existing situation and after a proposed change.

Economists do not ordinarily analyze all-or-nothing decisions but are concerned with decisions made at the **margin**—the additional costs or benefits of a specific change in the current situation. An individual consumer, for example, does not decide to spend his or her entire budget solely on food, cassette tapes, or weekends at the beach. Consumers purchase hundreds of goods and services. Their choice to purchase or not purchase additional units of any one good is based on the additional (or *marginal*) satisfaction that that single unit would bring to them.

Marginal analysis:
Looking at changes in the costs and benefits of a change from the status quo to a proposed new situation. These marginal changes in the costs and benefits are the basis for rational economic choice.

Marginal analysis is a method of finding the optimal, or most desirable, level of any activity—how much coffee to drink, how much bread to produce, how many store detectives to hire, and so on. In an economic sense, every activity we undertake involves *both* benefits and costs, so an optimal level of an activity is the point at which the activity's benefits outweigh its costs by the greatest amount. For example, the optimal level of coffee drinking is reached when coffee's total benefits (its taste and stimulating effects, perhaps) exceed its costs (the expense, the health risks, the acid indigestion) by the greatest degree.

Students make marginal decisions all the time, whether studying for exams, purchasing a new sweater, or maintaining a car. Clearly, additional study for a mathematics examination will improve the grade you receive. But doing your best will not mean devoting *all* available time to the project. The total gain in terms of grade achieved will rise, but the total costs due to the opportunity cost of time will rise also. Additional hours spent studying math may require forgone activities such as work, sleep, studying history, or even recreation. The rational student will stop studying for an examination when the *marginal* benefits from another hour of study equal the *marginal* costs of study. Beyond this point, additional study hours would likely raise the exam grade by a few more points, but the additional study would not be worth the additional cost in terms of other activities given up. The *net* benefits of studying math (net benefits = total benefits − total costs) are always maximized where the marginal benefits equal the marginal costs.

The marginal principle carries over into all we do. Regular automobile maintenance (for example, getting an oil change or having the tires rotated) costs money and time, but there are benefits in terms of the quality of the car's performance. What is the optimal amount of miles to drive between oil changes? As usual, marginal analysis helps us decide on an answer. Obviously a change every 1000 miles would produce some benefits in terms of the maintenance of the car's engine, whereas an oil change only every 20,000 or 25,000 miles would likely produce positive harm. Given the marginal costs (time and money) and the marginal benefits from periodic servicing, the car owner will probably choose a length of time between changes that is less than 25,000 miles but greater than 1000 miles. More frequent changes would increase total benefits but at higher total costs. The individual will maximize the *net* benefits of the service where the additional or marginal benefits of getting the oil changed just equal the marginal costs incurred.

The marginal principle in economics adds new meaning to the familiar statement "Whatever is worth doing, is worth doing well." We never want to maximize the total benefit or return from an activity—studying for an examination, purchasing and eating hamburgers, or getting an oil change—without weighing the cost. We "do well" by maximizing the *net* benefits from purchases or activities, which means that we follow the marginal principle. Rational self-interest requires isolating and considering the specific effects of specific changes—of choices at the margin, in the area of change. (Economics in Action at the end of this chapter provides further illustrations of marginal analysis.)

Prices Are Signals to Producers and Consumers

What products and services are produced in our economic system and how are they produced? Consumers decide what is to be produced—TVs, automobiles, beets—with the scarce resources in our society. Economists say that consumers transmit their desires through **markets,** which are simply arrangements where buyers and sellers exchange goods or services for money or some other medium. Buyers and sellers can be physically together in a market, as in a livestock market, or they can be separated by geographic distance or by wholesalers and other intermediaries, as when the buying and selling of a company's stock is carried out through stockbrokers. A market may even be an abstraction, as is the labor market, in which the supply of and demand for jobs and workers are juggled on a broad scale. The prices established in these markets (through mechanics to be explored in Chapter 4) are the key to understanding what gets produced and how much is produced in our economic system. Economists, therefore, give a great deal of attention to the role and function of prices and markets in explaining how things get done.

In a market economy **prices** are the essential signals that tell producers and resource suppliers what and how to produce. Take, for example, a fairly new product, the compact disc (CD) player. Scarce resources—integrated circuits, electronic components, lasers, and fabricated metals—are used in producing CD players, and someone finds it profitable to do so.

What happens if consumers suddenly want CD players instead of cassette decks or turntables in their homes and automobiles? Consumers express this desire by buying many more CD players and leaving cassette decks and turn-

Market:
A collection of buyers and sellers exchanging resources, goods, or services.

Prices:
The market-established opportunity costs of goods and services obtained through exchange.

tables to gather dust on store shelves. Meanwhile, the relative unavailability of CD players causes their price to rise, because, temporarily, there are insufficient resources and production to meet the new demand. Manufacturers observe the increased sales and rising prices and realize that producing more CD players will be profitable. They react by producing more players, which means ordering more electronics and circuitry and plastics, and hiring more labor and machinery. Higher prices for integrated circuits, fabricated metals, and wiring give producers in Silicon Valley and other resource suppliers a signal to supply more of their inputs and services. Why do they do it? Because higher prices mean greater profitability to resource suppliers as well. Resources are diverted to CD players as both demand for and production of cassette decks and turntables decline.

Consumers also view prices as signals that help them decide what, and how much, to buy. Prices are both a mechanism that signals the degree of scarcity of goods and services to consumers and an allocator of the available quantities of goods and services among consumers.

Suppose, for example, that one-half of Brazil's coffee crop is destroyed by frost. Less coffee would be available, and coffee would become scarcer on supermarket shelves in the United States. The economic system informs consumers of the scarcity by a rise in the price of coffee. The economic system also allocates the smaller amount of coffee among consumers through a price increase. Consumers will purchase a smaller amount when coffee becomes more expensive. Prices ration the available quantity among consumers by influencing the amount consumers will want to buy. Prices perform this rationing function no matter how much coffee is actually available. Likewise, a decrease in price signals consumers that a good has become less scarce. Price reductions allocate or ration increased amounts of goods by making them less expensive and by encouraging larger purchases.

Prices serve two basic functions in an economy. They serve to determine how much and what goods and services are produced by producers. They also serve to ration available commodities among different consumers and competing end uses.

Economists Do Not Decide Who Gets What

Economists study poverty and wealth; but as economists they have no unique knowledge to comment on how rich people should be or how much poverty is tolerable. Economists do not decide whether a college football coach deserves $16 million on a five-year contract or whether a Nobel Prize–winning physicist deserves more. Economists basically explain that the economic value of all individuals—expressed as their income—is determined by the relative desires for their services and by the relative scarcity of their talents and abilities. Perhaps good football coaches are relatively more scarce and more highly desired than good physicists.

Most products and services—such as food, vacations, and domestic help—are allocated to those with the greatest desire and ability to pay for them. Our ability to pay is determined by the economic value of our own particular services or resources in the marketplace. This value depends on our education, on-the-job training, health, luck, inheritance, and a host of other factors.

The distribution of "public" goods and services—such as highways and bridges, space weapons, and "free" movies on campus—is conducted by national, local, and student governments through the filter of politics and voting. A decision whether to add seating capacity to the football stadium or to double the size of the English department at a public university may be made by a university committee appointed by the president and board of trustees, who may be appointed by the governor, who is elected by the citizens of the state. Ultimately, therefore, decisions on how resources are to be distributed are made by voter choices. If voters do not like the decisions made in the political process, they have a right to change the decision-makers. Chosen by voters, politicians make economic decisions based on their perceptions of costs and benefits to the public—as well as to their own chances of reelection. In government, as in the workings of the market, the chief role of economists is not to say who should get what, but to describe and analyze the process—the costs, benefits, and incentives—through which the distribution of all products and services takes place.

We All Need Money, But Not Too Much

Barter:
Direct exchange of one good or service for another without the use of money.

Economists also place a special significance on the role of money in our lives. The trade of goods for goods, called **barter,** will not work in any economy that completes billions of transactions every day. Barter may have been sufficient in primitive societies where few things were produced and traded, but as individuals became specialized, using more and more of their talents and skills, the number and kind of traded commodities and services grew. As the number of commodities grew, the cost of transacting by barter grew enormously. A common denominator, acceptable to all, developed within economic societies to reduce the costs and inconveniences of barter. That common denominator is **money,** which serves as a medium of exchange.

Money:
A generally accepted medium of exchange.

Money is not limited to coins and paper dollars. Throughout history many things—shells, feathers, paper, gold, and cattle, for instance—have served as money. The important point to economists is that money, whatever it is, reduces the costs associated with barter and increases specialization and trade. At the same time, economists are concerned that money should not be available in such quantities as to become unacceptable and valueless to people who produce, buy, and sell. For society, at least, huge increases in the money supply may be too much of a good thing. For example, in post–World War I Germany the government attempted to solve the nation's economic problems by printing more money. Eventually, money was worth more as paper than as a medium of exchange; buying a loaf of bread required a wheelbarrow full of money.

Inflation:
A sustained increase in the general level of prices; inflation reduces the purchasing power of money.

When the quantity of money increases beyond its use as a means of making transactions, confidence in the medium of exchange and its value (in terms of the quantity of goods and services a unit of it can purchase) deteriorates. Economists call this phenomenon **inflation.** Inflation was an especially sad fact of American life during the 1970s, and it is a persistent element in nations around the world. Inflation, if left untamed, can result in the collapse of entire economies with reversion to primitive barter conditions. Economists therefore are very concerned with the relation between the production and trade of goods and the quantity of money available to facilitate these crucial activities. Breakdowns must be prevented, and economists have valuable insights on preventive measures.

Voters Choose the Role of Government—The Economist Analyzes

In a functioning democratic system, society chooses an economic role for government by electing politicians. In general, that role has included such activities as taxation for and provision of collective goods such as national defense, highways, and education; the regulation of monopoly; pollution control; control of the money supply; and alleviation of poverty through welfare programs. In its economic role of taxing and spending, government can affect economic factors such as inflation, the degree of unemployment, economic growth, and international trade.

Economists have always been concerned with the effects of government activity in these areas. In the United States, economists are in the thick of government. Since 1946 an official Council of Economic Advisers has been appointed by the president to aid in the formulation and implementation of economic policy. Almost every agency of government employs economists to give advice in their areas of expertise.

In their role as advisers, economists primarily evaluate, from the perspective of economic theory or analysis, the effects of proposals or, more correctly, of marginal changes in economic policies. Economists do not argue, for example, that additional funds should be allocated to Social Security and taken away from water reclamation projects. They simply evaluate and communicate the costs and benefits of such proposals.

Economists are not confined to giving advice on specific issues such as the Social Security program or the effects of advertising regulation by the Federal Trade Commission. Larger issues are within economists' purview as well. Predicting the effects of government taxing and spending policies on employment, interest rates, and inflation is a very large part of economists' role. Economists might predict, for example, the impact of a tax cut on private spending, interest rates, the private production of goods and services, and inflation. As such, economists are concerned with *economic stabilization*.

Despite economists' influence, however, the economic role of government is ultimately decided by voters in periodic elections. Specific economic functions are not decided in elections, but politicians run on platforms pledging to "increase social welfare spending," "increase defense spending," "reduce the debt," "balance the budget," and "increase environmental regulation." In a loose sense, then, voters decide economic policies. Economists evaluate the implications of government's economic policies. Economists advise. They do not make ultimate decisions about what the government should do.

THE ROLE OF THEORY IN ECONOMICS

Economists must be able to discern fundamental regularities about human behavior. Only if behavior is regular and consistent, on average, among individuals or from generation to generation will economists be able to predict

Model:
A simplified abstraction of the real world that approximates reality and makes problems easier to analyze; also called a theory.

the results of behavior. Economists organize their thoughts about human behavior and its results through **models.** Economists, like all scientists, construct models to isolate specific phenomena for study. Constructing models requires assumptions and abstractions from the real world.

The Need for Abstraction

The economist, the biochemist, or the physicist could never handle all the details surrounding any event. Thousands of details are involved in even the simple act of buying a loaf of bread. The friendliness of the clerk, the way the buyer is dressed, and the freshness of the bread are all details surrounding the purchase, and these details may be different each time a buyer makes a purchase. Likewise many details surround a particular chemical reaction or an astronomical event like the appearance of a comet. Economists, like chemists or astronomers, are interested in particular details about an event, such as how much the bread cost or how many loaves the buyer purchased.

Economists must *abstract* from extraneous factors to isolate and understand some other factor because, as one economist put it, people's minds are limited and nature's riddles are complex. Economists must assume that the extraneous factors are constant—that "other things are equal"[8]—or that, if altered, they would have a predictable effect on the relations or model under consideration. Humanity has never progressed very far in understanding anything—be it chemistry, astronomy, or economics—without abstracting from many factors that are not central to a given problem. *Thus, all economic models are of necessity abstractions. Good models, those that perform and predict well, use relevant factors; poor models do not.*

An economic model (or, essentially the same thing, a theory) can be expressed in verbal, graphical, or mathematical form. Sometimes verbal explanation is sufficient, but graphs or algebra often serve as convenient shorthand means of expressing models. Economics is like other sciences in this regard. A complicated chemical or physical process can be described in words, but it is much more convenient to use mathematics. All methods of expressing models will be used in this book, but we rely primarily on words and graphs. The appendix to this chapter explains how to read and interpret graphs.

The Usefulness and Limitations of Theory

In recognizing the regularities of human behavior and in committing them to a model, economists or scientists do not have to rethink every event as it occurs. Theory saves time and permits extremely useful predictions about future events based upon regularities of human behavior.

Economic theory has its limits, though. Since a complex world is the economist's workshop, economic theory cannot be tested in the way chemical or physical theories can. Economists can seldom find naturally existing conditions that provide a good test of a model, let alone a sequence of such conditions, and it is difficult to conduct controlled laboratory experiments on

---

[8]The Latin phrase *ceteris paribus,* meaning "other things being equal," is common economic shorthand for this assumption about human behavior.

human beings to determine their economic behavior. Because of the difficulties of testing, economists are less certain than, say, geneticists or biologists. The accuracy of economics is somewhat more like that of meteorology. Total accuracy is not within the meteorologist's abilities. At least, total accuracy is not worth what it would cost to obtain in either weather forecasting or economics. The unusual weather conditions of 1988, including a severe drought in the far western and southwestern parts of the United States, were caused by a complicated host of factors related to air currents, stalled high-pressure fronts, and other weather phenomena. It took meteorologists a good deal of time to sort out the relevant causes by testing and applying their models.

In economics, the problem of imperfect conditions for testing is a limitation to theory, but theory is essential nonetheless. Nothing can substitute for the usefulness of theory in organizing our thoughts about the real world and in describing the regularities of economic behavior.

In constructing models, moreover, economists and all other scientists must be careful to follow the rules of logic and to avoid common fallacies. Two of these are the **fallacy of composition** and the *post hoc* **fallacy.** The fallacy of composition involves generalizing based on a particular experience. Suppose that you had never seen a fox, and then the first one you saw was white. Should you conclude that all foxes are white? If you did, you would commit the fallacy of composition. The conclusion that if everyone stands up at a crowded football game, each will get a better view founders on the same fallacy.

The *post hoc* fallacy (from *post hoc, ergo propter hoc,* "after this, therefore because of this") is the faulty reasoning of cause-and-effect relations between events. The ancient Aztec Indians of Mexico believed that the spring ritual of sacrificing children and virgins appeased the gods of agriculture, bringing a bountiful harvest. When crops appeared in the fall, high priests insisted that the good crop was caused by the sacrifice. If the crop was insufficient, more children and virgins had to be wary the following spring. In economic analysis, the *post hoc* fallacy may be involved in statements such as "high interest rates cause inflation" or "after hoarding sugar, the price of sugar rises" or "the government subsidy to Chrysler Motor Company saved the business." Economists and all who are interested in sound thinking must constantly guard against such fallacies.

Positive and Normative Economics

Economics is usually a positive rather than a normative science. Positive statements describe what is or predict what will be under certain circumstances, whereas normative prescriptions entail value judgments about what should be. For the most part, economists confine themselves to positive statements. Individual values, concepts of justice, or tastes are normative matters and generally do not enter economists' analyses of issues. These matters are not testable in any accepted scientific sense and are therefore excluded from economics.

Consider U.S. welfare programs. To say that additional tax dollars should be spent on welfare would involve a normative judgment on the part of economists. Once society has decided to spend more on welfare, however, economists can make positive statements about the effects of such spending. Or economists may observe the welfare system and analyze how the system could

Fallacy of composition: Incorrectly generalizing that what is true for a part is also true for the whole.

Post hoc **fallacy:** The incorrect linking of unrelated events as a cause-and-effect relationship simply because one event happens after the other.

Positive economics: Observations, explanations, or predictions about economic life; scientific economics.

Normative economics: Value judgments based on moral principles or preferences about how economic life should be.

work more efficiently in achieving its goals. In other words, economists must show, once society has decided on a welfare system and on some dollar amount to be devoted to welfare, how alternative systems of welfare distribution would alter the effectiveness of the program. Economists make positive statements in presenting alternatives and their effects so that society might get the most for the dollars spent.

On the smaller scale, imagine a student facing an afternoon choice between watching soap operas and studying for an economics quiz. In positive terms, economists can only describe the alternatives open to the student. An observer would be on normative grounds if he or she insisted that the student should avoid TV all afternoon and spend the time preparing for the quiz. Free choice is, in this as in all cases, the prerogative of the economic actor. Economists can only array the alternatives. On occasion, normative statements slip into economic discussion, as they undoubtedly do in this book. Beware of them and learn to distinguish them from positive economics.

Microeconomics and Macroeconomics

The first half of this book concerns what economists call microeconomics, and the second half deals with macroeconomics. **Microeconomics,** like microbiology, concerns the components of a system. Just as a frog is made up of individual cells of various kinds, individual sales and purchases of commodities from potatoes to health care are the stuff of which the whole economy is composed. Microeconomists are thus concerned with individual markets and with the determination of relative prices within those markets—the price of potatoes versus the price of hot dogs. Supply and demand for all goods, services, and factors of production are the subject matter of microeconomics. Microeconomists address questions such as the following: Will the use of larger quantities of solar energy reduce the total energy bill of Americans? Will an increased tax on cigarettes increase or decrease federal revenues from the tax? Will the quality and quantity of nursing services in the state of Wyoming be changed by the licensing of nursing in that state?

Microeconomics:
Analysis of the behavior of individual decision-making units, including individuals, households, and business firms.

Macroeconomics is the study of the economy as a whole. The overall price level, inflation rate, international exchange rate, unemployment rate, economic growth rate, and interest rate are some issues of concern to macroeconomists. Macroeconomists analyze how these crucial quantities are determined and how and why they change.

Macroeconomics:
Analysis of the behavior of an economy as a whole.

Some issues contain elements of both microeconomics and macroeconomics—for instance, a proposed U.S. tariff on Japanese auto imports. Microeconomists would be interested in the effects of the tariff on auto prices, on the American auto industry, and on the quantity of cars bought by U.S. consumers. Macroeconomists would be primarily interested in the effects of the tariff on international trade, the balance of payments, and total spending. They might address such questions as: Would the tariff increase or decrease economic growth in the United States and in Japan? Would total employment in the United States or Japan change because of the tariff?

Daily television reports and newspapers are filled with discussions of both macroeconomic and microeconomic issues: Do tax cuts to business spur investment and economic growth? Will an OPEC price decrease or an alteration in supply affect oil and gas prices in America? Is the economy headed for more inflation, greater unemployment, or both? Will a tightening of the money supply cause an increase or decrease in interest rates? Does foreign competition mean fewer jobs for domestic autoworkers? Will price competition cause some airlines or trucking firms to shut down? Should the federal government balance the budget or not? A mastery of the fundamental and general principles of economics will give you a good foundation for formulating intelligent and reasoned answers to important questions such as these.

Why Do Economists Disagree?

Government or academic economists are forever predicting economic doom or economic prosperity for the same future time period. If economics contains fundamental principles agreed on by all, why do economists always seem to be arguing over predictions or over causes and effects? Why do economists disagree? One of the limitations of economic science is its inability to test theory. This imperfection means that alternative theories may be offered to explain the same events, such as the effects of government budget deficits or of the Great Depression of the 1930s. Alternative theories mean divergent policy prescriptions and different perspectives on the effects of policy prescriptions.

Even when economists agree on theoretical apparatus, they may differ on the magnitude of the effects suggested by the theory. And secondary effects—effects not considered in a theory—can occur after the initial impact of a policy change has taken place. Economists often disagree on the nature and importance of these secondary effects. Would new monetary incentives for an all-volunteer army increase or decrease our military effectiveness? Economists of good faith and common fundamentals might disagree. We do not

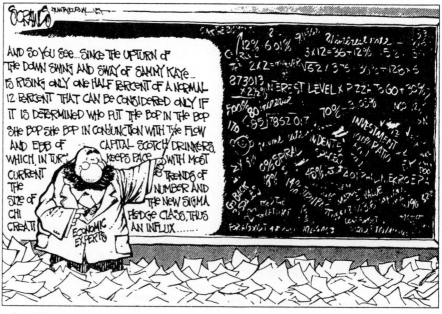

© Sam C. Rawls 1984.

wish to overemphasize economists' disagreements or the ambiguous nature of economics. Meteorologists of equal training and ability might well disagree over whether it will rain tomorrow.

Economics, like meteorology, is an inexact science, and it is likely to remain so. But economic theory and prediction are accurate and testable enough to provide extremely important insights into numerous issues that touch our lives. And the science of choice and scarcity is (like meteorology) constantly being improved from both theoretical and empirical perspectives. The well-established power of economic thinking is the result of two hundred years of such continuing improvements. Sound understanding of the principles of economic thinking will improve your understanding of the world.

SUMMARY

1. Economics is basically concerned with three questions: What goods and services are produced? How are goods and services produced? For whom are goods and services produced?
2. Economics is the study of how individuals and societies choose to allocate scarce resources given unlimited wants.
3. Scarce resources include human and nonhuman resources as well as time and technology. Human resources consist of labor, including entrepreneurship, and management. Nonhuman resources include land and all natural resources such as minerals, technology, information, and capital.
4. All scarce resources bear an opportunity cost. This means that individuals or societies forgo other opportunities whenever scarce resources are used to produce specific goods and services.
5. Economic behavior is rational: Human beings are assumed to behave predictably by weighing the costs

and benefits of their decisions and their potential actions.
6. Economic choices are made at the margin—that is, the additional costs or benefits of a change in the current situation. Prices are the signal that indicates individual and collective choices for goods and services as well as the relative scarcity of the resources necessary to produce the goods and services.
7. The study of prices of individual products and inputs is called *microeconomics,* and the study of inflation, unemployment, and related problems is called *macroeconomics.*
8. Economics is a more inexact and imprecise science than chemistry or physics. It is accurate enough to predict much economic behavior, however, and to provide insight into a large number of important problems.

KEY TERMS

goods	information	marginal analysis	*post hoc* fallacy
services	property rights	markets	positive economics
resources	institutions	prices	normative economics
scarcity	accounting costs	barter	microeconomics
economic goods	explicit costs	money	macroeconomics
free goods	implicit costs	inflation	
human resources	opportunity costs	models	
nonhuman resources	rational self-interest	fallacy of	
technology	margin	composition	

QUESTIONS FOR REVIEW AND DISCUSSION

1. What problem creates the foundation of economic analysis? Is this problem restricted to the poor? Why or why is it not relevant to the animal kingdom?
2. Can wants be satisfied with existing resources?
3. What are resources? How is the resource capital different from the resources land and labor?
4. What is the difference between behaving in one's self-interest and behaving selfishly?
5. What functions do prices have in the economy? Why were things rationed during World War II?
6. You have already paid your tuition. What does it cost you, at the margin, to attend your afternoon economics class on Friday? On Tuesday? (*Remember: The margin refers to the additional cost of attending one additional class.*)
7. Is air a free good? Is clean air a free good? Is cleaner air a free good?
8. Why do economists abstract from reality when formulating theories? Does this imply that their theories have no relevance in the real world?
9. "The stock market crash of 1929 preceded the Great Depression. Therefore, the fall in stock prices caused the Great Depression." "Periods of inflation are frequently followed by increases in the stock of money. Therefore, inflation causes increases in the money supply." "*A* occurs after *B*. Therefore, *B* causes *A*." These statements violate which fallacy? How?
10. "The distribution of income in the United States is not fair." What type of statement is this? Can "fair" be used to describe something without being normative?

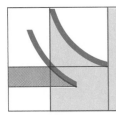

ECONOMICS IN ACTION
Marginal Analysis in Business and Politics

Far from being an abstract, theoretical exercise, marginal analysis—making decisions at the margin—is central to the everyday life of individuals, businesses, governments, and politicians. Suppose you manage a large department store and want to reduce the amount of shoplifting that takes place. By hiring additional store detectives, you will benefit from fewer thefts. But the detectives must be paid, so the net benefit is the amount you save minus the costs of the detectives. You might perform an experiment to determine whether you have enough detectives. Hire an additional detective and see whether losses from shoplifting fall by more than the $300 per week you pay each detective. If losses decrease by more than $300, hire additional detectives; if not, let detectives go. Stop hiring when the reduction in losses per week (the marginal benefit) is exactly equal to the weekly wage of detectives (the marginal cost to the store). (Note that the optimal level of shoplifting you will permit is not zero! Something worth doing is not necessarily worth doing well if "doing well" means eliminating *all* shoplifting.)

Suppose you are the manager of a large grocery store close to campus. On what basis would you decide to stay open all night rather than close at midnight and open at 6 A.M.? The costs would include the additional electricity required to stay open later plus the additional labor cost of cashiers and stock persons. The additional benefit is the sales revenue the store would make from staying open six more hours each day. In other words, the decision would not be based on the costs of building the grocery store, installing shelves, and so on. The decision, like all decisions, will be based on marginal, forward-looking considerations.

Government, through the political process, also makes decisions at the margin. The completion of the Strategic Defense Initiative ("Star Wars") program or the decision to finish a nuclear power plant are pertinent examples. These decisions will not be made on the basis of how much has already been spent on the projects but on the additional costs and benefits attached to completion. Political opposi-

tion, for example, will increase the marginal costs to those who vote to complete the "Star Wars" project, whereas political (voter) support will increase their marginal benefits. If the benefits of completing a nuclear power plant no longer outweigh the costs of ample electric power, then the plant will probably sit half-finished.

Politicians also gauge costs and benefits in running for election. In a presidential election, a candidate cannot campaign continuously all over the country. He or she must make marginal decisions about where to spend scarce campaign time and funds based upon factors such as the strength of support in various states and regions, the likelihood that undecided voters will commit in any particular area, and the number of electoral votes obtainable in any "noncommitted" state or region. Each political party conducts polls to determine this sort of information. Some states or areas may be "given up as lost," which means, in economic terms, that the marginal costs far outweigh the marginal benefits of campaigning there. As election day approaches and time becomes more scarce, candidates usually visit states and regions where the marginal benefits (in terms of the probability of obtaining electoral votes) to campaigning exceed the marginal costs. The marginal principle holds true for state and local politicians.

Every one of these decisions, and millions more like them, employ marginal analysis. It is one of the foundations of economics.

Questions
1. In the store detective example, why wouldn't it be considered optimal to permit no shoplifting at all?
2. On what will you base your decision whether to eat another piece of pizza at a pizza parlor that advertises "all you can eat" for $5?
3. Would a rational person in a hurry ever give away money to a beggar on the street? Use both the concepts of opportunity cost and marginal analysis to explain your answer.

Working with Graphs

Economists frequently use graphs to demonstrate economic theories or models. This appendix explains how graphs are constructed and how they can illustrate economic relations in simplified form. By understanding the mechanics and usefulness of graphs, you will find it much easier to grasp the economic concepts presented in this book.

THE PURPOSE OF GRAPHS

Most graphs in this book are simply pictures showing the relation between economic variables, such as the price of a good and the quantity of the good that people are willing to purchase. There are many such pairs of variables in economics: the costs of production and the level of output, the rate of inflation and the level of unemployment, the interest rate and the supply of capital goods, for example. Graphs are the most concise means of expressing the variety of relations that exist between such variables.

Figure 1 illustrates these ideas. It is a bar graph that shows the relation between the U.S. gross national product (GNP), a measure of the value of all goods and services produced annually, and time, in this case, the period between 1960 and 1990. The GNP variable is plotted along the vertical line on the left side of the graph. The time variable is plotted along the horizontal line at the bottom of the graph. From this graph you can roughly estimate the level of GNP for each year between 1960 and 1990. For instance, GNP in 1967 was somewhere around $800 billion. You can also see that GNP tended to increase over the years 1960–1990. By working with the graph, you could estimate the rate of increase of GNP from year to year or the percentage increase over a particular period, such as 1965–1970.

This one concise picture—the graph—contains a great deal of information. Aside from economy of expression, graphs have a great deal of cognitive appeal: People can more easily grasp concepts demonstrated through pictures than concepts demonstrated through words.

Some of the graphs in this book are bar graphs; many others use the Cartesian coordinate system, which consists of points plotted on a grid formed by the intersection of two perpendicular lines. See Figure 2. The horizontal line is the **x-axis,** and the vertical line is the **y-axis.** The intersection of the two lines is the point 0, called the *origin.* Above the origin on the vertical axis, all values are positive. Below the origin on the vertical axis, all values are negative. Values to the right of the origin are positive; values to the left are negative. The economic variables we use in this book are usually positive; that is, to plot economic relations we will usually use the upper-right portion, or quadrant, of a graph such as the one in Figure 3.

FIGURE 1

This graph shows the levels of U.S. GNP between the years 1960 and 1990 at five-year intervals. (1990 figure is an estimate.)

Source: Council of Economic Advisers, *Economic Report of the President* (Washington, D.C.: U.S. Government Printing Office, 1990) p. 294.

A Bar Graph

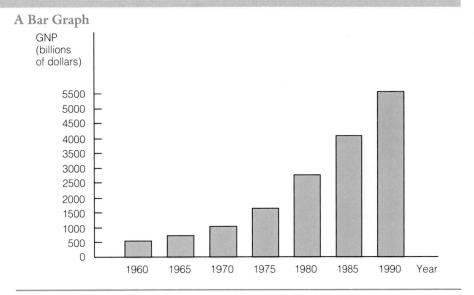

FIGURE 2

Any pair of numerical values can be plotted on this grid. The upper-right quadrant, shaded here, is the portion of the graph most often used in economics.

A Grid for Plotting Graphs

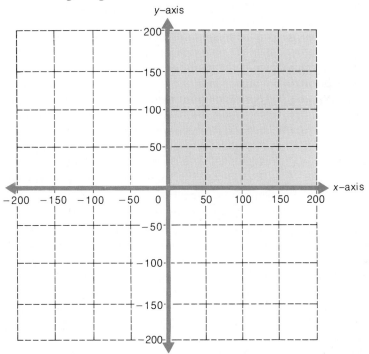

FIGURE 3

A Simple Line (or Linear) Graph

Curve *AE* shows the essential relation between two sets of variables: the number of words memorized and the number of minutes spent memorizing. The relation is positive; as the variable on the *x*-axis increases or decreases, the variable on the *y*-axis increases or decreases, respectively. A positive relation is shown by an upward-sloping line tracing the intersection of each pair of variables.

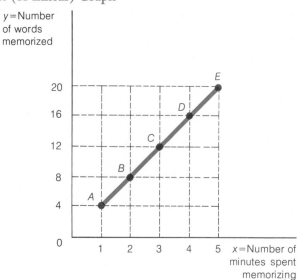

HOW TO DRAW A GRAPH

Suppose you wish to graph the relation between two variables. Variable *y* is the number of words memorized, and variable *x* is the number of minutes spent memorizing words. Table 2 presents a set, or schedule, of hypothetical data for these two variables.

We can plot the data from Table 2 on a graph using points in the upper-right quadrant formed by the *x*-axis and the *y*-axis. See Figure 3. The variable, number of words memorized, is measured along the *y*-axis and is considered the *y* value. The variable, number of minutes spent memorizing, is measured along the *x*-axis and is the *x* value. From the data in Table 2 we see that each increase of 1 minute of memorizing resulted in 4 more memorized words. The graph in Figure 3 illustrates this relation.

The points marked as large dots in Figure 3 represent pairs of variables. Point *A* represents the pair on the first line of Table 2: 4 words and 1 minute. Point *B* represents 8 words and 2 minutes, and so on. When we connect the points, we have a straight line running upward and to the right of the origin. Lines showing the intersection of *x*- and *y*-values

on a graph are referred to as **curves** in this book, whether they are straight or curved lines.

Curves show two types of relations between variables: positive and negative. The relation between the *x* and *y* values in Figure 3 is positive: as the *x* value increases, so does the *y* value. (Or, as the *x* value decreases, the *y* value decreases. Either way, the relation is positive.) On a graph, a **positive,** or **direct, relation** is shown by a curve that slopes upward and to the right of the origin. In a **negative,** or **inverse, relation,** the two variables change in op-

TABLE 2
Schedule of Hypothetical Data

Number of Words Memorized (*y*)	Number of Minutes Spent Memorizing (*x*)
4	1
8	2
12	3
16	4
20	5

posite directions. An increase in *y* is paired with a decrease in *x*. Or a decrease in *x* is paired with an increase in *y*. Figure 4 shows a negative, or inverse, relation on a graph. The curve for a negative relation slopes downward from left to right—the opposite of a positive relation.

General Relations

Throughout this book, some graphs display general relations rather than specific relations. A general relation does not depend on particular numerical values of variables, as was the case in Figure 3. For example, the relation between the number of calories a person consumes per week and that person's weight (other things being equal) is positive. This suggests an upward-sloping line, as shown in Figure 5a, with calories on the *x*-axis and weight on the *y*-axis. Figure 5 represents a general relation, so it does not need numerical values on either axis. It does not specify the particular number of calories required to maintain a particular body weight; it simply shows that an increase in the number of calories consumed increases body weight. Figure 5b shows an inverse relation between body weight and the amount of exercise per week, again a general relation. Sometimes two variables are not related. Figure 5c shows that a person's weight is independent of a neighbor's caloric intake. Thankfully, no matter how much your neighbor eats, it has no effect on your weight.

At this point you should be able to construct a graph showing simple relations. For example, graph the relation between the weight of a car and the miles per gallon it achieves or between the length of the line at the school cafeteria and the time of day. If the relationship between any two variables you select is a straight line, it is said to be **linear.** A linear relationship means that for every unit change (increase or decrease) in one of the variables (the weight of a car), the other variable (miles per gallon of gasoline) changes (increases or decreases) by some fixed amount.

Nonlinear Relations

Often, relations between two variables are not the simple linear relationships depicted in Figures 3, 4, and 5. For example, unlike in Figure 3 where each additional minute spent studying enables one to memorize 4 additional words, it may be that the number of additional words memorized changes as the number of minutes changes. Such a **nonlinear** relationship is depicted in Figure 6. There, 1 minute of studying enables a student to memorize 6 words, but 2 minutes of studying enables a student

FIGURE 4   A Negative Relation Between Two Variables

As the price of a cup of coffee increases, the number of cups drunk each day decreases. When variables move in opposite directions, their relation is negative, or inverse. Negative relations are shown by a curve that slopes downward and to the right of the origin.

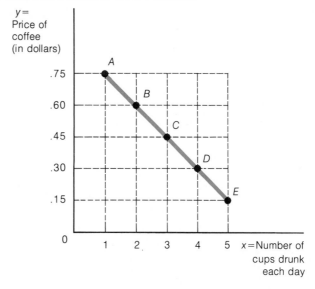

FIGURE 5   General Graphical Relations

General relations are (a) positive, (b) inverse, or (c) independent. General relations are not measured numerically on the y- or x-axis.

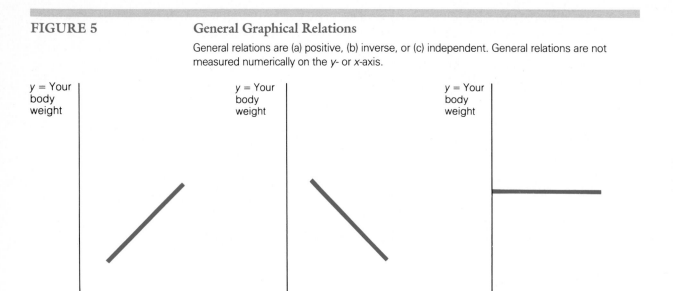

(a)   (b)   (c)

to memorize only 11 words—the second minute adds only 5 additional words to the total. Additional minutes of studying beyond 2 lead to even smaller increases in the total number of words memorized. Therefore, there is a positive relationship between the two variables, but the relationship is *nonlinear.*

Occasionally nonlinear relations are more complex than the one depicted in Figure 6 and do not fall into the simple category of positive or negative. Figure 7 shows that for some relatively low x values, the variables on the graph are positively related, but as the x value increases, a point is reached where the two variables become inversely related. In Figure 7 from the origin to x^* the curve slopes positively. But for values greater than x^*, the curve slopes negatively. To illustrate, we let the x-axis show the number of pieces of pizza that a friend consumes in an evening and the y-axis show the total amount of pleasure she receives from each additional slice. At first, the more she eats, the happier she becomes, but eventually a critical point is reached, after which the more she eats, the less pleasure she receives from each additional slice.

FIGURE 6
A Nonlinear Graph

Curve *AE* shows the nonlinear relation between the number of minutes spent studying and the number of words memorized.

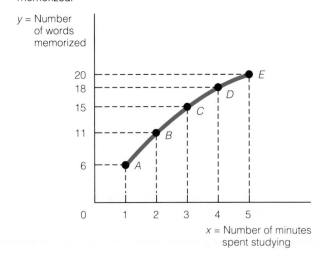

FIGURE 7

For lower values of x—in this example, the number of pizza slices eaten—the y value—the amount of satisfaction—increases. After some point, say 3 slices, the y value decreases with increasing values of x.

Variables Both Positively and Negatively Related

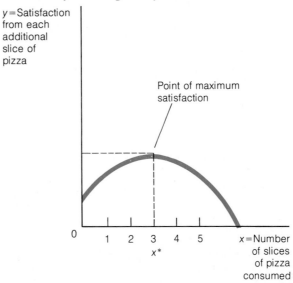

FIGURE 8

Some relations yield a U shape. Variables along the x- and y-axes are inversely related at first, but after some critical value, here shown as x*, they become positively related.

A U-shaped Curve

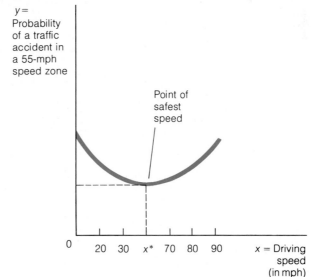

Many other relations can exist. A U-shaped curve, as graphed in Figure 8, shows that the x value is at first inversely related to the y value and then positively related. After some critical value, x^*, the y value begins to rise as the x value increases. The y-axis in this example might represent the probability of having an accident on an interstate highway and the x-axis might show the miles per hour at which a car travels. To avoid accidents, x^* is the optimal, or "best," speed. Driving at speeds lower than x^* increases the probability of an accident, but rates faster than x^* mph also increase the chances of an accident.

SLOPE OF THE CURVE

In graphical analysis the amount by which the y value increases or decreases as the result of an increase or decrease in the x value is the **slope** of the curve. The slope of the curve is an important concept in economics. Much economic analysis studies the margin of change in a variable or in a relation between variables, and the slope of a curve mea-

sures the marginal rate of change. In Figure 3, for example, every change in the x value—every increase of 1 minute—is associated with an increase of 4 words memorized. The slope of the curve in Figure 3 is the rate of change. Economists express the concept "change in" with the symbol Δ. So in Figure 3 the slope of the line AE is $\Delta y/\Delta x$, or $4/1 = 4$.

For the straight-line curves in Figures 3 and 4, the slope is constant. Along most curves, however, the slope is not constant. In Figure 8, an increase in driving speed from 55 to 60 mph may increase the probability of an accident only slightly, but an increase from 60 to 65 mph may increase the probability by a greater amount. Not only does the probability increase for each mile-per-hour increase in driving speed, but it increases by a greater amount. This indicates that the slope not only is positive but also is increasing.

The slope of a curved line is different at every point along the line. To find the slope of a curved line at a particular point, draw a straight line tangent to the curve. (A tangent touches the curve at one point without crossing the curve.) Consider point A in Figure 9. The slope at A on the curved

---

FIGURE 9   Slope Along a Curve

The slope of a curve at a particular point is the slope of a straight line tangent to the curve at that point.

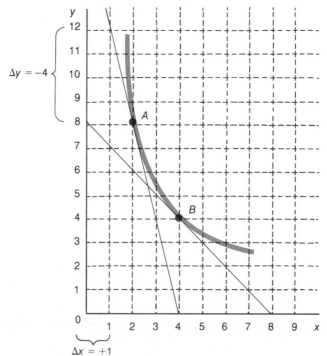

FIGURE 10   A Curve with an Increasing Slope

As the *x* variable increases, the change in the *y* variable increases.

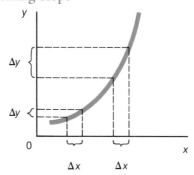

line is equal to the slope of the straight line tangent to the curved line. Dividing the change in the *y* variable (Δ*y*) by the change in the *x* variable (Δ*x*) yields the slope at *A*. In Figure 9, every change in *x* from 0 to 1 and 1 to 2, and so on, results in a change in *y* along the curve. At point *A,* the change in *y* = −4. So Δ*y*/Δ*x* = −4/1 = −4. At lower points along the curve, such as *B*, the curve is flatter—that is, less steep. The line tangent at *B* has a slope of −1. As we move from point *A* to point *B*, equal increases in *x* result in smaller and smaller decreases in *y*. In other words, the *rate* at which *y* falls decreases as *x* increases along this particular curve.

Other relations lead to different slopes and different changes in the slope along the curve. Along the curve in Figure 10, not only does the *y* value increase as the *x* value increases but the slope increases as the *x* value increases. For equal increases in the *x* value, the incremental changes in the *y* value become larger.

Interpreting the essential concepts illustrated in graphs is a necessary part of learning economic principles. Should you encounter difficulty in interpreting any of the graphs in later chapters, a brief review of this Appendix will prove helpful.

SUMMARY

1. Graphs are a concise expression of economic models, or theories. Graphs usually show the relation between two variables, such as price and quantity.
2. Linear graphs are drawn with two perpendicular lines, called axes. The *x*-axis is a horizontal line. Variables measured along the *x*-axis are called *x* values. The *y*-axis is a vertical line. Variables along it are called *y* values.
3. Lines showing the correlation between *x* and *y* values are called curves. An upward-sloping curve indicates a positive, or direct, relation between variables: As the *x* value increases or decreases, the *y* value does likewise. A downward-sloping curve indicates a negative, or inverse, relation between variables: As the *x* value increases, the *y* value decreases and vice versa.

4. Relations between variables may be specific or general. Specific relations are based on numerical quantities measured on either the *x*- or *y*-axis or both. General relations are not based on specific numerical quantities.
5. Relations between two variables can be either linear or nonlinear.
6. Variables can be both positively and negatively related. In such complex relations, the curve is either bow-shaped or U-shaped.
7. The slope of a curve measures the ratio of change in the *x* value to changes in the *y* value, expressed as Δ*y*/Δ*x*. Along a straight-line curve, the slope is constant. Along a curved line, the slope is different at every point.

Key terms

x-axis, y-axis

curve

positive, or direct, relation

negative, or inverse, relation

linear relation

nonlinear relation

slope

Questions for review and discussion

1. Explain how the slope of a line tells you whether the relation between the two variables illustrated is direct or inverse. If you drew a line illustrating your score on a history test as you study more hours, which would its slope be?

2. Plot the following points on a graph with X on the horizontal axis and Y on the vertical axis. Connect the dots to show the relation between X and Y.

	X	Y
A	0	2
B	2	4
C	4	8
D	6	14
E	8	22

What is the slope of the line between the points A and B? What is the slope between C and D? Is this a straight line?

3. Curves can be represented in algebraic form by an equation. For example, the points along a certain line can be demonstrated by the equation

$$Y = 10 - 2X.$$

The value of Y can be found by inserting different values of X and solving the equation for Y. Some of the values of Y for different values of X are shown in the following table. Fill in the blanks by solving the equation for the values of Y for each value of X given.

X	Y
0	10
2	6
4	—
6	—
8	—
10	—
12	—

Draw this set of points on a graph. Does this show a direct or inverse relation between X and Y? What is the slope of this line between the first and second points? Between the second and third? Is this a straight line?

4. If you measured body weight on the horizontal axis and the probability of dying of heart disease on the vertical axis, what would be the slope of a curve that showed the relation between these two variables?

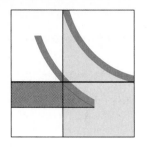

2

Economic Principles

The essence of the economic problem is how to get as much value as we can from limited and costly resources. To do so, we constantly make choices. One college student may choose to spend a weekend at the beach rather than buy a new sweater and skirt. Another may choose to sleep late rather than attend an eight o'clock chemistry class. Every choice must be made at some cost.

Economists emphasize that decisions to use scarce resources bear an opportunity cost. The **opportunity cost** of a decision is the next most preferred or next-best alternative to a good or activity (the new clothes or the class instruction) that one must forgo in order to obtain some other good (a beach weekend or extra sleep). Economists have developed tools for expressing the choice and opportunity cost that are central to all decisions. After reading Chapter 2 you should understand

- how individuals and societies actually make decisions given that they are always costly.
- how individuals make practical decisions, since all-or-nothing choices are rare.
- how specialization and trade increase quantities of output for parties who exchange goods and services.
- how exchange, transaction costs, and other barriers reduce the benefits from specializing and trade.

Opportunity cost:
The highest-valued alternative forgone in making any choice.

OPPORTUNITY COST: THE INDIVIDUAL MUST CHOOSE

Suppose that a student is trying to decide what to do with 4 hours of time on a Sunday evening. One alternative is to work at the library, where the student earns $4 per hour. The other choice is studying for an economics quiz to be given Monday morning. The student views these two activities as the highest-valued uses of the 4 hours of time on Sunday evening. Table 1 depicts five different ways the student can allocate the 4 hours of time. Also depicted are

TABLE 1   **The Individual Chooses: Working or Studying**

Individuals must make choices from many alternatives available. In this example, the individual has choice options involving various combinations of studying and working in the library. These options range from no studying and all work to no work and all studying, with various other options in between these two. The trade-off involved in these choices is clear—more work (and more income) comes at the expense of less study time and a lower grade, and vice versa.

Choice of Time Allocation	Income Earned (in dollars)	Grade Earned (in percent)
(1) 0 hours working, 4 hours studying	0	100
(2) 1 hour working, 3 hours studying	4	90
(3) 2 hours working, 2 hours studying	8	75
(4) 3 hours working, 1 hour studying	12	55
(5) 4 hours working, 0 hours studying	16	0

five different combinations of income earned and percentage quiz scores the student could "produce" with the five different allocations of time. Choice (1), no work and 4 hours of study, yields the student a perfect quiz score but no income. Choice (2), allocating 1 hour to library work and 3 hours to study, produces an income of $4 and a score of 90 percent. The third, fourth, and fifth alternative choices mean still more income but lower quiz scores. Choice (5) involves no study time at all—and a score of 0 percent—but the student earns the highest income possible for the evening's work, $16.

Table 1 sets forth an important point. The student must spend time working and studying to obtain some income and a positive quiz score. The student's scarce resource, time, is used to produce two economic goods, grades and income.

Consider the two right-hand columns in Table 1. These two columns show the five different combinations of income and grades that the student can obtain from allocating the evening's available 4 hours of time five different ways. In Figure 1 these combinations are plotted as black dots and connected with a smooth curve. Choice (3) from Table 1, $8 of income and a score of 75 percent, is shown as point (3) in Figure 1. This particular combination of goods produced implies 2 hours of time allocated to library work and 2 hours to study.

Several aspects of Figure 1 are important. *All possible combinations* of income and quiz scores that the student could conceivably earn are represented by the curved line. This means that the choices between working and studying are *continuous*. Continuous choice implies that the five combinations in Table 1 are not the only ones available with 4 hours of time. The student could choose any combination of income and quiz score that together required 4 hours of time to produce—say, $2 of income for ½ hour worked and a score of 95 percent with 3½ hours of study. If choices were *discrete*, the student would be limited to only the five choices labeled (1) through (5). (Discrete

FIGURE 1

As the hours spent working increase, the score on the economics quiz falls.

The Individual Chooses: Income or Grades

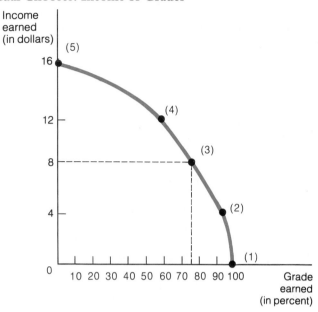

choices are fixed in number.) For convenience, economists ordinarily assume that economic relations are continuous.

A second crucial point is that Figure 1 and Table 1 constitute what economists call a *model*. Economists construct models to isolate specific phenomena for study. The model summarized in Figure 1 and Table 1 assumes a number of things about the student in the example. First, as just explained, the choices are continuous rather than discrete. Second, we assume as given that the total amount of time that the student has available for both activities combined is fixed—in this case, 4 hours. The general relationship governing the amount of time put into an activity and the resultant amount of the activity produced is also assumed given. Each hour worked yields $4 and only $4 of income. The first hour of study always yields a score of 55 percent, never 60 or 50 percent. Two hours of study produce a grade of 75 percent, not 74 or 76 percent. Other factors, such as the total amount of time the student has already put into the course before Sunday evening and the student's IQ, are assumed given. Does the student have the flu, a factor that would detract from performance on the quiz? Is the income more important to the student than the economics quiz? Are there other alternatives such as washing a car or spending time in language lab? Is the fact that one alternative has a future payoff, such as a job, relevant to the choice? Certainly matters such as these are significant, but we assume them as given with respect to the choice at hand.

Economists also emphasize that the decision to study or to work is made at the margin. Practically, making decisions at the margin means that we are faced not only with all-or-nothing choices but also with degrees of balancing units of one choice against another. Each choice would be made in terms of the costs of an additional hour of study or work forgone. Satisfactions from both activities are thus balanced **at the margin.** For example, suppose the

Choices at the margin: Decisions based on the additional benefits and costs of small changes in a particular activity.

student had originally planned on working 2 hours and studying 2 hours. This division of the evening's time would produce $8 of income and a grade of 75 percent on the economics quiz. Suppose the student considers choosing to earn $4 more income. This would entail working 1 additional hour, which means studying 1 less hour. A reallocation of the time resource means that a quiz grade of 55 percent will be earned rather than 75 percent. The student must make a decision at the margin. Does the additional satisfaction of the extra $4 of income outweigh the quiz score falling by 20 percentage points? The drop of 20 points is the opportunity cost of choosing to earn an additional $4 (whether or not the extra $4 is "worth it" to the student is a question to be addressed in Chapter 6).

In making decisions at the margin we assume that all other factors are equal, or fixed. Each time we make a decision some fixed or given factors resulting from previous decisions come into play. In our example, the student would weigh, for instance, the amount of previous study, a fixed factor in choosing work or study on the evening in question.

Previous decisions cannot be changed and are gone forever, but that does not mean that they have no impact on current choices. It simply means that we make choices in the present with unchangeable past choices as given and unalterable. This is another aspect of making choices at the margin.

OPPORTUNITY COST AND PRODUCTION POSSIBILITIES: SOCIETY MUST CHOOSE

So far we have focused on individual choices, but the same principles apply to society's choices. Just as an individual is limited by the scarcity of time in choosing among options, society is constrained by scarce resources in producing and consuming alternative goods. Let us examine an abstract example. Suppose a society produces only two goods—oranges and peanut butter—and that all its resources and technology are fixed and constant in amount and level.

Given the state of technology and assuming that the society uses all its resources, the society could produce either 100 million jars of peanut butter or 16 million tons of oranges (see Table 2). Or the society may choose to

TABLE 2

Society Decides: Oranges or Peanut Butter

Society must choose among many alternative combinations of goods to produce. The cost of one good is the lost production of other goods.

Choice	Peanut Butter (millions of jars)	Oranges (millions of tons)
A	100	0
B	90	4
C	75	8
D	50	12
E	0	16

devote some of its resources to producing peanut butter and some to producing oranges. These choices, called society's *production possibilities,* are listed *A–E* in Table 2. From this information a production possibilities curve can be constructed (see Figure 2). A production possibilities curve depicts the alternatives open to society for the production of two goods, given full utilization of all existing resources, human and nonhuman, and an existing state of technology. When resources are fully employed, moreover, society is said to be producing on its **production possibilities frontier.**

At choice *A* in Figure 2, society produces 100 million jars of peanut butter and no oranges, while at choice *E* society uses all its resources in orange production. Choices in between, with some of both commodities produced, are shown at points *B, C,* and *D.* Continuous choices of all other possible combinations are shown along the curve; resources are assumed to be fully employed at all points on the curve. The curve therefore shows all of the possibilities for the production of oranges and peanut butter, assuming resources are fully employed. Points such as *G* lie beyond the production possibilities frontier. The country's resources and technology do not permit it to produce at points such as *G* that lie outside the frontier.

Production possibilities frontier:
The curve that graphs all the possible combinations of two goods that an economic entity can produce given the available technology, the amount of productive resources available, and the fact that these resources are fully utilized.

The Law of Increasing Costs

Just as there was an opportunity cost to the student in choosing to study for the quiz or to work in the library, there is an opportunity cost for society in any choice between producing oranges and peanut butter.

Consider a society that produces nothing but peanut butter, choice *A* in Figure 2. The opportunity cost of that choice is that no oranges can be produced. A move to choice *B,* representing a shift of some resources from

FIGURE 2   **Production Possibilities Curve**

As more and more oranges are produced, the opportunity cost per orange increases. The opportunity cost of producing the first 4 million tons of oranges is 10 million jars of peanut butter. The opportunity cost of producing the next 4 million tons of oranges is an additional 15 million jars of peanut butter, and so on.

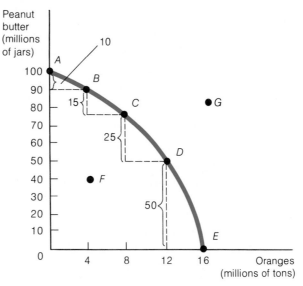

peanut butter production to orange production, means a sacrifice of 10 million jars of peanut butter, but society gains 4 million tons of oranges. Thus the opportunity cost of producing the first 4 million tons of oranges is 10 million jars of peanut butter. To get the second 4 million tons of oranges, however, a larger quantity of peanut butter must be given up—15 million jars. Thus as society becomes more specialized in production of either oranges or peanut butter, the opportunity cost per unit of the good rises. This effect is called the **law of increasing costs.**

Law of increasing costs: As more scarce resources are used to produce additional units of one good, production of the other good falls by larger and larger amounts.

Why does the law of increasing costs hold? Resources, training, and talents are not all alike and are not perfectly adaptable to alternative uses. Land suited to orange growing is not equally suited to peanut farming and vice versa. Orange pickers are not equally adept at the manufacture of metal lids for peanut butter jars or even peanut farming without additional training. The most-suited human and nonhuman resources are moved into production first, but as production of a good increases and becomes more specialized, less-adaptable resources must be used to produce it. The costs of producing additional units of the good rise because it requires larger amounts of these increasingly less-adaptable resources to produce each successive unit. This means that greater quantities of another good do not get produced and must therefore be sacrificed in the process. A society of peanut butter lovers might be growing peanuts in greenhouses in North Dakota, and concert pianists and nuclear technicians might be operating machinery in peanut butter processing plants.

Unemployment of Resources

The law of increasing costs always applies when resources are fully employed. When there is a degree of **unemployment of resources,** however—such as a certain amount of land lying idle—society finds itself producing at a point *within* the production possibilities curve. Point *F* in Figure 2 represents such a situation. From point *F* to the curve, additional oranges or peanut butter can be produced without any increase in opportunity costs until resources become fully employed. The production possibilities curve is thus referred to as a *frontier* because it represents full employment of resources. Full employment means that society is realizing its maximum output potential. Many economic problems are the result of unemployment.

Unemployment of resources: A situation in which some human and/or nonhuman resources that can be used in production are not used.

Choices Are Made at the Margin

As with individuals, society's choices are made at the margin. Suppose, for example, that a society has for years been one of peanut butter lovers and orange haters. Suppose further that long-time devotion of society's resources to peanut butter production "warped" resources—made them more adaptable over time—to peanut butter production. Past decisions to warp the resources would make current additional orange production more costly. A sudden decision by society to produce more oranges would have to be made at the present—not some past—margin. Thus past decisions obviously affect current costs, but past decisions cannot be changed.

WHY THE PRODUCTION POSSIBILITIES FRONTIER SHIFTS

If we keep in mind the meaning of the production possibilities frontier, we will also understand that an increase or decrease in society's human or non-human resources can shift society's output potential. An understanding of such changes is central to the understanding of economic growth—or the lack of it.

The Shifting Frontier

The production possibilities frontier can only shift leftward or rightward in response to any change in the quantity of human resources, any change in the quantity of nonhuman resources, or any change in technology. Changes in these factors shift the production possibilities frontier because we previously assumed they were constant.

Suppose a technological improvement occurs in peanut butter production that increases the productivity of peanut harvesters—perhaps a fertilizer or new crop techniques. In such a case, society's production possibilities relating to peanut butter are increased without a similar decrease in orange production. The result is a shift rightward on the peanut butter end of the production possibilities curve. Such a change is shown in Figure 3a as a shift from the PP_1 curve to the PP_2 curve.

In Figure 3b, a productivity change brought about by technological improvement occurs in orange production. Here the production possibilities curve shifts rightward on the orange end; if society prefers, additional oranges can be produced without any sacrifice of peanut butter.

In Figure 3c, a general change in productivity, technology, or resource supply is assumed. An increase in the quantity of labor (through a simple growth in population), for example, shifts the entire production possibilities frontier rightward from PP_1 to PP_2. Suppose society now chooses the peanut butter/orange combination A_1. More of both goods are produced and consumed as a result of the technological improvement. But society faces new trade-offs once it is producing on its new frontier. Opportunity costs arise again in resource utilization, just as they did at combination A on production possibility curve PP_1. Society cannot escape scarcity, yet it can improve its production possibilities through growth in technology, quantity of human or nonhuman resources, or resource productivity.

Economic Growth: How Economies Progress

We can understand the nature of economic growth with the aid of the production possibilities curve model. The key to economic growth in society is related to the growth or change in capital stock and other crucial resources.

The creation of **capital stock** (a supply of items used to produce other items) takes time and bears an opportunity cost in present consumption. The benefits of creating capital, however, are in increased amounts of future consumption. In other words, forming new capital stock requires that people save—that is, abstain from consuming in the present. When investment in

Capital stock:
The amount of nonhuman resources available in the economy. These include tools, land, machinery, equipment, and so on.

FIGURE 3   Shifting the Production Possibilities Frontier

(a) A technological improvement in peanut butter production shifts the production possibilities curve outward at the peanut butter end. (b) A technological improvement in orange production shifts the production possibilities curve outward at the orange end. (c) A general increase in technology or resource supply shifts the entire production possibilities curve outward.

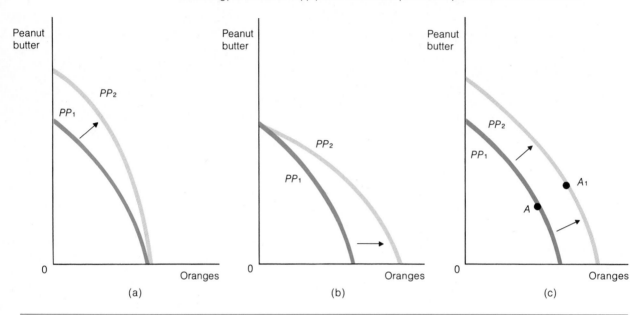

Economic growth:
A permanent increase in the productive capacity of the economy.

capital stock results from this saving, capital formation and growth occur. The formation of capital goods—tools, tractors, computers and so on—requires a redirection of resources from consumption of goods to production of capital goods. The opportunity cost of acquiring capital is thus consumption goods forgone, but the reward for society is an increase in future productive capacity in consumption goods, capital goods, or both.

We can illustrate this phenomenon with the production possibilities curve. Figure 4 shows two production possibilities frontiers that contrast capital goods production (the vertical axis) with consumption goods production (the horizontal axis) for two hypothetical societies with initially similar production possibilities curves. Consider society A's choice of consumption and capital goods in 1990, represented by point E_A in Figure 4a. Clearly, society A devotes a larger proportion of its resources to capital goods production than to consumption goods production. Saving (abstaining from current consumption), investing, and capital formation are all high in that society. The payoff for society A will come later, say in 2000, with vastly enlarged productive capacity, designated by the shift of the production possibilities curve to PP_{2000} in Figure 4a.

Society B chooses to use almost all of its resources in 1990 for consumption goods, with only a small quantity of resources devoted to capital goods, a combination represented by point F_B in Figure 4b. The consequence of this choice is low economic growth over the following decade. By 2000, the production possibilities of that society have grown by only a small amount, as curve PP_{2000} in Figure 4b indicates. Thus **economic growth** in the future is

FIGURE 4   Growth Choices on the Production Possibilities Curve

(a) By producing more capital goods, E_A, in 1990, society A can produce more consumption goods in the future than (b) society B, which produces only F_B capital goods in 1990.

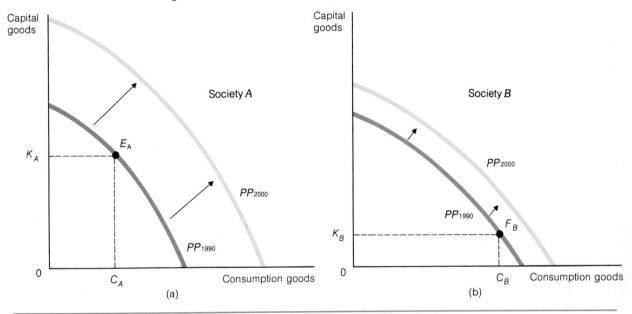

(a)   (b)

largely determined by current decisions about production. Technological changes are important factors in the progress of society, but to take advantage of technology, society must sacrifice some present consumption. (See Focus, "How Societies Can Regress and Progress: Black Death in the Middle Ages.")

In addition to choosing to put some resources into the creation of capital stock, societies can increase their output by specializing in and trading, or exchanging, goods and services. **Specialization** simply means that the tasks associated with the production of a product or service are divided—and sometimes subdivided—and performed by many different individuals to increase the total production of the good or service. The principles of specialization are therefore related to how all societies and economic organizations try to overcome the basic problem of scarcity.

Specialization:
An economic entity producing only one good or service or the performance of a single task in a production process by an individual.

SPECIALIZATION AND TRADE: A FEATURE OF ALL SOCIETIES

Virtually all known peoples have engaged in specialization and trade, and theories and principles related to specialization and trade have been part of economists' tool kits for more than two hundred years. Adam Smith (1723–1790), the Scottish philosopher and recognized founder of economics, published his great work *An Inquiry into the Nature and Causes of the Wealth of Nations* in 1776 (a year of declarations). It formally established the science of what we now call economics. (For more on Adam Smith, see Point-Counterpoint, pp. 142–144.)

FOCUS   How Societies Can Regress and Progress:
Black Death in the Middle Ages

As we know from the ancient Greek and Roman experiences, civilization and its production possibilities can decline or be lost. Perhaps the greatest calamity ever visited on the Western world was the bubonic plague—the so-called Black Death. Between 1347 and 1350, rats infested with plague-ridden fleas spread death throughout Europe; between 33 percent and 65 percent of the population perished.

In 1300, before the Black Death, Europe's production possibilities (even given feudal institutions and technology) were considerably larger than after the catastrophe. The Black Death, by decimating a large percentage of the working population, reduced the production possibilities frontier of European society. It did not, however, eliminate the trade-off between consumer goods (goods in the present) and capital goods (goods for producing more goods in the future). (See Figure 5.)

Since labor had been cheap and plentiful relative to other resources before the plague, agricultural methods had been oriented to the large, untrained labor supply. The scarceness of labor following the plague—even given the smaller number of mouths to feed—meant society had to devote a large proportion of its resources to consumption goods (such as food) to survive. In 1350, European society was forced to a point such as B on the innermost production possibilities curve in Figure 5.

Relatively expensive labor, brought about by the general population reduction, meant that businesses "economized" or "rationed" labor by trying to substitute capital and other resources for it. In this process, many "labor-saving" inventions were discovered (new uses for water power, new agricultural implements, and so on). Later, steam power supplemented or replaced water power. The Black Death of the fourteenth century may have ultimately made the production possibilities curve PP_{1700} possible for Europeans.[a] At points such as C on the furthermost production possibilities curve in Figure 5, the choices available to society between

FIGURE 5
Production Possibilities and the Black Death

The loss of labor resources caused by the bubonic plague shifts the production possibilities curve toward the origin for 1350. Technological advances in and inventions of labor-saving capital, in part created by the shortage of labor, created a huge rightward shift in the production possibilities curve by 1700—the beginning of the Industrial Revolution.

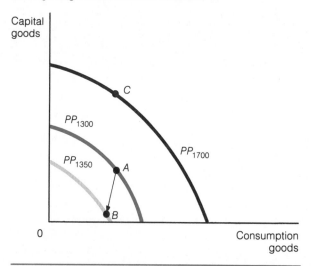

consumer and capital goods were greatly enhanced. It is an ill wind that does not blow some good ultimately (somewhere).

[a]This position is developed in Charles Maurice and Charles W. Smithson, *The Doomsday Myth: 10,000 Years of Economic Crises* (Stanford: Hoover Institution Press, 1984), pp. 86–91.

At the very core of economics, according to Smith, is the ability of individuals and societies to deal with the facts of scarcity through specialization and trade. In the *Wealth of Nations,* Smith used the example of a pin factory, a seemingly trivial manufacturing activity he had observed directly, to evaluate specialization. Smith observed that pin making was no longer a trade peculiar to a single individual but instead was "divided into a number of branches, of which the greater part are likewise peculiar trades."[1] Straighten-

---

[1]Adam Smith, *An Inquiry into the Nature and Causes of the Wealth of Nations,* ed. Edwin Cannan (1776; reprint, New York: Modern Library, 1937), pp. 4–5.

ing wire, cutting it, putting a point on it, constructing a head to the pin, and inserting the pins into paper for ease in handling were all separate "trades" performed by individuals. (Smith, in fact, counted up eighteen distinct operations in some pin factories.)

How does Smith's description of a pin factory promote an understanding of output growth? Smith's point is that when tasks are divided, permitting each individual to concentrate on a single element in the production of a good, output increases over what it would be if each individual produced the entire good. Specialization and the **division of labor** led to increased output. As a result, people became more dependent on one another for all goods. We may work in an automobile plant, for example, but we still want eggs for breakfast. Smith recognized that mutual dependence could be a problem but thought that the potential for increased output with given resources was well worth the cost.

If an analysis of a pin factory does not stir your imagination, think of any organization and try to list the number of distinct divisions of labor in it. Think of a larger factory, a steel mill, a football team, a fraternity, a church. Specialization exists in almost everything we do. (See Focus, "Economic Specialization in Everyday Life: Marriage and Roommate Selection," for illustrations.)

All modern nations, states, firms, and individuals specialize in the production of economic goods and services, in varying degrees. The individual, the most basic economic entity, specializes to the greatest extent. Your teacher for this course specializes in economic research and teaching. Other people specialize in mechanical engineering services or in breeding thoroughbred racehorses. Some businesses produce only one product, whereas others offer a multitude. One very critical point must be made about all specialization and trade—it is as significant as having more and better resources or improved production techniques. As Smith noted, specialization and division of labor leads to increased output and it does so without any additional resources. The gains from specializing in and exchanging goods and services are, in effect, *equivalent* to acquiring or developing additional natural resources or capital.

The notion of specialization can also be applied to entire nations. Table 3 shows that large percentages of many of the goods consumed by Americans are obtained from other countries. For commodities like crude rubber and diamonds, there is no domestic production; the entire supply is imported. While nations specialize in the production of a multitude of goods, patterns of specialization across countries may be observed nonetheless. Exotic spices are not commercially grown in Canada, for example, although they *could* be grown there with greenhouses, sufficient heating expenditures, and so on. Canada does produce a fair proportion of the world's wheat. Likewise, no fine silk is produced on the tiny Caribbean island of Grenada, but nutmeg and other spices are. The explanation for such general production patterns across countries and more complete patterns of specialization among individuals resides in concepts that are at the very core of economics—comparative advantage, specialization, and trade.

Comparative Advantage

While Adam Smith developed the fundamentals underlying specialization and trade, it was left to his English followers David Ricardo (1772–1823) and Robert Torrens (1780–1864) to develop the critically important principle of

Division of labor:
Individual specialization in separate tasks involved with a production process; the result of specialization.

TABLE 3

Selected Imports and Exports as a Percentage of the U.S. Market

A look at leading U.S. exports and imports provides an indication of how specialization and trade apply to every country of the world. The nature of these tradables changes over time with shifting comparative advantage. (Data are for 1976.)

Industry	Exports as a Percentage of Output	Industry	Imports as a Percentage of New Supply
Wheat	66%	Crude rubber	100%
Oilfield machinery	63	Diamonds	100
Missiles, space vehicles	62	Bauxite	94
Milled rice	58	Crude petroleum	53
Medicinals, botanicals	47	Motorcycles, bicycles, and parts	51
Construction machinery	43	Finfish, shellfish	47
Aircraft	41	Potash	47
Corn	39	Raincoats	47
Soybeans	38	Zinc	47
Tobacco	37	Radios and TVs	43
Pulpmill products*	35	Iron ore	39
Solid-state semiconductor devices	34	Pulpmill products*	33
Turbines	32	Watches and clocks	32
Cotton farm products	29	Textile machinery*	30
Textile machinery*	28	Sugar	29
Electronic computing machinery	26	Women's shoes	27
Industrial trucks, tractors	20	Passenger cars	20

Source: U.S. Department of Commerce, Bureau of the Census, *U.S. Commodity Exports and Imports as Related to Output, 1976 and 1975* (Washington, D.C.: Government Printing Office, 1980), pp. 1–4.

*Note that textile machinery and pulpmill products are significant on both sides of the international market.

specialization—the theory of comparative advantage. Comparative advantage (and its relation to specialization and trade) is best understood with a simple, hypothetical example. Table 4 describes three production combinations of silver and lumber for two different locales, Canada and Mexico. The production possibilities information in Table 4 is reproduced graphically in Figure 6. The production possibilities curves of Figure 6 do not look exactly like the production possibilities curves we have discussed so far. For simplicity, we have temporarily assumed that the law of increasing costs does not hold in the two locales—at least not where lumber and silver production are concerned. Instead, we assume that in each locale both silver and lumber production are subject to constant opportunity costs of production.

Table 4 indicates that production of the first 30,000 ounces of silver in Canada means 300,000 board-feet of lumber do not get produced. Moving from point *A* to point *B* on Canada's production possibilities curve reduces the production of lumber from 1 million to 700,000 board-feet. In such a move, each additional ounce of silver produced has an opportunity cost of 10

FOCUS Economic Specialization in Everyday Life:
Marriage and Roommate Selection

Specialization and trade has increased economic welfare and human progress from the very beginning of time. These gains have depended on the diverse talents of individuals as well as the different resources of great nations. Consider two examples that do not often come to mind when considering the economic principles of specialization—the selection of a marriage partner and selection of a roommate.

Although relationships like marriage have many bases—love, security, etc.—one of them is surely economic. The greatest gains from trade occur when individuals (or countries) with widely differing skills or resources trade. In a society in which males and females acquire widely different skills, the incentive to marry is quite strong. If, as in primitive society, women do not know how to hunt or fish and men cannot prepare food or make clothing, the gains to both partners in a marriage relationship are immense. In fact, survival outside of a marriage-type relationship may be impossible. In such societies, nearly everyone would marry, and individuals would abandon a marriage relationship only to enter another one.[a] In societies where men and women acquire similar skills, the gains from exchange between marriage partners are much smaller. Individuals, therefore, have a weaker incentive to marry or to remain married. The slowing marriage rate and the growing divorce rate in Western societies in recent decades may partly be attributed to greater occupational equality. As the incomes of women rise (the opportunity cost of child rearing) a lower birth rate may be expected. Specialization may even be reversed, with

men taking more active roles in raising children. "Mr. Mom" may become more common due to economic specialization and trade.

Roommate selection, an activity perhaps closer to your experience, also takes place, in part, on the basis of economic specialization and trade. Students room together to save money, but they also do so, in part, because of the gains from specialization and trade. Communal arrangements ranging from fraternities and sororities to clubs and study groups work best when the participants have tradable skills. Ideally, then, one roommate would be an excellent cook, say, while another roommate would be an expert carpenter, and yet another would be adept at yard work. Even if individuals' skill levels are pretty much the same, trade is still profitable when roommates' tastes and preferences for specific jobs differ and trade is possible. Problems and disputes arise most often between roommates when trade agreements or "contracts" are not enforceable. You may do the cooking, but can you "force" your roommate to clean up the kitchen—assuming you both agreed she would?

The benefits of specialization and trade are not just of academic interest, nor do they pertain only to trade in goods and services between nations such as Japan and the United States. As workers, club members, marriage partners, roommates, or friends, these principles affect us every day.

[a]For some fascinating details of the emergence of modern humans and the family, see Richard E. Leakey, *The Making of Mankind* (London: Abacus, 1982).

Marginal opportunity production cost:
The number of units of one good that do not get produced when one additional unit of another good is produced.

Comparative advantage:
An economic entity's ability to produce a good at a lower marginal opportunity production cost than some other entity.

board-feet of lumber. If Canada is producing 30,000 ounces of silver and shifts productive resources from the lumber industry to produce 70,000 more ounces of silver (for a total of 100,000 ounces), lumber production drops by 700,000 board-feet. Each additional ounce of silver produced has a constant opportunity cost of 10 board-feet of unproduced lumber, regardless of how many ounces of silver are already being produced.

The situation may be viewed from another angle, and the same information may be expressed in a different manner. In Canada, the additional, or **marginal opportunity production cost** of 1 board-foot of lumber is constant and equal to $\frac{1}{10}$ of an ounce of silver. Silver and lumber production in Mexico are also subject to constant (marginal opportunity) production costs. For each additional ounce of silver produced, only 1 board-foot of lumber goes unproduced. The marginal opportunity cost of producing 1 ounce of silver in Mexico, 1 board-foot of lumber, is *less* than it is in Canada, where it is equal to 10 board-feet of lumber. Mexico is said to possess a **comparative advantage** over Canada in producing silver. A comparative advantage exists because the marginal opportunity cost of producing an ounce of silver in Mexico (1 board-

TABLE 4   Production Possibilities in Canada and Mexico

Canada has a comparative advantage in lumber. If Canada were to move to producing combination A instead of B, 300,000 board-feet of lumber could be had at an opportunity cost of 30,000 ounces of silver. Each board-foot of lumber has a marginal opportunity cost of $\frac{1}{10}$ of an ounce of silver going unproduced. If Mexico were to move from B to A, 40,000 more ounces of silver could be had at an opportunity cost of 40,000 board-feet of lumber. Each ounce of silver costs Mexico 1 board-foot of lumber. Likewise, Mexico has a comparative advantage in producing silver. In Canada an extra ounce of silver costs 10 board-feet of lumber.

	Canada's Production Possibilities			Mexico's Production Possibilities		
	A	B	C	A	B	C
Silver (ounces)	0	30,000	100,000	0	40,000	80,000
Lumber (board-feet)	1,000,000	700,000	0	80,000	40,000	0

foot of lumber) is less than it is in Canada (10 board-feet). So, any locale with a lower marginal opportunity cost of producing a good possesses a comparative advantage over some other locale in producing that good.

Canada has a comparative advantage over Mexico in lumber production, as indicated in Table 4. Canada can produce lumber at a lower marginal opportunity cost ($\frac{1}{10}$ of an ounce of silver) than can Mexico (1 ounce of silver). If Canada has a comparative advantage in lumber production, this necessarily means that Mexico has a comparative advantage in silver production. One ounce of silver costs Mexico only 1 board-foot of lumber, whereas in Canada the cost is 10 board-feet. Each country has a comparative production advantage over the other, but in a different good.

Suppose that both Mexico and Canada are initially self-sufficient in silver and lumber. That is, each locale produces and consumes some of both goods and does not trade with the other nation. Specifically, suppose that both countries produce and consume the combination of silver and lumber labeled B in Table 4 and Figure 6. We assume that combination B represents the most desirable consumption combination for both Canada and Mexico that is attainable from self-production.

How might Mexicans and Canadians be made better off economically? The residents could consume more of both goods or more of one good and the same quantity of the other good. Economic growth, either from technological improvement or from increased quantities of productive resources in each country, would shift the production possibilities curve rightward, enabling greater quantities of silver and lumber than those represented by B in Figure 6 to be produced and consumed. Economic growth would, therefore, make residents of either country better off in economic terms.

Excluding economic growth, residents of each locale could improve their economic situation through specialization and trade. Each could specialize in producing the good for which that locale has a comparative advantage and then *trade* some of its output for the other good.

FIGURE 6

Both locales agree that each 1000 ounces of silver trades for 5000 board-feet of lumber, or a board-foot of lumber for ⅕ of an ounce of silver. Each agrees to trade on these terms because obtaining a good through trade is less costly than obtaining the good by producing it at home. After specialization and trade, each locale will consume combination *D,* a combination that lies beyond each country's production possibilities curve.

Canada's and Mexico's Production Possibilities Curves

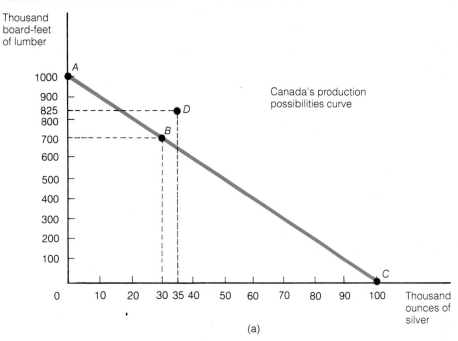

(a)

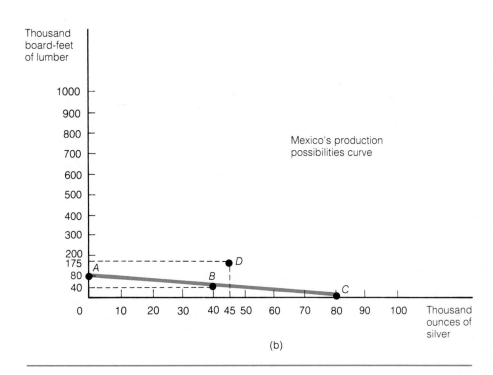

(b)

Specialization

Suppose that Mexico and Canada happen to hire the same economic consultant to help them improve their respective economic fortunes. After a study of each economy, the consultant brings representatives of both locales together and suggests a plan that will leave each economically better off: Specialize according to comparative advantage and trade with each other.

The benefits of specialization and trade are shown in the four parts of Table 5. Table 5a shows the situation in each locale before specialization and trade occur. Specifically, it reproduces combination *B* from each locale's production possibilities curves shown in Figure 6a and b. Combination *B*, recall, is assumed to be the most desirable consumption combination for each locale. Also shown in Table 5a is the sum total of both locales' production and consumption of each good. It is assumed that Canada and Mexico constitute the "world."

Table 5b depicts the production situation in each locale, and, therefore, the world, after Canada and Mexico have specialized in production according to comparative advantage. After specialization, total world output of silver is 10,000 ounces *greater* than it was at combination *B* on the production possibilities curves in Figure 6. World production of lumber has also increased. It is 260,000 board-feet more than before specialization. The world is economically better off (more of both goods), but we have yet to show that each individual locale is made better off as a result of specialization according to comparative advantage.

There is one more step to the process, that of trade.

TABLE 5a

Canada and Mexico Before Specialization and Trade

The amounts actually produced and thus consumed in Canada and Mexico are the combinations labeled *B* in Table 4. Amounts of each good for the "world" are the sums of the two countries' production.

	Canada Produces and Consumes	+	Mexico Produces and Consumes	=	World Produces and Consumes
Silver (ounces)	30,000		40,000		70,000
Lumber (board-feet)	700,000		40,000		740,000

TABLE 5b

Canada and Mexico After Specialization but Before Trade

Specialization in production according to comparative advantage yields a world gain in the output of both goods.

	Canada Produces	+	Mexico Produces	=	World Produces	World Gains
Silver (ounces)	0		80,000		80,000	+10,000
Lumber (board-feet)	1,000,000		0		1,000,000	+260,000

Trade: The Fruits of Specialization

Our consultant realizes that neither Canada nor Mexico would voluntarily agree to an exchange that would leave them worse off (than before trade). For voluntary exchange to take place, each nation must end up economically better off. With this in mind, the consultant proposes that Canada trade 175,000 board-feet of lumber to Mexico in exchange for 35,000 ounces of silver, or 5 board-feet of lumber for each ounce of silver. The Canadians would agree to this trade since domestic production of the 35,000 ounces of silver would cost them 10 board-feet of lumber each, for a total of 350,000 board-feet. This exchange allows the Canadians to obtain silver from the Mexicans cheaper than to produce it themselves.

The Mexicans would also agree to the proposed trade. Each board-foot of lumber costs them 1 ounce of silver to produce, but the proposed trade allows them to obtain each board-foot for $\frac{1}{5}$ of an ounce of silver. The trade with Canada enables Mexico to obtain 175,000 board-feet of lumber for 35,000 ounces of silver. The opportunity cost to Mexico of producing 175,000 board-feet of lumber would be 175,000 ounces of silver. It is less costly for Mexico to obtain lumber through trade than through self-production. This trade is depicted in Table 5c.

Terms of trade:
The number of units of one good that exchange in the market for one unit of some other good. Although not expressed in terms of money, it is a price nonetheless.

The number of board-feet of lumber that trade for an ounce of silver is called the **terms of trade.** The terms of trade is really a price that is not measured in terms of either country's money. In this example, Canada pays Mexico 5 board-feet of lumber for each ounce of silver. Mexico pays $\frac{1}{5}$ ounce of silver for each board-foot of lumber. The terms of trade is a price that defines the number of units of one good that exchange for one unit of some other good. The terms of trade will always fall somewhere between the mar-

TABLE 5c

The Trade Between Canada and Mexico

Canada and Mexico agree that each ounce of silver trades for 5 board-feet of lumber, or a board-foot of lumber trades for $\frac{1}{5}$ of an ounce of silver. Each agrees to trade on these terms because obtaining a good through trade is less costly than obtaining it by producing it at home.

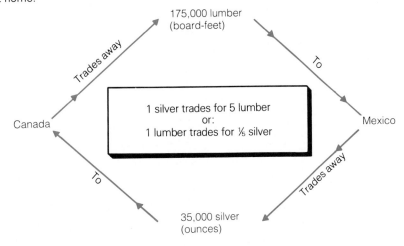

ginal opportunity production costs of a given good in each of the two countries. In this case an ounce of silver has an opportunity cost of 10 board-feet of lumber in Canada and 1 board-foot of lumber in Mexico, so the terms of trade will be at least one board-foot of lumber for an ounce of silver, but at most 10 board-feet of lumber for 1 ounce of silver. Terms of trade outside these limits would cause trade to be counter to the interests of citizens in one of the countries—for instance, Canadians would be better off producing their own silver than paying more than 10 board-feet per ounce for Mexican silver.

Table 5d summarizes the economic positions of Canada and Mexico after specializing in production and trading. Most important, both countries end up with more of both the goods to consume than before trade. Canada consumes 125,000 more board-feet of lumber than it did initially and Mexico an additional 135,000 board-feet. Both enjoy 5000 more ounces of silver than in the prespecialization and trade period. In Figure 6a and b, both locales are consuming combination *D*—combinations of goods that lie beyond the respective production possibilities curves. Without specialization and trade, these combinations could only be attained through economic growth. It is as if additional resource quantities of silver and lumber were actually created through specialized production and division of labor. Residents at *each* locale are economically better off. Specialization according to comparative advantage and trade has led to increased living standards in both parts of the world.

Factors Explaining Comparative Advantage

There are basically two reasons why a locale would have a comparative advantage over some other locale in producing any given good relative to other goods—differences in technology or differences in the quantities of productive inputs in the two locales. Relative differences in production technologies of the goods in the two locales can lead to a comparative advantage for each locale. With a given level of productive resources, Mexico might be able to produce an ounce of silver relatively more cheaply than Canada owing to technological differences in each good's production process in the two locales.

TABLE 5d   **Canada and Mexico After Specialization and Trade**

Specialization in production according to comparative advantage and trading yields a world gain and a gain for each locale.

| | Canada | | | | | Mexico | | | | |
	Produces	Trades For (+) Away(–)	Consumes After Trade	Consumed Before Trade	Gains From Trade	Gains From Trade	Consumed Before Trade	Consumes After Trade	Trades For (+) Away (–)	Produces
Silver (ounces)	0	+35,000	35,000	30,000	+5,000	+5,000	40,000	45,000	–35,000	80,000
Lumber (board-feet)	1,000,000	–175,000	825,000	700,000	+125,000	+135,000	40,000	175,000	+175,000	0

Lumber production technology may be identical in each locale, but the technical know-how of making silver may be more advanced in Mexico.

Alternatively, if production technologies are identical in both locales, an abundance of the productive resources used in producing lumber in Canada compared to Mexico's amounts of these resources could exist. This would give Canada a comparative advantage in lumber. But a relative abundance of lumber-producing trees in Canada implies a relative abundance of silver inputs in Mexico. These relative, or comparative, differences in the amounts of productive resources in the two locales can produce the pattern of comparative advantage shown above. Patterns of comparative advantage may, of course, shift over time with either natural or artificially induced changes in resource prices and supplies or with changes in technology. (See Economics in Action, "When Is a Rose Not a Rose? Shifting Comparative Advantage in the Flower Industry," at the end of this chapter.)

Consider another aspect of the situation in Mexico and Canada. Table 5 indicates that Canada has the ability to produce more lumber in absolute numbers than Mexico if each country produces only lumber (1 million board-feet versus 80,000 board-feet). Canada also has the capacity to produce absolutely more silver (100,000 ounces versus 80,000 ounces) than Mexico. Canada has what economists call an **absolute advantage** in production of both goods. That is, Canada can specialize in silver production and simply produce more silver than Mexico. The same holds for lumber production. Any time a country can specialize in producing a good and produce absolutely more of it than some other country, the first country has an absolute advantage over the second. An absolute advantage can arise because of technological factors or from one country being larger in terms of the quantity of productive resources it possesses. Although Canada has an absolute advantage in producing both goods, it has a comparative advantage only in lumber. Mexico has an absolute disadvantage in both goods, but it still can produce silver at a lower marginal opportunity cost than Canada. Both countries still benefit from specialization and trade according to comparative advantage.

Finally, we must clearly understand the simplifications attached to the discussion. Differences in marginal opportunity costs explain comparative advantages, but the economic system does not actually require an "economic consultant" to tell locales (or businesses or individuals) about the potential gains from specialization and trade. Relative scarcities based on differences in marginal opportunity costs are transmitted to producers and consumers through the price system. Prices "inform" producers and consumers about what, how much, and when to supply and consume millions of goods and services. The details of how prices are formed through the interaction of supply and demand are reserved for Chapter 4. Nonetheless, it is useful to remember that prices, not hypothetical economic consultants, "discover," signal, and reflect the comparative advantages that exist between nations, states, locales, businesses, and individuals.

Absolute advantage:
The ability of an economic entity to specialize and produce a greater amount of some good than another entity can.

Exchange Costs

The model of comparative advantage and trade—along with all other economic models—is a simplification of reality. A number of important assumptions hide behind our simple discussions. But there are also costs to the process of the exchange that must be accounted for when calculating the benefits of specialization and trade. We classify these **exchange costs** as transaction costs, transportation costs, and artificial barriers to trade.

Transaction Costs. Transaction costs are all the resource costs (including time-associated costs) incurred because of exchange. Transaction costs occur every time goods and services are traded, whether exchanges are simple (purchase of a pack of gum) or complex (a long-term negotiated contract with many contingencies).

Here's a simple example: Gwen goes to the supermarket to purchase a pound of coffee. What are the costs of the transaction? Gasoline and auto depreciation must of course be considered as resource costs, but the principal cost is the opportunity cost of Gwen's time. Gwen might have spent this time working or playing tennis instead of grocery shopping. Gwen's wage rate might then serve as her opportunity cost. If the shopping trip takes 30 minutes and if Gwen's wage rate is $15 an hour, the time part of her transaction costs is $7.50.

In this simple case the contracting and negotiating are instantaneous—Gwen simply gives the money to the checkout person, takes her coffee, and the transaction is complete. In other, more complex exchanges—such as the purchase of a house, a car, or a major appliance or the negotiation of a long-term labor contract—contracting and negotiating costs can be substantial. Think of the time and other resource costs associated with long-term supply contracts such as U.S. arms deals with allies or negotiations for ammonia plants in China. Every detail must be studied, formulated, and then spelled out.

The important point is that transaction costs include resources used by each party to the exchange. The higher the resource costs, the lower the benefit that comes from specialization and trade. Institutions—new legal arrangements, new marketing techniques, new methods of selling—have emerged, and are continually emerging, to reduce all forms of transaction costs. Gwen could have purchased coffee at a convenience store nearer to her house. The price of the coffee might have been somewhat higher, but Gwen's time costs, and therefore her total transaction costs, would have been lower. In a broader sense, laws about contracts, and law itself, are means by which transaction costs are reduced. The invention of money and the development of various forms of money and financial instruments are responses to transaction costs associated with barter and more primitive means of exchange.

In addition to money, intermediaries such as wholesalers and advertisers developed over the ages to facilitate exchange. The creative marketing of goods and services from bazaars to discount stores to media advertising has increased consumer information and thus reduced the costs of making transactions. Middlemen have lowered transaction costs by decreasing the risk of exchange. The production of some goods entails some risk and uncertainty on the part of buyers and sellers. Planting wheat in the spring for sale in the fall obviously entails some uncertainty about what prices will be at harvest. Middlemen-speculators who deal in futures provide sellers and buyers assurance of prices in the future. This type of middleman makes profit on the miscalculations of buyers and sellers but reduces uncertainty and thereby increases trade and specialization.

Transportation costs:
The value of resources used in the transportation of goods that finalize any trade.

Transportation Costs. A second impediment to trade is transportation costs, resource costs associated with the physical transport of products from place to place. The higher these resource costs, the lower the benefits from specialization and trade.

We did not include transportation costs in our initial examples of comparative advantage with Canada and Mexico. Let's do so now. Suppose that transportation costs associated with the trade amounted to 10,000 board-feet of lumber to each country. Even after paying these transportation costs, Canada and Mexico still enjoy more lumber than they did before specializing and trading (see Table 5d). Even if the "consultant," or the intermediary who organized trade, also charged a fee of 5000 board-feet of lumber to each country, both would still gain from specialization and trade. If transportation costs were high enough, possible advantages to specialization and trade could be wiped out completely. Cheaper transportation costs permit more trade and open up opportunities for new forms of and increases in specialization. The invention of the railroad in the nineteenth century, the spread of the automobile and the truck, and the dawning of air freight transport in the twentieth century were all boons to specialization and increased output.

Artificial barriers to trade:
Restrictions created by the government that inhibit or prevent trade; includes import quotas and tariffs.

Artificial Barriers to Trade. The final impediments to specialization and trade are government-imposed restrictions such as tariffs, quotas, and outright prohibitions on the import or export of goods. More localized restrictions include minimum-wage laws and specific restrictions on an industry or in an area. Such impositions, known as artificial barriers, either reduce or eliminate the benefits of specialization and trade.

Governments always have reasons for these restrictions, but the reasons must be closely scrutinized because the benefits from international and domestic specialization and trade are potentially huge for all consumers. Artificial barriers have the power to reduce economic welfare by reducing or eliminating the benefits of specialization according to the law of comparative advantage.

The possible effects of restrictions on trade can be seen in the growing volume of trade between Japan and the United States in commodities such as TVs, automobiles, stereo equipment, and musical instruments. Special-interest groups—such as American autoworkers and manufacturers—have lobbied for import tariffs and other trade restrictions to protect their own interests, which include increased demand for American-made products and therefore increased domestic production. Government-enforced tariffs make Japanese goods more expensive, however, causing a reduction in the general well-being of Americans. Artificial restrictions on trade, whatever their purpose, reduce the advantages of specialization and trade. As a matter of economic principle, therefore, most economists generally advocate free trade over any type of trade restriction. Further, any institution or mechanism that reduces the costs of exchange usually gets the support of economists because greater specialization permits better utilization of scarce resources. Specialization, in other words, helps us get more of what we want, given a limited amount of resources.

Real-World Patterns of Trade. The previous sections suggest that trade occurs between two countries when the countries have differences in opportunity costs of producing various goods (when comparative advantages exist), when transaction costs and transportation costs are small, and when the countries promote free trade. Real-world evidence reported in Table 6 and Figure 7 supports these arguments. For example, Canada is the leading trade partner of the United States. Transportation costs between the two countries are very low, and the two countries have one of the freest trade relationships in the world. In contrast, the United States trades substantially less with the United Kingdom because its trade policies are more restrictive and transportation costs are much greater than those with Canada.

The same factors explain the relative importance of foreign sales in the economies of different nations. Foreign trade is more important to the Dutch economy than to the New Zealand economy largely for geographic reasons that affect transportation costs. In addition, the Netherlands has historically pursued less restrictive trade policies.

The tremendous volume of trade between Japan and the United States is best explained by the strong comparative advantages between the two countries. Because the types of productive resources found in the two countries differ greatly, certain goods that have high opportunity costs in Japan have low costs in the United States, and vice versa. A huge trade volume, therefore, exists between the two countries, even though they both pursue policies to restrict foreign trade, and despite the large transportation costs of moving goods between the two countries.

TABLE 6   **Leading Trading Partners of the United States, 1987**

In terms of exports, Canada is the biggest customer of the United States. However, Americans import more goods and services from Japan than from any other country.

Country	Value of U.S. Imports (in billions)	Value of U.S. Exports (in billions)
All countries, total	$405.9	$252.9
Canada	71.1	59.8
Japan	84.6	28.2
West Germany	27.1	11.7
United Kingdom	17.3	14.1
Mexico	20.3	14.6
France	10.7	7.9
Netherlands	3.9	8.2
South Korea	17.0	8.1
Hong Kong	9.9	4.0
Singapore	6.2	4.1

Source: U.S. Bureau of the Census, *Statistical Abstract of the United States* (Washington, D.C.: U.S. Government Printing Office, 1989), pp. 788–791.

FIGURE 7

Foreign Trade as a Percentage of Gross Domestic Product (1987) in Various Countries

International trade is clearly more important in percentage terms to some countries—Korea or Belgium—than to others, such as the United States and Japan.

Source: International Monetary Fund, *International Financial Statistics Yearbook* (Washington, D.C., 1988).

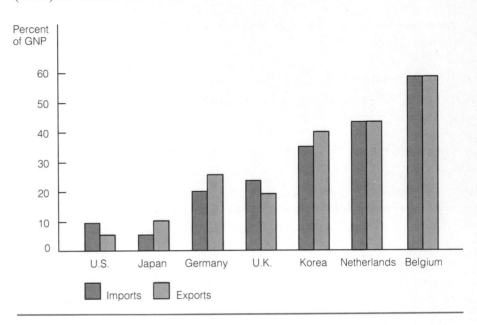

SUMMARY

This chapter described several principles that provide a foundation to economic thinking.

1. Economic choices, both for the individual and for society, always involve an opportunity cost.
2. Opportunity cost is the highest-valued alternative forgone in the decision to engage in a particular activity.
3. The law of increasing costs means that as more of one good is produced by a society, the opportunity costs of obtaining additional units of that commodity rise. The increase in cost is the result of resources becoming less adaptable as production becomes more specialized.
4. Choices are ordinarily made not in all-or-nothing fashion but at the margin. Both individuals and societies, therefore, calculate the cost of consuming additional units of some good or service.
5. The production possibilities curve shows the possible quantities of two goods that could be produced given the state of technology and society's scarce resources.
6. Changes in technology or increases (or decreases) in the amount of resources cause rightward (or leftward) movements in the production possibilities frontier.
7. Greater quantities of output can be obtained with society's scarce resources when people specialize and trade. Trade takes place according to the principle of comparative advantage.
8. Trade can take place between two individuals or economic entities even if one of the entities is more efficient at producing all goods. All that is required is that each entity be relatively more efficient than the other in some production.
9. Transaction costs, transportation costs, and artificial trade barriers such as tariffs and quotas reduce the benefits obtainable from specialization and trade.

KEY TERMS

opportunity cost	economic growth	absolute advantage
choices at the margin	specialization	exchange costs
production possibilities frontier	division of labor	transaction costs
law of increasing costs	marginal opportunity production cost	transportation costs
unemployment of resources	comparative advantage	artificial barriers to trade
capital stock	terms of trade	

QUESTIONS FOR REVIEW AND DISCUSSION

1. What did reading this chapter cost you? Did you include the price of the book? What will reading the next chapter cost? Does that include the price of the book?

2. Do government-sponsored financial aid programs for college students influence the amount of education produced? Do these programs shift the production possibilities curve?

3. What does a movement along the production possibilities frontier suggest? What does a point inside the curve suggest?

4. A subsidy to farmers who purchase tractors and combines increases the production of this farm machinery. Does this cause an increase in the production possibilities curve or just a movement along the curve? Can subsidies cause economic growth?

5. Why would a country with an absolute advantage in the production of all goods be willing to trade with other countries?

6. Alpha can produce 60 bottles of wine or 40 pounds of cheese. Beta can produce 90 bottles of wine or 30 pounds of cheese. Both have constant costs of production. Draw their production possibilities curves. What is Alpha's cost of 1 bottle of wine? What is Beta's cost of 1 pound of cheese? If they trade, who should specialize in cheese?

7. What are the costs of going to college? Does the marginal benefit outweigh the marginal cost?

8. Is the lost present consumption associated with the production of capital goods worth the benefit of the new capital?

9. Does Japan have an absolute advantage over the United States in the production of televisions and stereo equipment, or is it just a comparative advantage?

10. Who is hurt by and who benefits from an import quota on foreign beef?

11. How does the cost of purchasing a loaf of bread at a supermarket compare with the cost of purchasing a loaf of bread at a convenience store?

PROBLEMS

Countries A and B both produce golf balls and golf clubs. The table shows what each country can produce at full employment.

1. Graph the production possibilities curve of each country.

2. Do both production functions exhibit constant costs?

3. Who has the absolute advantage in both golf ball and golf club production?

4. Who has the comparative advantage in the production of golf balls?

5. Who has the comparative advantage in the production of golf clubs?

A		B	
Golf balls	Golf clubs	Golf balls	Golf clubs
1200	0	900	0
1000	50	750	25
800	100	600	50
600	150	450	75
400	200	300	100
200	250	150	125
0	300	0	150

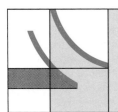

ECONOMICS IN ACTION
When Is a Rose Not a Rose? Shifting Comparative Advantage in the Flower Industry

Changes in technology, in capital investment, and in resource prices will often alter comparative advantage and trade in surprising ways. Consider conditions in the American flower industry, particularly among flower and plant growers.

Imported plants and cut flowers were a mere trickle in 1973 compared to recent years. Colombia, Mexico, the Netherlands, and Israel have made huge incursions into U.S. wholesale and retail markets for fresh cut flowers (especially roses, carnations, and chrysanthemums), and Belgium, Canada, Denmark, the Netherlands, Israel, and Costa Rica have done the same in the plant market. Colombia, America's largest foreign source of cut flowers, exported almost 73 million roses to the United States in 1982 and half a billion carnations. In fact, cut flowers were second only to coffee as Colombia's leading legal export item in recent years. Israel also has come on strong as a rose supplier to the United States with the aid of Israeli government subsidies. A survey taken by Professor Kenneth Sanderson of Auburn University in 1986 revealed that 82 percent of the roses, 79 percent of the carnations, and 41 percent of the chrysanthemums used by Alabama retail florists were imports.[a]

A number of reasons related to shifting comparative advantage can be offered for the lower prices and increased supplies of cut flowers and plants from foreign sources. The energy crisis of the 1970s raised the price of heating greenhouses, putting a cost squeeze on many domestic growers, especially those in the colder climates of North America. In 1986, according to U.S. Department of Agriculture (USDA) estimates, the states of Florida and California combined accounted for approximately half of the entire U.S. greenhouse and permanent-cover growing area. Under the high energy price conditions of the 1970s and early 1980s, nations such as Colombia had a new source of comparative advantage in flower growing—no heating of greenhouses is necessary.

A second reason for the new strength of imports is the technical possibility of avoiding historical restrictions on the importation of plants potted in soil. Modern techniques permit plant cultivation in such media as sphagnum moss, unused peat, plastic particles, glass wool, and inorganic fibers. Dutch growers have become especially adept at these new techniques for commercial propagation. Such plants (with some limitations) are allowed into the United States under a USDA regulation called Quarantine 37. Under Quarantine 37, plants grown under very rigid specifications in foreign countries may be preinspected by USDA teams in the foreign country and admitted into U.S. markets.

While higher energy prices might help explain the initial shift in comparative advantage from the United States to Colombia and other nations in flower and plant growing, it does not explain why comparative advantage has not been regained by the United States since the collapse of OPEC and lower energy prices in recent years. Other factors related to comparative advantage are clearly relevant. An important factor is that foreign growers are able to use insecticides and chemicals that are not allowed in the United States. Environmental Protection Agency (EPA) and Occupational Safety and Health Administration (OSHA) regulations on plant and flower growers may, in part, explain why the United States is not recapturing comparative advantage. Flower growers also may be hurt relatively more than greenhouse plant and food growers if blanket restrictions apply to all greenhouse propagation.

More important, perhaps, is the fact that significant technological advances occurred in flower growing and transportation during the 1970s and 1980s. Growers in such nations as Colombia started up with state-of-the-art capital and growing techniques. In the case of Canada, the low price and high quality of flower and plant products were "the outcome of general improvements pushed by former European growers who had emigrated to Canada" in the 1960s and 1970s.[b] Modernization of greenhouses and equipment together with a willingness to risk capital will be required before the United States can recapture its comparative advantage.

Predictably, efforts to institute artificial barriers to trade, such as tariffs and quotas, have been made by lobby groups and trade organizations of the various segments of the American flower industry in the late 1980s. Protectionists, especially those representing flower growers, drew battle lines, declaring "cheap foreign labor," "inferior-quality products," "unemployment in the flower industry," "foreign government subsidies," and "health hazards through damaging

---

[a]Market Letter, News Edition, *Florist's Review* (September 29, 1986), p. 1.

[b]Rick Davis, "Canadian Imports Up as Relations Strain," Market Letter, Market Edition, *Florist's Review* (August 25, 1986), p. 2.

insect pests." Leading the fight in 1986 and 1987 was the Washington-based lobby group of the industry called the Society of American Florists (SAF). Roses, Inc., a floral trade association, called for legislation against countries who supposedly sell ("dump") flowers in the United States below their costs of production.

These groups have had a measure of success. In March 1987 a thinly disguised protectionist "Anti-Dumping Duty" was imposed on U.S. importers of carnations and pompon chrysanthemums from several Latin American countries and in January 1989 duties were imposed on flower containers and silk flowers imported from South Korea, Taiwan, Hong Kong, and Singapore (all formerly duty-free nations). Industry experts estimated an increase of flower costs to American consumers of $4 million dollars in 1987, with equal or higher losses calculated for 1988 and 1989.[c] The price of flower arrangements to consumers rose by approximately 33 percent in 1989, with further increases predicted.

None of the reasons given by the flower industry, except the possible problem of the importation of damaging insects, holds a drop of water when compared to the benefits of comparative advantage, specialization, and free trade. If Colombian or Israeli roses are of inferior quality, as U.S. growers allege, the market soon adjusts prices and quanti-

ties accordingly. (In fact, Colombia's initial stock of the Visa rose, the hearty mainstay of its export trade, had to be imported from France because American rose propagators refused to trade.) If other nations wish to subsidize exports of flowers to the United States, American consumers gain.

It is as yet unclear how much more protection will be supplied in the flower industry. Not all interests in the U.S. flower business are the same. Flower growers and other groups such as container manufacturers favor protection, while flower importers are, in general, fighting it. Politicians and government agencies have demonstrated that they will respond to protectionist pleas from the industry. The economic principles of comparative advantage, specialization, and trade suggest that gains to one small group of producers would be more than offset by higher prices and welfare losses to other industry segments and to flower consumers as a whole.

Question

Suppose that Japan has a comparative advantage in certain types of automobiles and that the elimination of all quotas and tariffs on U.S. imports of Japanese automobiles would reduce employment in the American automobile industry by 200,000 jobs. Would you support the immediate elimination of all artificial barriers to trade? Would you support a gradual elimination? No elimination? Would you support the implementation of retraining programs and subsidies to auto workers? Answer the questions on the basis of comparative advantage. Are there other problems to consider?

---

[c]"Duty Debate Continues," *Florist's Review* (January 1988), p. 46; Spencer, Elaine, "Christmas Costs Climb Higher and Higher," *Florist's Review* (July 1988), p. 16.

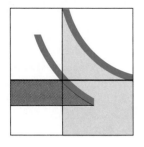

3

Economic Institutions and the Role of Government

The vehicles for economic growth, as we have seen, are technology and resource development, specialization, and trade. But what makes these vehicles possible? Why are they more apparent in some societies than in others? To better understand the answers to these questions and the workings of the American market economy, we give an overview of the American economic system and contrast it to other contemporary economic systems and societies. When you finish Chapter 3 you should know

- the major institutions of market, socialist, and mixed economies that channel the problems of scarcity and unlimited wants.
- the roles governments play in the major economic societies and nations of the world.
- the specific role government plays in the U.S. economy with respect to free markets, property rights, law, and public goods and services.
- whether expanding government's role in mixed economies enhances or detracts from production and economic well-being.

THE U.S. MARKET SYSTEM IN PERSPECTIVE

Economic system:
The part of the social system determining what, how, and for whom goods and services are produced.

Rice paddies in China, nut-and-fruit-gathering societies in Africa, government enterprise in Russia, free-trade zones in Hong Kong, computer hardware development in California's Silicon Valley—all these arrangements represent different answers to the "what," "how," and "for whom" questions under different economic systems. An **economic system** is the particular form of social arrangements through which the three fundamental questions are answered. In this chapter we focus on the capitalist system as it exists in the United States.

Comparative Systems

Two basic types of economic systems have emerged in response to scarcity of resources: capitalism and communism. All societies, including the United States, actually contain some elements of each type. It is very difficult to identify a pure type of economic system in contemporary societies.

Capitalist, Communist, and Mixed Economies.   The comparison of economic systems in different countries is made easier by the classification of systems along a spectrum that ranges from pure capitalism to pure communism. A **pure capitalist** economy is one in which most property is owned and most economic decisions are made by private individuals and in which government economic control is minimal. An economic system characterized by common ownership of productive resources, both human and nonhuman, is called **pure communism.** A **pure socialist** economy is one in which most of the nonhuman resources are owned by the state, which in turn makes most production and some consumption decisions.

The real world is complex, however; there simply are no examples of pure capitalist, pure socialist, or pure communist systems (although there are examples that come fairly close to each). Moreover, it would be a mistake to draw a single line between pure capitalism and pure communism and attempt to place various countries on either side of it. Some countries have economic systems in which most property is privately owned but in which government regulation and control is extensive; in other countries the opposite is true. For example, Sweden permits free ownership of resources, but a very high share of the economy's total output goes to taxes. In Poland there are still extensive controls of property, but people are relatively free to spend incomes as they choose. Ranking economic systems with respect to degrees of economic freedom is problematic. Distinctions may be made about the degree of capitalism and communism or socialism in *many* dimensions. What's more, many economic and political systems are now in a state of flux; a distinction that holds today may not hold tomorrow. Figure 1 illustrates the differences between existing economic systems in just two dimensions—degree of economic freedom and per capita GNP. The per capita GNP is shown on the horizontal axis and the degree of government control is shown on the vertical axis.

Mixed Capitalism.   To varying degrees, the economies of France, Canada, and England display the characteristics of **mixed capitalism.** In such systems, the state is an important participant in the economy, but by and large the bulk of productive activity is undertaken by private firms and individuals. (One economy in Figure 1—that of Hong Kong—does come close to the pure capitalism model.)

In a large number of countries the dominant economic institutions are fundamentally different from those in capitalist societies. These are the socialist economies, such as in China and the Soviet Union. Socialism is basically a system of economic organization in which resource allocation is determined by central planning rather than by market forces. Many socialist economies are undergoing rapid change, however—mainly in the direction of capitalism. (See Focus, "Capitalism: Wave of the Future?")

Pure capitalism:
An economic system in which most resources are owned, and most relevant decisions are made, by private individuals.

Pure communism:
An economic system in which most productive resources, both human and nonhuman, are publicly owned.

Pure socialism:
An economic system in which most nonhuman productive resources are owned by the state.

Mixed capitalism:
An economic system in which most economic decisions are made by the private sector but in which government also plays a substantial economic and regulatory role.

FIGURE 1   Economic Systems and Per Capita Income

Figure 1 links the per capita income produced in various economies, shown on the horizontal axis, to the degree of government control in them, shown on the vertical axis. No economies exactly fit the extremes of pure capitalism and pure communism, but China and Hong Kong come close. Furthermore, there is no exact relation between per capita income and the type of economic system in countries.

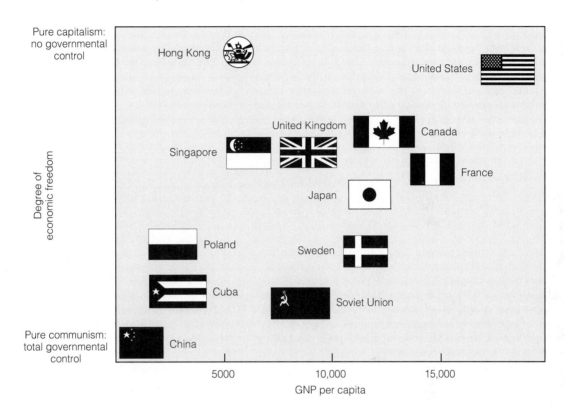

Market society:

An economic system in which individuals acting in their own self-interest determine what, how, and for whom goods and services are produced, with little government intervention.

Market Societies. In a **market society,** personal and impersonal forces lead consumers and producers to answer the three fundamental questions of production. Consumers answer the "what" question through their participation in the marketplace. Production of goods and services such as personal computers and auto repair is determined by "dollar votes." Just as political votes elect a president, dollar votes—or money spent on products and services—express consumers' demands. Suppliers of products and services, interested in making profits, respond to these votes by providing the products and services in just the right quantities. (Chapter 4 explains exactly how this occurs, through the laws of supply and demand.)

The "how" question in the market society is, at any one time, answered by available technology and by suppliers' profit-motivated desire to produce goods most cheaply given the price of resources. Most goods can be produced by a variety of methods. Avocadoes, for example, can be picked by hand or by harvesting machines. The avocado grower will choose whatever method min-

FOCUS   Capitalism: Wave of the Future?

Historically, the economic experience of most societies has been one of government controls, economic stagnation, and abysmal living conditions. In ancient Egypt, in Rome, and in France under Louis XIV the privileged few reached economic and cultural highs, but the dreadful conditions of the average citizen were the shameful downside of such opulence. In contrast, eighteenth-century capitalism emphasized free, unregulated markets in a new industrial setting and a government that was small relative to the private economy. This new system of Adam Smith replaced a system of controls in Great Britain and eventually in the United States and parts of Western Europe. To this day, most economic systems are based on government controls in the form of regulation of the private sector, plus outright government ownership and direction in some sectors of the economy.

Ideas and policies, however, come and go. Following a period of increased government controls in most Western nations after World War II, the United States, Great Britain, and France have recently taken steps to deregulate their economies. For example, the shift away from regulation and control has dramatically affected the transportation and banking industries in the United States, and the full effects are not as yet completely known. However, the most startling experiments with capitalism are taking place in societies that previously had very tight economic and political controls. The Soviet Union, China, Poland, Hungary, and many Third World nations are trying a system of freer markets along with alternative, or freer, political systems.

In a number of cases, the changes represent dramatic reversals of long-standing policy. The Soviet Union is attempting, through *perestroika* and *glasnost* (openness), to increase free farm production (which was tightly controlled in the past) and to pursue freer trade with Western nations. In some cases, the "new openness" in the Russian economy is merely the legalization of activities that were taking place in the "second economy," where markets previously functioned in an illegal or quasi-legal environment. China, too, has moved toward capitalistic production and trade. Specifically, the Chinese government has established clearer property rights in land and embraced Western technology and business practices in an attempt to foster economic growth. The Beijing Kentucky Fried Chicken restaurant—at 500 seats, the world's largest—opened in 1987. It is a symbol of new directions for the Chinese economy, although political repression continues.

Countries from the Third World and Soviet bloc have also taken steps to deregulate their economies. In 1988 the government in Poland passed laws that, for the first time, enabled business firms to be established with relative freedom. The communist government in power has since opted to relinquish control to popularly elected leaders. In Latin America, Chile relaxed many restrictions on domestic businesses and experienced a period of rapid economic growth. Countries as diverse as Pakistan and New Zealand have similarly removed many long-standing economic controls and adopted free-market policies.[a]

The motives for adopting new policies differ from country to country. Much of the change in Poland has been forced on the government by popular uprisings and open dissent. In the Soviet Union, change seems to have been imposed from the very top of the Soviet government with little evidence of popular support. In nearly every case, supporters of free enterprise have convincingly argued that their policies are essential to the economic well-being of average citizens. Although there are exceptions, evidence generally supports that argument. Factors such as climate, natural resources, and history undoubtedly play important roles in determining a country's production level, but Figure 1 indicates a strong connection between a country's degree of economic freedom and its economic success as measured by GNP per capita. People throughout the world will be paying close attention to the economic successes or failures that occur in countries where freer markets have been permitted. Depending upon the economic experiences of these countries, capitalism may again be the wave of the future.

[a]These and other matters are discussed by Nobel laureate Milton Friedman in "Why Liberalism Is Now Obsolete," *Forbes* (December 12, 1988), pp. 161–68.

---

imizes the cost of production. In a market economy prices are the signals not only for what to produce and how to produce now but also for how new technologies and new resources can be brought into production over time.

When one highly demanded resource becomes scarce and therefore high-priced, producers will attempt to substitute other resources for it. If possible substitutions are limited, alternative technologies and new types of resources may be developed. In mid-nineteenth-century America, for example, whale oil—used primarily for lighting—became scarce and high-priced as the supply of whales depleted. Price provided the incentive to develop alternative lighting fuel such as fossil fuels. Some historians believe that the depletion of the whales encouraged both the discovery of petroleum and the widespread use of oil derived from petroleum.

Prices also answer the "for whom" question in a market society. Just as the prices and quantities of all goods and services available in a market system are determined by the demands of buyers and sellers, so are the "prices" (such as wage rates, rental rates, and interest rates) of resources used to produce them. The value of particular resources in general depends on the demand for the product that the resource helps produce. For example, the owner of property bordering Central Park in New York City may expect to receive a higher rental than one who owns desert property in Nevada. Luciano Pavarotti, a world-renowned operatic tenor, may be expected to receive a higher wage than a college president. The money rewards to these resources are determined not only by the demand for them but also by their relative scarcity. First-class tenors are scarcer than college presidents.

Most Western economists see the market system as the greatest force for economic growth within the context of political and economic freedom. The U.S. market economy—its functioning and its problems—therefore receives the lion's share of attention in this book. The American economy is one of a kind, but it shares some important features with other, similar market systems. One shared feature is the use of money and a circular flow between money, goods, and resources.

Money in Modern Economies

Barter:
The trading of goods for other goods without using a medium of exchange such as money.

Despite their differences, a feature of all economic systems is the use of money. **Barter**—the exchange of goods for goods—is cumbersome and costly. For a system to take advantage of specialization, output must grow steadily. For output to expand, trade must take place at a low cost. But the costs of bartering goods are numerous, for the value of each good must be recorded in terms of the other goods traded. As the number of goods traded increases, calculations become overwhelming. Money was invented as a medium of exchange and as a unit of accounting. It is a good in terms of which the value of all other goods can be calculated. Money lowers the cost of transacting and is therefore essential to any modern society.

We can think of money as a substitute for real things traded. Wages, for example, represent a trade of the output of a worker for the goods and services consumed by the worker. We may earn wages as a bricklayer and purchase fried chicken at a fast-food establishment. In a real sense, we are bartering bricklayer labor for fried chicken. Money simply substitutes for real trades.

The Circular Flow in a Market Economy

Circular flow of income:
The movement of real goods and services, payments, and receipts between households and business firms.

The exchange of money for goods and services takes place throughout the United States and other developed economies. One can conceptualize this exchange as a **circular flow of income** (Figure 2), a cyclical pattern of money payments and goods and services produced.

In Figure 2 the arrows on the outer circle represent the flow of real goods and services between business firms and households, while the arrows on the inner circle represent the reciprocal flow of money payments. In the circular flow of products, business firms produce products and services with resources

FIGURE 2   The Circular Flow of Income

Economic activity between business firms (producers) and households (consumers) takes place in a cyclical pattern. The arrows on the outer circle represent the flow of real goods and services (consumer products and factors of production such as labor); the arrows on the inner circle represent the reciprocal flow of money payments for real goods and services.

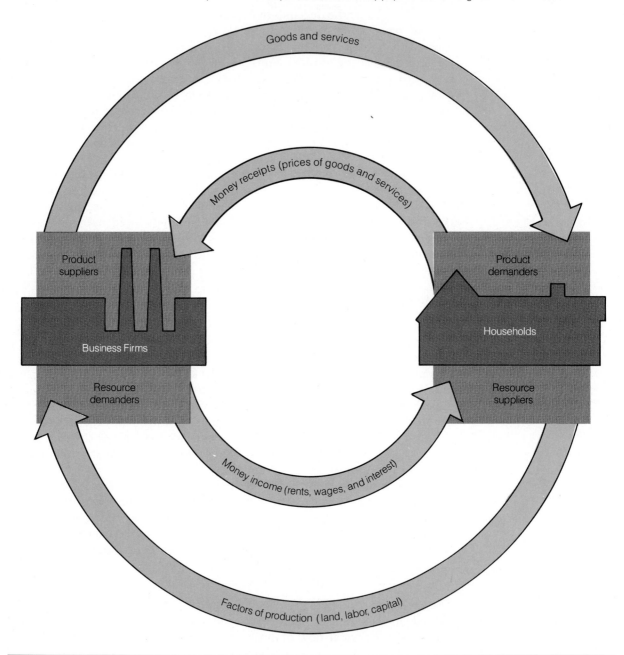

(land, labor, and capital) from resource suppliers. To complete the circle, households that purchase products and services are virtually all resource suppliers—of labor, land, or capital. The flow of products has a corresponding and counterbalancing money flow in the opposite direction. For goods and services, firms receive money payments (business receipts) from households, and for resources (labor, land, and capital), resource owners receive money income in the form of rents, wages, and interest from firms. The quantities and the mix of resources used and products produced are determined by price signals. These signals, as we will show more clearly in Chapter 4, are the result of the impersonal forces of supply and demand.

Figure 2 is not meant to depict a functioning economy in detail but to serve as a model for product and money flows. Missing are the complexities of flows by which producers supply goods to other producers and of the tax and expenditure flows by which government provides public goods and services.

INSTITUTIONS OF AMERICAN CAPITALISM

While money and real goods circulate through all modern economic systems like blood through the veins and arteries of the body, societies vary in the institutions they create for ownership and use of goods and money. A *capitalist economy* relies primarily on market forces and the profit motive for production, distribution, and consumption of goods and services. Capitalism is characterized by individual ownership of property, free enterprise, open competition, and a minimal role for government.

Property and the Law

In the American economy the individual's right to own and dispose of property is regarded as basic. Property includes both physical property (such as houses and automobiles) and intellectual or intangible property. For example, the ownership of poems, songs, and books by their authors is protected by copyright laws; inventions are protected by patents. The legal apparatus set up to protect such rights may even make a distinction between property and property rights. Rental of a carpet cleaner from U-Rent-Um gives the renter certain property rights over the cleaner but not ownership of the property itself. In all societies, rights to use property are limited. For example, the Environmental Protection Agency has used its legislatively derived power to limit the rights of businesses to pollute air and water and has established worker protection standards (such as those limiting the use of asbestos) that restrict businesspeople's free use of property.

In a capitalist society, the law protects property rights; the proper assignment of property rights is thought to be a key to economic efficiency. (See Focus, "Property Rights, Incentives, and Economic Development.") Without some guarantee that property rights will be protected, there would be little incentive to accumulate capital stock and, therefore, to grow economically. Without state guarantees of rights to property, individuals would have to protect their own property at high personal cost.

FOCUS   Property Rights, Incentives, and Economic Development

Why does rental property, jointly owned property, leased equipment, or public parkland tend to be abused or used inefficiently compared to the property of an individual owner? Economists argue that resources attain economic efficiency when governments or legal systems assign few or no limits to property use. Consider what this means in terms of practical examples of property rights assignment.

In past centuries, property rights to land were limited or restricted by tradition or by law. One institution that emerged in Western Europe and the American South—sharecropping—illustrates the economic point about rights and efficiency. Under sharecropping, tenants do not *own* the land but are given rights by the owner to farm it, with certain terms and conditions attached. In return for these temporary rights, owners receive a portion (typically, one-half or one-third) of the product or its value. Unfortunately, tenants have no incentive to conserve property (land, capital, and other resource inputs) to maximize production under this system. When users do not own the capital or land they employ, there are few incentives to conserve resources, which may lead to overutilization (overfarming) of land, little conservation, or lack of capital improvements (deterioration of plows, fences, or other farm implements). Although owners and tenants might create contracts to try to avoid problems, maximum output and full economic efficiency in resource use is not expected without complete ownership.

These problems apply to many current land reforms undertaken by developing nations. Concentrations of land ownership are, in some cases, dissolved by governments only to be replaced with systems that do not produce economic efficiency. Farmers and peasants are often given limited terms of ownership or limited rights to farm or develop land and other resources. If the property, for example, is leased for a specified number of years or over the farmer's lifetime (restricting or eliminating rights of survivors), there will be no incentive to farm efficiently and to maximize output over the life of the lease. (If restrictions on the *use* of the property limit land use to agricultural production or to a certain type of agricultural output, even less efficiency may be expected.) The point is that the incentive to conserve property and to use it efficiently is directly related to the user's ability to own the property. Economic theory teaches us that, in general, a full assignment of property rights—with full costs and benefits assigned to the owner—is necessary for maximum economic efficiency.

Legal protection of property rights often emerges as a response to market activities. Consider an example from the American frontier West. In the early days of silver and gold prospecting, individuals were forced to protect their own mining claims. As their claims grew, individual protection entailed higher opportunity costs—that is, higher costs in time spent away from mining or prospecting and in potential loss of equipment or mined ore. Thus, the collective benefits of enforcement through police, courts, and prisons outweighed the costs of such enforcement to individual prospectors—paying taxes, serving on posses, and the like. Property rights and the laws that protect them emerge when benefits to the parties involved begin to exceed the costs of acquiring and enforcing the rights. Such rights to private property, established by law, have been a part of American capitalism since the founding of the nation.

Free Enterprise

Free enterprise:
Economic freedom to produce and sell or purchase and consume goods without government intervention.

Free enterprise, the freedom to pursue one's economic self-interest, is an intrinsic part of the capitalist system. Men and women are free to choose their line of work with few or no governmental restraints or subsidies, and businesspeople are free to combine any resources at their command to produce products and services for profit. Laborer-consumers are free to produce, purchase, and exchange any good or service so long as their activity does not infringe on other's rights. (Bear in mind that participants are also *not* free of the constraints of limited resources and unlimited wants.) Free enterprise, in sum, means that

1. Laborers are free to work at any job for which they are qualified;
2. Business firms and entrepreneurs can freely combine resources, at competitive market prices, to take advantage of profit opportunities;
3. Consumers can decide what products and services will be produced; and
4. There is freedom within constraints (for example, within a rule of law).

Competitive Economic Markets

Competition:
A market situation satisfying two conditions—a large number of buyers and sellers and freedom to enter and exit the market—and resulting in prices equal to the costs of production plus a normal profit for sellers.

The American economic system is characterized by free competitive markets. **Competition** entails two important conditions: a large number of buyers and sellers and free entry and exit in the market. When these two conditions are met, the self-interested actions of buyers and sellers tend to keep prices of goods and services at a reasonable level, usually the costs of production plus a normal profit for the sellers.

When the number of buyers and sellers is large, no individual buyer or seller can affect the market price of a product or service. Many millions of individuals purchase canned soup, for example, but no one buyer purchases enough to affect the market price of the soup. Likewise, the existence of competing suppliers means that no individual seller can acquire enough power to alter the market for his or her gain. Sellers of canned soup are numerous enough that no one seller can affect the price of soup by increasing or decreasing output.

Crucial to the effects of large numbers is the condition that firms be free to enter and leave markets in response to profit opportunities or actual losses. New firms entering particular lines of business, bankruptcies, and business failures are expected consequences of a competitive system. New fast-food restaurants open every day in anticipation of profits. Airlines declare bankruptcy and leave the industry—a sure sign of losses. Competition requires that entry and exit into business be free and unregulated. The Focus, "Adam Smith's 'Invisible Hand,' " discusses the competitive system.

Coordinating the billions of individual decisions involved in competition is an interconnected system of prices for inputs and outputs that is so complex that no individual or computer can fully comprehend it. We begin to study the intricacies of the price system in Chapter 4.

The Limited Role of Government

Laissez-faire economy:
A market economy that is allowed to operate according to competitive forces with minimal government intervention.

American capitalism as an economic system requires an attitude of laissez-faire (from the French, meaning roughly "to let do"). Laissez-faire has come to mean minimum government interference and regulation in private and economic lives. In a pure **laissez-faire economy,** government has a role limited to setting the rules—a system of law establishing and defining contract and property rights, ensuring national defense, and providing certain goods that the private sector cannot or would not provide. The last category includes roads, canals, and national defense.

THE MIXED SYSTEM OF AMERICAN MARKET CAPITALISM

In truth, no society ever conforms totally to the laissez-faire ideal. The ideal is modified in two ways: in an altered notion of the competitive process and in an expanded role for government. Such a modification is called *mixed capitalism*.

An Evolving Competitive Process

Was any country ever composed of so many competing buyers and sellers to become, in Adam Smith's phrase, a "nation of shopkeepers"? Although historical data are less than perfect, we are fairly certain that purely competitive market structures did not exist even in Adam Smith's time. With the Industrial Revolution, capital requirements of firms were such that the most efficient firms—those producing goods at lowest cost—became larger. Certain industries and markets no longer had large numbers of competing sellers. Economists call such markets imperfectly competitive. They are also called *oligopolies* (characterized by a few competitors) or *monopolies* (having a single producer).

Some economists have argued that the decline in the number of competitors in some markets has led to concentrations of economic power in the hands of a few and to the demise of the laissez-faire competitive system. Modern economic research into the competitive process disputes this position, however. In the new view, competition is not to be described by a given number of sellers and buyers but rather by a rivalry for profits—that is, a process. Such rivalry—or even the potential for it, as long as individuals and businesses are free to enter and exit the market—produces results similar to competition among many buyers and sellers. One or two sellers in an industry can be competitive as long as entry and exit in the market is possible.[1]

The Expanded Role of Government

The most important modification in the traditional conception of laissez-faire capitalism is an expanded social and economic role of government. Since the turn of the century, and especially since the 1930s, the relative size of government in the United States has grown dramatically in both social and economic spheres. In the 1960s and 1970s we saw large increases in government payments to individuals through Social Security, Aid to Families with Dependent Children, Medicare and Medicaid, unemployment compensation, and other welfare programs. The direct economic activity of government has grown apace.

Public Goods and Externalities. Theoretically, underlying the government's role in economic life is the failure of a free-market society to satisfy all of its

---

[1]See Israel M. Kirzner, *Competition and Entrepreneurship* (Chicago: University of Chicago Press, 1973), for more details on rivalrous competition.

FOCUS   Adam Smith's "Invisible Hand"

Economists tend to praise a free and unfettered competitive market system because the rational and self-interested forces that characterize economic behavior lead not to a permanent state of chaos but to a harmony of interests. Adam Smith had great insight into the matter more than two hundred years ago in his "invisible hand" message in the *Wealth of Nations:*

> Every individual necessarily labours to render the annual revenue of the society as great as he can. He generally, indeed, neither intends to promote the public interest, nor knows how much he is promoting it. By preferring the support of domestic to that of foreign industry, he intends only his own security; and by directing that industry in such a manner as its produce may be of the greatest value, he intends only his own gain, and he is in this, as in many other cases, led by an invisible hand to promote an end which was not part of his intention. Nor is it always the worse for

the society that it was no part of it. By pursuing his own interest he frequently promotes that of the society more effectively than when he really intends to promote it. I have never known much good done by those who affected to trade for the public good.[a]

Smith felt that individuals' tendency to act in their own self-interest is a natural law and a natural right that precedes the existence of government. The exertion of these individual rights in a competitive market setting, furthermore, creates the greatest good for the greatest number in society. Smith's view, although a mainstream perspective in American capitalism, has been amended to accommodate government provisions of goods when the market fails to provide them in sufficient quantities.

[a]Adam Smith, *An Inquiry into the Nature and Causes of the Wealth of Nations,* ed. Edwin Cannan (1776; reprint New York: Modern Library, 1937), p. 423.

Public goods:
Goods that no one individual can be excluded from consuming once they have been provided to another, such as national defense.

members' needs. The market society can fail in its ability to provide **public goods** such as national defense. Since national defense protects all citizens regardless of whether they pay for it, no one is likely to contribute to defense voluntarily. The private market fails in the sense that public goods such as defense would not be provided (or provided in sufficient quantity) unless government assumed responsibility.

Another cause for government intervention in a free-market economy is what economists call an *externality.* An externality is an unintended by-product of some activity, and it often involves environmental protection. A beautiful

Positive externality:
A benefit of producing or consuming a good that does not accrue to the sellers or buyers but can be realized by a larger segment of society, such as vaccinations.

garden creates a **positive externality** in that it confers benefits to neighbors for which they do not pay. A **negative externality** might arise from a factory belching smoke or a firm dumping chemical wastes into a stream. In such a case, costs are imposed on members or segments of society, for which they are not compensated, rather than limited to the perpetrators of the externality. Both positive and negative externalities involve inefficient allocations of resources. Externalities have led to various government interventions to correct the inefficient resource allocations of the market. Taxes, subsidies, quotas, prohibitions, and assignment of legal liability are examples of government intervention (see Chapter 20).

Negative externality:
A cost of producing or consuming a good that is not paid entirely by the sellers or buyers but is imposed on a larger segment of society, such as pollution.

Many problems that justify government intervention involve negative externalities. Regulations prohibiting overfishing in the open seas attempt to limit the externalities imposed by self-interested commercial or sport fishermen. Elimination of garbage and industrial waste at sea, highlighted in the summer of 1988 by the medical waste that washed ashore on the east coast of the United States, is another example of an externality. Climatologists warn of a very difficult and complex negative externality—a worldwide "greenhouse effect." The greenhouse effect is a persistent rise in global temperature caused by the human use and production of products that emit carbon dioxide, fluorocarbons, and other gases. Overuse of these gases lets sunlight in but does not let heat out of the earth's atmosphere. Self-interested actions contribute to the possibility that the earth may eventually warm up between three and nine degrees Fahrenheit. Some scientists fear that this warming could shift weather patterns, causing devastation in the form of droughts in once fertile regions and excess rainfall in deserts. Melting glaciers could raise the sea level as much as six feet, disrupting agriculture, coastal economic activity, and water resources. All of the consequences of continued global warming are not known at present. These kinds of negative externalities, like the problem of acid rain in the northeastern United States and Canada, require multinational political solutions.

Income Distribution. The price system, where goods and services are produced and distributed within markets, does not necessarily produce what society might regard as a "just" distribution of income. In the market system, individuals earn income according to their abilities, education, and drive. Inheritance augments the incomes of some individuals. Some individuals, as a result of economic discrimination, poor education, or lack of abilities or incentives, earn less income or no income at all. Other people are poor because they are physically or mentally handicapped, indigent, old, or unable to work. We are, sadly, all familiar with poor and homeless people. Our society, like most others in history, is unwilling to endure a high degree of such income disparity.

At times, and in different degrees, the market system fails to provide the amount of income equality desired by society. When this happens, provisions for the poor, indigent, and needy are made through the political process, primarily through tax redistributions. These provisions take a number of forms. Until the Tax Reform Act of 1986 income tax rates were sharply graduated upward. In this progressive system of income taxation, the rich (higher-income individuals and families) were taxed at higher marginal tax rates than the poor (lower-income individuals and families). One of the stated objectives of the Tax Reform Act of 1986 was to simplify the tax system (basically to two income tax rates) and, at the same time, to remove approximately six million of the poorest families from the tax rolls altogether. Public goods and other government expenditures will still be paid for by wealthier, higher-income individuals and families, which is, in effect, an income redistribution through the governmental process.

The government administers other more direct forms of income redistribution in society. **Public assistance,** or welfare, **programs** are designed to aid the needy, the indigent, the handicapped, and the unemployed with income assistance derived from government taxation. Programs such as Aid to Families with Dependent Children, the food stamp program, and Medicaid bring relief to those who have little or no income. The Medicare and Social Security programs are designed to supplement the fortunes of the old, the retired, and the ailing members of society. Other kinds of assistance and subsidies are available to specific groups in society. Direct farm subsidies were oriented as a price support system for certain agricultural commodities when prices fell below that deemed "fair" in the political process. (The recent reduction or elimination of these subsidies has caused disruptions in the farm sector.) Finally, artificial barriers to trade, including quotas and tariffs on imported

Public assistance programs: Efforts by government to provide a more equitable distribution of income.

goods, form a "subsidy" to domestic producers. In many cases, such as in the plant and flower industry (see Economics in Action, Chapter 2), in textiles, and in the automobile industry, the government redistributes income from domestic consumers of products to businesses and laborers in the protected industries.

Government has always functioned as a redistributor of income in the United States, but that role has expanded greatly in the past twenty-five years. As always in economics, the question is not essentially *whether* income should be redistributed to the poor, sick, and needy, but *how much* should be transferred within the political process. President George Bush called for a new initiative of private charity to care for those in need (a "thousand points of light"), but critics charge that an entirely private redress of the problems of the poor will always be insufficient. Economists do not ordinarily comment on the normative aspects of such policies. The economist, however, has a role to play in assessing the problems of income distribution. As we will see in Chapter 18, the economist analyzes income distribution and the costs and benefits of initiating, expanding, or contracting specific welfare programs.

Antitrust and Monopoly Regulation. Another broad area of increased government participation in the U.S. free-market economy is **industry regulation.** Early in this century, antitrust laws prohibiting price discrimination, collusion among producers, and deceptive advertising practices were passed in an attempt to restore competition where it no longer existed. Such laws continue to be enforced today.

Industry regulation: Government rules to control the behavior of firms, particularly regarding prices and production techniques.

Even earlier, however, economists and politicians believed that government had a role whenever competition could not exist, perhaps because of economies of large-scale production, or what economists call *natural monopolies.* Such monopolies are created when each seller can produce more and more output at lower and lower costs. Eventually it becomes profitable for only one seller to supply the *total* quantity demanded of a good, thereby creating a monopoly. Federal, state, and local governments undertook the regulation—not the ownership or operation—of transportation, communications, energy, and many other industries that were regarded as natural monopolies. Government regulation was considered a substitute for competition where viable competition could not exist because of industry production and cost conditions.

Some economists have strongly disputed this view (see Chapter 19) and question the existence of large-scale economies (natural monopoly) in many of these regulated industries. Some contemporary economists believe that regulation of prices and profits must fail, either because regulation has been ineffective or because these industries are more competitive than previously thought. Questions have been raised about the self-interested supply of regulation by politicians combined with the self-interested demand for regulation by firms and industries. Do industries and other interest groups use the government regulatory apparatus for their own benefit? Should broad areas of regulation of industry, such as regulation of transportation and communications be eliminated? Has the deregulation of airlines fostered competition and benefited consumers, as many economists allege? These and many other issues concerning the expanded role of government are in hot debate. A firm foundation in economic theory is required to answer these important questions.

Economic stabilization:
The goal of governments' attempts to prevent adverse swings of inflation rates, interest rates, unemployment rates, and economic growth rates over time in the economy.

Economic Stabilization.　A final, but crucially important, part of the expanded role of government is in macroeconomic **stabilization** of the economy—that is, the government's efforts to promote full employment of resources without creating increases in the price level (or inflation). Taxation, expenditure policies, and the money supply can be intentionally changed by the federal government to help maintain full employment and promote economic growth at noninflationary levels.

Whether the government is capable of achieving macroeconomic goals of full employment without inflation is a subject of debate among economists. The mission to stabilize business cycles of inflation and unemployment has been a generally accepted role of government since the 1930s—the years of massive unemployment of resources known as the Great Depression. Much of the impetus to assign this new function to government came from the writings of the British economist John Maynard Keynes (1883–1946). Keynes believed that government could actually influence employment and inflation through spending and taxing policies and could thereby prevent depressions or severe reductions in economic activity.

The role of government in American economic life is much larger than it was fifty years ago. The American market system is modified laissez-faire. Government has provided a large number of social and economic goods, regulated markets and externalities such as pollution, and attempted to establish a high rate of economic growth through full employment without inflation. These microeconomic and macroeconomic functions of government receive a great deal of attention later in this book. A brief look now at the relative size of government's role in the private economy will provide some perspective on the modified system of laissez-faire that constitutes the American market system.

GROWTH OF GOVERNMENT

Private sector:
All parts of the economy and activities that are not part of government.

How big is government in our mixed American economy? Should the economic role of government be larger or smaller in relation to that of the **private sector**—all nongovernment activities? This is the subject of an ongoing debate among political candidates, members of Congress, journalists, intellectuals, academics, and private citizens. Rather than developing value judgments about how big government should be, economists analyze the probable effects of political decisions on the past and present role of government. To provide background information for such an economic analysis, we examine the size of the U.S. government's economic role by looking at its expenditures and the taxes it levies to support them, contrast the level of U.S. government taxation and spending with that of some other developed nations, and then relate this information to patterns of economic growth.

The Size of the Federal Budget

We can get an overview of the role of the federal government in the U.S. economy by looking at a gross measure of government expenditures and receipts over the past four decades. Figure 3 depicts the federal budget (expenditures and tax receipts) for the years 1950–1991 (estimated). After a slow

FIGURE 3

Growth of the Federal Budget, 1950–1991

Since 1950 the federal budget (the total of expenditures and receipts) has grown both absolutely, in total dollars, and as a percentage of the gross national product. Federal deficits grew dramatically in the first half of the 1980s but have begun to decline since then. The deficits for 1990 and 1991 are estimates.

Sources: Board of Governors of the Federal Reserve System, *Historical Chart Book* (Washington, D.C.: U.S. Government Printing Office, 1986); Council of Economic Advisers, *Economic Report of the President* (Washington, D.C.: U.S. Government Printing Office, 1990), p. 383.

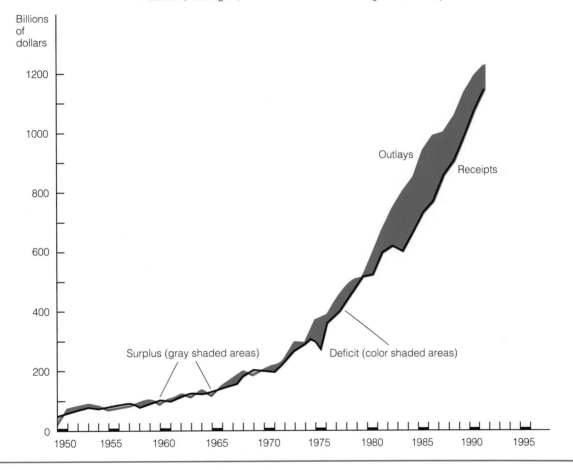

rate of growth through the mid-1960s, expenditures and tax receipts began to increase at a faster pace.

The Great Society welfare programs begun by President Lyndon B. Johnson in the mid-1960s and the defense expenditures of the Vietnam War were partly responsible for the absolute increases in government spending and taxation. Especially during the 1970s, deficits appeared when expenditures exceeded tax revenues. The government's growth is not only of recent origin, however. The Franklin D. Roosevelt administration's social and economic programs in the 1930s—a response to the largest worldwide depression in modern history—were an initial and important force for the expansion of government into a mixed economy. The participation of government at all levels—federal, state, and local—has increased dramatically since 1930.

Since prices of goods and services have risen considerably during the twentieth century, the absolute dollar increase in government expenditures

Gross national product (GNP):
The dollar value measured at market prices of all final goods and services produced in an economy in one year.

does not necessarily indicate whether government has grown bigger relative to the private sector. For this information, economists often look at government expenditures as a percentage of the **gross national product,** or GNP. The GNP is the aggregate value of all goods and services produced in the country over some period, usually a year. Using this measure, economists have found that while the government accounted for less than 10 percent of all purchases of goods and services as a percent of gross national product in 1929, by 1989 government purchases of goods and services were responsible for more than 20 percent of GNP. Since 1960, government's percentage of purchases of goods and services has remained fairly constant at 20 percent, but this constancy understates the growth of the government's role in the economy. The government's tax receipts at all levels in 1989 accounted for more than 32 percent of GNP. We can understand the discrepancy between expenditures and receipts and the expanding role of government by examining the kinds or distributions of expenditures at the various levels of government and then looking at the ways the government collects revenues.

Government Expenditures

Direct government purchases:
Real goods and services, such as equipment, buildings, and consulting services, purchased by all levels of government.

Government transfer payments:
Money transferred by government through taxes from one group to another, either directly or indirectly; also called income security transfers.

There are two kinds of government expenditures: direct purchases of goods and services and transfer payments. **Direct purchases** of newly produced goods and services include such items as missiles, highway construction, police and fire stations, consulting services, and the like. In other words, the government purchases real goods and services. **Transfer payments** are the transfers of income from some citizens (via taxation) to other citizens; these are sometimes called *income security transfers* or payments. Examples of transfer payments are Social Security contributions and payments, Aid to Families with Dependent Children, food stamp programs, and other welfare payments. These transfers do not represent direct purchases by the government of new goods and services, but they influence purchases of goods and services in the private sector. They are a growing part of government's role in the mixed economy.

The Distribution of Federal Expenditures. Out of the thousands of items in the federal budget, we can use six major categories to compare expenditures as a percentage of the total federal budget in 1960 and 1989 (see Figure 4). Since providing national defense is one of the major functions of the federal government, we would expect defense to account for a large proportion of federal outlays, and it does. National defense expenditures represented about one-quarter of all federal outlays in 1989. The largest single item in the 1989 federal budget, however, was not defense expenditures but income security transfers, which made up 33 percent of total outlays. Expenditures on interest service of the federal debt, education, and natural resources ranged from almost 15 percent to about 1 percent, respectively. The remainder, accounting for only 10 percent of the federal budget, went to such activities and projects as the administration of justice, science and technology, transportation, agriculture, international affairs, energy, the environment, revenue sharing, and the running of general government.

A mere recital of the proportions of outlays in the 1989 budget is not as interesting as a more dynamic picture of how these outlays changed over the preceding three decades. Using Figure 4, compare the distribution of expenditures in 1960 and 1989. In 1960, fully 50 percent of federal expenditures

FIGURE 4

These two illustrations show percentage shares of federal spending. Expenditures at the federal level between 1960 and 1989 underwent dramatic changes. The percentage spent on defense was cut in half and the percentage of the budget spent for income security transfers increased by 14 percent. Education and health also received increased shares of expenditures.

Source: Council of Economic Advisers, *Economic Report of the President* (Washington, D.C.: U.S. Government Printing Office, 1990), p. 385.

Federal Expenditures, 1960 and 1989

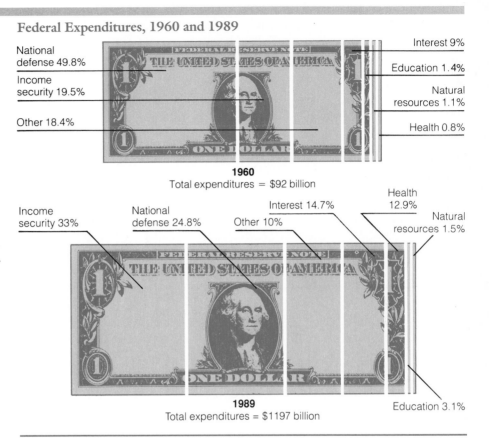

National defense 49.8%
Income security 19.5%
Other 18.4%
Interest 9%
Education 1.4%
Natural resources 1.1%
Health 0.8%

1960
Total expenditures = $92 billion

Income security 33%
National defense 24.8%
Interest 14.7%
Other 10%
Health 12.9%
Natural resources 1.5%

1989
Total expenditures = $1197 billion
Education 3.1%

went to national defense, while only 19 percent went to income security. Health-related expenditures have grown from less than 1 percent in 1960 to more than 12 percent in 1989.

Changes in defense spending and in transfer payments between 1960 and 1989 are part of a clear trend over the period, shown in Figure 5. Over most of the 1960s, transfer payments grew at a faster rate than defense purchases, reflecting the decisions of President Johnson and Congress to attack poverty and social imbalance. In spite of the fiscal pressures of the Vietnam conflict, transfer payments overtook defense purchases in absolute amounts—that is, in actual billions of dollars spent—in about 1970 and have exceeded them every year since.

Will this trend continue? Ronald Reagan campaigned for and won the presidency in 1980 and 1984 partly on this issue, promising to slow the growth rate in income security expenditures and to raise it on defense expenditures. To an extent he succeeded, but President George Bush, promising to work toward budget balance, has had to moderate all spending. The final outcome is still unclear.

State and Local Expenditures. Figure 6 shows that the primary public goods provided by state and local government are education, highways, public welfare, health and hospitals, police and fire protection, and other goods and services. Economists, voters, and other observers view the federal government as the principal economic agent in the mixed economy. The truth is, however,

FIGURE 5

The dramatic growth rate in transfer payments over the 1960s and 1970s is shown in the figure. Absolute amounts spent on transfer payments overtook defense expenditures in about 1970.

Sources: Board of Governors of the Federal Reserve System, *Historical Chart Book* (Washington, D.C.: U.S. Government Printing Office, 1984), p. 53; Council of Economic Advisers, *Economic Report of the President* (Washington, D.C.: U.S. Government Printing Office, 1990), p. 389.

Growth in Government Expenditures, 1950–1989

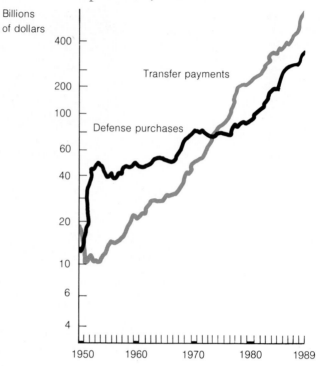

FIGURE 6

Principal expenditures at the state and local levels of government are on education, highways, public welfare, and health and hospitals.

Source: Facts and Figures on Government Finance (Washington, D.C.: The Tax Foundation, 1988), p. 168.

State and Local Expenditures by Category

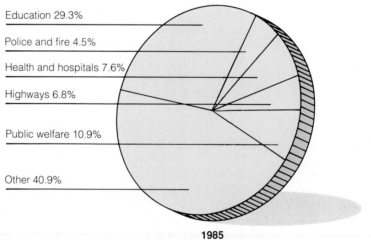

Education 29.3%

Police and fire 4.5%

Health and hospitals 7.6%

Highways 6.8%

Public welfare 10.9%

Other 40.9%

1985
Total state and local outlays = $658 billion

that state and local governments combined approximate the level of goods and services provided by the federal government. The big difference between the economic impact of the federal government and state and local governments is the huge federal redistribution of funds through the tax system from some citizens to others. When income security transfers are included, the economic impact of the federal budget is larger than that of state and local governments.

Government Receipts: The U.S. Tax System in Brief

Goods and social transfers provided at all levels of government are paid for out of taxation. The type of taxes levied at federal, state, and local levels varies a great deal.

Federal Taxation. The principal source of federal revenues, as shown in Figure 7, is the individual income tax. In 1990, the individual income tax is expected to account for 45.6 percent of total federal receipts.

Second in order of importance at the federal level, representing 35.9 percent of receipts in 1990, are receipts from social insurance taxes and other contributions. These taxes are, principally, the payroll taxes paid jointly by employees and employers that finance Social Security, disability compensation, and other payments. Receipts from these taxes have grown, dramatically, from less than $10 billion in 1950 to more than $600 billion in 1990.

Taxes on corporate income accounted for about 10 percent of revenues in 1990 and have generally declined since 1970 as a percentage of federal revenue. Other sources of federal revenues include federal excise taxes on goods such as liquor, tobacco, and gasoline, customs deposits paid on imports and exports, and estate and gift taxes.

FIGURE 7

Social insurance tax receipts have more than doubled as a percentage of total receipts between 1959 and 1990, while the relative contribution of the individual income tax has remained almost constant. (Data for 1990 are estimated.)

Source: Council of Economic Advisers, *Economic Report of the President* (Washington, D.C.: U.S. Government Printing Office, 1990), p. 385.

Distribution of Federal Tax Receipts, 1959 and 1990

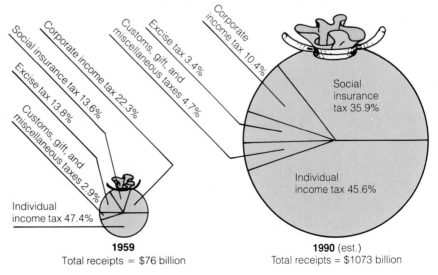

Social insurance tax 13.6%
Corporate income tax 22.3%
Excise tax 13.8%
Customs, gift, and miscellaneous taxes 2.9%
Individual income tax 47.4%

Customs, gift, and miscellaneous taxes 4.7%
Excise tax 3.4%
Corporate income tax 10.4%
Social insurance tax 35.9%
Individual income tax 45.6%

1959
Total receipts = $76 billion

1990 (est.)
Total receipts = $1073 billion

State and Local Receipts.   State and local governments rely primarily on property taxes and sales taxes for revenue. Additional revenue sources, of varying importance from state to state, are the state income tax and state lottery. Only about 10 percent of state receipts were from state income taxes in 1990. Transfers of revenue from the federal to state and local governments, called *grants-in-aid*, have assumed increasing importance over the past twenty years. In 1990, for example, federal grants accounted for the highest single percentage of revenue for states and municipalities.

The United States and Other Mixed Economies

The preceding discussions indicate the kinds of activities pursued by government in a mixed economy as well as the kinds of taxes the government relies on for revenue. The relative size of government is only hinted at by the breakdowns of outlays and receipts, however. To understand how mixed the American economy is, we can consider some international comparisons.

Figure 8 shows the growth of the government's public expenditures as a percentage of gross domestic product for five Western industrialized nations

FIGURE 8

Relative Growth Rates of Government Public Expenditures in Five Western Democracies, 1965–1988

The bars represent government expenditures as a percentage of gross domestic product (GDP). By this measure, the U.S. economy is the least mixed of five Western democracies.

Sources: Organization for Economic Cooperation and Development, *Main Economic Indicators,* various issues; *Government Finance Statistics Yearbook* (Washington, D.C.: International Monetary Fund, 1989).

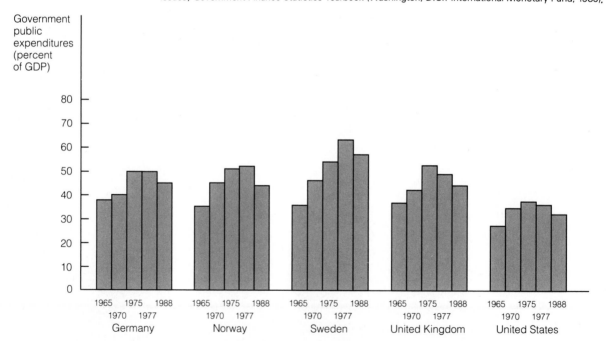

Gross domestic product (GDP):
A measure of the final goods and services produced by a country with resources located within that country.

between 1965 and 1988. **Gross domestic product** (GDP), like GNP, is a measure of a country's production of goods and services, but GDP measures final goods and services produced using domestic resources. (GDP is determined by subtracting income earned by foreign investments from the GNP.)

Public expenditures as a percentage of GDP grew between 1965 and 1977 in all of the countries shown in Figure 8, although the percentage has declined since 1985. The percentage of government expenditures in Sweden almost doubled between 1965 and 1977. By 1977, more than 60 percent of spending in Sweden was directed by the government. Germany, Norway, and the United Kingdom were about evenly divided in their mix between public and private participation in the economy by 1977. The trend over the past fifty years, until the 1980s, at least, has been toward more government participation in Western democracies. The bottom line: Of the leading Western industrialized nations, the U.S. economy is the least mixed in that the government directs only one-third of the country's spending.

The Economic Effects of Increased Government

Do economists care about how mixed economies are? Most economists believe that rational self-interested forces and private enterprise are the key factors leading to maximum output, growth, and efficiency. In their view, government-directed enterprises—of self-perpetuating bureaucracies—do not normally provide maximum incentives for work, creativity, technology, and economic progress.

An ever growing federal debt, the result of previous deficits, is also a major feature of the increased size of government in the United States. The sheer size of the debt is staggering—over three *trillion* (3319 billion) dollars in 1990. Growing deficits (the difference between government expenditures and tax collections) create this debt, which must be financed through borrowing from individuals or from banks. Government borrowing competes with businesses who borrow and use the private savings of individuals for investment. Some economists argue that the pressure of government debt finance reduces private investment and the future production possibilities of society. Further, there is the important question of whether and in what manner future generations will be burdened by the debt. There are alternative views on these complicated issues. At this point it is important to remember that an enormous federal debt has accompanied the recent progress of American capitalism; that debt, and the growth in deficits that created it, may alter that progress.

Government, as we have seen, has important and legitimate functions. Few economists, moreover, would question some redistribution of income based on a concept of justice since a market system does not automatically produce a just distribution of income or wealth. The question plaguing economists is a marginal one: Will added government control over a given amount of private resources increase or decrease satisfaction and economic incentives to work, produce, and invest? Is the relative size of government a tonic to economic society or a sedative? These are extraordinarily difficult questions to answer. Much of this book is devoted to both microeconomic and macroeconomic analyses of these critical questions since American capitalism is a blend of larger government combined with free-market forces.

SUMMARY

This chapter discussed alternative economic systems and their characteristics, with particular emphasis on the American economy.

1. Specialization and trade, which are responses to the problem of scarcity, take place within economic systems. The two main types of economic systems are socialist and capitalist.
2. Market societies allocate resources and consumer goods and services through the interplay between consumers' dollar votes and the free and unregulated decisions of producers and resource suppliers.
3. All real-world systems are combinations of socialist and capitalist characteristics. Further, modern economic systems are mixed economies because they contain elements of both free-market forces and government provision of goods, services, and income security transfers.
4. Some of the important features of American capitalism include the individual's right to own and dispose of property, a legal system protecting property and contracts, free enterprise, competitive economic markets, and a traditionally limited economic role for government.
5. An expanded economic role for government characterizes contemporary American capitalism. The basis for this role is the provision of goods such as national defense that would not be produced in sufficient quantity by the private sector. Government also intervenes in the market to block the effects of negative externalities, to regulate industry competition, and to help achieve economic stabilization.
6. Local, state, and federal governments directed about one-third of America's resources in 1990 through purchases of goods and services and through the redistribution of income. Income security transfers are, in absolute terms and as a percentage of total spending, the largest item in the federal budget, whereas expenditures on defense are half the percentage today that they were in 1960.
7. Economists study mixed economies and the role of government to determine whether an enlarged public sector increases economic well-being or reduces incentives to work and to invest capital.

KEY TERMS

economic system
pure capitalism
pure socialism
pure communism
mixed capitalism
market society
barter
circular flow of income

free enterprise
competition
laissez-faire economy
public goods
positive externality
negative externality
public assistance programs
industry regulation

economic stabilization
private sector
gross national product
direct government
  purchases
government transfer
  payments
gross domestic product

QUESTIONS FOR REVIEW AND DISCUSSION

1. How are the "what," "how," and "for whom" questions determined in a market society and in a command society?
2. "They don't build cars like they used to. These days cars wear out before they are paid for." This type of statement is heard frequently. Who determines the quality and durability of products?
3. What is capitalism and what does it have to do with property rights and economic freedom?
4. What are some of the roles of government in the U.S. economy? Has the role of government increased in size and scope? Does this hinder or help the rate of economic growth?

5. What are the primary activities of state and local governments?
6. Can free enterprise exist in a country where a dictator or king has absolute power?
7. "The local cable TV company provides slower services, and it doesn't have many channels." If this cable company has a monopoly granted by the government, is Adam Smith's invisible hand at work?

8. The Baltimore city government was disappointed when the Colts, a professional football team, moved to Indianapolis. Is a professional football team a public good? Explain.
9. Does individual self-interest hinder economic growth and well-being if there is competition?
10. What can government do to improve the general economic welfare? Has it done such things?

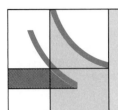

ECONOMICS IN ACTION
Contrasts in Economic Institutions: The Two Koreas

Can differences in social, political, and economic institutions be pinpointed as a major cause of differences in economic development? The experiences of North Korea and South Korea—neighboring countries with vastly different institutions—suggest the answer to this question is yes.

The two Koreas were one nation for hundreds of years. When the two separated in 1950, they adopted diametrically opposed paths to economic development. The People's Democratic Republic of (North) Korea has adhered strictly to the central planning model. It has one of the world's most highly socialized and centrally planned economies. All industrial enterprises are either directly owned by the state or are cooperatives owned indirectly by the state. Agriculture is carried out on either collective or state farms. Following the Soviet model (that is, the Soviet model *before* Gorbachev's economic reforms), the central planning system has allocated priority to investment in heavy industry at the expense of consumer and agricultural sectors. Despite this emphasis, the performance of the industrial sector has been disappointing. Productivity is low, and virtually all plants and equipment are obsolete, although North Korea has recently begun to purchase Western equipment and technology, including complete plants. Nominal per capita income in 1988 was approximately $1200 per year. There is little variety in consumer goods, and quality is uniformly low. Shortages are common, and standing in long lines to purchase basic necessities is a way of life. Consumer durables like appliances are usually unavailable.

Although the land, climate, and people of South Korea are similar to those of North Korea, there are dramatic dif-

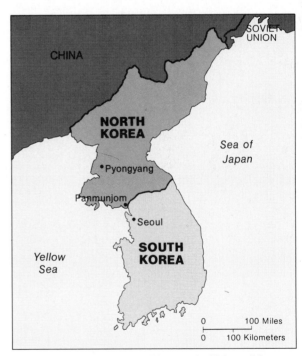

The arbitrary political division of Korea at the 38th parallel following World War II produced two very different nations.

ferences between the two countries. The Republic of (South) Korea has an economy based on private enterprise and a market economy. In a little over twenty years South Korea transformed itself from an economy dominated by subsistence agriculture (which is characteristic of most poor nations) to a modern economy with an emphasis on light industry. A thriving export market has led to South Korea's surge of development, and exports increased annually between 1974 and 1989. This growth reflects, in part, the improving quality of its exports, which include many finished goods, such as Hyundai automobiles and trucks and Reebok shoes. The standard of living is among the highest in modern Asia; per capita income for South Koreans in 1988 was over $2000, with a diverse array of high-quality consumer goods available. Interestingly, South Korea has only 10 to 20 percent of the Korean peninsula's deposits of mineral resources.

Similar contrasts may be made between the ethnically and culturally identical mainland Chinese and their freer neighbors in Hong Kong and on Taiwan. Estimates of GNP per capita in 1985 put China at $253, Taiwan (1986) at $3784, and Hong Kong at $6258. The standard of living in the latter two countries is high and visibly improving with relatively low levels of government regulation and thriving entrepreneurship. Despite some continued political repression, communist China is currently experimenting with capitalist elements in its own economy (as you discovered in Focus, "Capitalism: Wave of the Future?").

Such real-world examples suggest that different systems of property rights and incentive structures play a vital role in relative economic development. In other words, economists believe that many differences in economic development between North and South Korea can be explained on the grounds of different institutions. These institutional differences, especially those relating to political controls or to regulation of markets and economic processes, are often more important than the endowment of resources in determining economic progress.

Question

Why do you think countries with centrally planned economies typically have lower output and standards of living than countries with a free-market economic system, even when the countries have similar natural resources?

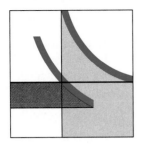

4

Markets and Prices: The Laws of Demand and Supply

Simple specialization began to take place in primitive cultures as individuals recognized unique abilities in themselves and in others. As we have seen, increasing specialization led to organized markets where people bought and sold goods, to the use of money, and to increasingly large groups of buyers and sellers. Economists define these organized markets—such as bazaars, the stock exchange, or Saks Fifth Avenue—as places or circumstances that bring together demanders (buyers) and suppliers (sellers) of any goods or services.

After reading Chapter 4 you should understand

- the motivations of demanders and suppliers in the exchange of goods and services in markets.
- how and why some goods and services get produced and sold at certain prices while other items are not produced or sold at all.
- what happens to demand and supply when governments or other agencies institute price or rent controls.
- that the full price we pay for goods and services includes the money price and such things as time and the other costs involved in a transaction.

AN OVERVIEW OF THE PRICE SYSTEM

Every day the news media provide dramatic evidence of the workings of the market system. The price of silver rises by 45 percent in one day as massive investments in silver futures by two of the world's richest oil magnates trigger a bandwagon effect. Leak of a technological breakthrough in a certain computer firm creates a frenzy of stock buying, driving up the price of the firm's stock overnight. Crude oil prices fall sharply when the OPEC cartel has trouble policing its members.

In the familiar economic transactions of everyday life, we too enter markets where buyers and sellers congregate to buy and sell a great variety of products and services. The typical American supermarket sells thousands of products, and as we wander through the store we can view a price system in action. In the produce section, for instance, quantities and prices of fruits and vegetables depend on the quantities consumers want and on the season. Early crops usually bring in the highest prices. Watermelon may sell for more than two dollars a pound in March but only fifteen cents a pound by the Fourth of July.

What determines who will get the early melons or how they will be rationed among those who want them? Why are prices and quantities constantly rising and falling for millions of goods and services in our economy? How do new products find their way to places where buyers and sellers congregate? The answers are simple. In a market society, the self-interest of consumers and producers, of households and businesses, determines who gets what and how much. To paraphrase Adam Smith, it is not to the benevolence of the butcher and the baker that we owe our dinner but to their self-interest. The primary way that consumers and producers express their self-interest is through the economic laws of supply and demand. Sticking a price tag on a product does not imply price-setting power, as anyone who has run a garage sale knows. In a market system, demand and supply determine prices, and prices are the essential pieces of information on which consumers, households, businesses, and resource suppliers make decisions. High melon prices in March will encourage suppliers and discourage demanders, whereas low prices in July will encourage demanders and discourage suppliers. Before investigating the mechanics of these laws of supply and demand, we consider a simple overview of the price system.

As market participants, households and businesses play dual roles. Businesses supply final output of products and services—rock concerts, bananas, hair stylings—but also must hire or demand resources to produce the outputs. Households demand rock concerts, bananas, and hair stylings for final consumption. But they also supply labor and entrepreneurial ability as well as quantities of land and capital to earn income for the purchase of products and services.

As Figure 1 shows, businesses and households are interconnected by the **products** (outputs) **market** and by the **resources** (inputs) **market.** Each market depends on the other; they are linked by the prices of outputs and inputs. The particular mix of goods and services exchanged in the products market depends on consumer demands in that market plus the cost and availability of necessary resources. For example, which groups are featured at a rock concert will depend on what the targeted audience wants to hear plus the ability of that audience to pay the price asked by the groups and the groups' availability on the chosen date. Similarly, the particular mix of resources available at any one time or through time is determined by what households are demanding—subject also to the availability of the resources. If land suitable for banana growing is available, it is most likely to be sold for banana plantations if households are demanding a lot of bananas, thereby making it possible for banana growers to pay landowners handsomely for their land.

Prices are the impulses of information that make the entire system of input and output markets operate. Take the prices of fad goods: At times, certain goods or services—such as hula hoops and Nintendo video games—have quickly appeared and then disappeared. When a fad begins to catch on, prices tend to be high because there is a high and rapidly growing demand and because resources necessary to produce the good may be scarce and command a high price. It takes time to adapt resources to the production of

Product market:
The forces created by buyers and sellers that establish the prices and quantities exchanged of goods and services.

Resource market:
The forces created by buyers and sellers that establish the prices and quantities exchanged of resources such as land, labor services, and capital.

FIGURE 1   The Product and Resource Markets: A Circular Flow

Businesses play a dual role in the market economy: They are the suppliers of goods and
services as well as the demanders of resources. Households also have a dual role: They are
both demanders of goods and services and suppliers of resources.

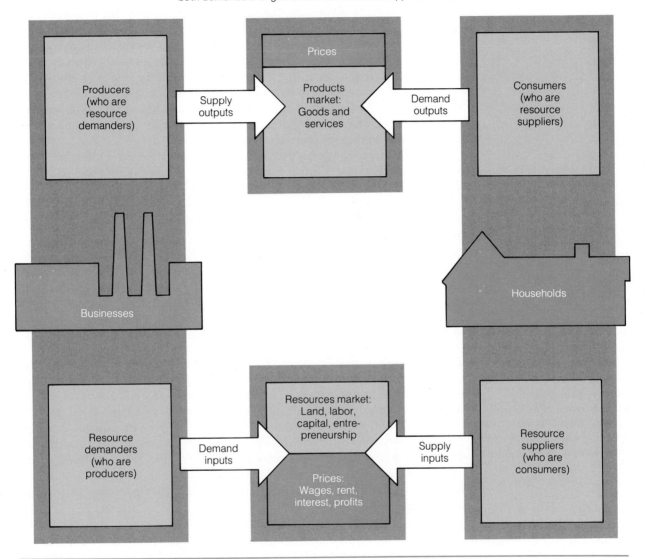

the fad good. Labor must be drawn from other uses and trained in the new
production techniques. Marketing channels must be established so that sellers
and buyers can converge at convenient points of trade. Demand for the fad
good is transmitted through businesses to the factors of production through
a system of prices. Initially high prices signal the scarcity of goods and resources. As more entrepreneurs and businesses perceive the profit opportunities associated with the fad and as more resources are discovered or
developed to produce it, prices of both the inputs and the outputs change
accordingly.

The price system reacts similarly with goods that remain in the market for a longer time. Consider the development of computers and computer technology in the 1960s. Initial investments by producers were substantial as businesses rushed to introduce computer systems. In particular, the wages of computer programmers and technicians were high because there was a relative scarcity of workers possessing the skills necessary to use and produce computers. High demand and relative scarcity mean high wages. However, high wages are also an excellent piece of information that may encourage changes that ultimately lower wages. From the 1960s to the present, many schools teaching computer technology have emerged, reducing the scarcity of this resource. Demand for computer technology, however, has grown over time. The wages for people supplying services essential to production depend on consumers' demand for computers and on price(wage)-signaled supply conditions in the market for these services.

The informative signals of a price system work whether goods have short or long lives. The prices formed in both product and resource markets reflect the relative desires of consumer-demanders for particular goods and services as well as the relative scarcity of the resources required to produce them. The very fact that a product or service bears a price means that scarcity exists. Supply and demand in all markets is at the core of scarcity and, therefore, of economics. These critical notions must be understood with the greatest possible clarity. We begin with demand.

THE LAW OF DEMAND

Relative price:
The price ratio or "trade-off" in consumption between one product (or service) and another product (or service) or between one good and other goods taken as a whole.

The concept of demand is intuitive. The notion that the amount of goods sold depends on the prices charged seems to "just make sense." The amount of any one good bought during a sale, for example, depends upon the **relative price** of the good on sale—the price in relation to the price of some other good or of goods as a whole. The actual money price of the good in isolation does not determine what we purchase. If the relative price of shoes declines—that is, the item is put "on sale"—the price has fallen relative to other shoes, shirts, or camcorders. Intuitively, we understand that more shoes will be purchased. By formally expressing this easily understood relationship, economists merely make intuition more rigorous.

Law of demand:
The price of a product or service and the amount purchased are inversely related. If price rises, then quantity demanded falls; if price falls, quantity demanded increases, all other things held constant.

What determines how much of any good or service—camcorders, compact discs, or hair styling—consumers will purchase during some period of time? Economists have answered that question for hundreds of years in the same manner—by formulating a general rule, or law, of demand. The **law of demand** states that, other things being equal or constant, the quantity demanded of any good or service increases as the price of the good or service declines. In other words, **quantity demanded** is inversely related to the price of the good or service in question.

Quantity demanded:
The amount of any good or service consumers are willing and able to purchase at various prices.

The relation between price and quantity demanded is a fact of everyday experience. The reaction of individuals and groups to two-for-the-price-of-one sales, cut-rate airline tickets, and other bargains is common proof that quantities demanded increase as prices decrease. Likewise, gas price hikes will lower the quantity of gasoline demanded. The formalization of the inverse relation between price and quantity demanded is called a law because econo-

Demand curve:
A graphic representation of the quantities of a product that people are willing and able to purchase at all possible prices.

mists believe it is a general rule for all consumers in all markets. Imagine a graphic representation of the law of demand—called a **demand curve**—for two hypothetical consumers.

The Individual's Demand Schedule and Demand Curve

Suppose that we observe the behavior of Dave and Marcia over one month. These two music lovers own compact disc players and are willing and able to purchase, or demand, CDs. To determine Dave's and Marcia's demand for CDs, we need only to vary the price of discs over the month, assuming that all other factors affecting their decisions remain constant, and observe the quantities of CDs they would demand at various prices. This information is summarized in Table 1.

Table 1 shows a range of CD prices available to Marcia and Dave over the one-month period and the quantities (numbers) of discs that each would purchase, all other things being equal. (For simplicity we have kept CD prices low.) Given factors such as their income and the availability of other forms of entertainment, neither person would choose to purchase even a single CD at $10 per disc. Dave, however, would buy one CD per month at $9 and two at $8. Marcia would not buy her first CD until the price was $7. Each would purchase more discs as the price falls. Thus, Dave's and Marcia's CD-buying habits conform to the law of demand.

We obtain the individuals' demand curves by simply plotting or transferring the information from Table 1 to the graphs in Figure 2a and b. The prices of CDs are given on the vertical axis of each graph, and the quantities of CDs demanded per month are given on the horizontal axis. The various combinations of price and quantity from Table 1 are plotted on the graphs. Each demand curve is then drawn as the line connecting those combinations of price and quantity. For both Dave and Marcia, the demand curve slopes

---

TABLE 1

Two Consumers' Demand Schedules

While individuals' demand schedules may differ, they do not violate the law of demand. For both people, the quantity demanded increases as the price falls.

Price of Compact Discs (dollars)	Quantity Demanded (per month)	
	Dave	Marcia
10	0	0
9	1	0
8	2	0
7	3	1
6	4	2
5	5	3
4	6	4
3	7	5
2	8	6
1	9	7
0	10	8

FIGURE 2

A consumer's demand for a product is the quantity that he or she is willing to purchase at each price. The demand curve is downward-sloping for both Dave (a) and Marcia (b): As the price falls the quantity demanded increases, and as the price rises the quantity demanded decreases.

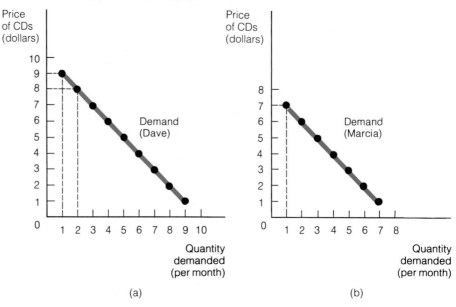

Demand Curves for Two Consumers

(a)   (b)

downward and to the right (a negative slope), indicating an increase in quantity demanded as the price declines and a decrease in quantity demanded as the price rises.

Factors Affecting the Individual's Demand Curve

In addition to the price of a good or service, there are dozens, perhaps hundreds, of other factors and circumstances affecting a person's decision to buy or not to buy. These **factors affecting demand** include income, the price of related goods, price expectations, income expectations, tastes, the number of consumers, and time. Even when the list of other factors is limited, as here, it is not possible to handle simultaneous variations among all factors in expressing a demand curve or schedule.

Factors affecting demand: Anything other than price, such as consumer income and preferences, that determines the amount of a product or service that consumers are willing and able to purchase.

Holding Factors Other Than Price Constant. To isolate the effect of price on quantity demanded, the nonessential factors must be stripped away. We want to know what quantity of CDs Dave and Marcia would choose to purchase in a month at various possible prices, given that other factors affecting their decision do not change. This condition is called *ceteris paribus* ("other things being equal") by economists. It is essential to the development of any economic theory or model dealing with real-world events since all events cannot be controlled. Economists hold factors such as income and the price of related goods constant when constructing a demand schedule or curve.

Ceteris paribus: The Latin phrase for "all other things held constant."

This does not mean that these factors cannot change, but if they do change, the demand schedule or curve must be adjusted to account for them. Laboratory scientists are in a better position than economists to hold conditions constant. Chemists can perform controlled experiments, but economists, like weather forecasters, deal with a subject matter that can rarely be controlled. Economics, after all, is a social science; it deals with human nature and with people in society. The very subject matter of economics makes most factors affecting demand difficult to control. But like their scientific counterparts, economists must use scientific methods to organize real-world events into theories of how things work. The economist can use these theories to predict some of the effects on the demand schedule of changes in factors other than price.

Changes in Demand Versus Changes in Quantity Demanded. A simple but crucial distinction exists between a change in Dave's or Marcia's *demand* for CDs and a **change in** their **quantity demanded** of CDs. Other things being equal, a change in the price of CDs will change the quantity demanded of CDs, as we have seen. Figures 3 and 4 illustrate an increase and a decrease in quantity demanded, respectively. The graphs illustrate a movement along a single demand curve, indicating that factors like buyers' incomes and preferences are held constant. Figure 3 shows that a decrease in the price of discs leads to an increase in the quantity demanded. Figure 4 shows that an increase in the price of discs reduces the quantity demanded. A change in any factor other than the price will shift the entire demand curve to the right or left. Economists call this a **change in demand.** An increase in demand is shown as the rightward shift of the entire demand curve in Figure 5. A decrease in demand, shown in Figure 6, is a leftward shift in the entire demand curve.

Change in quantity demanded:
A change in the amount of a good a consumer is willing and able to purchase that is caused by a change in the price of the good or service.

Change in demand:
A shift of the entire demand curve to the right or left.

FIGURE 3
Increase in Quantity Demanded

Holding Marcia's demand constant, a decrease in the price of CDs from $4 to $3 will lead to an increase in the quantity of CDs demanded from 4 to 5 per month.

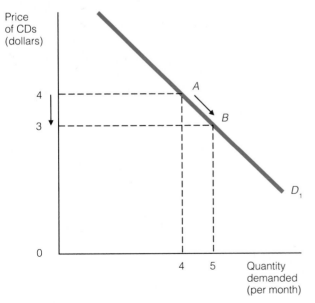

FIGURE 4
Decrease in Quantity Demanded

Holding Marcia's demand constant, an increase in the price of the CDs from $4 to $6 will cause Marcia to decrease the quantity of CDs demanded from 4 to 2 per month.

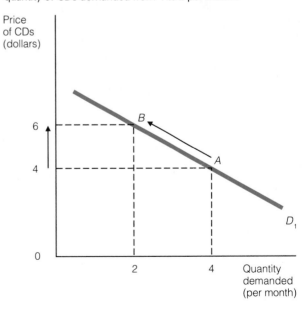

FIGURE 5
Increase in Demand

A change in any factors affecting demand causes a shift to the right or left in the demand curve. In this case, Marcia's income increases, causing an increase in her quantities demanded for CDs at every price. The demand curve shifts to the right. At a price of $4 per disc, Marcia previously would purchase 4 CDs, but given her increased income, she would now purchase 8 CDs. In this representation, D = demand.

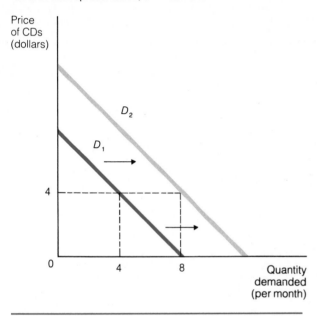

FIGURE 6
Decrease in Demand

A leftward shift of the demand curve indicates a decrease in demand. In this case, the price of a substitute good decreased, causing Dave to demand fewer discs at every price. The demand curve shifts to the left. Before the price change in the substitute good, Dave would purchase 5 CDs at $5 each, but given the change in the substitute good's price, he would purchase only 2 CDs at $5 each.

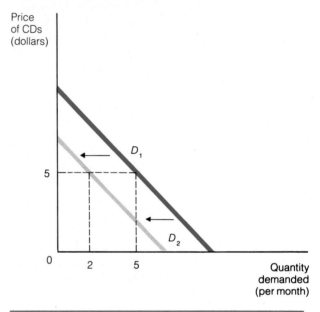

Normal good:
A good that a consumer chooses to purchase in smaller (larger) amounts as income falls (rises).

Inferior good:
A good that a consumer chooses to purchase in smaller quantities as income rises or in larger amounts as income falls.

Change in Income. Marcia's or Dave's income may change, and such a change would necessitate a redrawing of the entire demand curve for CDs. For most goods, a rise in income means an increase in demand. For instance, if Marcia's income increases from $1500 to $2000 a month, she will demand more CDs at every price because she can afford more. Figure 5 shows that, given a new, higher income, Marcia's demand curve shifts to the right for every price of CDs. When demand increases, quantity demanded is increased at every price.

Although the theory that rising income means greater demand for goods holds true for most goods, it does not apply to all goods. Economists distinguish between normal goods and inferior goods. **Normal goods** are those products and services for which demand increases (decreases) with increases (decreases) in income; the demand for **inferior goods** actually decreases (increases) with increases (decreases) in consumers' income. Joe's demand for Honda automobiles may decrease as his income increases; a Honda automobile is an inferior good to him. Beth purchases less Häagen-Dazs vanilla ice cream as her income falls, indicating that Häagen-Dazs ice cream is a normal good for her.

The terms *normal* and *inferior* contain no implications about intrinsic quality or about absolute standards of goodness or badness. Indeed, a good or service that is normal for one consumer in a given income range may be inferior for another consumer in the same income range. It is even possible for a good to be normal for an individual consumer at certain levels of income and inferior at other levels. As one's income rises, for example, hamburgers or compact cars may change from normal to inferior. We will discuss this distinction in more detail later, but it is important to note that a change in income will produce a shift in the demand curve.

Substitutes:
Products that are related such that an increase in the price of one will increase the demand for the other or a decrease in the price of one will decrease the demand for the other.

Complements:
Products that are related such that an increase in the price of one will decrease the demand for the other or a decrease in the price of one will increase the demand for the other.

Prices of Related Goods. Suppose that the price of a good closely related to CDs—such as cassette tapes or CD players—changes during the month for which Dave's and Marcia's demand curves are drawn. What happens? Clearly, one of the assumptions about other things being equal has changed, and the demand curve will shift right or left depending on the direction of the price change and on whether the closely related good is a **substitute** for or a **complement** to the product under consideration.

Suppose that other forms of entertainment can substitute for CDs in Dave's or Marcia's budgets. If ticket prices for movies or tape prices decline during the month, the demand curve for CDs for both consumers would shift to the left; that is, the demand for CDs would decline. For every price of CDs, the quantity demanded would be lower. This shift is represented in Figure 6. If the price of a substitute good increased during the month, the demand for CDs would increase.

If the price of a good or service complementary to CDs rises or falls, the demand curve for CDs would shift. Such a complementary good or service might be compact disc players for home or auto. If the price of the complement increases, the demand for CDs would decrease (shift left). If the price of the complement decreases, demand for CDs would increase (shift right).

Other Factors Shifting the Demand Curve. A number of factors other than income and the price of related goods can cause a shift in the demand curve. Among these are consumers' price and income expectations and consumers' tastes. If the price of CDs or the income of consumers is expected to change in the near future, the demand for CDs during the month will be altered. Marcia may discover during the month that she will receive an inheritance. The basis under which her original demand curve was derived changes because she anticipates a change in income. Or back-to-school CD sales might be announced for August during the middle of July, causing a decrease in demand during July. Likewise, any alteration in the time period under examination—changing from a month to a day, week, or year—will alter the construction of the demand curve. A purchase of four pizzas per month at a price of $6.95 each would be represented differently than a weekly consumption of one pizza. A change in the time period requires a redrawing of the demand curve. Also held constant is the quality of the good or service. Changing the amount of ice in a 10-ounce soft drink, for example, will alter the quality of the drink. The change in quality will alter quantity demanded at any price.

Reviewing the Law of Demand

The demand curve expresses an inverse relation between the price of a good and the quantity of the good demanded, assuming a number of constant factors affecting demand. As price rises, quantity demanded falls; as price falls, quantity demanded rises. When any of the other factors affecting demand change, we must reevaluate the demand schedule and curve. In general, we identify only the most important factors affecting demand curves. If we have missed some important factor affecting demand—Dave's carburetor unexpectedly burns out in the middle of the month, for example—that factor must be accounted for in analyzing demand.

Economists predict that individuals (and collections of individuals), all things being equal, will purchase more of any commodity or service as its price falls. To verify this prediction, the individuals in question do not even have to be fully aware of their behavior; they need only act in the predicted manner. Individuals' response to sales of any kind—they buy more when price declines—is evidence that a general and predictable law of demand exists. That law is a fundamental tool of economists' analyses of real-world events.

From Individual to Market Demand

Market demand:
The total amount consumers are willing and able to purchase of a product at all possible prices, obtained by summing the quantities demanded at each price over all buyers.

While an individual's demand curve is sometimes of interest, economists most often focus on the **market demand** for some product, service, or input such as automobiles, intercontinental transport, or farm labor. Market demand schedules are simply the summation of all individual demand schedules at alternative prices for any good or service. An increase in the number of consumers increases the market demand curve and a reduction decreases market demand. The key is to add up the quantities demanded by all consumers at alternative prices for the good or service in question.

We can use the CD demand example to understand market demand. We constructed individual demand schedules for Dave and Marcia by varying the price and observing the quantities of discs that they would buy at those prices, other things being equal. To determine the market demand schedule we simply observe the behavior of all other consumers in the same market situation.

Table 2 begins with the data on Dave's and Marcia's demand from Table 1. The table also contains a summary of quantity demanded for all other

TABLE 2   Market Demand Schedule

The total market demand for a product is found by summing the quantities demanded by all consumers at every price.

Price of CDs (dollars)	Quantity Demanded (per month)			
	Dave	Marcia	All Other Consumers	Total Market Quantity Demanded
10	0	0	0	0
9	1	0	39	40
8	2	0	78	80
7	3	1	116	120
6	4	2	154	160
5	5	3	192	200
4	6	4	230	240
3	7	5	268	280
2	8	6	306	320
1	9	7	344	360
0	10	8	382	400

consumers at every price and, finally, the total quantity demanded for all consumers, or the total market demand. At a price of $10 no one, including Dave and Marcia, wants to buy CDs. At a slightly lower price, $9 per disc, Marcia does not choose to buy, but Dave and 39 other consumers buy 1 disc. The total market demand is, therefore, 40 discs at a price of $9. (Note that actual numbers of discs sold to all consumers would be much higher. We use low numbers for simplicity. The important point is that the market demand schedule for CDs or any other privately produced product or service is constructed in precisely this manner.)

The market demand schedules can be represented graphically as market demand curves (see Figure 7). Dave's and Marcia's demand curves are repeated from Figure 2. The demand of all other consumers, taken from Table 2, is plotted in Figure 7c. The total market demand, shown in Figure 7d, is simply the horizontal addition of the demand curves of Figure 7a, b, and c.

As in the case of individual demand curves, the market demand curve is downward-sloping (negatively sloped) and drawn under the assumption that all factors other than the price of CDs remain constant. If the incomes of consumers change, or the price of goods or services closely related to CDs is altered, the market demand would shift right or left, as in the individuals' demand curves. Economists must focus closely on these related factors in any real-world application. Changes in the demand for any product—compact cars, energy, crude oil—will be closely related to factors such as income changes and the price of substitutes and complements.

The important concept of market demand summarizes only half of the factors determining and affecting prices. Like the cutting blades of a pair of scissors, two sets of factors—demand and supply—*simultaneously* determine price.

FIGURE 7 — Market Demand Curve

The total market demand curve for a product is obtained by summing the points on all the individual demand curves horizontally. This is accomplished by selecting prices and summing the quantities demanded by all individuals to obtain the total quantity demanded at each price.

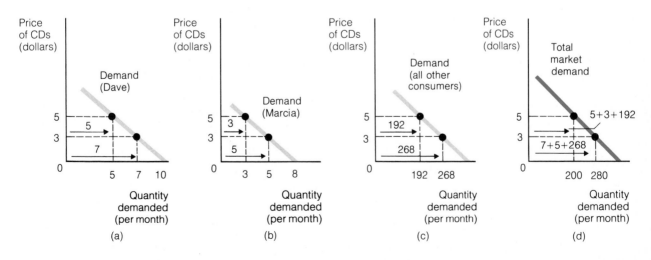

SUPPLY AND OPPORTUNITY COST

Indirectly, we have already encountered a supply concept—that of opportunity cost along a production possibilities frontier, which we discussed in Chapter 2. We will briefly review those concepts before shifting attention from the behavior of the consumer to that of the producer.

An opportunity cost—the highest-valued alternative product forgone—is incurred whenever any good or service is produced. Consider the trade-off between producing automobiles and wheat in a two-good world. See Figure 8a. A given stock of resources is available for the production of these two goods. Society, of course, will choose some combination of the two, and there is an opportunity cost in terms of automobiles forgone making a choice of more wheat.

Marginal opportunity cost:
The extra cost associated with the production of an additional unit of a product; this cost consists of the unproduced amounts of some alternative product.

Consider what the real **marginal** (or additional) **opportunity cost** of producing more automobiles is in terms of wheat forgone. The marginal cost (short for marginal opportunity cost) of more automobiles is simply the amount of wheat sacrificed to produce the additional automobiles. This is plotted in Figure 8b. From Figure 8a we see that society's choice of the first million automobiles is made at a cost of 10 million tons of wheat (point *G* in Figure 8b). An additional, or marginal, million automobiles can be produced

---

FIGURE 8

The marginal opportunity cost of a product rises as more and more of that product is produced. This is shown in the production possibilities curve as well as in the marginal opportunity cost curve.

Production Possibilities and Marginal Opportunity Cost

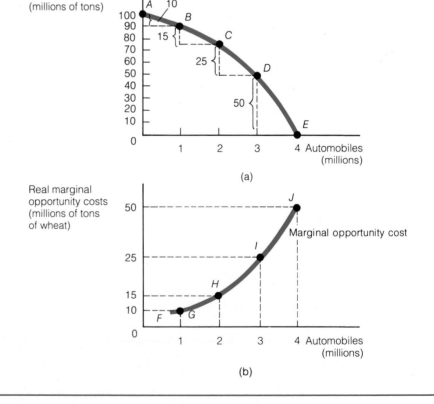

(a)

(b)

at an additional cost of 15 million tons of wheat (point *H*). Additional automobiles will be produced at higher and higher opportunity costs of wheat. Figure 8b gives the marginal cost curve in terms of real opportunity cost. Note that marginal cost increases as more automobiles are produced. Why? Common sense suggests that there are increasing costs of transforming resources from wheat production to automobile production. At first the resources drawn from wheat are easily adapted to producing automobiles (that is, there is a low opportunity cost); as more and more automobiles are produced, less-adaptable and less-talented resources must be used. The concept of the law of supply is totally analogous to this real opportunity cost except that prices (or opportunity cost in money terms) serve as the proxy for the real output of some good given up (wheat) to produce another good (automobiles).

Thus, any production involves a real opportunity cost to society. The increasing money costs of producing additional CDs, for example, is merely a reflection of the higher real opportunity costs of drawing resources from other productions. Money prices, which represent real opportunity costs, are merely representations of the real factors underlying the economy. Scarcity and opportunity cost do not vanish, in other words, in a highly developed economy. Relative resource prices and, consequently, costs of production are but relative signals of scarcity.

THE LAW OF SUPPLY AND FIRM SUPPLY

Law of supply:
The price of a product or service and the amount that producers are willing and able to offer for sale are positively related. If price rises, then quantity supplied rises; if price decreases, then quantity supplied decreases.

Quantity supplied:
The amount of any good or service that producers are willing and able to produce and sell at some specific price.

Supply curve:
A graphic representation of the quantities of a product or service that producers are willing and able to sell at all possible prices.

The **law of supply** states that, other things being equal, firms and industries will produce and offer to sell greater quantities of a product or service as the price of that product or service rises. There is a direct relationship between price and quantity supplied: As price rises, **quantity supplied** increases; as price falls, quantity supplied decreases. The assumption of other things being equal is invoked, as in the case of demand, so that the important relation between price and quantity supplied may be specified exactly. This relation, called a **supply curve,** shows the quantities of any good that firms would be willing and able to supply at alternative prices over a specified time period.

The method for constructing an individual firm's (and the market's) supply schedule is identical to the method we used for individual and market demand. All factors affecting supply except the price of the good or service are held constant. The price of the good or service is varied and the quantities that the firm or the industry will supply are specified.

To see how the supply curve is drawn, we turn to the supply side of CDs. Suppose that there are a number of firms supplying CDs in a given geographic area and that the output per month of two typical firms (Oranges Inc. and Joe's Audio) and all other firms combined is as shown in Table 3. The supply schedules of Oranges Inc. and Joe's Audio are given in the table by the combination of price and quantity supplied. That is, given alternative prices of CDs and the assumption that all other things are equal, Oranges Inc. and Joe's Audio specify the quantity of CDs that they would be willing to supply during a one-month period. (Again, numbers are kept arbitrarily low for simplicity.)

TABLE 3   **Individual Firm and Market Supply Schedules**

Individual firms' supply schedules follow the law of supply: As the price of the product increases, the quantity supplied increases. The total market supply is obtained by summing the quantities supplied by all firms at every price.

	Quantity Supplied (per month)			
Price of CDs (dollars)	Oranges Inc.	Joe's Audio	All Other Firms	Total Market Quantity Supplied
10	24	16	410	450
9	21	14	365	400
8	18	12	320	350
7	15	10	275	300
6	12	8	230	250
5	9	6	185	200
4	6	4	140	150
3	3	2	95	100
2	0	0	50	50
1	0	0	0	0
0	0	0	0	0

At a price of $10 per disc, Oranges Inc. would be willing and able to supply **24** discs, but if the price falls to $3 per CD, Oranges Inc. will supply only **3** discs.

As in the case of demand schedules, the information from supply schedules can be graphically expressed as supply curves (see Figure 9). The individual supply curves for Oranges Inc. and Joe's Audio conform to the law of supply—other things being equal, as price rises, the quantity supplied increases and as price falls, quantity supplied decreases. Note that the supply curve for the individual firm is sloped upward and to the right. This is because the marginal opportunity cost of resources used for increased CD production rises as more discs are produced. As more CDs are produced, less-adaptable resources are drawn into disc production, just as in the case of wheat and automobile production. To increase the quantity of CDs supplied, a firm may have to enlarge its quarters by buying and converting buildings formerly used for other purposes, incur the costs of hiring and training workers who have never made CDs before, and perhaps redesign its product to use alternative materials as original materials become more scarce. These increases in marginal costs may make it unprofitable for the firm to supply more CDs unless the price of CDs rises.

Change in quantity supplied:
A change in the amount of a good a producer is willing and able to produce and sell that is caused by a change in the price of the good or service.

Change in supply:
A shift of the entire supply curve to the right or left.

Changes in Quantity Supplied and Shifts in the Supply Curve

As in the case of demand, a change in price will alter the quantity that producers are willing to supply, indicated by a movement along a given supply curve, and a change in any other factor will cause a **change in supply,** indicated by a shift in the supply curve either right or left. An increase in price will increase the quantity supplied, but a decrease in price will reduce the quantity

FIGURE 9

Market Supply Curves

The market supply curve of a product is obtained by summing the quantities that will be supplied by the two individual firms and by all other firms at every price. For example, at a price of $7 the total quantity supplied is 300 (15 + 10 + 275).

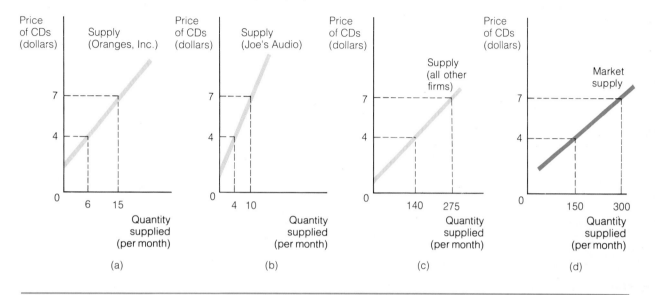

(a)   (b)   (c)   (d)

supplied. The supply curve is positively sloped—upward and to the right—and, as we saw, the demand curve is negatively sloped—downward and to the right. When **factors affecting supply**—that is, factors other than the price of the good—change, the whole curve shifts.

Factors affecting supply: Anything other than price, such as technology or input costs, that determines the amount of a product or service that sellers are willing and able to offer for sale.

Changes in Cost of Production. The most important influence on the position of the supply curve is the cost of producing a good or service. The price of resources—labor, land, capital, managerial skills—may change, as may technology or production or marketing techniques peculiar to the product. Any improvement in technology or any reduction in input prices would increase supply; that is, it would shift the supply curve to the right.

Suppose that the price of plastic materials used in compact disc construction falls or that the wages of salespeople available to CD stores decline. As the production or sales costs to firms producing and selling CDs decline, the quantity supplied increases and the supply curve shifts to the right for every price of CDs. An increase in supply is shown in Figure 10a. At price P_0, the firm was willing to supply quantity Q_0 of discs when the supply curve was S_0. After the firm (and all other firms) experiences a reduction in costs, the supply curve shifts rightward to S_1, indicating a willingness to supply a quantity Q_1 at price P_0. An improvement in production or sales techniques or a reduction in the price of some resource shifts the supply curve to the right. A decline in production or sales or an increase in any input cost shifts the supply curve to the left, as shown in Figure 10b.

Other Determinants of Supply. Factors other than cost of production changes can affect the location of the supply curve. One such factor is changes in

FIGURE 10

As factors other than price change, the supply curve shifts. When input costs fall, the quantity supplied increases from Q_0 to Q_1 at the price P_0, shifting the supply curve to the right from S_0 to S_1. An increase in input costs causes a decrease in quantity supplied from Q_0 to Q_2, and the supply curve shifts to the left, from S_0 to S_2.

A Shift in the Supply Curve

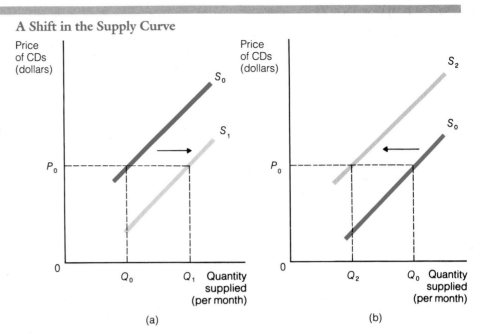

(a)   (b)

---

producer-seller price expectations. The supply curve, like the demand curve, is drawn for a certain time period. If expectations of future prices change drastically in a market—for example, prices of the good or service are expected to rise suddenly—suppliers would withhold current production from the market in anticipation of higher prices. The current supply would be reduced, causing the supply curve to shift to the left, as in Figure 10b.

One other factor deserves mention. The supply curve is drawn for a given time period. A change in the time period (from one month to one week or one year) will alter the dimensions of the supply curve; it must be redrawn if the time period changes.

Market Supply

Market supply:
The total amount producers are willing and able to offer for sale of a product at all possible prices, obtained by summing the quantities supplied at each price over all producers.

Market supply is simply the addition of all firms' quantities supplied for every price. If the number of firms in a given market increases or decreases, the supply curve would increase or decrease accordingly because the market supply curve is constructed by adding all the supply curves of individual firms. The market supply of CDs represented by the price-quantity combinations of the first and last columns of Table 3 is plotted in Figure 9d. The market supply curve is obtained by plotting the total quantities of CDs that would be produced and sold at every price during the time period.

The market supply curve is positively sloped—that is, total quantity supplied increases with increases in price—because the real marginal opportunity cost of CD production rises as more discs are produced. Resources become more costly as more and more inputs are diverted from other activities into CD production. Remember that money cost is simply a proxy for real marginal opportunity cost.

MARKET EQUILIBRIUM PRICE AND OUTPUT

Market:
The interaction of buyers and sellers producing and buying goods and services. Prices tend towards equality through the continuous exchange between suppliers and demanders.

Perfect market:
A market in which there are enough buyers and sellers that no single buyer or seller can influence price.

Law of one price:
In perfect markets, the market forces of supply and demand produce a single, equilibrium price for a good or service.

We now put the concepts of supply and demand together to understand how market forces work to establish a particular price and output. A **market** is any area in which prices of products or services tend toward equality through the continuous interactions of buyers and sellers. Competitive (self-interested) forces of both buyers and sellers guarantee this result. All other things being equal, a buyer of dog food will always choose the seller with the lowest price, whereas a seller will choose if possible to sell at higher prices. Buyers will not pay more than price plus transportation costs, and sellers will not take less. Only one price is possible.

In a **perfect market,** both buyers and sellers are numerous enough that no single buyer or seller can influence price. In addition, buyers and sellers are free to enter or exit the market at any time. In this case of perfect competition, no single seller sells enough of the commodity and no buyer buys enough of the product or service to influence price or quantity. In a perfect market the **law of one price** holds: After the market forces of supply and demand, of buyers and sellers, are at rest or in equilibrium, a single price for a commodity (accounting for transportation and other costs) will prevail. If a single price did not prevail, someone could get rich by buying low and selling at a higher price, thereby driving prices to equality. The self-interested, competitive forces of buyers and sellers acting through supply and demand guarantee this important result.

The Mechanics of Price Determination

Price and output are determined in a market by the simple combination of the concepts of supply and demand already developed in this chapter.

Tabular Analysis of Supply and Demand. Table 4 combines the data on the market supply and demand for compact discs and contrasts the quantities supplied and quantities demanded at various prices. The numbers used in Table 4 come from Tables 2 (market demand for CDs) and 3 (market supply of CDs). The principles discussed here apply to supply and demand functions in any market.

Consider a price of $10 for CDs in Table 4. At the relatively high price of $10, the quantity of discs supplied would be 450 while quantity demanded would be zero. That is, suppliers would be encouraged to supply a large number of CDs at $10, but consumers would be discouraged from buying CDs at that high price. If a price of $10 prevailed in this market, even momentarily, a **surplus** of 450 CDs would exist and would remain unsold on the sellers' shelves.

Surplus:
The amount by which quantity supplied exceeds quantity demanded at a price above the equilibrium price.

These unsold inventories of CDs would create a competition among sellers to rid themselves of the unsold discs. In this competition sellers would progressively lower the price. Consider Table 4 and assume that the price is lowered to $7. At $7 the quantity supplied of discs is 300, while the quantity demanded is 120—a surplus of 180. Only when price falls to $5 per CD is there no surplus in the market.

TABLE 4

Market Supply and Demand

The equilibrium price is established when quantity supplied and quantity demanded are equal. Prices above equilibrium result in surpluses; prices below equilibrium result in shortages.

Price (dollars)	Quantity of CDs Supplied (per month)	Quantity of CDs Demanded (per month)	Surplus (+) or Shortage (−)
10	450	0	450 (+)
9	400	40	360 (+)
8	350	80	270 (+)
7	300	120	180 (+)
6	250	160	90 (+)
5	200	200	0
4	150	240	90 (−)
3	100	280	180 (−)
2	50	320	270 (−)
1	0	360	360 (−)
0	0	400	400 (−)

Shortage:
The amount by which quantity demanded exceeds quantity supplied at a price below the equilibrium price.

Equilibrium price:
The price at which quantity demanded is equal to quantity supplied; other things being equal, there is no tendency for this price to change.

Now consider a relatively low price: $3 per CD. As the hypothetical data of Table 4 tells us, the quantity demanded of CDs at $3 would far exceed the quantity that sellers would willingly sell or produce. There would be a **shortage** of 180 CDs—that is, 280 minus 100. Clearly some potential buyers would be unable to buy CDs if CD prices remain at $3. In fact, some buyers would be willing to pay more than $3 per CD rather than go without music. These buyers would bid CD prices up—offer to pay higher prices—in an attempt to obtain the product.

As the price bid by buyers rises toward $5, sellers will be encouraged to offer more CDs for sale; simultaneously, some buyers will be discouraged (will buy fewer CDs) or drop out of the market. For instance, at a price of $4 per disc, sellers would sell 150 CDs while buyers would demand 240, creating a shortage of 90 CDs. The shortage would not be eliminated until the price reached $5.

Equilibrium price in this market is $5; equilibrium quantity is 200 compact discs supplied and demanded. At this price there is no shortage or surplus. A price of $5 and a quantity of 200 is the only price-output combination that can prevail when this market is in equilibrium—that is, where quantity demanded equals quantity supplied. The very existence of shortages or surpluses in markets means prices have not adjusted to the self-interest of buyers and sellers. *Equilibrium* means "at rest." In economic terms, equilibrium is that price-output combination in a market from which there is no tendency on the part of buyers and sellers to change. It is the price-output combination that clears the market. The free competition of buyers and sellers leads to this result.

Graphic Representation of Supply and Demand. The most common and useful method of analyzing the interaction of supply and demand is with graphs.

Figure 11 displays the information of Table 4 on a graph that combines the market demand curve of Figure 7d with the market supply curve of Figure 9d.

The interpretation of Figure 11 is identical to the interpretation of Table 4, but the point of equilibrium is pictured graphically. Equilibrium price and quantity for CDs is established at the intersection of the market supply and demand curves. The point where they cross is labeled *E*, for equilibrium. At equilibrium, both demanders and suppliers of CDs are mutually satisfied. Any price higher than $5 causes a surplus of CDs; that is, a higher price eliminates some demanders and includes more suppliers. Any price below $5 eliminates some suppliers and includes more demanders so that a shortage of CDs results.

The theory of supply and demand is one of the most useful abstractions from the world of events that is available to economists. Here we will discuss a few of the implications of supply and demand for society and for public policy.

Price Rationing

Prices, which are formed through the interaction of supply and demand, are **rationing** devices. Scarce resources are channeled to those who can produce a desired product in the least costly fashion for demanders who most desire the product. Another way of saying this is that resources flow to their most highly valued uses. Consider our hypothetical market for compact discs again. Suppliers who are able and willing to produce or sell CDs at a cost below $5

Rationing:
The allocation of goods among consumers with the use of prices. The equilibrium price rations the limited amount of a good produced by the most willing and able suppliers, or sellers, to the most willing and able demanders, or buyers.

FIGURE 11

The equilibrium price is established at the point where the demand and supply curves intersect. At this price, quantity demanded equals quantity supplied. At prices below equilibrium, the quantity demanded exceeds the quantity supplied and the price is bid upward. At prices above equilibrium, the quantity supplied exceeds the quantity demanded and the price is bid downward.

Equilibrium Price and Quantity

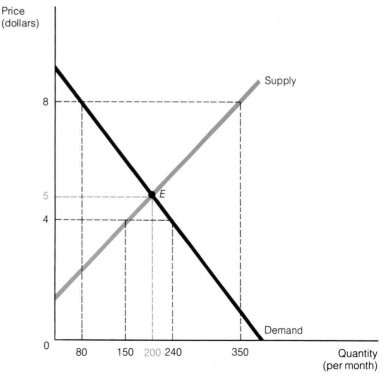

(including a profit) are "successful" in that their discs will be purchased. Demanders who are willing and able to purchase CDs at a price at or above $5 are the successful buyers of CDs. Only the most able sellers and buyers of CDs are successful in this market. High-cost producers (above $5) and buyers with a low preference for CDs (below $5) are eliminated from the market. CDs and all other goods are rationed by a price system—by the free interplay of supply and demand. In such a system no conscious attempt is made by any organization (such as government) to allocate scarce resources on the basis of factors such as presumed need, eye color, morals, skin color, or ideas of justice. As such, the market system plays no favorites. A price rationing system ensures that only the most able suppliers and demanders participate in markets.

Effects on Price and Quantity of Shifts in Supply or Demand

Both individual and market supply and demand functions are constructed by assuming that other things are equal. What happens if other things do not remain equal? We can summarize these other factors and indicate their influence on equilibrium price and quantity in any market obeying the law of one price.

Demand Shifts. Any change in a factor other than the price of a good will alter the basis on which a demand curve is drawn; that is, it will shift the curve left or right. (Remember the difference between a change in demand, which is caused by a change in other factors, and a change in quantity demanded, which is caused by a change in price.) A number of shifting factors are summarized in Table 5, which indicates the nature of the change, the direction in

TABLE 5   Factors Shifting the Demand Curve

Changes in factors other than the price of a good or service will shift the demand curve either to the right or to the left, changing equilibrium price and quantity.

Factors Changing Demand	Effect on Demand	Direction of Shift in Demand Curve	Effect on Equilibrium Price	Effect on Equilibrium Quantity
Increase in income (normal good)	Increase	Rightward	Increase	Increase
Decrease in income (normal good)	Decrease	Leftward	Decrease	Decrease
Increase in income (inferior good)	Decrease	Leftward	Decrease	Decrease
Decrease in income (inferior good)	Increase	Rightward	Increase	Increase
Increase in price of substitute	Increase	Rightward	Increase	Increase
Decrease in price of substitute	Decrease	Leftward	Decrease	Decrease
Increase in price of complement	Decrease	Leftward	Decrease	Decrease
Decrease in price of complement	Increase	Rightward	Increase	Increase
Increase in tastes and preferences for good	Increase	Rightward	Increase	Increase
Decrease in tastes and preferences for good	Decrease	Leftward	Decrease	Decrease
Increase in number of consumers of good	Increase	Rightward	Increase	Increase
Decrease in number of consumers of good	Decrease	Leftward	Decrease	Decrease

which demand will shift, and the effects on equilibrium price and quantity. Note that when demand changes, equilibrium price and quantity move in the same direction.

These facts can be seen graphically in Figure 12. Factors causing an increase in demand from Table 5 will have the effects on price and quantity shown in Figure 12a. An increase in demand shifts the whole demand curve rightward from D_0 to D_1. A shortage appears at price P_0. All the self-interested market forces that we discussed earlier now come into play. Demanders bid price up to P_1, where additional quantities are supplied by firms and where a new equilibrium, E_1, is established. Thus, an increase in demand has the effect of increasing the equilibrium price and the quantity of the product demanded and supplied. A decrease in demand causes the demand curve to shift leftward (shown in Figure 12b). This has the effect of reducing equilibrium price and quantity demanded.

Supply Shifts. The effect of supply changes are summarized in Table 6. Any increase or decrease in a factor such as resource prices or price expectations will cause increases or decreases in the whole supply schedule. Effects of such changes are shown graphically in Figure 13.

Figure 13a shows the effects on price and quantity of an increase (rightward shift) in the supply schedule. At price P_0 a surplus is created and self-interested competitive firms and buyers bid price down to P_1. Note, however, that while equilibrium price decreases, equilibrium quantity *increases* from Q_0 to Q_1. A price decline from P_0 to P_1 means that an additional quantity of the product or service will be demanded by consumers. Figure 13b shows the effects on price and quantity of a factor that decreases the supply curve (shifts it leftward). A decrease in supply has quantity-decreasing (from Q_0 to Q_1) but

FIGURE 12

(a) An increase in demand from D_0 to D_1 will increase equilibrium price and equilibrium quantity. (b) A decrease in demand from D_0 to D_1 will decrease both equilibrium price and quantity.

Shifts in the Demand Curve

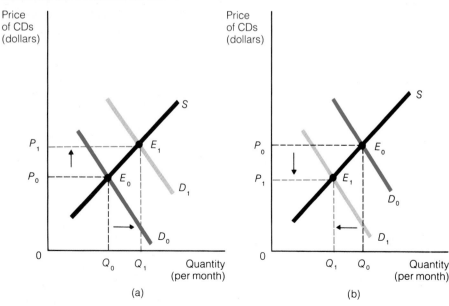

TABLE 6	**Factors Shifting the Supply Curve**				

Factors changing the supply schedule will change equilibrium price and quantity in opposite directions.

Factors Changing Supply	Effect on Supply	Direction of Shift in Supply Curve	Effect on Equilibrium Price	Effect on Equilibrium Quantity
Increase in resource price	Decrease	Leftward	Increase	Decrease
Decrease in resource price	Increase	Rightward	Decrease	Increase
Improvement in technology	Increase	Rightward	Decrease	Increase
Decline in technology	Decrease	Leftward	Increase	Decrease
Expect a price increase	Decrease	Leftward	Increase	Decrease
Expect a price decrease	Increase	Rightward	Decrease	Increase
Increase in number of suppliers	Increase	Rightward	Decrease	Increase
Decrease in number of suppliers	Decrease	Leftward	Increase	Decrease

price-increasing (P_0 to P_1) effects, as Figure 13b shows. With supply shifts, unlike demand shifts, equilibrium price and quantity change in opposite directions.

Shifts in Both Supply and Demand. In the previous two sections, shifts in either the demand curve or the supply curve were considered; however, simultaneous shifts in both curves are also possible. If both curves shift simultaneously, changes in both equilibrium price and quantity are possible, but it will only be possible to predict the direction of change for one of the two— not both. In Figure 14 initial positions of demand for wheat (D_0) and supply of wheat (S_0) are shown with the equilibrium price of $6 per bushel and the equilibrium quantity of 240 tons per year. Suppose there is an increase in the number of farmers who grow wheat, causing the supply curve to shift from S_0 to S_1 in Figures 14a and 14b. If demand remained unchanged, the increase in supply would unambiguously lead to a decline in the equilibrium price to some level below $6 and an increase in the equilibrium quantity above 240 tons per year. Suppose, though, that during the same time period that supply increases, Russian buyers arrange to purchase wheat, which leads to an increase in the demand for U.S. wheat. Figure 14a depicts this as a shift in demand to D_1. The new equilibrium point is where D_1 intersects S_1. If we compare the new equilibrium with the old one, we can see that the equilibrium quantity has increased. Since both increases in demand and increases in supply lead to higher equilibrium quantities, simultaneous increases in both also lead to a higher equilibrium quantity. However, it is impossible to say what happens to equilibrium price when both supply and demand increase. The increase in demand raises equilibrium price, but the increase in supply lowers it. Depending on which shift is greater, equilibrium price can increase, decrease, or remain unchanged. In Figure 14a, equilibrium price appears to remain unchanged. If the increase in demand were greater, the equilibrium price would

FIGURE 13

(a) An increase in supply from S_0 to S_1 will lower the equilibrium price and increase the equilibrium quantity. (b) A decrease in supply from S_0 to S_1 will increase the equilibrium price and lower the equilibrium quantity.

Shifts in the Supply Curve

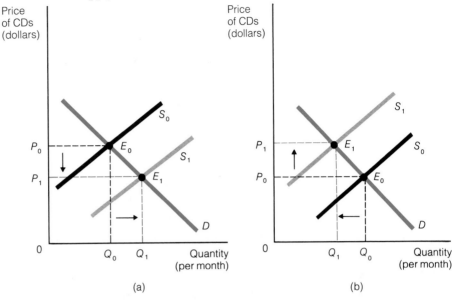

(a)

(b)

FIGURE 14

Simultaneous Demand Shifts and Supply Increases

(a) When the supply curve shifts to the right and demand increases, quantity will always increase, but the price change will depend on the size of the two shifts. (b) When demand decreases and supply increases, price will always decline, but the new equilibrium quantity will depend on the size of the two shifts.

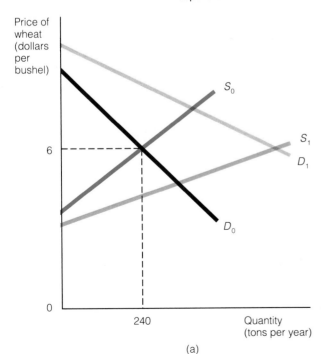

(a)

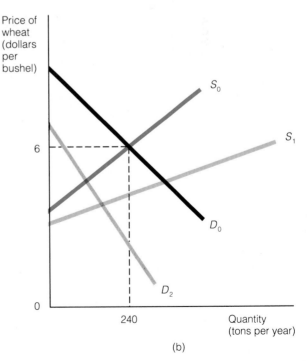

(b)

rise; it would fall if the increase in demand were smaller than that depicted in the diagram.

It is also possible that when the supply of wheat increased, demand for wheat decreased—perhaps because of a change in taste by wheat buyers who, for example, now prefer corn. In Figure 14b these changes are depicted by a shift in supply from S_0 to S_1 and a shift in demand from D_0 to D_2. Since each of the shifts occurs independently of the other and each causes the equilibrium quantity to fall, the price will fall below $6 per bushel. In this case, it is impossible to say what will happen to the equilibrium quantity—the decrease in demand causes it to fall, but the increase in supply causes it to rise. Depending on the magnitude of the two shifts, the equilibrium quantity can increase, decrease, or remain unchanged.

The same complexities arise if a decrease in supply is accompanied by changes in demand. Figure 15 depicts initial positions of demand and supply of wheat. Instead of considering an increase in supply of wheat, imagine that the price of inputs used in wheat production rises. This will cause the supply of wheat to fall from S_0 to S_1 in the diagrams. If demand for wheat simultaneously increases (see Figure 15a), the equilibrium price of wheat will rise, but the equilibrium quantity can rise, fall, or remain unchanged. Figure 15b shows that a simultaneous decrease in demand and supply will cause the equilibrium quantity to fall since both changes have this effect. However, price

---

FIGURE 15   **Simultaneous Demand Shifts and Supply Decreases**

(a) A simultaneous supply decrease and demand increase will have the effect of raising prices, but the change in quantity will depend on the size of the shifts. (b) A decrease in both supply and demand will always reduce quantity, but the effects on price will depend on the size of the shift.

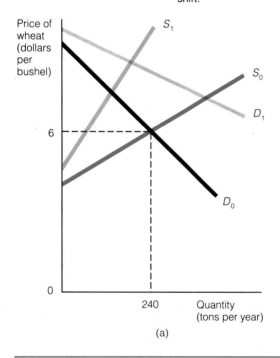

(a)

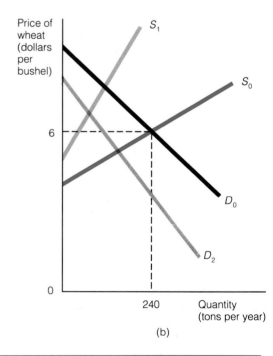

(b)

can rise, fall, or remain unchanged depending on the size of the two shifts. If the decrease in supply is large relative to the decrease in demand, the equilibrium price will rise. The price will fall if there is a small reduction in supply and a large reduction in demand.

SIMPLE SUPPLY AND DEMAND ANALYSIS: SOME FINAL CONSIDERATIONS

Many real-world events—new entrants into markets, oil price increases, new computer technology—can be analyzed using the simple laws of supply and demand. Some seemingly unrelated events also affect supply and demand. (See Economics in Action, "Global Problems in the Cashmere Market.") The theory of supply and demand is one of the most powerful tools the economist has to analyze the real world. It is important to understand some limitations and some possible applications and extensions of the simple mechanics described in this chapter.

Price Controls

Price control:
The setting, by government, of a price in a market different from the equilibrium price.

As we have seen, a major effect of the free interplay of supply and demand is the rationing of scarce goods by a system of prices. One of the best ways to understand price rationing and its usefulness is to examine what happens when government intervenes with regulation in freely functioning markets. One such intervention into the natural functioning of supply and demand is called a **price control.** Rent controls, price controls, agricultural price supports, usury laws (controls on interest rates), and numerous other policies are examples of such tinkering in free markets. We deal with many of these matters elsewhere in the book, but simple supply and demand analysis provides the basis for an initial discussion of the rationing of goods and services by non-price means.

Price ceiling:
A form of regulation in which a maximum legal price is established by government above which exchange between buyers and sellers is illegal.

Price Ceilings and Price Floors. Imagine a hypothetical market for wheat. The market demand and supply curves are depicted in Figure 16. Without government interference, the equilibrium price of $7 per bushel would be reached with 12 million bushels of wheat being bought and sold each month. Government officials could become concerned about the high price of food and impose a **price ceiling** of, say, $5 per bushel. The government is declaring that wheat can be sold only at prices of $5 per bushel or less. While the intent of the legislation is to enable buyers to obtain all the wheat they want at a lower price, Figure 16 shows that at the ceiling price of $5 per bushel, the number of bushels that buyers would like to buy (14 million bushels) exceeds the quantity that sellers are willing to sell (9 million bushels) by 5 million bushels. In other words, at the $5 price, there will be a shortage of wheat equal to 5 million bushels. Clearly, the desires of buyers and sellers are not synchronized at that price. Wheat buyers who cannot obtain desired quantities of wheat will offer to pay more than $5 per bushel (in some cases even more than $7 per bushel) rather than go without.

To prevent the price from rising above legal levels, the government must engage in potentially costly enforcement activities. If the government succeeds in preventing illegal price increases, some other means will be used to determine which buyers get wheat. Any number of allocation plans could be used. Sellers could make the wheat available on a first-come, first-served basis, in which case long lines would form. Consumers could buy wheat at a reduced dollar price, but they would also pay with their time. Alternatively, the government could impose rationing so that each consumer is restricted to buying a fraction (nine-fourteenths) of their desired quantity of wheat. Other possibilities would be for government to establish priority schemes, with some consumers being permitted to buy and others being denied that opportunity. At any price below the equilibrium level there is an insufficient amount of wheat to meet demand, and some nonprice rationing scheme must be used to determine who does and does not obtain wheat.

Alternatively, given the same circumstances, government officials might decide that the equilibrium price of $7 per bushel is too low to assure prosperity to wheat growers. They might decide to keep the price of wheat up by imposing a **price floor**—a minimum legal price of perhaps $9 per bushel—on the sale of wheat. Figure 17 shows that at $9 per bushel, the quantity supplied of wheat (16 million bushels) exceeds the quantity demanded (10 million bushels) by 6 million bushels. In this case, a *surplus* of wheat of 6 million bushels exists. Wheat producers would find it difficult to locate buyers at the legal price, and they would have an incentive to reduce the price (in the absence of government enforcement). With effective enforcement, only 10 million bushels will be purchased at $9 per bushel; the government would be forced to use taxpayers' money to buy the surplus.

Price floor:

A form of regulation in which a minimum legal price is established by government below which exchange between buyers and sellers is illegal.

FIGURE 16
A Shortage Caused by a Price Ceiling

When the price of wheat is not allowed to rise above $5 per bushel, quantity demanded exceeds quantity supplied, creating a shortage of wheat.

FIGURE 17
A Surplus Caused by a Price Floor

When a price floor above equilibrium price is placed on any commodity, quantity supplied exceeds quantity demanded.

The U.S. government has supported prices of products such as milk, cheese, and peanuts, and these purchase and storage programs can be costly. This experience also shows why world trade of agricultural products has caused serious disputes among countries. For a variety of reasons, governments in Great Britain, Japan, the United States, and several Western European countries have imposed price floors on various agricultural products. As a consequence, the cost of storing surpluses has grown dramatically. Each of the governments, therefore, is eager to get rid of domestic surpluses by selling in world markets. Simultaneously, each government wants to prevent the inflow of foreign agricultural products. An inflow will force the government to purchase larger quantities of its own product to keep its price from falling below the price floor. For example, the Japanese government has a strong incentive to prevent American rice from entering the Japanese market; the U.S. government has an equally strong motive for providing American growers access to Japanese markets.

Price Controls and Quality Changes. One additional implication of price controls is interesting and relevant to understanding the competitive market process. We have assumed in the foregoing that the quality of goods and services produced remains the same when price controls are established. This is not generally the case.

Consider the recent deregulation of the airline industry. Prior to deregulation in the late 1970s, airline fares were controlled (regulated) by the Civil Aeronautics Board, a government agency, at levels above equilibrium. This price floor created a surplus of passenger seats and unfilled airplanes. The reaction of the airlines, since they were by law forbidden to lower airfares, was to alter the quality of passenger air service in an effort to compete. Higher quality is more costly to suppliers, in effect shifting the supply curve to the left. Higher quality is, at the same time, more valuable to consumers, shifting the demand curve to the right. Both effects tend to eliminate the surplus. In the case of airlines, gourmet meals, more frequent flights, and other extras were offered a pampered flying public. These activities increased the quality of air travel at the controlled fares. Quality competition, which eventually became too costly for airlines and contributed to their deregulation, sidestepped the money price control imposed by the government and effectively lowered the price of air services to customers through increased quality.

Price ceilings also may be avoided through quality changes. New York, Washington, D.C., Los Angeles, and a host of other U.S. cities impose rent controls on apartments and other rental housing. This means that the rental price of these apartments is fixed by law. While such price controls are often enacted to "protect" low-income families, quality changes may often mean lower quality to these groups over time. When landlord-owners cannot by law raise rents as the demand for housing increases or as the cost of supplying housing rises, equilibrium rents rise above the controlled ones. If these rates are adequately enforced, the available housing will be rationed to housing demanders as a result of the shortage. Since some of the demanders will be willing to pay higher prices than the controlled rate for the lower available quantity of housing, *black markets* (extralegal markets) may develop. Illegal side payments to landlords, known as "key money," are common in rent-controlled cities.

FOCUS   Palace Ruins, Key Money, and "Togetherness": Price Controls in Lisbon

Rent controls were instituted in Lisbon in 1948 and were applied in all of Portugal in 1974. The freezes brought about a dreadful housing situation and serious decay of large numbers of once-glorious old buildings because landlords' maintenance costs exceeded rental income received. Prior to 1986, rents ranged from 40 to 1000 escudos per month (200 escudos is currently approximately equivalent to $1.35).

The effects of rent control on Lisbon's rental housing were predictable. Buildings decayed over time as a result of the controls, which left landlords with not only insufficient income but also insufficient incentives for repairs. Once-elegant palaces and apartment buildings have been left crumbling and in ruins despite persistent tenant complaints.

The reactions to quality decline also were predictable. Those lucky enough to find an apartment "sublet" to other tenants. Although the practice was (and is) strictly illegal, as many as 20 lodgers were crowded into cheap flats, each paying thousands of escudos per month. Little new housing was built, since both new and old housing were subject to rent controls. Those seeking new housing could obtain it only after paying millions of escudos to landlords in key money. Such paid-in-advance key money compensated owner-landlords for future rent depreciations from inflation. Many new buildings remained empty and thus decayed because tenants preferred not to pay.[a]

In 1986, new rental laws went into effect as worsening conditions were partially recognized. New levels were established, with as high as 300 percent rent increases and yearly adjustments for inflation. Many observers do not believe that Lisbon's (and Portugal's) rental problems are over or that progress has been made. A 1000-escudo apartment before rent control cost $6.75 per month. Assuming the worst, a 300 percent increase would be to 3000 escudos, a rent of $20.75 per month. This amount would likely not cause landlords to order mortar and hire stonemasons. It is not clear that, over the long run, most Portuguese consumers will benefit from rent controls.

[a]"Rent a Ruin," *The Economist* (July 12, 1986).

Another possibility exists, however. If controls are effectively enforced and black markets are prohibited, landlords have little incentive to maintain rental property. Excess demand for apartments at the controlled price makes it possible to obtain tenants even if the unit deteriorates. For example, imagine a landlord in a college town who is compelled by law to lower the rent on a unit from $550 per month to $300 per month. Unless the unit is allowed to deteriorate to the point that it is no longer worth $300 to any potential tenant, the owner will receive $300 per month in rent. It will be in the landlord's interest to save money on maintenance and to allow the unit to deteriorate until it is worth no more than $300. Regulations that prevent prices from adjusting to equilibrium levels cause predictable changes in quality. Experience with rent controls in cities as diverse as New York City and Lisbon (see Focus, "Palace Ruins, Key Money, and 'Togetherness': Price Controls in Lisbon") shows that such programs produce low prices and substandard housing. Markets can clear at very low prices if quality can be reduced to a sufficiently low level. This type of nonprice competition has thwarted the best intentions of many regulators.

Static Versus Dynamic Analysis

The analysis discussed in this chapter is called *static equilibrium analysis*. This means that (1) time does not enter into the discussion—it is not dynamic; and (2) price-quantity combinations move from one equilibrium to another (E_0 to E_1, for instance, in Figure 13) with no indication of the process by which firms and consumers actually move. The *dynamic analysis* of market supply and demand considers the time and process involved in moving from one equilibrium situation to another. How long, for example, does it take for a world oil price increase to influence prices in the various markets that use oil as an input? A static analysis cannot tell us. It can indicate only the probable direction of change in price and quantities. What is the role of the entrepreneur in seeking profit opportunities when demand or supply schedules shift and markets are in disequilibrium—that is, in markets that experience shortages or surpluses? Again, static analysis provides no method for answering questions about disequilibrium. A number of these issues will be discussed and supply and demand will be analyzed more thoroughly in a real-world context in the following chapters.

Full Versus Money Prices

Money price:
The dollar price that sellers receive from buyers; a price expressed in terms of money, not in terms of an amount of another good.

Full price:
The total opportunity cost to an individual of obtaining a good; includes money price and all other costs such as transportation costs or waiting time costs.

Another distinction must be made about prices resulting from the forces of supply and demand: There is a difference between the **money price** of a product or service and the **full price.** Consider the money price of a haircut for which the customer pays $12.50 in cash. Is this the full price of a haircut?

Money price is often not the only cost to consumers. In the case of a haircut, we must account for the time spent traveling to and from the salon, the time spent waiting, and the time spent with the hairdresser. The economist accepts the truth of the adage "time is money." Time, like diamonds, is a scarce resource, and it bears an opportunity cost. Time costs are often estimated in terms of the wage rate forgone, the leisure time forgone, or, generally, as the opportunity cost of the consumer's next-best alternative. Thus the full price of a haircut or any other good or service includes the price in money terms plus any other resource costs required in the purchase of the commodity. (See Focus, "Full Price and a New Orleans Restaurant.") Prices as interpreted in the simple model of demand and supply of this chapter are to be regarded as full prices. Consumers react to full prices, not money prices. No one, for example, should take an advertisement for "free puppies" or "free kittens" literally. There is no such thing! Do consumers react to the money price of products and services or to what economists call the full price? The theory of supply and demand discussed in this chapter has not explicitly stressed the distinction between money prices and full prices. But it is important to interpret even basic supply and demand theory as a theory of full, not money, prices. With this distinction taken into account, the theory of supply and demand forms the foundation for understanding how markets function and, therefore, for the whole science of economics.

FOCUS   Full Price and a New Orleans Restaurant

New Orleans is considered a restaurant town by gourmets. Restaurants such as Le Ruth's, Antoine's, Brennan's, and Commander's Palace consistently offer some of the best cuisine to be found anywhere. One of our favorite French Quarter restaurants, however, is Galatoire's. Galatoire's has earned a reputation for producing some of the highest-quality meals in the city. Menu prices, however, have remained low relative to other famous establishments over the past several decades.

Have both menu prices and full prices remained low at Galatoire's? If not, why not? Finally, what evidence might be offered for a real price increase? How would an economist view the matter?

The economist would focus on elements in the full price of a meal at Galatoire's. The restaurant has not enlarged its classic physical plant over the years but, over time, longer and longer lines form outside the door during the day and evening. Galatoire's, unlike most of its competition, does not take reservations or accept credit cards—only cash will do. Moreover, Galatoire's enforces a dress code—tie or coat for men (evenings and all day on Sundays) and, until a few years ago, dresses (no pants) for women.

All these factors would tend to increase the full price of

dining at Galatoire's. There are opportunity costs to waiting for a table (time is a scarce resource); the time and resources spent dressing for dinner are also applicable to the full price. The length of the line at the restaurant can also make the real price higher or lower than anticipated, although diners can form hunches about when the line is apt to be shortest or nonexistent.

These additional costs mean that the full price exceeds the money price printed on the menu. However, the economist must calculate all benefits as well as all costs associated with purchasing products or services. Consider the possibility that some customers get positive benefits from dressing for dinner and from being surrounded by those similarly attired. Others may value the prestige or satisfaction of dining at the legendary restaurant. Such factors would tend to increase the benefits to these consumers. The full price paid for a meal at Galatoire's varies among consumers, depending on opportunity cost. However, consumers will marginally balance the perceived costs of buying products and services with the perceived benefits associated with consumption. When price or price formation is discussed in this book, it is therefore the full price, not the nominal or money price, that is being considered.

SUMMARY

1. The extension of specialization from earlier societies is the modern market society, where individuals and collections of individuals buy and sell—demand and supply—millions of products and services.
2. Demand can be expressed as a schedule or curve showing the quantities of goods or services that individuals are willing and able to purchase at various prices over some period of time, all other factors remaining constant.
3. Supply can be expressed as a schedule or curve of the quantities that individuals or businesses are willing and able to sell at different prices over a period of time, other factors remaining constant.
4. Equilibrium prices and quantities are established for any good or service when quantity supplied equals quantity demanded.
5. A change in the price of a good or service changes the quantity demanded or quantity supplied along a given demand or supply curve. A change in demand or supply occurs when some factor other than price is altered. When these factors change, the demand or the supply curve shifts to the right or left, either raising or lowering equilibrium price and quantity.
6. The market system, through supply and demand, rations scarce resources and limited quantities of goods and services among those most willing and able to pay for them. Products and services, moreover, appear and disappear in response to the market system of supply and demand.
7. Price controls instituted by governments tend to create shortages or surpluses of products. Market forces usually result in some form of rationing other than price rationing under such circumstances.

KEY TERMS

product market
resource market
relative price
law of demand
quantity demanded
demand curve
factors affecting demand
ceteris paribus
change in quantity
  demanded
change in demand
normal good
inferior good

substitutes
complements
market demand
marginal opportunity cost
law of supply
quantity supplied
supply curve
change in quantity
  supplied
change in supply
factors affecting supply
market supply
market

perfect market
law of one price
surplus
shortage
equilibrium price
rationing
price control
price ceiling
price floor
money price
full price

QUESTIONS FOR REVIEW AND DISCUSSION

1. What happens to demand for a product if the price of that product falls? What happens to the quantity demanded?
2. What happens to the supply of coal if the wages of coal miners increase?
3. If income falls, what happens to the demand for potatoes? Are potatoes inferior goods?
4. If price is above equilibrium, what forces it down? If it is below equilibrium, what forces it up?
5. What is a shortage? What causes a shortage? How is a shortage eliminated?
6. If the demand for compact disc players increases, explain the process by which the market increases the production of CD players. What are the costs of CD players?
7. A price ceiling on crude oil has an effect on the amount of crude oil produced. With this in mind,

explain what happens to the supply of gasoline if there is a price ceiling on crude oil.

8. What happens to the supply of hamburgers at fast-food restaurants if the minimum wage is increased?

9. What is the full price of seeing a movie? Is it the same for everyone?

10. "Lately the price of gold keeps going up and up, and people keep buying more and more. The demand for gold must be upward-sloping." Does this statement contain an analytical error?

PROBLEMS

Examine the data in the table below.

1. Graph the supply and demand curves.
2. What is the equilibrium price?
3. What is the equilibrium quantity?
4. At what price does a shortage of 280 exist?
5. At a price of $19, how much of a surplus exists?

Price	Quantity Demanded (per month)	Quantity Supplied (per month)
$0	400	0
3	340	60
5	300	100
8	240	160
10	200	200
13	140	260
16	80	320
19	20	380

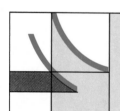

ECONOMICS IN ACTION
Global Problems in the Cashmere Market

A formal discussion of the factors that affect demand and supply rarely includes real events that affect market prices and quantities traded. Yet the factors that affect supply and demand, such as changes in income or in the price of related goods, always occur in some framework of social, political, and economic institutions. As an example, let's consider how international events affect the market for a popular gift item—the cashmere sweater.

Cashmere is a wool fiber derived from the down (found under the coarse outer hair) of goats raised in mountainous or arid regions. It has long been the material of choice for fine garments, especially sweaters, jackets, and coats. The world supply of cashmere comes almost exclusively from three countries: Iran, Afghanistan, and China, which alone has produced 75 to 80 percent of the world's supply of raw cashmere. The material is precious, indeed; the down output of approximately four goats is required to make one pullover sweater. Fibers are woven into fabric, and one yard of 100 percent cashmere can cost as much as $140 from an American mill. Products such as sweaters or coats are then constructed from the fabric by clothing manufacturers.

Worldwide demand for cashmere products rose by 25 to 40 percent in early 1989.[a] Increased affluence in Japan and Western Europe played a role in the increase, as did supply

[a]Lena H. Sun, "A Crisis Is Shaping Up for Cashmere," *Washington Post* (December 21, 1988), pp. G1, G4.

restrictions. Figure 18 shows how demand increase shifts the demand curve rightward from D_0 to D_1. If supply had remained constant, price would have risen and the world quantity traded of cashmere would have increased. But supply did not remain constant. The supply of cashmere has diminished, shifting the supply curve to the left, from S_0 to S_1. If demand had remained constant, the equilibrium price would have increased and equilibrium quantities of cashmere would have declined. With the two influences—a simultaneous demand increase and supply decrease—price will definitely rise, but the resulting equilibrium quantities traded are unpredictable. The effects of these changes on quantity are unpredictable because they depend upon the size of the relative shifts in demand and supply. If the demand change is greater, quantity will rise; if the supply shift is greater, as we assume to be the case in Figure 18, quantity will fall. Price will rise in either event.

Why has the supply of cashmere shifted leftward? The curve shifts when any nonprice factor affecting supply, such as costs of production, changes. Costs of production are determined by many factors, including the availability of raw material resources. When raw materials, such as cashmere fibers, become scarce, costs of production rise. Higher-priced fibers mean higher-priced fabric, which inevitably means higher-priced cashmere sweaters. But this does not explain why cashmere fibers are less available. For that, we must consider the real-world institutional framework in which the fibers are produced.

Political disruptions in Iran and Afghanistan occurred throughout the 1980s. The Russian occupation of Afghanistan and Iran's war with Iraq brought chaos to those countries and dislocated local producers of goats. Such dislocations decreased the availability of cashmere fiber from these countries. An entirely different institutional change reduced the supply of fiber from China. The "capitalist revolution" in China—the partial conversion of some controlled markets to free production and exchange—reduced the supply of cashmere. Goat and fiber producers in many Chinese localities were no longer forced to sell to government "marketing collectives." Instead, they chose to follow market instincts and establish their own factories to process fiber, manufacture fabric, and produce final goods. Traditional channels for marketing fiber to producers in the developed nations have been disrupted. The overall effect has been a reduction in the supply of cashmere garments, including sweaters.

Along with a demand increase, these political and economic factors explain the worldwide price increase of cashmere products. That price increase may be modified with changes in the circumstances affecting supply. For instance, the price increase has encouraged other countries such as Australia, New Zealand, and even the United States to at-

FIGURE 18　　　　**Demand and Supply in the Market for Cashmere Products**

In 1989, demand increases for cashmere and cashmere fibers along with decreased supplies created an increase in the price of cashmere sweaters and other products. Supply decreases were caused by political and market disruptions in Afghanistan, Iran, and China.

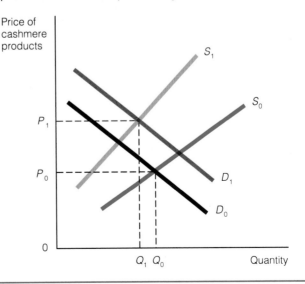

tempt to breed cashmere-producing goats. Success would have price-reducing effects on world markets; however, agricultural experts believe that the climates and terrain in these countries may not be suitable. Though goats may be raised successfully under lush agricultural conditions, fat goats produce little down. Also, when marketing channels develop for sale of finished products from China, price will tend to fall.

Some important lessons may be learned from the example of cashmere. Although a solid knowledge of demand and supply is essential to understand real-world market functioning, a keen knowledge of complex economic, social, and political factors is important as well. The theory of demand and supply is an invaluable tool in helping us to organize our thoughts about how prices and quantities behave in any actual market. As critical in analyzing any particular market is an understanding of the factual institutional framework through which demand and supply function.

Question

If a synthetic fabric were developed that was relatively inexpensive to produce and possessed similar characteristics to cashmere, what changes would occur in the cashmere market? Include supply, demand, price, and quantity in your answer.

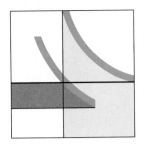

5

Elasticity

Studying the laws of supply and demand helps economists organize their thoughts about real-world problems. But it is not enough to understand that an inverse relation exists between price and quantity demanded or that a decrease in supply causes price to rise in a market. For supply and demand theory to explain and predict economic events, economists must be able to say how much the quantity demanded or supplied of a product will change after a price change. The laws of supply and demand tell us nothing about how responsive quantity demanded or quantity supplied is to a price change. But if, for example, you owned a fast-food restaurant, you would be very interested to know how responsive your customers would be to a hamburger price discount. The law of demand tells you that you would sell more hamburgers, but it does not tell you how many more.

Economics does provide a means of determining how many more (or less) goods and services will be bought when prices or other factors change: the application of the concept of **elasticity.** When you finish Chapter 5 you should understand

Elasticity:
A measure of the relative responsiveness of one variable to a change in another variable; the percentage change in a dependent variable divided by the percentage change in the independent variable.

- the general nature of elasticity and how it is measured.
- how elasticity relates to the impact of a percentage change in prices on the percentage change in quantity demanded.
- how elasticity relates to many quantifiable economic events and relations.
- what factors determine elasticity of demand and supply.
- how time affects consumers' responses to changes in prices.

THE CONCEPT OF ELASTICITY

The following examples—one relating to drugs and the other to the business world—demonstrate the practical nature of the questions that the concept of elasticity allows us to answer.

The Drug Enforcement Administration initiates a crackdown on the import of illegal drugs such as crack cocaine. With stepped-up enforcement, a smaller quantity of higher-potency drugs is smuggled into the country by organized crime. As a result, the money price of these drugs goes up steeply. Will the revenues of organized crime increase or decrease? There will be some reduction in quantity demanded; that is, fewer drugs will be sold at higher prices. The important question is, how much of a reduction? The answer will depend on the responsiveness of drug users to the increase in price.

You are contemplating two business alternatives: buying a gourmet delicatessen or opening a new travel agency. Best estimates tell you that consumers' incomes are expected to rise by 5 percent per year over the next eight years. On these grounds, which business should you enter? By what percent will an increase in consumers' incomes increase the amounts of gourmet foods purchased compared to the amounts of travel and leisure services consumed?

To answer these questions we must gauge the relative responsiveness of decision-makers—consumers—to changes in price or income, or the elasticity. Elasticity is calculated as the ratio of the percentage change in some effect (quantity demanded of illegal drugs; quantity demanded of gourmet food or travel services) to the percentage change in the cause (price change, income change, or any other change). You should keep in mind that while elasticity most often relates changes in demand to changes in price or income, the calculation may be applied to *any* cause-and-effect relationship. Elasticity is *always* a percentage change divided by a percentage change, resulting in a number that is independent of any *absolute* change in a cause or an effect.

Consider the relation between egg production and the weather. Assume that egg production falls with increasing henhouse temperatures. The elasticity of egg production with respect to changes in temperature is calculated by dividing the percentage change in production by the percentage change in temperature. If, according to a farmer's records, a 10 percent increase in henhouse temperature resulted in a 30 percent reduction in egg production, we say that the chickens are very responsive to temperature changes; that is, egg production dropped by a larger percentage than temperature rose. If a 10 percent increase in temperature reduced egg production by only 2 percent, we say that the chickens are not very responsive to temperature changes.

All kinds of elasticities are measured in the same way. More drug enforcement reduces supply and increases prices by some percentage. Drug purchases are reduced by some percentage depending on buyers' responsiveness to the price change, but, given the effects of addiction on drug users, the decrease in purchases will probably be small. Percentage increases in income will, similarly, cause percentage increases in gourmet food and travel consumption. The percentages of these changes can be estimated from similar past experiences, and businesses can use the information to make decisions.

PRICE ELASTICITY OF DEMAND

Elasticity, as these examples suggest, is a general and wide-ranging concept with many applications. The most common and important applications relate to demand.

Formulation of Price Elasticity of Demand

Price elasticity of demand:
A measure of buyers' relative responsiveness to a price change; the percentage change in quantity demanded divided by the percentage change in price.

The formal measurement of demand elasticity, like the generalized concept itself, is simple and straightforward. **Price elasticity of demand** is the percent change in quantity demanded divided by the percent change in price.

$$\epsilon_d = \frac{\text{price elasticity of}}{\text{demand coefficient}} = \frac{\text{\% change in quantity demanded}}{\text{\% change in price}}$$

Demand elasticity coefficient:
The numerical representation of the price elasticity of demand: $\epsilon_d = (\Delta Q/Q) \div (\Delta P/P)$.

Price elasticity of demand is expressed as a number. If, for example, a 10 percent reduction in the price of jogging shoes causes a 15 percent increase in the quantity of jogging shoes demanded, then the ratio, called the **demand elasticity coefficient,** ϵ_d, is

$$\frac{15\%}{10\%} = 1.5.$$

This elasticity coefficient or ratio, 1.5, and the percent changes in price and quantity demanded from which it was calculated are independent of the absolute prices and quantities of jogging shoes. If a 10 percent rise in the price of jogging shoes causes a 2 percent decline in sales, the price elasticity coefficient is calculated in the same way:

$$\frac{2\%}{10\%} = 0.2.$$

The price elasticity of demand coefficient (or, more simply put, the demand elasticity coefficient) always measures consumers' responsiveness, in terms of purchases, to a percent change in price.[1] To determine the effect of price changes alone, all other changes—such as differences in the quality of goods—must be held constant.

Elastic, Inelastic, and Unit Elastic Demand

Elastic demand:
A situation in which buyers are relatively responsive to price changes; the percentage change in quantity demanded is greater than the percentage change in price: $\epsilon_d > 1$.

The size of the elasticity coefficient is important because it measures the relative consumer responsiveness to price changes. If the number obtained from the elasticity calculation is greater then 1.00, we say that demand is **elastic** over the given price and quantity range; the percent change in quantity

---

[1]Notice that in actual calculation, the demand elasticity coefficient will always be negative owing to the inverse relation between price and quantity demanded (the law of demand). If price goes up, quantity demanded for a good or service goes down, and vice versa. Unless otherwise noted, this point is irrelevant to the interpretation of elasticity. We will accordingly eliminate use of a negative sign before the demand elasticity coefficient.

demanded is greater than the percent change in price. Above a coefficient of 1.00, degrees of elasticity vary. A demand elasticity coefficient of 1.5 for jogging shoes means that consumers are somewhat responsive to a price change. A coefficient of 6.0 for pizza means that buyers of pizza are much more responsive to a change in pizza price than they are to a change in the price of jogging shoes (four times more responsive, in fact). The larger the demand elasticity coefficient is above 1.0, the more elastic demand is said to be. (*Remember:* Price elasticity of demand measures the *relative* response of quantity demanded to a price change, the percentage change in quantity demanded caused by some percentage change in price.)

Unit elasticity of demand means that the elasticity coefficient equals 1. In this case, a given percent change in price is exactly matched by the percent change in quantity demanded. If, for example, a 2 percent increase in the price of candy bars causes a 2 percent reduction in purchases, demand would be of unit elasticity. The same would be said if an 8 percent decrease in the price of Volkswagens caused an 8 percent increase in quantity demanded.

An **inelastic demand** coefficient is a number less than 1, meaning that a percent change in quantity demanded is less than the percent change in price that caused the change in quantity. If the price of salt increases by 5 percent and the quantity demanded decreases by 2.5 percent, the demand elasticity coefficient would be 0.5, placing it in the inelastic category. An elasticity number lower than 0.5 for salt would mean that demand is relatively more inelastic.

The various categories of price elasticity of demand can be shown with demand curves. Figure 1 depicts three responses to a 20 percent increase in pizza prices over a given time period in a small college town. In Figure 1a, a 20 percent increase in price causes a 5 percent reduction in quantity demanded. This means that pizza consumers are not very responsive to a change in price: ϵ_d is inelastic—it equals 0.25, which is less than 1. In Figure 1b, a 20 percent increase in pizza price reduces pizza consumption by exactly 20 percent, meaning that demand is of unit elasticity: $\epsilon_d = 1$. Figure 1c shows an elastic demand—a 20 percent price increase causes a 50 percent reduction in the quantity of pizzas demanded: ϵ_d is 2.5 (greater than 1).

The elasticity of two special forms of the demand curve is also of interest in analyzing economic problems. Figure 2 shows a completely inelastic and a completely elastic demand curve. Total or complete price inelasticity means that consumers are not responsive at all to price changes, a condition that is seldom met in the real world. Increases or decreases in price leave quantity demanded unchanged—the demand curve is vertical, as in Figure 2a. One might think of the demand for addictive drugs—at least for certain price ranges and certain levels of use—as being completely inelastic. The price elasticity of demand coefficient is zero along such a curve: $\epsilon_d = 0$.

A completely elastic demand curve—along which an infinitely large or small quantity is demanded at a given price—is shown in Figure 2b. Individual businesses in competitive markets view the demand for their products as totally elastic. In a competitive market, producers are so numerous that they are unable to affect prices. The huge number of wheat farmers, for example, means that a single small producer cannot affect the market price by altering production. If the wheat farmer raises his or her price by even a small amount, buyers will not purchase any of the farmer's production. Buyers can get all the wheat they want at the (lower) prevailing market price. In these competitive circumstances, a single wheat farmer faces an infinitely elastic demand curve

Unit elasticity of demand: A condition where the percentage change in quantity demanded is equal to the percentage change in price: $\epsilon_d = 1$.

Inelastic demand: A situation in which buyers are relatively unresponsive to price changes; the percentage change in quantity demanded is less than the percentage change in price: $\epsilon_d < 1$.

FIGURE 1

Price Elasticity of Demand

(a) The percent reduction in quantity demanded (from Q_0 to Q_1, 5%) is less than the percent increase in price (from P_0 to P_1, 20%). Demand is inelastic, $\epsilon_d < 1$. (b) The percent reduction in quantity demanded equals the percent increase in price. Demand is unit elastic, $\epsilon_d = 1$. (c) The percent reduction in quantity demanded is larger than the percent increase in price. Demand is elastic, $\epsilon_d > 1$. The same relations hold for reductions in price or increases in quantity demanded.

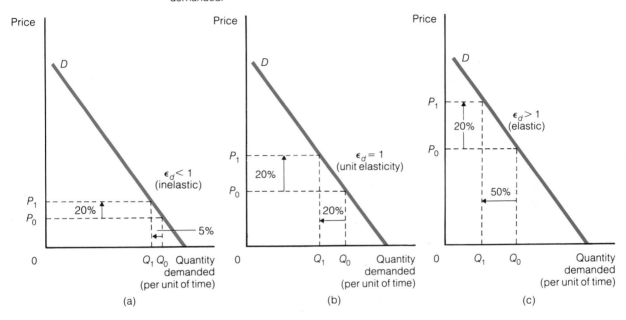

FIGURE 2

(a) Quantity demanded is unresponsive to price changes (totally inelastic). (b) Quantity demanded is completely responsive to price changes (totally elastic); a small increase in price will cause quantity demanded to disappear. Perfectly competitive suppliers view the demand for their output as totally elastic.

Demand Curves May Be Totally Inelastic or Totally Elastic

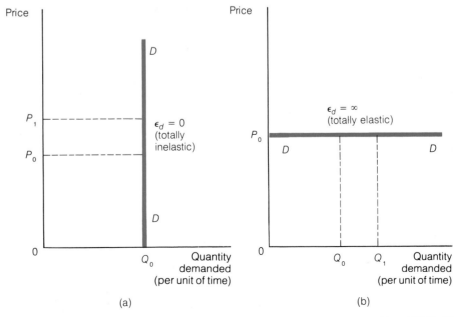

($\epsilon_d = \infty$). Quantity demanded is supersensitive to price increases. The farmer can sell as much or as little as he or she desires at the market price.

To summarize, an elasticity coefficient less than 1.0 means that demand is inelastic, and a coefficient greater than 1.0 means that demand is elastic. A coefficient equal to 1.0 indicates unit elasticity of demand. In all cases, elasticity values apply over a given range of prices. The demand curve can, under certain circumstances, be completely elastic or completely inelastic.

Elasticity Along the Demand Curve

Our discussion of demand elasticity has contained a crucial qualification: that the coefficient (whether elastic, inelastic, or unitary) has meaning only over certain (or relevant) price ranges. We now investigate exactly what this means. To do so requires that we be even more specific about the basic elasticity concept and its algebraic formulation.

Table 1 and Figure 3 show the market demand function—or price quantity pairs—that constitute the demand schedule for cassette tapes. (Table 1 and Figure 3 are similar to Table 2 and Figure 5d of Chapter 4, which relate to the market demand curve for compact discs.)

Is it ever correct or meaningful to ask, "What is the elasticity of this or any other demand curve?" Some simple calculations from the market demand function of Table 1 or Figure 3 will tell us that the answer is no. Remember that demand curves are downward-sloping because quantity demanded drops as price rises. Every negatively sloped demand curve will, in general, contain portions that are elastic, unit elastic, and inelastic. The elasticity coefficient will vary along any straight (linear) or curving (nonlinear) demand curve in

TABLE 1
Market Demand Schedule for Tapes

Price of Tapes (dollars)	Quantity Demanded (per month)
10	0
9	40
8	80
7	120
6	160
5	200
4	240
3	280
2	320
1	360

FIGURE 3

The elasticity of demand is different between various points along a downward-sloping demand curve. If prices fall by $1 between A and B, demand is elastic. If prices fall by $1 between C and D, demand is inelastic. The calculated elasticity is different depending on whether it is measured from A to B and C to D or from B to A and D to C.

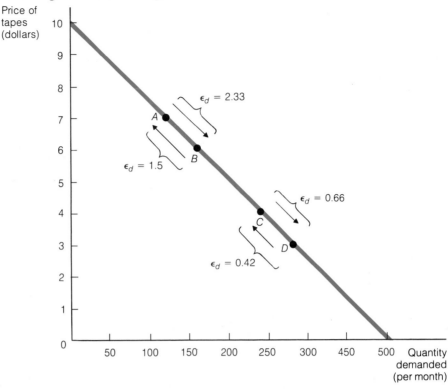

Differing Elasticities Along a Market Demand Curve

all but a few special cases. To verify this fact, consider the simple elasticity expression and its algebraic counterpart once more.

$$\epsilon_d = \frac{\% \text{ change in quantity demanded}}{\% \text{ change in price}} = \frac{\Delta Q/Q}{\Delta P/P}$$

In the algebraic expression, Q means quantity, Δ means "a change in," and P means price. In the numerator, percent change in quantity demanded is determined by dividing the change in quantity demanded by the initial quantity demanded ($\Delta Q \div Q$). The same is done in the denominator for initial price and change in price to determine the percent change in price. Then elasticity can be expressed as the percent change in quantity demanded ($\Delta Q/Q$) divided by the percent change in price ($\Delta P/P$). This formulation can be rearranged thus:

$$\frac{\Delta Q/Q}{\Delta P/P} = \frac{\Delta Q}{Q} \times \frac{P}{\Delta P}.$$

We will use this expression to make some calculations.

Suppose from Table 1 and Figure 3 that the price of tapes declines from $7 to $6. Quantity demanded would increase from 120 to 160 tapes. How would elasticity be calculated? Returning to our simple formula, we can calculate the elasticity across this price range as follows:

$$\epsilon_d = \frac{\Delta Q/Q}{\Delta P/P} = \frac{\Delta Q}{Q} \times \frac{P}{\Delta P} = \frac{40}{120} \times \frac{7.00}{1.00} = 2.33.$$

The number of tapes sold increased by 40 over the original quantity of tapes, those purchased at $7 (120). Thus, 40/120 is multiplied by the ratio of the original price, $7, to the change in price, $1. The elasticity coefficient is 2.33, which means that demand is elastic over this range of prices. Consumers are responsive to a price reduction from $7 to $6.

Now assume that tapes are selling at $4 and that the price is reduced to $3. Using the same method, we see that

$$\epsilon_d = \frac{\Delta Q/Q}{\Delta P/P} = \frac{\Delta Q}{Q} \times \frac{P}{\Delta P} = \frac{40}{240} \times \frac{4.00}{1.00} = 0.66.$$

The coefficient indicates that for a decline in price over the price range from $4 to $3 demand is inelastic. Consumers are far more responsive to a one-dollar price reduction from $7 to $6 than they are to a one-dollar price reduction from $4 to $3.

The formula for elasticity used above may be simplified even further. It can be reorganized

$$\epsilon_d = \frac{\Delta Q}{\Delta P} \times \frac{P}{Q}.$$

This equation tells us that elasticity and slope are different concepts.[2] The slope of the demand curve is $\Delta P/\Delta Q$; slope shows how price changes with unit or other changes in quantity. Elasticity is the inverse of the slope ($\Delta Q/\Delta P$)—that is, the slope "turned upside down"—multiplied by the ratio of some specific price and quantity (P/Q) that varies along the demand curve. So elasticity may be expressed

$$\epsilon_d = \frac{1}{\text{slope}} \times \frac{P}{Q}.$$

If a demand curve is a straight line (linear), its slope is negative and constant; therefore, the value of the slope divided into 1 is also constant. However, the *ratio* of price to quantity changes along the demand curve, meaning that elasticity also changes up and down the demand curve.

---

[2]You might want to reread portions of the Appendix to Chapter 1 on the value of slopes in linear and nonlinear situations. Along nonlinear demand curves, the slope changes along with the ratio of price to quantity, which (ordinarily) gives different values to the elasticity coefficient.

Again, suppose that $7 tapes are reduced in price to $6 and that $4 tapes are reduced to $3. As determined from the data in Table 1, the slope of the demand curve for tapes is 1/40, so the reciprocal of the slope (1/slope) is 40—a number that does not change as we calculate different elasticities along the demand curve. The *ratio* of price to quantity, the other part of the elasticity calculation, does change—from 7/120 in the first calculation to 4/240 in the second. The first calculation produces a number greater than 1 (40 × 7/120 = 2.33), or an elastic demand; the second yields a number less than 1 (40 × 4/240 = 0.66). The demand for any item—salt, cigarettes, tapes—cannot be called elastic or inelastic without first identifying some specific price range for that item.

The knowledge that elasticity changes along demand curves suggests another difficulty in accurately calculating elasticity. Since elasticity varies at all points along the demand curve, it also varies along the arc, or length, *A* to *B* or *C* to *D*. In other words, there will be different elasticity coefficients for price changes *between* $4 and $3, such as a price increase from $3.25 to $3.75. We will even get a different elasticity coefficient for a price *increase* from $3 to $4, as we verify in the following calculation (also see Figure 3):

$$\epsilon_d = \frac{\Delta Q/Q}{\Delta P/P} = \frac{\Delta Q}{Q} \times \frac{P}{\Delta P} = \frac{40}{280} \times \frac{3.00}{1.00} = 0.42.$$

Whereas a price decrease from $4 to $3 yielded an elasticity of 0.66, a price increase from $3 to $4 yields an elasticity of 0.42, a more inelastic consumer response. The difference reflects the fact that *initial* prices and quantities are plugged into the formula.

One compromise solution to the problem of determining the exact elasticity of demand over such a price range is to find the **arc elasticity,** or the average elasticity within the arc between the two price-quantity combinations.[3] There are other methods of calculation as well. Naturally, the smaller the price change, the more precise the simple formula $\epsilon_d = (\Delta Q/Q) \div (\Delta P/P)$ is at estimating the true elasticity between two points.

There are several means of calculating elasticity. While all these calculations (as with many other representations of actual economic data) are approximations, elasticity is often useful in assessing real-world problems and policies. We will continue to use the simple formula as our approximation.

Arc elasticity:
A measure of the average elasticity between two points on the demand curve.

---

[3]To calculate the arc elasticity in the $3 to $4 price range for tapes, the prices $3 and $4 and the quantities 240 and 280 are given equal weight. To express the formula algebraically, we can call one quantity Q_1 and the other Q_0. The price at Q_1 is P_1; the price at Q_0 is P_0. The average elasticity of their relation can then be calculated as:

$$\epsilon_d = \frac{\dfrac{Q_1 - Q_0}{(Q_1 + Q_0)/2}}{\dfrac{P_1 - P_0}{(P_1 + P_0)/2}} = \frac{Q_1 - Q_0}{Q_1 + Q_0} \times \frac{P_1 + P_0}{P_1 - P_0} = \frac{280 - 240}{280 + 240} \times \frac{3 + 4}{3 - 4} = 0.53.$$

The average elasticity coefficient is thus between those calculated for a price increase and for a price decrease. This is one method of handling the difference in elasticity between two points.

Relation of Demand Elasticity to Expenditures and Receipts

It is often necessary to estimate the effect of a proposed increase or decrease in price on total revenue—how much for instance, a fast-food chain will make (or lose) by offering a half-price sale on hamburgers. Estimates of elasticity from previous experience can make such projections possible. Or, if the price change and consumer response have already occurred, we can look at what happened to determine the elasticity of demand by examining either what customers have spent for a good or what businesses have received for it.

Common sense tells us that an industry's revenues are the same as consumer's expenditures for the industry's product. The number of items bought by all consumers multiplied by the price paid for each item is the same as the number of items sold by all producers multiplied by the average price charged for the items. Elasticity, therefore, is related both to **total expenditures** of customers and to **total revenues** or receipts of businesses.

To understand how elasticity is related to consumer expenditures, we return to the example from Chapter 4 of a single consumer purchasing compact discs. Table 2 reproduces Dave's demand and total expenditures (quantity times price) for CDs, and Figure 4 reproduces his demand curve with the associated elasticities. Dave's total expenditures on CDs begin to rise as the price of CDs falls below $10. As the price falls to $9, $7, and $5, Dave's quantity demanded *and* his total expenditures on CDs rise. For decreases in price, if elasticity is greater than 1, total expenditures will increase. Why?

Total expenditure:
The total amount spent by consumers on a good or service; calculated as equilibrium price times equilibrium quantity.

Total revenue:
Total receipts of businesses; always equal to total expenditures by consumers.

TABLE 2   **Elasticity and Consumer Expenditures**

The average elasticity of demand is greater at higher prices and falls as price falls. At the midpoint (near $5), the elasticity is equal to 1 and total expenditures are at a maximum.

Price of CDs (dollars)	Quantity Demanded (per month)	Total Expenditure	Average Elasticity of Demand
10	0	0	
			–19
9	1	9	
			5.66
8	2	16	
			3
7	3	21	
			1.85
6	4	24	
			1.22
5	5	25	
			0.81
4	6	24	
			0.53
3	7	21	
			0.33
2	8	16	
			0.17
1	9	9	
			0.05
0	10	0	

FIGURE 4

The elasticity of demand varies along a downward-sloping demand curve. As price falls, the elasticity falls.

An Individual's Elasticity of Demand

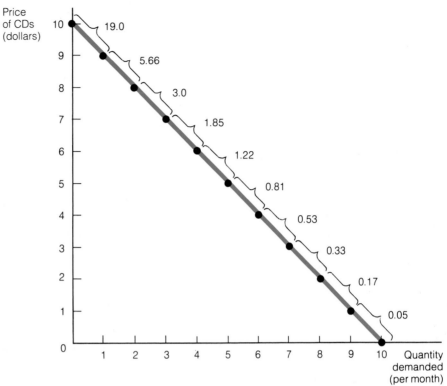

When demand is elastic, there is an inverse relation between price and total expenditures because the percent change in quantity demanded dominates (is larger than) the percent change in price. But as price is reduced below $5, Dave's total expenditures begin to decline, even though his consumption of CDs continues to increase. In the price range in which demand is inelastic (a coefficient of less than 1) total expenditures decrease as price falls. Here the percent decline in price dominates the percent increase in quantity, and total expenditures fall. In other words, prices and total expenditures change in the same direction if demand is inelastic.

The same relation between price and total expenditures is found when prices increase. If demand is inelastic, expenditures rise as prices increase from some low level, say $2, to a new level or over a range. If demand is elastic for that price range, total expenditures actually fall as prices increase. At some price-quantity combination, demand is unit elastic, $\epsilon_d = 1$. For Dave in Figure 4, unit elasticity of demand occurs around $5, when Dave's total expenditures for CDs will remain constant whether price is increasing or decreasing by some minuscule amount. At this point Dave's expenditures are at a maximum.

Being able to estimate the ways that price elasticity of demand affects the total expenditures of consumers is of obvious value to businesses seeking to maximize revenues.

If total expenditures are known, the relations between the direction of the price changes and total expenditures can be used as an informal method for determining elasticity, though not of calculating elasticity coefficients. The relations between the direction of the price change, the elasticity, and total expenditures (or revenues) are summarized in Figure 5. As the price falls from P_1, where consumption of the good is zero, to P_2, the midpoint on the demand curve, demand is elastic; total expenditures (TE) and therefore total receipts (TR) are rising. At P_2, price elasticity of demand is unitary, and total receipts and expenditures remain constant as the price rises or falls around this price. As the price falls below price P_2 (where quantity Q_2 is demanded), the demand elasticity coefficient falls below 1. Below P_2, total expenditures and receipts fall, and demand is inelastic, becoming more inelastic as the price approaches zero.

The major point to remember is that elasticity varies along any ordinary demand curve. It makes no sense to say, for instance, that salt is an inelastically demanded commodity without reference to some price range. The demand for salt may be elastic over some price range and inelastic over another. In the next section we consider what makes the demand elasticity coefficient greater than, equal to, or less than 1 and what factors determine consumer responses to price changes. (See Focus, "How to Tell Who Your Friends Are," for a broad application of elasticity.)

FIGURE 5

Total Expenditures and Total Receipts Along a Demand Curve

As the price falls ($P \downarrow$) along the demand curve, both total receipts (TR) and total expenditures (TE) rise, indicating that elasticity is greater than 1. At the point of unit elasticity, TE and TR remain constant. As the price falls from the midpoint, TE and TR decline owing to inelasticity of demand. Rising price ($P \uparrow$) has the opposite effects on expenditures and receipts.

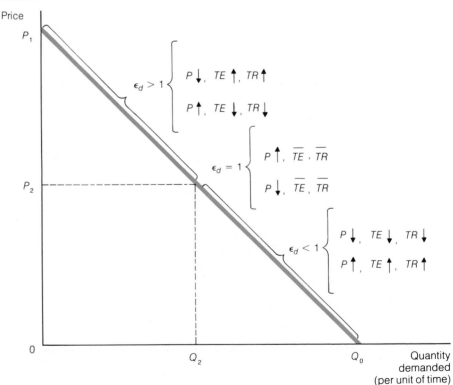

FOCUS How to Tell Who Your Friends Are

Elasticity is a general measure of the responsiveness of one thing relative to another. In economics we speak of price elasticity of demand, income elasticity of demand, elasticity of supply, and so on. The concept of elasticity is more than an intellectual device to examine strictly economic data. It can be useful to you in a practical manner. It can help you classify the quality of your friends.

Friendship elasticity can be interpreted from an economic perspective. A "good friend" is someone who has a low price elasticity of demand for your companionship. In other words, the person in question desires your company pretty much independently of what it costs him or her. You can raise the "price" of your friendship to a friend by behaving badly—being late for dates, being loud and obnoxious, grinding your teeth, not keeping your word, lying, and so on. But your friend will not desert you at the higher "price." The demand for your friendship is inelastic; consumption of your friendship does not change much at all when its price rises.

Other people will not pass the friendship test. Their demand for your companionship will be very elastic. If things get even slightly more difficult, they will desert you. Perhaps there are larger numbers of substitutes for your friendship available.

Figure 6 illustrates this phenomenon. The "price of friendship" on the vertical axis is what it costs an individual to be your friend—Are you easy to get along with? Are you fun? Are you a good conversationalist? Are you trustworthy? and so on. Higher or rising prices mean that being your friend becomes more costly in terms of your behavior. The quantity of friendship on the horizontal axis may be thought of as the amount of time you spend with a friend. The two demand curves in Figure 6 illustrate two types of behavior. The steeper demand curve D_F is relatively less elastic than D_{NF} (NF = no friend). Demand curve D_F represents the behavior of someone who is a "true friend." At high prices or low that person has a fairly constant desire to be around you. Demand curve D_{NF} proxies a "fickle friend." At a slightly higher

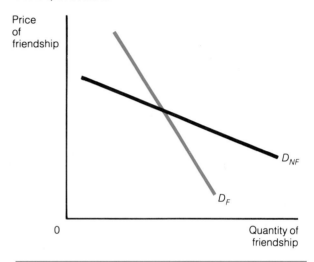

FIGURE 6
Demand Curves for Friendship

Good friends express demand curves of relatively lesser elasticity for your friendship. Poorer friends show more elasticity of demand.

price (suppose you get sick), the demand for your company is radically reduced. Friendship is an inelastic demand curve for you; a relatively higher elasticity of demand implies a weaker concern.

Think of your own personal relationships. Do you know of people who have a high elasticity of demand for you? How do they behave—missed phone calls, only call when they need something, always insisting on doing what they want to do? And what about your good friends? Need we say more? Elasticity can be applied to the interpretation of friendships. Indeed, is not "love" a relatively inelastic demand curve?

DETERMINANTS OF PRICE ELASTICITY OF DEMAND

There are three major determinants of price elasticity: (1) the number and availability of substitutes, (2) the size and importance of the item in the consumer's budget, and (3) the time period involved. Since all three factors interact, the condition of other things being equal must be invoked to determine the specific effect of any one factor.

Number and Availability of Substitutes

By far the most important predictor of demand elasticity is the ability of consumers to find good substitute products. If the price of one brand of toothpaste rises, many consumers may respond by switching to a different brand. This substitution will happen only when alternatives are available.

Food is a vital commodity. Everyone must eat; elasticity of demand for nutrients in general is probably very low over relevant price ranges. For most of us, there is no substitute for food. But it is possible to substitute between kinds of food. While the demand for food as a whole tends to be inelastic, the consumer may substitute between broad food groups such as meat and seafood and also between foods within the broad groups. Consumers of meat, for instance, have a wide choice of substitutes, such as chicken, beef, pork, duck, possum, or alligator. Consumers are far more sensitive to changes in the price of beef when other substitutes are available. Elasticity of demand for meat itself is lower than that for kinds of meat over the same price ranges.

What about the elasticity of demand for beef versus beef products such as hamburger, sirloin steak, oxtails, and so on? The consumer can substitute among beef products. When the price of sirloin rises relative to hamburger, the consumer can substitute hamburger for sirloin. The elasticity of demand for hamburger is therefore higher than the elasticity of demand for meat. By now, the general rule must be apparent: The broader the product or service group, the lower the elasticity because there are fewer possibilities for substitution. We expect the elasticity of demand for Budweiser beer to be more elastic than the demand for beer, just as the demand for a Ford or Mercedes-Benz is more elastic than the demand for automobiles. Ordinarily, the wider the selection and substitutability of similar products and services, the larger the elasticity of demand for those products.

In Chapter 9 we will see that elasticity is a crucial factor in determining how competitive markets are structured. One view of competition is that it exists when products are perfectly substitutable—one seller's wheat is identical to another seller's, for example. A number of closely substitutable products—such as hair stylists in a large city—would also indicate a very competitive market. When goods are demanded and produced with few or no close substitutes, the market changes from competition to monopoly.

The Importance of Being Unimportant

The size of the total expenditure within the consumer's budget is another determinant of elasticity. Ordinarily, the smaller the item in the consumer's budget, the less elastic the consumer's demand for the item will be over some price ranges. A salt user may be insensitive to price increases in salt simply because expenses for salt are a small part of his or her budget. If the price of salt were to rise too high, the user might substitute alternatives, such as artificial salt or lemon juice. Thus, in calculating elasticity it is important to analyze both substitutability and the size of the item in the consumer's budget.

On the other hand, the effects of size in one's budget and substitutability may offset each other in determining elasticity of demand. Take, for instance, the demand for electricity by the poor and the aged living on Social Security or other transfer payments. Inflation and rising energy costs caused electricity rates to soar during the 1970s. How would such consumers respond to rising electricity prices, which take up a large portion of their total budget? We might be tempted to say that their demand for electricity is highly elastic. But economic theory and common sense tell us that electricity consumers will not be very responsive to price increases because there are few viable substitutes for electricity (except perhaps for intolerable house temperatures or highly expensive conversion to oil heat, when electricity is used for heating and cooling). Thus, substitutability—the second determinant of elasticity—outweighs the importance of being unimportant.

The condition of other things being equal clears up our understanding of the elasticity determinants. Given some constant degree of substitutability, the more unimportant the commodity is to a consumer—that is, the smaller the item in the consumer's budget—the lower demand elasticity will be. This indicates that tastes, substitutability, and importance of the commodity in the consumer's budget must all be examined in gauging the demand elasticity of products over given price ranges.

Time and Elasticity of Demand

Time is the final factor affecting the elasticity of demand. We alluded to this at the beginning of the chapter, but now we expand on the effects of time.

Let's assume a local market for tennis rackets is represented in Figure 7. (For simplicity, we may neglect the supply function.) Assume that the initial price is P_0 and the initial quantity demanded is Q_0. What happens to elasticity of demand over time if tennis rackets go on sale—that is, if that price falls to P_1 per unit, a 15-percent decline?

FIGURE 7

As time goes by, a given price change (ΔP) may be associated with larger and larger changes in quantity demanded (ΔQ). Since the percent change in quantity demanded grows over time, the elasticity of demand grows as well.

Elasticity of Demand over Time

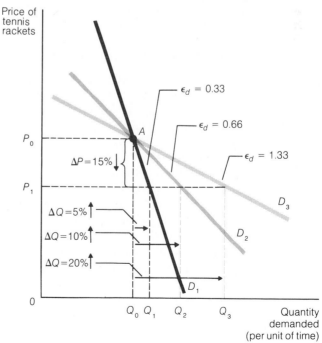

The answer depends on how long it takes for consumers and potential consumers to adjust to the new price. If the sale is totally unpublicized, there may be no immediate reaction to the new price. As consumers gain information, however, demand increases. Thus, we may think of the demand curve as rotating around a point (*A* in Figure 7) as news of the sale becomes more widespread. Greater quantities (Q_1, Q_2, and so on) will be sold *through time* at the new lower price. For the given price change, the elasticity of demand will be different at different times—that is, it will depend on whether it is calculated on the first day of the sale ($\epsilon_d = 0.33$) or one week ($\epsilon_d = 0.66$) or one month later ($\epsilon_d = 1.33$). Percent changes in quantity demanded are greater as time passes, meaning that the demand elasticity coefficient is larger and larger (up to some limit). The general rule holds: Given quality and consumer preferences, elasticity of demand increases the longer any given price change is in effect.

The time period of adjustment is a crucial factor in calculating or estimating all types of actual elasticities. Not only do tastes, substitutability, and size within the consumer's budget affect elasticity, but the ability of consumers to recognize and adjust to changes also plays a part.

OTHER APPLICATIONS OF ELASTICITY OF DEMAND

The concept of elasticity is not restricted to price elasticity of demand. In general, we can calculate an elasticity of any dependent variable (effect) to a change in any independent variable (cause). We will consider two other important applications of this versatile and useful economic concept: income elasticity of demand and cross elasticity of demand.

Income Elasticity of Demand

Income elasticity of demand:
A measure of consumers' relative responsiveness to income changes; the percentage change in quantity demanded divided by the percentage change in income, holding price constant.

As you will recall from Chapter 4, a consumer's income is an important determinant (independent variable) of the demand for goods and services. It is often very informative to inquire about consumers' **income elasticity of demand.** Producers of all kinds are interested in the magnitude of consumption changes as incomes rise or in consumption habits within various income groups. Budget data compiled by the government and other sources can be used to calculate recent and historical trends in changing consumption patterns as incomes change.

The mechanics of income elasticity of demand are identical to those involved in the calculation of price elasticity; only the independent variable changes. With price held constant, income elasticity is the percent change in quantity demanded resulting from (divided by) a given percent change in income. It is expressed as ϵ_y, with Y representing income.

$$\epsilon_y = \frac{\% \text{ change in consumption of a good}}{\% \text{ change in income}} = \frac{\Delta Q}{Q} \div \frac{\Delta Y}{Y}$$

The income elasticity coefficient, ϵ_y, may be positive or negative depending on whether the good is normal or inferior. (Recall from Chapter 4 that a good is normal if an increase in income results in greater consumption and inferior if an increase in income results in a reduction in product consumption.) When applying the income elasticity formula, if ϵ_y is greater than zero, the good is normal; if ϵ_y is less than zero, the good is inferior. For the moment we discuss only normal goods.

If the elasticity coefficient ϵ_y is greater than 1, demand (or consumption) is said to be income elastic; if ϵ_y is less than 1, the product is income inelastic; and if ϵ_y equals 1, income is unit elastic. Suppose that income in the United States rises by 10 percent in 1990 and that the quantity of new automobiles consumed over the year increases by 8 percent. New automobiles are a normal good since their consumption increases along with the increase in income. But what is the income elasticity? The simple computation is

$$\epsilon_y = \frac{8\%}{10\%} = 0.8.$$

The income elasticity of demand for automobiles in this hypothetical calculation is less than 1 but greater than zero. What does this mean for the auto industry? Other things being equal (such as price and tastes), the demand for automobiles will rise, but at a slower pace than income. This fact is important to groups such as auto manufacturers, investors, boat dealers, and airlines.

Income elasticity for a particular good may be determined for any individual consumer or for consumers as a group. The practical importance of this calculation is undeniable. An individual deciding between opening a gourmet food shop and a travel agency during a period of rapidly rising income would be very interested to know, for example, that income elasticity for gourmet foods is perhaps 0.2, while the same coefficient for Mediterranean vacations is 6.2. However, to achieve accuracy in actual use, all other factors, such as substitutability and the price of the product, must be kept constant. If these factors vary, as they often do in the real world, their impact on consumption must be determined and integrated into the analysis.

Cross Elasticity of Demand

Cross elasticity of demand:
Measures buyers' relative responsiveness to a change in the price of one good in terms of the change in the quantity demanded of another good. The percentage change in the quantity demanded of one good divided by the percentage change in the price of another good.

Substitutes:
Two goods whose cross elasticity of demand is positive; $\epsilon_c > 0$.

Cross elasticity of demand reveals the responsiveness of the quantity demanded of one good to a change in the price of another good. As such, a cross elasticity coefficient can define either substitute or complementary products or services. In more general terms, cross elasticity is an extremely useful economic tool for identifying groups of products whose demand functions are related. Cross elasticity is calculated as the ratio of the percentage change in the quantity demanded of one good, *A,* to the percentage change in the price of another good, *B,* or

$$\epsilon_c = \frac{\Delta Q_A}{Q_A} \div \frac{\Delta P_B}{P_B}.$$

If the price of one good rises and, other things being equal, the quantity demanded of another good increases, those products are **substitutes.** If Dorothy's demand for Bayer aspirin rises 85 percent following a 10 percent rise in the price of Bufferin, her cross elasticity of demand for aspirin is $+8.5$. The coefficient of cross elasticity of demand is calculated thus:

$$\epsilon_c = \frac{\text{\% change in quantity demanded of Bayer}}{\text{\% change in price of Bufferin}} = \frac{85}{10} = +8.5.$$

For substitute commodities, the cross elasticity coefficient is positive because an increase in the price of one good causes an increase in the quantity demanded of the other. The larger the elasticity coefficient (in absolute terms), the more substitutable the products or services are.

Some items that are complements in consumption—bacon and eggs; gasoline and automobiles; light bulbs, lamps, and electricity. Goods are **complements** when an increase in the price of one good results in a decrease in the quantity demanded of the other. Gin and vermouth are the two essential ingredients (besides olives) in a martini. If there is a 4 percent increase in the price of vermouth and a 16 percent reduction in the quantity consumed of gin, other things being equal, we can call gin and vermouth complementary products. Note that the cross elasticity coefficient is negative.

$$\epsilon_c = \frac{\text{\% decrease in quantity demanded of gin}}{\text{\% increase in price of vermouth}} = \frac{-16}{4} = -4.0$$

A negative number is obtained for the cross elasticity coefficient for complementary goods, since the increase in the price of one is always associated with a decrease in the demand for the other.

In calculating cross elasticity, therefore, a positive sign indicates that goods are substitutes and a negative sign indicates that they are complements. The absolute size of the coefficient, moreover, tells us the degree of substitutability or complementarity. A coefficient of -28.0 indicates a greater degree of complementarity than one of -4.0, for example.

ELASTICITY OF SUPPLY

The versatile concept of elasticity, applied thus far only to demand, can also be applied to problems related to supply. **Elasticity of supply** is the degree of responsiveness of a supplier of goods or services to changes in the price the supplier receives for those goods or services.

A price elasticity of supply coefficient can be mechanically calculated in the same manner as all other elasticities. To determine the relation between a change in quantity supplied and a change in price, this simple formula can be applied:

$$\epsilon_s = \frac{\text{\% change in quantity supplied}}{\text{\% change in price}} = \frac{\Delta Q_s}{Q_s} \div \frac{\Delta P}{P} = \frac{\Delta Q_s}{Q_s} \times \frac{P}{\Delta P}.$$

Such a simple coefficient or some more elaborate "average elasticity" can be calculated for any supply curve at any instant in time just as it can be for the elasticity of demand. Elasticity of supply can also be applied to any kind of supply curve, from beets to ball bearings. We turn to an input supply curve—a labor supply curve.

Complements:
Two goods whose cross elasticity of demand is negative; $\epsilon_c < 0$.

Elasticity of supply:
A measure of producers' or workers' relative responsiveness to price or wage changes; the percentage change in quantity supplied divided by the percentage change in the price or wage rate.

The Elasticity of Labor Supply

A labor supply curve, such as the one shown in Figure 8, simply shows the amount of work (measured in number of hours) that a laborer, whom we will call Sam, would be willing to supply at alternative wage rates. Factors such as the worker's wealth, tastes, preferences, and other factors affecting work decisions are held constant. Each person's labor supply function differs because of these factors.

Ordinarily the labor supply curve is positively sloped, like the supply curve for any commodity or service. An increase in the wage rate from W_0 to W_1 in Figure 8 causes Sam to increase the number of hours he is willing to work from L_0 to L_1; likewise, a wage increase from W_2 to W_3 increases Sam's quantity of work supplied from L_2 to L_3. What is the elasticity of the labor supply schedule and what does it tell us?

The elasticity of labor supply shows the responsiveness of labor supply to a percentage change in the wage rate. It is calculated

$$\epsilon_{L_s} = \frac{\%\ \text{change in quantity of labor supplied}}{\%\ \text{change in the wage rate}} = \frac{\Delta L}{L} \div \frac{\Delta W}{W} = \frac{\Delta L}{L} \times \frac{W}{\Delta W}.$$

We can make an elasticity calculation for two different segments of Sam's supply curve. Starting from a relatively low wage rate, W_0, an increase in wages of 10 percent will produce a 25 percent increase in the number of hours worked. The coefficient ϵ_{L_s} is 2.5, which indicates an elastic supply of work effort (because it is greater than 1).

But notice what happens to an identical wage rate increase (10 percent) starting from a higher wage, W_2. Sam increases the number of hours worked

FIGURE 8

Starting from a relatively low wage rate (W_0), a 10 percent increase in Sam's wage leads him to supply 25 percent more work, an elastic response. A 10 percent rise at a higher wage (W_2) increases Sam's hours worked by only 3 percent, an inelastic response.

Elasticity of Labor Supply

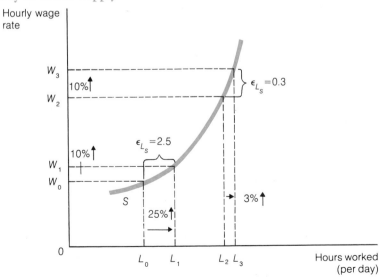

by 3 percent, producing an elasticity coefficient, ϵ_{L_s}, of 0.3—clearly an inelastic response. Why the drastic change in Sam's response to wage increases?

Some personal reflection will give us clues to Sam's work behavior. Work and leisure are two ways of using the scarce resource of time. The more hours we work, the less time we have for leisure. As we work more hours per day in response to wage rate increases, the relative opportunity cost of working (leisure forgone) begins to increase. At some point, laborers start to substitute leisure for work and income. Elasticity of labor supply is one method of calculating this trade-off (although other factors such as income level also shape labor supply). Other things being equal, an inelastic labor supply coefficient for a given wage rate change means that the laborer demonstrates a preference for leisure over work (nonmarket time over market time).

Time and Elasticity of Supply: Maryland Crab Fishing

An extremely important issue concerns the time dimension over which the economist calculates supply elasticities. A time dimension exists in all facets of life and human activity, and it is important in the economic activities of suppliers and producers.

A supply elasticity coefficient would not ordinarily capture the full response of suppliers over time to a given price change. To illustrate, consider a crab fisherman from Chesapeake Bay who daily brings in a catch and offers it for sale. The supply curve for crabs on any given day would be totally inelastic. On any given day, the quantity supplied of crabs would be completely unresponsive to price changes.

How then does the market establish a price? Price is determined by the interaction of supply and demand. If the demand for crabs on some particular day happens to be D_0 in Figure 9, price will settle at P_e and the entire quantity of crabs (a commodity that we assume, unrealistically, is not storable) will be sold.

Now suppose there is a change in consumers' taste. Maryland crabs become more desirable, and the demand curve shifts permanently to D_1. The fisherman's good fortune is revealed when his usual catch of Q_0 crabs brings a higher price P_0. How will the fisherman respond? If the price P_0 is higher than his average production costs, meaning a higher-than-normal profit, the fisherman will adjust by shifting available resources into crab fishing as soon as possible. If he has idle boats or nets and if there is plenty of labor available, all will be put to use. The act of producing more crabs takes time because resources are not instantly adaptable to crab fishing.

During ensuing days, weeks, or months, more crabs will be offered for sale per day, resulting in a more elastic supply curve for crabs. Such a supply curve over the initial adjustment period may look like S_1 in Figure 9. The price may temporarily fall to P_1 given that the demand for crabs remains stationary at D_1. Comparing the quantity Q_1 sold at price P_1 with the previous quantity of crabs sold, Q_0, shows us that over some adjustment period the supply curve for crabs is not completely inelastic but that quantity supplied is responsive to the initial price change. The response of the fisherman to price changes on any given day will still be nil; but over time, he will adjust resources to increase the amount of crabs he offers for sale.

FIGURE 9

If the demand for crabs shifts from D_0 to D_1, then price rises quickly to P_0. As time goes by and crab fishermen are able to adjust inputs, the price begins to fall to P_1. After a long period of time and all adjustments are made to the increased demand, price falls to P_2. Over time, elasticity of supply increases.

Time and Elasticity of Supply

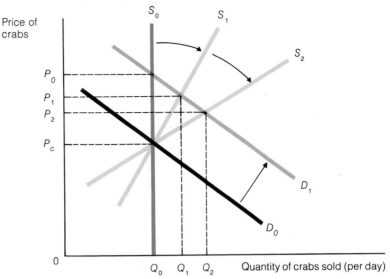

If price P_1 is still abnormally profitable, the fisherman will continue to shift resources into crab production by purchasing new boats and equipment and by training new workers. Again, such activity takes time, but the effect will be to increase crab supply (perhaps to S_2). The end result in the crab market will depend on the adaptability and availability of resources for crab fishing and on the cost of producing new inputs. But the general rule is that elasticity of supply will tend to increase over time. The longer the time period of adjustment to an initial change in price—whether price is rising or falling— the more elastic supply schedules will be. This principle applies to all supply curves, including market or industry supply curves. In the case of market supply curves, the adjustment to a change in demand and price will depend on how long it takes to draw on unused or idle capacity or on resources from other industries; in the case of a permanent price drop, the adjustment will depend on the time it takes to decrease the use of resources. The full impact of economic policy changes—levying taxes on industries, for example—often hinges on the elasticity of supply over time.

Real-world events are seldom so isolated and data so accurate as to provide the economist with means to calculate elasticities precisely. It is nonetheless important to a great number of economic and practical problems that elasticities can be estimated. To estimate elasticities, the economist must apply precise analytical tools to often complicated policy situations. In Economics in Action, "Cigarettes, Gasoline, and Elasticity: The Effects of an Excise Tax," we provide an example of two such situations.

SUMMARY

1. Elasticity is the ratio of the percent change in effect to the percent change in some cause. If changes in quantity demanded (the effect) are caused by changes in price, elasticity of demand is the percent change in quantity divided by the percent change in price. This ratio is called the demand elasticity coefficient (ϵ_d).

2. A demand elasticity coefficient greater than 1 means that consumers are responsive to price changes; demand is elastic. When $\epsilon_d = 1$, demand is unit elastic. When ϵ_d is less than 1, consumers are not very responsive to price changes; demand is said to be inelastic.

3. Elasticity can also be derived (in a general, short-hand manner) by examining total expenditures (or total revenues) as price rises or falls. If total expenditures rise (fall) as price rises (falls), ϵ_d is less than 1. If total expenditures remain constant as price rises or falls, $\epsilon_d = 1$. If total expenditures fall (rise) as price rises (falls), the demand elasticity coefficient is greater than 1—that is, it is elastic.

4. There are three major determinants of demand elasticity: (1) the number and availability of substitutes; (2) the size and importance of the item in the consumer's budget; and (3) the time period over which the coefficient is calculated.

5. Other applications of the elasticity concept related to demand are the relation between income changes and changes in quantity demanded (income elasticity of demand) and between price changes for one good and changes in quantity demanded for another complementary or substitute good (cross elasticity of demand between two goods).

6. An elasticity coefficient can be calculated for all kinds of supply curves. A supply elasticity coefficient is simply the percent change in quantity supplied divided by the percent change in price. The concept can be applied to all input and output supply curves, including labor supply.

7. Time is at the center of most important economic calculations, including elasticity. A general rule regarding time and elasticity is that the elasticity of demand and supply increases with the time that a change (in price, for instance) is in effect.

KEY TERMS

elasticity
price elasticity of demand
demand elasticity coefficient
elastic demand
unit elasticity of demand

inelastic demand
arc elasticity
total expenditure
total revenue
income elasticity of demand

cross elasticity of demand
substitutes
complements
elasticity of supply

QUESTIONS FOR REVIEW AND DISCUSSION

1. The formula for elasticity is

$$\frac{\%\Delta Q_d}{\%\Delta P} = \frac{\Delta Q_d/Q}{\Delta P/P} = \frac{\Delta Q_d}{Q} \times \frac{P}{\Delta P}.$$

Using this formula, derive the elasticity of demand for a product when the price changes from $1 to $1.50, $2 to $2.50, $3 to $3.75, and the change in quantity demanded is 15 to 10, 25 to 5, 50 to 30, respectively.

2. What are the three determinants of consumers' sensitivity to a change in price? Do these always work in the same direction?

3. Is it feasible to talk about *an* elasticity all along a single demand or supply curve? Why or why not?

4. Given that a price change remains in effect over a period of time, will elasticity increase or decrease? Why?

5. What is meant by cross elasticity? How is it algebraically different from elasticity of supply and elasticity of demand, which we calculated earlier?

6. What do cross elasticities indicate about relations between two goods?

7. What might reports about the link between aspirin consumption and heart attacks do to the elasticity of demand for aspirin?

8. Is the demand elasticity coefficient for large industrial consumers of electricity larger or smaller than that for residential users? If electric companies lower the price to both groups, would total revenues from each group change in the same direction?

9. Suppose a friend has an allowance of $25 per week. She spends all of her weekly income on banana splits. What is her income elasticity of demand for banana splits?

10. A college town pizza parlor decides to offer a back-to-school two-for-one special, in effect cutting the price of pizza in half. More pizzas will be sold according to the law of demand. Will the total receipts of the parlor increase, decrease, or remain the same if pizza consumption increases by 30 percent? By 80 percent?

PROBLEMS

1. Compute the price elasticity of demand for a change in price from $5 to $3.

2. Is the resulting value elastic, inelastic, or unit elastic?

3. Will the firm's total revenue rise or fall from such a price change?

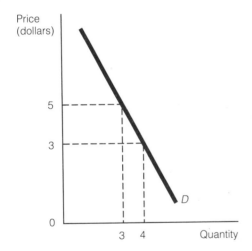

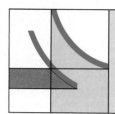

ECONOMICS IN ACTION
Cigarettes, Gasoline, and Elasticity: The Effects of an Excise Tax

An excise tax is a simple per unit tax on the sale of a particular item. Tax collectors determine the amount of the taxable good sold by a retail or wholesale firm and require that the firm pay the amount of the tax times the quantity sold.

The equilibrium effects of an excise tax on cigarettes are shown in Figure 10. The hypothetical supply and demand curves for cigarettes before the excise tax are S_1 and D. The equilibrium price, E_1, is $1.75 per pack and the quantity is 50 million packs per day. The effect of a 30-cent-per-pack excise tax can be shown by shifting the supply curve vertically upward by 30 cents to S_2. For each quantity along S_2 the price at which producers were willing to offer that quantity has now increased by 30 cents. Producers were previously willing to offer 50 million packs for $1.75 each, but now they must receive $2.05 per pack to offer 50 million packs.

The new equilibrium quantity, E_2, is lower, at 40 million. This change occurs because buyers respond to price changes; their elasticity of demand for cigarettes is greater than zero. As the excise tax puts upward pressure on the price, a smaller quantity is demanded. Producers were willing to offer 40 million packs at a price of $1.60 before the tax. The posttax equilibrium price to consumers, P_c, is $1.90. From this price, producers must pay the 30-cent excise tax and receive the net price, P_p, of $1.60 per pack.

The total revenues received by the government from the tax may not be as great as some politicians expected. Before the tax was instituted, the quantity bought was 50 million. A simple multiplication of 30 cents times 50 million would yield an overestimate of tax revenues. The actual tax revenues are 30 cents times 40 million, the new equilibrium quantity. For any excise tax the elasticity of supply and demand must be taken into account before a projection is made for tax revenues.

The elasticities of supply and demand also determine the relative burden of the excise tax. Who actually pays the tax—producers or consumers—is shown by the change in price to the buyers and sellers. In this example, the price to consumers increased 15 cents and the net price to producers fell 15 cents. Here the burden is shared equally by consumers and producers, but this is not necessarily the case.

If demand had been relatively less elastic, then price would have increased more to consumers than it fell to producers. Figure 11a shows that with less elastic demand, more of the burden is shifted to consumers. Also, Figure

FIGURE 10
Effect of an Excise Tax on Cigarettes

When a 30-cent excise tax is added to the price of a pack of cigarettes, the entire supply curve for cigarettes shifts from S_1 to S_2. At the new equilibrium price, $1.90, the elasticity of demand is greater than zero; specifically, consumers will reduce their consumption of cigarettes by 10 million packs and total tax revenues will equal 40 million times the tax. The shaded area represents government tax revenues, the 30-cent excise tax per pack multiplied by the number of packs of cigarettes sold after the tax is imposed.

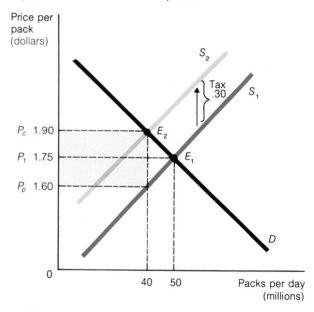

11b shows that if supply had been less elastic, more of the burden would have shifted back to the producers. Figure 11c shows that a more elastic demand also shifts more of the burden to producers.

Similarly, the effect of proposed changes in excise taxes on gasoline depends on demand and supply elasticity. In view of the large federal deficit and the stated opposition of the Bush administration to increased taxes, considerable attention is being given to raising federal excise taxes on gasoline by 15 to 20 cents per gallon, calling the tax a "user

FIGURE 11 — Elasticity and the Relative Burden of a Tax

(a) With less elastic demand, more of the burden of an excise tax is shifted to consumers: At Q_1 consumers pay the equilibrium price P_1, but at Q_2 following a tax, consumers must pay P_c.
(b) With less elastic supply, more of the burden of a tax is shifted to producers. (c) More elastic demand also shifts more of the burden to the producers.

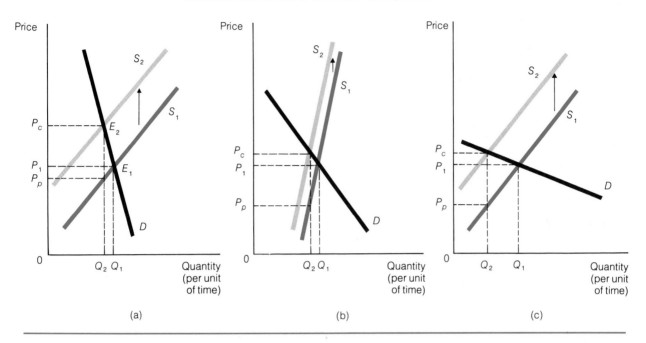

(a)   (b)   (c)

fee." Given the nature of elasticities, such an increase would likely generate increased federal revenue. This is less certain to be the case, however, for states considering increases in gasoline excise taxes. If federal taxes are increased, gasoline prices will tend to rise uniformly in all states. This will induce consumers everywhere to conserve gasoline, but it will provide no incentive for consumers to switch gasoline purchases between states. In contrast, if a single state increased its excise taxes, gasoline prices there would rise. Consumers in that state would have an incentive both to conserve gasoline and to purchase gas in neighboring states. For certain regions, many buyers either reside in other states or can conveniently travel to adjacent states. Delaware officials, for example, should expect significant interstate substitution if they were to raise gasoline taxes. Demand for gasoline in Delaware (where substitutes are readily available in New Jersey or Maryland) is more elastic than demand in Montana, where most buyers must travel great distances to escape state taxes. Therefore, gasoline tax increases in states like Montana would likely prove more successful in generating tax revenue than they would in states like Delaware.

What would be the effects of a new and higher federal excise tax on gasoline? The price would rise, but not by the full amount of the increase. Producers and consumers would share the burden of the tax. However, the burden might not be shared equally. The tax revenues would equal the amount of the tax times the quantity sold *after* the tax was instituted. The change in price, the burden of the tax, and the level of tax revenues all would be determined by the elasticity of supply and demand.

To summarize the effects of an excise tax: The lower the elasticity of demand, the greater the price increase or tax burden to consumers. The lower the elasticity of supply, the greater the net price decrease or burden to the producers. And the greater the elasticity of supply or demand, the lower the total tax revenues.

Question

Why are federal and state taxes on alcoholic beverages so prevalent? If "moral objections" to such beverages are the reason for raising excise taxes, do you believe that the taxes have had the desired effects? Why or why not?

Adam Smith

Karl Marx

Adam Smith and Karl Marx: Markets and Society

ADAM SMITH, one of the most important figures in the history of economics, actually began his career as a lecturer in moral philosophy at Scotland's Glasgow College in 1751. Moral philosophy in Smith's time encompassed a wide range of topics, including natural theology, ethics, jurisprudence, and economics. In 1776, coincident with the Declaration of Independence, Smith published his second book (his first was a treatise on moral behavior), *An Inquiry into the Nature and Causes of the Wealth of Nations,* known usually by the shorter title *Wealth of Nations.* The book won much attention from scholars of the day, and it brought together most of what was then known about the workings of the market system. Smith was one of the most eloquent defenders of free markets and the promise of capitalism. More than two hundred years later, his insights are still being taught.

Smith was born in Kirkcaldy on the east coast of Scotland in 1723 and lived most of his life in his native country. Although known for his brilliant lectures (and for his many eccentricities), Smith did not devote his entire career to teaching. In 1778, he accepted a well-paying job as commissioner of Scottish customs, a post in which he remained until his death in 1790.

KARL MARX "*looked* like a revolutionary," writes Robert Heilbroner in *The Worldly Philosophers.* "He was stocky and powerfully built and rather glowering in expression with a formidable beard. He was not an orderly man; his home was a dusty mass of papers piled in careless disarray in the midst of which Marx himself, slovenly dressed, padded about in an eye-stinging haze of tobacco smoke."[a]

Marx wrote in response to the miseries of the European working class during the Industrial Revolution of the late eighteenth and nineteenth centuries. Coauthor with Friedrich Engels of the *Communist Manifesto,* which predicted the inevitable downfall of capitalism and the triumph of communism, Marx spent most of his life in difficult circumstances. His activities as a radical in the communist movement caused his exile from his native Germany as well as from Belgium and France. In 1849, a year after the publication of the *Manifesto,* he settled in London, where he and his family survived through the benevolence of Engels and where Marx researched and wrote *Das Kapital,* a theory and history of capitalism and its ills. Marx died in 1883 in London at the age of sixty-five.

[a]Robert L. Heilbroner, *The Worldly Philosophers* (New York: Simon and Schuster, 1953), p. 131.

THE "INVISIBLE HAND"

Smith's views of the free-market system are summarized in a passage from the *Wealth of Nations* in which he writes that individuals pursuing their own self-interest are "led by an invisible hand to promote an end which was no part of [their] intention."[b] Smith believed that by freely exchanging goods and services across markets, individuals contribute to the public good—the aggregate wealth of society—even though they act from purely self-interested motives. In other words, markets cause individuals to benefit others even though they intend only to benefit themselves.

To Smith, voluntary market exchange coordinated the decisions of consumers and producers and generated economic progress. Producers compete with one another to satisfy consumers with the most appropriate and cheapest goods and services, not out of the goodness of their hearts, not because government planners instruct them to do so, but simply because they maximize the profits of their enterprises by doing so. Markets coordinate supply and demand by way of the price system. Consumers express their preferences in their decisions about what to buy; producers attract customers by producing goods at the least cost. In this system of coordination without command, individuals pursuing their own interests are led "as if by an invisible hand" to mesh their interests with those of other individuals trading across markets.

Smith was not opposed to government, but argued that its proper role in society was to provide a legal framework—police and courts—within which the market could operate, as well as to provide certain other services (including national defense, highways, and education) that the market itself would either not supply or would tend to supply in inadequate amounts. Smith also felt that government should provide welfare services for the poor. But he strongly believed that government could best assist the market economy achieve growth by stepping out of the way—that is, by not regulating and by not granting monopoly privileges to favored groups and individuals.

In Smith's view, income was distributed in a market economy by the production of wealth. An individual's income was a strict function of the value of his or her output. Smith did not feel that income inequality by itself was unfair because the invisible hand ensured that individuals' wealth (or lack of it) was a measure of how much their efforts benefited society as a whole. Anyone can increase his or her income in a free market by serving the consumers in a new, better, or faster way.

THE "ANARCHY OF PRODUCTION"

Karl Marx rejected Smith's view of the market process. In *Das Kapital* he argued that Smith's writing represented merely the interests of the ruling capitalist class. To Marx, the market process was a system of exploitation by which owners of capital robbed their employees by paying them wages less than the worth of their labor (a situation he termed the *alienation of labor*).

The alternative social system that Marx thought would eliminate this exploitation and at the same time greatly increase the efficiency of production was a "general organization of the labor of society . . . [that] would turn all society into one immense factory."[c] He viewed the market economy as one of general disorganization. Its main feature was "the anarchy of production" where producers overproduced and consumers were forced to accept goods they neither wanted nor needed. He claimed that the market process, left to itself, could not coordinate diverse individual plans.

In Marx's view, Smith's "invisible hand" was a euphemism for describing the economic system in which "chance and caprice have full play in distributing the producers and their means of production among the various branches of industry. . . . [T]he division of labour within the society [the theme of much of Smith's *Wealth of Nations*] brings into contact independent commodity-producers, who acknowledge no other authority but that of competition, of the coercion exerted by the pressure of their mutual interests. . . . [T]he same bourgeois mind which praises division of labour in the workshop [as a conscious organization that increases productivity] denounces with equal vigour every conscious attempt to socially control and regulate the process of production."[d] Smith's "invisible hand" was not only invisible but also unbelievable to Marx. Only the central planning of economic activity by society (government), which owned all means of production, could coordinate the needs of consumers and producers and eliminate the wastefulness of capitalism. To Marx it was nonsense to describe the market as organized economic activity because there was no organizer. Coordination of economic activity requires the conscious, centralized control of the economy.

While Adam Smith described the emerging market economy of his day and offered reforms (mostly summarized by the phrase *less government*), Marx offered a vision of economic organization that did not exist at the time he wrote but that he maintained was the inevitable wave of the future. In a sense he was proven correct. Followers of the teachings of Marx and his admirer Lenin (who filled in many details of

[b]Adam Smith, *An Inquiry into the Nature and Causes of the Wealth of Nations,* ed. Edwin Cannan (1776; reprint, New York: Modern Library, 1937), p. 423.

[c]Karl Marx, *Das Kapital,* ed. Max Eastman (1867; reprint, New York: Modern Library, 1932), p. 83.

[d]Marx, *Das Kapital,* p. 83.

what a central planning system would look like in practice) imposed avowedly Marxist-socialist, centrally planned economies on Russia (1917), China (1949), most of the countries of Eastern Europe, and some African and Latin American nations.

In another sense Marx's teachings appear to have failed, as recent developments in the Eastern bloc have demonstrated. The centrally planned economies seem to function poorly—providing low per capita income and poor rates of economic growth—relative to the modern versions of the capitalist economies whose central principle of market organization was so clearly seen by Smith.

Macroeconomics: Key Concepts

We have culled some of the most important principles of macroeconomics from the pages of this book for presentation in this section. Separating these important concepts from the text and presenting them as a group serves two purposes. First, it gives beginning students an idea of the scope of macroeconomics and sets them on the road toward an economic way of thinking. Second, it provides students who are familiar with the basics of macroeconomics an opportunity for review and—with an expanded use of color, especially—an opportunity to see new relationships.

Aggregate Supply and Aggregate Demand

The aggregate supply curve shows the relation between real output and the price level. The slope of the aggregate supply curve depends on economic conditions. The horizontal portion of the curve, called the *Keynesian range,* represents supply during times of severe unemployment and underutilization of resources. In this range, an increase in output will not be accompanied by an increase in the price level. The upward-sloping portion of the curve, the *intermediate range,* represents supply under normal or nearly normal conditions. The economy has not reached its production possibilities frontier (represented by Q_F, full employment), but neither is it depressed. In this range, any real increase in output will be accompanied by higher price levels. The vertical portion of the curve, the *classical range,* represents the economy at full employment. In this range, output cannot increase, and supply is perfectly inelastic in relation to the price level.

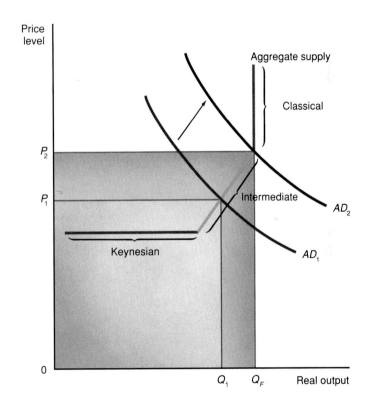

One goal of macroeconomic policy is maintaining full employment. If aggregate demand is not sufficient to achieve full-employment output, depicted by AD_1 in the figure, then demand-increasing monetary or fiscal policies may be used. An easy money policy or an expansionary fiscal policy may shift aggregate demand from AD_1 to AD_2. The movement from AD_1 to AD_2 will increase output from Q_1 to the full-employment level and increase price from P_1 to P_2.

The Federal Reserve System

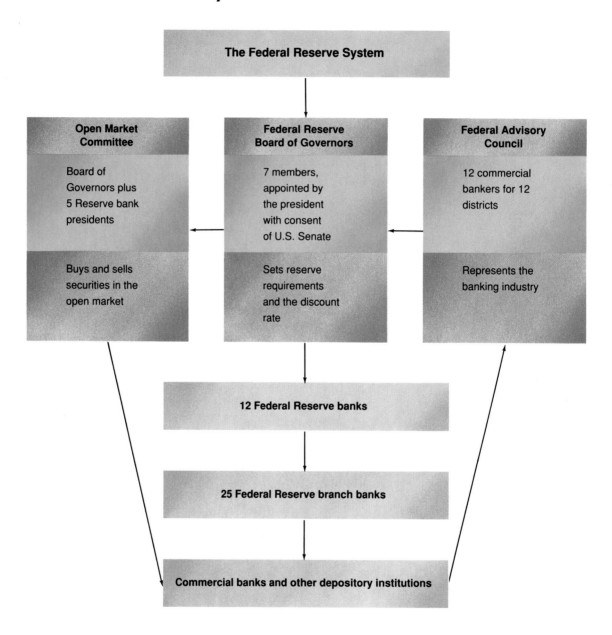

The commercial banking system and other financial institutions that issue checkable deposits are regulated and controlled by the Federal Reserve System, which is composed of twelve Federal Reserve banks and twenty-five branch banks. Monetary control is exercised through the Board of Governors in Washington, D.C., by means of reserve requirements and the discount rate. The major tool of monetary policy, open market operations (the buying and selling of securities on the open market), is overseen by the Federal Open Market Committee. The Federal Advisory Committee is the banking industry's voice in the monetary policy-setting process.

Keynesian and Monetarist Transmission Mechanisms

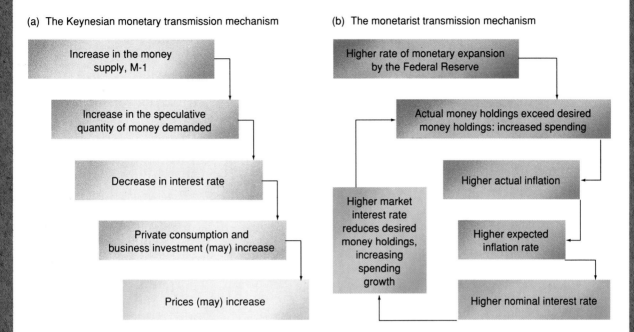

(a) The Keynesian monetary transmission mechanism

Increase in the money supply, M-1

Increase in the speculative quantity of money demanded

Decrease in interest rate

Private consumption and business investment (may) increase

Prices (may) increase

(b) The monetarist transmission mechanism

Higher rate of monetary expansion by the Federal Reserve

Actual money holdings exceed desired money holdings: increased spending

Higher actual inflation

Higher market interest rate reduces desired money holdings, increasing spending growth

Higher expected inflation rate

Higher nominal interest rate

Keynesians and monetarists differ on the effects of an increase in the money supply on prices. Despite a shared starting point—the increase in M-1—and shared focus (both approaches focus on money holders and the uncertainty that drives money holders to act), the monetarist model predicts inflation, while the Keynesian model predicts modest or negligible price increases.

Economists differentiate between types of demand for money: transactions demand, precautionary demand, and speculative demand. With regard to M-1 and inflation, Keynes was interested primarily in speculative demand. Speculators are constantly reevaluating their holdings—deciding sometimes to hold money, while opting at other times to hold less-liquid assets, such as bonds. (a) In Keynes's view, an increase in the money supply will decrease interest rates and increase bond prices, thereby increasing the speculative demand for money. Since people may tend to hold money rather than to spend it in uncertain economic times, speculative demand short-circuits the normal cause-and-effect relation between money supply and prices. In a depressed economy total expenditures and, therefore, prices may not rise—or may rise only slightly—along with the money supply. Individuals and businesses may view the higher bond prices as abnormal and so may avoid capital losses when bond prices drop by holding money instead. (b) Monetarists ignore distinctions between types of money demand. Instead, they view money as something held in response to independent variables such as real income and interest rates. In the monetarist view, the increase in money supply will be spent away in an attempt by individuals and businesses to restore equilibrium between quantity demanded of money and quantity supplied. The increased spending will push up prices, or increase the actual rate of inflation. Eventually, the public will accept the new rate of inflation and adjust expectations accordingly. Since nominal interest rates are the sum of the constant real rate of inflation and the expected inflation rate, nominal interest rates rise. Higher interest rates will prompt businesses and consumers to again rid themselves of cash balances. (Money is a poor store of value in inflationary periods.) The monetarists see the process as continuing until the Fed stabilizes the rate of monetary growth.

The Effects of a Tariff

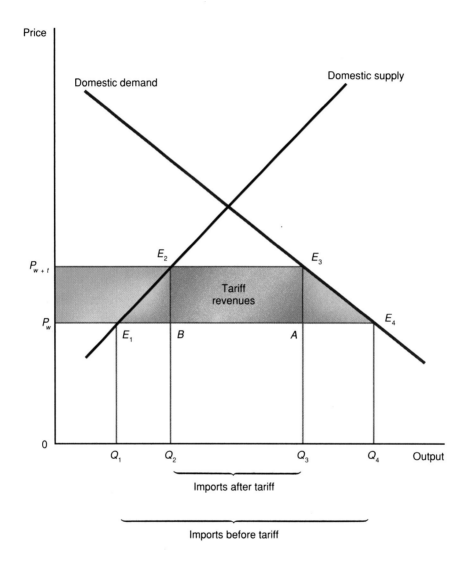

The world price of a good or service is determined by global supply and demand. Consumers and producers in individual countries may buy or sell all they wish at the world price. Here, we show the domestic demand and supply curves. A world price of P_w results in domestic production of Q_1 and domestic consumption of Q_4, with the difference, $Q_4 - Q_1$, made up by imports. A tariff on imports in the amount of t per unit of output effectively raises the world price to P_{w+t}. At the higher price, producers increase their output to Q_2, and consumers decrease their purchases to Q_3. Imports of the foreign-made good fall to $Q_3 - Q_2$; government receives tariff revenue in the amount of t times the amount imported, $Q_3 - Q_2$ (represented here by E_2E_3AB); producers' increased benefits are represented by the area $P_{w+t}E_2E_1P_w$. The gains received by producers and government come at the expense of domestic consumers; the total loss to consumers is represented by $P_{w+t}E_3E_4P_w$. Imposition of a tariff results in a net loss to society equal to the sum of the areas E_2BE_1 and E_3E_4A.

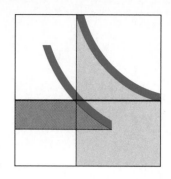

PART TWO

Private-Sector

and Public-Sector

Macroeconomics

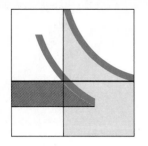

6

Macroeconomics: Contemporary Problems and Issues

Today's local newspaper or the evening television newscast is likely to contain much economic news. There might be stories on conditions in microcomputer markets or on the migration of agricultural labor from Minnesota to South Dakota. By far the most consistently reported economic news relates to the overall health of the economy.

The media pay careful attention to monthly and quarterly statistics on such measures as the inflation rate, the unemployment rate, and the growth rate in gross national product (GNP). Government economic policies to remedy macroeconomic problems are also heavily reported.

Topics such as the real rate of growth in the economy may seem abstract and distant, but they do have an immediate and lasting impact on individual economic well-being. Economists have spent more than two hundred years seeking to understand how the macroeconomy—the large-scale economy—shapes our lives.

Think for a moment about how the major macroeconomic issues—inflation, unemployment, and growth—are likely to influence your future. Will economic conditions affect your ability to repay your college loan? Will you enter the job market during a time of high unemployment? Will your hopes for a high-paying job, a comfortable home, a promising future for your children be realized? The study of macroeconomics certainly cannot answer these questions for you, but it can better equip you to plan for the future, whatever the future may hold. Likewise, this chapter is not intended to begin our formal study of macroeconomics. Instead, we present an overview of basic macroeconomic policy goals and introduce much of the terminology employed by macroeconomists. When you complete Chapter 6 you should understand

- the overall goals of macroeconomic policy and the trade-offs between goals.
- the nature of unemployment and inflation and their effects on economic growth.
- how, in general terms, fiscal and monetary policies are used to achieve the goals of macroeconomic policy.
- the essential tools of aggregate demand and aggregate supply that economists use to analyze the macroeconomy.

THE GOALS OF MACROECONOMICS

In Chapter 1 we defined *macroeconomics* as the analysis of the economy as a whole. When working with macroeconomic theory, the focus is on whole quantities, or what economists call aggregate quantities. Macroeconomics concerns not just one market but all markets; not just one price change but all price changes; not just one firm's employees but all employment.

As with any discipline, the field of macroeconomics is made up of many specialized areas, competing theories, and ongoing debates. Consistent throughout macroeconomics, however, is a shared set of goals. Both macroeconomists and the politicians who heed (or disregard) their advice are interested in achieving three separate, sometimes conflicting, objectives: full employment, price stability, and economic growth. We discuss each of these goals separately, but you will soon see they are closely intertwined.

The Full-Employment Goal

Full employment is a primary goal of any economic society for obvious reasons. The more fully resources are employed, the greater the levels of output of goods and services, and the higher the prosperity.

Social Concern over Unemployment. Not only does high unemployment threaten to bring poverty to millions of citizens, but it also can lead to political upheaval. During the Great Depression of the 1930s, for example, signs of social and political unrest appeared in the United States. Farmers marched on Washington, D.C., makeshift camps of the poor and out-of-work dotted the nation's cities, and mass migrations of the jobless from the Dust Bowl of the Midwest to the Promised Land of California took place. When World War II mobilized the economy, full employment was restored before serious political and social upheaval could erupt.

Other nations of the world have not been spared such upheavals. Witness the frequent changes of government and political systems in developing nations, where poverty—much of it caused by widespread unemployment—is rampant. Increased crime and even violent revolution can result from failure to attain the macroeconomic goal of full employment.

The purely human costs of unemployment on individuals, families, and society itself can be devastating. Unemployment is a primary cause of poverty, dislocations of families, and, in extreme cases, homelessness. It puts extraordinary pressure on social and welfare services that are funded with taxes. More important, unemployment represents resources *not used* to produce goods and services—perhaps the ultimate inefficiency.

In recognition of the social and political implications of unemployment, the U.S. government passed the Employment Act of 1946 on the heels of the Depression and World War II. The act recognized and enshrined maximum employment as a macroeconomic goal of the federal government. The meaning of the term *maximum employment* has been modified in the intervening years, but policy-makers still respect the intent, if not the letter, of the law. Unemployment rates of 10 percent and more, for example, which characterized the U.S. economy in 1982 and 1983, brought great concern to the U.S. Congress and to the Reagan administration. Unemployment rates also ran high in Europe during the early 1980s, reaching over 13 percent in England and close to 10 percent in Italy by 1984. In all nations, the goal of full employment is critical. Social programs such as unemployment compensation and food stamps ease the burden of unemployment, but they cannot substitute for the economic benefits of full employment.

Defining the Levels of Employment and Unemployment. Some unemployment in specific markets is always expected. In a dynamic economy, demand grows for some goods and services and declines for others. In recent years, for example, the demand for high-technology outputs such as microcomputers, lasers, and fiber optics has outpaced demand for the products of heavy industry, and temporary unemployment in heavy industries such as steel and machine tools has been very high. Some workers may develop new skills, however, and temporarily unemployed resources may flow into new areas of production.

From an economic perspective, there is little reason to be concerned with the temporary periods of unemployment that workers in specific fields experience as the economy undergoes change. In such cases, **unemployed** workers generally remain out of work for relatively brief periods of time before they succeed in obtaining a job. However, there *is* reason for concern when numerous workers in many different industries simultaneously become unemployed. When this happens, output levels fall far below potential, and families of the unemployed workers experience real hardship over extended periods of time. For this reason, the federal government keeps close tabs on the **unemployment rate** each month.

A random sample from 55,800 household units is surveyed each month to calculate unemployment. Household members who are under sixteen years of age are not counted as members of the labor force, nor are nonworking full-time students, the hospitalized, or the incarcerated. Qualifying individuals are asked a series of questions to determine whether they are employed, unemployed, or not in the labor force. A person is considered to be employed if, during the survey week, he or she did any work at all as a paid employee or for a personally owned business or a profession. Unemployed persons are all civilians who had no employment during the survey week, who were available for work (except, perhaps, for temporary illness), and who had made specific efforts to find employment some time during the prior four weeks. Persons who are neither employed nor unemployed (those not working and either unable to work or not looking for employment) are not deemed to be members of the labor force.

The labor force is therefore defined as the total of employed and unemployed persons. To calculate the unemployment rate, the number of unemployed persons is divided by the total labor force. This method of measuring unemployment is not without problems. During periods of high unemployment, unemployed workers become discouraged and stop searching for jobs. Once they stop looking, they are no longer considered members of the labor force. This behavior causes measured unemployment to fall. (The opposite is true during periods of unusually low unemployment, when people are enticed into the labor market.) For reasons such as these, the unemployment rate may not provide a perfect picture of what is happening in the economy.

Unemployed:
A labor-force status characterized by an individual who is actively seeking employment but is not working.

Unemployment rate:
The percentage of the labor force without jobs.

Figure 1 shows the growth of the labor force and the fluctuations in employment and unemployment since 1950. Table 1 presents data on the unemployment rate, the number of unemployed workers, and the size of the labor force since 1975.

The Bureau of Labor Statistics also breaks down the unemployment rate into rates for various demographic groups to show the *differing rates* of unemployment for particular groups in the economy. Figure 2 shows the total unemployment rate in the U.S. economy for the period 1960–1989 and the corresponding unemployment rates by race, sex, and age. Some facts about the composition of the unemployment rate are apparent: (1) Minority groups

---

FIGURE 1   The Labor Force, Employment, and Unemployment

The national labor force is the sum of the employed and the unemployed. The labor force has increased steadily because of population growth, but the level of unemployment has fluctuated with changes in the overall economy.

Sources: U.S. Board of Governors of the Federal Reserve System, *Historical Chart Book* (Washington, D.C.: Board of Governors of the Federal Reserve System, 1984); Council of Economic Advisers, *Economic Report of the President* (Washington, D.C.: U.S. Government Printing Office, 1990), pp. 330, 338.

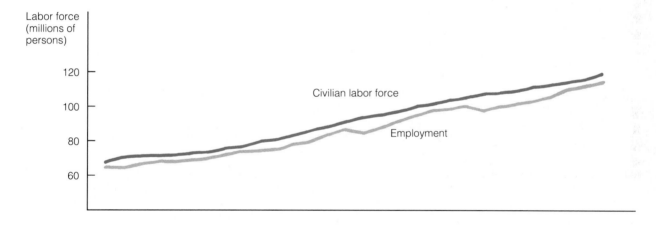

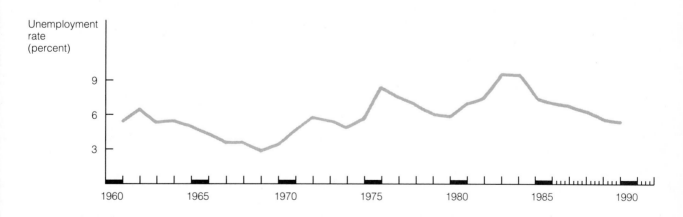

TABLE 1

Unemployment, Unemployment Rate, and the National Labor Force, 1975–1989

Year	Unemployment Rate (percent)	Unemployment (thousands of persons)[a]	Civilian Labor Force (thousands of persons)[a]
1975	8.5	7,929	93,775
1976	7.7	7,406	96,158
1977	7.1	6,991	99,009
1978	6.1	6,202	102,251
1979	5.8	6,137	104,962
1980	7.1	7,637	106,940
1981	7.6	8,273	108,670
1982	9.7	10,678	110,204
1983	9.6	10,717	111,550
1984	7.5	8,539	113,544
1985	7.2	8,312	115,461
1986	7.0	8,237	117,834
1987	6.2	7,425	119,865
1988	5.5	6,701	121,669
1989	5.3	6,528	123,869

Source: Council of Economic Advisers, *Economic Report of the President* (Washington, D.C.: U.S. Government Printing Office, 1990), p. 330.

[a]Age sixteen and over.

have experienced a higher unemployment rate than whites, (2) teenagers in the 16–19 age group have experienced a higher unemployment rate than any other age group, and (3) women over twenty years of age have generally experienced higher unemployment rates than men of the same age.

Despite the presence of unemployment, **full employment** remains a political goal. As we have seen, the Employment Act of 1946 charged the federal government with the responsibility of promoting maximum employment. In 1978, Congress passed the Full Employment and Balanced Growth Act, which committed the government to full employment, defined as an unemployment rate of 4 percent. The goals of the act have been modified in the intervening years, with the goal being adjusted upward over the 1970s and 1980s.

How can full employment be defined as allowing for any unemployment? Some economists feel that there is a **natural rate of unemployment** (or employment), the rate that would exist under long-run equilibrium conditions because of the time needed for adjustments in the labor market, the lag in matching vacancies and workers, the costs of hiring and firing and of changing jobs, regulations affecting structural changes in labor markets, and so forth. Market forces and institutions, not individuals, determine the natural rate of unemployment at any given time. The actual rate of unemployment can be compared to the theoretical concept of the natural rate, as in Figure 3. Note that the actual unemployment rate has fluctuated around the natural rate, with cycles of business activity producing unemployment below the natural rate in some periods and above the rate in other periods. In the most direct sense, macroeconomics deals with why the actual rate of unemployment differs from the natural rate and with what might cause the natural rate to change over time.

Economists debate, sometimes hotly, what the appropriate level of full employment is. In fact, the unemployment rate has not fallen below 5 percent

Full employment:
A situation in which unemployment exists only because of normal market adjustments to changing demand or supply or to outmoded skills of workers; also a numerical federal government goal for the unemployment rate.

Natural rate of unemployment:
A theoretical concept; the unemployment rate that coexists with macroeconomic stability or labor-market equilibrium in the long run.

FIGURE 2

Unemployment Rates

The unemployment rate (the number of persons unemployed divided by the labor force) rises and falls with other economic activity. However, blacks and teenagers consistently have higher rates of unemployment than other groups.

Source: Council of Economic Advisers, *Economic Report of the President* (Washington, D.C.: U.S. Government Printing Office, 1990), p. 338.

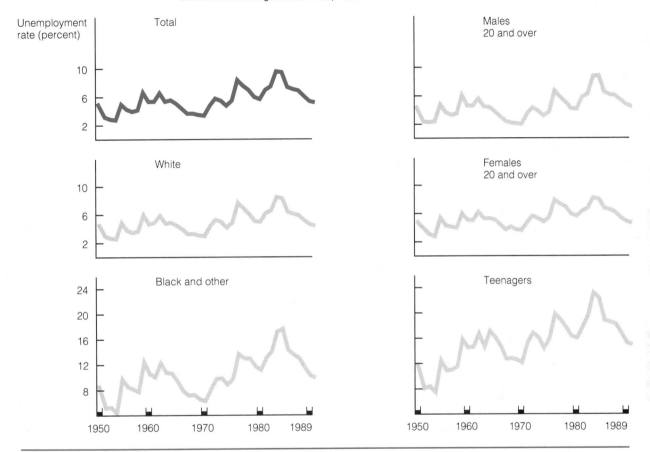

since 1973, and many economists now think that the "full-employment" unemployment rate should be in the 5–7 percent range, a range close to the theoretical concept of the natural rate of unemployment. Unemployment is a familiar problem in economies, even in rapidly growing countries (see Focus, " 'Floating Waves' of Unemployed in Japan").

The Goal of Price Stability

Price stability:
A situation of no inflation or deflation in the economy; no change in the overall level of prices of goods, services, and resources.

The second major macroeconomic goal is **price stability**—the absence of inflation or deflation in the overall level of future prices. Inflation is a process of price level increases that take place over time. Inflation can be stable and predictable or unstable and unanticipated—in either case, bringing higher costs to consumers and producers, and to buyers and sellers. Inflation is far more disruptive when it arrives unannounced, however.

FIGURE 3

Rate of Unemployment, 1890–1989

The actual rate of unemployment has fluctuated widely since 1890. The unemployment rate rose to dangerous levels during the 1930s but has stayed within narrower limits since World War II. The actual unemployment rate has fluctuated around the natural rate of unemployment, a theoretical concept that depends on the situations and institutions surrounding the demand and supply of labor.

Source: Robert J. Gordon, *Macroeconomics,* 5th ed. (Glenview, IL: Scott, Foresman, 1990), p. 14.

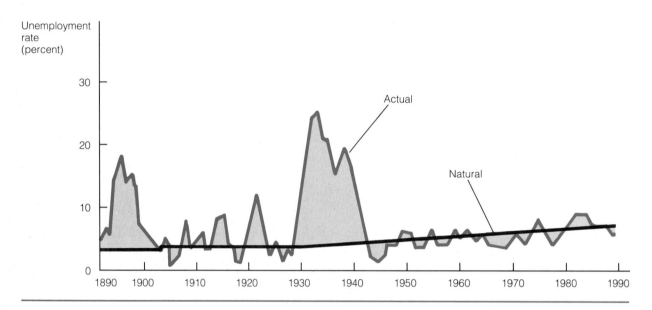

Inflation is not simply a rise in the price of gasoline or chicken. Rather, inflation is a macroeconomic situation characterized by sustained and continuous increases in the overall level or average of all prices. One way to measure inflation is to look at the average of prices for some representative collection, or market basket, of goods and services that people buy. An increase in this average, or general, level of prices over some given time period (a month or a year) indicates the presence of inflation in the economy.

Suppose that food was the only good people bought. A 2 percent increase in the average level of food prices during the month of March means that the consumer must spend $1.02 at the end of March to buy the same market basket of food items that $1.00 would purchase in February. Never mind that bacon prices actually fell in March and that potato chip prices rose by 10 percent. Inflation is measured by considering the average prices of some representative bundle of goods at some given level—such as the retail, wholesale, or producer level.

If the cost of some market basket of goods and services was, say, $200 in one month and $210 in the next month, then prices in general would have risen by 5 percent during the month. When the change in prices over any period of time (a month here) is expressed as a percentage, the number calculated is called the **inflation rate.** The inflation rate is the speed at which

Rate of inflation:
The percentage change in the average level of prices over a period of time; the speed at which prices in general are rising.

FOCUS   "Floating Waves" of Unemployed in Japan

Popular wisdom has it that Japan's postwar economic "miracle" provides jobs and prosperity for all in society. Although formal unemployment does exist in Japan, a generous social safety net provides for the unemployed. A recent article disputes the conventional wisdom about the magnitude of unemployment in Japan.[a] The *furosha,* or "floating waves" of homeless street people, wander day and night through the parks, streets, and rail stations of Japan's major cities—despite free medical care from the government, subsidies of up to $1000 per month per person for food and shelter, and subsidized housing. How is such homelessness to be explained in a prosperous and growing nation?

As in the United States, many who find their way to the streets are old, infirm, or addicted to alcohol or drugs; they are unable to raise themselves to a level of self-support. Many of the unskilled day laborers who helped build the infrastructure of Japan in the 1960s are now too old to find work. In addition, residents of outlying areas often move into the cities, hoping to secure a job with a salary that will allow them to send money back home.

Important cultural differences between Japan and the United States may explain why the Japanese homeless problem may be more entrenched, despite the considerable social safety net provided. The rigid employment track, where job entry to retirement is carefully planned within an employment "family," means that job mobility is not as fluid as in the United States. On-the-job skills are important; older workers may find it difficult to secure new jobs if employers think there is a need for significant retraining and projected work years for the workers are few. Japanese unable to find work have access to welfare and social services but apparently do not use them. The shame associated with failure—losing one's job, falling into debt, or the simple inability to find work—is far more culturally ingrained in Japanese than in Americans. In Japan, a governmental investigation into family finances is required before subsidies will be paid. In the United States, this kind of scrutiny would represent merely a minor structural impediment to the unemployed; in Japan, the impediment is cultural and moral as well, and of great importance in explaining the *furosha.*

[a]Neil Gross, " 'Floating Waves' of Homeless in a Sea of Prosperity," *Business Week* (September 12, 1988), p. 50.

prices in general are increasing. In this example, the inflation rate calculated is 5 percent per month. If prices continued to increase at the same speed for an entire year, the inflation rate would be 80 percent per year (5 percent per month compounded for 12 months). A statistic calculated by the federal government's Bureau of Labor Statistics called the consumer price index (CPI) is used to measure the overall average level of prices in the United States. By calculating the percentage changes in the CPI, the inflation rate in the U.S. economy can be measured. (The CPI will be explained and discussed fully in Chapter 7.)

Deflation:
Sustained decreases in the average level of prices.

Deflation is a decrease in the general price level. Since World War II, price instability has been due to inflation rather than deflation. During the 1970s, for example, the United States experienced double-digit inflation rates reaching almost 14 percent per year in 1980.

Certainly we have plenty of evidence that inflation can get out of hand. Like severe unemployment, runaway inflation can wreak havoc in a society, causing social and political disintegration. A classic example occurred in post–World War I Germany when the inflation rate was as high as thousands of percentage points *per day*. Eventually, the German mark was worth more as paper—it was actually used as wallpaper—than as money. As a result, goods disappeared from markets and people starved. Looking farther back in time, economic historians claim to have evidence that runaway inflation was partly responsible for the breakdown of the Roman Empire's economic and political institutions.

Many of the costs of inflation and deflation can be traced to the inability of various economic institutions to adjust quickly to unanticipated price changes. When inflation is fully anticipated, personal savings for education, retirement, or vacations; tax codes; and financial contracts may be adjusted. But when inflation is unanticipated, adjustments become costly and difficult. People who live on fixed incomes—many of them elderly and poor to begin with—are particularly hard hit by inflation, as we will see in Chapter 17.

Historically, inflation has been a problem in the United States during postwar periods. Even then, as Figure 4 shows, the inflation rate has seldom risen above 10 percent per year. In the period of inflation following the Vietnam War, the inflation rate rose to 13.5 percent in 1980, before falling sharply. Increases in the inflation rate late in the 1980s again generated fears of serious inflation. Other countries have had much worse inflation problems in recent years. For example, the inflation rate in Argentina and Brazil reached annual levels in excess of 1000 percent during the 1980s. In Bolivia, the annual inflation rate exceeded 20,000 percent in 1985. Mexico had inflation rates in excess of 150 percent but has since adopted policies that sharply reduced the inflation rate to less than 25 percent per year.

Real income:
The purchasing power of money income; the quantity of goods and services that money income can buy.

Even when the rate of inflation stands at relatively modest levels, it can pose problems for the economy. First of all, inflation has peculiar redistributive effects. That is, it enhances some people's real incomes at the expense of others'. **Real income** is the quantity of goods and services that can be bought with an individual's **nominal,** or money, **income.** In other words, real income is the real purchasing power of one's nominal income. For example, if a person was earning $10,000 per year in 1975 and continued to do so in 1990, a modest inflation rate of 6 percent per year from 1975 to 1990 would mean that the person's real income, or purchasing power, would have fallen by more

Nominal income:
Income measured in terms of money, not in terms of what the money can buy.

FIGURE 4

The inflation rate is measured by calculating the yearly percentage changes in the CPI. Inflation rates varied greatly over the period 1950–1989, although the trend since 1950 has been toward average higher rates. Notice, however, the downward trend in the inflation rate since 1980.

Source: Council of Economic Advisers, *Economic Report of the President* (Washington, D.C.: U.S. Government Printing Office, 1990), p. 364.

The Rate of Inflation, 1950–1989

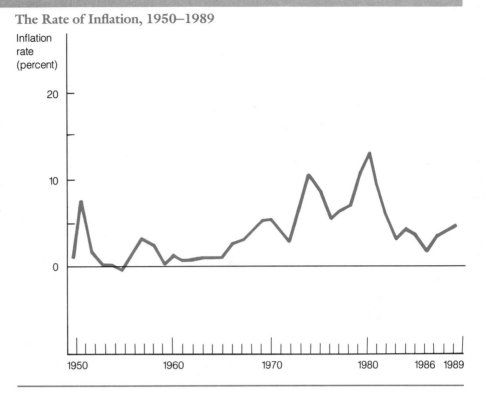

than 50 percent, despite the fact that the nominal income remained the same. This loss of real income is all too familiar to people on fixed money incomes—those on fixed pension plans, for example. When prices of the goods and services consumed by these groups rise, but their nominal incomes remain the same or do not rise as fast as prices, the real income of these consumers falls. Naturally, consumers whose income is rising at a faster rate than prices are better off during inflationary periods. Under such circumstances, arbitrary redistributions take place, with those on fixed incomes bearing the costs.

Uncertainty about future prices also results from price instability. Debtors and creditors, for instance, must guess at future prices and charge or pay interest rates that may or may not cover the real change in the value of money. Inflation also disrupts decisions of producers and consumers. Consumers' expectations about future prices and future real incomes are especially important. Consumers may adjust to their expectations, buying today if they expect prices to push higher tomorrow or if they think that inflation will reduce purchasing power in the future. (Likewise, if consumers expect deflation at some point in the future—far less likely, given U.S. experience—they would be more likely to postpone purchases, especially of durable goods.) While fully expected inflation may cause some transaction costs, unanticipated inflation and an unstable, unpredictable inflation rate greatly disrupt the plans of buyers and sellers. Before 1981, consumers also faced the possibility of real income erosion due to the tax structure. When nominal income increased as a result of attempts to maintain real income, income earners were forced into higher

Tax indexation:
The basing of income taxes on real income instead of nominal income.

tax brackets. This "bracket creep" occurred because tax rates have been levied on money income received, not on real income earned. **Tax indexation** is one way to curb this detrimental effect of inflation. Under tax indexation, the federal tax tables are tied to the inflation rate. Tax indexation was first implemented in 1981 and was preserved in the Tax Reform Act of 1986.

Producers are also profoundly affected by unanticipated inflation. With uncertainty about inflation, producers may withhold output of goods and services from the market. Under extreme uncertainty, the plans of investors and business entrepreneurs can be badly upset, causing postponement or abandonment of projects that enhance employment and economic growth. High, unpredictable rates of inflation help explain the low rates of capital formation and slow economic growth in some developing nations.

The Objective of Economic Growth

Economic growth:
A sustained increase in the overall productive capacity of an economy over time.

The third major macroeconomic issue is growth in the economy. **Economic growth** refers to any increase in the productive capacities of the economy, whether as a result of an increase in the labor supply, an increase in the productivity of labor (the output per worker), or a net increase in the quality or quantity of the nation's capital stock, the wherewithal of production.

The labor supply grows through increases in population, immigration, or the number of people willing to work. Increased productivity of labor in output per worker is achieved through improvements in education and human capital or through a higher quantity and quality of capital stock supplied to labor. Writers and secretaries, for instance, may increase their productivity by switching from typewriters to word processing systems. Additions to the nation's capital stock are made through new investment in capital goods— word processors in offices, robots in factories. This investment arises from another macroeconomic variable, private saving. To save, individuals must forgo present consumption. Under favorable economic conditions, when the two goals of price level stability and full employment are achieved, any given rate of private saving is more likely to generate new investment, capital formation, and economic growth than would otherwise be the case.

Gross national product (GNP):
The value of all the final goods and services produced in an economy during a year.

Real economic growth, measured in terms of changes in **gross national product (GNP)**, has averaged about 3 percent per year in the United States over the past hundred years. However, this rate of growth has slowed somewhat in the last two decades. Another related problem in recent U.S. experience has been slowed growth in productivity—a reduction in the ratio of total output to the number of employed workers. While the reasons for a slowdown in productivity growth are complex—as are the relations between economic growth and changes in productivity—one major problem has been a reduced rate of technological development in the United States. Reduced productivity may translate into much slower economic growth in the future and a lessened standard of living for Americans.

Although politicians often express concern over the slow rate of productivity growth and the somewhat lessened rate of economic growth over the past few decades, this issue tends to be given low priority in policy decisions. After all, the effects of these slower growth rates are not immediately apparent. However, the cumulative effect of a slower growth rate can become stagger-

Nominal GNP:
The economy's total production of final goods and services measured in dollars unadjusted for changes in the price level.

Real GNP:
The total production of final goods and services measured in dollars that have been adjusted for changes in the price level.

ingly large in just a generation. For example, if a country's rate of growth is 8 percent per year instead of 10 percent per year, real GNP will be only half as large within thirty-six years as it would have been at the slightly higher annual rate. Except for the period of the Great Depression, for over one hundred years each generation of Americans has had reason to believe that it would have a markedly higher standard of living than the preceding generation. If U.S. productivity and economic growth fall to low levels, this expectation may no longer be realistic for many Americans. Figure 5 shows two measures of aggregate economic growth between 1950 and 1988. One line measures **nominal GNP;** the other line, **real GNP.** Nominal GNP for each of the years is measured in terms of prices that prevail in that year. Therefore, increases in nominal GNP can be caused either by increases in output or by increases in prices. Real GNP is a measure of the economy's output adjusted for general price level changes. The measures of real GNP in Figure 5 reflect the quantities of goods that are produced in the various years in constant dollars, or in prices that existed in some given year (1982 in Figure 5).

FIGURE 5

Real and Nominal GNP

The black line shows the rising level of GNP. Most of this increase is caused by rising prices. The colored line shows the trend of real GNP by removing the effects of inflation on prices. GNP, in other words, rises less rapidly in terms of constant 1982 dollars.

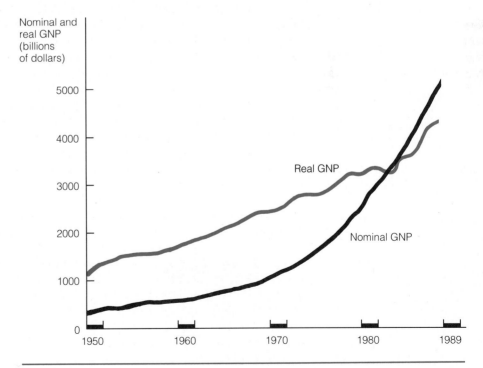

The distinction between real GNP and nominal GNP is important: Price changes cloud the picture of the value of output over time. Nominal GNP can increase between any two years even if production levels fall because the effect of rising prices can offset the effect on nominal GNP of falling levels of production. Therefore, we focus on real GNP, not nominal GNP, in measuring the rate of economic growth.

ECONOMIC STABILITY AND BUSINESS CYCLES

Economic stabilization:
A situation in which the price level and the unemployment rate vary from desired levels only temporarily and by small amounts.

The overall goal of macroeconomic policy is to achieve **economic stabilization.** By stabilization, we do not mean *no* economic growth. Instead, the term describes an environment in which price changes (resulting either from inflation or from deflation) are moderate and in which the unemployment rate differs little from the full-employment level. In such an environment, the prices of individual goods will change, leading to changes in employment levels, as existing industries grow and contract and as new industries arise. However, neither a persistent change in the price level nor excessive unemployment will upset overall consumption and production and disrupt economic growth under stabilization.

Economic stability thus means the achievement of full employment under inflationless or near inflationless conditions to attain maximum economic growth in the present and future. Stabilization is a tall order in a modern economy, where economic activity is subject to fluctuations. These fluctuations, called **business cycles,** are the result of severe variations in the plans of buyers and sellers beyond those variations necessary for changes and improvements in production and consumption.

Business cycles:
Recurrent, systematic fluctuations in the level of business activity; usually measured by changes in the level, or rate of growth, of real GNP over time.

Business cycles are made up of, at one extreme, peaks and, at the other extreme, recessions or depressions. At the peak of a business cycle, the economy is expanding rapidly, with employment at or near capacity. In a recession or depression, resources—especially human resources—are grossly underused. In the expansionary phase of a cycle, increased demand for goods and services causes rapidly increasing demand for all resources, putting pressure on the supplies of labor, capital, and raw materials. One signal that the economy is in the expansionary phase is that business inventories are rapidly being depleted. This period of a business cycle is often characterized by increased inflation, as business activity and employment expand. After the peak of the cycle, the economy enters a contractionary phase. As production of goods exceeds demand for them, inventories build up—one signal of contraction. This phase is characterized by stable or falling prices, excess production capacities, and unemployment. When depression or recession is reached, the economy experiences negative real economic growth rates and stagnation. When recovery is relatively quick in arriving, the period of stagnation is termed a *recession*. A *depression* is a longer, more damaging period of stagnation. Eventually, however, growing demand for goods and services will pull the economy out of any slump. Figure 6 shows cycles of business activity as measured by real GNP growth rate since 1950. Figure 7 illustrates a typical business cycle. (In Chapter 19 we examine a number of explanations for the nature of and turning points of business cycles.)

The goals of macroeconomic policy are to even out or counterbalance the opposing forces of the business cycle. Such policy is therefore called countercyclical policy. Its role is to counter the business cycle to produce inflationless economic growth with full employment. The role of macroeconomic and monetary theory is to understand the causes of changes in business activity—that is, the causes of the business cycle.

AGGREGATE DEMAND, AGGREGATE SUPPLY, AND MACROECONOMIC POLICY

Identifying goals is only the first step. Questions abound: How can full employment be reached? How can inflation be tamed? How can economic growth be sustained? Questions such as these require both theoretical and political answers. In this section we briefly introduce two of the most important macroeconomic theoretical tools—aggregate demand and aggregate supply—and the two most important types of macroeconomic policy.

FIGURE 6

Cycles of Real Annual Growth Rates in GNP, 1950–1989, in Constant (1982) Dollars

Periods of economic expansion and contraction have varied a great deal in this century. Note the roller-coaster path since 1960, punctuated by sharp recessions in 1974–1975, 1980, and in 1981–1982.

Sources: U.S. Board of Governors of the Federal Reserve System, *Historical Chart Book* (Washington, D.C.: Board of Governors of the Federal Reserve System, 1984), p. 12; Council of Economic Advisers, *Economic Report of the President* (Washington, D.C.: U.S. Government Printing Office, 1990), p. 297.

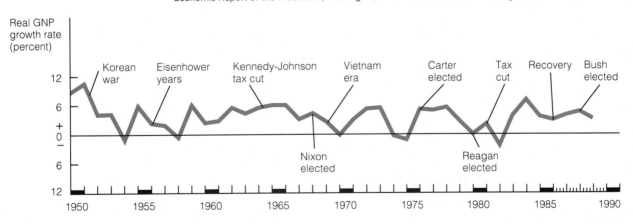

FIGURE 7

Most business cycles vary in length and intensity. A typical cycle includes an expansionary phase of rising business activity and growth, a peak of activity, a contractionary phase of falling activity, and a low point, usually referred to as a recession or depression.

A Typical Business Cycle

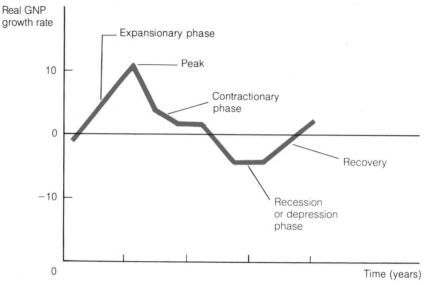

Aggregate demand:
The total spending that occurs in an economy at various price levels during a specified period of time.

Aggregate supply:
The total output that will be produced by an economy at various price levels during a specified period of time.

Aggregate Demand and Aggregate Supply

In examining macroeconomic phenomena, it is often useful to conceive of aggregate demand and aggregate supply curves. In the abstract, **aggregate demand** represents all components of expenditure on domestically produced goods and services. Like an ordinary demand curve, which shows the quantity of a particular good or service that buyers as a group are willing to purchase at each possible price, an aggregate demand curve shows the value of all goods and services that buyers (domestic consumers, business firms, government agencies, foreign buyers) are willing to purchase at each price level over a specific period of time. Similarly, the **aggregate supply** curve shows the time-specific value of all goods and services that producers as a group are willing to offer for sale at each possible price level. In drawing an aggregate demand or supply curve, price level is measured on the vertical axis, and aggregate output is measured on the horizontal axis. Typical aggregate demand and supply curves are depicted in Figure 8.

Although the analogy between demand and supply in an individual market (such as the market for CDs) and the aggregate demand and supply of all goods and services is not perfect, the concepts are similar. Both the demand curve for an individual product and the aggregate demand curve are negatively sloped; as price declines, quantity of goods and services demanded rises. Several factors lead to larger aggregate demand at lower price levels. One of the most obvious is an increase in export sales to foreign buyers. A decrease in prices in this country is likely to make American goods more attractive to foreign buyers, causing the foreign component of aggregate demand to rise. Spending by domestic buyers is also likely to increase, for reasons we will detail in Chapter 11.

FIGURE 8

Like the demand and supply curves for a single good, the aggregate demand and aggregate supply curves for all goods and services determine a price level and a level of output for all goods produced and consumed. Equilibrium is achieved at the point where aggregate demand equals aggregate supply.

Aggregate Demand and Aggregate Supply Curves

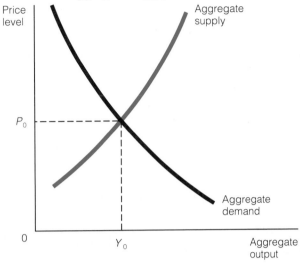

Like a typical supply curve in an individual market, the aggregate supply curve shown in Figure 8 is positively sloped. Producers as a group are revealed in Figure 8 to be willing to supply larger quantities of goods and services at higher price levels, presumably because higher price levels yield higher rates of profit. A detailed discussion of the forces underlying aggregate supply will also be presented in Chapter 11.

Equilibrium occurs where aggregate demand equals aggregate supply. This occurs at a price level of P_0 and an output level of Y_0 in Figure 8. At price levels above P_0, aggregate supply of goods and services exceeds aggregate demand. This surplus of goods and services in aggregate exerts downward pressure on prices, causing the price level to fall to P_0. At price levels below P_0, aggregate demand is greater than aggregate supply. General shortages of goods and services cause prices to rise, driving the price level up to the equilibrium at P_0.

Aggregate demand and supply curves are useful for examining the issues of unemployment, price stability, and economic growth. Depending on the positions of aggregate demand and supply, the equilibrium level of output can be at high or low levels. Unemployment becomes a serious problem when the equilibrium level of production is too low, causing many workers to lose their jobs.

To consider the goal of price stability, it is necessary to consider shifts in aggregate demand and supply over time. Such shifts can lead to price instability—changes in the equilibrium price level above or below P_0 in Figure 8. Price stability occurs if neither of the curves shifts or if both shift rightward or leftward at the same rate. However, suppose aggregate demand increases more rapidly than does aggregate supply. In this case, the economy will experience inflation, as the price level rises to an equilibrium level above P_0. Similarly, the economy would experience deflation if aggregate supply rose relative to aggregate demand.

Comparing the equilibrium level of output over time provides a picture of economic growth. Shifts to the right in either aggregate demand or aggregate supply will cause economic growth, the pace depending on the rate at which aggregate demand or supply increases.

MACROECONOMIC ISSUES: ACHIEVING GOALS IS NOT EASY

Unfortunately, policies to achieve full employment, price stability, and economic growth often fail. One explanation for this is that macroeconomic policies that might work beautifully in isolation sometimes can conflict with each other. For example, policies that shift aggregate demand rightward to attain full employment will tend to cause price increases rather than price stability. Also, certain policies to contain inflation will increase unemployment. In such cases, decision-makers are faced with a **policy trade-off;** they are forced to decide which of the economic goals is more important to attain.

Additional problems in implementing macroeconomic policy arise from political considerations. Certain policy changes, such as reductions in government spending or tax increases, are politically unpopular. Therefore, such policies tend not to be implemented or tend to be delayed, even when economically desirable.

Policy trade-off:
A situation in which a policy that promotes the attainment of one macroeconomic goal necessarily implies that the attainment of another macroeconomic objective becomes more difficult.

Can Discretionary Macroeconomic Policy Work?

A more fundamental macroeconomic issue relates to the advisability of using **discretionary policies** (monetary or fiscal adjustments in the economy). Some economists question whether the economy can be managed at all by fallible public officials who possess imperfect information. **Fiscal policy**—taxing and spending policy—is controlled by Congress and the president. **Monetary policy**—control over the growth in the money stock—is controlled by the politically appointed Federal Reserve Board. The issue is whether these groups could ever know enough about the economy or react quickly enough to disturbances to direct and control the economy in discretionary fashion. If mistakes are possible, could not discretionary policies create so much uncertainty and confusion that they might sometimes have the opposite effects to those intended?

Some contemporary macroeconomists believe that, for reasons such as conflicting goals and imperfect information, discretionary fiscal and monetary policies have built-in side effects that make them worse than useless. These economists call for the use of policy rules such as predetermined growth in the money supply and balanced federal budgets instead of discretionary control of the macroeconomy. Rules and balanced budgets would, in the view of some, take policy out of error-prone human hands, leading to more certain expectations among consumers, producers, and investors in the economy.

Underlying a faith in establishing rules rather than discretion in enacting policy is the belief, held by early classical economists and upheld by their

Discretionary policy:
A policy or change in policy that is determined by choices or decisions of policy-makers.

Fiscal policy:
The use of government spending and taxation to effect changes in aggregate economic variables.

Monetary policy:
The use of money supply changes to effect changes in aggregate economic variables.

followers today, that the economy, if left undisturbed by government, will automatically achieve the goals of full employment, price stability, and maximum economic growth. Much of the policy controversy discussed in ensuing chapters centers on issues such as these. Can discretionary policy work? How automatic are free-market forces in achieving macroeconomic goals? Are rules preferable to continual alterations in fiscal and monetary policies?

Demand-Side Versus Supply-Side Policies

Demand-side policy:
Fiscal or monetary policy intended to alter the overall level of spending, or aggregate demand.

Most contemporary macroeconomic theory and policy, originating in the 1930s in the writing of John Maynard Keynes, is directed toward manipulating aggregate demand, either in discretionary fashion or with rules designed to produce full employment, price stability, and growth. This approach is now referred to as **demand-side policy.**

Supply-side policy:
Fiscal or monetary policy intended to directly alter the incentives to produce output; policies designed to shift aggregate supply.

Some economists, notably those associated with the Reagan administration, have focused instead on some of the factors related to output response or to aggregate supply changes. As noted earlier, output response is largely determined by factors related to resource supply and to investment and capital accumulation. The **supply-side** view of the macroeconomy emphasizes the possible effects of taxes on work effort, labor supply, and investment. High tax burdens on consumer-workers and on investors mean that the economy's output response is constricted. A lower output response creates rigidities in the economy, limiting the attainment of macroeconomic goals. Indeed, one of the goals of the Tax Reform Act of 1986 was to stimulate output by lowering the federal income tax rates individuals and businesses face. Institutional changes surrounding the work decision—such as an increase in the number of women in the work force—plus government social programs and minimum-wage laws may also play a role in influencing aggregate supply.

A focus on aggregate supply should not be taken to mean that aggregate demand theory or policy is unimportant. As we will see, both aggregate demand and aggregate supply play critical roles in explaining success or failure in obtaining macroeconomic goals.

MODERN MACROECONOMICS: A MIXED APPROACH

Our brief look at the confusing and often conflicting issues surrounding the attainment of macroeconomic goals should not discourage you. Rest assured that modern economists can lay claim to a practical understanding of the basic functioning of the aggregate economy.

Still, economists often take different policy positions based on alternative outcomes—and different magnitudes of outcomes—predicted by different theories. One rather unsettling fact will become clear as we go on: No single theory tells us everything we want to know. Rather, there is some truth in a number of theoretical approaches that may be viewed as alternative or complementary to each other.

SUMMARY

1. Macroeconomics studies the effects of the interplay between aggregate demand and aggregate supply on inflation, unemployment, and economic growth, whereas microeconomics is concerned with the functioning of supply and demand in specific markets.
2. The overall goal of macroeconomic theory and policy is economic stabilization. Specifically, macroeconomic policy aims at an inflationless and fully employed economy with maximum economic growth. Some unemployment is expected in any fluid, dynamic economy, as individuals change jobs and other resources adapt to changing market conditions.
3. Inflation and unemployment are the enemies of economic growth because they create an environment within which private saving and new investment are reduced. A reduction in new investment means lower capital formation and reduced growth prospects.
4. Runaway inflation can have disastrous social and economic effects in an economy. Redistributions of real income from those on fixed incomes, often the poor and elderly, extreme variations in buyers' and sellers'

plans, and arbitrary increases in taxes required by government are among the problems created by inflation.
5. Trade-offs may exist between the achievement of two or more economic goals such as inflation and unemployment.
6. Fiscal policy and monetary policy are the two major means for manipulating aggregate demand and aggregate supply. Fiscal policy is the alteration in tax or spending activities by government. Monetary policy is control of the money supply and interest rates.
7. Economists have differing opinions about whether discretionary macroeconomic policy is stabilizing or destabilizing in promoting economic goals. In the view of some economists, rules should be substituted for authority in the quest for economic stabilization.
8. Supply-side economists have shifted attention to the factors affecting output response in the economy, such as the effect of taxation on work effort, new investment, and labor productivity.

KEY TERMS

unemployed
unemployment rate
full employment
natural rate of
    unemployment
price stability
rate of inflation
deflation
real income

nominal income
tax indexation
economic growth
gross national product
    (GNP)
nominal GNP
real GNP
economic stabilization
business cycles

aggregate demand
aggregate supply
policy trade-off
discretionary policy
fiscal policy
monetary policy
demand-side policy
supply-side policy

QUESTIONS FOR REVIEW AND DISCUSSION

1. What is price stability? Is a constant rate of inflation at 10 percent less harmful to people than an inflation rate that randomly fluctuates between 2 percent and 8 percent?
2. What are the three major goals of macroeconomic policy? Why have politicians in the past been less concerned with policies aimed at achieving sustained long-run growth than achieving the other two goals?
3. Why do economists disagree on macroeconomic policies? Does this imply that economists do not understand macroeconomics?
4. What is discretionary-demand management policy? Can discretionary fiscal policy eliminate swings in the business cycle?

5. Suppose that the economy is experiencing less than full employment. Utilizing the aggregate demand and aggregate supply theory developed in this chapter, explain the possible trade-offs that would have to be made to attain full employment.
6. What is necessary to achieve economic growth? Do inflation and unemployment hinder this process?
7. Can discretionary-demand management cause aggregate supply problems? What other trade-offs exist for policy-makers?
8. Which do you suppose is better for the economy, an increase in aggregate demand or an increase in aggregate supply? What is the difference?

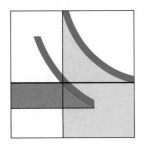

7

Measuring the Macroeconomy

Chapter 6 presented recent data on the American economy, including statistics on gross national product, unemployment, and inflation. In this chapter we look at these measures in more detail, examining the components of gross national product, the relation between GNP and national income, and the methods through which economists derive these aggregate data. We also look at the methods for measuring inflation in the economy and at how a price index is compiled. Statistics such as GNP and the rate of inflation are the bread and butter of macroeconomic study and of policy debate. Price changes are revealed monthly and real GNP performance is revealed quarterly. Consumers and businesses, not to mention many world markets, react to each announcement of the data. When you complete Chapter 7 you should recognize

- what aggregate measures of economic well-being include (and what they do not include).
- why no measure of an economy's progress is perfect and why all measures must be qualified.
- the methods upon which economists and statisticians build the national income accounts.
- how price changes and inflation or deflation relate to aggregate measures of economic progress.

AGGREGATE ACCOUNTING AND THE CONCEPT OF GNP

National income accounting—and macroeconomics itself—was born in the seventeenth-century endeavor to develop a "political arithmetic." Chief among the writers in this tradition were Sir William Petty (1623–1687) and his follower Charles Davenant (1656–1714). "By Political Arithmetick," wrote Davenant, "we mean the art of reasoning by figures upon things relating to government. . . . The art is undoubtedly very ancient. . . . But Petty first gave it that name and brought it into rules and methods."[1] Petty tried to estimate the national income of England as early as 1665, and economists have attempted to measure the economic performance of economies ever since.

Although economists have long been interested in aggregate economic statistics, it was not until the 1930s in both the United States and Great Britain that economists and government agencies began to collect such data. At that time, Congress instructed the Department of Commerce to assemble and report on the national accounts. Modern **national income accounting,** or the statistical measuring of the nation's economic performance, was officially born.[2] These principles were, in large measure, the legacy of two Nobel Prize–winning economists—Simon Kuznets in the United States and Sir Richard Stone in Great Britain. (See Focus, "Pioneers in Social Accounting: Kuznets and Stone.")

National income accounting:
The process of statistically measuring the nation's aggregate economic performance.

Before we examine the process of national income accounting, consider the concept of **gross national product (GNP)** in more detail. GNP is the most comprehensive national income statistic, and the one that usually gets the most public attention. Gross national product is the market value of all the final goods and services produced in an economy over a given period. As we shall see in more detail later, the word *gross* means that the total market value of all goods produced, including the production of capital goods, is included in GNP. GNP therefore does not account for the wear and tear on physical assets—called depreciation—that takes place during a given period. The word *national* means that GNP covers the whole economy. The word *product* refers to the market value of final goods and services. We cannot sum physical amounts of goods because many goods simply cannot be added together. What, for example, is the total of ten haircuts plus thirty hamburgers? Also, there are goods and services for which data on the total number of units produced do not exist. We can, however, sum the money or market values of different goods and services because businesses keep records of their receipts for tax purposes. GNP is thus the sum of the final market values of all goods and services sold.

Gross national product (GNP):
The market value of all final goods and services produced in an economy over a given period of time, usually a year.

Two other elements of the definition are important. First, only sales of *final* goods and services are counted in GNP. To do otherwise would be to double-count. The value of McDonald's or Burger King's purchases of raw meat would be added to consumers' purchases of hamburgers and thus be double-counted if all purchases of goods and services sold in the economy were used to calculate GNP. The flow of inputs and outputs in the economic system that creates double-counting problems also permits an alternative means of calculating GNP, as we shall see presently.

A second point involves the time period. GNP ordinarily refers to final sales over the period of a year. GNP and other national income accounts are measures of what economists call *flows*. Flows are processes taking place

---

[1]Charles Davenant, quoted in Joseph A. Schumpeter, *History of Economic Analysis* (New York: Oxford University Press, 1954), pp. 210–11.

[2]Economists use the term *national income* both as a generic term encompassing all of the national income accounts (gross national product, net national product, national income, and so on) and as a specific term referring to the total compensation of all the factors of production (labor, capital, and so on) in the economy over some period.

FOCUS   Pioneers in Social Accounting: Kuznets and Stone

Prior to World War I very little was known about income and output (GNP), although the quest among economists for an accurate measure of national economic performance goes back several centuries. One of the first to fill in the facts and figures about the aggregate economy was Simon Kuznets (1901–1985). In a series of studies from the mid-1920s until the 1950s, the Russian-born Kuznets developed and made estimates of total output (GNP) and income, measured by final product, industry of origin, and type of income. Further, Kuznets provided methods of estimating savings and capital formation and a means for estimating the income distribution between the rich and the poor. The Great Depression of the 1930s, the development of Keynesian economics in the 1930s, and World War II spurred Kuznets's inquiries into aggregate consumption, savings, and investment statistics, which he developed under the auspi-

ces of the National Bureau of Economic Research. For his work on business cycles and comparative economic growth among nations, Kuznets was awarded the Nobel Prize in 1971. Sir Richard Stone (b. 1913), who won the Nobel Prize for economics in 1984, is another innovator in the area of national income accounting. Along with collaborators, Stone was the first economist to officially estimate British national income and expenditure (in 1944). More important, he provided a theoretical model and specified a scrupulously accurate statistical method for calculating his integrated system of balanced national income accounts on a worldwide basis.

No one would argue that the actual numbers produced through the social accounting system are perfect. Economists make constant refinements, but they build on the enormous advances of pioneers such as Kuznets and Stone.

through time and, as such, are measured per unit of time. GNP is the total output of an economy *per year*. A stock, such as the capital stock of an economy, is the total amount of something in existence at a point in time. Additionally, economists also discuss the rates at which variables such as GNP are changing. These growth rates are measured by calculating percentage changes of the variables from one period to the next.

What GNP Does Not Count

Official statistics on GNP are far from perfect. The most serious shortcoming is that they fail to include the value of certain types of production. Goods and services produced for home consumption are omitted, for example. This category includes such activities as backyard vegetable gardens, do-it-yourself home repair, and the myriad services provided by homemakers. Since the value of such goods and services is so hard to estimate, national income accountants omit the value of this kind of production in their calculations of GNP.

A second category of production that does not appear in official GNP estimates is the underground economy. Various goods and many services, such as yard work or maid service, are paid for in cash and are not reported for tax purposes. Also, some business firms avoid paying taxes by not recording all sales. GNP accountants elect to omit such transactions because it is so difficult to estimate their magnitude. (See Focus, "The Underground Economy.")

The third major category of omitted production is illegal goods and services. As you know, profits from illegal drug sales run into the billions worldwide each year. These transactions are omitted from official statistics—again, because the magnitude of drug sales is difficult to judge; but there is also a reluctance to view the production of illegal goods as an addition to national income.

FOCUS   The Underground Economy

The underground economy refers to all the transactions between individuals and firms that are not officially recorded in the government's national income accounts. Unrecorded transactions are not limited to illicit transactions such as gambling, prostitution, and the drug trade. They also include the summer yard work that children and teenagers do for pay, baby-sitting and daytime child-care services that are paid for in cash and not reported to the Internal Revenue Service (IRS), the many kinds of barter transactions that occur, and a multitude of other exchanges that take place in economies that simply do not get entered on the official books. Most of us have participated in the underground economy at one time or another.

One factor responsible for the existence of the underground economy is the income tax and all other taxes levied at all levels of government. Individuals act in their own self-interest, and some will choose to evade paying a portion of their taxes in order to increase their wealth. Some professionals, for example, simply do not declare all their earned income on their income tax forms. Waiters and waitresses occasionally understate their tips to the tax authorities. One result is that the value of these services does not enter the government's official income accounts. Nonetheless, the services these people perform make the economy wealthier and should be reflected in GNP. Quite often these unreported transactions are purely cash transactions. Checks or credit cards leave a paper trail, whereas cash is much harder for income tax auditors to trace.

Income tax rates have traditionally played a major role in determining the extent and size of the underground economy. When people barter or swap goods and services, the value of the transaction goes unreported in GNP but still enhances the barterer's economic welfare. When all relevant tax rates that individuals face are lower, the incentive to barter is diminished, and the underground economy will shrink in size. Indeed, this was one of the reasons that the top federal income tax rate was reduced from 70 percent in 1981 and further reduced from 50 percent in 1986. (The top rate in 1990 was 33 percent.) Other taxes at all levels, including Social Security taxes, have been rising over recent years, however.

A third explanation for the existence of the underground economy is that artificial entry barriers exist in many occupations. Factors such as a person's age, immigrant status, union status, or other legal requirements may prevent employment in the regular economy. Illegal aliens may work as domestics for unreported income in order to avoid detection and deportation. Hundreds of "gypsy cabs" operate in New York City; these private automobiles that ferry passengers about the city are driven by people unable to obtain a license for an official taxicab. Doubtless, many such transactions go unreported. These people work in the underground economy because they can earn larger incomes than they could by working in the official economy.

Just how big is the underground economy? No one knows for sure, but some economists have used various techniques to measure its size. One method is to compare Department of Commerce data on GNP to the IRS's income data. Another approach looks at government-reported data concerning the proportion of the population that is officially reported as employed. This figure can be compared to the number that could reasonably be expected in calculating the size of underground income earned. A third method tracks the total amount of cash, as well as the amount of "large" bills, circulating in an economy and compares it with total checking accounts and credit purchases. Unusually large amounts of cash or large bills indicate a large underground economy.

Estimates on the size of the underground economy in the United States for the late 1970s range from 4 to 25 percent of GNP. If 10 percent of all economic activity were hidden from official view in 1989, then underground GNP would total more than $500 billion. While this is large in absolute terms, some have estimated Italy's underground economy to amount to about 35 to 40 percent of that country's official GNP. Japan, however, appears to produce only about 1 to 2 percent of its total output in an underground economy. Clearly, such factors as tax rates, cultural attitudes, laws, and resources devoted to uncovering the underground economy will influence the extent of such activity across countries.

There are positive and negative aspects to an underground economy. Government clearly loses tax revenue that could be used to finance social goods and national defense. Additionally, macro variables calculated by the government, such as the unemployment rate, are not as accurate as economists would like them to be. On the other hand, the underground economy provides jobs and income for literally millions of people. Some of these jobs constitute full-time employment, while some represent only moonlighting and part-time work. Either way, many households benefit from income earned underground.

Such glaring omissions caution against making sweeping statements about international comparisons of GNP. In developing countries a huge percentage of all production may be used by the large rural population for home consumption. In other countries, a majority of all production may be sold in the underground economy. Official GNP statistics understate actual levels of production in all economies, though not necessarily to the same degree. Official statistics showing the GNP of the United Kingdom to be slightly larger than the GNP of Italy are not conclusive evidence that actual production is larger in the United Kingdom. It may simply be that a smaller proportion of Italian production is included in GNP statistics.

Other transactions are excluded from GNP calculations because they do not represent purchases of current goods or services. For example, the purchase of stock or other securities is not included because it represents a transfer of assets and not production of goods or services. Similarly, real estate transactions involving old homes are not counted. However, any fees paid to stock brokers or real estate agents would be included, since they represent payment for current services.

GNP as a Measure of Economic Welfare

It is tempting to use readily available GNP statistics to measure economic welfare. Even if the problem of uncounted production were solved, however, GNP still would not accurately measure worldwide economic welfare. GNP statistics do not account for pollution and congestion costs, which go hand in hand with economic growth in most developed countries. Also, the average work week in industrial countries has declined markedly in this century, but GNP statistics do not capture the value of increases in leisure time. Actually, GNP never was intended to be a measure of economic welfare. GNP is a measure of production—without any indication of who gets the goods and services produced or what the goods and services are. GNP is indifferent between the provision of handguns or health care. Nonetheless, some economists have attempted to compute a **measure of economic welfare (MEW)** based on GNP statistics (see Economics in Action, "GNP, Leisure, and Social Welfare," at the end of this chapter).

Measure of economic welfare (MEW):
A concept of social and economic well-being that accounts for the production of all goods and services, not just those transacted for in markets.

Final goods:
Goods sold to the final consumers of the goods.

Intermediate goods:
Goods used as inputs in the production of final goods.

Final-Goods Versus Value-Added Approaches

GNP may reflect either market values of all final goods and services or the value added at each stage of production because both sums are identical. **Final goods** and services are end products in the economy; **intermediate goods** go into the production of end products. McDonald's meat purchases to produce hamburgers are purchases of intermediate goods. In the final-goods approach, the purchases of intermediate goods are excluded from GNP to avoid the problem of double counting. For example, cigar making is a multi-step operation. If we counted the value of the tobacco sold by the farmer to the cigar maker and the value of the cigar sold to the cigar store by the cigar maker, as well as the price consumers pay for the finished cigars, we would have counted the value of the tobacco three times. This is an example of double counting or, we should say, triple counting. The value of the tobacco should be counted only once. One way to avoid double counting is to count only the price of the final good; the other is to count only the value added at each stage of production. **Value added** is the difference between the revenues the firm receives from selling its product and the cost of inputs that it has purchased from other firms.

Value added:
The increase in value or market worth of a good associated with each stage of production.

To better understand value added, consider the making of a cigar in more detail. Suppose that the farmer sells a quantity of tobacco to the cigar maker for $3. The value added by the farmer is thus $3, which covers the farmer's costs of producing the tobacco (wages, rent, interest, and profit). In the second stage, the cigar maker sells a certain number of cigars, produced from the quantity of tobacco, to the cigar store for $8. Since the cigar maker paid the farmer $3 for the tobacco, the value added at the second stage by the cigar maker is $5 ($8 − $3). In the final stage, the cigar store sells the cigars to smokers for $15. Since the cigar store paid $8 for the cigars, the value added in the third stage is $7 ($15 − $8). Table 1 illustrates the value-added approach to GNP with the example of cigars.

Summing the value added at each stage of production, we find that $15 equals the market price of the final good. If we had instead added the sales price at each stage of production ($3 + $8 + $15), we would have double-counted. The correct measure of GNP is $15, not $26. The value-added approach is logically equivalent to using the market price of final goods and services to estimate GNP. The final-goods approach is easier to calculate, but the value-added approach serves as a useful check on other methods of estimating GNP.

NATIONAL INCOME ACCOUNTING

Although we have thus far spoken only of the market value of goods, aggregate value in the economy can actually be derived either by summing all expenditures for final goods or by summing all income received. The following sections explain why these constructs should yield identical results and what factors must be taken into account to arrive at identical sums.

| TABLE 1 | **Value-Added Approach to GNP** |

When GNP is estimated by the value-added approach, the extra value added at each stage of production is summed. At the first stage, the farmer adds $3 in value; at the second stage, the cigar maker adds $5 in value; and, finally, the cigar store adds $7 in value. The sum of the three values added is $15, which is identical to the final sale price.

Stage of Production	Seller	Buyer	Sale Price of Good	Value Added
First	Farmer	Cigar maker	$3	$3
Second	Cigar maker	Cigar store	$8	$5
Third	Cigar store	Smoker	$15	$7
				$15

The Circular Flow of Economic Activity

Flow of expenditures:
Total spending of consumers, businesses, and government on final goods and services during any given time period.

Flow of earnings:
Total income received by resource suppliers during any given time period.

National income (GNP) can be measured in two ways: the flow of expenditures approach and the flow of earnings, or income, approach. The **flow of expenditures** approach looks at national income as the total amount spent on final goods and services. The **flow of earnings,** or income, approach looks at national income as the amount earned by factors of production (land, labor, capital, and the entrepreneur).

Logically, the two approaches have to yield the same figure for national income: All income earned by all factors in the production of goods and services is spent on those goods and services. Figure 1 is a circular flow diagram for an economy with only two sectors—a household, or consumer, sector and a firm, or business, sector. In the inner loop of the upper part of

FIGURE 1   The Circular Flow of Economic Activity

The circular flow diagram is portrayed with only a business and a household sector. The upper loop is the flow of final output and expenditures on final output. The lower loop is the flow of input factors of production and the return flow of factor incomes. By definition, the value of the upper and lower loops must be equal. Therefore, GNP as measured by the flow of expenditures approach and GNP as measured by the flow of earnings approach must be identical.

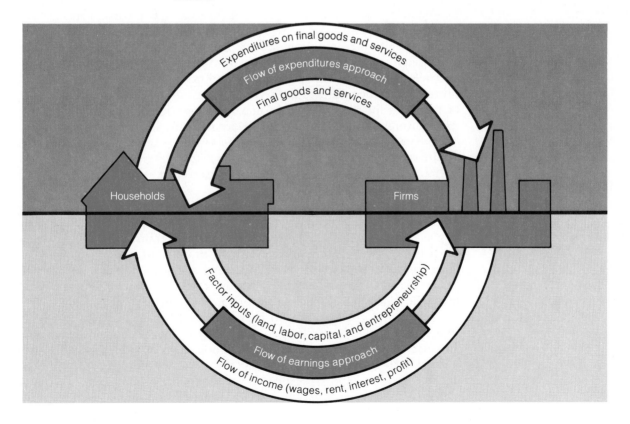

the diagram, firms (suppliers) produce goods for sale to consumers (demanders). The flow of goods to households is matched by a return flow of expenditures, indicated by the outer flow line. Businesses use the revenue from final sales to cover their costs of operation.

The inner part of the lower loop shows businesses or firms (demanders) employing factors of production from the household sector (suppliers). The factors of production are paid incomes that reflect their productivity in producing final output. Firm revenues are exhausted by factor payments because any left over, or residual, portion accrues to the entrepreneur or owners of the firm in the form of profit, which is a type of income.

The upper and lower loops of the circular flow diagram illustrate the identity of the two approaches to measuring national income. The revenues from producing final goods and services are transformed into payments to cover the costs of producing the output. Total revenues from producing goods break down into profits, wage payments, interest, and land rent. By necessity, the dollar value of the expenditure flow on goods and services equals the dollar value of the income, or earning, flow to the factors of production. The important point is that national income can be measured with either approach, and the results will be identical. The flow of expenditures approach is formally identical to the flow of earnings, or income, approach.

Leakages and Injections: Some Complications

Before using these equivalent approaches to national income, consider some complications. The simple case described by Figure 1 excludes such features as saving and other important sectors of the economy such as government or the foreign sector. Without them, the flow of income to factors of production matches the flow of expenditures on final goods and services to firms. But since the excluded features and sectors are part of the economy, Figure 1 does not account for certain leakages out of and injections into the simple flow of expenditures and receipts. A leakage occurs when spending is diverted from the income stream. Household or business saving is a leakage from the expenditure stream. When processed through banks and other financial institutions or intermediaries, such saving becomes investment, an injection or addition to the expenditures flow.

Likewise, government expenditures are injections into the simple flow of expenditures, since the government, like households and businesses, makes expenditures on goods and services. Government transfers income to recipients through welfare and other programs as well. All such expenditures are injections into the circular flow. Financing such expenditures, however, requires the taxation of households and businesses. Taxation represents a leakage from the expenditure stream of the private economy.

The U.S. economy is also heavily involved in international trade and exchange, but the simple flows shown in Figure 1 do not include exports and imports. Exports—the sale abroad of goods and services produced in the United States—are an injection into the circular flow of expenditures and income, while imports—expenditures on goods and services produced abroad—are leakages from the simple income-expenditure flow.

In short, the simple income-expenditure model of Figure 1 does not account for certain leakages and injections. Government expenditures and exports must be counted as injections into the expenditure stream of private household and business spending. Likewise, household and business savings, along with government taxes and imports, are leakages from the simple circular flow of economic activity (see Figure 2).

The Flow of Expenditures Approach

National income accounting puts into practice the principles of the simple, two-sector circular flow diagram as amended by injections and leakages. The national income accountants apply the flow of expenditures approach to measuring GNP by breaking the economy down into four sectors: household, business, government, and foreign. Individuals in the economy are assigned among the four sectors, and GNP is estimated by adding the amount spent on final output by individuals in each sector. Table 2 gives the 1989 data on spending in each sector. Figure 3 compares the flow of expenditures to the flow of earnings.

FIGURE 2   **Leakages from and Injections into the Circular Flow**

The simple two-sector economy portrayed in Figure 1 does not include the leakages represented by savings, taxation, and imports and injections represented by investment, government purchases, and exports. When these additional concepts are included, economists speak of a four-sector economy, including firms, households, government, and foreign markets.

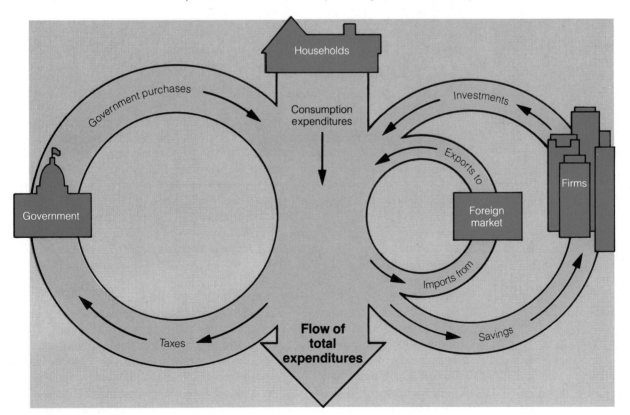

TABLE 2

Gross National Product, 1989: The Flow of Expenditures

Total expenditures in the economy are broken down into four basic groups: private consumption expenditures; private domestic investment expenditures by businesses; government expenditures; and net exports (foreign purchases of U.S. goods minus U.S. purchases of foreign goods).

	Expenditures (billions of dollars)	
Personal consumption expenditures (C)		
Durable goods	473.6	
Nondurable goods	1122.6	
Services	1874.1	
Total		3470.3
Gross private domestic investment (I)		
Fixed investment	747.7	
Change in business inventories	29.4	
Total		777.1
Government purchases (G)		
Federal	404.1	
State and local	632.5	
Total		1036.7
Exports and imports of goods and services		
Exports (X)	624.4	
Imports (M)	675.2	
Net total (X − M)		−50.9
Total expenditures in GNP		5233.2

Source: Council of Economic Advisers, *Economic Report of the President* (Washington, D.C.: U.S. Government Printing Office, 1990), p. 294.

Note: GNP is in 1989 nominal dollars. Subcategories may not total because of rounding.

Personal consumption expenditures (C): Total spending by households on final goods and services.

Personal Consumption Expenditures. Expenditures by individuals and non-profit institutions are called **personal consumption expenditures (C).** These expenditures are broken down into spending on durable goods, on nondurable goods, and on services. Durable goods are items such as refrigerators that are expected to last for more than three years. Nondurable goods are such things as food and clothes that are not expected to last for more than three years. Services are intangible items such as travel, car repair, entertainment, and medical care. Personal consumption expenditures represent the largest expenditure component of GNP ($3470.3 billion in 1989).

Gross private domestic investment (I): Total spending by private businesses on final goods, including capital goods and inventories.

Gross Private Domestic Investment. Expenditures on final output by private business firms (including resource-owning households) are called **gross private domestic investment (I).** Investment expenditures include spending on capital goods such as machinery and warehouses, new residential construction, improvements to existing houses, farm investments, and inventories. These expenditures were 777.1 billion in 1989. The qualifier *gross* is used because these expenditures include spending on new plant and equipment as well as on the replacement of worn-out plant and equipment. Business inventories are an investment in the holding of finished goods, semifinished goods,

FIGURE 3   Total Expenditures Equal Total Income Plus Adjustments

In any given year, total expenditures, composed of consumption, investment, government, and net foreign spending, must equal the income to the factors of production plus corrections. This income is composed of wages, rents, interest, proprietors' income, and corporate profits. The flow of total expenditures must equal the flow of total earnings.

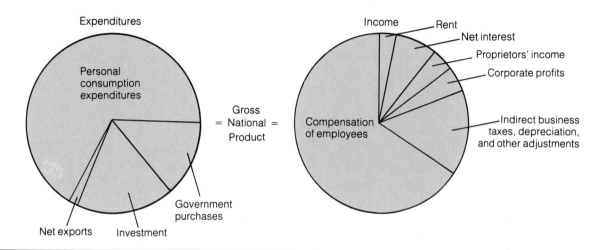

or raw materials by business firms. Investment in business inventories can vary greatly; that is, inventories can be built up or drawn down. For example, firms often draw down the level of their inventories in a period when business is bad, such as a recession. They hold fewer goods in inventory in the anticipation of decreased demand for the goods by consumers. Conversely, businesses will add to inventories in anticipation of sales increases and prosperous times.

Government purchases (G): Total spending by federal, state, and local governments on final goods and services.

Government Purchases. The third component in the expenditure approach to GNP is **government purchases (G)** on final goods and services at the federal, state, and local levels. Government spending was $1036.7 billion in 1989. Government transfer payments, such as Social Security and veterans' benefits, are not included in this figure because such payments are not made to individuals for current productive activities.

Net exports (X − M): Total spending by foreigners on domestically produced goods and services minus total spending by domestic residents on foreign-produced goods and services.

Net Exports. The final category of spending in the expenditure approach to GNP is **net exports (X − M)**. **Exports (X)** are domestic goods purchased by foreigners. **Imports (M)** are foreign goods purchased by U.S. citizens. The purpose of GNP accounting is to measure current production in the economy. Thus, we must add the value of domestic goods purchased by foreigners and subtract the value of foreign goods purchased by Americans in calculating GNP by the expenditures approach. In other words,

Exports (X): Total spending by foreigners on domestically produced goods and services.

Net exports = total exports (X) − total imports (M).

Imports (M): Total spending by domestic residents on foreign-produced goods and services.

Net exports can be negative or positive. Obviously, if we spend more on imports than we sell in exports, net exports are going to be negative. In 1989, net exports were negative. We imported more than we exported by $50.9 billion.

The flow of expenditures approach to measuring GNP is quite simple.

GNP = personal consumption expenditures (*C*)

+ gross private domestic investment (*I*)

+ government purchases (*G*)

+ net exports (*X* − *M*), or

$$GNP = C + I + G + (X - M)$$

By this method, GNP was $5233.2 billion (over 5 trillion dollars!) in 1989, as shown in Table 2. Keep in mind that the expenditures approach is the national income accounting measure of the upper loop in the circular flow model of economic activity.

The Flow of Earnings Approach

The flow of earnings approach should give us the same value for GNP as does the expenditures approach. Table 3 gives the categories used in the flow of earnings approach. (Refer also to Figure 3.)

National Income. The most inclusive figure in the flow of earnings approach to GNP is specifically called **national income (NI).** NI is determined by adding the income earned by factors of production (land, labor, capital, and entrepreneurship) used to produce final goods and services during a given period. Table 3 shows national income of $4265.0 billion for 1989, the sum of income items 1 through 5: compensation of employees, proprietors' income, rental income of persons, corporate profits, and net interest.

National income (NI):
Total earnings of resource suppliers during a given period of time.

TABLE 3

Gross National Product, 1989: The Flow of Earnings

GNP can be calculated by summing the incomes received by suppliers of resources. Labor income, interest income, rental income, and profits are all summed—with adjustments for indirect business taxes and depreciation—to obtain the same level of GNP as found by the expenditures approach.

	Earnings (billions of dollars)
1. Compensation of employees	3145.4
2. Proprietors' income	352.2
3. Rental income of persons	62.9
4. Corporate profits	298.2
5. Net interest	324.0
National income (NI) (total of 1–5)	4265.0
6. Indirect business taxes and other adjustments	434.2
Net national product (NNP)	4699.2
7. Capital consumption allowances (depreciation)	552.2
Gross national product (GNP)	5233.2

Source: Council of Economic Advisers, *Economic Report of the President* (Washington, D.C.: U.S. Government Printing Office, 1990), pp. 318–21.

Note: GNP is in 1989 nominal dollars. Subcategories may not total because of rounding.

Compensation of Employees. Compensation of employees is the largest component of national income. It is the sum of wages and salaries paid to employees plus employer contributions to Social Security and employee benefit plans. In 1989, this category amounted to $3145.4 billion.

Proprietors' Income. Proprietors' income is the net income earned by sole proprietorships and partnerships. Both proprietorships and partnerships are mainly small businesses that are not incorporated. Proprietors' income in 1989 amounted to $352.2 billion.

Rental Income of Persons. Rental income of persons is the income of individuals from renting property, like a house or a car, as well as returns to individuals who hold patents, copyrights, and rights to natural resources, such as an oil or timber lease. National income accountants also estimate a rental value to owner-occupied houses. In other words, home ownership is treated like a business that produces a service sold to the owner. All these forms of rental income yielded earnings of $62.9 billion in 1989.

Corporate Profits. Corporate profits are the net income of private corporations, including profits on foreign operations. The total of corporate profits was $298.2 billion in 1989.

Net Interest. Net interest consists of the interest received by U.S. households and governments minus the interest paid by these households and governments. Some interest payments are not counted as a part of national income because they are not considered payment for current production. Net interest totaled $324.0 billion in 1989.

From National Income to Gross National Product. The figure for national income in Table 3—the sum of income items 1 through 5—does not equal the 1989 figure for gross national product in Table 2 figured by the flow of expenditures approach. Yet we know by the principle of the circular flow model that both approaches to measuring GNP must yield the same result. The problem is that there are two items—items included in total expenditures that are not income to anyone—that must be added to national income to obtain GNP. Let us examine these adjustments in detail.

Indirect Business Taxes and Other Adjustments. Indirect business taxes and other adjustments must be added to national income to determine GNP because such taxes are part of the total expenditures on goods and services but are not received by anyone as income. These include sales and excise taxes paid by purchasers of goods and services; property taxes; business transfer payments such as corporate donations to charitable institutions; government subsidies; and other minor statistical adjustments.

Capital Consumption Allowances. Capital consumption allowances, or depreciations, are an adjustment made for the wearing out of capital goods such as plant and equipment during the current production period. Capital consumption allowances, like indirect business taxes, enter the flow of earnings approach to calculating GNP even though they do not truly represent earnings. They do represent, however, part of the resource cost of producing

GNP, but not an expenditure on final output. For this reason, these items are included in the flow of earnings calculation of GNP. In Table 3, depreciation is equal to $552.2 billion. With adjustments for indirect business taxes and capital consumption allowances, GNP figured by the flow of earnings approach is $5233.2 billion, the same estimate derived from the flow of expenditures approach given in Table 2. Using the flow of earnings method of accounting, GNP is, in short, the sum of returns to the factors of production (wages, proprietors' income, rents, interest, and corporate profits) plus indirect business taxes and depreciation.

Net National Product

Net national product (NNP):
GNP minus capital consumption allowances (depreciation); the value of total output less the value of the capital used up in producing output.

Another useful national income concept can be derived from the statistics of Table 3. Net national product is equal to GNP minus depreciation, the value of the capital consumption allowances. In Table 3, the net national product for 1989 can also be determined by adding to the national income of $4265.0 billion the indirect taxes and other adjustments of $434.2 billion. Net national product in 1989 was $4699.2 billion. **Net national product (NNP)** is the net market value of goods and services produced in any economy in a given period. It tells us the value of all cars and houses and such produced during a certain period minus the value of the capital, plant, and equipment used up in this production. Since such capital is constantly being used up or transformed into current production of goods and services, it must be subtracted to get the net value of current production.

Other National Income Concepts

Macroeconomics is often concerned with the amount of income that goes to the household sector in an economy. By adjusting the figure derived for national income—income earned by factors of production—we can arrive at the concepts of personal income and disposable personal income.

Personal income (PI):
Total earnings resource suppliers actually receive during a given period of time plus transfer payments.

Personal Income. **Personal income (PI)** is the amount of income that households receive during a certain period. There is a difference between income earned and income received. A writer, for example, may not receive royalties on the great American novel until years after writing the book because of the time lags in the production and marketing processes. Current production does not necessarily translate instantly into current income. The major categories of situations in which household earnings do not coincide in time with household income are given in items 1, 2, and 3 in Table 4.

To determine personal income, items 1, 2, and 3 must first be subtracted from national income because they represent income earned but not directly received by households in the current period. Corporate profits do not flow directly to individuals, but instead to firms. Net interest, because it refers to interest earned by businesses, also must be subtracted from national income in calculating personal income. Contributions for social insurance ($479.3 billion)—such as payroll deductions for Social Security—are also excluded from personal income because they are earned but not received by workers in the current period.

TABLE 4

National Income, Personal Income, and Disposable Personal Income, 1989

National income minus income not received (items 1, 2, 3) plus income received (items 4, 5, 6, 7) yields personal income. Subtracting personal taxes from personal income yields disposable personal income.

		Value (billions of dollars)
National income		4265.0
1. Minus: Corporate profits[a]	−298.2	
2. Minus: Net interest	−461.1	
3. Minus: Contributions for social insurance	−479.3	
4. Plus: Government transfer payments	+600.3	
5. Plus: Personal interest income	+657.8	
6. Plus: Personal dividend income	+112.4	
7. Plus: Business transfer payments	+31.8	
Personal income		4428.7
8. Minus: Personal taxes	−513.4	
Disposable personal income		3780.0

Source: Council of Economic Advisers, *Economic Report of the President* (Washington, D.C.: U.S. Government Printing Office, 1990), pp. 319, 324.

[a]Includes inventory valuation and capital consumption adjustments.

Note: Disposable personal income is in 1989 nominal dollars.

Items 4 through 7 are received by households in the current period and are therefore counted as part of personal income. These include government transfer payments, such as Social Security payments, personal interest income, dividends, and business transfer payments.

Depending on the magnitudes of the minuses and pluses, national income can be larger or smaller than personal income. In a period of declining business activity, for example, national income can fall below personal income because corporate profits go down while government transfer payments go up. Personal income in 1989 was $4428.7 billion, an amount greater than national income.

Disposable personal income:
Personal income minus taxes; income available to spend.

Disposable Personal Income. Disposable personal income—what income receivers have left to spend or save after taxes—is found in Table 4 by subtracting certain personal taxes from personal income. These personal taxes include income and property taxes. In 1989, disposable personal income was $3780.0 billion.

Personal Saving

Personal saving:
Disposable personal income less personal consumption expenditures.

Personal saving, another important economic statistic, represents the funds provided for investment by the saving of individuals and unincorporated businesses in the economy. Their choice to refrain from spending all they receive is a crucial ingredient in economic growth. Table 5 shows the calculation of personal saving as $206.3 billion in 1989.

TABLE 5

Personal Saving, 1989

Disposable personal income may be saved or spent by households. In 1989, households chose to save $206.3 billion and spend $3573.7 billion of their disposable personal income.

	Value (billions of dollars)
Disposable personal income	3780.0
Minus: Personal outlays	−3573.7
Personal saving	206.3

Source: Council of Economic Advisers, *Economic Report of the President* (Washington, D.C.: U.S. Government Printing Office, 1990), p. 324.

Note: Personal savings in 1989 nominal dollars.

THE MEASUREMENT OF PRICE CHANGES

Was GNP in 1989 greater than in 1980? To answer this question, we might simply compare GNP for 1980 and 1989. Yet changes in prices make such comparisons difficult. Think of a simple world in which only chocolate fudge is produced. The fact that total expenditures on fudge rose from $5 million in 1980 to $10 million in 1989 tells us very little. Total expenditures will increase if (a) more fudge is produced, (b) the price of fudge rises, or (c) both (a) and (b) happen at the same time. The same facts hold for changes in GNP. GNP can change over time because total output increases, prices increase, or both happen at the same time. Thus, since we are interested in comparing differences in aggregate output over time when using national income statistics, a means has to be found to adjust GNP data for changes in prices. (The more difficult issue of changes in the type and quality of goods over time is treated in Focus, "GNP and Economic Change.") The **price level** is the average of the prices of all goods and services. It is not to be confused with relative prices, which show the price of one good in terms of another.

Economists and national income statisticians approach the problem of detecting price level changes by constructing **price indexes.** All indexes use a base year, against which subsequent changes in prices are measured. The most common method of measuring price change uses base-year quantities as weights for the price indexes of ensuing years.[3] Any price index compares the

Price level:
The average of the prices of all goods and services in the economy; used for calculating the inflation rate and for converting nominal into real values.

Price index:
A statistic used to calculate the price level and the rate of inflation.

---

[3]An understanding of the base-year index calculation can be reached with a simple example. Assume that the consumer price index is composed of only two goods, beer and pizzas, and that the relevant data on prices, outputs, and expenditures are as follows.

Commodities	Price (per unit)	Quantity Sold	Total Expenditures
Beer (six-packs)			
1989	$2.00	2 million	$ 4 million
1990	$3.00	3 million	$ 9 million
Pizza (each)			
1989	$4.00	3 million	$12 million
1990	$5.00	5 million	$25 million

FOCUS GNP and Economic Change

Comparisons of GNP over time are even more complicated than controlling for price changes with a price index. Such comparisons are fundamentally difficult because entrepreneurs introduce new and improved goods and services to the economy. For example, how useful is it to compare GNP in 1890 with GNP in 1990? The United States at these two time periods comprised two different economies. In 1990, there were cars, fast-food restaurants, televisions, computers, and liver transplants. These goods and services did not exist in 1890. On the other hand, there was a great deal of open land, a relatively low crime rate, and little or no acid rain in 1890. These conditions largely no longer existed in 1990.

The goods available to consumers—that is, the final outputs of the economy—change over time. Even someone with a lot of money in 1890 could not have purchased what the average middle-income family purchases today. The point is simple but profound. An economy changes across time, and comparisons of GNP therefore lose much of their relevance.

So, while we know that the U.S. economy has grown remarkably over its history, the fact that the bundle of goods available to consumers has changed over time makes the measurement of this growth difficult. For example, real per capita GNP in 1950 was $3535. In 1980, it was $6645. Does this mean that workers in the United States produced roughly twice the amount in 1980 as they produced in 1950? The problem is that GNP cannot give a clear answer to this type of question. (Remember: A change in GNP does not necessarily measure a change in welfare.) The goods pro-

duced in each period have changed. We do not now produce twice the amount of the *same* goods produced in 1950. Our capacity to produce goods and services has increased, no doubt, but the exact amount of this growth is not measured by the growth of real GNP.

The farther apart in time that comparisons of GNP are made, the more severe is the problem caused by the differences in economies in the two periods. However, even over a short period, GNP comparisons are difficult because of changes in the quality of existing goods. In a span of a little more than ten years, consumers in the United States have gained access to improved goods such as cable television and more efficient computers. Do these improvements in quality mean growth in the value of the economy? If so, how could it possibly be measured? These complications indicate that GNP comparisons over time are useful, but not perfect.

Finally, exactly the same point can be made about the difficulty of comparisons of GNP across countries. Countries obviously produce different bundles of goods, and for the reasons just given, international comparisons of GNP are difficult and subject to interpretation. Different tastes for goods and services likely exist across countries, further complicating simple GNP comparisons intended to reflect differences in economic well-being. None of this argues that comparisons of GNP are meaningless. The point is that such comparisons should be made carefully and conclusions drawn about economic growth only after a careful study of all the relevant information about the economy or economies concerned.

Assume that the base year is 1989 and that we are interested in how prices have changed in 1990; that is, has there been inflation or deflation? A base-year quantity weight index for beer and pizza can be expressed

$$\text{Price index} = \frac{q_b^{89} p_b^{90} + q_p^{89} p_p^{90}}{q_b^{89} p_b^{89} + q_p^{89} p_p^{89}}.$$

The superscripts denote the relevant year (1989 or 1990), and the subscripts denote beer (b) or pizza (p). Price is p and quantity is q. Using this price index formula with 1989 as the base year, the price index is equal to 1.31. That is,

$$\text{Price index} = \frac{\$(6 + 15) \text{ million}}{\$(4 + 12) \text{ million}} = 1.31.$$

The value of the index is always equal to 1.0 in the base year (try the calculation). When the index is greater than 1.0, it tells us that prices are, on average, higher than they were in the base year. When the index is less than 1.0, the average of prices is lower than it was in the base year. The inflation rate is the percent by which the index changes from one year to the next. In this example, the inflation rate in the beer-and-pizza economy was 31 percent (1.31 minus 1.00 divided by 1.00).

average level of prices at a given point in time (be it today or 1947) to the average level of prices at some specific point in the past (the base year or period). If the ratio is greater than 1, then prices in general are greater at the time for which the index is calculated than they were in the base year. If the ratio is less than 1, then prices are generally lower than in the base period. (The consumer price index formula is multiplied by 100.)

Price indexes serve two very important functions. Above all, they give us a measure of what is happening to the overall level of prices. By calculating the percentage change in a price index, the inflation rate over any given time period is measured. Additionally, a price index can be used to convert nominal variables, such as GNP, to real variables. Suppose the price index is based in 1982. Dividing nominal GNP in 1990 by the price index in 1990 (based in 1982) gives a measure of the total output of the economy in 1990 measured in 1982 prices. This allows more accurate comparisons of GNP between years, comparisons that are not biased by price changes. This gives a more accurate picture of how aggregate output changes over time. Almost all nominal variables can be converted to real variables by dividing by a price index. Government statistics calculate several indexes for the American economy.

The Consumer Price Index

Consumer price index (CPI):
A price index that uses the prices of goods and services consumers generally buy to calculate the price level and the rate of inflation.

The **consumer price index (CPI)** measures price changes in a typical market basket of goods purchased by urban wage earners and clerical workers. This "market basket" was developed from a survey of about 20,000 families, who provided information on their buying habits. The market basket includes food, housing (rental costs), apparel, transportation, health and recreation, and miscellaneous services. To measure price changes in the market basket, the Bureau of Labor Statistics at the Department of Labor collects data every month from a wide variety of retail stores and service establishments. The CPI is issued monthly, and its base period is 1982–1984. Current prices are compared to average base-period prices. In the CPI, 1982–1984 = 100.

Figure 4 shows the movement of the CPI for the period 1970–1989. Notice that the CPI for all items has been broken down into two categories: food and rent. Each of these categories fluctuates over time; one may be rising while another is falling during a given period.

The Producer Price Index

Producer price index (PPI):
A price index that calculates the general level of prices and the rate of inflation of goods businesses purchase.

The Bureau of Labor Statistics also publishes statistics known as the **producer price index (PPI),** previously known as the wholesale price index. This index excludes consumer prices and instead covers about 2800 industrial commodities, from raw materials to finished goods. For the PPI the Bureau of Labor Statistics collects about 10,000 price quotations each month from companies that sell goods to producers.

The Implicit Price Deflator

Implicit price deflator:
A price index that uses the most comprehensive set of prices to calculate the level of prices and the rate of inflation facing households, businesses, and government; also called the GNP deflator.

The final major index is the **implicit price deflator,** often called the GNP deflator. This index goes to the heart of the problem of measuring price changes over time. As we have seen, it is impossible to add the different outputs

FIGURE 4   **The Consumer Price Index, 1970–1989**

The consumer price index measures the average change in price of a bundle of consumer goods. The prices of goods in the categories of food or rent change at different rates. However, the overall CPI has increased fairly consistently. The base period for constructing the price indexes measured on the vertical axis is 1982–1984 (1982–1984 = 100).

Source: Council of Economic Advisers, *Economic Report of the President* (Washington, D.C.: U.S. Government Printing Office, 1990), pp. 359–60.

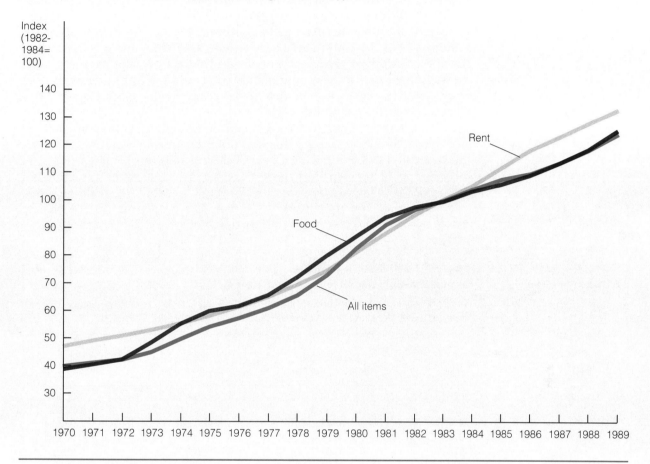

of goods over time. Rather, we add the dollar amounts spent on commodities. But since both prices and quantities of commodities can change over time, the comparison of GNP at different points in time is difficult. Remember that the economist is interested in measuring the economy's real output. Therefore, the GNP statistician must be careful to distinguish current or nominal GNP, which is evaluated in current dollars, from real or constant GNP, which is evaluated in constant dollars. The implicit price deflator is a means to convert nominal GNP values into real GNP values.

The GNP deflator is similar to the CPI in that it is a price index. However, the GNP deflator is a broader index of prices than the CPI. The CPI pertains only to goods and services purchased by consumers; the implicit price deflator also takes into account goods and services generally consumed by producers and government. A major weakness of price indexes is the noncompatability of base years. Government agencies that collect and publish various statistics often change the base year used, causing potential confusion. Nominal GNP is converted to real GNP by use of the GNP deflator—by dividing nominal GNP by a constant GNP value for the same base-year prices. For example, Table 6 shows that in 1989 the GNP implicit price deflator was 1.263. This number tells us that, on average, prices were 26.3 percent higher in 1989 than in 1982 (1982 being the base year). Nominal GNP for 1989, $5233.2 billion, divided by the GNP deflator for 1989 gives the real GNP for 1989—$4143.5 billion ($5233.2/1.263). This figure reveals what the value of GNP would have been in 1989 if prices had not changed since 1982. Put another way, it measures the value of the output of final goods and services in terms of 1982 prices. (For examples of price changes for selected goods, see Focus, "Price Changes from Truman to Bush.")

Table 6 shows GNP in both constant-dollar and current-dollar, or nominal, terms, using the varying implicit price deflator for GNP for the years 1972 to 1989. One interesting aspect of these data is that between 1973 and 1975 and again between 1981 and 1982, GNP in current terms was rising but real GNP was falling. In other words, growth in the GNP was due to inflation in prices rather than to increases in output. The proper measure of the real performance of the economy is the movement of real GNP over time.

TABLE 6

Nominal GNP, GNP Deflator, and Real GNP, 1972–1989

The GNP deflator is used to convert nominal GNP into real GNP. By dividing any year's GNP by that year's GNP deflator, one can estimate real GNP in terms of 1982 dollars.

Year	Nominal GNP (billions of dollars)	÷	GNP Deflator (1982 = 1)	=	Constant GNP (billions of 1982 dollars)
1972	1212.8		0.465		2608.1
1973	1359.3		0.495		2746.1
1974	1472.8		0.540		2727.4
1975	1598.4		0.593		2695.4
1976	1782.8		0.631		2825.4
1977	1990.5		0.673		2957.7
1978	2249.7		0.722		3115.9
1979	2508.2		0.786		3191.1
1980	2732.0		0.857		3187.9
1981	3052.6		0.940		3247.4
1982	3166.0		1.000		3166.0
1983	3405.7		1.039		3277.9
1984	3772.5		1.077		3502.8
1985	4014.9		1.109		3620.3
1986	4231.6		1.138		3718.5
1987	4524.3		1.174		3853.7
1988	4880.6		1.213		4023.6
1989	5233.2		1.263		4143.5

Source: Council of Economic Advisers, *Economic Report of the President* (Washington, D.C.: U.S. Government Printing Office, 1990), pp. 296, 298.

Note: Nominal GNP is in billions of dollars, the GNP deflator is 1982 = 1, and constant GNP is in billions of 1982 dollars.

FOCUS Price Changes from Truman to Bush

Are historical contrasts valid or misleading? A recently released movie has grossed over $100 million and now ranks ahead of such classics as *Gone with the Wind* in terms of all-time box-office receipts. The average salary among major league baseball players is now more than three times as high as the highest salary ever paid to Babe Ruth. A house in California purchased at the end of World War II for $10,000 sells for $885,000. When adjustments to reflect changes in purchasing power are made, prices such as the $15 million paid for the Louisiana Purchase may not be so surprising.

Let's focus on Babe Ruth's salary. In 1933, he earned a salary of $90,000. By 1988, the average major league salary stood at about $270,000. Using the implicit price deflator to measure average price changes, prices in 1988 were about 11.1 times as high as in 1933. In other words, Babe Ruth's 1933 salary had roughly the purchasing power of $1,000,000 in 1988. Although he was not paid as much as modern stars, Ruth's real pay was nearly four times as high as today's average player's. To compare the total receipts of *Gone with the Wind* and, say, *Raiders of the Lost Ark,* it would be necessary to ascertain annual sales since each was released before making appropriate adjustments.

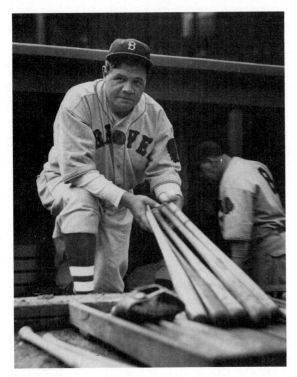

Babe Ruth

TABLE 7
Prices of Selected Goods in 1949 and 1989

While the price of each of the selected goods increased between 1949 and 1989, the rate of increase was far from uniform. Had the price of flour risen at the same rate as prices in general over the forty-year period, ten pounds of flour would have cost $4.34 in 1989. The actual price in 1989 was $2.99.

Item	1949 Price (Truman Dollars)	Equivalent Number of Bush Dollars	1989 Price (Bush Dollars)
Flour (10 lb)	$.83	$4.34	$2.99
Eight O'Clock coffee (1 lb)	$1.15	$6.01	$8.39
Lean ground beef (1 lb)	$.45	$2.37	$1.69
Dozen eggs (large)	$.57	$2.98	$1.03
Coca-Cola (12 oz)	$.05	$.26	$.50
Wool suit	$39.75	$207.89	$210.00
Muffler	$4.95	$25.89	$39.95
Movie ticket (adult)	$1.32	$6.96	$4.50
Washing machine (Hotpoint)	$119.95	$627.33	$439.00

Price indexes reflect average price level changes, but it is important to realize that the prices of all goods do not change uniformly over time. Using the implicit price deflator to measure price level changes, prices were about 5.23 times as high at George Bush's presidential inauguration in 1989 as they were in 1949, when Harry Truman took the same oath of office (the index had risen from 23.6 to 123.6, using 1982 as the base year). In other words, the *Truman Dollar*—the purchasing power of the dollar in 1949—had 5.23 times as much purchasing power as the *Bush Dollar.* Table 7 shows the 1949 prices of selected goods, the equivalent number of Bush Dollars, and the actual prices of the goods in 1989. Prices were taken from advertisements in local newspapers on the inaugural dates discussed. While all prices increased over the period, the rate of increase was not, as you might expect, a uniform 5.23 percent.

SUMMARY

1. National income accounting is concerned with the measurement of the aggregate performance of the economy.
2. Gross national product (GNP) is the market value of all the final goods and services produced in an economy during a given period. It includes only currently produced goods and services, and it excludes such items as illegal transactions and household production.
3. GNP is not a measure of economic welfare. It does not count social costs such as pollution, which lowers economic welfare, or such goods as leisure, which raises economic welfare.
4. Gross national product can be measured by the value-added approach, the final-goods approach to expenditures, or the income paid to factors of production to produce final outputs. The latter two methods are the most useful.
5. Gross national product can be computed in two ways: by adding expenditures on final goods and services produced during a given period or by adding the earnings or incomes of the factors of production used to produce final goods and services during the period. The two approaches, subject to a statistical discrepancy, yield the same result for GNP.

The Flow of Expenditures Approach

$$\text{Personal consumption expenditures } (C) + \text{gross private domestic investment } (I) + \text{government purchases of final goods and services } (G) + \text{Net exports } (X - M) = \text{GNP}$$

The Flow of Earnings Approach

$$\text{Wages} + \text{proprietors' income} + \text{rents} + \text{net interest} + \text{corporate profits} + \text{indirect business taxes} + \text{depreciation} = \text{GNP}$$

The flow of expenditures approach focuses on buyers' evaluations of goods produced during a year. The flow of earnings approach concentrates on the cost of production of goods and services. The circular flow of economic activity, therefore, ensures that the two approaches are identical. That is,

$$\frac{\text{Dollar spending}}{\text{on final outputs}} = \text{GNP} = \frac{\text{dollar costs of}}{\text{producing final outputs}}.$$

6. Other important national income accounting concepts are personal income, disposable personal income, and personal saving. Each provides important information for the macroeconomist in analyzing economic stability and growth.
7. To compare GNP in different time periods, some method must be used to control for price changes. The government uses various price indexes, including the consumer price index, the producer price index, and the implicit price deflator for GNP.

KEY TERMS

national income accounting
gross national product (GNP)
measure of economic welfare (MEW)
final goods
intermediate goods
value added
flow of expenditures
flow of earnings

personal consumption expenditures (C)
gross private domestic investment (I)
government purchases (G)
net exports (X − M)
exports (X)
imports (M)
national income (NI)
net national product (NNP)

personal income (PI)
disposable personal income
personal saving
price level
price index
consumer price index (CPI)
producer price index (PPI)
implicit price deflator

QUESTIONS FOR REVIEW AND DISCUSSION

1. Why does GNP count only the production of final goods and services? Why aren't intermediate goods and services counted?
2. What are the relations among gross national product, net national product, national income, personal income, and disposable personal income?
3. List three reasons GNP should not be considered an overall indicator of society's well-being.
4. What are the three approaches used to estimate GNP?
5. American society has become more urbanized and industrialized since 1930. Other things being equal, do you think this means that our measurement of GNP is more or less precise? Why?
6. What is GNP in constant dollars and how is it calculated?
7. Why might GNP be a misleading statistic with which to compare the economy of the United States with that of the Soviet Union?
8. Which of the following are counted in the calculation of this year's GNP: (a) the services provided by a homemaker; (b) the wage paid to a maid; (c) Sam's purchase of an antique desk; (d) Joan's purchase of ten shares of stock; (e) Social Security checks received by the elderly; (f) Social Security taxes paid by workers?
9. Can a price index be calculated for the commodities in Table 7 of this chapter? If so, make up some numbers and calculate an index.

PROBLEM

Suppose that nominal GNP in 1995 totals $8475 billion and rises to $12.5 trillion ten years later. If the GNP deflator for 1995 is 1.85 and for 2005 is 2.75, in what year is real GNP greater? By how much?

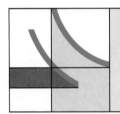

ECONOMICS IN ACTION
GNP, Leisure, and Social Welfare

As you know, GNP is not a perfect measure of economic well-being. GNP statistics exclude the value of goods produced for home consumption, the value of increases in leisure time, and the value of goods produced in the underground economy. In addition, some of the costs that are often associated with economic development, such as pollution and congestion, are not subtracted from GNP in measuring economic well-being. If one is willing to assume that all such omissions are proportional to measured GNP, then changes in GNP can be considered an excellent measure of changes in economic well-being. However, if this assumption is viewed as unrealistic, then there is reason to have serious reservations about using measured GNP to determine economic progress.

Some scholars have tried to overcome these problems in measuring GNP by proposing alternative measurements of an economy's performance that would more closely re-

flect the underlying welfare or happiness of its people. William Nordhaus and Nobel laureate James Tobin have proposed the use of measure of economic welfare (MEW) as such a measure. Their MEW would modify the traditional measurement of GNP in the following ways.

1. Measures of the value of leisure time and household production and consumption would be added to GNP.
2. The costs of pollution and congestion would be subtracted from GNP.
3. Expenditures on goods produced by government, such as national defense and police protection (which are intermediate goods that are inputs to other end-product activities), would be subtracted from GNP.

By their calculations, MEW has grown slower than GNP since 1965, which implies that official GNP statistics have overstated the rate of economic improvement. This is largely attributable to rapid increases in the costs of pollution in recent years.

The use of MEW by national income scholars remains controversial, although it represents a step toward more accurate measurement of the macroeconomy. However, it should be noted that MEW does not attempt to adjust GNP figures to account for goods produced in the underground economy. Although it is extremely difficult to obtain any reliable estimates concerning the size of the underground economy, many observers believe that it has grown in relative importance in recent years, as Americans have increasingly become a nation of tax evaders. If this observation is true, then official GNP statistics would tend to understate the extent of economic progress in recent years.

In comparing official measures of economic production across countries, it is important to keep in mind that all countries (even totalitarian ones) have underground economies. Therefore, some goods and services that are produced and consumed will not be included in official statistics. Accordingly, some differences in measured GNP among countries may be caused by differing abilities to record production. This problem was made clear at the July 1989 summit meeting between the five leading free-market countries (the United States, France, Japan, West Germany, and Great Britain). Government leaders in Italy were offended by being excluded from the meeting, arguing that they, not Great Britain, deserved an invitation. The Italians claimed that production in Italy was greater than in Great Britain, despite official statistics to the contrary. According to the Italian officials, the amount of output that was omitted in Britain's official GNP statistics was quite small, since the British are meticulous record keepers and, further, a nation of law-abiding citizens not given to tax evasion. In contrast, omitted output in Italy was large, Italy being a country with a lax system of records keeping and massive tax evasion. Therefore, since official statistics indicated that Britain's production was slightly larger than Italy's, it must be the case that Italy in fact outproduced Britain. Although the dispute was never settled, Italy was invited to a follow-up meeting.

If the problem of uncounted output creates confusion in comparing the success of the economies of highly developed countries, the problem is much greater for Third World countries. In developing countries, the economic system is based on production for home use, and a huge proportion of total production takes place in the uncounted underground economy. Official GNP statistics for such countries can be highly misleading.

Question

How would one go about estimating the value of leisure or the extent of production for home consumption?

Source: William Nordhaus and James Tobin, "Is Growth Obsolete?" in *Economic Growth,* Fifteenth Anniversary colloquium (New York: National Bureau of Economic Research, 1972).

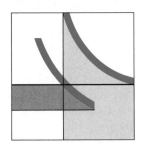

8

Classical Theory

$\mathbf{M}$easuring the rise and fall of macroeconomic variables such as the rate of inflation, GNP, and unemployment is only a first step toward understanding why these economic indicators fluctuate and what measures, if any, are needed to maintain stability and growth.

The next four chapters survey some of the major theoretical tools of macroeconomics to discover the conditions under which the economy can achieve stability and growth. We concentrate on both aggregate demand—the spending side of the economy—and aggregate supply—the producing side of the economy. This chapter and Chapters 9 and 10 develop economic principles pertaining to aggregate demand. Chapters 11 and 12 deal with the interaction of aggregate demand and aggregate supply.

Some simplifications are necessary to understand how aggregate demand and supply interact to sustain full employment, economic growth, and low levels of inflation. This chapter and the next concentrate on two views of consumer and business spending—the private or nongovernment part of aggregate spending. The first view is the classical notion of a self-regulating aggregate economy; the second is the perspective of John Maynard Keynes, who focused attention on how spending changes cause prosperity and depression. To simplify our development of aggregate demand and supply theories, we only briefly cover here important but complicating variables such as the money supply. We defer our in-depth analysis of money until Part Three.

The classical view sees the economy as self-regulating, without need of large-scale government intervention. A full appreciation of the classical view is the starting point for understanding how and why Keynes and others modified macroeconomic theory. When you complete Chapter 8 you should understand

- why the classical writers had faith that a nonregulated economy could fully employ all resources in the long run.
- the four essential components of the classical view that the economy would function at or near full employment over time.
- the basic classical view that government intervention should be minimized in the private economy.
- how classical macroeconomic theories and their policies interrelate.

CLASSICAL THEORY

Can the economy remain as close as possible to its production possibilities frontier? Can it manage to keep all resources, human and nonhuman, fully employed? More fundamentally, can the economy automatically produce full employment, a maximum GNP, and price stability? If not, what actions are necessary to maintain these important goals?

Historically, economists have given many different answers to these difficult questions. **Classical macroeconomic theory** stems from Adam Smith's pioneering work, *An Inquiry into the Nature and Causes of the Wealth of Nations*, published in 1776. Smith and those who followed in the classical tradition believed that, given laissez-faire government policies and enough time, the economy would achieve the goals of price stability, full employment, and economic growth through its own ability to correct short-run unemployment and inflation. In other words, the classical theorists believed that unemployment and inflation were temporary phenomena. In the long run (a period of time that is hard to specify), the economy would remain close to or on its production possibilities frontier and enjoy a stable level of prices. This classical tradition lasted for well over 150 years (the last great neoclassical economist, A. C. Pigou, died in 1959). The theory that grew from Smith's faith in a self-adjusting market mechanism was the work of many economists who wrote at different times in response to different conditions. The following simplified discussion of classical macroeconomics is a composite of various individual contributions. First, consider the classical engine of economic growth.

The Classical Blueprint for Economic Growth

The classical economists were writing at a time of rapid technological advance. Attitudes toward the Industrial Revolution—the catchphrase for the technological advances of the eighteenth and early nineteenth centuries—undoubtedly colored the classical economists' conception of how the economy works and grows. The **classical process of economic growth** conceives of a circular flow of human activities leading to growth in per capita output and economic well-being for the average citizen of the economy. The circular flow of this classical process of economic growth—like the one already considered in Chapters 3 and 7—focuses on the real factors and activities leading to economic growth.

The heart of Adam Smith's view of economic progress is the natural tendency for society to divide tasks. The **division of labor** in producing some output creates enormous advantages for society. A modern assembly line or fast-food production by McDonald's, Wendy's, or Burger King are excellent examples of the division of labor. Given enough time, a single worker could certainly build an automobile from scratch. Only the hobbyist would approach car building this way, however. Adam Smith hit on the critical idea (from observation) that the division of tasks (in the context of automobile manufacture, fitting parts, welding motor parts, installing windshields) educates workers in some critically important ways. The repetition of specific tasks in production leads to increased skill and dexterity in every worker, thereby increasing human capital and productivity. The repetition of specific tasks also fosters invention and creativity in workers—an advantage encouraged by the

Classical macroeconomic theory:
A view of the macroeconomy as being self-adjusting and capable of generating full employment and maximum output in the long run without government intervention; dominant from the late eighteenth century through the early twentieth century.

Classical process of economic growth:
A process based on the division of labor but also involving increases in saving, investment, capital accumulation, and, ultimately, growth in real GNP.

Division of labor:
An economic principle whereby individuals specialize in the production of a single good, service, or task, thereby increasing overall productivity and economic efficiency.

narrow focus of the individual's attention on particular job tasks. Moreover, while training and retraining for specific tasks takes time, on balance the application of the division of labor saves time in that workers need not move from task to task.

Figure 1 shows, in simplified form, how the division of labor leads to the growth of real output as it works its way through production processes in an economy. As the circular flow progresses, increased real GNP creates higher real wages and higher per capita incomes. Higher wages and incomes permit individuals to consume and save more annually. But, as we will see in more detail later in the chapter, saving by some individuals is translated directly into investment by other individuals. At low interest rates, individuals want to invest more, and savers want to save less. High rates encourage savers and discourage investors. There is a point at which the desires of savers and of investors are in equilibrium.

The process depicted in Figure 1 is continuous; there is no starting point. Each element is equally important to the process, and each can serve as the "first step." For ease in understanding, however, we may think of the process as beginning with increased demand (consumption) for goods. The saving of consumers permits, through the link to investment, additional capital accumulation. An increase in the (net) capital stock raises the productivity both of labor and of natural resources, permitting more division of labor. The result of greater application of capital and enhanced division of labor is higher real GNP. Wages rise, as do per capita incomes, leading to more consumption, saving, and investment. The process continues until, in Adam Smith's words, the extent of the market is reached—that is, until domestic and international markets are saturated with goods and services.

It is worthwhile to remember that, in this simple process, savings are translated *automatically* into the exceptionally important mechanism of investment. Through investment, capital is accumulated. Capital—broadly defined to include factories, machinery, tools, and human skills—is a force for

FIGURE 1

Enhanced division of labor in the classical growth process leads directly to increased output of goods and services. The division of labor is directly fueled by capital accumulation in the circular flow.

The Classical Process of Economic Growth

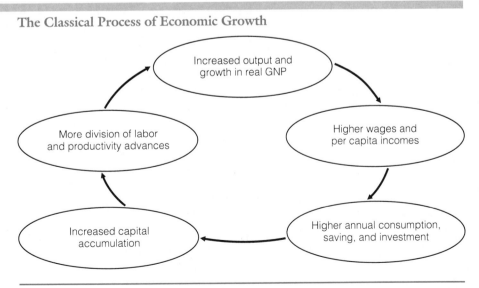

growth because it permits and facilitates the division of labor. Increased capital accumulation, as shown in the circular flow of Figure 1, allows division of labor and, along with it, *productivity of labor and capital*. Using Smith's words again, the "wealth of a nation"—GNP—is the annual product of the raw materials, land, and labor of a society, assisted, critically, by the accumulation of capital goods and the division of labor.

Many of the classical economists' predecessors equated the accumulation of gold and other precious metals with the wealth of a nation. Instead, according to the classical economists, human capital and resource development, assisted by growing capital and the division of labor, produced the wealth of the nation and contained the keys to economic growth. The division of labor gives rise to increased output and economic growth. Higher per capita wages and incomes result from increased real output. Higher incomes produce higher consumption and savings. Additional savings lead to additional investment in capital and in capital accumulation. Capital accumulation enhances and facilitates a greater division of labor, and the process continues.

Limits to Growth. The process depicted in Figure 1 is neither instantaneous nor limitless. As we already mentioned, the growth process may be limited by the "extent of the market." Profitable investment outlets may dry up as demand, both foreign and domestic, for goods and services becomes saturated. The classicals knew that the economy's maximum attainable output is limited by its actual supply of human and nonhuman resources, the state of technology, productivity, and population. The classical view of the macroeconomy was a **long-run equilibrium** conception. In other words, classical theory was concerned with how an economy adjusts to some hypothetical equilibrium given some actual supply of resources, level of population, technology, or state of specialization.

Classical long-run equilibrium:
The hypothetical adjustment of an economy to full employment given an actual supply of resources, population, technology, and degree of specialization.

The classicals believed that mechanisms within the economy were self-adjusting—in other words, that self-adjusting mechanisms automatically brought full employment in the long run. Full employment of resources in the long run is, of course, tantamount to being on the economy's production possibilities curve (see Figure 2a). Society's choice between capital and consumer goods in the present has an effect on future economic growth. In the classical context, a choice of more capital goods relative to consumer goods means encouraged investment and capital accumulation, which produces a greater division of labor and more rapid future economic growth. The point to remember, however, is that the attainment of any point such as A on PP in Figure 2a is the result of self-adjusting forces in the economy in the long run. The exact point chosen on any production possibilities curve also depends on society's relative demands for present and future consumption. The society that chooses more capital goods at the expense of consumer goods will enjoy more future growth potential. The society that chooses more consumer goods in the present will enjoy more goods and services now but will have less growth potential.

Points such as A on PP_0 in Figure 2a also imply that *all* resources are fully employed in the economy. At the risk of getting a little ahead of ourselves, we should note that later economists, including Keynes, challenged the belief that automatic, self-adjusting forces could be relied upon to get the economy to points such as A on PP_0. They believed that certain short-run factors, such as wage and interest-rate inflexibility inhibited the classical mechanism. For

FIGURE 2

Production Possibilities and the Aggregate Supply Curve

In the long-run adjustment mechanism of classical economics, attainment of points such as A on production possibilities curve PP_0 of Figure 2a translate to vertical aggregate supply curves, such as AS_A at output level Y_0 in Figure 2b. In the classical model, there is no unemployment in the long run. Technological advances or discovery of new resources could be part of the long-run economy-wide adjustments that shift the production possibilities frontier and aggregate supply curve rightward.

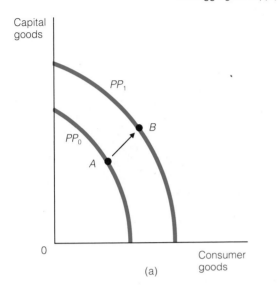

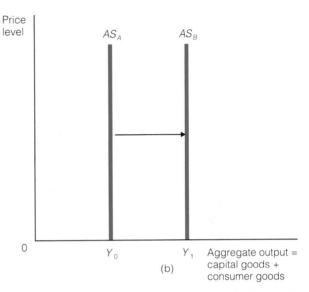

(a)

(b)

now, just keep in mind that points such as A in Figure 2a are attained only after adjustments take place in the long run and full employment is reached in the entire economy.

Economic Growth and Aggregate Supply. Economic growth, as summarized by a production possibilities model, may also be related to the aggregate (economy-wide) supply curve developed in Chapter 6. If production possibilities curve PP_0 is drawn under assumptions of constant technology, possibilities for the division of labor and economic growth are limited. The attainment of point A in Figure 2a may be viewed as equivalent to a level of income, Y_0, that defines the aggregate supply curve AS_A in Figure 2b. At any given moment, then, the growth process is limited by, among other things, the state of technology. The maximum amount of output that can be had out of the economy, irrespective of the price level, is designated AS_A or Y_0. Note that the vertical supply curve of Figure 2b differs from the upward-sloping aggregate supply curve in Chapter 6 because the attainment of any point on production possibilities curve PP_0 means that consumer and capital goods production is maximized. The upward-sloping aggregate supply curve indicates that some unemployment of resources exists—in other words, that the outer limits of the production possibilities curve have not been reached.

A change in technology or the augmentation of resources (perhaps through international trade or through resource discoveries) would shift the production possibilities curve rightward. Attainment of a new equilibrium point such as B in Figure 2a through long-run, economy-wide adjustments would shift the aggregate supply curve rightward. All points on new production possibilities frontier PP_1 contain higher total production of consumer and capital goods than on PP_0. In terms of Figure 2b, aggregate supply shifts to AS_B at output level Y_1. In short, the aggregate supply curve of any economy is based on the "possibilities" of attaining maximum production. A vertical aggregate supply curve means that society has reached the production possibilities curve of the economy. We must now investigate how the classicals arrived at the rather startling conclusion that the economy would adjust itself to full employment in the long run if left unassisted by an outside force such as government.

Cornerstones of Classical Macroeconomic Theory

Classical economic theory primarily concerned itself with how economies grow and prosper. Imbedded within the elements of economic progress they described, however, is a theory of macroeconomic functioning. Taken as a group, the classicals developed an exact theory of how the economy adjusts in the long run to reach a point on the production possibilities or aggregate supply curve. The classical economist's belief that the economy self-adjusts in response to short-run disturbances and produces full employment and economic growth without government interference rests on four cornerstones:

1. Say's law;
2. Interest rate flexibility;
3. Price-wage flexibility; and
4. Quantity theory of money.

The first three cornerstones deal with the flexibility of the macroeconomy in maintaining full employment. The fourth concerns the determination of the price level and the control of inflation.

Say's law:
A proposition of the classical economists that the production of goods and services will generate incomes sufficiently large that those goods and services will be purchased.

Say's Law. Say's law is an economic principle first attributed to Jean Baptiste Say (1767–1832). According to Say's law, diagrammed in Figure 3, the act of supplying goods, or total real output, is the equal but opposite side of demanding goods, or total real expenditures. Say's law implies that full employment is a permanent, built-in feature of the macroeconomy. Resource unemployment is impossible because the act of producing goods is the same act as demanding goods. In other words, supply creates its own demand.

Say's law is most easily understood in a barter economy, where goods are exchanged for goods. Suppose, for example, that a chicken farmer supplies eggs and demands auto parts. If a deal can be worked out with an auto parts supplier, the farmer's act of supplying eggs is simultaneously the act of demanding auto parts. Likewise, the auto parts supplier's demand for eggs is reflected in his supply of auto parts. What is true for the farmer and the auto parts supplier is also true for all traders in the economy.

Say's law also applies to an economy using money. When money is used as a common denominator or as a medium of exchange for all goods and services, the egg supplier does not deal directly with the auto parts seller, but he or she does exchange goods indirectly through the use of money. Money in this system is merely a veil that hides the real workings of the economic system.

FIGURE 3

In the circular flow of income and output, the act of supplying goods and services is necessarily equal to the act of demanding goods and services.

Say's Law

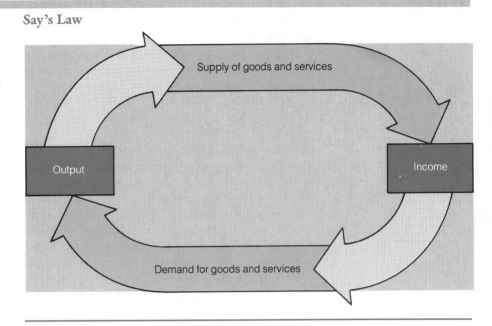

Say believed that in a money economy the aggregate demand for goods and services is financed through the earning of income, as in the circular flow diagram in Figure 1 of Chapter 7. How do productive factors earn wages, rents, interests, and profits? They do so by producing goods and services. In this system, as in a barter system, the act of producing specific goods and services results in the demand for other goods and services.

According to Say, supply creates its own demand, since the income generated in the act of producing (or supplying) goods would always be used to buy (or demand) goods of equal value. Say's law may seem perfectly sensible, but what happens when consumers choose to save part of their income? The act of saving—the sacrifice of present consumption for larger future consumption—disrupts the perfect balance between income and output.

Saving is a leakage, or withdrawal, from the circular flow of income and spending. If this withdrawal from spending is not matched by an injection—another form of spending to compensate for the saving withdrawal—underconsumption and unemployment result and Say's law does not work. Investment spending is one form of injection into the circular flow to make up for a savings leakage. But how do private saving—the leakage—and investment—the injection—become linked? Can Say's law be vindicated? The answer, the classical economists thought, lay in the mechanism of interest rates.

Interest Rate Flexibility. People save, or postpone current consumption, because of a reward for doing so. Interest paid on savings is their reward, enabling savers to consume more goods later. This important relation may be expressed

$$S = s(r),$$

or saving (S) is a function of the real rate of interest (r). The rate of interest is both the percentage that savers earn annually on their savings and the percentage that borrowers must pay to use funds deposited in savings insti-

Real rate of interest:
The nominal interest rate minus the inflation rate; the interest rate that measures the true incentives and costs that savers and investors face.

tutions. The **real rate of interest** is the nominal rate of interest minus the annual rate of inflation. The real rate reflects the fundamental forces of saving and investment in the economy.

Classical economists believed that saving was positively related to the real interest rate: A rise in the interest rate increased the amount saved. For example, when the real interest rate increases from r_0 to r_1, depicted in Figure 4, consumer-savers in the economy are encouraged to save more for future consumption. The higher the interest rate, the less you must sacrifice today in order to increase consumption by a given amount in the future for a new car, a college education, a new house. A high interest rate encourages savers to devote greater amounts to saving out of current income because future goods become "cheaper" relative to current consumption. Any increase in attitudes encouraging saving would cause the S curve in Figure 4 to shift to the right, indicating more saving at all rates of interest. If attitudes toward thrift become discouraged, of course, the whole curve would shift to the left.

Keep in mind that increases in saving are accompanied by simultaneous decreases in current consumption. In other words, according to the classical model, aggregate demand falls by the amount that saving increases. Will an increase in saving mean that aggregate supply will not call forth enough aggregate demand? Will goods remain on shelves, inventories pile up, and thousands of workers be laid off? To both of these questions, the classical economists answered no—with the qualification that the economy must be allowed to reestablish its equilibrium. Not only does the interest rate paid to savers determine their choices, but the interest rate charged on loans determines the behavior of investors. Investment is a flow of expenditures to repair or replace capital goods or to make additions to the capital stock of the nation. Investment spending, just like consumption spending, generates income and employment.

In classical theory, a lower rate of interest makes more investment projects—such as expenditures for warehouses and machinery—profitable. Since interest payments factor into the cost of new investment, higher interest rates make new investment more costly, other things being equal. Investments become more attractive when the interest rate falls. The interest rate may be thought of as the price of loanable funds to investors (whereas the price level is the price of commodities to consumers). As this price (the interest rate) rises, investors are discouraged from engaging in new investment projects. As it falls, investors spend more on capital goods. Technically, this relation can be expressed

$$I = i(r),$$

or investment (I) is a function of the real rate of interest (r). However, unlike the relation between saving and interest, investment and the real rate of interest are negatively related. Rises in r cause declines in the amount of I, and reductions in r provoke increases in the amount of I.

This inverse relation is depicted in Figure 5. As the real rate of interest declines, the investment spending represented by curve I increases. Conversely, when the rate of interest rises, fewer and fewer investment projects become profitable, and investment spending declines. Increases in the productivity of capital—through inventions or improvements in technology—would increase the level of investment at every rate of interest, shifting the whole curve to the right.

FIGURE 4
The Classical Concept of Saving

Saving and interest rates are positively related. As the real rate of interest rises, from r_0 to r_1, the level of saving in the economy rises from S_0 to S_1. An increase in the amount saved means that present consumption, or demand, is diminished by an equal amount.

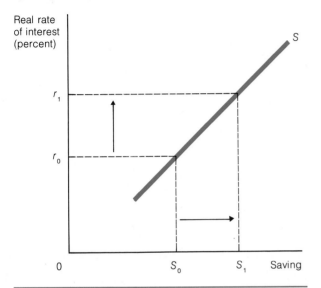

FIGURE 5
The Classical Concept of Investment

The amount invested (I) and the real rate of interest (r) are negatively related, given a constant rate of return on investment in capital goods. As the rate of interest falls from r_0 to r_1, businesses invest more in capital goods. The increase in investment expenditures from I_0 to I_1 represents a net increase in demand.

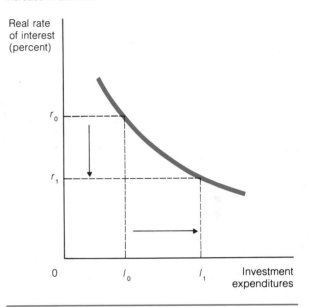

According to the classical system, saving and investment are balanced by means of the interest rate. Figure 6 reproduces the saving and investment curves already discussed. An initial economy-wide equilibrium is established where saving equals investment at interest rate r_0. At interest rate r_0, in other words, the amount that individuals in society wish to direct from consumption to savings is S_0. Real interest rate r_0 is the savers' reward for their thrift. At interest rate r_0, moreover, investors find I_0 worth of investment projects to be profitable—no more, no less. Given curves S and I, no other interest rate is compatible with equilibrium. Why? Because an interest rate lower than r_0 would create a shortage of investment funds, and one higher than r_0 would mean a surplus of funds. In the former case, according to the law of supply and demand, investors' demand would force the interest rate up to r_0; in the case of a surplus of funds, savers' demand would force the interest rate down to r_0. To put the matter formally, macroeconomic equilibrium requires that the amount of saving equals the amount of investment, or, in terms of the above expressions, that

$$S = I.$$

What happens if the whole saving curve or investment curve shifts, reflecting a sudden change in society's underlying attitudes toward thrift (increased saving for retirement or expectations of hard times) or a technological

FIGURE 6

Initial equilibrium E_0 is established at interest rate r_0 with saving and investment curves S and I. An increase in thrift will cause the saving function to shift rightward from S to S_1, lowering the rate of interest from r_0 to r_1. As the interest rate declines, the amount of investment spending increases. Reduction in the amount of consumption spending brought about by increased saving is therefore accompanied by a counterbalancing increase in the amount of investment spending.

The Relation Between Rate of Interest, Saving, and Investment in the Classical System

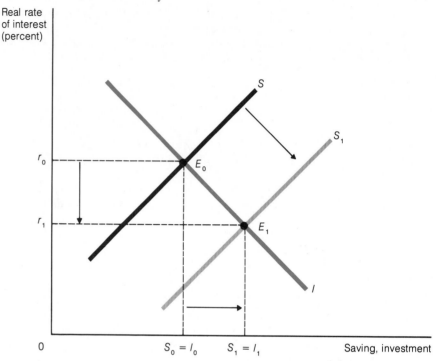

breakthrough that increases the productivity of investments? Suppose, for example, that individuals wish to save more at every rate of interest, shifting the saving function rightward from S to S_1, as shown in Figure 6. A surplus of saving develops at interest rate r_0, forcing the rate of interest down. As the rate falls, investors take advantage of new, profitable investments. Finally, at the new equilibrium interest rate, r_1, a new higher quantity of savings, S_1, equals a new, higher level of investment expenditures, I_1.

If Say's law is true, all leakages from the income stream must be replaced by injections. According to classical economics, increases in saving (leakage) are replaced by increases in investment (injection) through the mechanism of the real rate of interest. Aggregate demand for goods and services would fall short of aggregate supply were it not for the mechanism of interest rates. In other words, the classical economists believed that Say's law is valid if the interest rate is able to adjust freely upward or downward without regulations or restrictions. Consumption spending plus investment expenditures will be sufficient to purchase all of the output produced by the economy.

Price-wage flexibility:
An economic principle whereby prices and wages can fluctuate with changing economic conditions; thus the economy will be self-adjusting toward full employment even in response to shocks in supply and demand.

Price-Wage Flexibility. The validity of Say's law requires another cornerstone of classical thought: **price-wage flexibility.** To understand this second concept, suppose that future economic conditions appear very uncertain. There might be expectations of war, of a coming depression, or even of an overall decrease in prices. In response to this uncertainty, individuals seek greater immediate economic security. A drastic increase in saving at such a time of crisis will have the effect of lowering the interest rate; the price of loanable funds is reduced to investors, encouraging more investment and additions to the capital stock and making up the difference for the reduction in consumption. But in the event of a sudden surge of saving, investors might not be able or willing to adjust their spending quickly enough to make up the difference in total spending. Aggregate demand would be insufficient to carry off the aggregate supply of goods and services and Say's law (temporarily) would not hold; supply would not be creating its own demand. Unemployment would increase disastrously, leaving the economy vulnerable to collapse. According to classical theory, however, any such reduction in demand would also provoke another mechanism—price-wage adjustment.

With a (temporary) reduction in total spending, prices and wages would be expected to fall in the economy in proportion to the size of the reduction. As the prices of shoes, pizzas, hair stylings, and all other goods and services decline, additional quantities of goods will be demanded, and all excess production will quickly be bought up by consumers. Wages of laborers and the prices of all raw materials and other inputs will also decline, encouraging their employment by businesses. Nominal wages and the price level (for commodities) will both decline, helping to preserve the purchasing power of the new, lower nominal incomes. The flexibility of prices and wages in a competitive market helps guarantee full employment, even in the event of a sharp and protracted reduction in aggregate demand.

It must be emphasized that the classical cornerstone of price-wage flexibility applies when aggregate demand is insufficient to maintain full employment for *any* reason. Natural disasters and wars were thought to pose no threat to full employment in the long run, as long as prices and wages were allowed to adjust. The purely competitive market system—an assumption of classical economists—is the fail-safe mechanism through which unemployment over long periods of time was thought to be impossible. For the system to operate properly, of course, there could be no restrictions on prices (such as price controls) or wages (such as a minimum wage) in either product or resource markets.

The Quantity Theory of Money. In the long run, real GNP and employment would be maximized in a laissez-faire economy. Thrift, the productivity of capital investment, and Say's law guaranteed maximum output in the classical economist's theoretical system. The price level and the nominal wage level were explained in the classical system by a theory that, in the long run, viewed output and employment as independent of the money supply—the **quantity theory of money.** The quantity theory of money simply states that, in the long run, there is a clear and proportional relation between the money supply and the price level in the economy.

Quantity theory of money: A theory stating that in the long run with output and velocity fixed, changes in the money supply cause proportional changes in the price level.

While we postpone a detailed discussion of money and prices until Part Three, it is useful at this point to understand some of the principles that underlie the formation of prices and inflation. The classical economists (like modern economists) used certain relationships in the real world to explain and predict how the price level is formed. Specifically, they began their argument by noting that the following relationship existed:

Money supply × velocity = the price level × real GNP.

In symbols,

$$MV = PY,$$

where M = the money supply, consisting of currency in the hands of the public plus all checkable deposits (all checkbook money) used in transactions by the public (in the U.S. monetary system, M is determined by the Federal Reserve System, an agency of the federal government);

V = velocity, or the average number of times a unit of money changes hands per year (or other time period) in financing the purchase of real output by the public;

P = the price level of all output (goods and services); and

Y = the final real output of goods and services produced and sold in the economy over some time period. (Y, in other words, is real GNP.)

Velocity:
The average number of times a unit of money changes hands per year in financing the purchases of GNP.

If money is defined as currency plus checkable deposits held by the public, the public, at any given time, will hold a certain portion of their wealth in the form of money, in addition to houses, goods, and other types of assets. They will demand money (currency and checkable deposits) to facilitate transactions as a proportion of their total income. For example, if income in the economy was $900 billion in 1990 and the public demands one-third of this amount to facilitate all transactions in the economy, the average dollar exchanged hands or "turned over" three times in the economy in 1990. This means that **velocity** (necessary to facilitate the purchase of yearly GNP) was 3. The classical economists thought that this proportion was a constant over specific time frames, such as a year, and that velocity changed slowly due to (slow-changing) institutions in the economy.

If we consider the above equation and believe, along with the classical economists, that money serves individuals only as a medium of exchange, we may understand that increases in the *supply* of money will cause the price level to rise in the same proportion. That is, by assuming velocity and real GNP constant, the equation $MV = PY$ becomes an expression of the quantity theory of money. If the money supply, M, were to double, the equation indicates that the price level, P, also would double. More money in the hands of individuals means that too much is being held to facilitate their level of goods and services transactions. What will people do? They will increase their demands for these goods and services by offering larger amounts of money for them. But recall from the other three foundations of the classical system that *real* output of these goods and services is always (over the long run) at a maximum. When no more goods can be obtained, prices must rise. If the velocity of money, which is another way of expressing individuals' money demand behavior, is constant, and if real income is already at a maximum, the only possible effect of an increase in the money supply is to cause an increase in the price level.

If resources were for any reason unemployed in the short run, and if, as this implies, real output (real GNP) were not at a maximum, increases in M with constant velocity would imply that real output and employment could be brought to a maximum. New spending created by increases in M would increase society's real output of goods and services and employ the resources necessary to produce them. This means that velocity is a key to understanding why increases in the money stock could be used in a short-run situation of unemployment to return the economy to full employment. The classical economists assumed that the public's money demand (which determined velocity) was stable and did not change when the money supply was altered. Thus, the strict quantity theory relationship—for example, a doubling of M causing a doubling of P—held only in the long run, when real output and employment were at a maximum and velocity was constant.

Throughout the nineteenth century and into the twentieth, the size of the money supply was, in the main, determined by gold and silver stocks. The discovery (or hoarding) of precious metals had a profound impact on the price level at any time (and on the rates of inflation or deflation). In the modern U.S. system, the money supply is independent of the amount of gold or silver in the economy. It is controlled by the Federal Reserve System, an agency of the federal government. The Federal Reserve directs the money supply by regulating lending and other activities of banks in our economy. All of these matters will be carefully discussed in Part Three, but it is useful to remember that the classical writers thought that resources were fully employed and real output was maximized in the normal state of the world.

CLASSICAL THEORY AND POLICY: THE MEANING OF A SELF-ADJUSTING ECONOMY

Classical self-adjustment mechanism:
The theory that, through Say's law, full employment will be reached given interest rate flexibility and price-wage flexibility.

The cornerstones of classical macroeconomic theory imply that self-adjusting forces in the economy will guarantee full employment. Long-run unemployment is simply not possible if the economy functions as the theory predicts. Consider the meaning of the **classical self-adjustment mechanism** in a real-world context.

The classical economists knew that adjustments due to supply "shocks" such as rapid technological change or new inventions, weather conditions, or wars were not instantaneous. Suppose, for example, that a drought occurs. A sharply reduced supply of grain and other foodstuffs means that the price of food will rise (given some inelasticity of demand). But given the logic of the quantity theory of money, the prices of other goods that are consumed in the economy must fall! Adjustments of nominal prices in all of the various markets of the economy will be accompanied by changes in the nominal wage rates associated with each production. While all of these prices and wages are changing, the economic system will be in disequilibrium, with temporary surpluses and shortages of some goods and with excess demand for or supplies of labor in various markets. Unemployment of labor and other resources, as a temporary *and necessary* phenomenon, will take place, a fact the classical economists freely acknowledged. If wages and/or prices were "sticky"—that is, if they were not allowed to rise—unemployment would be more persistent. A critical question is, How long will the economy have to endure this temporary phenomenon in actual time? Two months? One year? Ten years?

While never directly answering this question, the classical economists did offer some important insights, based on the understanding that any interference by government or private coalitions would make the problem of adjustment worse. In other words, although natural and unfettered market forces would not restore equilibrium instantaneously, reliance on market forces was the best choice in an imperfect world. The setting of wage or price controls of any kind, such as minimum wages or union-controlled wage rates, would only impede flexibility in the marketplace. Market forces would eventually conquer the controls, extending the time period for adjustment. Unemployment would last longer if wages, prices, and interest rates were not permitted to adjust through unregulated market forces. The long run over which the market will adjust to changing underlying conditions in the economy (a drought, perhaps, or technological changes) was an indeterminate period of time that was minimized by the absence of controls in the economy.

John Maynard Keynes took exception to classical economic theory's conception of the nature of actual conditions in the economy—specifically, the issue of how rigid or flexible prices and wages are in the real world. The logic of classical economics led to the conclusion that market forces, in and of themselves, are the best means of providing adjustments in prices, wages, employment, and output. All adjustments take time, of course, but in the classical view free-market adjustments minimize the time necessary for full employment of resources to take place.

Classical Policies for Rapid Self-Adjustment

The classical economic policy recommendations fit hand in glove with the theoretical cornerstones. If the logic of their system required full flexibility of prices, wages, and interest rates—as well as the encouragement of industry—then their economic policy had to promote free markets. On practically every point of economic policy, the classicals supported economic freedom. Consider some of the chief tenets of their economic policy.

Balance the Budget. Classical economists emphasized the need for a balanced government budget for a number of reasons. If government is allowed to spend more than it receives in taxes, the government will be forced to compete with investors to borrow available funds. Such competition will tend to increase real interest rates, choking off private investment, capital formation, and economic growth. Financing deficits by printing money—an attractive option when governments have access to the presses—would have equally bad effects on the private economy. As we will discuss in Chapter 17, increases in the money supply can create inflation, which is tantamount to a tax on the private sector.

Keep Government Small. High levels of taxes necessary to finance big government reduce incentives to private saving from which new investments are made. Big government, in the classical view, short-circuits the mainspring to progress.

Moreover, large-scale government includes domestic or international regulations that tend to reduce trade, productivity, and consumers' well-being. In the classical laissez-faire view, the government should be restricted to providing national defense, a legal system, and few other functions. Over the past two centuries, a number of policy-makers have pursued these classical economic conclusions, as described in Economics in Action, "Macroeconomic Theories and Policies in Classical and Modern Economics."

Laissez-faire. Capitalism requires well-defined property rights. The classical economists underscored this belief by promoting policies that encouraged individual ownership and increased incentives to save and invest. These were primarily "hands-off" policies, or laissez-faire. The theory is that most regulation in the workplace, business, and in financial markets should be dismantled; also, all newly proposed regulations should be viewed with extreme skepticism. The classicals also adhered to the belief that much regulation was inspired by interest groups who wanted to capture the political process for their own gain. A good example of this is the factory legislation of early nineteenth-century England, which, supposedly, was passed to protect children from exploitation. (See Focus, "The Factory Acts and the Macroeconomy of Nineteenth-Century England.") Any laws or regulations that reduced saving, investment, or capital formation—domestic or international—were opposed by classicals.

Free Foreign Trade. The self-adjusting macroeconomy and economic growth were also believed to be fostered by international free trade. The free-trade philosophy espoused by nearly all classical economists brought about calls for the elimination of all barriers to free exchange, such as tariffs and quotas. A major strand of classical economic policy, then, was the removal or reduction of all impediments to both internal and external trade—in other words, anything in the way of the gains from specialization and comparative advantage.

Classical Theory and Policy: Summary

The classical cornerstones of macroeconomic theory were part of a long-run view of economic activity. Yet the classical writers never stated the actual time period needed for the economy to self-adjust. They merely emphasized that any short-run government tinkering with the private economy in either a macroeconomic or a microeconomic sense would have negative long-run effects. In their view, the best long-run economic hope for all members of society—laborers, households, consumers, businesspeople, investors, savers— was to let unfettered market forces work in the private economy, unassisted by government.

Recessions, depressions, or periods of high unemployment caused by massive shifts in consumption spending, natural disasters, or wars all could wreak short-run havoc and temporary unemployment in the economy, as all classical economists knew. Society's members, however, would all be better off to suffer the temporary consequences rather than demand that government intervene. In the classical view, nearly all short-run actions of government in the aggregate economy only made problems worse, prolonged recessions or depressions, and created built-in instabilities in the macroeconomic system. Capitalism was not perfect, but society's inability to endure the short-run pains of recession and unemployment (reflected in demands for government to do something) meant that there would be greater economic pain in the long run.

FOCUS The Factory Acts and the Macroeconomy of Nineteenth-Century England

In general, policy recommendations of the classical economists were based on the notion of a self-adjusting economy. The vehemence of the classical economist Nassau Senior's (1790–1864) objections to factory legislation is not unusual.

The Factory Acts, enacted between 1833 and 1850, were a series of restrictions on the employment of women and children in the British textile industry. While many historians believe that these acts were passed for humanitarian reasons, Senior saw more rhetoric than genuine concern for working women and children. He identified an interest group—primarily, male workers—as the real agitator for factory legislation. If competing suppliers of labor—women and children—were eliminated from the work force and if hours of work were shortened or regulated, the wages of male workers would rise. Senior believed that the actual efforts to pass factory legislation had little to do with the "public interest."

Senior's second reason for opposing the Factory Acts rested on the impact on the macroeconomy of legislatively mandated reductions in work hours and labor participation in the textile industry. Senior interviewed mill owners on the matter of the proposed restrictions, quoting one as having said, "When a laborer lays down his spade, he renders useless, for that period, a capital worth eighteen pence. When one of our people leaves the mill, he renders useless a capital that has cost 100 pounds."[a] In other words, restrictions on labor contracts idled capital and reduced the marginal efficiency of capital, thereby reducing the efficiency of resource allocation. Senior knew that a legislated reduction in the efficiency of capital would lower the rate of return on capital investment in the textile industry below that which

could be earned outside the industry. Higher-cost producers would leave the industry, reducing employment and granting a competitive advantage to foreign producers not subject to legislated restrictions on work hours and labor participation. Senior therefore complained that "the English capitalist using his machinery for only 10 hours a day will be undersold by the German or the American who employs his for 12, 13, 14 and even 15," and that "the factories which work for the foreign market must be closed, and with them the means of clothing, feeding, and supporting many hundreds of thousands of workpeople [in England]."[b]

Senior's point, shared by most classical economists, was that regulations that had negative effects on investment, capital formation, and domestic employment were detrimental to maximizing society's total income. A modern parallel of this argument is the U.S. Environmental Protection Agency's regulations on the sulphuric content of coal. This legislation has adversely affected the demand for coal extracted in Appalachia by coal demanders such as electrical utilities in the northeastern United States. The response of these utilities has been to import coal (of lower sulphuric content) from western Canada (via the Panama Canal) and from Latin American countries. Economists, of course, do not dispute the fact that clean air has value or that some humanitarian purpose might have been accomplished by the Factory Acts. Rather, they point out that rules and regulations have costs—costs that are often ultimately reflected in the self-adjusting character of the economy and in the economy's attainable output and income potential.

[a]N. W. Senior, *Selected Writings on Economics* (New York: Augustus Kelley, 1966), p. 14.

[b]N. W. Senior, *Industrial Efficiency and Social Economy*, vol. 2 (New York: Henry Holt, 1928), p. 309. Also see Gary M. Anderson, Robert B. Ekelund, Jr., and Robert D. Tollison, "Nassau Senior as Economic Consultant: The Factory Acts Reconsidered," *Economica* 56 (February 1989), pp. 71–81.

SUMMARY

1. The classical blueprint for economic growth consists of progressive extensions of the division of labor, private savings and investment, and capital accumulation.

2. Economic growth in any economy is limited by, among other things, the economy's actual supply of human and nonhuman resources, the state of technology, productivity, and population.

3. Given the factors that limit growth at any one point in time, the best the economy can attain is a point on the production possibilities curve. The point of attainable possibilities corresponds to a vertical aggregate supply curve for the economy.

4. Classical macroeconomics consists of four cornerstones: Say's law, price-wage flexibility, interest rate flexibility, and the quantity theory of money. From

these foundations, classical economists concluded that the economy would self-adjust to reach a full-employment level of production and income.

5. Say's law states that the act of supplying goods creates an automatic demand for the goods. The act of saving or hoarding does not mean that overproduction will occur. If prices and wages are flexible downward, price and wage declines will ensure that all units of production will be sold. Further, the linkage between the rate of interest and saving and investment guarantees that what is removed from the income stream (saving) will be returned in a different form of spending (investment). The quantity theory of money indicates that the price level is proportional to the nominal money supply and suggests an avenue by which prices change when the money supply changes.

6. Classical economic policy, in the main, reflected the classical economists' theoretical view of the macro-

economy. They supported policies that promoted the flexibility of prices, wages, and interest rates in the face of ever-changing conditions.

7. In the classical view, maximum price and wage flexibility would be promoted by the reduction both of internal and external regulations and by minimal government involvement in the economy and a balanced budget.

8. Classical macroeconomic theory was a long-run theory that emphasized the self-adjusting character of the economy as the least-cost means for arriving at the economy's production possibilities curve. In the classical view, all economies must go through adjustments, and the best way to let all markets adjust is through reduction or elimination of government interference.

KEY TERMS

classical macroeconomic theory
classical process of economic growth
division of labor
classical long-run equilibrium
Say's law

real rate of interest
price-wage flexibility
quantity theory of money
velocity
classical self-adjustment mechanism

QUESTIONS FOR REVIEW AND DISCUSSION

1. According to Say's law, under what circumstances would the quantity of goods demanded be less than the quantity of goods supplied?

2. Will people be willing to save money when the real rate of interest is equal to zero? What is the real rate of interest on a passbook savings account if the inflation rate is 7 percent and the bank pays 5½ percent interest?

3. According to the classical view, why does an increase in the level of saving not decrease the total level of spending? Would this be true if interest rates were not flexible?

4. What is the importance of price and wage flexibility under the classical system? What would be the consequence of rigid wages or prices if the macroeco-

nomic system were disturbed by, say, poor grain crops?

5. Does the self-adjusting mechanism of classical economics indeed guarantee full employment of labor and other resources at all times? (Remember the distinction between the short run and the long run.)

6. How were classical macroeconomic theories and economic policy recommendations related?

7. Why did classical economists recommend small balanced budgets for government? Why did they suggest that large budget deficits would lead to lagging economic growth?

8. Why did the classical economists oppose regulations on business behavior? What did laissez-faire mean to classical economists?

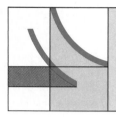

ECONOMICS IN ACTION
Macroeconomic Theories and Policies in Classical and Modern Economics

Numerous parallels exist between classical and modern macroeconomic theory and policy. The self-adjusting economy is a major tenet of several modern schools of thought. The monetarists and new classical economists, whose theories we will develop at length in Chapters 17 and 18, both hold to the classical idea that government interventions in markets will, at best, do little good and, perhaps, will reduce output potential in the economy. While these theories of how the economy functions are complex extensions on classical ideas, they are based on the persistent notion that maximum output results from free-market functioning with minimal government interference.

Classical writers and policy-makers insisted on balanced budgets and minimal government intervention. Consider the policies of William Gladstone, appointed vice-president of the Board of Trade in England under the Conservative government of Prime Minister Robert Peel in 1841. Designed to eliminate as much government intervention in the private sector as possible, Gladstone's policies included a reduction in import tariffs and the abolition of the income tax. Before Gladstone's reductions, approximately four hundred products were subject to import tariffs, a form of excise tax on imported goods; Gladstone removed the tariffs on all but about fifteen items.

Major tariff reductions resulted in a temporary government deficit. To balance the budget, Gladstone called for a 10 percent income tax. The income tax rate was reduced in subsequent years, before being eliminated altogether. The income tax was a temporary measure and disappeared from the budget after its aims had been achieved.

Certain more recent policies bear a resemblance to Gladstone's. President Jimmy Carter's administration achieved significant deregulation in the economy—for example, in the airline industry. President Ronald Reagan's *original* economic proposals emphasized less total government spending and lower taxes to increase private saving and investment, although lower total spending proved to be unfeasible politically. Reagan, like Carter before him, sponsored reductions in domestic regulation in, notably, the transportation and communications industries. Reagan's policies, moreover, had a long-run orientation; the slogan employed at the midway point of Reagan's first term—"Stay the Course"—implied both a direction for and the duration of his administration's economic policies. Certainly, the Reagan administration's so-called trickle-down theory (the idea that prosperity follows a downward course from increased in-

dustry to the poor) is a long-run view with origins in classical macroeconomics.

The supply-side economics that surfaced in the 1980s also has its origins in classical ideas. Stated simply, supply-side economics means that taxes and/or restrictions on individuals and markets must be eliminated to increase aggregate supply of goods and services in the economy. Higher tax rates on individual work effort reduce the incentive to work and produce. Higher tax rates on capital investment mean less investment and less capital accumulation. The Tax Reform Act of 1986 was inspired in large part by the classical principle that lower tax burdens on individuals mean greater work effort. Similarly, the Bush administration's calls for a reduction in the capital gains tax (a lower tax rate on capital gains from investments than on ordinary income) are consistent with the classical notion that investment and capital accumulation are key elements leading to the increased wealth of a nation.

Despite the ongoing goal of marginally lower levels of government involvement in the economy, total federal government outlays grew between 1980 and 1990, partly as a result of a large defense buildup, partly as a consequence of the increased burden of social programs. At the same time, huge deficits began to worry financial markets and citizens.

A key to classical laissez-faire policy is the denial of permanent political access to tax revenues—this to guard against entrenched government intervention. Today, the role of government in the economy—efficient or inefficient—is so pervasive that even marginal changes are considered radical. Recent administrations' policies aimed at lowering the financial base of the federal government have been less successful than those aimed at deregulating some critical industries and transferring control over resources from the public to the private sector and from federal to state and local governments. Whether modern economic policies filtered through a political process can achieve, have achieved, or will achieve critical macroeconomic goals and objectives in an efficient manner remains a matter of great debate.

Question

This discussion has depicted the Reagan administration and others as having reduced the scope of government. Is there any evidence that the scope of government has in fact declined?

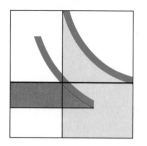

9

Introduction to Keynesian Economics

Classical economic theory, the topic of the previous chapter, dominated the economic debate until the early twentieth century, when a series of catastrophic events sorely tested economists' faith in a self-adjusting economy and the validity of Say's law. After the extraordinarily prosperous 1920s, the United States and the rest of the world fell into the deepest and most prolonged depression in modern history.

In September 1929, the market for stocks and other securities began to fail. On what has come to be known as Black Thursday, October 24, 1929, stock prices plummeted and thousands of investors lost hundreds of millions of dollars' worth of securities. The stock market crash ushered in (though it did not necessarily cause) steep declines in industrial production, real income, and civilian employment. For more than a decade, between 1929 and 1940, industrial production in the United States failed to exceed its 1929 level. Real GNP (expressed in 1982 dollars) was about $700 billion in 1929, a level unmatched until 1939. Most important, civilian unemployment rose to more than 30 percent by 1933.

The exact causes of the Great Depression are still a matter of debate among macroeconomists, but the prolonged economic chaos is a matter of fact. The Depression and the unemployment that accompanied it brought ruin for millions of Americans and similar hardships around the world. The classical self-adjusting macroeconomic system did not appear to work. In this chapter we present the theory of John Maynard Keynes, which was a reaction to the apparent failure of the macroeconomic system to adjust to the problems of the Depression. After reading Chapter 9 you should understand

- Keynes's criticisms of the self-adjusting classical principles of macroeconomics.
- how Keynes evaluated classical ideas to construct his own model of macroeconomics.
- how total private expenditures by consumers and businesses form the basis for Keynes's model of income determination.
- the role of saving and investment interactions in producing equilibrium income in the private economy (with no government assumed).

KEYNES AND THE CLASSICALS

Economists were among the first to recognize that the catastrophic events of the Great Depression appeared to overwhelm theory. In particular, some economists at Cambridge and Oxford universities in England began to question and analyze the cornerstones of classical economics. Economists Richard Kahn, Joan Robinson, R. G. Hawtrey, Roy F. Harrod, Friedrich Hayek, and John Maynard Keynes met regularly during the early 1930s to discuss reasons for the apparent failings of the classical system.

J. M. Keynes (1883–1946) was particularly vocal. In open letters to President Franklin D. Roosevelt, published in the *New York Times,* Keynes advocated the use of government spending and taxation policies to supplement private spending as a cure for the ailing economy. (Roosevelt, clinging to more traditional thinking, heeded Keynes's advice guardedly and hesitantly.) Keynes was firmly convinced that, contrary to classical theory, private market forces would not be sufficient to regain full-employment equilibrium in the depressed economy. He dismissed the long-run self-adjustment theory of the classical economists with scorn. As he said in another context, "In the long run we are all dead." The economy could be stuck at some equilibrium characterized by high levels of unemployment for an extended period of time, as it seemed to be in the early 1930s.

Since the classical theory, in Keynes's view, did not offer rescue from the Depression, Keynes sought a better model from which to interpret events. In 1936, Keynes published his *General Theory of Employment, Interest and Money,* which established a new theory of how the economy functions—a new macroeconomics. In proposing this theory, Keynes had to counter the foundations of the classical macroeconomic system.

Keynes's Evaluation of Classical Theory

Recall that Say's law states that supply creates its own demand if savings (a leakage) can be transformed into investment expenditures (a compensating injection) through a flexible interest rate and if prices and wages are flexible when aggregate demand is exceeded by aggregate production. Keynes took exception to Say's law and to the two other cornerstones that support it—the belief that price-wage flexibility and interest rate flexibility will cure any temporary disruptions in the economy.

First, Keynes argued that saving and investment are determined by a host of forces in the economy in addition to the rate of interest. In Keynes's view, savers and investors are different groups with different sets of motivations and interests. Savers, he thought, are more responsive to their amount of personal disposable income than to the rate of interest in deciding how much to save. Higher interest rates, thought Keynes, might even mean less saving if people were saving toward a particular goal—such as some fixed retirement income—since a high interest rate means that less saving is required per period.

Similarly, investment was not very responsive to the short-run interest rate, in Keynes's view. Much investment, especially in large projects, takes place over long periods. Once investment decisions are made, the investment is autonomous, unrelated to the interest rate or other variables. The point is that the different motivations of savers and investors mean that saving and investment plans could become unlinked. A flexible interest rate, responsive to the desires of savers and investors, would not guarantee that the saving leakage would automatically be turned into the investment injection. There was no built-in assurance that savings would equal investment at a full-employment, growth-maximizing level of economic activity.

Second, Keynes argued that in reality the internal structure of the economy was not competitive enough to permit prices and wages to fall in response to insufficient aggregate demand. To Keynes, the existence of monopoly and union pressures in the economy had to be taken into account. If demand fell off, monopolies would let output fall rather than accept price reductions. Workers, moreover, would refuse to take cuts in their money wages, thereby creating unemployment and layoffs by businesses. Even if workers did take money wage cuts, the reduction in income would further reduce the demand for goods and services, probably reducing output and employment even more. The conclusion: *Classical self-adjusting mechanisms in the private economy would not lift us out of a depression.*

The Relative Unimportance of Money

Money does not play the same role in relieving economic distress in the Keynesian system as it does in classical economics. The classical economists believed that the quantity theory mechanism could, in the event of short-run unemployment of resources, help return the economic system to full employment and maximum income. Their view was premised upon a constant demand for money that resulted in constant velocity. With constant velocity, aggregate spending would increase with increases in the money supply. This would increase the production of goods and services in the economy and the employment of resources that would be necessary to produce them.

Keynes had no such faith in the use of money to cure recessions or depressions characterized by low production and low employment. He did not adhere to the classical notion of the quantity theory—that there was a predictable relation between the money supply and prices in the long run or between money and output and employment in the short run. His reasoning was somewhat complex, but it depended on the notion that money was not simply held by individuals to act as a medium of exchange (as the classicals believed). People held money for other purposes—for a "rainy day" or in order to take advantage of profitable investments in the present or future. This meant that under conditions of short-run economic distress, an increase in the money supply would not necessarily increase total spending and create new production and employment. Money, or the intentional alteration in the quantity of it, was, to Keynes, relatively unimportant.

In the terms of classical economics, an increase in M could be accompanied by a fall in V or, what is the same thing, a rise in the demand for money. To Keynes, people might simply hold more money when economic conditions were poor, meaning that the average dollar would circulate more slowly as the money stock increased. These effects, according to Keynes, would short-circuit the link between money supply increases and increases in real GNP. Monetary policy could not cure unemployment problems; it could not increase the aggregate demand for goods and services. Only government, in

Keynes's view, was powerful enough to affect aggregate demand by changes in spending or taxing policies to restore the economy to full employment. Before we consider government's role in the Keynesian model, we will examine the Keynesian theory of spending—specifically, the interrelation of income, consumption, saving, and investment—in more detail.

The Importance of Income

Keynes believed that a prolonged depression proves that the economy can establish equilibrium at less than full employment. The classical economists, as we have seen, placed their confidence in a flexible price system—flexible prices, wages, and interest rates—as the self-adjusting mechanism that would assure full employment when aggregate demand got out of kilter with aggregate supply.

Income-expenditures model:

A theory suggesting that private expenditures are basically determined by the level of national income and that these expenditures in turn determine the levels of output and employment in the economy.

Keynes argued instead that aggregate demand and economic activity in general were determined by income and by changes in income. He thereby developed an **income-expenditures model** of macroeconomics. The income-expenditures model shows that private expenditures (the same as aggregate demand) are primarily determined by the level of national income and that such expenditures, in turn, establish equilibrium (or nonequilibrium) levels of output and employment in the economy. Other factors, as we will see, may help determine expenditures, but they are unimportant as short-run determinants of what people spend.

In the Keynesian view, equilibrium output would occur when demand for goods and services just equaled the production of goods and services. At lower output levels, production would fall short of demand, and this would lead to increases in production until the equilibrium level was reached. If production temporarily took place at a level above the equilibrium level, production would exceed demand, inventories of unsold goods would accumulate, and businesses would contract production. Again, the level of production would adjust to the equilibrium level. However, unlike the classical system, in which the equilibrium level of production implied full employment, the Keynesian model allowed for equilibrium at any level of production. Should conditions arise under which demand was low, the equilibrium level of production would coincide with high unemployment.

THE INCOME-EXPENDITURES MODEL

Keynes focused on aggregate demand or spending because he viewed rapid aggregate demand changes as the villain in recessions and depressions. Keynes believed that aggregate supply factors—large-scale changes in productivity, such as new technology and inventions and changing incentives to work and produce—changed slowly and could therefore be neglected when considering short-run macroeconomic problems. (Aggregate supply factors will be considered in Chapters 10 and 11.) In the short run, the time period most relevant to Keynesian macroeconomics, the economy's production or supply of goods and services seemed to react passively to changes in total expenditures.

Assumptions of the Income-Expenditures Model

The Keynesian view of total spending is quite complex. In its most complete form, total spending for goods and services is viewed as coming from domestic households, domestic business firms, domestic units of government, and from foreign buyers. Therefore, in the complete Keynesian model, the equilibrium level of production occurs when production equals the spending by these four groups of buyers. We will develop the Keynesian model in steps. Initially, for example, buyers will be assumed to consist only of domestic households and business firms. We make several other assumptions.

1. Government spending and taxation as well as foreign trade (exports and imports) are excluded from the basic model of private spending. Taxes, transfer payments (such as Social Security payments), and any other government activities are not considered. Depreciation is also ignored. Income or output is produced and consumed only in the private sector of the economy. This simplification also means that national income and disposable after-tax income are the same.
2. The purely monetary side of the economy is excluded from the basic model. The interest rate and any possible effects of interest rate changes are therefore excluded from consideration. This assumption makes sense if we accept Keynes's basic point that real income, not the interest rate, is the principal determinant of both consumption and saving. (Keynes did believe that money and interest rates play some role in explaining total spending in the economy, but we will defer discussion of these factors for the time being.)
3. We assume that, over the short run, prices and wages remain constant. This assumption means that total income or output will increase or decrease solely in response to changes in aggregate spending and not to price or wage changes. This also means that we do not need to distinguish nominal from real income, consumption, saving, or investment. With the price level fixed, changes in the nominal values of these variables are identical to changes in their real values.

In subsequent chapters these simplifying assumptions will be dropped, and a complete model will be developed.

Given these assumptions, the equilibrium level of output will occur when production equals household spending (consumption) plus business spending (investment). An understanding of consumer spending behavior and business spending behavior needs to precede any effort to understand how the equilibrium level of output is determined.

Private Consumption Expenditures

The classical writers, as we saw earlier, placed primary emphasis on the real rate of interest in determining the relation between savings (income reserved for future consumption) and expenditures (income used in current consumption). One of Keynes's basic criticisms of classical theory was that the rate of interest could not always enable us to predict how much of current income an individual would choose to save or to spend. Keynes believed that current income was the most reliable and predictable determinant of consumption expenditures. Private saving, the residual of income after consumption, was also a function of, or was explained by, income. The simple Keynesian model of consumption and saving, in other words, does not account for any factors other than current income. Consider how these relations between consumption and income and between saving and income might be expressed and analyzed.

Consumption and Saving Functions and Schedules

Keynes constructed consumption and saving functions and schedules based on income. The consumption function and the saving function can be expressed simply as

$$C = C(Y) \quad \text{and} \quad S = S(Y).$$

In other words, consumption (C) is a function of income (Y), and saving (S) is a function of income, which simply means that consumption and saving are related to income in some way. Both consumption and saving, as we will see, are positive functions of income, meaning that an income increase will increase both consumption and saving, and an income decrease will decrease both consumption and saving.

Consumption and saving relations can also be regarded as schedules. A consumption-income schedule shows the amount that households would desire or plan to consume at every level of income. Likewise, a saving-income schedule shows the desired or planned level of saving that households would undertake at various levels of income.

In the basic Keynesian model, income can be disposed of by households in only two ways: They may consume it or save it. This observation means that

$$Y = C + S,$$

and it also means that consumption and saving are related in a unique way.

Numerous studies have attempted to relate saving and consumption to family income. The evidence provided by these studies shows that as income increases, families increase both saving and consumption. Further, richer families tend to save a higher proportion of income than do poorer families.

The Marginal and Average Propensity to Consume and Save. Macroeconomists are often interested in knowing how consumption or saving will change with a change in income. The two concepts that give us this answer are the marginal propensity to consume and the marginal propensity to save. The **marginal propensity to consume (MPC)** is defined as the ratio of the change in consumption (ΔC) to the change in income (ΔY) that causes the change in consumption, or

Marginal propensity to consume (MPC):
The percent of an additional dollar of income that is spent on consumption; change in consumption divided by change in income.

$$MPC = \frac{\Delta C}{\Delta Y} = \frac{\text{change in consumption}}{\text{change in income}}.$$

Marginal propensity to save (MPS):
The percent of an additional dollar of income that is saved; change in saving divided by change in income.

The **marginal propensity to save (MPS)** is the ratio of a change in saving (ΔS) to a change in income that causes the change in saving, or

$$MPS = \frac{\Delta S}{\Delta Y} = \frac{\text{change in saving}}{\text{change in income}}.$$

Since households in the simple Keynesian model dispose of income only by consuming or saving, any change in income will be completely exhausted by the resulting changes in consumption and saving. This means that because the *MPC* measures the change in consumption resulting from a change in income and the *MPS* the change in saving arising from the same change in income, the *MPC* plus the *MPS* must add to 1:

$$MPC + MPS = 1.$$

Average propensity to consume (APC):
The percent of a particular level of income that is spent on consumption; total consumption divided by total income.

Average propensity to save (APS):
The percent of total income that is saved; total saving during any given period divided by total income in the same period.

Economists are also interested in how much, on average, households consume and save at various income levels. The **average propensity to consume (APC)** is the proportion of income consumed at any income level, or *C/Y*. Likewise, the **average propensity to save (APS)** is the ratio of saving to income at any level of income, or *S/Y*. Since consumption and saving are the only two ways that households can dispose of income, a unique relation exists between the *APC* and the *APS*:

$$1 = \frac{\text{consumption}}{\text{income}} + \frac{\text{saving}}{\text{income}},$$

or

$$1 = APC + APS.$$

Keynes's Theoretical Model of Consumption and Saving

The features of actual household consumption and saving behavior can be translated into a theoretical model of consumption and spending for the entire economy—how the country as a whole would choose to spend or save at different levels of national income. (Using hypothetical data for the entire economy, we abstract essential information from the actual behavior of households.) To make this model easier to comprehend—with no important loss in accuracy—we will assume that the consumption-income and saving-income relations are in the form of straight lines. This assumption means that the *MPC* and the *MPS* are constant. No matter what the level of income, the *MPC* will be the same number. If, for example, the *MPC* were 0.8 at the $100 billion level of income, it would be 0.8 at the $300 billion and the $750 billion levels also. The same relationship holds for the *MPS*. This simplifying assumption does no damage to our conclusions, and it greatly facilitates understanding of these crucial ideas.

Hypothetical information about economy-wide consumption and saving is given in Table 1. The hypothetical data of Table 1 show, in billions of dollars, what private consumption and private saving would be at alternative levels of income. Consider, for instance, a year in which national income is $100 billion. How would households plan to divide this income between purchases of consumption goods and saving? Consumption expenditures at a $100 billion

TABLE 1

Hypothetical Consumption and Saving Data for the Economy

The economy consumes and saves more as income increases. Further, the average propensity to consume declines and the average propensity to save rises with increases in income. For the sake of simplicity, the MPC and the MPS are assumed to be constant.

National Income (billions of dollars) (Y)	Planned Consumption Expenditures (billions of dollars) (C)	Planned Savings (billions of dollars) (S)	Average Propensity to Consume (APC = C ÷ Y)	Marginal Propensity to Consume (MPC = ΔC ÷ ΔY)	Average Propensity to Save (APS = S ÷ Y)	Marginal Propensity to Save (MPS = ΔS ÷ ΔY)
0	40	−40	—	0.8	—	0.2
100	120	−20	1.2	0.8	−0.2	0.2
200	200	0	1.0	0.8	0	0.2
300	280	20	0.93	0.8	0.07	0.2
400	360	40	0.90	0.8	0.10	0.2
500	440	60	0.88	0.8	0.12	0.2
600	520	80	0.87	0.8	0.13	0.2
700	600	100	0.86	0.8	0.14	0.2

Dissaving:
Occurs when consumption is greater than income; the use of previous years' savings or borrowing to finance consumption expenditures that are greater than income.

Autonomous consumption:
Consumption expenditures that are independent of the level of income.

Consumption function:
The positive relationship between levels of consumption expenditures and levels of income, holding all other relevant factors that determine consumption constant.

level of national income would exceed income by $20 billion. This − $20 billion would be **dissavings.** To consume $120 billion at an income level of $100 billion, in other words, households would have to draw down $20 billion in previous savings. A special interpretation is given to dissaving at a zero income level. Note that all households would consume at the level of $40 billion even if no income were earned; this $40 billion is independent of income. Such **autonomous consumption** expenditures are independent of income. At levels of income higher than zero, consumption expenditures increase until they are equal to income. If national income were $200 billion, all income would be devoted to consumption. At income levels higher than $200 billion, consumption expenditures fall short of current income, and the remainder is devoted to saving.

Consumption and the 45-Degree Line. An important method for understanding how consumption is related to income is to compare historical consumption levels with a hypothetical relation in which consumption spending is always equal to income. When consumption spending always equals income, graphing the two variables yields a straight 45-degree line like that in Figure 1. The positive slope of the consumption schedule graphed in Figure 1, $C(Y)$, reflects Keynes's basic notion that the larger our income, the larger will be our consumption expenditures.

Examine Figure 1, on which national income levels are displayed on the horizontal axis and consumption expenditures on the vertical axis. At every point on the 45-degree line in Figure 1, total spending—in this case, consumption spending—*equals* total income. The extent to which actual consumption levels for particular periods differ vertically from this 45-degree line indicates the degree to which consumption does not equal income. Points along the **consumption function** above the 45-degree line indicate dissavings;

FIGURE 1

The Level of Consumption as a Function of the Level of Income

The consumption function $C(Y)$, shows that the level of consumption expenditures rises as income rises. When income is $100 billion, consumption spending is $120 billion; when income is $200 billion, consumption is $200 billion; and when income is $300 billion, consumption is $280 billion. Along the hypothetical 45-degree line, consumption expenditures are exactly equal to income. The degree to which consumption differs from income indicates dissaving or saving by society as a whole. In this example, consumption spending is equal to income only at the $200 billion income level. Along the consumption function and above the 45-degree line, society dissaves; along the consumption function and below the 45-degree line, positive saving takes place.

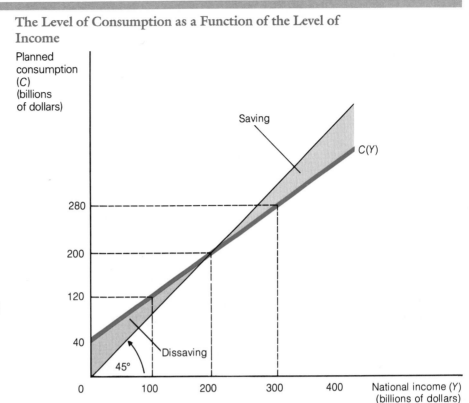

points below it indicate savings. In Figure 1, actual consumption is equal to income only at the $200 billion income level. At a national income below this break-even point, society would go into debt or dip into past savings; above it, society would save some of its income.

The Consumption Schedule. Household consumption is the major factor in total spending, spending that creates jobs and production in the economy. Macroeconomists are therefore very interested in how much household consumption will change with changes in national income. The value of the marginal propensity to consume tells us how much more will be consumed out of an additional dollar—or an additional 100 billion dollars—in national income.

The marginal propensity to consume is of course different for different individuals and for different groups in society. Some of us are more likely than others to spend every dollar we have. In this example, we simplify the variations by choosing an *MPC* value of 0.8 for society as a whole and by holding this value constant across varying national income levels. In Figure 2, an increase in national income from $300 billion to $400 billion will increase the level of consumption spending from $280 billion to $360 billion, an increase of $80 billion. Likewise, an increase from $400 billion to $500 billion will cause

FIGURE 2

Along a straight-line consumption function, $C(Y)$, the MPC is constant. In this graph, $MPC = 0.8$. Each time income rises by $100 billion, the level of consumption rises by $80 billion. Or, for every $1 increase in income, consumers increase expenditures by $0.80.

Marginal Propensity to Consume

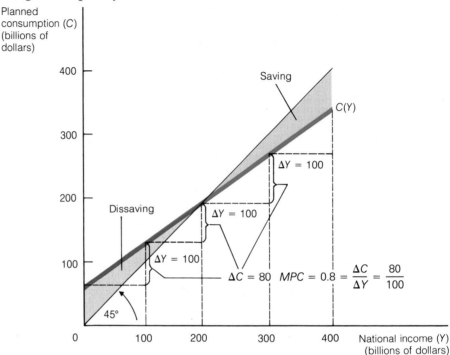

consumption spending to increase by another $80 billion. The MPC is, therefore, the ratio 80/100 or 80 percent or 0.8, as indicated in Table 1.

Though the actual relation of the MPC to national income is a matter of debate, we know that the average propensity to consume changes as income levels change. In general, as income rises, the APC, or the ratio of consumption to income, falls. At a $300 billion income level, for instance, consumption expenditures are $280 billion and the APC equals 280/300 or 0.93. On average, the population would be spending 93 percent of its income. But if national income rose to $600 billion, households would spend only 87 percent of their income (520/600).

The Saving Schedule. Like consumption, saving is a positive function of income. That is, the more income we have, the more we save; the lower our income, the less we are able to save. In the hypothetical **saving function** in Figure 3, at a national income level of $400 billion, desired saving is $40 billion. In fact, saving becomes positive rather than negative at all levels of income greater than $200 billion in this example.

The marginal and average propensity to save are also illustrated in Figure 3. Remember, the MPS is the ratio of a change in saving to a change in income. As shown in Figure 3, incremental changes of $100 billion change saving by $20 billion, so

Saving function:
The positive relationship between levels of current saving and levels of income, holding constant all other relevant factors that determine saving.

$$MPS = \frac{20}{100} = 0.2.$$

FIGURE 3

A Saving Function

The saving function, $S(Y)$, shows that the desired or planned saving is positively related to the level of national income. At a low level of income (below $200 billion), there is dissaving. As the level of income rises from $200 billion to $300 billion, the level of saving rises from $0 billion to $20 billion. At $Y = 400$, $S = 40$, and at $Y = 500$, $S = 60$. The figure also illustrates the marginal propensity to save. Along a straight-line saving function, the MPS is constant. Here the MPS is equal to 0.2. For each increase in income of $100 billion, the level of saving increases by $20 billion.

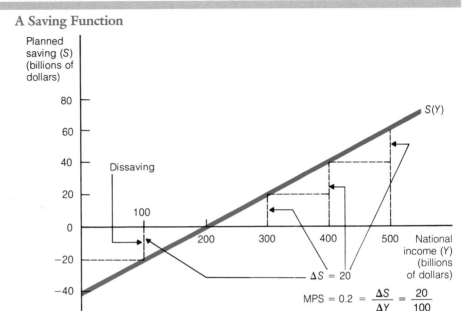

The average propensity to save is the ratio of savings to income at any level of income. The APS rises as income rises, as you can see in Table 1, from which the data in Figure 3 are taken.

Assuming straight-line consumption and saving functions and the use of all income as either saving or spending,

$$1 = MPC + MPS \quad \text{and} \quad 1 = APC + APS,$$

or

$$MPS = 1 - MPC \quad \text{and} \quad APS = 1 - APC.$$

The values of MPC, MPS, APC, and APS are very important for economic policy. A high MPC means that increases in income will generate a large amount of additional private spending. A low value for the MPC (or, exactly the same thing, a high MPS) means that increases in income will generate only small increases in consumption. (Keep in mind that the values of MPC and MPS given in Figures 2 and 3 are based on hypothetical data.) These features of the consumption function will have an extremely important impact on the model of total expenditures developed in the following chapters.

Nonincome Factors Influencing Consumption and Saving

Although Keynes's basic argument involved the effects of income levels, income is not the only factor affecting consumption expenditures. A host of nonincome factors also determine the amount of planned consumption spending by all households. If any nonincome determinant of consumption spending changes, the entire consumption function shifts upward or downward. The amount of planned consumption changes at every income level when a nonincome element affects consumption changes. In contrast, a change in income simply changes the amount of income consumed, expressed graphically as a movement along a given consumption function.

In Figure 4, assuming an initial consumption function $C_0(Y)$, a change in any nonincome factor affecting consumption will shift the consumption schedule either upward to $C_2(Y)$ or downward to $C_1(Y)$. (The break-even level of income, where consumption spending equals income—on the graph, the point where the consumption function intersects the 45-degree line—also changes to Y_2 with consumption C_2 or to Y_1 with consumption C_1.) By contrast, if income increases from Y_0 to Y_2, consumption increases along consumption function $C_0(Y)$ from point A to point F.

In this section, we address seven of the most important nonincome factors that may affect consumption: wealth; the price level; price and income expectations; credit and the interest rate; taxation; age, geographic location, and population; and the distribution of income.

Wealth or the Stock of Assets. People consume not only on the basis of the flow of current income but also on the basis of a previously accumulated stock of wealth. Purchase of real goods—such as precious stones or a painting by Andrew Wyeth—takes place at a given time. As the money value of such assets increases over time, people feel richer and consume more, even though their incomes do not increase. Conversely, reductions in the money value of assets

FIGURE 4

Any change in nonincome factors affecting consumption spending will shift the consumption function, $C_0(Y)$, either upward or downward. An increase in consumption means that consumption spending rises for every level of income (from A to B); a decrease in spending creates a fall from A to D in the figure. By contrast, a change in income, all other factors being equal, moves consumers along a given consumption function. For example, increasing national income from Y_0 to Y_2 would move consumption from point A to point F in the figure.

Shifts in the Consumption Function

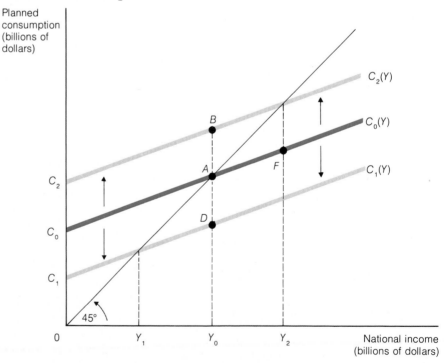

reduce wealth and tend to reduce consumption at every level of income. (Wealth effects are treated in detail in Chapter 11.)

The Price Level.   Some assets—money or assets denominated in money terms, such as bonds—change value with changes in the price level. If you hold a given stock of money, a halving of the price level would double the real value or purchasing power of the money assets you hold. Since you would then be richer, your desired consumption would increase. For the opposite reason, rising prices reduce consumption expenditures.

Price and Income Expectations.   We all have anticipations about our economic lot in the future. If we expect prices to be higher in some future period, we will tend to increase consumption expenditures in the present to beat price hikes. Expectations of lower prices will reduce present consumption. Likewise, if we expect higher future incomes, our present consumption will rise. Expectations of harder economic times will reduce present consumption and increase present saving.

Credit and the Interest Rate.   Two closely interrelated factors affecting consumption are the availability of credit and the interest rate. The number of institutions offering credit in the economy has increased dramatically since World War II. The overall effect of increased credit availability, along with improved terms of credit (longer payback period, lower down payment), is to make consumption higher at any given level of income.

Along with credit availability and improved credit terms, an important factor affecting consumption is the cost of credit, determined by the interest rate. As the interest rate rises or falls, other things such as credit terms being equal, consumers will reduce or increase their present consumption expenditures. A higher rate of interest, moreover, will mean a higher level of saving in the present because reduced consumption will lead to increased saving. As indicated earlier, Keynes did not believe that the interest rate had predictable effects on consumption and saving. His view was in direct contrast to the classical writers, who thought that the interest rate was central to explaining saving and consumption behavior.

Taxation.   As we will see more fully in Chapter 10, consumption and saving behavior are also affected by taxation and government transfers. An increase in income taxes, for example, reduces the amount of income available to a family and thereby tends to reduce both consumption and saving. Similarly, an increase in government transfer payments such as Social Security payments has the effect of increasing spendable income and raising both consumption and saving.

Population, Age Distribution, and Geographic Location.   An increase in population will obviously shift the consumption schedule upward over time. The age distribution of the population—the proportion of young, middle-age, and older citizens to the total population—is a slowly changing but important factor affecting consumption. (For details, see Economics in Action, "The Life Cycle and Consumption Behavior," at the end of this chapter.) Both the young and the old have a tendency to spend a larger portion of their income than do people in their middle years. An age distribution shift to the middle years will therefore tend to reduce consumption and increase saving.

Factors such as geographic location may also affect consumption spending. A large population movement from rural to urban areas may increase present consumption, for example, if city dwellers have a higher tendency than country dwellers to consume their income.

Distribution of Income. A final factor affecting planned household consumption is how income is distributed among different income levels. Low-income, middle-income, and high-income households may have different marginal propensities to consume and to save. Specifically, low-income families may have generally higher *MPCs* than high-income families. In the Keynesian analysis of consumption, a permanent redistribution of income from high-income families to low-income families may cause an increase in total consumption; that is, it may shift the consumption schedule upward, because low-income families have higher marginal propensities to consume than high-income families.

Although Keynes envisioned differences in the *APC* between income groups, empirical evidence on actual consumption functions over the long run suggests that a long-run proportionality exists between consumption and income; society seems to consume the same proportion of income at low as well as at higher levels of income, indicating a more or less constant *APC*. A number of economists have attempted to reconcile data showing short-run nonproportionality with long-run proportionality, although explanations vary. At bottom, it is not clear how a redistribution of income from rich to poor families would affect aggregate consumption spending at any one time or over a long period of time.

Consumption spending is affected by a large number of nonincome determinants. A change in any one of them will shift the consumption function either upward or downward. A single consumption function, however, is constructed by holding all the factors constant and by varying income.

Investment Expenditures

So far, we have looked at household consumption and its relation to income. Private spending in the economy also includes investment spending. In a macroeconomic context, **investment spending** means spending by the private sector—mainly businesses—on capital goods. Public investment in goods such as schools, water reclamation projects, or dams is not included in private investment expenditures. Public investment expenditures are categorized as government spending and will be covered in Chapter 10. Rather, private investment refers to the national income category gross private domestic investment, defined previously as including fixed investment in plant and equipment, all private-sector residential and nonresidential construction, and changes in business inventories (increases or decreases in stocks of finished goods, semifinished goods, or raw materials).

Clearly, there are two effects on the capital stock of the nation at any given time: Some of it is being used up or depreciated, and new net investment

Investment spending:
Expenditures made by businesses on capital goods plus any change (positive or negative) in business inventories.

is creating additions to it. Businesses usually replace their worn-out capital stock and add to their stock of capital with new investments.

Autonomous Short-Run Investment Spending

Keynes argued that in the short run, investment expenditures could be viewed as autonomous—independent of the level of income, profit expectations, the interest rate, and all of the other factors possibly affecting investment. The idea that investment could be autonomous in the short run stems from the fact that most investment expenditures in any current period have been determined by past investment decisions.

Businesses, in fact, make investment decisions from a long-run perspective. The building of new plants and the installation of sophisticated equipment typically take a number of years to complete. During the investment period, planned investment expenditures are often carried out regardless of current business conditions. Planned investment expenditures are those that businesses desire to undertake. (Planned investment expenditures may not be the same as actual expenditures, as we will see later in this chapter.) These investment expenditures are then independent of the level of income.

Autonomous investment:
Investment expenditures that are independent of the level of income.

The concept of **autonomous investment** spending can be analyzed within the framework of the simple Keynesian model of private spending. If I stands for investment spending by businesses, autonomous investment is simply described as some constant level, I_0, or

$$I = I_0,$$

where the subscript 0 means that expenditures are constant at some specified level—$20 billion, $50 billion, $100 billion—during the period under consideration.

If we assume that autonomous investment expenditures are constant at $20 billion, we can express investment this way:

$$I = I_0 = \$20 \text{ billion.}$$

Figure 5 shows the relation between income levels and autonomous investment. Autonomous investment is constant at every level of income. An increase or a decrease in autonomous investment shifts the flat **investment function** upward or downward, respectively, by the amount of the increase or decrease.

Investment function:
In the income-expenditures model, all investment is autonomous, or independent of the level of income. The investment function is horizontal when plotted against income.

In short, planned investment expenditures, while volatile and changing from period to period, may be assumed constant over any given short-run period. They provide, in addition to consumption spending, the means of arriving at the Keynesian concept of total expenditures in a purely private economy.

Long-Run Factors Affecting Investment. While investment is considered autonomous in the Keynesian context, it is subject to a number of rapidly changing factors, including the rate of interest, the cost of capital, and current and expected sales.

Rate of Interest and the Cost of Capital. Ultimately, profitability—or expectation of future profits—determines the amount of investment that bus-

FIGURE 5

The horizontal investment function, *I*, shows that the level of planned investment expenditures is independent of the level of income. As income changes, the level of investment remains constant. An increase in investment caused by factors such as a change in interest rates is shown as a parallel shift upward.

Autonomous Investment Expenditures

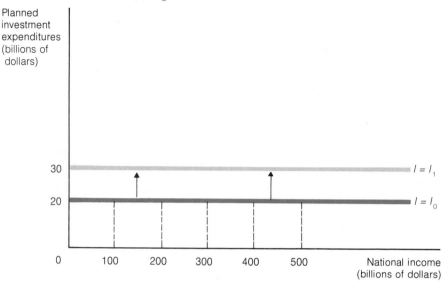

inesses will undertake. Profitability is, in simple terms, the difference between a firm's revenues and its costs.

The cost of capital investment is heavily dependent on the rate of interest. Whether a business uses its own internal funds or borrows to make an investment, it incurs an opportunity cost in the form of interest lost. An increase in the interest rate, other things being equal, will reduce the amount of investment; a reduction in the interest rate will increase investment. The cost of the capital equipment itself is also important in determining the amount of desired investment. An increase in costs, other things being equal, reduces the amount of investment.

Current Sales and Expected Sales. The other side of the profitability of business investment is sales. If a large capacity to produce already exists, an increase in current sales will not encourage new investment expenditures very much. If businesses are operating close to the limits of their ability to produce, an increase in current sales will cause current investment spending to rise.

Expectations are also a central feature of Keynes's theory of investment. Sales expectations require estimates of future business conditions and tend to vary greatly and quickly over time. Optimism concerning future sales and business conditions will mean increases in capital investment in the present. Pessimism will have the opposite effect.

As we will see in later chapters, the volatility of profit expectations is a principal cause in the creation of unstable income levels, unemployment, and cycles of business activity. Before turning to these issues, however, we must first understand how income equilibrium is defined in a purely private economy.

PRIVATE INCOME-EXPENDITURES EQUILIBRIUM

The classical economists argued that full employment would be achieved automatically simply through the activity of supplying goods in an essentially private economy, an economy theoretically free of government intervention. Should difficulties in adjustment to this full-employment equilibrium take place, prices, wages, and interest rates would change to bring the aggregate output of goods in line with aggregate expenditures.

For reasons already outlined, Keynes did not agree that wages, prices, or interest rates would change in any predictable way to bring the demand for goods in line with the supply of goods. How could a depression economy reach equilibrium with high unemployment? Keynes argued that levels of private spending (consumption and investment) determine the output of goods produced in the economy. In other words, businesses react to any level of total expenditures by producing the quantities demanded. If households want more kitchen appliances, they are produced; if businesses demand less computer software, less is produced. Since it obviously takes more or less labor and other resources to produce more or less total output, the level of employment is also affected.

Keynes's theory of output and income determination can be expressed in symbolic terms using the tools of private spending analysis developed previously. Since total private expenditures are a function of income, and since these total private expenditures consist of consumption and investment spending, we can express the Keynesian equilibrium as follows:

$$Y = C + I = \text{total expenditures.}$$

Private-sector equilibrium:
A situation of equality between total private expenditures and output. In this equilibrium, there is no unplanned investment and no tendency for the level of output to change.

Private-sector equilibrium, or equilibrium output, occurs when $C + I$ equals income. In other words, equilibrium output in the economy exists when total expenditures equal what is produced.

An alternative way to define the establishment of equilibrium output involves the relation of income to expenditures. We know that income received by all factors of production may be disposed of in two ways, or

$$Y = C + S.$$

That is, income may be used for consumption spending or for savings, the residual of consumption spending. Equilibrium will occur when income received is equal to total expenditures:

$$C + S = C + I, \quad \text{or} \quad S = I.$$

Total Expenditures Equal Total Output

Keynes's theory—that equilibrium income (or, its mirror image, equilibrium GNP or output) is a function of total expenditures—can be expressed numerically and graphically using tools already at our disposal. All of our previous consumption, investment, and income figures are reproduced in Table 2. Total expenditures, shown in the fourth column, are equal to the sum of consumption and investment expenditures. Recall that planned consumption depends di-

TABLE 2 Planned Total Expenditures Determine Total Output and Equilibrium Income

For equilibrium in the private economy, planned total expenditures, $C + I$, must equal total income or output, Y. In this example, equilibrium is reached at a national income (or output) level of $300 billion. At national incomes less than $300 billion, total expenditures exceed total income. At national incomes higher than $300 billion, total expenditures are less than total income.

	(1) National Income or Output (Y)	(2) Planned Consumption Expenditures (C)	(3) Planned Investment Expenditures ($I = I_0$)	(4) Desired or Planned Total Expenditures ($C + I_0$)	(5) Difference Between Total Expenditures and Total Output ($C + I_0 - Y$)
	100	120	20	140	+40
	200	200	20	220	+20
Equilibrium	300	280	20	300	0
	400	360	20	380	−20
	500	440	20	460	−40

Note: All values are in billions of dollars.

Equilibrium level of national income:
In the income-expenditures model, the level of income at which total private expenditures equal total output.

rectly on the level of national income, reported in column (1). According to the circular flow model, the first column represents both the total output of goods and services in the economy as well as national income. Total expenditures may be greater or less than total production or output. The amount by which income or output exceeds expenditures is shown in the last column.

At an income level of $100 billion, for example, total expenditures are greater than total output by $40 billion. This situation is possible only if businesses draw down on inventories of goods. Producers react to such a situation by producing greater quantities of goods and services, thus generating additional income to workers and to the other factors of production. The resulting increases in income will change consumption plans. At incomes higher than $100 billion, households will spend greater amounts on goods and services, indicated in the second column of Table 2 and in Figure 6, which merely reproduces the information of Table 2 graphically. (Note in Figure 6 that investment is added vertically to the consumption function at an autonomous level of $20 billion in order to obtain the $C + I$ line.)

A new, higher level of output produced and income received at $200 billion creates higher total spending, but there is still an excess of total expenditures over output (amount FG in Figure 6). Inventories continue to be drawn down and production stepped up until an **equilibrium level of national income** of $300 billion is reached. Only at this level of income will production plans be in line with the plans of households and businesses to consume and invest.

What would happen at an income level greater than $300 billion, say $400 billion? If an income level of $400 billion were temporarily established, total output would temporarily exceed total expenditures by $20 billion, or AB in Figure 6. Unwanted inventories of goods would pile up unsold, and producers would cut back the rate of production. Since a cutback in production would reduce income, consumption plans of households would be revised downward. Equilibrium would again be achieved when the level of income dropped to $300 billion.

FIGURE 6

The equilibrium level of income exists when total private expenditures are just great enough to purchase the total output of the economy. At equilibrium, expenditures and output will meet at the point along the 45-degree line where they are exactly equal. At income level $Y = 300$, the economy is at equilibirum, E. At an income or output level of 400, desired total private expenditures at point B are insufficient to purchase the total output generated at point A. Inventories of goods will pile up, causing reductions in the rate of output and a lowering of income. These reductions will take place until income and output again equal the equilibrium level of 300. At this level, total expenditures equal total output produced in the economy. The reverse analysis applies to income and output levels that are less than the equilibrium level.

Private-Sector Equilibrium

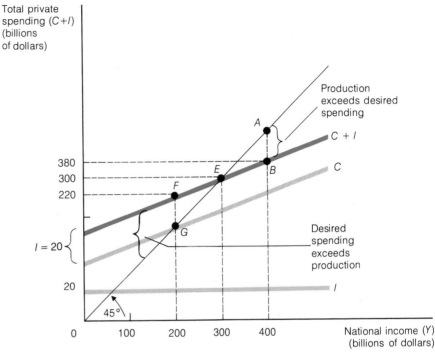

It is always worth remembering that the simple Keynesian model of total private spending is a short-run model. Prices, wages, and interest rates do not adjust as they do in long-run classical theory. The only factors that are adjusting are the real quantities of goods and services produced in the economy.

Desired Saving Equals Desired Investment: An Equivalent Method

An equivalent method for determining private-sector equilibrium is to equate private saving and private investment. This method is based on the fact that private saving is what is left over after planned private consumption is determined for various income levels.

Desired saving and desired investment concern the plans of households and businesses. Over any period and at alternative income levels, businesses plan to invest some amount—in the foregoing model, $20 billion worth of investment at every level of income. Households, likewise, plan to save some amount out of income for every level of income; but unlike business investment, household saving varies with income. Desired saving at an income level of $400 billion in our numerical example is a positive $40 billion. But it is a negative $20 billion at an income level of $100 billion; that is, $20 billion will be dissaved.

In other words, at an income level of $100 billion (see Table 3), businesses plan or desire to invest $20 billion. But because total expenditures draw down inventories by $40 billion, they actually end up with a negative $40 billion worth of unplanned investment. Recall that economists include business inventories in the measure of gross private domestic investment. Thus, in this example, when inventories are reduced by $40 billion, the $40 billion represents an unplanned reduction in investment. What do businesses actually invest? Actual investment is the sum of desired (planned) investment plus unplanned investment. In the numerical example of Table 3, actual investment is a negative $20 billion at the income level of $100 billion ($20 billion planned plus a negative $40 billion unplanned). In this situation of falling inventories (negative unplanned investment), businesses respond by increasing output. The increases in output drive up incomes, and thus saving, and move the economy toward its equilibrium level of output.

At the $500 billion level of income, consumption expenditures fall short of income-producing unplanned investment (inventory increases) of $40 billion. Total investment at the $500 billion level of income will then be $60 billion ($40 billion unplanned plus $20 billion desired). Businesses will cut back on production with the effect of lowered incomes. These lower incomes reduce saving, and once again, the economy moves back toward an equilibrium output, one at which planned saving and investment are equal. (For a discussion relating saving to economic progress, see Focus, "The Low Saving Rate in the United States.")

At alternative income levels, therefore, actual investment may diverge from desired or planned investment, but whenever this occurs, producers will change their rate of production. The important point is that actual investment will always equal the actual amount of savings. But when the plans or desires of savers and investors differ, income and output will increase or decrease. The only possible equilibrium will take place when the plans of both household savers and business investors are identical. As Table 3 and Figure 7 show, this equilibrium income occurs when $300 billion of output is consumed by consumers and investors.

TABLE 3   Equilibrium Income

The actual levels of investment and saving are accountings of the difference in total expenditures and total income. If total expenditures are greater than total income, then actual investment is below desired investment. In such cases, businesses increase output until their actual investment equals their desired investment. If total expenditures are less than total income, then actual investment is greater than total income, and businesses decrease output. Equilibrium occurs where desired and actual saving equals desired and actual investment.

	National Income (Y)	Desired Saving	Desired Investment	Unplanned Investment	Actual Investment	Actual Saving	Income Adjustment
	100	−20	20	−40	−20	−20	increase
	200	0	20	−20	0	0	increase
Equilibrium	300	+20	20	0	+20	+20	—
	400	+40	20	+20	+40	+40	decrease
	500	+60	20	+40	+60	+60	decrease

Note: All values are in billions of dollars.

FOCUS   The Low Saving Rate in the United States

According to the Council on Competitiveness, the greatest challenge facing the United States is reversing the decline in the national saving rate. This concern is based on the notion that a country's savings determines how much it has to invest in new plant and equipment. A decline in the saving rate therefore leads to less investment, which in turn reduces the ability of the economy to produce goods and services.

Although there is some controversy concerning the importance of the saving rate as a determinant of economic growth, two things are clear: The saving rate in the United States has declined sharply over the last fifteen years, and this decline has brought the U.S. saving rate to a level far below that of other major economic powers. In 1973, Americans were saving about 10 percent of their disposable income; this percentage fell to under 3 percent in 1987. Since then, the trend has reversed, and the saving rate reached 6 percent by 1989.

In explaining the difference between the saving rate in the United States and in other countries, much attention has been paid to the way that interest income is taxed in the United States. In the United States, interest earnings are taxable income. If a family has accumulated, say, $20,000 in savings that yields 9 percent interest, the $1800 in annual interest is an addition to taxable income. Assuming the family to be middle income, each additional dollar of taxable income will lead to a twenty-eight cent increase in federal taxes owed by the family. In addition, the interest earnings are also subject to state taxation. While the rate varies among states, this family probably would pay about five additional cents in taxes for each additional dollar in interest earnings. When state and federal taxes are combined, $600 of the $1800 earned in interest will go to pay taxes—in effect reducing the interest rate to 6 percent. By taxing interest income, the tax system in this country reduces the returns to saving and presumably causes the saving rate to be lower than it otherwise would be.

In addition to discouraging saving, the U.S. tax system subsidizes borrowing. If a family in this country borrows $100,000 to buy a new home, any interest that the family pays is tax-deductible. Assuming mortgage interest payments of $9000 per year on the loan, this debt enables the family to reduce taxable income by $9000, which lowers state and federal taxes by about $3000. In effect, the loan costs the family only 6 percent in interest. Until recently, all interest paid on consumer loans was tax-deductible. However, this deduction has been phased out, explaining in part the recent upturn in savings. Nonetheless, tax policy in this country still has the effect of reducing the return to saving and reducing the cost of borrowing.

In many countries, individuals do not pay taxes on interest earnings, nor can they use interest payments as a tax deduction. Many economists feel that the U.S. should adopt a similar tax policy.

Only where desired saving comes in line with desired investment does the process of adding to (or subtracting from) inventories stop. Only at an income level of $300 billion does desired saving of $20 billion equal desired investment of $20 billion. At this level, and only at this level, producers' motivations to increase or decrease production will cease. That is why it is called the equilibrium level of income. Only at an income of $300 billion is the behavior of savers or, more properly, consumer-savers, consistent with that of investors. Not only does $S = I$ in the actual accounting sense, but the desired economic behavior of savers and investors is mutually consistent. Thus, for equilibrium,

$$\text{Desired } S = \text{desired } I = \text{actual } S = \text{actual } I.$$

The condition that in equilibrium desired saving equals desired investment is equivalent to the condition stated earlier that total expenditure ($C + I$) equals total income for an equilibrium level of income to exist. Anytime desired saving and investment are not equal, unintended investment in the form of inventory changes is taking place. From our earlier discussion, unintended investment occurs only when total expenditure does not equal total income. Thus, to say that intended investment equals intended saving in equilibrium is also to say that total expenditure equals total income in equilibrium.

FIGURE 7

Saving-Investment Equilibrium

When $C + I = Y$ (at an equilibrium output equal to $300 billion in Figure 6), saving is equal to investment. The equilibrium level of income occurs where the saving function intersects the autonomous investment function (I_0)—in this case, at 300.

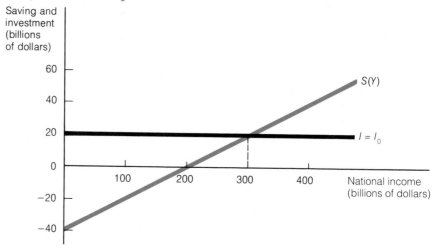

Private Equilibrium in the Keynesian System

Unlike the classical economists, who believed that the economy would self-adjust until full employment was reached, Keynes thought that the economy could adjust to an equilibrium level with widespread unemployment. In terms of the situation depicted in both Figure 6 and Figure 7, the $300 billion level of income is not necessarily the full-employment level of income. This unfortunate state of affairs, in Keynes's view, either was permanent or would last a long time. In either case, some action was demanded in the economy. That action, as we will see, was a role for the government.

SUMMARY

1. Theory clashed with events when, in the 1930s, a decade-long depression in output and employment took hold of the United States and other Western countries. The response of economists was to provide a new version of how the macroeconomy functions. The principal developer of the new macroeconomics was the English economist John Maynard Keynes.

2. Keynes criticized classical theory as being an inadequate description of events in the real world. For example, Keynes did not believe that prices, wages, and interest rates were flexible enough to create a permanent and sufficiently rapid tendency to private-sector full-employment equilibrium.

3. Keynesian economics is predicated on a model of total expenditures. In the simple private-sector model, consumption and investment spending determine equilibrium output and income.

4. Keynes argued that consumption was primarily a function of current income and that the marginal and average propensities to consume were related to in-

come in a stable and predictable manner. Investment, the other kind of private spending, was related to expectations and to a number of factors but could, in the short run, be considered autonomous of income.

5. The income-expenditures model of equilibrium output/income determination employs Keynes's arguments concerning the relationship of certain macroeconomic variables. The level of consumption spending is positively related to the level of income. The marginal propensity to consume (*MPC*) measures the change in consumption expenditure that results from a $1 change in income. The marginal propensity to save (*MPS*) measures the change in saving that results from a $1 change in income. Other factors, such as the price level, wealth, and taxation, help determine consumption and saving. Investment spending is assumed to be autonomous.

6. The level of equilibrium income or output in the private-sector model can be derived by either of two approaches, each yielding the same answer. In the

income-expenditures approach, the equilibrium level of income exists when total expenditure equals total income or output in the economy $(Y = C + I)$. In the desired saving–desired investment approach, the equilibrium level of income exists when desired saving equals desired investment output in the economy $(S = I)$.

7. Whenever total expenditure does not equal total income or whenever desired saving does not equal desired investment, unintended investment in the form of inventory changes exists. The unintended investment will drive income or output toward its equilibrium level. However, the equilibrium level of income may not be a level of income at which full employment occurs.

KEY TERMS

income-expenditures model
marginal propensity to consume
   (MPC)
marginal propensity to save
   (MPS)
average propensity to consume
   (APC)
average propensity to save
   (APS)

dissaving
autonomous consumption
consumption function
saving function
investment spending
autonomous investment
investment function
private-sector equilibrium
equilibrium level of national income

QUESTIONS FOR REVIEW AND DISCUSSION

1. How does Keynes's view of saving differ from the classical view of saving? How does Keynes's view of wage-price flexibility differ from the classical view?
2. Define marginal propensity to consume and average propensity to consume. What is the essential difference between the two?
3. If the MPC is 0.75 and national income increases by $200 billion, then by how much will consumption expenditures increase?
4. Can you think of any nonincome factors not listed in the text that might affect consumption decisions?
5. What is autonomous investment spending? Does it change as the level of income changes? Do you think that this is an accurate interpretation of how businesses make investment decisions?
6. When does equilibrium occur in the Keynesian income-expenditures model? What adjusts to obtain equilibrium?
7. Why does the level of actual investment always equal the level of actual saving, while the level of desired investment may not equal the level of desired saving?

PROBLEM

Consider a basic income-expenditures model (with no government sector and where $Y = C + I$) in which Y is real national income, C is real consumption expenditures, and I is real autonomous investment expenditures.

Let $C = \$40$ billion $+ (MPC)Y$ and $I = I_0$. If $I_0 = \$50$ billion and $MPC = 0.5$, compute the equilibrium levels of national income, Y; consumption, C; and saving, S.

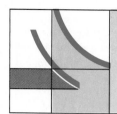

ECONOMICS IN ACTION
The Life Cycle and Consumption Behavior

The Keynesian consumption function used in this chapter is often called the absolute income hypothesis concerning the consumption behavior of members of society. The absolute income hypothesis suggests that current income determines the amount of household consumption. Keynes, however, did not base his theory of consumption on budget studies or on extensive economic reasoning about how and why individuals exhibit such behavior. Since Keynes, economists have developed a number of alternative theories about why individuals and households consume and save as they do. One of the most interesting concerns the human life cycle and our perception of it.

Originally developed by economists Albert Ando, R. E. Brumberg, and Nobel laureate Franco Modigliani, the life-cycle hypothesis is based on the idea that household income and wealth (income plus all accumulated assets) change through time.[a] Individuals and households, further, recognize

[a]Franco Modigliani and R. E. Brumberg, "Utility Analysis and the Consumption Function: An Interpretation of Cross-Section Data," in *Post-Keynesian Economics,* ed. K. K. Kurihara (New Brunswick, N. J.: Rutgers University Press, 1954); and Albert Ando and Franco Modigliani, "The 'Life-Cycle' Hypothesis of Saving: Aggregate Implications and Tests," *American Economic Review* 53 (March 1963), pp. 55–84.

this fact and consume and save depending on their life-cycle income and wealth, and, of course, on how long life is expected to be. Figure 8 depicts the notion graphically.

The average individual's income flow, in Figure 8, is much lower in early age (age t_0 through t_1) and in "old" age (t_2 through death, D) than in middle age (age t_1 through t_2). The consumption stream of the individual (as shown in Figure 8) is constant (or rising slightly) over time. This means that individuals (and households) consume more of the value of their (expected) lifetime income/wealth flow in early age and old age and less in middle age. In early age, individuals are net borrowers and dissavers. In middle age, they build up savings (consume less than their incomes) to pay off debts from early age and to provide "nest eggs" for retirement. In old age, the individual is again a dissaver. That is, he or she spends assets accumulated during middle age.

Students, for example, have some perception of the present value of expected lifetime income from property and from labor. This expected income is conditioned by many factors, such as educational level (or the one you hope to attain), the average expected earnings in the job or profession you expect to go into after graduation, expectations about longevity, probable inheritance, unexpected bequests, and so on. Consumption in the present is conditioned by the present value of this expected income. (Present value

FIGURE 8   Hypothetical Life-Cycle Consumption Behavior

The figure depicts a stylized profile of income, consumption, and savings. In the life-cycle theory, individuals consume and save on the basis of expected income over the life cycle. This implies that consumption is at a higher level than income in early age, is less than income in the middle years, and is again greater than income (people dissave) in retirement. In the figure, time t_2 represents retirement. After t_2, during retirement, the source of income becomes interest earnings from accumulated assets.

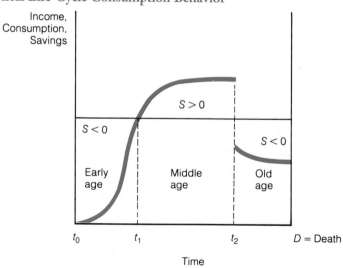

is today's value of income received in the future, or it is future income discounted by the rate of interest.) Some medical, law, or MBA students buy BMWs, Porsches, and fine wardrobes; these students are dissaving out of current income. They are, however, consuming in response to expected income over the life cycle.

The importance of the life-cycle hypothesis for macroeconomic theory is that it explains some rather apparent empirical contradictions. The consumption function, estimated over some short-run period, such as a year, shows that consumption is not proportional to income. People and households with lower incomes tend to consume a *larger* proportion of their incomes, whereas higher-income individuals and households consume a smaller proportion. How-

ever, when the consumption function is estimated over long periods of time, we find that, in the aggregate, consumption is proportional to income. This means that a relatively constant proportion of aggregate income is consumed from year to year. The life-cycle hypothesis explains this apparent anomaly by maintaining that consumption is a function of the present value of *lifetime* income and wealth, not short-term yearly income.

Question

How might a changing age distribution of the U.S. population toward (a) older citizens or (b) younger people affect consumption expenditures in the present?

APPENDIX

An Algebraic Treatment of Keynesian Theory

The tables in the text of this chapter provide useful information for several levels of national income. But what if the information you need cannot be obtained from these tables? At times, an algebraic version of the Keynesian model of equilibrium will prove useful to you.

Using the simplifying assumption that the marginal propensity to consume is constant regardless of level of income, a general consumption function can be expressed as

$$C = a + b(Y),$$

where b is the marginal propensity to consume and a is the consumption spending that would occur if national income were zero.

It is therefore reasonable to assume that a is some positive number and that b is a fraction. For example, the consumption function presented in numerical form in Table 1 in the text could be expressed as

$$C = 40 + 0.8(Y).$$

If some income level (say, $400 billion) is substituted into the equation, then the equation can be

solved for C to determine that planned consumption is $360 billion when income is $400 billion—exactly the answer provided in Table 1.

Similarly, an algebraic equation can be derived to express the saving function. Since, by definition,

$$Y = C + S,$$

S can be expressed as

$$S = Y - C.$$

However, $C = a + b(Y)$. Substituting in the previous equation yields

$$S = Y - [a + b(Y)],$$

or

$$S = Y - a - b(Y).$$

Rearranging terms,

$$S = -a + Y - b(Y),$$

or

$$S = -a + (1 - b)Y.$$

Here, $(1 - b)$ is interpreted as the marginal propensity to save, and $-a$ is the level of saving when income is zero.

The specific saving function presented in Table 1 is

$$S = -40 + (1 - 0.8)Y.$$

If specific numbers are substituted for Y, the above equation can be used to determine the level of planned saving at each income level. Doing so yields numbers identical to those presented in Table 1.

Finally, it is also possible to develop an algebraic expression of the equilibrium income. In the simple case presented in the text of this chapter, where demanders of goods and services are domestic households and business firms, the equilibrium level of production occurs when

$$Y = C + I_0,$$

or when

$$Y = a + b(Y) + I_0.$$

Rearranging,

$$Y - b(Y) = a + I_0,$$

$$Y(1 - b) = a + I_0,$$

or

$$Y = \frac{(a + I_0)}{(1 - b)}.$$

If we know the appropriate consumption function (the values of a and b) and the investment function (the value of I_0), we can substitute the values into the equation and solve for the equilibrium income level. For example, using the numerical example presented in Table 1, where $a = 40$, $b = 0.8$, and $I_0 = 20$, in equilibrium,

$$Y = \frac{40 + 20}{1 - 0.8},$$

$$Y = \frac{60}{0.2},$$

or

$$Y = 300.$$

We can see that at a production level of $300 billion, consumers will be willing to buy $280 billion of goods and services—$280 = 40 + 0.8(300)$—with the business sector preferring to buy the remaining $20 billion of goods and services. At that production level, total spending is equal to production.

We can also employ an algebraic approach to determine equilibrium income, using the savings and investment approach. At the equilibrium level of income,

$$S = I_0.$$

Since $S = -40 + (1 - 0.8)Y$ and $I = I_0 = 20$, then, in equilibrium,

$$-40 + 0.2(Y) = 20,$$

$$0.2Y = 60,$$

or

$$Y = 300.$$

With simple examples, the equilibrium level of income can be depicted with either numerical charts or with graphs. However, as the model is made more complete and realistic, these two approaches become cumbersome. The use of an algebraic equation can therefore be quite helpful.

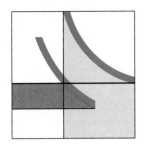

10

Output Fluctuations and the Public Sector

The last chapter focused on how equilibrium in the private economy is reached in the Keynesian model. In the classical view, discussed in Chapter 8, equilibrium was conceived from a long-run perspective, a period of time that could encompass short-run swings in income and employment. From a short-run perspective, however, equilibrium seems an illusive concept, for we commonly observe fluctuations in real GNP, employment, and inflation whenever the government releases its latest statistics on the economy. An essential part of the Keynesian model and Keynes's critique of classical economics was an explanation of how and why the economy in the short run increases or decreases its output in response to changes in spending. Keynes sought, in other words, the reasons for short-run economic instability and what can be done to correct it. In essence, Keynes argued that spending in the private economy would normally be insufficient to produce an economy characterized by full employment and little or no inflation. He felt that the public sector—the government—must pursue spending and taxation policies to ensure full employment and economic growth. After reading Chapter 10 you should understand

- the process through which changes in private spending are translated into changes in output and income.

- how the impact of spending changes on income described by Keynes is important in explaining cycles of business and economic activity.

- how foreign trade and government act as components of spending in the economy.

- how government spending and taxation in a Keynesian system are called upon to alleviate downturns and to modify inflationary pressures in the private economy.

FLUCTUATIONS IN THE PRIVATE SECTOR

Before we analyze the mechanics of the Keynesian model, let's review briefly. The private-sector equilibrium discussed at the end of Chapter 9 was based on Keynes's central assumption that total expenditures determine output and income. (Keep in mind that the terms *output* and *income* are used interchangeably in macroeconomics. In the circular flow of goods and services, one person's expenditures on output always represent another person's income. The final or total value of output must therefore equal the level of income in the economy.)

In the Keynesian model, output and income can increase or decrease in response to any change in the components of total expenditures. For example, if autonomous consumption or investment increases, income will increase. If the economy-wide marginal propensity to consume increases, income will increase. Table 1 summarizes possible changes in private expenditures and their effects on income and output.

To see how changes in these factors actually affect income and output, consider an increase in autonomous investment spending. Recall that autonomous investment spending is independent of income and depends instead on factors such as the cost of capital, expected sales, and business profits. What happens to income when investment spending increases? In the example illustrated in Figure 1, the initial level of income of $300 billion is determined by the private spending level $C + I_0$. Assume that investment spending then increases by $20 billion because of an increase in expected future profits. The total spending curve shifts upward to $C + I_1$ by the amount $\Delta I = \$20$ billion. Desired spending then exceeds the output of goods and services by $20 billion (distance AB in Figure 1). To meet the demand, inventories are drawn down, producers step up the rate of output, and income rises. The question is, What effect does a $20 billion increase in autonomous investment spending have on equilibrium income? Does income increase by $20 billion exactly or by a greater or lesser amount? As you may have noticed in Figure 1, income increases by $100 billion with an investment spending increase of $20 billion. Why does such a relatively small increase in investment result in such a relatively large increase in income?

TABLE 1

The Sources of Income and Output Changes in the Private Economy

Increases or decreases in autonomous consumption or investment spending or in the marginal propensity to consume (and save) will cause increases or decreases in the level of income and output in the economy.

Component Change	Change in Income and Output
↑ Autonomous consumption spending	Increase
↓ Autonomous consumption spending	Decrease
↑ Marginal propensity to consume	Increase
↓ Marginal propensity to consume	Decrease
↑ Autonomous investment spending	Increase
↓ Autonomous investment spending	Decrease

FIGURE 1

When the level of autonomous investment increases by $20 billion, from $60 billion to $80 billion (*AB*) in the figure, and the marginal propensity to consume is 0.8, equilibrium income rises by $100 billion— in this case, from $300 billion to $400 billion. The multiplier effect causes the level of income to rise by more than the amount of the increase in investment.

The Effects of an Increase in Investment Expenditures

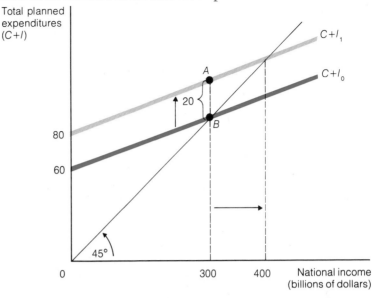

Investment multiplier: The multiple by which equilibrium income will change given a change in autonomous investment expenditure; 1/*MPS*.

The Investment Multiplier

The answer to this question is given by the value of the multiplier, a number found by dividing the change in income by the change in autonomous spending that caused the change in income. In Figure 1, we are looking at a change in autonomous investment spending. Thus the **investment multiplier** is found by dividing $100 billion by $20 billion or, if k_I represents the investment multiplier,

$$k_I = \frac{\Delta Y}{\Delta I} = \frac{100}{20} = 5.$$

If autonomous investment spending increases by ΔI, or $20 billion, the initial expenditure first generates an addition to income of $20 billion ($\Delta Y$) because expenditures on investment goods create returns (or income) to resources. However, the process does not end here, for all resource owners, laborers, holders of capital or land, and so on, are consumer-savers. New income will cause the consumer-saver to spend some and to save the rest. The *MPC*—the marginal propensity to consume—and the *MPS*—the marginal propensity to save—will always add to 1 out of total income. (What is consumed is not saved; what is saved is not consumed.) Consumption expenditures on goods and services, then, create additional income out of which another set of income recipients spend a portion and save the rest. In this process, the initial increase of $20 billion is multiplied at each stage.

This multiplier process is illustrated in Table 2. The initial injection of $20 billion in autonomous investment spending creates an addition to income (ΔY) of $20 billion. Assuming that the *MPC* is 0.8 and the *MPS* is 0.2, income recipients will spend 80 percent and save 20 percent of the new income. The new consumption thus creates an addition to total income of $16 billion on

---

TABLE 2   **The Workings of the Investment Multiplier**

Any change in autonomous investment spending changes equilibrium income by some multiple, depending on the value of the MPS. In this example, MPC = 0.8 and MPS = 0.2. The simple multiplier is the reciprocal of the MPS—in this case, 1/0.2 = 5. In a simple Keynesian framework, the change in equilibrium income is equal to the multiplier times the original change in spending, or 5(20) = 100.

Round of Spending	Increase in Autonomous Investment Spending (ΔI)	Increase in Income (ΔY)	Increase in Consumption (ΔC)	Increase in Saving (ΔS)
1	20	20	0.8(20) = 16	0.2(20) = 4
2		16	0.8(16) = 12.8	0.2(16) = 3.2
3		12.8	0.8(12.8) = 10.24	0.2(12.8) = 2.56
4		10.24	0.8(10.24) = 8.19	0.2(10.24) = 2.04
•		•	•	•
•		•	•	•
•		•	•	•
All others		40.96	0.8(40.96) = 32.96	0.2(40.96) = 8.19
		100	0.8(100) = 80	0.2(100) = 20

Note: All values are in billions of dollars.

the first round of consumption spending. The recipients of the $16 billion consumption spending in turn spend part of it—80 percent of $16 billion, or $12.8 billion—and save part of it—20 percent of $16 billion, or $3.2 billion. The multiplier process goes on until the total change in income equals $100 billion, of which $80 billion is composed of new consumption and $20 billion of new saving. It is no accident that the new savings are exactly equal to the initial amount of new autonomous investment spending. Why? Because only when the increase in desired investment is matched by an equal amount of additional desired saving will the initial disequilibrium caused by the new investment be corrected and equilibrium be restored.

The Multiplier Formalized

The value of the multiplier is determined by the MPC or MPS. A quick method of determining the multiplier, therefore, is to divide 1 by the MPS.

$$k_I = \frac{1}{(1 - MPC)} = \frac{1}{MPS}$$

Using an MPC of 0.8,

$$k_I = \frac{1}{(1 - 0.8)} = \frac{1}{0.2} = 5.$$

Any change in income caused by a change in an autonomous expenditure may then be determined by multiplying the autonomous expenditure change by the multiplier or, in the example,

$$\Delta Y = k\Delta I = \frac{1}{MPS}(\Delta I) = 5 \times \$20 \text{ billion} = \$100 \text{ billion}.$$

A change in the *MPS,* which also means a change in the *MPC,* will obviously change the value of *k,* the multiplier. The multiplier is the reciprocal of the *MPS.* If the *MPS* is 0.1, the multiplier is 10. Under these circumstances, a $20 billion injection of autonomous expenditures would increase income by $200 billion. Or, if Americans saved one-half of every additional dollar received in income, the multiplier would take on a value of 2. (On a piece of scratch paper, demonstrate to yourself why this is so.) In this case, a $20 billion increase in investment spending would raise equilibrium income by only $40 billion.

The Autonomous Consumption Multiplier

The **autonomous comsumption multiplier** applies to the autonomous portion of consumption, that portion of consumption spending independent of income and determined instead by variables such as thrift attitudes and the rate of interest on savings.

If autonomous consumption increases, income also increases by some multiple. If, for example, the autonomous component of consumption increases from $40 billion to $50 billion in a society with a marginal propensity to save of 0.2, equilibrium income would rise to $450 billion from its previous level of $400 billion. The change in income can be expressed as follows:

$$\frac{\Delta \text{Autonomous consumption}}{MPS} = \frac{\$10 \text{ billion}}{0.2} = \$50 \text{ billion.}$$

Thus the autonomous consumption multiplier, like the investment multiplier, is the reciprocal of the *MPS* (in this example, 1/0.2 = 5). The higher the *MPC* (or, what is the same, the lower the *MPS*), the higher the consumption multiplier and the higher the income change from a given change in autonomous expenditures.

To summarize, income will rise or fall by an amount greater than the expenditure change because of a multiplier process. The multiplier, which is simply the reciprocal of the *MPS,* magnifies the change in autonomous expenditures that creates the change in equilibrium income. Stated another way, changes in equilibrium income are calculated by applying the multiplier to changes in autonomous expenditures.

These concepts are of great importance for practical policymaking. The most significant effect of the multiplier is that very small changes in spending may be greatly magnified in resulting income and employment changes. For example, a small change in private spending could precipitate a relatively large economic contraction or reduction in employment and business activity. As we will see later in this chapter, Keynes recommended that government's fiscal actions be used to counteract the instabilities generated by the multiplier effects of private spending on GNP, employment, economic growth, and inflation.

The Multiplier and Private Income Equilibrium

Before turning to more elaborate models of the macroeconomy and the impact of prices in the Keynesian framework, it is useful to reflect on some crucial assumptions about the multiplier process and about the basic Keynesian private-sector model in general.

The multiplier process just described is a simplification. No time horizon is placed on the rounds of spending, and the process requires that income receivers who spend and save do so in the exact amounts given by the *MPC* and the *MPS*. In the simple model there are no other deductions from income except saving. Since there is still no role for government in the model, income receivers do not have to pay taxes on income received or on income spent, such as excise or consumption taxes. (As we will see later in this chapter, taxes are a leakage from income that has the effect of reducing the numerical value of the multiplier.)

In addition, the simple private model does not consider spending injections into the macroeconomy other than autonomous consumption and investment spending. As we will see in the next section, investment can be accelerated by changes in income, and there are other injections, such as government spending, to account for. Such additional spending tends to increase equilibrium income. In general, then, leakages—deductions from income such as savings and taxes—reduce equilibrium income, while injections—additions to spending—increase equilibrium income. Most of these factors are fully integrated into the basic macroeconomic model later in this chapter.

THE MULTIPLIER AND THE BUSINESS CYCLE

The income-expenditures approach to macroeconomic theory establishes an explanation for equilibrium levels of GNP and employment. As we have seen, the multiplier process explains how changes in autonomous consumption or investment spending change the equilibrium level of income. These models are extremely useful in organizing our understanding of how GNP and employment of resources are determined. However, data on unemployment, GNP fluctuations, and inflation suggest that our economy undergoes cycles of business activity. As indicated in Chapter 6, the business cycle consists of observed upswings and downswings in the production of goods and services and in the employment of resources to produce goods and services.

The Business Cycle

Business investment in a particular period is determined by the level of autonomous expenditures and by the growth or decline of sales. If sales are growing at a steady rate (for example, 3½ percent per year), only autonomous factors will affect investment. If all other factors affecting income growth remain constant, the economy will grow at a steady rate. Businesses, however, will seek to maintain additions to net investment (and hence their capital stock) in some proportion to the levels of their output of goods and services. These additions, above and beyond the ongoing autonomous investment spending that takes place in the economy, will rise when the amount of capital falls below the amount that businesses wish to maintain in proportion to their current output. When does this happen? This additional "kicker" of net investment can rise when actual sales of goods and services grow beyond some expected and predictable steady rate or when some other factor affecting new additions to net investment changes.

Consider some actual and potential reactions of businesses to increases or reductions in the demand for their products. In the short run, businesses with a relatively fixed capacity must either add labor and other variable resources when sales increase or lay off labor and other resources when sales decline (in which case business capital simply depreciates). In the short run, businesses have relatively few options. Decreases in sales will create unemployment of labor and other resources, as well as unused capacity; increases in output demand may lead to pressure on labor and other resources, accompanied possibly by a high rate of inflation. The result: In the short run, businesses may alter the rate of output of their plants, but actual increases in output are severely constrained because of the impossibility of adding capacity by building warehouses and plants or purchasing sophisticated equipment over a short-run period.

Figure 2 shows the path of real GNP through time; the straight line depicts a constant and steady growth rate in output. This straight-line path in output (about 3 percent growth, on average, over the past hundred years in the United States) would occur steadily and smoothly when all factors affecting the growth in investment spending remain the same. For example, when sales are assumed to be growing at a steady rate, as between hypothetical time periods t_0 and t_1 in Figure 2, income also grows at a steady rate. But what happens if actual sales outpace expected sales at some hypothetical point in time, t_1, and actual sales increases are expected to continue? Investment expenditures of the autonomous type will rise initially, raising income; but rising demand for and sales of goods and services will also signal new additions to net investment because businesses will want to maintain some desired ratio of capital stock to total sales volume.

This accelerated growth in investment expenditures in response to rising sales creates a business cycle. As income is increased through the multiplier

---

FIGURE 2

A jump in investment spending at time period t_1 due to an unexpected rise in sales of goods and services creates a business cycle; output rises sharply due to the multiplier effect. Eventually, the growth in output slows, and a peak is reached as resources such as labor and raw materials become scarce. Investment may then return to lower levels, causing the economy to contract. Since expectations about future business conditions change constantly, business cycles are a fact of life in market economies.

Changes in Autonomous Investment and the Business Cycle

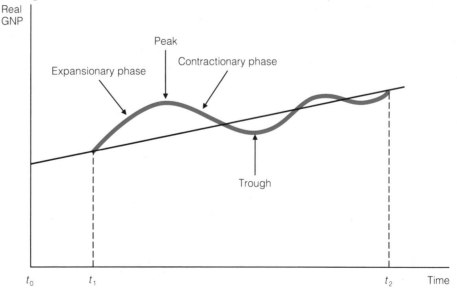

process, investment expenditures are magnified in the system *because* of the increased growth rate of output and sales. Additional capital investment creates an expansionary phase of the business cycle (again, see Figure 2). The expansionary phase is characterized by the struggle to hire more labor and other inputs in order to expand business activity and production; in addition, there are new net additions to investment and the capital stock.

If the economy is producing close to capacity—where labor, raw materials, and available capital goods are scarce—higher prices may accompany this phase (which is why the vertical axis of Figure 2 shows *real* GNP). With no influence other than a new, higher expected growth in sales, the rate of growth in real GNP eventually slows owing to these resource scarcities, and new investment expenditures slow. As actual sales of goods and services grow at a slower rate, businesses desire smaller new net additions to the capital stock and hence reduce investment spending. A peak of the cycle is reached, and business activity, measured in real GNP, begins to decline. Workers are laid off and plant production is reduced in this contractionary phase of the cycle. Existing capital depreciates, or "wears out" with no new net investment. At some point, the decline in real GNP finally slows down; a bottom, or trough, of the business cycle is experienced, and the process starts over again.

Figure 2 shows the cycle of output swings getting smaller, ultimately reaching stable equilibrium at hypothetical time t_2. However, is the steady state of GNP growth outcome likely in the real world? The answer is no; there is too much uncertainty about investment and income. The likely scenario is an economy in a perpetual state of flux, with recurring cycles of business expansion (and possible inflation) and contraction. In the Keynesian view of the world, even the act of saving may produce economic contractions.

Contractionary and Expansionary Gaps

Contractionary gap:
The amount by which total planned expenditures at the level of full-employment income fall short of the level required to generate full-employment income; also called a recessionary gap.

Expansionary gap:
The amount by which total planned expenditures at the level of full-employment income exceed the level required to generate full-employment without inflation; also called an inflationary gap.

Failure of the private economy to provide stable growth and predictable, stable levels of full employment led to Keynes's fundamental criticism of classical economics. Though Keynes himself did not discuss a business cycle, in his view the private economy was erratic and subject to long-run periods of large-scale unemployment and low production levels. In terms of Figure 2, the contractionary phase of the cycle would engender more and greater pessimism about future business conditions, keeping the economy in a contractionary phase of the cycle for a very long period of time. Only accident, not dependable market forces as the classical economists had maintained, would produce a stable equilibrium at full employment with no inflation.

For our more familiar income-expenditures approach to the macroeconomy, Keynes envisioned the economy as reaching, and remaining in, either a contractionary gap or an expansionary gap. A **contractionary gap** (sometimes called a recessionary gap) exists when equilibrium output is less than full-employment output. This is so because the level of total expenditures that would exist at full employment would be insufficient to purchase total output. Inventories would pile up, and the level of output would adjust to a lower equilibrium level as businesses cut back production. An **expansionary gap** (sometimes called an inflationary gap), the opposite situation, means that total private expenditures exceed those expenditures necessary to produce a full-employment level of income without inflation.[1] Excess expenditures, in other words, put pressure on the employment of resources. Since the economy cannot push output beyond its production possibilities frontier, inflation is created.

These gaps can be illustrated graphically. Figure 3 shows the two possible equilibrium positions for the private economy. In Figure 3a, private spending results in an equilibrium at point E. Private consumption and investment spending produce an equilibrium income (and level of employment) Y_E. Income level Y_E is not, however, a full-employment level of income. Workers are laid off and other resources are unemployed, as indicated by the spending or contractionary gap represented at income level Y_F, the level needed for full employment without inflation. The contractionary gap in the private economy (AB in the figure) presents the amount of additional consumption and investment spending that would be necessary to bring the economy to a full-employment equilibrium.

Figure 3b depicts the opposite situation. Consumption and investment spending produce equilibrium and a level of employment at Y_E. Full employ-

---

FIGURE 3

(a) A contractionary, or recessionary, gap exists when private spending is insufficient to bring the economy to full employment without inflation. Y_E is the equilibrium income reached by private spending and investment. Unemployment is high and production is low, however, with a contractionary gap AB represented at Y_F, the level needed for full employment without inflation. (b) An expansionary gap results when private spending exceeds the resource capabilities of the economy. Such excess spending creates inflation. Equilibrium at Y_E is in excess of the level Y_F needed for full employment without inflation. The excess spending creates pressure on the economy to expand, usually causing inflation.

Contractionary and Expansionary Gaps

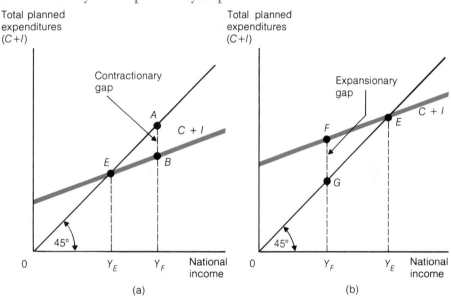

(a)   (b)

---

[1]The expansionary gap is also called an inflationary gap, but the amount of inflation produced by excess spending depends on how close the economy is to maximum capacity. When the economy is on its production possibilities frontier, no additional output is possible and the excess spending produces pure inflation.

ment without inflation occurs at the lower income level Y_F, however. Spending in excess of what is needed for the full-employment income level Y_F creates pressures on the economy to expand. Because resources are limited, these pressures usually create inflation, a general rise in prices. An expansionary gap exists in the amount represented by FG at full-employment income level Y_F. This gap represents the amount of excess consumption and investment that causes inflation at full employment.

GOVERNMENT SPENDING AND TAXATION

Keynes believed that the invisible hand—those forces that would return the economy to full-employment equilibrium without inflation—was seriously arthritic. Even if such forces on private spending did exist, in Keynes's opinion they would probably be unendurably slow in restoring equilibrium. Keynes argued that society should not have to endure contractionary or expansionary gaps of long duration. Since automatic forces were unreliable, he saw discretionary government interventions as necessary. Keynes felt that macroeconomic management should be entrusted to the central government, which theoretically has the ability to adjust aggregate spending in line with national economic goals by the use of its two major budget weapons: government spending and taxation. Changes in one or both of these areas constitute fiscal policy, the object of which is the manipulation of total spending in the economy. In this section we will examine the macroeconomic effects of government spending, taxation, and foreign trade; in the final section of the chapter, we will analyze how leakages and injections to total expenditures can be manipulated to control the whole economy.

Government Expenditures

In the context of the basic Keynesian income-expenditures model, government spending (G) is an addition to total private spending, represented graphically by raising the $C + I$ curve to account for the new source of spending. (In adding government spending, we are relaxing one of the simplifying assumptions of our basic model discussed in Chapter 9.)

Once a government sector is incorporated into the model, the equilibrium production level is that at which output is equal to consumption (demand from households) plus investment (demand from businesses) plus government spending on goods and services (demand from the government sector). Previously, we had operated under the assumption that the level of government purchases of goods and services was zero. Then, total spending consisted of household spending (consumption) plus business spending (investment).

Government spending can take many forms and have many (sometimes conflicting) objectives. For example, in one sense the government behaves like a business, purchasing inputs used in its daily operations, such as labor, machinery, and buildings. In another sense, the government acts like a consumer, purchasing products for its own use, such as missile systems, tanks, ammunition, and airplanes. An extensive and controversial type of government spending does not result in the outright purchase of goods and services:

transfer payments or "negative taxes" that redistribute income among various groups in society—from rich to poor, from able to disabled, from healthy to sick, from employed to unemployed. These transfer payments are not included in our definition of government purchases of goods and services; government spending, which we will designate as G, thus includes only purchases of goods and services.

Keep in mind that a government's decision about how much to spend is somewhat different from private decisions to consume or invest. A major difference is that the government is a not-for-profit sector of the economy. Its decisions are often not motivated by private profit or economic efficiency. Furthermore, its spending is not constrained by its income in tax receipts. Congress can, and often does, spend far more than it takes in in the form of taxes, issuing government bonds or creating money to cover the difference. Because government spending is not constrained by government tax collections, enormous budget deficits have built up in recent years, causing much concern among the electorate and in Congress. One reflection of this concern is the broad support for a balanced budget amendment to the Constitution (see the Economics in Action at the end of this chapter). It is dangerous to ignore the consequences of budget deficits, but in this first approach we will do so to keep the model simple.

To further simplify the analysis, we will assume that government expenditures to purchase goods and services actually are **autonomous government expenditures;** in other words, they do not depend in any predetermined way on national income. Thus we may write, as we did previously for investment, $G = G_0$ to indicate that government expenditures are independent of income. Total spending can now be redefined as follows:

$$C + I + G_0 = \text{total expenditures.}$$

Graphically, the addition of autonomous government spending, G, results in a parallel upward shift of the total spending function. In Figure 4a, the $C_0 + I_0 + G_0$ curve is higher than the $C_0 + I_0$ curve at each level of national income by whatever amount of G_0 government decides to spend. Notice that the addition of government spending to the total expenditures curve has the effect of moving the total spending curve to an intersection point higher up the 45-degree line. In other words, government expenditure, taken by itself, is expansionary; it leads to a higher level of equilibrium income.

Government expenditures are also an injection into the expenditures stream. In Figure 4b, government expenditures in the amount of G_0 are added vertically to private investment expenditures of I_0. Since there are no leakages in this simple model other than private saving, equilibrium occurs where saving—the leakage from the income-spending stream—is equal to the sum of investment and government spending injections into the income stream. The equilibrium level of income and output is equal to that produced in the total expenditures approach to income determination shown in Figure 4a.

The Effects of Taxation

To introduce the concept and effect of government spending, we merely acknowledged the impact of an injection of new spending on the macroeconomy. In fact, government spending decisions are rarely made in a budgetary vacuum. Decisions about taxes—both their level and their structure—almost always

Autonomous government expenditures:
Government expenditures that are independent of the level of income.

FIGURE 4

The introduction of government spending increases total spending and the equilibrium level of income. (a) With government spending of G_0 added to autonomous consumption and investment, $C_0 + I_0$, total income rises from Y_0 to Y_1. (b) An equivalent level of income appears in a leakage-injection analysis. The saving leakage, S, is equated to the investment and government spending injections, $I_0 + G_0$, to determine an equilibrium level of income.

Effects of Government Expenditures on Total Spending

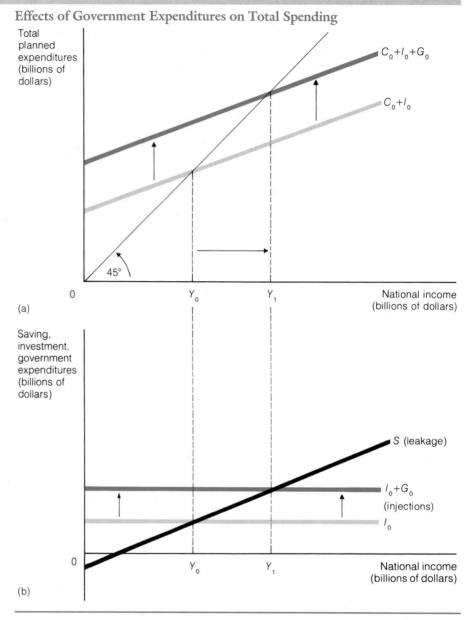

(a)

(b)

accompany decisions about government spending. We will disregard changes in tax structure and concentrate on the effects on output and employment of changes in the level of taxes. Taxes represent a leakage from the income-expenditures flow. In this respect they are like savings and for analytical purposes can be treated in the same way as savings. (You might think of taxes as "public saving" in conjunction with the private decision to withhold from spending a part of national income.) The fact that taxes represent involuntary saving does not concern us for the moment because the macroeconomic effects do not depend on whether saving is voluntary or involuntary.

To determine the effect of taxes on the macroeconomy we must ask, Who pays taxes? The answer, of course, is that consumers (and, to a lesser extent, businesses) do. The effect of taxes, therefore, is primarily to lower planned consumption insofar as taxes reduce the disposable income received by households, the income left after taxes. We must refine another assumption in light of government spending. As we saw earlier, when government is not a factor in the economy, several of the aggregate income measures are identical to each other. But once we subtract taxes from the national income, national income and disposable income are no longer the same. Disposable income is equal to national income minus the amount of taxes paid. Total spending is, therefore, a function of disposable aggregate income once taxes are admitted into the analysis. However, the purpose of the analysis is to determine equilibrium national income. As such, all of the figures and graphs we use measure national income on the horizontal axis. When the difference between national income and disposable income changes as a result of tax changes, the result is to alter consumption at every level of national income (and therefore total spending). When taxes change, the consumption function shifts when it is plotted against national income. This same explanation is, of course, applicable to the saving function.

Exactly how do taxes affect spending and saving levels? Let us assume for convenience that taxes are paid out of household income only and that businesses are not taxed. In Chapter 9 we saw that any increase in household income will be distributed between consumption and saving and that once we know the marginal propensity to save (*MPS*), we know the percentage of the change in income allocated to each use. What works for injections to household income works in reverse for leakages from household income. That is to say, facing a higher tax bill (a lower disposable household income), households will finance the higher level of taxes partly at the expense of current consumption and partly at the expense of future consumption, or saving. This is true of any kind of tax increase. But the effect of the tax on the shape of the consumption and saving curves depends on the type of tax levied.

Lump-Sum Taxes. In order to concentrate on the effect that taxation has on equilibrium output, assume that the type of tax the government levies is a **lump-sum tax,** whose effect is straightforward: Every income earner is taxed the same amount, say $100. Each dollar increase in lump-sum tax revenue collected by government results in a dollar lost from household disposable income. An increase in the lump-sum tax therefore shifts the consumption curve downward, but the curve does not shift downward by the full amount of the tax because the saving schedule is also shifted downward. If *MPC* equals 0.8 and *MPS* equals 0.2, then every dollar increase in the lump-sum tax will reduce consumption by 80 cents and reduce saving by 20 cents. The downward shifts in consumption and saving curves will be parallel; a lump-sum tax means that the tax amount is the same regardless of the level of income. Figure 5 shows the shifts in consumption and saving curves resulting from the imposition of a lump-sum tax.

In Figure 5a, the imposition of a lump-sum tax on each household causes household consumption to decline by 80 percent of the tax because the *MPC* is 0.8. (Given any level of nominal income, disposable income, *DI,* falls by the amount of the tax. Since consumption is dependent on disposable income, consumption falls by $MPC \times \Delta DI$.) If the lump-sum tax is $100, the shift from $C_0 + I_0 + G_0$ to $C_1 + I_0 + G_0$ represents an $80 cut in household expenditures at every level of aggregate income. In Figure 5b, the shift of the

FIGURE 5

A lump-sum tax decreases both consumption and saving. (a) The decrease in consumption from C_0 to C_1 is determined by the *MPC*. If *MPC* = 0.8, a lump-sum tax reduces consumption by 80 percent of each tax dollar paid. A lump-sum tax reduces equilibrium income—in this case, represented by the shift from income level Y_0 to Y_1. (b) Imposition of the lump-sum tax reduces saving by an amount equal to the *MPS* times the tax paid, *T*. The saving function shifts downward from S_0 to S_1. The total tax leakage, *T*, is then added vertically to saving function S_1, making the total leakage $S_1 + T$. When equated to the investment and government injections, $I_0 + G_0$, equilibrium income shifts to Y_1.

Effects of a Lump-Sum Tax on Aggregate Household Spending and Saving

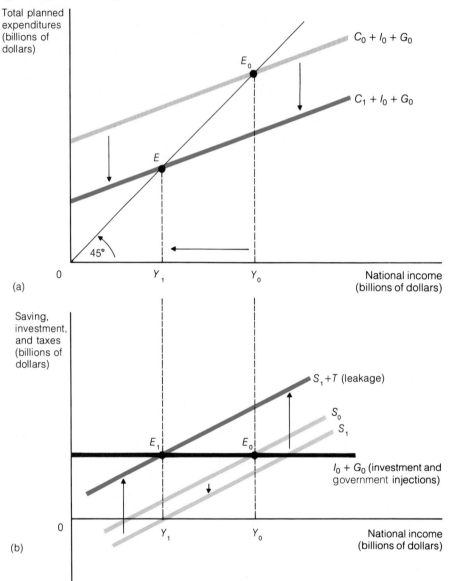

The effect of a tax increase, taken by itself, is contractionary. It causes a reduction in aggregate income and output. This point is readily seen in Figure 5a, where the effect of the tax is to reduce national income equilibrium from Y_0 to Y_1. Likewise, in the leakages-injection approach illustrated in Figure 5b, a new equilibrium is attained where the sum of the leakages, $S_1 + T$, equals the sum of the injections, $I_0 + G_0$. Equilibrium occurs at income level Y_1.

The Effects of Foreign Trade on Equilibrium Income

Previously, we have operated under the assumption that all goods produced in the United States are sold here and that all goods purchased by American households, business firms, and government agencies are made in the United States. There was a time when the foreign sector could be ignored without sacrificing believability; the United States used to be relatively self-sufficient. No more. Now, any realistic economic model must include a foreign sector. Fortunately, incorporating a foreign sector into our basic Keynesian model is easy to do. First, the notion of equilibrium income must be modified slightly. With foreign trade, equilibrium occurs when domestic production of goods and services is equal to total spending for those goods and services, including spending by foreign buyers. In other words **exports** (X), defined as spending by foreign households, business firms, or government agencies on goods produced in the United States, must be added to C, I, and G as a component of total spending. At the same time, the model must be altered to take imports into account. A portion of consumption spending, business spending, and government spending may be on goods produced abroad, and such expenditures do not represent demand for domestically produced goods. Therefore, if we define **imports** (M) as total spending on foreign goods, we must subtract M from total spending. Total spending, then, is equal to $C + I + G + (X - M)$, and the equilibrium level of national income is that level at which Y is equal to $C + I + G + (X - M)$.

It is also possible to use the injections and leakages approach to determine the equilibrium level of income in a model that contains a foreign sector. Total injections equal $I + G + X$, and total leakages equal $S + T + M$. Equilibrium income is where $(I + G + X) = (S + T + M)$.

The concept of a foreign trade component of total domestic spending is intuitive. The import of cashmere sweaters by consumers, computer chips by business investors, or titanium by the U.S. government replaces domestic spending by these groups and represents increased demands on *foreign* producers. Increased demand by U.S. consumers, investors, and by the U.S. government generates income in foreign countries. On the other hand, exports of American wheat, machinery, and airplanes represent demand for domestic products. These components of total spending (both positive and negative) must be compared before we can determine whether the trade sector contributes to or detracts from total expenditures in the United States. When imports exceed exports, total spending declines at home. The opposite occurs when our exports of goods and services exceed our purchases abroad.

In recent years, the United States was a net importer of goods and services to the tune of over $100 billion per year. This means that Americans collectively spent over $100 billion more on goods and services produced abroad than foreigners spent on U.S. products. In terms of the Keynesian model, this means that total domestic expenditure on all goods and services was billions of dollars less than it would have been had our exports equaled our imports. This international trade deficit has a number of implications for the U.S. economy, but we postpone a more complete discussion of foreign trade and its effects until Chapters 21 and 22, where both real and financial aspects of international transactions are considered.

Exports:
Expenditures by foreigners on domestically produced goods.

Imports:
Expenditures by domestic residents on goods produced in foreign countries.

Total Expenditures: A Recap

In summary, equilibrium income (and, by implication, the amount of employment hired to produce it) may be determined either by examining total expenditures, $C + I + G + (X - M)$, or by equating leakages to injections, $S + T + M = I + G + X$. Total income, the result of total planned or desired expenditures, can be viewed schematically in Figure 6 as subtractions from or additions to, leakages from or injections to, private consumption expenditures. The net effect of these leakages and injections from private consumption is that a specific level of total spending is determined, which in turn determines a specific level of income. This level of income is produced by some quantity of resources, including labor usage. Total employment or jobs filled is therefore the product of consumer spending modified by leakages and injections.

Countercyclical fiscal policy:
Changes in government expenditures or taxes that are designed to reverse changes in private expenditures or savings that produce unemployment or inflation.

COUNTERCYCLICAL FISCAL POLICIES

Having reached an understanding of how the presence of a government sector influences the economy, we now move the discussion toward a fuller understanding of the Keynesian prescriptions for **countercyclical fiscal policy.** Fiscal policy, as we have already noted, means budget actions: government expendi-

FIGURE 6

Total Planned Expenditures Determine Total Income and Employment

The Keynesian model of total spending can be viewed as a series of injections into and leakages from the flow of income. Savings, taxes, and imports are subtracted from private consumption expenditures; investment, government, and export spending injections are added, yielding total planned or desired expenditures. These expenditures determine an equilibrium income and output, at the level of income at which $S + T + M = I + G + X$.

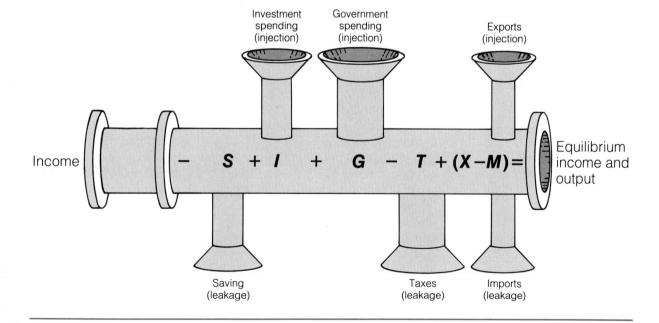

ture changes, tax changes, or a combination of the two. To say that a policy is countercyclical means that the policy seeks to correct whatever phase of the business cycle—contractionary or expansionary—the economy happens to be in. In a recession, for example, total spending, output, and employment are below the full-employment equilibrium level. In such circumstances, countercyclical fiscal policy would seek to raise the level of total expenditures to the full-employment level. During inflation, a countercyclical fiscal policy must try to induce a lower level of total spending. But knowing the appropriate direction of budgetary changes does not guarantee that the exact equilibrium target will be achieved. To do that, policy must be guided by knowledge of the relevant expenditure multipliers. Expenditure multipliers play a major role in the following analysis. Any autonomous expenditure is subject to the multiplier process; thus it is possible to identify consumption multipliers, investment multipliers, government spending multipliers, export multipliers, import multipliers, and so on.

Fiscal Policy to Deal with a Recession

To see how fiscal policies are used to change the direction of the business cycle, let us first suppose that the economy is in a recession. Imagine that government economic policy-makers have determined that the actual level of aggregate income-output is $50 billion below the full-employment level. In Figure 7, the government's problem can be seen as that of moving the economy from an income level of $2.50 trillion to one of $2.55 trillion (an increase of $50 billion). What is required in this case is an increase in G or a decrease in T, either of which would lead to an increase in total spending, $C + I + G + (X - M)$. If government simply increases G by $50 billion, it will overshoot

---

FIGURE 7

Government Spending to Eliminate a Contractionary Gap in Income

If total spending, $C_0 + I_0 + G_0 + (X_0 - M_0)$, is not great enough to achieve full employment, then an increase in government expenditures may restore full employment. In this example, initial expenditures, $C_0 + I_0 + G_0 + (X_0 - M_0)$, are insufficient to create a full-employment level of income. Government expenditures are increased to $C_0 + I_0 + G_1 + (X_0 - M_0)$, and, through a multiplier process, the contractionary gap, AB, is eliminated.

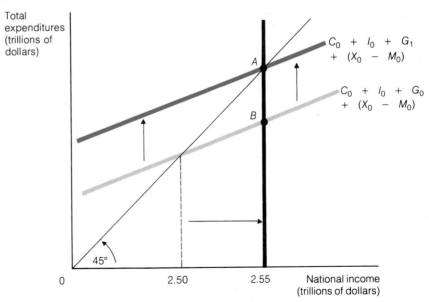

the desired target because the new additional expenditure of $50 billion will be multiplied through various rounds of spending into a much larger increase. What, then, is the appropriate fiscal stimulus?

The answer depends on the size of the contractionary gap, whether households or businesses are the ultimate recipients of government expenditures, and the value of the relevant multiplier. In the following analysis, assume (1) that only households will receive the government expenditures and (2) that *MPC* equals 0.8. We can determine the size of the contractionary gap, *AB,* and design a fiscal policy to eliminate it.

Since we know the value of the *MPC,* we can compute the consumption multiplier (the only relevant multiplier in this case):

$$ k = \frac{1}{1 - MPC} = \frac{1}{0.2} = 5. $$

We know the size of the income gap ($50 billion), and we know that whatever increase in government spending occurs will be multiplied by 5. Therefore, we can determine the size of the contractionary gap, *AB,* by the formula

$$ \text{Contractionary gap} = \frac{\text{income gap}}{k} = \frac{\$50 \text{ billion}}{5} = \$10 \text{ billion.} $$

In this case, an increase in total expenditures of $10 billion will, via the multiplier, produce an increase in aggregate income of $50 billion, thereby moving the economy to its full-employment equilibrium level.

There are two ways that fiscal policy could produce the additional $10 billion expenditure. The most direct way is to increase government expenditures, *G,* by $10 billion. We assume that this direct injection to the spending stream is not subject to any leakages. Therefore, the full $10 billion enters the expenditure flow at once.

An indirect way to accomplish the same thing is to cut taxes to stimulate consumption spending, as shown in Figure 8. Remember, however, that tax changes do not produce expenditure changes of the same dollar amount because taxes are paid partly at the expense of consumption and partly at the expense of saving. Against a contractionary gap of $10 billion, a lump-sum tax cut of $10 billion will only induce additional consumption of $8 billion ($MPC \times \Delta T$). To raise consumption spending by $10 billion requires in this instance a tax cut of more than $10 billion to offset the leakage of saving that occurs when household disposable income increases. A lump-sum tax cut of $12.5 billion, given that $MPC = 0.8$, would be required to raise aggregate consumption by $10 billion and thereby eliminate the $10 billion contractionary gap.

Government expenditure changes are more direct and more powerful, dollar for dollar, than tax changes of the same amount. This must be kept in mind when expenditures and taxes are changed simultaneously.

Fiscal Policy to Deal with Inflation

Once full employment is reached, further increases in total spending will tend to drive the price level upward, creating an expansionary gap. An expansionary gap develops because raw materials, labor, and inputs of all kinds become increasingly scarce. GNP, the economy's output, can be pushed only so far by excessive spending and only at the cost of causing inflation to accelerate. The

FIGURE 8

If total spending, $C_0 + I_0 + G_0 + (X_0 - M_0)$, is not great enough to achieve full employment, then total expenditures may be increased by a tax cut. In this example, if taxes fall, then consumption increases from C_0 to C_1 to achieve full employment. A tax cut increases the disposable income of consumers, causing them to spend more.

Taxation to Eliminate a Contractionary Gap

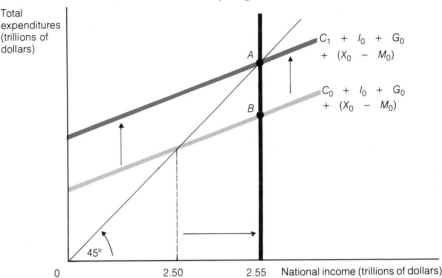

reverse of a given policy that works in one phase of the business cycle works for the opposite phase of the cycle. If the economy is characterized by inflation and full (or "overfull") employment, the appropriate fiscal response would be a decrease in government expenditures or an increase in taxes.

An expansionary gap, as discussed earlier, is the difference between the existing level of total spending and the desired level. The trick is to bring the actual level of total expenditure, $C + I + G + (X_0 - M_0)$, in line with the desired full-employment level. As in the case of contractionary gaps, the correction can be achieved in one of two ways: either a change of government expenditures or a change of taxes.

Assume that the economy is operating at a level of nominal output-income too high for full employment. (Since we are talking about the effects of inflation, the concepts of real and nominal come into play.) In what sense could the nominal level of income be too high? "More is better than less" when it comes to economic output, but there are two factors to consider. First, by definition, aggregate real output in the macroeconomy cannot increase after full employment has been reached because the economy is already at a point on the production possibilities frontier. Second, income measures beyond the full-employment level mean that a constant amount of goods and services is valued at higher unit prices, the effect of inflation. When the newspapers say that the economy is "overheating" they mean that a lower level of national income is preferred to the present higher one. Too high a level of total spending produces inflation.

The problem posed by inflation, then, is how to reduce the level of nominal income by some amount, say by $50 billion. With a multiplier of 5, a reduction in spending of one-fifth the observed income gap will produce the desired effect. This result can be achieved by cutting government expenditures by $10 billion, leaving taxes unchanged. Likewise, it can be achieved by leaving government expenditures unchanged and raising lump-sum taxes by $12.5 billion (to reduce the consumption component of aggregate demand by $10 billion). The mechanics of these changes are exactly the reverse of those used in the contractionary-recessionary situation. Changes in taxes or government expenditures therefore composed Keynes's arsenal of methods for counteracting severely contractionary or inflationary swings of the business cycle.

Keynesian Economics in Historical Context

Was Keynes right about the ability of government to use countercyclical fiscal policies to counteract extreme phases of the business cycle? Although the policy and theoretical issues are complex, it is probably the case that certain theoretical and political effects unforeseen by Keynes have inhibited the ability of government to control the business cycle and thereby guarantee continuous inflation-free levels of full employment and maximum economic growth.

Keynes was primarily concerned with the economic and human costs of economic depression (or, if you prefer, an extreme contractionary phase of the business cycle). His advice, though not fully implemented in Western democracies during the Great Depression of the 1930s and early 1940s, was at least partially responsible for the increased economic role of government at the time and, perhaps, for the absence of prolonged and serious depressions after World War II. But problems other than depression became paramount in the U.S. economy of the late 1960s, 1970s, and 1980s—particularly high rates of inflation combined with slowed economic growth. Keynesian economics was not explicitly designed to deal with these problems. Further, U.S. fiscal history since the beginning of the Vietnam War may have contributed greatly to contemporary difficulties. (In this regard, see Focus, "Deficits and Democracy.")

How could actual fiscal policy have caused these problems? The use of Keynesian countercyclical fiscal policy means that balancing government expenditures and receipts—a balanced budget—takes on secondary importance. The cumulative effect of unbalanced budgets is ignored by this approach. As we have seen, antirecessionary fiscal policy requires raising government expenditures or reducing taxes, either of which tends to produce a budget deficit. For reasons that will be explained more fully in Chapter 13, the history of fiscal policy in the United States has been one in which, since World War II, annual deficits have outnumbered annual surpluses by a margin of almost twenty to one, a policy that Keynes probably would not have supported. A deficit implies that government expenditures exceed revenues, further implying the need for creation of money and credit. Credit creation, in turn, has implications in the money markets of the macroeconomy, the most important of which is inflation.

A major deficiency of the income-expenditures model we have employed to this point is that it excludes monetary variables, particularly prices. Therefore, it does not tell all of the macroeconomic story. Prices affect both consumption and investment spending, which in turn affect macroeconomic activity. In other words, simple Keynesian economics leaves us ill-equipped to adequately analyze recent experience with unemployment and inflation. A more complete Keynesian theory of total expenditures, one including prices and other monetary factors, will help us better understand today's macroeconomic problems. This expanded theory will be presented in Chapters 11 and 12.

FOCUS Deficits and Democracy

Deficits occur when government expenditures exceed government income from taxation in any given fiscal year. The national debt is the sum at a certain point in time of all prior deficits. During the 1980s, huge deficits—on the order of $100 billion to $180 billion per year—were incurred by the federal government, which pushed the national debt over $2 *trillion* in 1990. Nondemocratic countries do not appear to experience deficits and debt to this degree.[a] Were these deficits, and the debt they created, the product of overt discretionary action to eliminate contractionary gaps as supported by Keynes or were they simply the products of institutions peculiar to democracy? While Keynes likely would not have supported such deficits, it may be that they are inevitable given the nature of the democratic political process; in other words, there may be an incentive to supply and demand deficits in a democracy.

The right to supply government products of all kinds is temporary, subject to renewal at election time and open to competition (Democrats versus Republicans). Once in office, a politician is confronted with a choice for financing the desired output of the public sector between raising taxes or borrowing funds and creating deficits. Naturally, this choice will be influenced by the preferences of voters, but there may be reasons for supplying deficits that are *independent* of voter choice. The key to understanding politicians' preferences for debt finance is the fact that responsibility for the

physical facilities (roads, buildings, bombers, national parks) owned by the community at large is assigned to politicians only temporarily. These temporary suppliers can issue outstanding claims (debt) without being personally liable for such debts—other than each politician's minimal *pro rata* share of the national debt as a taxpayer. Deficit finance may be preferred because it is less costly than the alternative—the decidedly unpopular tax increase.

Why would some voter-demanders of political products and services reveal a preference for deficit finance? Those who earn little or no income and who receive large net benefits from the government have little incentive to demand restraint from politicians. The taxes required to finance deficits and to fund the government's debt are applied either to human capital or to nonhuman capital. Since taxes fall disproportionately on human capital (in the form of income taxes) in most democracies, including the United States, some voters, especially *older* voters, have an incentive to support deficit finance over direct pay-as-you-go taxation to finance new government expenditures. In effect, these voters are electing to pass part of the burden of financing government expenditures on to succeeding generations of taxpayers.

There are incentives for both politicians and voters to prefer deficits over increased taxes to finance new expenditures. Politicians naturally want to get reelected; voters—some voters at least—would like to pass the bill for present enjoyment on to succeeding generations. Without an effective balanced budget constraint on federal politicians or on the financing process, democracies seem to have a built-in tendency to run deficits.

[a]See W. Mark Crain and Robert B. Ekelund, Jr., "Deficits and Democracy," *Southern Economic Journal* 44 (April 1978), pp. 813–28.

SUMMARY

1. A multiplier is calculated by dividing a change in income by the change in autonomous expenditures that caused the change in income. The multiplier is the reciprocal of the marginal propensity to save, or $1/MPS$.

2. A multiplier may be applied to any change in autonomous expenditures. For example, if the autonomous portion of consumption expenditures increases, income changes by the value of the expenditures multiplied by the reciprocal of the *MPS*.

3. Fiscal policy consists of budgetary action taken by the central government. More specifically, fiscal policy means congressional action to adjust either the level of taxes or the level of government expenditures to achieve a stable level of growth.

4. An increase in government expenditures, G, is expansionary. A decrease in government expenditures is contractionary.

5. An increase in the level of taxes, T, is contractionary. A decrease in the level of taxes is expansionary. Insofar as tax changes affect private spending only indirectly, a tax change is less effective than the same dollar amount of change in government expenditures.

6. Output effects from changes in G or T are multiplied. Although the value of the consumption multiplier ($1/MPS$) is the same in both cases, the output effects are different because a $1 change in taxes affects consumption less than a $1 change in government expenditures does.

7. Keynes's macroeconomic theory and his remedies for macroeconomic ills, while probably appropriate for periods of contraction and widespread unemployment, omitted crucial monetary variables, especially prices, from primary consideration. A modern and useful theory with a more complete ability to explain inflation and other contemporary macroeconomic problems requires the consideration of such factors.

KEY TERMS

investment multiplier
autonomous consumption multiplier
contractionary gap

expansionary gap
autonomous government expenditures
lump-sum tax

exports
imports
countercyclical fiscal policy

QUESTIONS FOR REVIEW AND DISCUSSION

1. What effect will a $30 billion decrease in autonomous investment have on total expenditures if the MPC is 0.9?
2. What is the essential implication of the investment multiplier? What is multiplied when autonomous investment changes?
3. How does the consumption multiplier differ from the investment multiplier? Will a $50 billion change in autonomous consumption expenditures have the same effect as a $50 billion change in autonomous investment expenditures when the MPS is 0.2?
4. Suppose autonomous consumption expenditures are $50 billion, autonomous investment expenditures are $20 billion, and the MPC is 0.8. What is the equilibrium level of income? What happens to the equilibrium level of income if autonomous consumption falls to $20 billion?
5. Does the full effect of changes in investment occur instantly? How long should it take?

6. What determines the level of investment expenditures? Does the level of investment expenditures determine the level of income or does the level of income determine the level of investment?
7. What was Keynes's basic dispute with the classical economists? What were his recommendations for smoothing out the business cycle?
8. What fiscal policy would Keynes recommend for large-scale unemployment? What would he recommend for inflation?
9. What can government do to offset a leakage from the income-expenditures flow? What can it do to offset an expansionary injection into the flow?
10. What effect does a lump-sum tax of $20 billion have on total expenditures if the MPC is 0.9? Would it have a greater effect if the MPC were 0.8?
11. Does an increase in government expenditures of $20 billion have the same effect on total expenditures as a $20 billion tax cut? Why?

PROBLEM

Suppose that total expenditures are $250 billion short of the full-employment level of income and that $MPC = 0.7$. In the Keynesian framework, by how much would government expenditures have to increase to bring the economy to full employment?

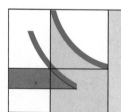

ECONOMICS IN ACTION
Should Congress Be Forced to Balance the Budget?

There is much grass-roots support for a constitutional amendment to balance the budget. Since 1977, thirty-two states (two short of the required number) have called for a constitutional convention to consider such an amendment.

In August 1982, the Senate approved the amendment by a vote of 69–31 with all senators present, but it was rejected in the House, 236–187, only 46 votes short of the two-thirds majority needed to amend the Constitution. In 1986, a Senate balanced-budget resolution came within one vote of passage (66–34). However, not until the summer of 1990 did the matter again reach the floor of either chamber for a vote.

In July 1990, the House rejected a balanced-budget amendment 271–150, seven votes short of approval. The House did approve a balanced-budget statute, which would require the president and the House and Senate budget committees to at least *present* a balanced budget every year (they could present unbalanced budgets as well). Support for a constitutional amendment persists, however, fueled by frustration and anxiety over Congress' seeming inability to do anything about budget deficits. What would be the economic effects of such an amendment? Consider the diverse views of three economists, all past members of the Council of Economic Advisers.[a]

William A. Niskanen, member of President Ronald Reagan's council, defends a constitutional amendment as appropriate and workable. It is appropriate, in Niskanen's view, as simply another economic rule like those already enshrined in the Constitution regarding property rights. A balanced budget rule is defensible, moreover, to help prevent the economic excesses of deficits and deficit finance. Niskanen argues that a constitutional amendment would not necessarily lead to a total abandonment of countercyclical fiscal policy by Congress; a supermajority in Congress could override the balanced budget in certain economic conditions, but violation of the balanced budget rule would require broad support in Congress. As Niskanen has argued: "Fiscal rules . . . are like a dam or like a fence—they can be valuable even if they have some openings."

James V. Tobin, Yale University professor and 1981 Nobel laureate in economics who served on President John F. Kennedy's Council of Economic Advisers, argues against the proposed amendment. How, asks Tobin, could the mid-1980s yearly budget deficits of approximately $200 billion be corrected without creating another Great Depression? Aside from the immediate problem of eliminating big contemporary deficits, Tobin believes that the amendment would actually increase economic instability. Escape valves to a strictly balanced budget would be open, but delays could be caused by minorities in Congress, which could be very costly for the economy. Tax receipts fall during business cycle contractions as incomes fall, and they rise during expansions as incomes rise, creating built-in stabilization in the economy. These stabilizers would tend to become ineffective over the business cycle, as deficits or surpluses would force Congress to enact procyclical spending and taxing policies. Def-

icits and surpluses, in other words, are themselves affected by business cycles. Tobin, in sum, thinks that abandonment of discretion in the use of fiscal policy would eliminate the insurance that has guarded the economy against depressions since the end of World War II.

Hendrik S. Houthakker, Harvard professor and economic adviser to President Richard M. Nixon, agrees with Tobin that a balanced budget amendment would be useless in view of the size of present deficits, but he argues that deficits must be harnessed. To Houthakker, broad-based public support for an amendment is merely an indication that the public is disenchanted with fiscal policy as it has been conducted over the past twenty-five years. Constant stimulus of the economy—witnessed by only one budget surplus (in 1969) in the previous twenty-eight years—has been self-defeating. Like overprescribed antibiotics, deficits will not work now when we really need them. As Houthakker says: "We have tried to prime the pump even when it was already working overtime."

The problem, in Houthakker's view, is that the federal budget does not follow sound budgetary principles. For one thing, it makes no distinctions between capital and current budgets. For example, on the assumption that bridges and highways will last forever, no provisions have been made for maintenance of the nation's capital stock. Budget reform is needed with respect to both revenues and expenditures. Both Social Security and Great Society income transfers and entitlements have grown dramatically without adequate provisions for financing. Fiscal reform, in other words, must take place before any sort of constitutional amendment could be successfully implemented.

In essence, economists are not in agreement as to the desirability of a balanced budget amendment or with respect to how such an amendment would affect the macroeconomy. Some are in favor of effective legal constraints, rules that allow little or no legislative or executive discretion concerning spending or taxes. One such rule was the Gramm-Rudman-Hollings Deficit Reduction Act, which attempted to force the Congress and the president to reduce the federal budget deficit. Others argue that these strict rules on spending and taxation will, by reducing the flexibility of policymakers to respond to changing economic conditions, impede the attainment of the macroeconomic goals of full employment and stable prices.

---

[a]These views are reported in "At Issue: The Balanced Budget Amendment," *Fiscal Policy Forum* (Washington, D.C.: Tax Foundation, January 1983).

Question

Would the passage of a balanced budget amendment likely lead to a smaller total size of the federal budget? Would politicians, in other words, be apt to find less support if they voted for policies and programs that must be immediately financed through taxation?

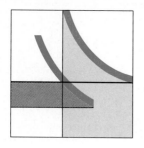

II

Aggregate Demand and Aggregate Supply

After World War II, a moderate inflation rate held off a doubling of the price level for twenty-five years. Less than ten years later, the price level doubled again. Since 1981, the acceleration of the inflation rate has slowed, but many economists believe there is a prospect of double-digit inflation in the future. By international standards, the United States has an enviable record of avoiding inflation. Peru, Mexico, Brazil, and Israel have experienced annual inflation rates in excess of 100 percent in recent years. In each case, runaway inflation has devastated the country's economy. Such experiences should teach us the importance of avoiding economic policies that lead to excessive inflation.

When we began our discussion of macroeconomics in Chapter 6, we included price stability in our list of primary macroeconomic goals. (The other two were full employment and economic growth.) Subsequent chapters developed a model that explained how the level of national income was determined. This model was used to explain unemployment and inadequate economic growth. However, in that model the price level remained unchanged; the model did not address the problems of inflation and deflation. This chapter develops a model of aggregate demand and aggregate supply in which the interaction of these two forces determines both the level of national income and the price level. We will show how shifts either in aggregate demand or in aggregate supply can cause inflation or deflation. After you complete Chapter 11 you should understand

- how price level changes cause changes in total real expenditures by consumers and businesses.
- how the aggregate demand curve relates national income and output to price level changes.
- how the aggregate supply curve is constructed and how its shape is determined by production and capacity levels.
- how shifts in aggregate demand and supply affect output and price levels.

PRICE CHANGES AND AGGREGATE DEMAND

We have defined the function $C + I + G + (X - M)$ as total expenditures. But an important distinction must be made between total expenditures and aggregate demand once the price level is explicitly recognized. The term *aggregate demand* refers to the relation between the price level of all output and the total quantity of all goods and services demanded. In other words, from here on, as we discuss contractionary and expansionary phases in the economy and proper macroeconomic policies to remedy such phases, we will be tying total real expenditures to a specific price level, a composite index of all prices in the economy. We will then vary the price level to see how such changes affect equilibrium output or income, since price level changes will affect total real expenditures.

The simple Keynesian model we have used up to this point assumes, correctly, that total expenditures are a function of national income. But it is also true that the price of something affects the amount that people choose to buy, so expenditures are determined by prices in addition to income. The factors affecting demand and supply for some particular good—textiles, Wendy's hamburgers—and the aggregate demand and supply for *all goods* are analogous. Both individual demand and aggregate demand are inversely related to price; both curves, therefore, are downward-sloping. In dealing with aggregate demand, however, we consider the effects of a declining price *level* on the aggregate demand, where each price level is associated with a different possible equilibrium of total expenditures and income. In contrast, the market for hamburgers shows how supply and demand interact to produce one possible equilibrium price and quantity in the hamburger market (see Chapter 4). Aggregate demand, as we will see in this chapter, is a locus of different points of equilibrium associated with different price levels. Aggregate supply of all goods and services produced in the economy is also shown as a function of the price level. Just as the interaction of supply and demand for hamburgers gives the equilibrium price and quantity of hamburgers, the interaction of aggregate demand and supply determines a unique price level and equilibrium quantity of *all* goods and services produced in the economy.

Price Changes and Changes in Purchasing Power

Chapter 6 defined the difference between nominal, or money, income—the income we receive in dollar terms—and real income—the purchasing power of those dollars. In times of inflation, nominal incomes may increase, yet real incomes may remain the same or even fall. Since inflation erodes the purchasing power of each dollar received, real income, or income adjusted for changes in the price level, is a more accurate measure of how the economy is performing.

Inflation affects more than income, unfortunately. It also affects wealth. The term *income* is usually taken to mean the sum of weekly, monthly, or annual earnings. **Wealth,** on the other hand, is the sum of all assets. Income is a flow variable; wealth is a stock variable. Flow variables are measured per unit of time. Speed, for example, is a flow variable—it is measured in feet per second

Wealth:
The total value of monetary plus nonmonetary assets in existence at a point in time; a stock variable.

or miles per hour. By contrast, weight is an example of a stock variable; it is defined independently of time. It is meaningful to say that someone weighs one hundred pounds without making any reference to time.

Wealth may be pecuniary (dollar-denominated, such as a savings account) or nonpecuniary (non-dollar-denominated, such as a house, auto, or Persian rug). The distinction between pecuniary and nonpecuniary wealth is important because the value of each type of wealth is affected differently by changes in the price level. Compare a $10,000 Persian rug with a $10,000 deposit in a savings account. When the price level doubles under 100 percent inflation, what happens to the real value of these two kinds of wealth? Dollar-denominated assets such as the $10,000 deposit in a savings account or a bond with a face value of $10,000 have a fixed dollar value. With a 100 percent increase in the price level, the value of a dollar-denominated asset has been cut in half, in terms of purchasing power. However, the higher price level implies that the nominal value of all non-dollar-denominated assets, including the Persian rug, has increased, assuming that prices of collectibles keep pace with the general price level. But the rug is still a rug: In real terms it is worth as much as it was before. It would now fetch $20,000 in the marketplace instead of $10,000, but the higher dollar amount would merely purchase the same amount of goods and services as $10,000 would have previously. In other words, the real value of many nonpecuniary assets (real estate, paintings, jewels) is unaffected by changes in the price level.[1]

Now contemplate the unfortunate effects of the same degree of inflation on the $10,000 savings deposit. Except in the unlikely case that the interest rate has kept pace with the 100 percent rate of inflation, the real value of the deposit will have declined. Assuming *no* interest return, the same $10,000 that would have purchased $10,000 worth of goods and services before inflation will purchase only $5,000 worth of goods and services now. In other words, price level changes bring about changes in the real value, or purchasing power, of pecuniary assets.

The Real Balance Effect

As inflation erodes the purchasing power of the money in our bank accounts and of our holdings of other dollar-denominated assets, we have to economize—buy fewer books, try to keep the old car running instead of buying an expensive new one. This change in consumption behavior that results from a change in the price level is sometimes called the **real balance effect.**

Real balance effect:
The effect on investment and consumption spending of a change in the price level that alters the real value of pecuniary assets.

If we let *MS* stand for society's entire stock of pecuniary, or dollar-denominated, assets and *P* for the aggregate price level, then the value of real balances can be expressed as MS/P. The level of real household consumption expenditures will be determined by the value of real balances as well as by the level of disposable income.

The relation between consumption and real money balances is positive, just as the relation between consumption and income is positive. If prices fall,

---

[1]The real value of nonmonetary assets can change. The belief, for example, that the purchase of Persian rugs would protect investors from inflation might mean brisk real demand increases. If the prices of Persian rugs were rising faster than the inflation rate, their real value would be increasing. Their increased real value would mean that they could be sold to purchase more goods and services than they did before the inflation.

assuming that MS remains the same, the value of real balances rises and consumers experience an enhanced wealth effect; that is, their money assets will purchase more goods and services than before. Thus, consumption will rise in response to greater real wealth. Graphically, the consumption function will shift upward, establishing a higher equilibrium level of output and employment. Conversely, if prices rise, the value of real balances declines, the consumption curve subsequently falls, and lower output and employment result. Changes in real balances are capable of inducing the same kinds of changes in total expenditures as fiscal policy manipulations (ΔG and ΔT).

We have already encountered this important concept. Recall that classical economists before Keynes generally believed that wage-price flexibility would automatically bring about total expenditure changes that would correct the cyclical swings of the macroeconomy. The logic behind this self-correcting view was as follows: If the economy slides into a recession and unemployment occurs, labor markets will be faced with an excess supply of workers. In competitive labor markets, this excess of workers will create downward pressure on wages. As wages fall, so will the unit costs of production; prices will therefore decline as well. The general decline in prices will sooner or later raise the real value of money balances, thus inducing consumers to spend more. The increased spending will thereby stimulate output and employment, lifting the economy out of the recession. In a similar fashion, the presence of inflation will eventually lead to a reduction in real balances and a consequent decline in total spending, thereby eliminating the inflationary tendencies. For the classical economists, the real balance effect on consumption helped explain the self-adjusting nature of the economy.

This important process can be fixed more precisely in graphical terms. In Figure 1, three total spending functions are shown for three alternative price levels. Given some price level P_0 and some constant level of pecuniary assets in the economy, real balances will produce some level of consumption, C_0. Consumption function C_0 and given levels of investment, government, and net foreign expenditures, I, G, $(X - M)$, produce an equilibrium level of real income Y_0.

What happens in the event of a price decline? A price reduction will increase the real value of pecuniary balances, causing an increase in the consumption component of total spending. In Figure 1, the original total spending function shifts upward to $C_1 + I + G + (X - M)$ at the new, lower price level. This new, higher total expenditures function is associated with a higher level of equilibrium income, Y_1. By the same reasoning, a rise in the price level above the initial level brings a reduction in equilibrium income to Y_2.

The Interest Rate Effect

We have seen that changes in the price level affect the purchasing power of our pecuniary assets and equilibrium income. Price level changes also affect income through the mechanism of interest rates.

Interest rates are always in the news. Consumers are highly interested in whether interest rates are high or low, rising or falling. Interest rates to some extent determine purchasing decisions—whether to buy a new car or to mortgage the purchase of a new home. Businesses are also very watchful of interest rate levels when deciding whether to make capital investments—build a warehouse, acquire new machinery, expand their inventories.

FIGURE 1

How Price Level Changes Alter Consumption Spending and Real Income

Any change in the price level from the initial level, P_0, will create a real balance effect on consumption, shifting the total spending curve upward or downward. A lower price level, P_1, is associated with a higher level of equilibrium real income, Y_1, and the total spending curve shifts upward to $C_1 + I + G + (X - M)$. A price level P_2 higher than the initial price level would, for similar reasons, be associated with a lower level of equilibrium income, Y_2, and a spending curve that shifts downward to $C_2 + I + G + (X - M)$.

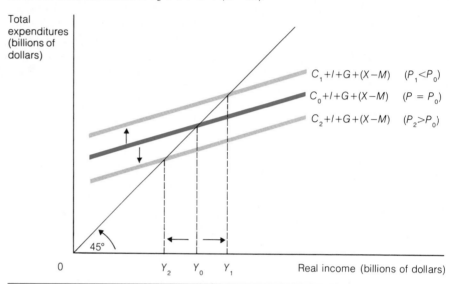

In general, interest rates depend on changes in the price level. When the price level rises, interest rates tend to rise; when the price level falls, interest rates tend to fall. As with all other goods, individuals will want to hold equilibrium quantities of real money—balances for transactions, for investments, or simply as a precautionary ("rainy day") measure. In other words, people are interested in the real value, or purchasing power, of their money balances, not in their nominal holdings of money. The value of dollar-denominated assets is inversely related to the price level, since these assets are fixed in money terms. The real supply of money is also altered by price level changes. The purchasing power of each dollar we hold rises when the price level falls and declines when the price level rises. In part, interest rates are the product of the demand for real money balances and their supply in real terms. Thus, as the real supply of these balances increases with reductions in the price level, the interest rate tends to fall. And, as the real supply of money balances declines with increases in the price level, the interest rate tends to rise. The details of this process are discussed in Chapter 17; at this point it is important to recognize that these interest rate changes affect the investment and consumption components of expenditures.

Figure 2 shows the effect of changes in the price level on interest rates. Investors react to these changes because the interest rate change alters the cost and profitability of investment projects; consumers react by changing expenditure plans, especially for durable goods (such as refrigerators) or homes. These changes in expenditures in turn cause changes in income and employ-

FIGURE 2

A rise in the price level may be related to a decrease in real income and employment via the process of investment and consumption spending. Conversely, a fall in the price level can lead to an increase in income. The lower half of the diagram shows that declines in the price level tend to lower the interest rate and expand investment and consumption expenditures. Increased production and jobs result.

The Interest Rate Effect

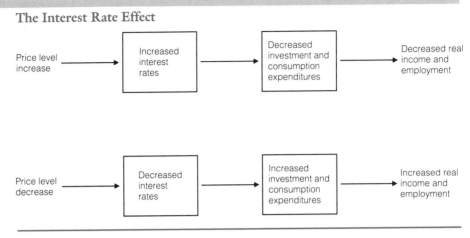

Interest rate effect:
The effect on investment spending that results from a change in the interest rate produced by a change in the price level.

ment. As prices rise (and the value of real money balances falls), output and real income decline; as prices fall, output and real income increase.

The **interest rate effect** can be viewed in the income-expenditures model depicted in Figure 3. With the price at some initial level, P_0, total expenditures equal $C + I_0 + G + (X - M)$. A decrease in the aggregate price level to P_1 will lower interest rates. Other things being equal, lower interest rates will lower the cost of all new investment projects. The consequent effect in the total expenditures model is to raise the investment function, thus stimulating the economy to a higher level of output and employment, Y_1.

Conversely, higher aggregate price levels tend to drive up interest rates. Now all new investment projects will be more costly than before, so a decline

FIGURE 3

Decreases in the price level from P_0 to P_1 lower interest rates and increase investment from I_0 to I_1. The higher level of investment increases real income from Y_0 to Y_1. Increases in the price level to P_2 increase interest rates and decrease investment to I_2 and income to Y_2.

The Price Level and Investment Spending

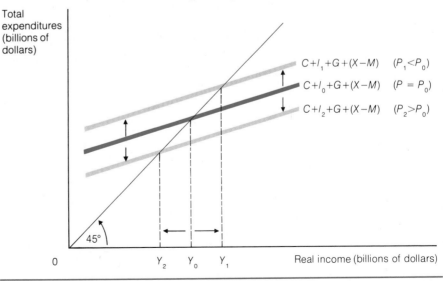

in the investment schedule can be predicted. In Figure 3, the total expenditure schedule will shift downward to $C + I_2 + G + (X - M)$ and establish a lower level of national income at Y_2.

To summarize, changes in the aggregate price level are likely to affect aggregate consumption (the real balance effect and the interest rate effect) and aggregate investment (the interest rate effect). The macroeconomy, viewed realistically, is a complex structure of relations in which the level of total expenditures is determined by the aggregate levels of income, wealth, and prices.

AGGREGATE DEMAND

Aggregate demand curve:
Graphical relation showing the different levels of national income that exist at different price levels.

In Chapter 4, we saw that all demand functions relating prices and quantity demanded are downward-sloping. This also applies to the **aggregate demand curve,** which captures the relation between the aggregate price level and real national income. The aggregate demand curve basically tells us that as the price level falls in the macroeconomy, other things being equal, households and businesses tend to buy more. Conversely, as the price level rises, other things being equal, households and businesses tend to decrease their spending. Again, a contrast between microeconomic supply and demand relations and the macroeconomic concepts is instructive. Recall from Chapter 4 that the demand curve for a particular good or service slopes downward because a price decrease for some good—say, football tickets—alters its *relative* price compared to all other goods. A lower relative price causes the student to substitute football tickets for all other goods in her budget; this substitution explains the negative slope of the demand curve. The negative slope of aggregate demand in macroeconomic theory does not depend on changes in relative prices but on changes in the price level—a relation that can be shown with the Keynesian income-expenditures model.

Deriving the Aggregate Demand Curve

Examine Figure 4, assuming that the macroeconomy is in equilibrium at Y_0. The $C_0 + I_0 + G + (X - M)$ curve in Figure 4a is constructed for a given price level, P_0 in Figure 4b. Starting from this point, we can hypothetically vary the price level up and down in Figure 4b, observing the corresponding income level produced. Matching pairs of P and Y will trace out the aggregate demand curve. For example, assume the price level falls from P_0 to P_1. The effect of this price decline will be to raise household consumption (the real balance effect) and to raise business investment (the interest rate effect). Thus, total expenditures will shift upward, establishing a higher income level at Y_1. A lower price level, P_1, therefore, matches a higher level of real income, Y_1. This matched pair of variables is plotted in Figure 4b as point F.

We can continue the conceptual experiment by raising the price level from P_0 to P_2. Inflation causes the consumption function to shift downward (the interest rate effect), moving the equilibrium income to Y_2. The combination (P_2, Y_2) is shown in Figure 4b as point B. The aggregate demand curve (AD) is the locus of all points generated in the manner of points B, A, F. The curve is downward-sloping, as stated at the beginning of this section.

FIGURE 4

A decrease in the price level from P_0 to P_1 creates an increase in consumption and investment spending. (a) A decrease from P_0 to P_1 increases real income from Y_0 to Y_1. Increases in the price level decrease C and I, so real income falls from Y_0 to Y_2. (b) The price and income combinations trace out the aggregate demand curve: Greater quantities of goods and services are demanded at lower prices.

Derivation of Aggregate Demand from Total Expenditures

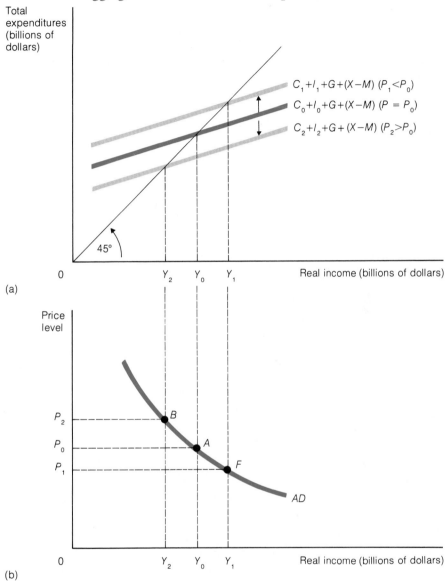

(a)

(b)

The Shape of the Aggregate Demand Curve

Both the real balance effect and the interest rate effect cause the level of aggregate demand to increase as the price level falls and to decrease as the price level rises. The shape of the aggregate demand curve depends on the magnitude of the two effects. If in Figure 4 a price level reduction from P_0 to P_1 causes a large increase in consumer wealth (perhaps because consumers have large holdings of dollar-denominated stocks), the total spending function will shift upward by a large amount. This in turn will result in a level of aggregate demand much greater at price level P_1 than at P_0. Accordingly, income level Y_1 will lie far to the right of Y_0, causing the aggregate demand curve to be flat. On the other hand, if consumers have few dollar-denominated assets, a fall in the price level will have little effect on total spending and the aggregate demand curve will be steep. In a similar fashion, the stronger the interest rate effect, the more elastic the aggregate demand curve.

The shape of the aggregate demand curve is important. With flat aggregate demand curves, shifts in aggregate supply will primarily affect the level of output, having little impact on the equilibrium price level. With steep aggregate demand curves, a shift in aggregate supply will have a large impact on price level but little impact on production level.

Shifts in the Aggregate Demand Curve

In tracing out the relation between the aggregate price level and the aggregate level of income, certain variables other than price are assumed constant. These constants are numerous. They involve all of those things that shift the demand function either rightward or leftward. The following list of factors capable of shifting aggregate demand is representative but not exhaustive.

household consumption (C): autonomous component
business investment (I): autonomous component
government expenditures (G)
saving (S): autonomous component
net exports $(X - M)$
the money stock (MS)
taxes (T)

A change in any of these factors will result in a different level of national income at the same level of prices. Graphically, a change in any of these factors will create a rightward or leftward shift in the aggregate demand function. Table 1 summarizes the effects on aggregate demand for each change listed, and Figure 5 shows the shifts graphically.

To test our understanding of the principles involved, assume some change in total expenditures, such as an increase in the net export balance. Spending increases at every price level, creating higher real income for every possible price level. In Figure 5, the aggregate demand curve shifts to the right from

---

TABLE 1   **Shifts in the Aggregate Demand Function**

A change in any of the listed variables will shift the aggregate demand function rightward or leftward, depending on whether the variable increases (↑) or decreases (↓).

Rightward Shift	Leftward Shift
Autonomous consumption ↑	Autonomous consumption ↓
Autonomous investment ↑	Autonomous investment ↓
Government expenditures ↑	Government expenditures ↓
Net exports $(X - M)$ ↑	Net exports $(X - M)$ ↓
The money supply ↑	The money supply ↓
Saving ↓	Saving ↑
Taxes ↓	Taxes ↑

FIGURE 5

Any change in a nonprice factor affecting total expenditures will shift the aggregate demand curve rightward or leftward. An increase in savings, for example, will reduce total expenditures and aggregate demand at each price level, causing a leftward shift from AD_0 to AD_2. A decrease in taxes or an increase in government expenditures will shift the curve rightward from AD_0 to AD_1, reflecting greater spending on goods and services at every price level.

Shifts in Aggregate Demand

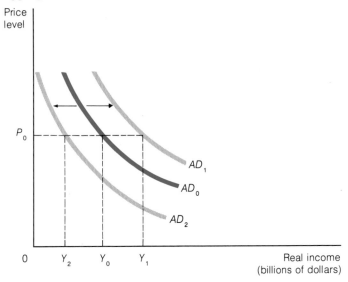

AD_0 to AD_1, illustrating that the real income at each price level increases. The same effect would occur with an increase in consumption (a reduction in saving), investment expenditures, or government expenditures.

Leftward shifts in the aggregate demand curve are likewise caused by both private-sector and government-controlled factors. Reductions in consumption (increases in saving), investment, or net exports would cause a leftward shift in the aggregate demand curve, from AD_0 to AD_2 in Figure 5, for example. An increase in taxes or a reduction in government spending would also shift the function leftward. These shifts occur due to a reduction in spending at every possible price level, meaning that the level of real income associated with any given price level falls.

As we have seen, many economic variables are capable of altering aggregate demand in the macroeconomy, thereby also altering the equilibrium levels of output, income, and employment. Some of these variables—such as household consumption and business investment—are determined by millions of decentralized, individual decisions. Others are determined by highly centralized government directives—decisions such as the appropriate level of government expenditures and taxes and the money supply. Among the latter set are various policy actions to combat the ups and downs of the business cycle.

The point of discretionary budget policies—manipulating taxes or government spending—is to stimulate the economy during periods of economic contraction and unemployment and to cool down the economy during periods of rapid expansion and inflation. Such efforts by the government to steer the economy are known as **discretionary fiscal policies.**

Discretionary fiscal policies: Government policy actions that attempt to influence aggregate demand.

Before we can discuss the possible effects of fiscal policy on aggregate demand, however, we must look at aggregate supply, the other major force determining the quantity of goods and services produced in the economy. We cannot determine the actual quantity of output produced through demand factors alone; we must also know what all businesses in the economy are willing to produce at alternative price levels.

AGGREGATE SUPPLY

Although higher price levels reduce the level of aggregate demand, they tend to have the opposite effect on aggregate supply. When producers receive higher prices for output, their profits rise, giving them an incentive to increase production. Furthermore, when producers attempt to increase production levels, they use existing resources more intensively, which drives up production costs. Producers are forced to charge higher prices to recover increased costs. The **aggregate supply curve** traces the relation between the price level and the aggregate level of production. A typical aggregate supply curve is shown in Figure 6.

Aggregate supply curve:
A graph showing the different levels of aggregate output produced at different price levels.

The Shape of the Aggregate Supply Curve

The shape of the aggregate supply curve depends on the state of the economy. When the economy is operating far below capacity with large quantities of unemployed resources, production can be increased without having much effect on input prices. Not only is it possible to employ workers of nearly all

---

FIGURE 6

The Aggregate Supply Curve

The aggregate supply curve, AS, shows the relation between real output, measured on the horizontal axis, and price level, measured on the vertical axis. The slope of the aggregate supply curve depends on economic conditions. The horizontal portion of the curve, called the Keynesian range, represents supply during times of severe unemployment and resource underutilization. In this range, any increase in output will not be accompanied by an increase in the price level. The upward-sloping portion of the curve, termed the intermediate range, represents supply under normal or near normal conditions. The economy has not reached its production possibilities frontier (represented by Y_F, full employment), but neither is it depressed. In this range, any real increase in output will be accompanied by higher price levels. The vertical portion of the curve, labeled the classical range, represents the economy at full employment. Output cannot increase and supply is perfectly inelastic in relation to the price level.

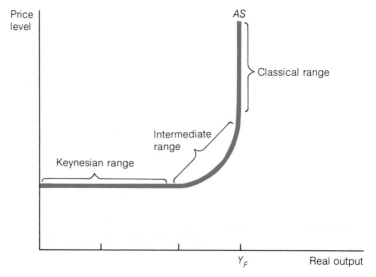

types, but productive inputs such as land and machinery are also readily available. This means that firms can hire more inputs without having to compete for them and that output can be expanded without much increase in average production costs. Therefore, small increases in the price level will lead to large increases in the level of production. This portion of the aggregate supply curve in Figure 6 is called the **Keynesian range,** reflecting Keynes's attention to large-scale unemployment in an economy.

When the economy is producing fairly close to capacity, the aggregate supply curve will be much steeper, as depicted in the **intermediate range** in Figure 6. In this range, attempts to increase production lead to shortages of certain inputs. Average production costs will rise, as firms are forced to pay more for scarce inputs. While it is possible to expand production, additional output can only be obtained at substantially higher price levels.

In the **classical range**—named for the classical economists, who described a full-employment economy—resources are fully employed and the economy is producing at some point on the production possibilities frontier. Since all available resources are employed, an individual producer can expand production only by bidding resources away from competing producers. The effect is to drive the price level up without increasing overall production. In this range, the aggregate supply curve becomes vertical.

Shifts in the Aggregate Supply Curve

In drawing an aggregate supply curve, certain variables other than price level are held constant. Should any of these variables change, the entire aggregate supply curve will shift. A complete list of variables that *might* cause aggregate supply to shift would be lengthy, but a relatively small number of variables have the greatest impact on aggregate supply—in particular, productive resource supply, technology, tax rates, and freedom to respond to economic incentives.

Resource supply often affects aggregate supply in obvious ways. For example, the discovery of new energy resources will cause energy prices to fall and productive capacity to rise; at all price levels, firms will have an economic incentive to increase output. Increases in resource availability, then, shift the aggregate supply curve to the right; decreases will cause a leftward shift. Let's consider a less obvious example—the recent criticism of the educational system in the United States and the many proposals for educational reform. Proponents of reform argue that improved education is necessary for the country to remain competitive in world markets. In terms of aggregate demand and supply, this proposal is an economic policy to increase the stock of human capital and, therefore, aggregate supply. (For an analysis of the effects of a decrease in the supply of a particular resource, see Focus, "Aggregate Supply Shifts: OPEC in the 1970s and 1980s.")

An improvement in technology affects aggregate supply in a way similar to an increase in resource availability. It also reduces production costs and increases the economy's capacity, shifting the aggregate supply curve to the right.

To understand how a change in tax rates affects the aggregate supply curve, keep in mind that in a free society aggregate supply is determined by the willingness of producers to produce, not just by the ability to produce. With high marginal tax rates, producers must pay a substantial portion of

Keynesian range:
A horizontal segment of the aggregate supply curve; shows that output can increase with no change in the price level because of some unemployment of resources.

Intermediate range:
A positively sloped segment of the aggregate supply curve; indicates that aggregate output and the price level will both change in the same direction.

Classical range:
A vertical segment of the aggregate supply curve; indicates that attempts to increase aggregate output will result only in a higher price level, since resources are fully employed.

FOCUS   Aggregate Supply Shifts: OPEC in the 1970s and 1980s

When the supply of any resource or the level of technology changes, the production possibilities of the economy expand and the aggregate supply curve shifts. In effect, for any given level of labor employment, more or less output can be produced. Supplies of resources can change for a variety of reasons. For example, the reduction in oil supplies imposed by the Organization of Petroleum Exporting Countries (OPEC) in the 1970s decreased the amount of oil available for the production of goods and services in the United States. Labor and other productive factors suddenly had less energy to work with, indicating that the productive effects of labor and other resources were lower, which in turn reduced the demand for labor. OPEC's action thus caused a "supply shock"—an unexpected, once-and-for-all leftward shift in aggregate supply, as illustrated in Figure 7.

A shift in aggregate supply from AS_0 to AS_1 in Figure 7, given a stable aggregate demand curve AD_0, meant that the price level rose permanently and output and employment declined. The emergence of the OPEC cartel contributed to the inflationary and recessionary pressures observed in the United States and in the world economy over the 1970s.

The 1980s witnessed a reversal of the OPEC supply shocks of the 1970s. Owing partially to price cutting by OPEC members and an inability to maintain and police output restrictions, the cartel lost much of its power. As a result, there was an increased availability of oil at lower prices to United States producers and consumers, as represented by the rightward shift in aggregate supply to AS_2 in Figure 7. To the extent that the formation of OPEC contributed to the inflationary and recessionary trends of the 1970s, its partial dissolution fostered lower inflation rates and higher output levels in the 1980s. The economy may respond to supply shocks by developing alternative resources. Part of the rightward shift to AS_2 has been due to the adaptation of production to the initial supply shock. New resource development,

FIGURE 7
Reduced Availability of Oil Shifts Aggregate Supply Leftward

The reduction in oil supplies in the early 1970s diminished the productive capacities of the United States with a supply shock, a sudden leftward shift in the aggregate supply curve. The effects were an increase in the price level from P_0 to P_1 and a reduction in real income and output from Y_0 to Y_1.

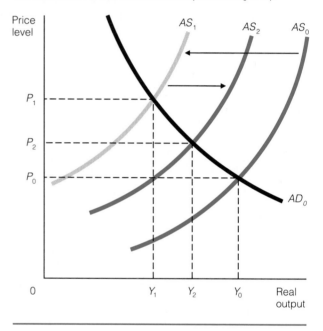

such as solar energy, and alternative production techniques also reduced the impact of the initial OPEC-induced supply shock.

their incomes in the form of taxes, and this reduces the incentive to produce. Workers in high tax brackets may chose to work shorter hours or retire earlier. Reductions in tax rates remove disincentives to work and shift the aggregate supply rightward. Similarly, many economists believe that certain governmental regulations form a barrier between individuals and the business activities in which they have economic incentives to engage. For instance, a teenager may see an opportunity to use his car as a taxi during rush hours, but he is prohibited from doing so because a government license is necessary. Removal of such regulation would increase the incentive to produce and cause aggregate supply to shift to the right. Much of the deregulation policy initiated during the Carter and Reagan administrations attempted to increase aggregate supply by reducing government red tape and, in Reagan's case, taxes.

THE EQUILIBRIUM LEVEL OF PRICES AND PRODUCTION

Since both the aggregate demand curve and the aggregate supply curve are plotted with real output on the horizontal axis and the price level on the vertical axis, both curves can be plotted on the same graph. In Figure 8, we see that AD_0 and AS_0 intersect at price level P_0 and output level Y_0. At any price level above P_0, the quantity of goods producers are willing to supply will exceed the quantity demanded by households, business firms, and so on. The excess demand for goods will cause prices to fall and drive the price level down to the equilibrium level, P_0. Aggregate demand and aggregate supply jointly determine the level of prices and output. Furthermore, any change in the equilibrium price level or output level can be viewed as being caused by a shift in either aggregate demand or supply. If, in Figure 8, the aggregate demand curve were to shift to AD_1 because of a change in one of the variables affecting aggregate demand, both the price level and the level of production would increase—to P_1 and Y_1, respectively. Had the aggregate supply curve been in the Keynesian range, output would have risen with little effect on the price level. The same increase in aggregate demand would have led to inflation but no increase in real output if aggregate supply had been in the classical range.

As depicted in Figure 8, an increase in aggregate supply would lead to an increase in equilibrium output and a decrease in the equilibrium price level. Decreases in aggregate supply have the opposite effects. Chapter 12 discusses specific government policies designed to shift either the aggregate demand curve or the aggregate supply curve.

FIGURE 8

With aggregate supply AS_0 and aggregate demand AD_0, the equilibrium price level will be P_0 and the equilibrium level of output will be Y_0. A change in any of the variables affecting aggregate demand that leads to increased aggregate demand shifts the curve rightward—in this case, to AD_1. This increase in aggregate demand increases the equilibrium price level to P_1 and raises the equilibrium level of real output to Y_1.

Equilibrium Price and Output Levels

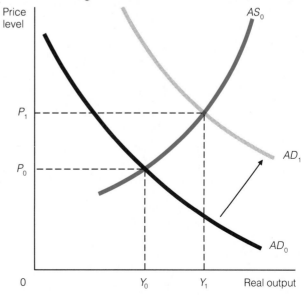

SUMMARY

1. The simple income-expenditures model is limited because it ignores monetary variables and price changes. These factors have become increasingly important since the late 1960s owing to inflation.

2. Price level changes affect household consumption by changing the real value of money balances held by consumers. This real balance effect means that price increases will decrease consumption spending and that price decreases will increase consumption spending. These spending changes affect the level of real income and employment, meaning that price changes may be related to the aggregate demand for output.

3. Price changes also alter business investment expenditures via the mechanism of interest rates. Investment spending will increase with declines in interest rates and decrease with increases in interest rates. The interest rate effect means that real income and employment are negatively related to prices through investment spending.

4. The aggregate demand function relates national income and output to changes in the price level; it is a downward-sloping function, like the demand curves discussed in Chapter 4.

5. Changes in both private and public nonprice variables (autonomous consumption, imports, government spending, taxation) cause the aggregate demand curve to shift rightward or leftward.

6. The aggregate supply curve relates the production of goods and services to the price level. It is a positively sloped function because higher prices increase the incentive to produce goods.

7. The shape of the aggregate supply curve depends on the level of production. At production levels that are low relative to capacity, the aggregate supply curve will be flat; its slope will increase until it becomes vertical as the production level reaches capacity.

8. The interaction of aggregate demand and aggregate supply determines the equilibrium level of output and the equilibrium price level, much like demand and supply for a particular good determine its equilibrium price and quantity.

KEY TERMS

wealth	discretionary fiscal policies	classical range
real balance effect	aggregate supply curve	
interest rate effect	Keynesian range	
aggregate demand curve	intermediate range	

QUESTIONS FOR REVIEW AND DISCUSSION

1. What macroeconomic goal does the simple Keynesian model of aggregate demand ignore? Why was this goal disregarded in the years immediately following World War II?

2. What effect does an increase in the price level have on the interest rate and, therefore, on the level of investment? Is this change in investment an example of the real balance effect?

3. Suppose that relatively small changes in the interest rate lead to large changes in business investment. Does this have any effect on the shape of the aggregate demand curve?

4. Moving from one point to another along the aggregate demand curve, what happens to exports? To government spending?

5. Can you think of two specific changes that would lead to a rightward shift of the aggregate demand curve? Two that would lead to a decrease?

6. As price level rises, what is likely to happen to business profits? To production levels?

7. Is it possible to solve major macroeconomic problems by inducing the aggregate supply curve to shift to the left?

8. If the government wanted to reduce the price level, would a reduction in aggregate demand be necessary?

9. What variable is likely to affect both aggregate demand and aggregate supply?

10. Under what circumstances is an increase in aggregate demand most likely to cause inflation? Least likely?

ECONOMICS IN ACTION
The Opening of the Iron Age: A Supply Shock in Ancient Greece

Americans had a number of long-run reactions to the energy crisis precipitated by the OPEC cartel in the 1970s. Initially, the supply shock caused a mass movement away from enormous, gas-guzzling American cars to small, fuel-efficient cars. After OPEC lost some of its power to control prices, gas prices stabilized, and larger automobiles were again in favor. Things were not the same after the supply shock, however, and will never be the same again. Today's full-size cars are relatively fuel-efficient; solar and other alternative forms of energy have found new uses; and production processes have adjusted permanently to oil shortages and to the possibility of future shortages. In sum, the doomsdayers who claim society will have to learn to live with less were not accurate. In fact, OPEC's supply shock may have had extremely beneficial effects on the American economy.

Two economists have taken the doomsdayers to task, examining a large number of supply shocks throughout 10,000 years of recorded history.[a] Supply shocks, they argue, never permanently reduce aggregate supply; instead, adjustments to supply shocks produce beneficial effects that reverse leftward shifts in aggregate supply.

Consider, for example, a supply shock in ancient Greece that marked the transition from the Bronze Age to the Iron Age. Why did our Greek ancestors switch from bronze to iron tools and weapons around 1000 B.C.? The reasons often given—that the Greeks didn't invent iron until 1000 B.C. and that iron was a much better metal than bronze—are questionable. People in ancient Greece had a knowledge of iron making as early as 3000 B.C. What's more, hammered bronze tools and weapons are almost as hard as iron ones and will hold an edge almost as well as iron tools. Since neither of these explanations is satisfactory, what other factor may have ushered in the Iron Age?

Consider some conditions existing during the Bronze Age. From trading records, we know that iron was extremely expensive during the Bronze Age. Records from the nineteenth century B.C. indicate that the exchange ratio of iron to silver was 1:40; in other words, one unit of iron cost 40 units of silver. Bronze is an alloy of about 90 percent copper

and 10 percent tin. At the time, copper was abundant, especially relative to iron—the trading ratio of copper to silver was 200:1. Tin was not so abundant and was probably imported into Greece from Iran, for there is practically no tin in the eastern Mediterranean area. During the Bronze Age, tin exchanged for silver at between four and ten units of tin to one unit of silver. Everything considered, the components for a bronze tool cost about 0.05 percent of what an iron tool would have cost. Small wonder the Greeks used bronze.

What happened to alter this situation? Around 1000 B.C. tin became extremely scarce in the Aegean. The Greeks experienced a supply shock of enormous severity owing to

Greek shoemaker's shop, 520–510 B.C. Black figured amphora. By the early 6th century B.C., the use of iron in toolmaking and weaponry had become commonplace.

[a]See S. Charles Maurice and Charles W. Smithson, *Doomsday: 10,000 Years of Economic Crises* (Stanford: Hoover Institution Press, 1985), pp. 95–105.

the wartime disruption of trade caused by the invasion of the Sea Peoples (the Philistines) into the eastern Mediterranean. These invasions, lasting from about 1025 to 950 B.C., led to the collapse of the major Bronze Age civilizations—Mycenean Greece, New Kingdom Egypt, and the Hittite Empire.

With tin no longer available, the price of bronze rose precipitously. Old bronze was melted down for its tin content and, because iron now became cheaper relative to bronze, ancient smiths began to forge iron tools and weapons. The Greeks responded to the tin crisis by ushering in the Age of Iron. Even when trade was reestablished and bronze prices fell, iron continued to be used. The crisis encouraged the smiths to learn ways to produce iron more cheaply. Iron continued to be used, even though the Greeks reverted in part to the use of bronze. In short, when resource crises or supply shocks occur, alternatives become cheaper and more attractive. Leftward shifts in aggregate supply create new circumstances that may mean vastly increased aggregate supply in the future. Within crises are the seeds of undreamed-of future economic possibilities.

Question

Assume that fires and disease destroy three-quarters of America's timber stock. What might be the effects of the catastrophe upon alternative resource development in the short run? Over a longer period of time?

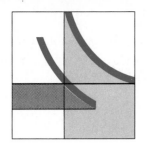

12

Aggregate Demand and Aggregate Supply Shifts: Fiscal and Supply-Side Policies

Contemporary macroeconomic theory and policy contain a large measure of both the classical and the Keynesian world views. Reserving an extended treatment of macroeconomic policy for Part Four, here we will briefly discuss how aggregate demand and aggregate supply can be used to understand macroeconomic policies. The major Keynesian prescription uses policies designed to manipulate aggregate demand to correct imbalances of employment and income growth in the economy. But in the debate over policy today, more and more attention is being paid to the concerns first expressed by Adam Smith and other classical economists. Labor productivity and capital accumulation were major concerns of the classical writers—the supply side of the economy. Supply-side economics, popular early in the Reagan administration, is based on the idea that overreliance on aggregate demand management, in the form of taxation and spending policies, has had ill effects on the growth of aggregate supply and has fostered much economic instability. This chapter considers the relation between aggregate demand and aggregate supply from both of these policy perspectives. When you complete Chapter 12 you will have insight into

- the role of government spending and taxing policies (fiscal policy) in Keynesian and new classical views of macroeconomics.
- using discretionary tools to affect the business cycle.
- how changes in fundamental factors affect the supply side of the economy on aggregate output and income.
- the interaction between policies designed to affect aggregate demand and the institutions and mechanisms that underlie aggregate supply.

POLICIES DESIGNED TO SHIFT AGGREGATE DEMAND

In large part, macroeconomic policy is an attempt to correct perceived failures in the private laissez-faire economy. When markets do not adjust automatically or adjust too slowly to correct imbalances in employment or economic growth, macroeconomic policies such as changes in taxes, government spending, or supply-side stimulation may be used as correctives. To assess the effects of macroeconomic policies, however, it is necessary to understand both the classical and Keynesian views of how the economy functions to correct imbalances.

Classical and Keynesian Perspectives

The classical economists' perspective on adjustments in the economy was long-run. Prices and wages were assumed to be flexible when there was an excess demand for or excess supply of labor in the labor market. These adjustments were not given an equivalent "clock time"; rather, classical theory assumed instantaneous adjustments. The result, as we noted in Chapter 8, was a vertical supply curve.

This classical supply curve can be matched with an aggregate demand curve, as in Figure 1. The elegant simplicity of the classical argument is revealed when aggregate demand is either increased or decreased from an initial equilibrium. Suppose, as in Figure 1, that the economy experiences a reduction in aggregate demand due to a fall-off in some component of private spending—the autonomous component of consumption, investment, or expenditures on exports. This reduction of aggregate demand is shown as a shift in the demand function from AD_0 to AD_1.

Equilibrium was established initially at E_0, where the economy was producing full-employment output (experiencing the natural rate of unemployment) at price level P_0. With the decrease in aggregate demand, we can think of the economy as moving to point A, where supply ceases to create its own demand. Demand is insufficient to purchase Y_F worth of output at price level P_0. Contraction of production and employment temporarily sets in, since prices (and money wages) will not totally and immediately adjust downward. Once prices start to fall from P_0 toward P_1, additional spending will result in

FIGURE 1   The Classical Long-Run Self-Adjustment Mechanism

In the classical view, when aggregate demand decreases, as from AD_0 to AD_1, the level of output temporarily falls from Y_F to Y_0, causing the level of employment to fall as well. The price level then falls from P_0 to P_1, and output rises back to Y_F. With flexible wages and prices, the economy returns to full employment.

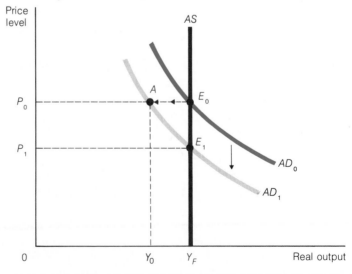

increased output back to the full-employment level. As noted in Chapter 11, falling prices will increase consumption spending *and* investment spending through increases in the real balances and decreases in the rate of interest.

When spending declines, unemployment is initially created. But in the classical version of events, wages also decline, so that all laborers seeking work find work, but at a lower nominal wage. In terms of Figure 1, prices and wages fall, so the economy rapidly ends up at a new full-employment equilibrium, E_1 at Y_F, but at a lower price level, P_1. In fact, the key to understanding the basically noninterventionist policies of the classical writers in macroeconomic affairs is the point that price, wage, and interest rate adjustments take place very rapidly.

Keynesians and the new classical theorists differ on many policy issues. One of the central differences rests upon the time required for automatic macroeconomic adjustment to take place. This difference is conceptualized in Figure 2. Once more, assume that autonomous consumption, investment, or export expenditures decline, causing the aggregate demand curve to shift from AD_0 to AD_1. Demand is again insufficient to purchase the full-employment output Y_F and to sustain full employment at price level P_0. In this case, the economy is in disequilibrium; aggregate supply, represented by point E_0, exceeds aggregate demand at point A for price level P_0. The degree and speed of wage and price level flexibility determines how quickly the economy will adjust to the excess supply at price level P_0. In the classical view, prices will

---

FIGURE 2

Demand Deficiency Unemployment: Short-Run Keynesian and New Classical Views

If aggregate demand falls from AD_0 to AD_1, unemployment will result. If prices and wages do not adjust at all, the short-run Keynesian view, a movement from point E_0 to point A takes place. The economy will produce a level of output equal to Y_1. The difference in employment levels at Y_F and Y_1 is the measure of demand deficiency unemployment. In the classical view, prices will adjust quickly to point B. Demand deficiency unemployment will be less—the difference between employment levels at Y_F and Y_0.

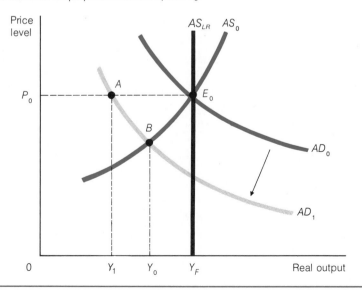

Demand deficiency unemployment:
A short-run situation in which the level of employment is less than if the full-employment level of output were produced; arises when aggregate demand is insufficient to purchase the full-employment output given the price level.

quickly adjust downward to point B, but Keynesians believe that downward adjustments in prices and wages can be slow, unpredictable, "sticky." Either drop—to A or to B—creates a certain amount of **demand deficiency unemployment,** unemployment that results whenever aggregate demand is insufficient to purchase the quantity of goods and services produced under full employment.

Under rigid Keynesian assumptions, prices and money wages are totally inflexible, meaning that the economy would move to point A with a relatively large amount of demand deficiency unemployment. Demand deficiency unemployment is measured as employment at the full-employment output, Y_F, minus the employment that will exist if the economy produces a level of output equal to Y_1. If prices and wages were somewhat flexible over a short period of time, however, a movement from E_0 to a point such as B on the short-run aggregate supply curve AS_0 would result. In this case, demand deficiency unemployment would equal the level of employment at Y_F minus the level of employment at Y_0.

Short-run unemployment of labor and reductions in real output are a fact of life for both modern Keynesians and for new classical theorists. But they differ widely in the kind of policies they would recommend. Keynesians favor the use of discretionary fiscal policy—the use of government expenditures and taxation or, to a lesser degree, discretionary monetary policy—to force the aggregate demand rightward from AD_1 back to AD_0 in Figure 2. According to Keynesian analysis, the economy is quasi-permanently stuck at point B, where unemployment exists. Government must do something about it.

By contrast, new classical economists believe that attempts to manipulate aggregate demand are doomed to fail. They feel that the discretionary actions of government—through fiscal and monetary policy—are unsettling and disruptive; they heighten fears about inflation and the economy in general, making the restoration of equilibrium even more difficult to achieve. They would prefer that government refrain from countercyclical fiscal policies except under certain conditions. Building on the simple concepts just outlined, we can describe some important aspects of the nature and practice of fiscal policy.

Fiscal Policy and Demand Management

Ordinarily, the economy's aggregate supply curve is positively sloped, meaning that, like the supply curves of individual products, higher price levels for all output are associated with higher levels of production. The positively sloped aggregate supply curve is midway between traditional classical assumptions and rigid Keynesian assumptions about the speed of price and wage adjustments to changes in the aggregate economy. In Figure 3, such a supply curve is reproduced along with the negatively sloped aggregate demand curve developed in the previous chapter.

Equilibrium output occurs initially at the intersection of the aggregate demand curve AD_0 and the aggregate supply curve AS along the ordinary, upward-sloping intermediate range of the supply curve. A level of real output or income is produced within the economy in the amount of Y_0 at a price level P_0. However, aggregate demand level AD_0 is insufficient to provide a level of

FIGURE 3

Assuming a positively sloped aggregate supply curve, *AS,* an increase in government spending or a decrease in taxes will shift the aggregate demand curve rightward from AD_0 to AD_1. The increase causes prices to rise as real income and employment rise to the full-employment level.

Fiscal Policy Shifts the Aggregate Demand Curve to Combat Recession

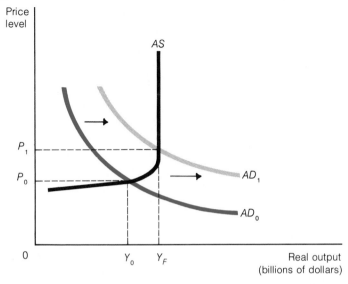

full-employment output, designated Y_F. What kind of macroeconomic policy would be called for? For fiscal policy, the government would attempt to stimulate spending by reducing taxes and thereby increasing consumption, by increasing government spending, or by stimulating consumption and investment spending. Demand management consists of manipulation of these politically controlled variables (the tax system and government spending) to shift AD_0 to AD_1, or to move demand in the opposite direction to combat rapid expansion and inflation. Fine-tuning the economy by shifting aggregate demand either rightward (to stimulate economic activity) or leftward (to cool down economic activity), the government thus manages aggregate demand to achieve economic goals of full employment and maximum economic growth. For an overview of the federal government's budgetary process, the method by which the federal government implements aggregate demand management policy through expenditure determination, as well as some suggestions for streamlining the process, see Economics in Action, "The Federal Budget: Process and Problems," at the end of this chapter.

Many government policies other than tax or spending changes and practices affect aggregate demand. Federal policies relating to international trade, for example, can affect aggregate demand. As noted in Chapter 11, *net* foreign spending—the difference between exports and imports—is a component of aggregate demand. Anything that affects either imports or exports, such as the erection or elimination of trade barriers, will shift the aggregate demand curve either to the right or to the left. Trade agreements with Japan to limit the American importation of automobiles or computer components will, for example, increase domestic aggregate demand by increasing *net* foreign spending (exports *minus* imports). Likewise, policies that encourage exports of American products will shift the aggregate demand curve rightward.

FOCUS Politics and Fiscal Policy

In any discussion of government economic policy, some allowance must be made for the possibility that policy-makers will not make the "right" response—namely, the policy change consistent with accepted countercyclical economic theory. Experience tells us that in the world of interest-group politics, economic considerations are not always uppermost in the minds of policy-makers. There is every reason to believe that, like everyone else, elected politicians are self-interested individuals. What is it that the self-interested politician seeks to maximize? Is it the public interest or job security (the probability of future reelection by voters)? Many economists believe it is the latter, so they recognize that knowledge of economic theory on the part of government policy-makers does not guarantee justifiable decisions. Political motives, in other words, frequently dominate fiscal policy decisions.

Consider the accepted "cure" for inflation, according to economic theory. In the Keynesian view, the appropriate fiscal response is a cut in government expenditures, an increase in taxes, or some combination of the two. But how many elected officials have the courage to vote for a tax increase in an election year? By the same token, reductions in government expenditures are politically unpopular with interest groups that receive these expenditures. What are politicians to do? If they wish to curry favor with the electorate—and what politician doesn't?—they will vote against unpopular fiscal measures, even though such measures may be sound countercyclical actions. Proof of this principle is the fact that the United States has incurred budget deficits in every year but two since World War II. If economic theory had dictated the deficits, their existence would imply that the U.S. economy has been in a quasi-perpetual state of recession, with Congress continually trying to spend us out of the slump. We know that this has not been the case. For many of the postwar years, Congress has actually pursued procyclical rather than countercyclical policy because politicians were unwilling to pay the political price for an unpopular though analytically sound economic policy.

One possible solution to this dilemma is to reduce the degree of autonomy that politicians have over fiscal policy, to take decisions out of their hands to a degree by placing fiscal constraints on the executive branch and the Congress. One such fiscal constraint is a balanced budget rule imposed by a constitutional amendment. This would prevent Congress and the president from spending amounts larger than tax revenues allow—in other words, no budget deficits. While a legal balanced budget requirement (or the pegging of government expenditures to a percent of GNP) could be procyclical, some argue that there would be less inflationary bias than under the current political system. Some type of constraint, the argument goes, would force Congress and the president to choose more carefully how to spend a more limited source of funds. A legal fiscal constraint may prevent, during periods of inflation, pork-barrel spending legislation; it might remove some of the built-in incentives politicians have to cast economically unsound votes.

Demand and Supply Interaction

Figure 3 shows that an increase in aggregate demand and an increase in real income and employment accompanies an increase in the price level. Whether or not prices will rise with increases in aggregate demand depends on the shape of the aggregate supply curve.

Figure 4 depicts aggregate demand shifts under alternative economic conditions summarized in the shape of the aggregate supply curve. With widespread unemployment of resources, as in the Depression of the 1930s, the economy is performing well within its production possibilities frontier. In Figure 4, an increase in aggregate demand from AD_0 to AD_1 through government fiscal policies will have the effect of increasing real output and employment *without* creating inflation by raising prices. Why? Because widespread resource availability permits increased real output without putting pressure on resources and output prices. This situation is close to the one Keynes described for the Depression world of the 1930s and 1940s. Under these extreme conditions, fiscal policy could achieve increases in output and employment without inflation.

The opposite extreme is also possible. When resources are fully and most efficiently employed, the economy is operating at or very near the production

FIGURE 4

The Effects of Demand Management and Alternative Shapes of Aggregate Supply

The effects of equal changes in aggregate demand on prices and output will be determined by the shape of the aggregate supply curve. Given the Keynesian case of depression and widespread unemployment, an increase in demand will increase real income with no increase in the price level. In a classical world of fully employed resources, an identical increase in aggregate demand will simply cause inflation with no increase in income. In the classical case, output cannot increase in real terms; it can, however, increase in nominal terms. In other words, the economy suffers inflation with no increase in output. In the intermediate case, both the price level and real income respond somewhat to aggregate demand increases.

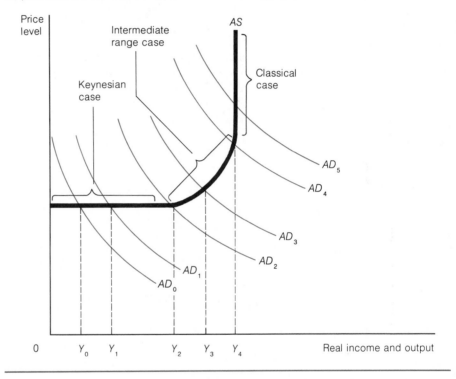

possibilities frontier. Given the state of technology, resources, and institutions, there is some maximum possible amount of real output and employment. If the economy is at this maximum point, the aggregate supply curve is vertical, as represented by the vertical section of the supply curve, the "classical case" in Figure 4. With a vertical supply curve, an increase in aggregate demand created by monetary or fiscal policies will be inflationary. In an increase of aggregate demand from AD_4 to AD_5, for example, real output would remain at a level Y_4 no matter what sort of discretionary demand management policies are followed. Demand management is unnecessary in the classical case because, as we saw in Chapter 8, the economy is self-adjusting and will produce full employment and maximum output automatically. Economists who adhere to classical principles or to modern versions of classical macroeconomics argue that discretionary demand management by government is unnecessary and possibly harmful to the economy.

Between the two extremes lies an intermediate case. Increases in aggregate demand will put some pressure on prices along with some increase in real national income and employment. This situation was depicted in Figure 3 and is shown as the intermediate case in Figure 4. An increase in demand from AD_2 to AD_3 will create some increase in prices, but real output and employment will also rise, from Y_2 to Y_3. However, shortages will develop in some resource markets, creating production bottlenecks and price increases. As the economy approaches full employment and the production possibilities frontier, prices will ordinarily rise at a faster rate and output increases will be smaller and smaller as resource shortages become more acute.

In sum, the effectiveness of managing demand by monetary or fiscal means depends in part on the shape of the aggregate supply curve. In the Keynesian case, reflecting depression conditions, demand changes will have their full impact on real income and employment with no effect on prices. In the classical case, demand management is virtually useless in affecting employment or output: Its sole effects are on the price level. The intermediate case contains elements of both Keynesian and classical conclusions. Aggregate demand changes will change real output and employment as well as the price level. The government's ability to adjust spending and aggregate demand to contractionary or expansionary gaps—to control unemployment and inflation and to promote economic growth—is therefore partially limited by the shape of the aggregate supply curve.

Possible Limits to Discretionary Demand Management

In addition to extreme shapes of the supply curve or the presence of stagflation, demand management by the government may be limited in its effectiveness by the realities of private decision making. About two-thirds of annual total expenditures in the economy come from the private sector—households and businesses. The private sector may have an ability to spend roughly equivalent to its income and wealth, and its desire to spend is not subject to direct government control. Thus it is possible for any governmental policy designed to accelerate or decelerate total expenditures to be thwarted by cumulative individual decisions to reduce or increase spending. In the context of the simple Keynesian model, for example, an increase in government spending could be partially or totally offset by a decrease in some autonomous component of private expenditures. By and large, the limits of discretionary demand management are related to expectations in the private economy and to the supply behavior of workers and other resource suppliers in the economy.

AGGREGATE SUPPLY POLICIES

Policies affecting the aggregate demand for goods and services in the U.S. economy are only one important part of macroeconomic policy. Throughout the 1970s and 1980s there was growing recognition that prolonged use of demand management might adversely affect aggregate supply. Many academic economists, for example, have been investigating the effects of tax rates on work incentives, the labor supply, and productivity. Some economists believe that tax rates, tax rate changes, and unpredictable changes in government spending affect the aggregate supply curve and thus employment and prices.

Others emphasize the impact of institutional factors, such as minimum-wage laws and income maintenance programs, on raising the natural rate of unemployment. This means that discretionary aggregate demand changes brought about by altering tax rates (as well as legislatively mandated institutional changes) might be partially offset by adverse shifts in aggregate supply. In that event, macroeconomic policy might be self-defeating.

Aggregate Supply and Resource Employment

Full employment:
To the classical economist, a situation in which all workers willing and able to work at the current market real wage rate are employed.

As Chapter 11 stressed, aggregate supply in the economy is related to the cost and availability of resources, especially labor resources. To classical economists, **full employment** meant that everyone who wanted a job had one; in other words, there was no excess demand for labor. In this view, the real wage established by the interaction of supply and demand for labor is the full-employment wage. Some unemployed workers would work for wages higher than the equilibrium real wage, but they are not considered unemployed because they voluntarily take themselves out of the labor force. All who would accept lower than equilibrium real wages are employed.

Today, economists prefer to talk of a natural rate of employment or unemployment. A certain amount of unemployment is expected in an economy at any given time. Because of changing demand conditions, resources are constantly shifted among producers. As Chapter 6 explained, a certain rate of unemployment arises from "friction" in the economic system, although the precise rate has changed over time and is a topic of debate among economists.

Natural rate of unemployment:
The rate of unemployment due to frictional unemployment plus structural unemployment; the rate of unemployment that will exist when expectations of inflation reflect actual inflationary conditions and all short-run macroeconomic adjustments have been made.

The **natural rate of unemployment** is easier to define than to measure: It is the rate of unemployment that exists when all unemployment is either frictional or structural unemployment. These two types of unemployment primarily result when there is imperfect labor market information, when the job search requires time, and when there is no match between the skill and location requirements of job openings and those of unemployed workers. The natural rate of unemployment stems from fundamental market and institutional changes that affect the decisions of workers to supply and employers to demand labor. Specifically, changes in minimum-wage laws, tax laws (especially income tax laws), and the availability and scope of retirement benefits affect workers' incentives to supply labor and thus the natural rate of unemployment. Another important factor is the increased participation rate of women in the labor force over the last twenty years.

The business environment also affects the natural rate of unemployment on the demand side of the resource markets. Taxes and tax laws affect business investments in capital and resources, including labor resources. Changes in tax laws or business regulations will affect the real demands for labor and other resources and ultimately affect the natural rate of unemployment in the economy.

Once these institutional factors are accounted for, the natural rate of unemployment may be interpreted as the rate of unemployment that occurs when full employment exists. This implies that the level of full-employment real output, Y_F, will be produced when the natural rate of unemployment exists. Any change in these institutional factors that affects either the supply of or the demand for resources will shift the aggregate supply curve either rightward or leftward. Supply-side economics, therefore, attempts to shift the aggregate supply curve rightward by changing policies and institutions that reduce the natural rate of unemployment. A rightward shift, for example, would enhance economic growth in terms of actual employment of resources and higher output.

The effects of supply-side or aggregate supply shifts may be shown utilizing the aggregate demand–aggregate supply apparatus from previous chapters. In Figure 5, long-run vertical aggregate supply curves are shown with an aggregate demand curve AD_0. Assume that initial equilibrium is associated with the intersection of the aggregate demand curve, AD_0, and aggregate supply curve AS_0. If the full-employment level of income produced by this intersection, Y_{F_0}, is insufficient, policy-makers might choose policies to increase income and employment growth. Policies that affect the natural rate of unemployment and aggregate supply will shift the aggregate supply curve rightward to new equilibrium positions. Two of these positions are shown in Figure 5. Tax reductions or deregulation in labor or product markets will decrease the natural rate of unemployment and increase the equilibrium income potential in the economy. In terms of Figure 5, policies designed to increase aggregate supply would increase the output potential of the economy from Y_{F_0} to Y_{F_1} or Y_{F_2}. These supply-side policies have been the concern of politicians and policy-makers in Congress for over a decade.

Supply-Side Economic Policies

Macroeconomic policy over recent political administrations (those of Presidents Carter, Reagan, and Bush) has been shaped by the recognition that excessive and prolonged use of demand management might have adverse effects

---

FIGURE 5

The Effects of Increases in Aggregate Supply

If government policies such as tax cuts and deregulation reduce the natural rate of unemployment, the aggregate supply curve will shift rightward—in this case, from AS_0 to AS_1 to AS_2. As a consequence, the price level will fall (below P_0) and real output will rise, from Y_{F_0} to Y_{F_2}.

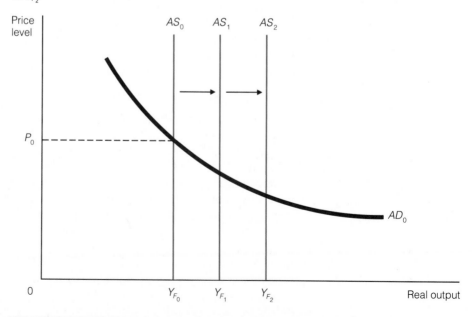

on the economy. Over the 1970s and 1980s, economists and policy-makers perceived that discretionary aggregate demand changes may have produced offsetting shifts in aggregate supply. Specifically, there was a realization that certain fiscal and legislative measures, particularly tax measures and regulatory changes, could alter incentives. Do businesses and workers respond to tax decreases by increasing investment in and production of goods and services? The Reagan administration made **supply-side economics**—the attempt to stimulate real production by providing new incentives to workers and businesses— a hallmark of its economic policy. (Although George Bush labeled Reagan's supply-side theory "voodoo economics" during the 1980 presidential campaign, Bush promised to embrace a similar approach as president.) Consider the nature of some of these policies.

Supply-side economics: Policy designed to stimulate production by altering incentives of producers; policy that has the purpose of shifting the aggregate supply curve to the right.

Policies to Increase Work Effort and Savings. Americans tend to save a smaller portion of their incomes compared to income earners in most other industrialized countries. However, Americans are not simply spendthrifts who live only for the present: We have been encouraged by the design of fiscal policies to borrow more and save less. Interest income from savings is taxed as ordinary income, while for many years interest *payments* were tax deductible. Under present law, interest earnings are still taxed as ordinary income, although deducting interest payments on loans for consumer goods purchases is no longer allowed. (Interest on home mortgages and home equity loans remains deductible.)

Policies enacted during the 1980s were directed at upgrading American saving and work habits, especially among low-income groups. Interest rate restrictions paid to small savers by banks and other financial institutions were loosened or removed, thereby encouraging private saving. The largest income tax cuts in recent history were passed in 1981 and 1986 to increase both saving and work incentives. Individual Retirement Accounts (IRAs), which allowed income earners to shelter some income from taxes for retirement purposes, were also instituted in the early 1980s. IRAs clearly encourage private saving, especially among lower- and middle-class income earners, although the tax deductibility of these instruments was limited by the Tax Reform Act of 1986. Policies to enhance saving may be working: Gross private personal savings rose (in real 1982 dollars) from $109.6 billion in 1986 to $158.7 billion in 1989.

Policies to Encourage Business Investment. Higher saving rates usually translate into higher investment rates by businesses. Institutional restrictions, such as high capital gains taxes and output-lowering regulations, have hampered productive investment in the past (and continue to do so today). Capital gains taxes are taxes on profits from the sale of stocks, real estate, and other investments. Prior to the Tax Reform Act of 1986, capital gains were taxed at a *lower* rate than ordinary income to encourage productive investment by small and large investors alike. These investments are an essential vehicle for creating higher employment and output growth.

The Tax Reform Act of 1986 increased the capital gains tax by treating capital gains from investments as ordinary income. That is, after 1986, capital gains were taxed at the same rates as earned income (15, 28, or 33 percent). Critics of this action claim that it had a chilling effect on investment—reducing the aggregate supply curve of the economy and thereby reducing economic growth potential. Institutional rigidities—in this case, a tax on investment—

may have a negative impact on aggregate supply and on economic performance.

Deregulation of Markets. Red tape and unnecessary regulations hamper economic performance in markets for goods and services or inputs, including labor. In the late 1970s, the federal government took steps to deregulate several industries, including the banking and financial services industry. The financial system that has emerged is more flexible and efficient, although the result has been tempered by widespread bankruptcies in the savings and loan industry, which may or may not be the result of deregulation.

Partial deregulation of transportation, including airlines, railroads and interstate trucking, began under President Carter and continued through the Reagan administration. Deregulation of these industries gave consumers lower prices, larger output, and greater choice of services. Elimination of institutional restrictions on businesses by government agencies, including the Occupational Safety and Health Administration (OSHA), increased the productivity of business capital and encouraged new investment during the 1980s. Recent changes in labor markets were also supply-oriented. For instance, modification of the minimum-wage law included a general increase in the minimum hourly wage but permitted the hiring of teenagers in need of job experience at lower-than-minimum wages for a limited "training period." The intended effect was an enhancement of aggregate supply and an improvement in long-run labor productivity.

There are indications that such institutional changes have produced a more efficient use of resources, but this is not to say that all supply-oriented changes have been beneficial. Because of federal deposit insurance, taxpayers are going to have to bail out the savings and loan industry—at a cost of perhaps $500 billion. Also, certain Reagan-Bush supply-side policies—for example, the elimination of job training programs and cuts in educational grants and loans—may have adversely affected labor-market institutions and skill levels of workers.

Trade Policies and the Supply Side. Protectionism has contradictory and self-defeating effects on the economy. The imposition of import tariffs or other trade restrictions may temporarily benefit the economy by providing a temporary increase in aggregate demand. However, the imposition of tariffs or other less formal trade restrictions will simultaneously reduce the long-run growth potential of the economy by reducing competition for domestic firms, input availability, and aggregate supply. While formal tariffs and quotas on goods and services are presently low (see Chapter 22), foreign cartels such as OPEC and "voluntary" trade agreements to restrict importation of foreign products or raw materials, which are more plentiful, have the same effects. As shown in a Focus of Chapter 11, the OPEC cartel created a negative supply shock in the U.S. economy, although its effects were mitigated somewhat over the 1980s. Likewise, import restrictions on inputs to protect domestic industries such as the computer and textile industries will reduce aggregate supply and the growth potential of the economy. While some protectionist agreements were reached during the 1980s, other trade agreements, such as the free-trade agreement concluded with Canada, will have significant effects on the aggregate supply curve.

The Impact of Supply-Side Policies

The results of supply-side policies enacted since the late 1970s have so far been mixed. A recession in the early 1980s, possibly precipitated by inflation-control measures, dampened enthusiasm for some such policies, although growth rates in real output and employment rose in 1983 and 1984. The economic growth rate in terms of real GNP was at a two-decade high in 1984 (6.8 percent); the rate has slowed to a little over 3 percent per year since 1984. Unemployment rates fell steadily after 1984. In 1988, Americans experienced the lowest unemployment rate (around 5½ percent) since 1972. Inflation was brought down from 18 percent in 1979 to little more than 6 percent in 1983 and ranged from about 2 percent in 1986 to a steady 4–5 percent in the late 1980s. Indeed, the U.S. economy suffered only one sharp but brief recession—in 1981–1982—throughout the 1980s.

DEMAND AND SUPPLY INTERACTION: PROBLEMS AND PROSPECTS

By the early 1980s, the ill effects of decades of countercyclical demand policies on aggregate supply were apparent to many economists. From the perspective of these economists, government at all levels tended to overspend and the increased taxation or inflationary tendencies created by deficit finance constrained work effort and private business investment. Aggregate demand policies by government may have worked faster than supply policies to alter inflation or unemployment, but their negative long-run effects on the economy's aggregate output of goods and services could no longer be ignored. Many economists now feel that quick-fix aggregate demand policies do not get at the long-run problems of economic growth and productivity. Aggregate supply policies—especially those relating to labor productivity, long-run business investment, and institutional change—will be more effective, but they also take more time. In this view, demand policies should receive consideration, but supply issues should be raised to equal importance.

Unfortunately, demand- and supply-side policies are enacted within a political process that often prevents or hampers coordination of macroeconomic policy goals. During the 1980s, tax cuts were enacted—a reasonable supply-side policy to enhance work effort, savings, and productivity. But at the same time, government expenditures were not reduced enough to cover increasing deficits in the federal accounts. These huge federal deficits were tantamount to an enormous Keynesian demand-side boost to total expenditures, which might explain the economic growth and general prosperity of the 1980s. But the federal deficit leads to uncertainty in private markets, which has a negative impact both on aggregate demand and aggregate supply. The deficit signals to potential savers and investors that inflation and/or government competition for private funds might soon be on the way. Deficits, then, have a dual impact: They increase the government portion of aggregate expenditures while reducing private expenditures through the creation of adverse expectations. These effects, and other economic impacts of deficits and debt, are the subject of Chapter 13.

SUMMARY

1. The interplay of aggregate supply and aggregate demand, in the long-run perspective of classical economists, produces full employment and economic growth at stable prices. Fiscal policy as a discretionary tool of government is largely unnecessary in the context of classical supply and demand interactions.

2. The Keynesian view of macroeconomics is that concerted discretionary policy is necessary to alleviate imbalances in aggregate demand and supply, since the private economy cannot produce equilibria at full employment with output growth.

3. Fiscal policy is the taxing and spending power of government. It can affect aggregate demand by increasing total government spending in the economy or by stimulating private consumption and investment spending (via tax cuts, for example). In the event of inflation, fiscal policy may also be used to reduce aggregate demand—that is, it can be contractionary as well as expansionary.

4. Policies other than tax and spending changes can also affect aggregate demand in the economy. Since *net* foreign spending is a component of aggregate demand, any policy change that affects imports or exports will shift the aggregate demand curve rightward or leftward.

5. The effects of fiscal policy by government depend on the shape of the aggregate supply curve. In the Keynesian range, demand increases cause increases in real income but not in prices; in the classical range, demand increases are inflationary, with no increase in income and employment; in the intermediate range, both prices and real income increase with increases in demand.

6. Supply-side economics is based on the idea that overreliance on aggregate demand management, in the form of tax policy, has had ill effects on the aggregate supply side of the economy.

7. Aggregate supply is related to the cost and availability of resources in the economy, especially labor resources. It is also related to the natural rate of unemployment, which exists when all unemployment is either frictional or structural in nature.

8. The natural rate of unemployment is dependent upon the institutions surrounding decisions to supply or demand labor. These institutions include but are not limited to tax policies on work and investment, the amount of government regulation, and trade policies.

9. Supply-side policies are designed to enhance work incentives, to increase productive investment, to eliminate regulations on businesses and workers, and to reduce formal or informal trade barriers.

10. Macroeconomic policies relating to both aggregate demand and to aggregate supply have been hampered by the existence of huge federal deficits.

KEY TERMS

demand deficiency unemployment
full employment

natural rate of unemployment
supply-side economics

QUESTIONS FOR REVIEW AND DISCUSSION

1. Discuss the classical long-run adjustment mechanism with regard to a decrease in aggregate demand.

2. What is demand deficiency unemployment? How might it arise in a short-run Keynesian context?

3. What, exactly, is demand management?

4. Why do modern Keynesians favor discretionary fiscal policies to address short-run unemployment problems?

5. In general, why do new classical or supply-side economists oppose demand management to address short-run problems of unemployment?

6. How would the elimination of all trade barriers with Japan affect aggregate demand and aggregate supply in the United States?

7. Suppose that demand management policies are effective in reducing aggregate demand. How will the price level be affected? Does your answer depend on the shape of the aggregate supply curve?

8. Define the natural rate of unemployment. How do market and institutional changes affect the natural rate?

9. How do policies related to saving and business investment affect output growth and employment in the economy?

10. Does the political process ever prevent or hamper the achievement of macroeconomic policy goals? How?

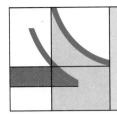

ECONOMICS IN ACTION
The Federal Budget: Process and Problems

Currently, federal government spending (including transfer payments) comprises nearly 25 percent of the United States' approximately $5 trillion GNP. The budget submitted to Congress by President Reagan in January of 1987 was the first ever to exceed $1 trillion. Clearly, expenditures of such magnitude will affect aggregate demand. The process by which the level of federal government expenditures is determined each year is complicated. These expenditures are not simply set by the president and implemented immediately; they must be proposed, debated, and approved in a complex budget process. This is a history of the technical budgetary process (the legal process by which federal government expenditures for any given year are established) up to the present. Some of the problems associated with the current process are discussed, as well as some popular suggestions for reform.

Prior to 1921, each major federal agency, such as the State Department, Department of War (now the Defense Department), the Treasury, and so on, submitted its own funding request to Congress for approval. In essence, there was no all-encompassing "federal" budget, but many federal budgets. Congress would either approve or modify and approve separate agency budgets through the voting actions of various committees. Determination of total federal government expenditures was a disjointed and uncoordinated process.

The Budget and Accounting Act of 1921 required, for the first time, that the president submit an executive budget to Congress for approval. All agencies were to submit their spending requests to the president. The newly created Bureau of the Budget, under the control of the president, would coordinate the various agencies' requests and prepare the president's expenditures requests. Thus, proposed agency spending became a direct responsibility of the president. The act also created the General Accounting Office (GAO) to provide Congress with an analysis of the president's budget. The Congress would then pass, with majority votes in both houses, a spending budget (usually the president's budget with some modifications). The president would either approve the federal spending legislation, thereby determining government expenditures, or veto the legislation and start the spending determination process anew.

With minor modifications, this process remained intact until the early 1970s. President Nixon, a Republican, faced Democratic majorities in both the House of Representatives and the Senate, hindering his ability to formulate and implement legislation. Differing philosophies of the two parties resulted in much disagreement over both the proper level of government expenditures and their composition. As a result, Congress often passed spending bills that contained items President Nixon did not want. Facing the options of vetoing congressional budgets (and starting the long budget process again) or accepting budgets for expenditures he did not want, President Nixon discovered a third alternative: He signed budget legislation passed by Congress but ordered agencies in the executive branch not to spend some of the funds appropriated by Congress. In short, he impounded funds that Congress voted to be spent, effectively altering the congressional budget to be more in line with his own budget, but without congressional approval.

These episodes resulted in the passage of the Congressional Budget and Impoundment Control Act of 1974. The stipulations set out in this act are still in effect today. The major effects of the 1974 act are to deny the president the authority to refuse to spend congressionally appropriated funds and to establish a specific timetable for all the steps of the budgetary process (see Table 1). The act also established the Congressional Budget Office (CBO) to specialize in budgetary analysis for the Congress. The GAO by this time had acquired so many other duties, and federal budgets had become so very large and complicated, that Congress felt better economic analysis of federal spending could be provided by an office for which this was the sole task.

Though the reforms established by the 1974 act were intended to make the budget process more efficient and streamlined, they had the opposite effect. Deadlines are seldom reached, deficits have ballooned, and, frequently, special temporary budgets have been approved to prevent the government from running out of money and ceasing operations. A number of proposals have been suggested for overcoming these problems.

Among the most popular is the line-item veto, a power given to most state governors. This would allow the president to veto specific parts, or line items, of budgets passed by Congress. One of the current problems with the budget process, as some see it, is that the president faces an all-or-nothing situation. The budget passed by Congress must be accepted intact or vetoed. This provides an incentive to attach special-interest spending bills, known as riders, to major spending bills. With a line-item veto, the president could dispose of riders and leave the major budget legislation intact; it also would provide greater flexibility in pinpointing federal spending the president would prefer to cut. Opponents of the line-item veto point out that it would alter

TABLE 1 — Timetable for the Congressional Budget Process

To pass a federal budget for government expenditures, the Congressional Budget and Impoundment Control Act of 1974 requires that these specific legal actions be taken by the president and Congress each year. The act also sets deadlines for each step.

Deadline	Action to Be Completed	Deadline	Action to Be Completed
November 10	President submits current services budget	Seventh day after Labor Day	Congress completes action on bills and resolutions providing new budget
Fifteenth day after Congress meets	President submits budget	September 15	Congress completes action on second required concurrent resolution on the budget
March 15	Committees submit reports to budget committees	September 25	Congress completes action on reconciliation bill or resolution, or both, implementing second required concurrent resolution
April 1	CBO submits report to budget committees		
April 15	Budget committees report first concurrent resolutions to their houses	October 1	Fiscal year begins
May 15	Committees report bills and resolutions authorizing new budget authority; Congress completes action on first concurrent resolution on budget		

the balance of constitutional power between the president and Congress by giving the president effective total control over federal government spending.

Other proposals consist of a two-year instead of a one-year budget, as well as dividing the budget into a current expense budget and a capital budget. With a two-year budget, Congress would go through the budget process only once every two years, rather than annually. Since the budget process has become a costly, drawn-out affair, this proposal has some merit. However, it reduces the flexibility and the ability to time federal fiscal policy properly. Dividing the budget into a capital budget for public goods, investment outlay,

(for example, highways), and a current expense budget for yearly operating expenses also may provide for greater fiscal flexibility as well as greater opportunity for the president and Congress to agree on compromise federal expenditures.

Question

If the federal government adopted a capital and a current expense budget, under which budget should federal spending on education be included?

Source: Budget Reform Proposals (Washington, D.C., American Enterprise Institute, 1985).

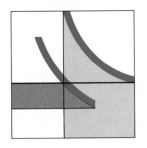

13

Public Finance and the Debt

Chapter 12 examined how fiscal policy could shift aggregate demand and supply curves to attain important macroeconomic goals. While fiscal policy may be a recommended stabilizing device, political pressures have led systematically to deficit spending. Since 1960, the U.S. government has run a surplus in only one year—1969. Government deficits were as large as $200 billion during the 1980s and could go even higher in the early 1990s. Despite political promises to balance the budget, the national debt has risen tenfold since 1960, to about $3 trillion in 1990. The Gramm-Rudman-Hollings legislation enacted in 1986 mandated that government deficits be eliminated over time. Nonetheless, it has failed to eliminate high deficits. The public, politicians, and economists are anxious about the effects of deficits and debt. This chapter examines the political foundation of federal deficits and debt. After reading Chapter 13 you should understand

- the proposed effects and the results of fiscal policy.
- features of government finance that automatically help control business cycles of recession and inflation.
- basic principles of public finance, especially as related to taxation.
- why deficits and debt concern economists and the public.

FISCAL POLICY IN PRACTICE

Fiscal policy is often difficult to implement—primarily because it must work through a political process. Inherent in this process are impediments to the smooth functioning of discretionary fiscal policy. It is often difficult to forecast economic downturns accurately or to implement appropriate fiscal policies in a timely fashion. In addition, political motives often cause politicians to favor fiscal measures. For now, though, we will focus on other aspects of fiscal policy that cause difficulties.

How Much Is Discretion?
How Much Is Automatic?

Governments continually levy taxes and make expenditures on a variety of goods and services, and all taxes and expenditures have fiscal effects. But most government taxes and expenditures are positioned in the budget no matter what the particular phase of the business cycle happens to be. The *level* of these tax receipts and expenditures varies with phases of unemployment and inflation in the economy, however, and these changes, called **automatic stabilizers,** are a part of fiscal policy.

Automatic stabilizers:
Taxes and government expenditures whose levels do not depend on decisions by policy-makers for change but instead change counter-cyclically in response to changes in the level of economic activity.

In order to understand the role of automatic stabilizers, consider the nature of certain types of taxes and expenditures. Prior to 1986, the personal income tax code in the United States was highly progressive (as opposed to proportional or regressive). Although we will explore the differences among types of taxes later in this chapter, it is important to recognize the nature of a progressive tax. A progressive tax taxes additions to income at higher and higher rates. For example, if Sam earns $15,000 per year, he pays 10 percent in taxes, or $1500. If Judy earns $30,000 per year, she would pay a greater total tax than $3000 (2 times $1500) in a progressive system. If Judy's total tax bill is $4500 on income of $30,000, her tax rate is 10 percent on the *first* $15,000 of earnings and 20 percent on the second $15,000 of income.

The advantage of a progressive structure (and other tax systems) is that it can act as a built-in stabilizer against inflation and recession in the economy. As money income rises—pushing the economy against its production possibilities frontier and fully employing resources—rising money incomes would push people into higher and higher income tax brackets. This, in turn, would withdraw some inflation-producing consumption expenditures from the economy. (This effect assumes that government does not spend the increased tax revenues.) As income falls, the total tax bill of individuals declines with lower and lower tax rates placed on declining incomes, causing unemployment-reducing purchasing power to be automatically injected into the economy. (In this case, the tax bill will also fall with a proportional tax, but it will fall faster with a progressive tax.)

Certain types of government expenditures, such as transfer payments from entitlement (aid) programs, also constitute an automatic stabilizer in the economy. Social Security payments, Aid to Families with Dependent Children, food stamps, unemployment compensation, and other such income security programs automatically inject purchasing power into the poorer and older segments of the economy in case of recession and unemployment. At federal, state, and local levels—but especially at the federal level of government—larger amounts of support flow through these programs during periods of unemployment, and smaller amounts are paid out during periods of fuller employment (and often inflation). Thus, both the tax structure and expenditure programs can be designed and set in place to act as moderating influences on adverse swings in the business cycle of unemployment and inflation.

What, then, is discretionary fiscal policy? If the Congress (with the help of the president) has previously decided the rules under which individuals will receive transfer payments and the rules under which individuals will be taxed, what is left to discretion? One obvious answer is that setting up the automatic stabilizers is itself an act of discretion. The Tax Reform Act of 1986 changed the automatic tax stabilizers that were part of the previous tax system, reducing the number of **marginal tax rates** from sixteen to three. The marginal tax rate is the percentage rate that applies to some additional amount of taxable income; it is figured by dividing the change in taxes by the change in taxable income. Welfare or entitlement program eligibility also may be changed periodically by Congress, and this has an impact on the countercyclical effectiveness of automatic stabilizers. Congress ordinarily decides on these matters from time to time by creating changes in the automatic stabilizers, but at any given time or phase of the cycle, many tax and expenditure programs are fixed.

At any point in time, some expenditures (and tax sources) are controllable and some are not. Approximately 25 to 35 percent of federal expenditures are fully discretionary—that is, not tied to ongoing, in-place programs such as Social Security, unemployment compensation and other income security programs, and interest payments on the federal debt. The bulk of these fully discretionary expenditures includes a large portion of national defense expenditures, public works programs, and appropriations to federal agencies and to state and local levels of government. Without question, Congress has the power and the responsibility to set up all tax and expenditure programs over the long run, but once many of these programs are set, room for short-run discretion is narrowed considerably. Over the short run, discretionary fiscal policy in the hands of Congress and the president is limited by the conditions attached to automatic stabilizers already in place. Some expenditures in the short run are controllable; some are uncontrollable.

Fiscal Policy and the Budget

As we have seen, discretionary fiscal policy suggests **budget surpluses** during periods of inflation and **budget deficits** over periods of unemployment and recession. While some classical economists advised strict balance in government accounts, the Keynesians argued that the budget should be balanced over the business cycle. A **cyclically balanced budget** in theory requires that budget surpluses run during periods of inflation match budget deficits run during periods of economic distress and unemployment. That is, economic contractions demand budget deficits that expand aggregate demand, and inflation demands a surplus in the federal accounts to reduce total spending on goods and services.

Unfortunately, the fiscal process has not worked exactly in this fashion over the past three decades. Deficits, which are supposed to be cyclically counterbalanced by surpluses, have been run by the federal government in twenty-nine of the past thirty years. These deficits have fiscal ramifications of their own. As we will see later in this chapter, a pile-up of deficits since 1960 pushed the **federal debt** over $3 trillion in 1990. It is most unlikely that such debt will bankrupt the United States, since the federal government has the power to tax and (unlike any individual or other unit of government) to create money. Economists do worry about other effects of deficits and debt. Such effects include adverse impacts on private spending in the present and possible reductions in economic growth and production possibilities in the future.

Marginal tax rate:
The tax rate, in percentage terms, that applies to additional taxable income; additional taxes divided by the additional income taxed.

Budget surplus:
The amount by which government's tax revenues exceed government's expenditures in a year.

Budget deficit:
The amount by which government's expenditures exceed government's tax revenues in a year.

Cyclically balanced budget:
A long-term view of the budget, in which surpluses generated during expansions match deficits created during recessions over a period of years.

Federal debt:
The total value of federal government bonds outstanding; arises from both current and past budget deficits.

PUBLIC FINANCE

Government expenditures obviously require some means, such as taxation, to finance them. When government finances the production of public goods or services—a local sewer system, a research program looking into the cause of acid rain, a nuclear warhead, a presidential limousine—it uses taxes to help pay the bill. In the United States, about 82,000 governmental bodies at federal, state, county, city, school district, municipal, and township levels have the power to establish taxes. As we saw in Chapter 3, the market fails to provide the optimal amounts of public goods such as national defense, police and fire protection, and education. In response, federal, state, and local governments traditionally have taken an active role in providing or influencing the production of such goods and services. In macroeconomic stabilization, government expenditures and taxation (especially at the federal level) take on new roles and new significance. Since the impact of fiscal policy is felt in the economy through government expenditures and taxation, it is important to understand some of the history and foundations of **public finance,** which is the study of government expenditures and revenue-collecting activities. Each and every government expenditure, along with the various tax schemes to finance it, has fiscal effects in terms of helping or hindering economic stabilization.

Public finance:
The study of how governments at the federal, state, and local levels tax and spend.

Government Expenditures

Chapter 3 reviewed some of the major categories of government expenditures and gave some statistics on the rate of government growth. There are two basic types of government expenditures: direct purchases of goods and services, and transfer payments, which are the redistribution of income from one group of people to another. Direct purchases involve spending on items such as defense, fire and police protection, and wages and salaries of government employees. Transfer payments include such expenditures as Social Security payments, Aid to Families with Dependent Children, and unemployment insurance.

The size of all government expenditures, adjusted for inflation, is shown in Table 1 for selected years from 1950 to 1989. Total government expenditures have increased dramatically since 1950 and are expected to rise even higher. These expenditures are ultimately determined by legislative decision, but about 70 to 80 percent are part of ongoing programs such as funds for police protection, water and sewer services (at the local level), military salaries, welfare entitlement programs, Social Security, and interest on the federal debt.

Trends in Government Expenditures. In Table 1, total expenditures are broken down into federal government expenditures and state and local government expenditures. Federal expenditures (which include grants-in-aid—cash distributions—to state and local governments) exceed state and local expenditures by a fairly constant proportion. Up to the early 1900s, local government expenditures exceeded the sum of federal and state expenditures. The Reagan administration attempted to return the provision and financing of many government goods and services to state and local entities, which caused many state and local governments to reorient their fiscal activities. This policy was dubbed the "New Federalism" because it sought a return to the fiscal system that existed prior to the 1930s in the United States.

TABLE 1

Real Federal, State, and Local Government Expenditures, 1950–1989

All government expenditures have increased over the past four decades, with real state and local expenditures increasing at about the same rate as real federal expenditures. This increase is not totally due to population growth; per capita real expenditures increased more than three-fold between 1950 and 1989.

	Expenditures (billions of 1982 dollars)			
Year	All Governments	Federal	State and Local	Total Per Capita
1950	266.5	172.4	94.1	1753
1960	465.4	303.9	161.5	2576
1965	594.1	370.7	223.4	3058
1970	813.8	494.8	319.0	3969
1975	1010.8	614.2	396.6	4680
1980	1141.5	717.7	423.8	5012
1981	1164.6	748.2	416.4	5060
1982	1195.5	781.2	414.3	5141
1983	1228.2	804.5	423.7	5231
1984	1273.5	831.6	441.9	5373
1985	1354.6	888.7	465.9	5661
1986	1403.8	908.6	495.2	5810
1987	1429.0	913.8	515.2	5982
1988	1459.3	921.9	537.4	5924
1989[a]	1502.4	947.3	555.1	6039

Source: Council of Economic Advisers, *Economic Report of the President* (Washington, D.C.: U.S. Government Printing Office, 1990), pp. 298, 387. Conversion to constant dollars provided by authors through use of the GNP implicit price deflator.

[a]Preliminary data.

Per household and per capita government expenditures at all levels have increased in the last few decades. Not only has the absolute level of expenditures increased, but the level of government expenditures as a percentage of GNP has simultaneously increased. Government expenditures at all levels increased from 21.3 percent of GNP in 1950 to 26.9 percent in 1960, 31.3 percent in 1970, and 35.3 percent in 1986; the percentage declined slightly in the late 1980s (see Figure 1).

Since the 1950s, federal government expenditures have increased most in the area of transfer payments, a trend that was sharply reinforced in the 1960s under the Great Society policies of the Lyndon Johnson administration. These Great Society policies expanded the welfare system, setting such expenditures at a sharply increasing rate of growth. As shown in Figure 2, the trend in federal expenditures on national defense declined as the percentage of outlays on social programs rose. Figure 2 also shows that the trend in these two broad expenditure classes reversed slightly under the Reagan administration, which emphasized defense readiness and military parity, or equality, with the Soviet Union.

Direct purchases of goods and services by the federal government also have increased in absolute terms but have decreased as a percentage of total expenditures. Direct purchases at state and local levels exceed those of the federal government. Such a result is not surprising when you consider the

FIGURE 1

Government expenditures at all levels have grown to well over 30 percent of GNP, although they have fluctuated widely—especially during wartime; note, for example, the huge increase during the World War II era due to defense spending.

Source: Council of Economic Advisers, *Economic Report of the President* (Washington, D.C.: U.S. Government Printing Office, 1990), pp. 294, 387.

Government Expenditures as a Percent of GNP, 1939–1989

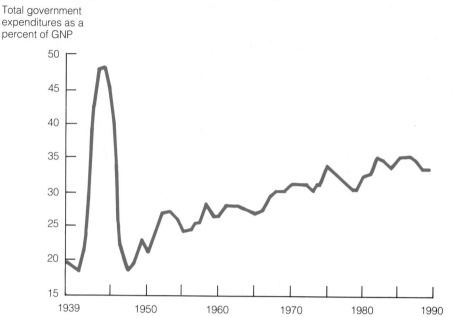

Total government expenditures as a percent of GNP

programs offered. Most streets, roads, and highways, police and fire protection, hospitals, education, and sewage and garbage disposal are provided by state and local governments. Indeed, state and local governments probably have a greater fiscal influence on our daily lives than does the federal government.

Discretionary Policy and the Level of Government Spending. Aspects of government finance at the various levels are critical to understanding the expenditure side of discretionary fiscal policy. Unquestionably, the expenditures of states, counties, townships, and cities have an impact on cycles of inflation and unemployment. Emphasis on the effectiveness of discretionary fiscal policy must be placed on *federal* policies, however, and the reason is not hard to understand. State and local governments, in most cases, *must* rely on tax sources to finance government expenditures. Most states and lower units of government, for example, are constitutionally forced to balance their budgets. (The predicament of states is this: A state cannot use its fiscal policy to help the country out of a recession, and it is difficult for a state to recover from a recession while the country is in one.) Although some governmental entities may borrow (largely through bond sales) to finance longer-term projects and budget deficits, their ability to sustain large debt is limited. Unlike the federal government, they do not have the power to print money and to engage in massive levels of debt. The result is that budget policy at the state and lower levels of government tends to be procyclical in character—expenditures are reduced on the downswing due to reduced tax collections and increased on the upswing when tax revenues are rising. In periods of economic distress and widespread unemployment, for example, these levels of government are forced

FIGURE 2

Defense and Social Programs as a Percent of Government Expenditures, 1920–1989

Expenditures in these two categories of government finance have fluctuated through time. In percentage terms, social programs have grown dramatically since the mid-1950s and the Great Society programs of the 1960s, while defense has generally declined since 1950.

Source: Council of Economic Advisers, *Economic Report of the President* (Washington, D.C.: U.S. Government Printing Office, 1990), p. 389.

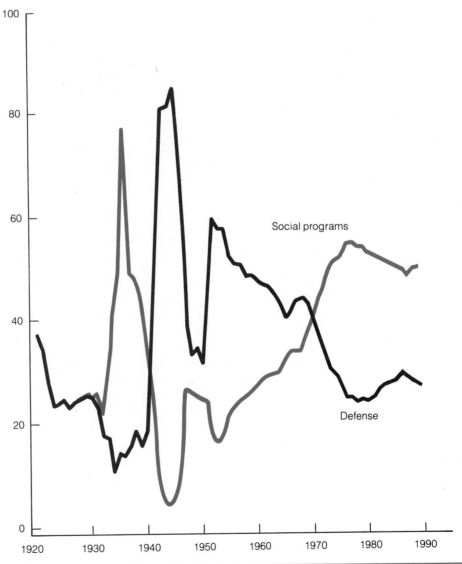

National defense and social programs as a percent of total government expenditures

to cut back on all kinds of goods purchases and services. For example, the weakening of OPEC in the early 1980s and the consequent fall in oil prices caused recessions and reduced tax revenues in Texas, Louisiana, and Oklahoma. These states' response was, at least in the short run, to reduce expenditures on goods and services, such as road repair, public education, and county and city services of all types. This response is said to be procyclical rather than countercyclical in character because discretionary policy would call for increased government expenditures and/or reduced taxes in the face of recession and unemployment. Indeed, the fact that state and local fiscal policy tends to be procyclical in nature is itself important for the conduct of discretionary policy at the federal level.

Tax Revenues

Bonds:
Financial instruments that create future obligations on the part of the issuers to make principal repayments and, in most cases, interest payments.

The two basic methods of financing public expenditures are taxing and borrowing. State and local governments usually borrow, as we have stated, by selling **bonds** to finance special projects such as highways, schools, or hospitals, but their access to such funds is limited by their ability to meet future obligations—that is, by their financial soundness and the faith that they will be able to pay off debt in the future. The federal government has come to use borrowing as a routine means of financing its burgeoning deficit, a practice that might eventually create economic problems of its own. Nevertheless, the largest portion of government expenditures is still financed by taxes. Table 2 shows the actual total tax receipts of the federal government from 1987 to 1989 and estimates for 1990 and 1991 from each source. The largest single source of federal revenues is the personal income tax, followed closely by Social Security taxes.

Property taxes and sales taxes are the two largest contributors to combined state and local government revenues, which are broken down in Table 3. The statistics reveal a recent trend in state and local financing: Property tax

---

TABLE 2

Actual and Estimated Tax Revenues of the Federal Government, 1987–1991

The federal government obtains most of its tax dollars from personal income and Social Security taxes. Total revenues are expected to increase by $180 billion between 1989 and 1991.

| | Total Revenues (millions of dollars) | | | | |
| | Actual | | | Estimated | |
Source	1987	1988	1989	1990	1991
Individual income taxes	392,557	401,181	445,690	489,444	528,489
Corporate income taxes	83,926	94,508	103,583	112,030	129,665
Social Security taxes	303,318	334,335	359,416	385,362	421,449
Excise taxes	32,457	35,227	34,084	36,154	37,634
Estate and gift taxes	7,493	7,594	8,745	9,279	9,809
Customs duties	15,085	16,198	16,334	16,785	18,615
Miscellaneous receipts	19,307	19,910	22,809	24,397	24,572
Total budget revenues	854,143	908,954	990,691	1,073,451	1,170,232

Source: Council of Economic Advisers, *Economic Report of the President* (Washington, D.C.: U.S. Government Printing Office, 1990), p. 385.

TABLE 3

State and Local Tax Revenues in 1977 and 1988

Unlike the federal government, state and local governments do not obtain the largest share of their tax revenues from individual income taxes. Since 1977, income and property taxes have fallen in relative importance, while sales and other miscellaneous taxes have risen.

| | Tax Revenues (millions of dollars) | | | |
| | 1977 | | 1988 | |
Type of Tax	Total Dollars	Percent of Total	Total Dollars	Percent of Total
Individual income	30,852	16.9	88,349	12.2
Corporation net income	9,709	5.3	23,741	3.3
Property	64,164	35.1	132,240	18.2
Sales and gross receipts	38,740	21.2	156,257	21.5
All other	39,307	21.5	326,558	44.9
Total tax revenues	182,772	100.0	727,145	100.0

Source: Council of Economic Advisers, *Economic Report of the President* (Washington, D.C.: U.S. Government Printing Office, 1990), p. 391.

revenues have not been rising as rapidly as sales and income tax revenues. This indicates that property owners are being taxed relatively less over time than other groups.

Equitable Taxation: Theories About Who Should Pay. Given the government's need for tax revenues, how should taxes be levied among the people? While voter-taxpayer resistance to specific forms of taxation is always a factor to consider since incumbent politicians must face voters after tax increases, the issue of tax equity is also important. Our society attempts to find an equitable way of distributing the tax burden, but there are no easy formulas for determining what is truly equitable. Theoretically, there are two basic methods by which we may determine who should be taxed and by how much: the benefit principle and the ability-to-pay principle. While these principles are not directly concerned with the impact of discretionary fiscal policy, they are worth mentioning briefly here.

Many taxes arise from the **benefit principle,** which means simply that individuals who receive the most benefits from government goods and services should pay the most for their production. Public transport facilities such as buses or subways, publicly owned electrical, water, and gas utilities, and toll roads charge users for the services provided. Many goods, such as national defense, interstate highways, and some educational facilities, provide indirect benefits to citizens that are not easily calculated. Some individuals receiving government benefits cannot always afford to pay an equitable share of taxes, even if the benefits they receive could be calculated exactly. For these reasons, most taxes are based on the ability-to-pay principle.

According to the **ability-to-pay principle** of taxation, those who are more able to pay should pay more taxes than those less able to pay. Under this principle, levels of an individual's income, wealth, or expenditures are measures frequently used for determining the level of tax obligation. There is general agreement that the wealthy should pay more taxes than the poor, but the question of how much more is not easily resolved.

Benefit principle:
A method of determining individuals' tax burdens on the basis of the beneficiaries of the expenditures that are financed by taxes; an example is a gasoline tax.

Ability-to-pay principle:
A method of determining individuals' tax burdens on the basis of those most capable of paying taxes.

Taxes and Ability to Pay. Three methods of relating taxes to ability to pay have been used in the past. Here, these methods of determining ability are applied to an income tax, but they also can be applied to other taxes.

Proportional Taxes. A tax that requires individuals to pay a constant percentage of income in taxes is a **proportional income tax.** If the proportion is 10 percent, a taxpayer earning $50,000 per year would pay $5000 (or 10 percent) in taxes. If a taxpayer earned $5000, his or her tax bill would be $500 (or 10 percent). Some states, such as Michigan, Illinois, and Indiana, levy a proportional income tax (with deductions and exemptions allowed).

Proportional income tax: A tax that is a fixed percentage of income for all levels of income.

Progressive Taxes. A **progressive income tax** requires that a larger percentage of income be paid in taxes as income rises. If the tax structure is based on this principle, an individual with a $15,000 income may pay only 5 percent of income in taxes, whereas an individual with a $30,000 income may pay 15 percent. Both the new and the old federal income tax systems are based on the principle of progressive taxation.

Progressive income tax: A tax that is a percentage of income and that varies directly with the level of income.

Regressive Taxes. With a **regressive income tax,** a lower percentage of income is paid in taxes as income rises. An individual with a $15,000 income may pay 10 percent in taxes, whereas an individual with a $30,000 income may pay 8 percent in taxes. While a regressive tax results in a lower percentage of income paid in taxes as income rises, people with higher incomes may pay higher taxes in absolute amounts. State and local sales taxes are good examples of regressive taxes, as are the more selective excise taxes on tobacco and alcohol.

Regressive income tax: A tax that is a percentage of income and that varies inversely with the level of income.

FEDERAL TAXATION, TAX REFORM, AND FISCAL POLICY

All taxation at federal, state, and local levels alike has a direct impact on the overall economy through its effect on individuals. The very *fact* of taxation means that income is withdrawn from the private sector of the economy, reducing aggregate demand. On the other side, the very *fact* that governments at all levels spend has an effect on aggregate spending. A *change* in government spending or taxation also will have effects on economic stabilization, *whether or not the effects are intended.*

When examining discretionary fiscal policy, however, we may provisionally ignore taxing and spending systems that are procyclical in nature and concentrate instead on those types of expenditures and taxes that may be used intentionally to affect aggregate demand. State and local spending and taxing policies certainly affect the economy. But such taxes and expenditures may be downplayed when discussing discretionary changes in the fiscal accounts because they tend to be procyclical in nature. Likewise, some taxes collected at the federal level, such as Social Security taxes, will clearly affect aggregate demand in the economy. But they are not, in the usual case, the taxes used to conduct discretionary policy in dealing with cyclical swings in unemployment and inflation.

Income and Corporate Taxes

Federal taxes both on individuals and on corporations were significantly altered in 1913 with the passage of the Sixteenth Amendment. This amendment allowed the federal government to levy income taxes on U.S. citizens. After its inception, the income tax system grew rapidly in size and complexity. By 1986, there were thousands of provisions for exemptions and deductions and sixteen income brackets, with marginal tax rates of 50 percent for the highest bracket. In the same year, taxes on corporate income stood at 46 percent of all business profits in excess of $100,000.

Beginning in 1966, the issue of tax reform was uppermost in some political rhetoric. In 1976, President Carter called the U.S. tax system "a disgrace to the human race" due to its confusing and complex provisions. The major criticism of the tax system was the number and kinds of items allowed both individuals and corporations as deductions from income. Rather than viewing the tax system as primarily a means of generating revenue, federal taxation was used for a number of other purposes. Special breaks were given to individuals and to corporations, for example, for investment purposes. The **investment tax credit** was instituted (in the early 1960s) on the principle that the tax code should encourage industrial modernization. Accelerated depreciation of business investments also was featured for the same purpose. Other deductions for both individuals and businesses were introduced, creating a tax code of incredible complexity and inequity.

Most economists believed that the tax code was inequitable and that it established counterproductive incentives for individuals and businesses. Tax "shelters" were sought and used to generate income losses to deduct from regular reportable income. The availability of tax shelters led to investments that generated loss potential rather than economic growth, which in turn weakened the economy. High marginal tax rates, moreover, may have caused individuals to work less or to work in an underground (untaxable) economy. Further, huge quantities of resources were employed in finding loopholes (tax provisions that generated tax-lowering deductions) in the tax laws.

Investment tax credit: A percentage or amount of new investment expenditure that is directly subtracted from the investor's tax bill in calculating total taxes.

The 1986 Tax Reform Act

In the largest tax overhaul since World War II, Congress passed the Tax Reform Act of 1986. One major thrust of the reform was to scale down both individual and corporate tax rates and to reduce tax complexity. Three tax brackets replaced the sixteen in place previously, with a maximum marginal tax rate of 33 percent. Under the reformed tax law, the top corporate income tax rate was reduced to 34 percent. (Figure 3 summarizes tax rates from 1913 to 1990.) Another major accomplishment of the new tax law was the reduction and standardization of exemptions.

While both individual and corporate rates fell under the 1986 legislation, more income was taxable. Many deductions—both for individuals and for businesses—were eliminated. The notorious "three-martini lunch" became a "2.4-martini lunch," since only 80 percent of business entertainment expenses could be deducted.

The new tax law was also designed to provide more equity. Partly as a result of increased personal exemptions, millions of low-income families were

FIGURE 3

A Summary of Individual and Corporate Tax Rates, 1913–1990

Individual and corporate tax rates have varied widely since 1913, with individual rates reaching a maximum marginal rate of 90 percent. After the Tax Reform Act of 1986, the maximum marginal rate on individuals is 33 percent, and corporations pay a maximum rate of 34 percent (with fewer deductions both for individuals and corporations).

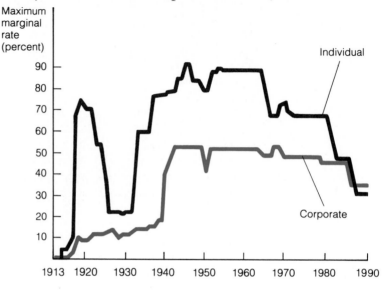

completely removed from the tax rolls. In addition, the elimination of many tax loopholes forced more well-to-do Americans to pay their fair share of taxes.

Economic Criticisms of the Tax Reform Act. The 1986 tax bill has been criticized on a number of fronts. First and foremost, the bill was designed to be revenue-neutral, meaning that the decrease in income tax collections of $121 billion (estimated over five years) would be exactly counterbalanced, or neutralized, by increased corporate and excise taxes of $120 billion. The shift in burden to corporations is incorrectly perceived, however, by the average citizen and journalist. Corporations do make tax payments, but corporations are simply legal entities owned by people who hire labor and other resources and sell output to customers. While corporations make tax payments to government, it is the owners, resource suppliers, and customers who bear the burden of the corporate tax. While economists cannot be certain of the exact shares of taxes shifted from corporations, the ultimate incidence of the "new" tax burden will not be on corporations, as it has never been, but on individuals (as workers, consumers, or stockholders).

Second, the revised tax code provided some simplification, but it fell short of the simplification that would pertain to a proportional tax, also called a flat-rate tax. While many deductions and exemptions were eliminated in the 1986 tax code, most economists point to the 2000-page (plus) document and argue that reform has not made the tax law much less complicated to adhere to or administer. As many resource costs—such as accounting costs and costs associated with preparing tax returns and keeping records—pertain to the new as to the old tax code.

Third, what Congress (and the president) does, it can undo. There is no guarantee that Congress will not alter the tax law again in coming years, perhaps reinstating pre-1986 complexities and inequities. Cynics view the 1986 tax law as little more than the foundation for new political campaign financing boondoggles. Nobel Prize–winning economists Milton Friedman and James Buchanan have argued that tax law changes have cleaned the slate so that future changes in the tax code will be available in return for political contributions from constituencies who would benefit from tax law changes.[1]

A final criticism of the tax reform act is that it provides no help in reducing the huge federal deficits, since it is revenue-neutral in character. Indeed, the likelihood that the law will be changed may be increased by the simple fact that it has not, at least in the short run, generated any help with high federal deficits.

DEFICITS, DEBTS, AND FISCAL POLICY

High deficits in the 1980s alarmed voters, economists, and politicians. Just what are the effects of huge deficits and the growing federal debt they have created?

Growing Deficits

As we have shown, deficits are created when government expenditures exceed taxation. Figure 4 provides a disturbing portrait of the emerging deficit situation. Since local and state governments tend to have balanced budgets, the

FIGURE 4   Deficits over Time and as a Percentage of GNP

While the size of deficits has grown over time, the federal deficit as a percent of GNP has remained fairly stable. This result is not surprising, since GNP is growing also.

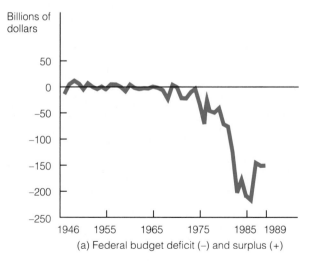

(a) Federal budget deficit (–) and surplus (+)

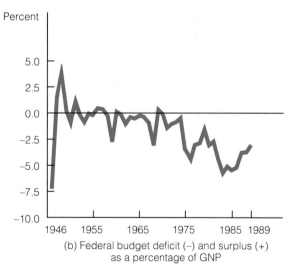

(b) Federal budget deficit (–) and surplus (+) as a percentage of GNP

[1]See, for example, Milton Friedman, "Tax Reform Lets Politicians Look for New Donors," *Wall Street Journal* (July 7, 1986).

overall government deficit is created primarily at the federal level. Large deficits have been a feature of federal finance since 1960, but in the mid-1970s, their magnitude mushroomed. From the middle to late 1970s, but especially in the 1980s, the federal deficit raced on uncontrolled. The deficit reached $200 billion in 1986 and has remained alarmingly high since then. Deficits of these magnitudes did not emerge overnight. The fiscal pressures of the Vietnam War, the social programs of the Great Society of the 1960s, the modernization of national defense by the Reagan administration, and so on—all added to contemporary deficit problems. There would be no deficit if Congress and presidential administrations were willing to tax in order to pay for government goods. Their unwillingness to do so means that the resulting deficits, or additions to the total federal debt, must be financed.

Deficits, Fiscal Policy, and Crowding Out

What other means might the federal government use to finance a deficit in its accounts? Since the federal government is allowed to print money, it could simply create money to finance the shortfall between expenditures and receipts. The creation of money, which will be discussed in the next four chapters, would erode the purchasing power of individuals' money holdings. Resources would be shifted from the private sector to the public sector due to the reduction in purchasing power in the private sector. The effect would approximate taxation, since resources are shifted to government from the private sector without the explicit consent of the governed.

Crowding out:
The competitive pressure exerted on private investment by government expenditures.

The federal deficit is financed primarily through the sale of bonds to individuals and to privately owned commercial banks. Predictably, increases in the supply of bonds resulting from deficit financing lower bond prices. As the price of a bond declines, however, its interest rate rises. Thus, increases in the supply of bonds raise interest rates and channel private saving from private investment into government expenditures. When bonds are sold directly to individuals (EE or HH savings bonds, Treasury bills and notes, and such) or to commercial banks, pressure is placed on private investment if additional funds are not saved. This phenomenon, known as **crowding out,** means that, depending on the reaction of savers and investors to the rise in interest rates, government borrowing may crowd out private investment. If private investment is discouraged, the rise in the interest rate may reduce the long-term growth prospects of the economy—unless individuals react to the increased deficit by saving more for future generations. (See Focus, "Do Deficits Matter? The Ricardian Equivalence Theorem.")

The high interest rates that result from government deficits may also lead to another type of crowding out—the displacement of domestically produced goods by foreign goods. As we will explain in more detail in Chapter 22, high interest rates in the United States make U.S. dollars attractive to foreign investors. This increase in demand for the dollar causes its price to rise in world markets; that is, the amount of a foreign currency that can be obtained for one dollar increases. For example, instead of getting 130 yen for a dollar, high interest rates in the United States may make it possible to obtain 140 yen. As a consequence, foreign goods become cheaper to Americans, but American goods become more expensive to foreign buyers. This leads to an increase in U.S. imports and a decrease in U.S. exports—both of which cause

FOCUS   Do Deficits Matter? The Ricardian Equivalence Theorem

Precipitously high deficits throughout the 1980s raised alarm in U.S. political and economic circles. Such deficits—yearly shortfalls in tax receipts necessary to finance yearly government expenditures—add considerably to the federal debt—the sum of past years' deficits. Do these deficits—for several years during the 1980s on the order of $150 billion to $200 billion per year—constitute or foretell a major economic crisis? Many observers and commentators have issued such warnings, despite reasonable annual economic performance. The inflation rate, the employment rate, industrial production, and other signals of economic growth were within tolerable limits between 1983 and 1990. So what is the issue—if indeed there is an issue?

For centuries, economists have debated the nature of deficits in government finance. Nineteenth-century economist David Ricardo argued that the effects of budget deficits and taxation were approximately the same. This idea—called the Ricardian equivalence theorem—suggests that individuals are indifferent between paying taxes in the present and paying taxes in the future (by incurring deficits and debt in the present to pay for government goods and services).

The best-known modern version of the theorem was presented by economist Robert Barro in 1974.[a] Barro argues that each individual has an "infinite" time horizon. This "infinite" time horizon assumes that the preferences or utilities of heirs in future generations are equal to those of the present generation. When the government issues bonds (or debt) to cover deficits in the present, the present generation compensates the next generation (one's heirs) with an increase in its bequest to cover the expected *future* tax liability. In other words, the present generation increases saving to make up for the future tax liability. In this sense, present taxation and budget deficits are equivalent because both result in a reduction in consumption in the present generation. A tax cut financed by an increase in the deficit will not shift aggregate demand or raise interest rates, in this view. The increase in demand for loanable funds by the government—through issuing bonds to finance the deficit increase—is exactly matched by increased saving on the part of the present generation (an increase in the supply of loanable funds). Since government spending and consumption spending remain the same, moreover, aggregate demand is unaffected.

Other economists, including 1986 Nobel laureate James M. Buchanan, oppose Barro's thesis on the basis that the present generation does not fully account for the future tax liability at the time debt is issued.[b] Present members of the economy behave as if government bonds add to net wealth. This perceived net wealth increase leads people to increase consumption and to reduce saving, which lowers capital accumulation and harms the heirs of the present generation. There is some empirical support for the view that taxation and debt are not equivalent and that the effects of bond-financed deficits are discounted in comparison with present taxation.[c]

Economists do not yet have a definitive answer concerning the full effects of deficits and debt. For many reasons, deficits and taxation might not be equal. Indeed, deficits may be the preferred method of financing federal expenditures by many groups in society. The age profile of U.S. citizens is an important component of this complex analysis. Older citizens are apt to prefer debt finance (bond issuance) to current taxation, as are single individuals and childless couples. Those in or expecting ill health (early death) might show similar preferences. In short, deficits may not be equivalent to taxation and may shift significant costs onto future generations of Americans. For some economists, debt and taxation are not equivalent, and the choice of more debt over higher present taxes must be carefully weighed.

To summarize: Deficits *do not* matter if our heirs are provided the financial wherewithal to pay them in the future. They *do* matter if Americans do not increase their bequests to future generations to cover the tax liability of current deficits.

[a]Robert J. Barro, "Are Government Bonds Net Wealth?" *Journal of Political Economy* 82 (November/December 1974), pp. 1095–1117; and "Budget Deficits: Only a Minor Crisis," *Wall Street Journal* (January 16, 1987), p. 22.

[b]James M. Buchanan, "Barro on the Ricardian Equivalence Theorem," *Journal of Political Economy* 84 (April 1976), pp. 337–42.

[c]Randall G. Holcombe, John D. Jackson, and Asghar Zardkoohi, "The National Debt Controversy," *Kyklos* 34 (1981), pp. 186–202.

aggregate demand to shift to the left. In this way, an increase in the government's budget deficit crowds out private spending by both domestic and foreign buyers.

Often when the Treasury finances a government deficit, the Federal Reserve attempts to prevent interest rates from rising by simultaneously buying bonds on the open market. This might temporarily keep interest rates down and prevent crowding out, but it causes the money supply to rise, which ultimately leads to inflation and higher interest rates.

Deficits and the Federal Debt

Large deficits have created a total federal debt on the order of $3 trillion in 1990. In order to assess its importance, it is instructive to see who owns the debt.

Table 4 shows the composition of debt ownership in 1988. Ownership of the federal debt is dispersed among private individuals, banks, and foreigners. Most of the debt is thus **internally held debt,** with a sizable portion held by individuals and banks outside the United States. (The importance of this **externally held debt**—claims or IOUs against U.S. resources by foreigners—is discussed in Focus, "Who Bears the Burden of the Debt?")

The Effects of the Federal Debt

Many economists, citizens, and politicians argue that the growing federal debt is a grave present and future problem for the economy and for economic growth. Their concerns relate to (1) the supposed relation between the size of the debt, inflation, and interest rates and (2) the possible burden of the debt on present and future generations.

Debt, Inflation, and Interest Rates. Depending on how government debt is financed, it tends either to raise interest rates or to cause inflation. When the

Internally held debt:
The amount of a country's total federal debt that is owned by the country's various governments, businesses, and individuals.

Externally held debt:
The amount of a country's total federal debt that is owned by foreign governments, businesses, and individuals.

TABLE 4

Ownership of the Federal Debt in 1988

The federal debt is owned, or held, by various groups. This table shows distribution of ownership of the federal debt as of the third quarter of 1988. All figures are in billions of dollars.

Type of Holder	Amount (billions of dollars)		
Total federal debt:	2602		
Total U.S. government ownership:		779	
U.S. government agencies			550
Federal Reserve			229
Total private ownership:		1823	
Commercial banks			203
Other U.S. financial institutions			232
Individuals			180
Foreign ownership			334
Other, including state and local governments			874

Source: Federal Reserve Bulletin (May 1989), p. A30.

FOCUS   Who Bears the Burden of the Debt?

Deficits occur when government expenditures exceed the taxes necessary to finance them. When the government borrows to finance these deficits, debt is created. The federal government has created debt from the very beginnings of the nation. Likewise, the debate over such policies is an ancient one among economists, politicians, and voters. In the nineteenth century and for part of our own, sizable debt was issued before and during wartime, with repayment effected through taxation after war's end. Modern times have witnessed the explosion of bond-financed deficits and a federal debt reaching more than $3 trillion in 1990. Does this seemingly astronomical debt matter to Americans? Does the sheer size of the debt forebode disaster? Are we burdening our children, grandchildren, and more remote descendants with the disastrous prospect of having to pay our debts back?

As a way to begin answering these questions, we again point out that it is most unlikely that the federal government of the United States will ever have to declare bankruptcy. Since the federal government is permitted (by the Constitution) to print money, the debt could be covered, if necessary and perhaps with ill consequences, in this fashion. Further, since the rate of growth in GNP exceeds the growth rate of the debt, the economy is (in a real sense of productivity) able to "stand" the growth in the debt. But problems associated with bankruptcy are not what economists contemplate when discussing the burden of the debt.

Economists usually think in intergenerational terms when discussing the possible effects of debt. They are concerned with whether government debt is borne solely or only partly by present or future generations. One idea prevalent in the post-Keynesian period is that "we owe the debt to ourselves" and that, therefore, it is not a problem to be very concerned about. A simplified version of this view, attributed to economist Abba Lerner, asks the questions, "Who owns the debt?" and "Who owes the debt?" Since the answer in both cases is "Americans," Lerner concluded that we owe the debt to ourselves.[a] While some of our children will inherit debt through taxation, others (or the same individuals) also will inherit claims (government bonds) to offset these debts.

However, a number of matters arise when we consider Lerner's proposition. In the first place, what if foreign individuals and governments hold some of our debt? Some $400 billion of the U.S. debt was so held in 1990. These foreign-held bonds represent real claims against the resources and output of the United States. The foreign-held proportion of the debt is small, however.

Another important matter is that the issue of debt by the federal government may have distributional effects over time. Bonds are usually purchased by high-income groups in our economy, but taxes are paid by all income ranges. Total economic well-being may be affected when a burden is placed on some Americans to the benefit of other Americans. Depending on propensities to consume, total private expenditures may be biased downward when debt is repaid from overall taxation to the upper-income groups over time.

Then there is the necessity of paying interest on the bonds that comprise the debt. Short of a declaration of bankruptcy, interest payments must be paid. They are, as Social Security has become, an untouchable area of the federal budget. During periods of high interest rates, this burden can become especially acute, putting demands on the tax system *or* on new debt finance. (In 1989, these interest payments were $174.4 billion, a significant part of the total federal budget.)

Nobel laureate James M. Buchanan argues that the effects taxation and debt have on present and future generations are *not* equivalent due to the fact that interest payments place a burden on present and future taxpayers.[b] When debt is created, buyers and sellers engage in voluntary exchange and therefore cannot be made worse off. But when it becomes necessary to pay interest on government bonds, taxation is required, and it is not voluntary. Future generations, therefore, do bear at least a portion of the burden of the debt.

Economists disagree over the question of where the burden of debt should be placed. The issue of whether our grandchildren will bear a portion of the burden of present government expenditures is an open one, but at least some effects of debt are passed on.

[a]Abba P. Lerner, "The Burden of the National Debt," in *Income, Employment, and Public Policy* (New York: W. W. Norton and Company, 1948).

[b]James M. Buchanan, *Public Principles of Public Debt* (Homewood, Ill.: Richard D. Irwin, 1958).

U.S. Treasury places bonds up for sale, it has no control over who the purchaser will be—that depends on who is willing to pay the most for the bonds. When the highest bidders are individuals, business firms, or financial institutions, the deficit will drive up interest rates by the amount necessary to attract these buyers. At other times, the bonds will be purchased by the Federal Reserve, the central banking authority in the United States. (The details of such purchases will be made much clearer in Chapter 16.) Purchase by the Federal Reserve tends to keep interest rates down (at least in the short run), but it can lead to higher inflation in the future. (Again, Chapters 14–17 will make it clear why this is likely.) The upshot is that financing the deficit inevitably leads to higher interest rates, inflation, or both—something to consider when such deficits are recommended.

Are Deficits and Debt a Burden on Future Generations? Economists are divided on the issue of whether the federal debt is a burden on future generations. The preponderance of opinion is that it is not, although the issue is far from settled.

How can this opinion be justified? First, the U.S. government will go bankrupt only if the government cannot meet all the debt claims that it issues. This is unlikely. If economic growth and the tax receipts that it brings continue at vigorous levels, the government will have no trouble meeting its obligations.

Other troublesome features of a large public debt are more subtle. Economic growth may be retarded if deficit and debt crowd out private investment expenditures. If private-sector expenditures are directed to more efficient and cost-effective investments, as they are under the revised tax system, productive expenditures might be crowded out by less-productive government expenditures through government bond sales.

Ownership of the debt, moreover, might create other problems. A portion of the debt is owned by middle- to high-income families, although pension funds, which tend to be owned by low- to middle-income families, also invest heavily in government bonds and notes. To the extent that future generations must finance present debt through tax payments, the burden of the debt will fall upon *all* future taxpayers. In other words, that portion of the debt owned by upper income groups will be paid for by *all* income groups in society in the future; some income will be intergenerationally redistributed from poor to rich.

Debt Management, Interest Payments, and Fiscal Policy. Discretionary fiscal policy may be influenced in several ways by the existence of a large federal debt. In 1989, almost 16 percent of total federal expenditures was composed of interest payments on the federal debt. A growing proportion of interest payments to total federal expenditures creates a growing problem with both the size of the annual deficit and the ability of Congress to manipulate expenditures and taxes to control periodic swings in the business cycle. At times, growing interest payments may help create larger deficits, which, in turn, create larger debt, and so on. The debt, in this view, may be self-perpetuating.

Can the Federal Deficits and Debt Be Controlled?

While it is easy to become unduly alarmed over deficits and the mounting federal debt, some real problems do exist. Economic growth and income distribution may be influenced in undesirable ways by growing debt and the problems (such as interest payments) that accompany it. Moreover, if discretionary fiscal policy is destabilizing, as some economists argue, efforts to balance the budget may bring some stability to the economy.

In late 1985, the U.S. Congress passed the Balanced Budget and Emergency Deficit Reduction Control Act (or Gramm-Rudman-Hollings) to deal

WHAT *YOU* CAN DO

Drawing by R. Chast; © 1984 The New Yorker Magazine, Inc.

with growing deficits and debt. Gramm-Rudman-Hollings "prorates," or automatically reduces, federal government expenditures when Congress does not come within preset deficit guidelines for the period 1986–1991. (For details, see Economics in Action, "Gramm-Rudman-Hollings and the Future of Macro Policy," at the end of this chapter.) While part of Gramm-Rudman-Hollings—the movement of congressional authority over spending to the executive branch of government—was challenged successfully in the legal system, the vigorous support and passage of the bill in the House and Senate by both political parties (and its legislative reassertion in 1987) may indicate a changing attitude toward the status of balanced budgets and discretionary fiscal policy in Congress. The entire question of whether discretionary fiscal policy can or will be effective in controlling unemployment and inflation is intimately bound to tax, spending, and budget policies, as well as to constraints at the federal level of government.

SUMMARY

1. Fiscal policy is the intentional manipulation of government expenditures and receipts to control cycles of unemployment and inflation in the economy. Its role is to help provide, along with monetary policy, stable growth in the economy without inflation.

2. While from a Keynesian perspective budgets are to be balanced over the business cycle, perennial deficits have been a feature of federal finance for the past thirty years. The mounting debt that these yearly deficits have produced has been a cause of concern.

3. Automatic stabilizers exist within the framework of government finance, wherein the levels of tax receipts and expenditures vary with rising and falling incomes in the economy, although they do not replace discretionary actions on the part of the president and Congress. They are not sufficient to produce a cyclically balanced budget.

4. Tax and spending policies of states, counties, townships, and cities have an impact on cycles of inflation and employment, but these entities have a limited

ability to engage in deficit finance. Budgets at these levels tend to be balanced and procyclical in character.
5. There are two basic principles of taxation: the benefit principle and the ability-to-pay principle, where those who are more able to pay actually pay more in taxes.
6. With a progressive tax, individuals pay a larger percentage of their income in taxes as their income rises. A proportional tax takes a constant percentage of income for taxes. A regressive tax takes a smaller percentage of income as income rises.

7. The Tax Reform Act of 1986 has simplified many aspects of the tax structure, including reducing the number of income tax brackets to three—with the highest marginal tax rate being 33 percent—and reducing the complexity of tax deductions.
8. Many economists and politicians warn that the growing federal debt created by massive deficits will create serious problems for economic growth and the distribution of income.

KEY TERMS

automatic stabilizers
marginal tax rate
budget surplus
budget deficit
cyclically balanced budget
public finance

federal debt
bonds
benefit principle
ability-to-pay principle
proportional income
    tax

progressive income tax
regressive income tax
investment tax credit
crowding out
internally held debt
externally held debt

QUESTIONS FOR REVIEW AND DISCUSSION

1. Mention and discuss three automatic or uncontrollable expenditures in the federal budget. How large are controllable or alterable federal expenditures relative to those that are less easy to change?
2. What are the major principles of discretionary budget policy?
3. Name and discuss two important trends in spending at the federal level. At the state and local levels of government.
4. What is public finance? Are the principles of public finance the same as those of personal finance? If not, how do they differ?

5. Clearly distinguish between progressive and regressive taxation, giving examples of each.
6. What are some of the economic advantages to society of the Tax Reform Act of 1986 over the previously existing tax code?
7. Economist Abba Lerner once observed that we owe the federal debt to "ourselves." Explain whether you agree or disagree with this proposition, and why.
8. How would you control deficits and debt at the federal level? Is a constitutional amendment the answer? Why or why not?

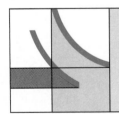

ECONOMICS IN ACTION
Gramm-Rudman-Hollings and the Future of Macro Policy

No economic issue has received more attention in the media recently than growing federal deficits. Deficits have long been a part of the American political and economic scene; the federal government ran a surplus in only two years out of the past thirty, as federal expenditures grew as a percent of gross national product. The problem became

critical after 1982, with an actual deficit in excess of $200 billion in 1986 and a projected deficit of over $250 billion in 1991.

In late 1985, in what some economists and observers branded an act of desperation, the U.S. Congress passed the Balanced Budget and Emergency Deficit Reduction Control Act (hereafter Gramm-Rudman-Hollings or GRH). While portions of the Gramm-Rudman-Hollings act were successfully challenged on grounds that it illegally transferred spending-cut authorization to the executive branch, the vigorous support of the bill throughout the House and Senate may be one indication of a changing attitude toward the status of discretionary fiscal policy in Congress. In fact, Congress passed a bill in 1987 that resolved the constitutional problems of the 1985 bill and set new deficit targets.

In essence, GRH prorated federal government expenditure cuts in the event that Congress itself did not come within deficit guidelines over the period 1986–1991. Actual deficits must, in any year, equal allowable deficits. Budget deficit limits were to be reduced by $36 billion per year in each fiscal year until the limit reached zero in 1991. Cuts were to be made automatically, when necessary, by the Office of Management and Budget, an agency of the executive branch. Gramm-Rudman-Hollings exempted some expenditures relating to the "social safety net" such as Medicare, food stamps, Aid to Families with Dependent Children, Social Security, and nutrition programs, as it did interest payments on the federal debt. Cutable expenditures include defense, transportation (Amtrak), education, foreign aid, agriculture, environment, and energy. To meet the GRH limits, Congress would either have to reduce expenditures or increase taxes.

Passage of GRH attempted to shift the mandatory and legal authority to cut budget deficits to the president when Congress cannot agree to do so. Opponents of the bill argued that it was unconstitutional because it violated the separation of powers. The Supreme Court agreed in 1986 and struck down the provisions mandating spending cuts by an appointee of the executive branch. No longer are cuts mandated by the Office of Management and Budget (OMB), a part of the executive branch, but violation of the limits imposed by GRH requires explicit congressional approval.

The passage of GRH carries some unmistakable implications. First, the act revealed that the political process is unable to balance the budget without some external constraint. Second, while some opponents argue that budget balancing would create economic instability, passage of the bill indicates that a majority of Congress believes that deficits per se have little or nothing to do with the business cycle. As Senator Phil Gramm (R., Texas) noted, deficits have co-existed with all phases of the business cycle—with falling interest rates, rising interest rates, growth in real income and employment, reductions in real income and employment, and so on.

The widespread support of GRH is consistent with the growing belief, both in and out of Congress, that there is a deficit bias in the political process. The persistence of pork-barrel legislation—where representatives and senators swap votes to provide vote-getting (but less necessary) projects for home constituents—and the unwillingness of politicians to raise taxes (for obvious political reasons) means that the probability of a balanced budget by an unconstrained Congress is virtually nil. In this view, supporters of GRH were trying to improve their reelection prospects by "passing the buck" to the executive branch of government, confident that the budget act would be rescinded or become ineffective, enabling them to return to spend and spend again.

An even more cynical interpretation is that Congress was trying to forestall a convention that could amend the Constitution to provide for a balanced budget—an event that many believe will be necessary in the long run. Since 1977, thirty-two states (only two short of the required number) have called for a constitutional convention to consider the matter. The passage of GRH could be an indication that politicians and those who elect them are losing confidence in the possibilities of discretionary policy implemented by the U.S. Congress and in the present fiscal system itself. Keynes believed that the private economy was unstable and required discretionary policies to moderate business cycles. In this system, budgets would be balanced over the business cycles (not necessarily in every year). Passage of GRH indicates the opposite conclusion—that governmental manipulations may be creating instability in the economy. Passage of GRH highlights the fact that, at one point in time, the vast majority of Americans, acting through their representatives, favored clear limits to the size and functions of the federal government.

At present, Congress is morally bound to the goals of GRH, although a vote could override the targets. Since, as many believe, Congress passed GRH to look as if it was addressing the problem without actually cutting spending or increasing taxes, such an override might not be politically popular. Other observers believe that GRH, while no panacea for the problem of deficits, at least defines the problem for Congress and the American people. Gramm-Rudman-Hollings might have been, as one observer put it, "a bad idea whose time had come."

Question

Do you believe it is possible to balance the federal budget given the "realities" of the reelection process, and given the fact that a large number of American voter-taxpayers would prefer reductions in government expenditures (on defense, domestic spending, and so on) to increases in taxes?

John Maynard
Keynes

Joseph A.
Schumpeter

J. M. Keynes and Joseph Schumpeter: Intervention or Innovation?

JOHN MAYNARD KEYNES (1883–1946) was the son of John Neville Keynes, a famous logician and writer on economic method. Educated at Eton and later at King's College, Cambridge, the younger Keynes developed interests in literature, mathematics, and, later, economics. One of his teachers at Cambridge, the neoclassical economist Alfred Marshall, was much impressed with Keynes's precociousness and strongly urged him to become an economist.

As an undergraduate, Keynes became an integral part of a small coterie of British intellectuals known as the Bloomsbury Group. Its members included novelist Virginia Woolf and biographer and literary critic Lytton Strachey. The group provided Keynes with an arena for intellectual debate, but he still had to decide on a career. Self-confidently, he wrote to Strachey, "I want to manage a railway or organize a Trust." Neither option materialized, and Keynes entered London's India Office of the British civil service in 1907.

Soon bored with civil service duties, Keynes returned to Cambridge and became editor of the prestigious *Economic Journal,* a post he held for thirty-three years. He joined the British treasury in 1915 as a monetary expert and became a key figure representing Britain at the Versailles Peace Conference at the end of World War I. In 1919, he wrote *The Economic Consequences of the Peace,* a condemnation of

the Versailles Treaty, which brought him international recognition. He went on to write a *Treatise on Probability* (1921) and to amass a personal fortune in the risky game of speculating in foreign exchange markets.

In the late 1920s, Keynes's interest turned increasingly to the theory and practice of macroeconomics. His productivity was enormous: Major works of the period include the *Treatise on Money* (1930), *Essays in Persuasion* (1931), and *Essays in Biography* (1933). In 1936, Keynes published the work for which he is most famous, *The General Theory of Employment, Interest, and Money.* In this book, Keynes rejected the idea of automatic adjustment in the economy and maintained that public policy and government expenditure are required for the prevention of economic stagnation and excessive unemployment. During World War II, Keynes negotiated lend-lease programs and was a leading figure in plans to restore the international monetary system. He died of a heart attack soon after the war ended.

JOSEPH A. SCHUMPETER (1883–1950) and Keynes were born only a few months apart. Schumpeter was raised in a provincial town in Austria (then Austria-Hungary) and studied law at the University of Vienna, where he also attended seminars on economics led by Carl Menger and Frederick von Weiser, two founders of the neoclassical Austrian school of economics. In 1906 Schumpeter earned his law degree and practiced law for a short time before deciding to devote himself to economics. At age twenty-eight he produced a brilliant doctoral dissertation, *The Theory of Economic Development* (1911), which brought him recognition as a first-rank theorist. After World War I and the breakup of the Austro-Hungarian monarchy, Schumpeter served as Austria's minister of finance. Throughout the 1920s he lectured throughout Europe. In 1932, as Fascism began its rise in Central Europe, he emigrated to America and became the senior economics faculty member at Harvard, where he remained until his death.

Schumpeter stands out as an extremely innovative thinker. He rejected many contemporary approaches to macroeconomic theory partly because they were based on pure mathematical insight. Schumpeter preferred to base his theory of economic change on the creative force of the individual, whose social, historical, and psychological dimensions are largely ignored by strict mathematical formulas. Schumpeter is also known for his broadly historical views of the discipline itself, which are presented in the posthumously published *History of Economic Analysis* (1954). Another work, *Capitalism, Socialism, and Democracy* (1942), is famous for its prediction that capitalism will eventually destroy itself, not because of its failures (as a Marxist would contend) but because of its successes.

FINE-TUNING THE ENGINE OF DEMAND

Keynes's central work, *The General Theory of Employment, Interest, and Money,* shared one important characteristic with the work of economist Alfred Marshall: a love for abstraction. Robert Heilbroner calls the *General Theory* "an endless desert of economics, algebra, and abstraction, with trackless wastes of the differential calculus, and only an oasis here and there of delightfully refreshing prose."[a] Beneath the calculus, however, were ideas capable of influencing an entire generation of economists and affecting the economic fortunes of millions of people.

Keynes's great insight rested upon his central abstraction, aggregate demand—in shorthand, $C + I + G + (X - M)$. Unlike his classical and neoclassical forebears, Keynes believed that insufficient demand, or spending, by consumers would leave the economy in disequilibrium, stagnating permanently below full employment. Accordingly, Keynes focused on means to increase demand through government policies and interventions in the economy.

In Keynesian terms, the economy is inherently unstable yet manageable. Guided by economic variables such as national income and business investment, government policy-makers can rely on fiscal measures to increase or decrease aggregate demand in amounts sufficient to restore equilibrium. Individual, or microeconomic, decisions to spend, invest, or save could predictably follow whatever course the fiscal and monetary planners design.

Despite the increased role he recommended for government, Keynes was mistrustful of overreliance on central planning. He was not attempting to redraw capitalism but to rescue it. (When the *General Theory* appeared, unemployment in the United States was close to 25 percent.) Keynes wrote the following in response to criticisms by economist Friedrich Hayek that an overplanned economy represents tyranny.

> Moderate planning will be safe enough if those carrying it out are rightly oriented in their own minds and hearts to the moral issue (of tyranny).[b]

CREATIVE DESTRUCTION

Whereas Keynes could be said to honor the economist's role in rescuing a stagnant economy, Schumpeter honored the entrepreneur's role. In many respects Keynes viewed the economy from above, from the heights of abstraction. Schumpeter looked from below, from the vantage point of individuals whose risk-taking and profit-seeking behavior spurred innovations and new growth opportunities. Accordingly, Schumpeter looked for ways to ensure free enterprise, not manage it.

To Schumpeter, the tendency of an economy to fall below levels of full employment resulted from shrinking opportunities for profits. As breakthroughs in technology or production occur, inspiring new investment and greater opportunities for profit, the economy generates growth. Schumpeter called the process *creative destruction* of profit opportunities, the continual rebirth of production frontiers.

Schumpeter naturally argued against government intervention and central control of the economy. He was much more mistrustful of the results of fiscal management than Keynes and felt that governmental tyranny would be its inevitable result. The first victim of such tyranny, in Schumpeter's mind, would be the entrepreneurial spirit. As Schumpeter summarized the matter: "The problem that is usually being visualized is how capitalism administers existing structures, whereas the relevant problem is how it creates and destroys them."[c]

[b]Heilbroner, p. 244.

[c]Joseph A. Schumpeter, *Capitalism, Socialism, and Democracy,* 3rd ed. (New York: Harper & Row, 1950), p. 81. Also see the excellent article by Peter Drucker, "Schumpeter and Keynes," *Forbes* (May 23, 1983), pp. 124–28, on which some of the themes of this section are based.

[a]Robert Heilbroner, *The Worldly Philosophers,* rev. ed. (New York: Simon & Schuster, 1961), p. 235.

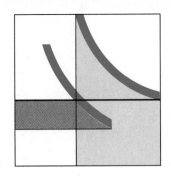

PART THREE

Money:

Its Creation

and Management

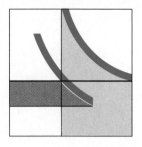

14

An Introduction to Money and the Banking System

As suggested in our discussion of macroeconomic theory, money is a vital link in our economy. This chapter and the three that follow it explore the nature of money and its economic role. We look at how economists define money, how money functions within the economy, and the reasons people hold and use money. Further, we see how money is related to the banking system and how the banking system itself is regulated by the government.

Money and monetary control are intimately related to the major goals of economic stabilization. Conversely, lack of monetary control can contribute to a society's economic downfall. Before we delve into these issues, our goal in the present chapter is to lay the groundwork for an understanding of money.

Familiar quotations point up the fascination—and the suspicion—that surrounds money. Shakespeare wrote that the person who wants money, means, and content is without three good friends. George Bernard Shaw noted, contrary to a certain religious teaching, that the *lack* of money is the root of all evil. And, in a cynical reversal of the notion that money cannot buy happiness, it has been said that happiness cannot buy money either.

Economics, of course, is not interested in the moral questions that money provokes, but it is interested in the nature of money and its role in our individual and collective lives. When you complete Chapter 14 you should understand

- why money emerged in economic life.
- the various ways in which money functions to increase specialization, the division of labor, and economic growth.
- the definition of money and the role of commercial banking and other financial institutions in the monetary system of the United States.
- the structure and basic economic functions of the Federal Reserve System.

FUNCTIONS OF MONEY

Barter economy:
An economy in which money is not used to facilitate exchange between individuals and firms; goods trade directly for other goods.

To understand the essential functions of money, try to imagine what a society would be like without it. Without the use of money all goods or services would be traded for other goods or services—a **barter economy** would exist. A visit to a psychiatrist, for example, would require a trade of some good or service for an hour on the couch. Suppose that you are the psychiatrist and three potential clients are waiting for your services, each with his or her own item of specialization to trade. Sam offers four hours of typing services, Bill three Persian kittens, and Judy, a farmer, one fully dressed hog. Will the demanders of psychiatric services be able to trade with you?

The result would depend on whether you, the psychiatrist, demand those goods or services in exchange for your own skills and on whether a price—a certain quantity of pork or kittens per hour of psychiatry—could be agreed on. In other words, a **double coincidence of wants**—a cat breeder wanting psychiatry and a psychiatrist wanting cats—would be required for a mutually satisfactory exchange to take place. It may be that, although not a cat lover yourself, you know someone who would be willing to exchange cassette tapes for Persian cats. In that event, a more complicated set of exchanges might be arranged. But these sorts of trades would require either luck or a great deal of information gathering. Transaction costs—the costs of getting buyers and sellers together for mutually advantageous exchanges—are astronomical in a barter economy. Many mutually beneficial transactions in a money economy could never take place in a barter economy due to high transaction costs.

It is not surprising that where barter is practiced, specialization and trade tend to be at relatively low levels. The high transaction costs associated with barter inhibit specialization and trade. A modern free-trade economy could not be founded on a system of barter because of the system's limiting effects. Money emerged to overcome these limitations. (The spontaneous emergence of money in a prisoner of war camp is the subject of Economics in Action at the end of this chapter.) In economic terms, money serves four separate functions: as a medium of exchange, as a unit of account, as a standard of deferred payments, and as a store of value.

Money as a Medium of Exchange

The evolution of money as a **medium of exchange,** or means of payment, came about from the desire to avoid the transaction costs associated with barter and to achieve greater economic efficiency. The need for a coincidence of wants between traders is avoided by the introduction of money. Once money is generally accepted as a means of payment, the hog or kitten owners sell their output in hog and kitten markets. They are willing to accept money in exchange for their products or services because they know that psychiatrists and sellers of all other items they consume are willing to do likewise. No longer is the psychiatrist required to search out demanders for psychiatric services who are simultaneously suppliers of goods or services that the psychiatrist demands. Use of money as a means of exchange fosters specialization and economic efficiency.

Commodity Money. Virtually anything can serve as money if it is generally accepted as a means of exchange or payment. Historically, an incredible assortment of items has served as **commodity money** within different societies, including horses, cowrie shells, elephants, stone wheels, cigarettes, colored beads, slaves, gold and other precious metals, cows, paper, and feathers. Most of the items that various societies have adopted to use as commodity money have had some common characteristics. Generally, commodities that have served as money have been scarce relative to other commodities. Scarcity

Double coincidence of wants:
A situation in trading in which each party to the trade has what the other wants and wants what the other has.

Medium of exchange:
An item that is generally acceptable as payment for goods and services.

Commodity money:
An item that serves as a medium of exchange and that is also a good itself.

ensures that only a fairly small quantity of the commodity money will be needed to make most purchases. Such items also were easily authenticated or readily identifiable as the commodity that actually served as money. Commodity monies also were divisible, so that a variety of sizes of transactions could take place, as well as highly portable, so that buyers and sellers were not severely limited in geographical market area. Physical durability is a characteristic common to the vast majority of commodities that have served societies as a money. Also, any commodity serving as money would need to be comparatively stable in supply; large fluctuations in supply of a commodity money would result in large fluctuations in the prices of other goods and services. (For a discussion of a somewhat unusual commodity money still in use today, see Focus, "The Stone Money of Yap.")

Most important, a commodity serving as money should be relatively scarce. The feathers of the extremely rare and beautiful quetzal bird would not have made a good medium of exchange in pre-Columbian Central America if the birds and their feathers had been in abundant supply. A sudden growth in the quetzal population would have produced inflation in the feather prices of goods—too many feathers available to exchange for too few goods. (Indeed, this is what inflation means—that money becomes overabundant in relation to the goods and services it can purchase.)

Yet another and possibly more important problem associated with all commodity monies, including quetzal feathers, is that there is an opportunity cost to using any commodity as money. A moment's reflection tells us what that cost is. Use of a commodity as a monetary medium of exchange means that it cannot simultaneously serve other uses. If quetzal feathers are used as money, they cannot simultaneously be used in headdresses.

Gold is perhaps the most familiar commodity money. The opportunity cost of using gold as money is particularly important. Most societies have valued gold highly as decoration, as an object of possession, and, more recently, in industrial or medical uses such as dentistry. Gold that is used for money cannot simultaneously be used to produce jewelry or to serve any other purpose. The value of gold in nonmoney uses is precisely the value given up when gold is used as money. When this opportunity cost rises above the value of gold in use as a medium of exchange, gold will be converted—coins melted down—to the uses of higher value.

History is peppered with such conversions resulting from changes in the opportunity cost of using gold or other precious metals as money. And social visionaries, seeking to abolish the "tyranny" of gold as money, have naively sought to demonetize gold by decree. Lenin once said that the first goal of his revolution would be to use gold in the manufacture of toilets. It does not appear that there are any gold-plated toilets in the Soviet Union today, and opportunity cost provides the explanation.

Fiat Money. Two problems—the opportunity cost of using commodities as money and instabilities in the exchange value of the commodity used as money—contributed to the emergence of fiat money. **Fiat money** is paper (or some other inexpensive, low-cost item such as lead or nickel) that is certified by government decree, or fiat, to be money. Dollars, pesos, rubles, and yen are all fiat money. Fiat money is not backed by a commodity such as gold; that is, it is not freely and perfectly convertible into that commodity. A system of paper backed by a commodity functions exactly the same as commodity

Fiat money:
Money, usually paper, that is made acceptable in exchange by law; usually not backed by any commodity such as gold.

FOCUS   The Stone Money of Yap

Yap is a tiny, thirty-seven-square-mile island in the South Pacific about 500 miles southwest of Guam. In the past, like many other peoples, the Yapese used commodity monies in order to facilitate trade among themselves and with the occasional foreign trader. Unlike in most parts of the world today, commodity money still plays a major role in expediting exchange among the Yapese. Such items as *yar* (pearl shell), *gau* (shell bead necklaces), *mbul* (woven mats), and bottles of beer all serve the citizens of Yap in making trades. U.S. dollars also circulate in Yap and are widely used in daily commerce.

In Yap, however, one commodity has served people as a money for some two thousand years and continues to do so today. A *rai* is a circular piece of limestone with a hole in the center; it looks like a washer. *Rai* range in size and weight from a few inches across and several ounces to twelve feet across and more than a thousand pounds. A very large *rai* can be carried only by nearly a dozen men shouldering a pole placed through the center of the stone.

Until the twentieth century, the stone money of Yap was used in many types of transactions, ranging from everyday trade to paying for tribal feasts and financing island wars. Today, its use has dwindled but has not disappeared. *Rai* have been used in modern times as partial payment for house construction and for some large purchases such as land transactions. Their use also seems rooted deep within Yapese culture and traditions. Yapese men still offer payments of *rai* for the right to marry to the fathers of prospective brides. An offer of dollars would be considered bad manners and an insult. The stone money also is used in making payments to settle disputes that have arisen among the islanders. It is by no means merely ceremonial, however. *Rai* still trade for many goods and services. This is, of course, the major reason that *rai* still actually functions as a money rather than a mere historical artifact.

The exchange value of any particular stone is unusually determined. Size is not the only factor determining what any particular stone will command in the Yapese marketplace. The age of the stone seems to matter most. The first *rai* were transported to Yap from the neighboring island of Palau by raft. Generally, these are the most valuable in terms of their command over goods. In the 1870s, a shipwrecked sailor transported a large number of *rai* to the island. Today,

Limestone money used on the island of Yap

these stones are worth about half as much as the earlier ones. Currently, there are about 6500 stones used as money in Yap.

The stones have, at first glance, some characteristics that a good commodity money would not possess. For example, *rai* are not easily transported. The Yap islanders avoid this nuisance by simply assigning ownership rights to the stones. The stones therefore need not be physically moved in facilitating exchange; only the ownership rights are transferred. Divisibility does pose a problem sometimes, which is the reason that other commodity monies have developed in Yap and the *rai* are used today in a limited range of transactions.

There are advantages, though, that go along with the stone money. The money is easily identified. Counterfeit *rai* do not pose a problem, nor do pickpockets. *Rai* are also fairly stable in supply as well as relatively scarce. Perhaps most important, they have served as a means of preserving the culture and customs of the Yapese. In fact, as a goodwill gesture, a representative from Yap has even offered a *rai* to the United States government as a contribution to help reduce the budget deficit.

Sources: Art Pine, "Fixed Assets, Or: Why a Loan in Yap Is Hard to Roll Over," *Wall Street Journal* (March 29, 1984); and Cora Lee C. Gillilland, *The Stone Money of Yap: A Numismatic Survey* (Washington D.C.: Smithsonian Institution Press, 1975).

money: The commodity must be stored for instant convertibility, thereby incurring an opportunity cost.

Even though fiat money is not backed by a commodity, governments have various ways of giving the money a generally accepted value as a medium of exchange. Fiat money sponsored by government is issued under closely enforced monopoly restrictions by the state. As long as the state does not allow the quantity of fiat money to grow too rapidly, the public generally remains willing to accept the money. Each individual remains confident that any fiat currency received will be accepted by others as payment for goods and services. The government contributes to the general acceptability of fiat money by declaring that debts are forgiven if the creditor refuses to accept fiat money as payment and by accepting fiat money as payment for taxes.

Use of fiat, nonconvertible paper money has one great benefit: It releases valuable resources—gold, silver, or other items—to other uses. But like all commodities, paper is not perfect money. Although it is easily transferable, divisible, and portable, it is less durable than some other forms of money such as gold. Paper money must be periodically replaced by the government, so replacement is a cost of using it. Another important cost is that the government monopoly might overissue paper money relative to the demand for it, thereby creating inflation. However, the widespread use of fiat money indicates that the benefits from using it outweigh the costs.

The reader may object: Is not paper a commodity and is there not an opportunity cost to using paper as fiat money? Paper is a commodity, but the price and thus the opportunity cost of using paper as money is extremely low relative to other possible forms of money. The important point is that the paper money must be generally acceptable as a medium of exchange. If a base metal or anything else meets this criterion, it also can serve as money.

A Medium of Exchange in International Markets. To understand how the use of a common medium of exchange facilitates exchange, it is useful to consider transactions between citizens of different countries. What is commonly accepted as a medium of exchange in one country is unlikely to be used in another. An American merchant offered payment in Japanese yen is in the same position as the psychiatrist offered payment in Persian kittens. The merchant will accept the yen only if there is a direct use for them (something that can be obtained in exchange for yen) or if the yen are easily converted to dollars. For this reason, transaction costs tend to be higher on international sales than on domestic ones—a situation that would be eliminated with the adoption of a common currency. At various times, certain currencies have come to be widely accepted in world markets. The British pound played such a role earlier in this century, but it was replaced by the U.S. dollar after World War II. However, rapid inflation in the United States in the late 1970s eroded some of the world's confidence in the dollar, and it became less widely accepted. As the U.S. dollar declined, currencies such as the German mark and the Japanese yen rose in importance. As part of the economic unification of Western Europe, plans are underway for a common currency—the European Currency Unit, often referred to as the European dollar. While there is a strong economic incentive for the European countries to use a common currency, nationalist forces in several of the participating countries actively oppose a common currency. Though unlikely to be adopted in the near future, a common European currency would be a strong candidate for an international medium of exchange.

Money as a Unit of Account

Money transactions are preferred to barter partly because money reduces the cost of economic transactions. To illustrate, a leathersmith in a small-scale barter economy produces tanned leather in exchange for blankets, gunpowder, food, alcohol, and metal traps. Without a money serving as a unit of account, the leathersmith (and anyone else who trades) must calculate relative prices of goods in terms of other goods in order to make rational trades. To allocate exchanges rationally, the leathersmith must consult four separate markets to find out the leather price of blankets, of food, and so on. Each trader must do the same. As the number of traders and the number of goods rises, the number of calculations rises exponentially.

Unit of account:
A standard measure, such as the dollar, that is used to express the values of goods and services; a function of money.

The use of money as a **unit of account** helps solve such problems. When money is introduced, all goods are valued in a common measure. Thus, if Jane knows that leather coats cost $4 each and that alcohol costs $2 a bottle, she will also automatically know that her can of gunpowder, worth $8, will trade for two leather coats or four bottles of alcohol or any other combination of goods equaling $8. The function of money as a unit of account means that the number of mental calculations required to determine the relative prices of all traded goods is vastly reduced. This function of money was called the *numeraire* by the French economist Léon Walras (1834–1910). The numeraire is the unit in which the prices of all other goods are stated. Prices are ordinarily stated in the society's monetary unit, such as dollars, sous, or pounds, but there is no reason why any other commodity could not serve as the numeraire. Prices may be reckoned through a leather unit of accounting or through an alcohol standard. The important point is that some *thing* serves to reduce the number of mental calculations required for rational trade. Money has often served in this capacity.

Money as a Standard of Deferred Payments

Money not only helps us keep track of the relative prices of goods, it also serves as a standard for payments that are deferred from the present to the future. When we borrow money for a Caribbean vacation, a home, or a new car, we are using money as a **standard of deferred payment.** Money is used as a standard of deferred payment when a debt or obligation is expressed in terms of dollars, pounds, or any other medium of exchange.

Standard of deferred payment:
A standard measure for expressing contractual values over time, such as the future payments associated with loans and debts; a function of money.

Contracts to buy or sell in the future use money as a standard of deferred payment, and there are potential costs in doing so. One of them is inflation—a reduction in the value of money. When money is used as a standard of deferred payment, there are potential gainers and losers. A contract to pay for a new car two years hence means an inflation risk for the lender. If the inflation rate depreciates the value of money by 10 percent in two years, the lender would receive dollars that would buy 10 percent fewer goods and services. Lenders will therefore try to protect themselves by charging interest to cover the risk of inflation.

Money as a Store of Value

Store of value:
The ability to own wealth in the form of some item, such as money; a function of money.

Individuals who want to save must store wealth, and one way to store it is in the form of money. Money's role as a **store of value** is its least exclusive function. Virtually all commodities, including furniture, houses, stamps, Pekinese puppies, and money, serve as temporary storehouses of wealth or value. But there are better and worse keepers of value. Commodities such as perishable foods are used up relatively quickly. Other commodities, such as land, precious metals, works of art, or buildings, tend to change value relatively slowly.

While any commodity is a store of value, not all commodities are instantly salable. The salability of commodities is called **liquidity,** the ease or rapidity with which any commodity can be converted into a medium of exchange. Money is the most liquid asset—the one most readily accepted in exchange for other goods and services. All other commodities take varying amounts of time to be converted into money. When cash is needed, land or warehouses cannot easily be converted into cash, but stocks and bonds (which are not money) can. Land is therefore less liquid than stocks and bonds.

Money has its own advantages and disadvantages as a store of value. It may retain its value over long periods, but during periods of inflation it may be a poor store of value. Under extreme conditions, as when a nation at war is forced to make huge expenditures to defend itself, money may lose its value or purchasing power very rapidly through inflation. Such was the case during the American colonial period, when paper money was known as Continentals. The phrase "not worth a Continental" refers to a rapidly depreciating store of value. In fact, inflation, or currency depreciation, has occurred during or after every American war, including the Vietnam War.

In general, money has served fairly well as a store of value in the United States, although its performance over the last several decades has been uneven. The holding of money, therefore, is both safe and risky. Money is instantly convertible to other goods and services, but it may lose its value more or less rapidly than other commodities. When a person holds any other asset (an interest-bearing savings account, IBM stock, a Picasso painting), liquidity is sacrificed.

THE OFFICIAL DEFINITION OF MONEY

Now that we have gained some understanding of money by examining its various functions, we can define more carefully what we mean by the word *money*. Of the various functions that money serves, its use as a medium of exchange is of greatest economic importance. Therefore, our definition of **money** was along these lines: Money is anything that is generally acceptable as a medium of exchange. Since coins and currency and checkbook money are widely accepted for payment, they must be considered money. To these, we want to add all close substitutes. Since how close a substitute certain assets are to currency is a matter of judgment, various official definitions of the money supply have emerged.

Possible confusion caused by the terminology surrounding checkbook money can be avoided by remembering that any accounts from which payments or funds transfers may be made are called **transactions accounts.** These include all demand deposits and checkable deposits managed by banks and other financial institutions. **Demand deposits** are those transactions accounts against which an unlimited number of checks may ordinarily be written. **Checkable deposits** often carry restrictions on transferability—a maximum number of checks may be written per month without penalty, and so on. Both demand deposits and checkable deposits are "checkable" in the sense that either may be utilized as a medium of exchange.

Though the "general acceptability" definition is reasonably clear-cut, a number of assets, such as noncheckable savings accounts, may have important effects on the behavior of investors and consumers and, therefore, on the economy. These less-liquid assets, sometimes called "near-monies," are there-

Liquidity:
The ease with which any asset or commodity can be converted into money with little or no risk of loss to the holder.

Money:
Anything that is generally acceptable as a medium of exchange.

Transactions accounts:
Demand deposits or other checkable accounts that allow the transfer of funds by writing a check.

Demand deposit:
A type of transaction account with virtually no restrictions as to the size, timing, or number of checks that can be written on the account.

Checkable deposits:
Demand deposits plus other types of transaction accounts that pay interest but that may carry some restrictions on use, including minimum balance and limits on the number of checks that can be written per month.

fore included in some statistical compilations. Thus the nation's money supply is officially measured in a number of ways.

Four major measures of money developed by the Federal Reserve System, the nation's central bank, are described in Table 1. Notice that the M-1 measure corresponds to the definition of general acceptability. M-1 is composed of coins and currency in the public's hands and most checkable deposits.

The measures are arranged from M-1 to L in order of decreasing liquidity. Small savings deposits, included in M-2, are ordinarily more liquid than large-denomination time deposits, included in M-3, since convertibility of the latter into cash often requires advance warning to the financial institution. U.S. government securities, included in measure L but not in M-3, are less liquid still, and so on. Conceptually there is no limit to these distinctions (Is the Brooklyn Bridge a more or less liquid asset than the Hoover Dam?), but these three measures plus M-1 are sufficient for most important economic calculations.

You may be wondering why credit card balances have not been included in any of our definitions of the money supply. After all, if money is viewed as *anything* that is generally acceptable as a medium of exchange, credit card balances should qualify. Having $500 in unused credit card balances is as useful in making purchases as having $500 in a checkable account. Albeit indirectly, unused credit card balances are included in each of our money supply definitions. One component of M-1 (and therefore of the other money supply measures) is deposits in checkable accounts. Credit cards operate this way: The issuing company maintains checkable balances that are transferred to the merchant's account whenever the merchant accepts one of the company's cards as payment. It would be double counting to include both these deposits and the unused balances held by cardholders.

Definitions of *money* and *near-monies* evolve with new developments, like the recent emergence of checkable accounts at nonbank financial institutions such as credit unions. Various items in the Federal Reserve System's definitions are lumped together because they are more alike than other possible groupings. Each definition has its own strengths and weaknesses as a tool for measuring the nation's money stock. M-2, for example, may be used in analyzing economic problems where a broader view of liquidity is appropriate.

Lest the reader get the impression that money is the economist's elusive cat in the hat, calculation of the various measures produces real numbers. Figure 1 graphically presents money supply data for October 1989. These figures, calculated in billions of dollars by the Federal Reserve System, correspond to the definitions given in Table 1. The figure shows that M-2 is almost four times the size of M-1, and L, the broadest definition of money, is almost six times the size of M-1. In general, however, economists consider "money" or the "money supply" to be M-1, which consists of assets that are generally accepted as a medium of exchange.

MONEY AND THE BANKING SYSTEM

The largest components of M-1 are bank deposits. As indicated in Figure 1, commercial bank demand deposits were worth $280.4 billion at the end of October 1989. Checkable deposits at other financial institutions accounted for another $280.3 billion. Together these bank deposits are more than two

TABLE 1 Four Measures of the Money Stock

Federal Reserve System classifications of money stock range from M-1 to L, in order of decreasing liquidity. The most liquid measure is M-1, which includes currency in the public's hands, most checkable and demand deposits at financial institutions, and travelers' checks. Although L is many times greater than M-1, as shown in Figure 1, economists often identify money as only assets that are generally accepted as a medium of exchange—that is, M-1.

Measure	Components	Definitions
M-1	Currency, including coins and paper money held outside banks	
	Checkable and demand deposits at commercial banks, savings institutions, and credit unions	
	NOW and super-NOW accounts	NOW (negotiable order of withdrawal) account: Interest-earning account on which owner may write checks; super-NOW account: NOW account with higher interest and additional restrictions on withdrawals.
	ATS accounts	ATS (automatic transfer savings) account: Interest-earning account, the contents of which are automatically transferred to an individual's checking account when the checking account falls to a minimum level.
	Travelers' checks	
	Checkable money market accounts	
M-2	M-1	
	Savings deposits and small-denomination time deposits in both commercial banks and savings institutions	Time deposit: Large savings deposit requiring notification (usually 30 days) or interest penalties for early withdrawal.
	Certain money market mutual funds	Money market mutual funds: Investment funds managed by banks or investment companies whereby investors' money is pooled and used to buy or sell bonds or other interest-earning investments; investors generally can write checks against their fund balances under some restrictions.
	Overnight Eurodollars	Overnight Eurodollars: Short-term dollar-denominated deposits held in foreign banks.

and a half times the size of the holdings of currency (including coins) by the nonbank public. We are all accustomed to accepting currency and coin as money. But how did bank money—that is, checkable deposits—evolve?

The Evolution of Banking

The emergence of banks and checkable deposits was intimately linked with the origins of fiat money. Before the Renaissance and the emergence of a modern market society, commodity money, usually gold or silver, circulated as a medium of exchange.

Use of gold, for all its advantages as a medium of exchange, had some drawbacks in actual trade. As Eastern and Western trade routes expanded and as exchange became less localized, merchants were forced to transport gold overland and overseas. A sale of goods by a merchant in Constantinople to

TABLE 1   **(Cont.)**

Measure	Components	Definitions
	Overnight repurchase agreements	Overnight repurchase agreements: Overnight loans of idle funds, in which Treasury bills serve as collateral.
M-3	M-2	
	Large-denomination time deposits ($100,000 or more) at commercial and savings institutions	
	Term repurchase agreements	Term repurchase agreements: Short-term loans of idle funds, in which Treasury bills serve as collateral.
	Eurodollar deposits held by U.S. individuals	Eurodollars: Deposits denominated in U.S. dollars held by individuals and nonbank businesses in banks located abroad (mostly in Europe), as opposed to overnight Eurodollars.
L	M-3	
	U.S. savings bonds	
	Short-term U.S. government securities	
	Bankers' acceptances	Bankers' acceptances: Notes that are issued by businesses to obtain short-term credit and that are accepted by a bank or other financial institution. Acceptance by the bank indicates that the bank stands ready to pay the principal of the note to the holder at maturity. At maturity the bank pays off the note, charges the business issuer's account, and charges a fee for its services.
	Commercial paper	Commercial paper: Short-term (up to six months) financial obligations (notes) of large corporations traded among finance companies and companies dealing in installment loan credit. Commercial paper may be placed in the market by corporations directly or through specialized dealers.

buyers in Venice required a corresponding payment in gold. But traders soon recognized the safety and convenience of not actually transporting gold at all.

Gold "warehouses" developed, often run by people whose job it was to certify the gold or silver content of coins and to stamp the coins accordingly. These warehouses were a primitive though essentially complete form of the modern bank. Goldsmiths stored the precious metal for traders, issuing a receipt representing the quantity of gold on deposit. These warehouse receipts, which were claims to gold, soon became acceptable as the medium of exchange in both local and international commerce.

This acceptability was a giant leap toward the development of nonconvertible, nonredeemable fiat money, although a commodity standard was still in existence at the time since these receipts were instantly convertible into gold or silver. Traders acquired faith in the goodness or ready convertibility of their warehouse receipts into gold, and with general acceptance, the receipts

FIGURE 1   Numerical Measures of the Money Stock, October 1989

The Federal Reserve System has calculated numerical measures of the money supply for October 1989. As the numbers indicate, L includes the largest numbers and amounts of assets, and the range from M-1 to L is in order of decreasing liquidity of assets. M-1, consisting of currency, all demand and checkable deposits except money market mutual funds, and travelers' checks, is the most useful measure of money. The *Federal Reserve Bulletin* does not report numerical values of all components of a measure; those reported for M-2, M-3, and L are thus selected portions of the measures.

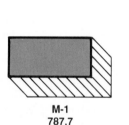
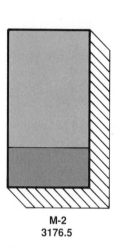
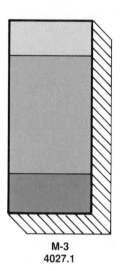
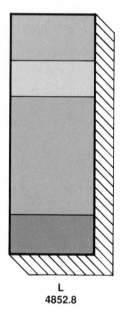

M-1	M-2	M-3	L
787.7	3176.5	4027.1	4852.8

Currency (held
  outside banks)   219.7
Demand Deposits 280.4
Travelers' Checks   7.3
Other Checkable
  Deposits   280.3

M-1 +
Savings Deposits 301.6
Small-denomination
  Time Deposits   882.5
Money Market
  Mutual Funds   241.0

M-2 +
Large-denomination
  Time Deposits 436.6

M-3 +
U.S. Savings
Bonds, Short-term
Government Securities,
Bankers' Acceptances,
Commercial Paper and
European Deposits
Held by U.S.
Individuals

Note: Amounts in billions of dollars. Totals do not necessarily sum due to the provisional nature of the data.

themselves became money. Currency had thus arrived; and modern checkbook money was only a small step away.

Accepting deposits is one of the two essential functions of banks, and the early goldsmith-warehousers originated the practice. A second major role of commercial banks is to make loans, a profitable but sometimes dangerous practice that was also devised by early bankers. In the beginning, the warehouser undoubtedly earned some income solely by guarding the deposited gold and charging a fee for risk and insurance. The warehouser's receipts were backed by 100 percent of the deposited gold. Soon, however, the primitive banker recognized that not all depositors presented receipts for payment at the same time. On the average, perhaps half the receipt holders demanded their gold during any given day or week. The ever-present profit motive took over. Gold (or gold receipts) could be lent to borrowers at some rate of interest, as long as some "safe" percentage of gold holdings was kept in reserve

Fractional reserve banking system:
A banking system in which banks hold only some percentage of deposits as reserves.

for conversion on demand. In this way, a **fractional reserve banking system,** in which banks maintain only a fraction of cash reserves against deposits, was born. The early goldsmiths issued more receipts than the actual value of gold in their vault. They kept a fraction of gold reserves in their vaults against the likelihood that depositors would demand their specie (gold and silver). The rest was lent at interest, creating another source of profit.

In performing the banking functions of accepting deposits and making loans, early goldsmith-bankers also encountered dangers similar to those inherent in modern fractional reserve banking. Greed in the form of lending too much money for profit—that is, underestimating the fraction of total gold reserves demanded by depositors at any given time—brought disaster. Bank runs occurred when customers became fearful that the goldsmith's deposits were not safe and immediately sought to withdraw their funds.

Two crucial points related to early banking are central to understanding modern banking systems: (1) The practice of lending at interest in a fractional reserve system meant that goldsmiths could actually alter the money supply, expanding it by lending, reducing it by calling in loans; and (2) goldsmiths could place all deposits and banks in jeopardy by misjudging the fraction of depositors' liabilities that would be presented for payment at one time. The first matter—multiple expansion and contraction of checkable deposits by commercial banks in a modern fractional reserve system—is the subject of Chapter 15. The second issue—the safety of the banking system and its regulation by the Federal Reserve System—is treated in Chapter 16. Before investigating these topics in detail, we take a brief overview of the contemporary banking system.

The U.S. Banking and Financial System

Commercial bank:
Chartered financial institution that accepts deposits of various types, especially demand deposits, and that makes commercial and consumer loans.

There are currently about fifteen thousand commercial banks in the United States. **A commercial bank** is a privately owned but publicly regulated financial institution whose primary role is accepting checkable deposits and making business and consumer loans. For years, there was a clear distinction between commercial banks and other financial institutions: Only banks could issue checkable accounts. However, during the 1970s, other financial institutions found ways to circumvent rules preventing them from offering checking privileges. Since then, regulations have been changed so that checking services can now be offered by the seventeen thousand credit unions and the three thousand savings and loans in this country. Since 1980, regulatory changes have brought these nonbank institutions increasingly under the control of the Federal Reserve System.[1] Today, the primary difference between banks and nonbanks lies in the types of loans in which they specialize (see Table 2). However, it is still informative to focus on commercial banks in discussing the role of financial institutions in money and money creation.

---

[1]Do not confuse the Federal Reserve System with the U.S. Treasury Department. The U.S. Treasury handles the budget, issues U.S. government bonds and securities to make up the difference when the budget is in deficit, and issues small amounts of money, mainly coins. The Federal Reserve System does not issue securities and does not act as the fiscal agent for government. It is primarily responsible for control and stability of prices and employment in the economy through control of the money stock.

TABLE 2   Major Types of Selected Financial Institutions in the United States and Assets, 1987

Type of Institution	Major Activities	Total Number[a]	Total Assets (billions of dollars)
Commercial banks	Accepting checkable deposits; making business loans	14,473	2743
Savings and loan associations	Accepting time deposits and NOW accounts; making residential mortgage loans	3513	1263
Life insurance companies	Issuing insurance policies; buying corporate bonds; and making commercial mortgage loans	2125	1000
Private pension funds	Issuing pension plans; buying corporate stocks and bonds	Not known	986
Money market funds	Issuing shares in fund; buying short-term liquid securities	670	316
Mutual savings banks	Accepting time deposits and NOW accounts; making residential mortgage loans	393	263
Credit unions	Accepting savings deposits and NOW accounts; making consumer loans	15,877	184
Mutual funds	Issuing shares in fund; buying corporate stock	1026	453

Source: Data from *Statistical Abstract of the United States,* 1989 (Washington, D.C.: U.S. Government Printing Office, 1989), p. 487.

[a]Data for 1984.

Federal Reserve System:
The central bank of the United States; regulates financial institutions and establishes and conducts monetary policy.

Both the individual states and the federal government charter, or license, privately owned commercial banks. National bank charters are issued by the Comptroller of the Currency (an official of the U.S. Treasury Department), while state banking commissions or similar bodies issue state bank charters. By law, all national banks must belong to the **Federal Reserve System,** whereas state banks may elect membership in "the Fed" subject to the approval of the Federal Reserve System. The basic role of the Federal Reserve System, a system of banks organized by geographic region, is to regulate member banks and other financial institutions. About two-thirds of all banks do not belong to the Federal Reserve System, but as we will see, this limited membership does not prevent the Federal Reserve System from overseeing and regulating the activities of all banks.

Statistics on commercial bank assets and liabilities provide an idea of the overall importance of the commercial banking system in our economy. Table 3 shows the balance sheet (total assets equal total liabilities plus net worth) of all domestically chartered commercial banking institutions in the United States as of the end of May 1990.

A glance at Table 3 reveals that the major functions of the U.S. commercial banking system—accepting deposits and making loans—are identical to those of the early gold warehousers. Modern U.S. banking follows the same

TABLE 3

The Balance Sheet of All Commercial Banks, May 1990

The aggregate balance sheet of all commercial banks highlights the major assets and liabilities of commercial banks. Major assets are cash and income-earning loans and securities. Major liabilities include demand, savings, and time deposits. Double-entry bookkeeping guarantees that total assets equal liabilities plus capital or net worth. Aggregate data include all Federal Reserve System member and nonmember commercial banks, mutual savings banks, and non-deposit trust companies in the United States, except branches of foreign banks.

Total Assets (billions of dollars)		Total Liabilities and Capital (billions of dollars)	
Total cash assets	245	Total deposits	2288
Currency and coin	30	Transactions	618
Reserves with the Federal Reserve banks	28	Savings	554
		Time	1117
Balances with depository institutions	32	Borrowing	543
Cash items in process of collection/other cash assets	155	Other liabilities	235
Loans and securities	2831		
Loans, excluding interbank loans	2037		
U.S. Treasury securities	417		
Other securities	377		
Other assets	202	Residual assets (assets less liabilities)	212
Total assets	3278	Total liabilities and capital	3278

Source: Federal Reserve Bulletin (August 1990).

tradition, but it is far more complex in that many financial instruments—variants of the early bankers' warehouse receipts—have evolved. Regulations to prevent problems in the banking system have also evolved; in the United States the Federal Reserve System, which was created by the Federal Reserve Act of 1913, makes and enforces such regulations.

Assets. Many of the assets and liabilities of the commercial banking system are self-explanatory, but some require comment. In Table 3, total commercial bank cash assets in May 1990 were $245 billion. The first but smallest category of cash assets is vault and till cash (currency and coins). The second and third cash assets are currency deposits that commercial banks have in other banks, including the Federal Reserve banks. Commercial banks often have financial arrangements with other commercial banks (and other depository institutions, such as savings and loans). These are called correspondent relations with correspondent banks. A special type of correspondent relation exists between commercial banks and the Federal Reserve banks: Commercial banks are required to keep a percentage of their deposit liabilities—a fractional reserve—available at all times. Some of this reserve is deposited in the Federal Reserve banks. The last cash asset, cash items in process of collection, refers to temporarily uncleared checks held by banks that, when cleared, will give the banks control over cash assets.

Loans and purchases of government securities and other interest-bearing instruments are the two most important means by which commercial banks earn returns and, presumably, profits. Loans include commercial, industrial, and private loans. Other assets ($202 billion in Table 3) include accrued interest on notes and securities, Federal Reserve bank stock (a required purchase by member banks), and real estate—bank premises, furniture and fixtures, and long-run real estate mortgages.

Liabilities. The major liabilities of commercial banks are deposits of several kinds. Transaction and demand deposits are checkbook money—generally acceptable orders by one business or individual depositor to pay another. Recall that such checkable deposits are included in M-1 and are therefore money as we have defined it. Savings deposits and time deposits include passbook savings deposit accounts, time deposits of various long-run durations, and interbank deposits (deposits held by one bank at another bank). Most time deposits require notification of intended withdrawal or invoke interest penalties for early withdrawal. If savings accounts are checkable or instantly transferable to checkable deposits, they are money in the M-1 sense.

The borrowing category includes borrowings from other banks, financial institutions, or the Federal Reserve System. Commercial banks often borrow from each other and from the Federal Reserve to invest in interest-earning assets such as loans or securities.

The Federal Reserve System

The Federal Reserve System is the basic regulatory agency in the business of commercial banking and other financial intermediaries. Its relation to the banking system is similar to that of the Federal Communications Commission and the radio and television industry. One might assume that the main purpose of the Federal Reserve System is to harness the activities of overzealous bankers, who might act in the manner of overzealous gold warehousers—that is, lending out too much money at interest and thereby being unable to meet commitments to depositors. Bank and depositor safety, however, is not a primary or even essential function of the Federal Reserve.

The Federal Reserve System, or any other modern central bank such as the Bank of England or the Bank of Sweden, has two essential functions. One is the older function of serving as a lender of last resort to commercial banks and other lending institutions—to respond quickly and adequately to bank runs, panics, or liquidity crises by providing currency or specie to meet withdrawals. The other, more modern function is to control the money supply to affect the business cycle and economic activity—to produce significant short-run effects on the rates of employment, inflation, and real income growth. This latter function developed slowly and has come into prominence only since the Great Depression of the 1930s, but it is now the major purpose of the Federal Reserve System. The Federal Reserve also conducts other service functions such as issuing currency and holding deposits of the federal government and its agencies.

The following chapters discuss monetary economics in detail—how the Federal Reserve controls the money supply and how changes in the money supply affect employment, inflation, and real income. As an introduction, we consider now the structure and membership of the Federal Reserve System.

Structure. Failure of the old National Banking System, established in 1863, to act as the lender of last resort led to the creation of the modern Federal Reserve Banking System in 1913. The system began operation with the following purposes: (1) to provide an elastic currency to help eliminate panics and bank runs: (2) to supervise the banking system at the federal level; (3) to provide facilities for the buying and selling of financial assets, a means of providing funds to banks at an interest rate called the discount rate; and (4) to enlarge facilities for check clearance. A formal structure within which these functions were to be performed was also established. The original structure survives almost unchanged today, although concentrations of power over monetary policy have developed within the system over the years of its existence. These power concentrations will become apparent in our discussion of the formal structure.

The structure of the Federal Reserve System is shown in Figure 2. The Federal Reserve System is composed of two basic units: the decentralized twelve Federal Reserve banks (see Figure 3 for their locations) and the central node of power, the Board of Governors in Washington, D.C. The Board of Governors consists of seven members appointed by the president, with six

FIGURE 2

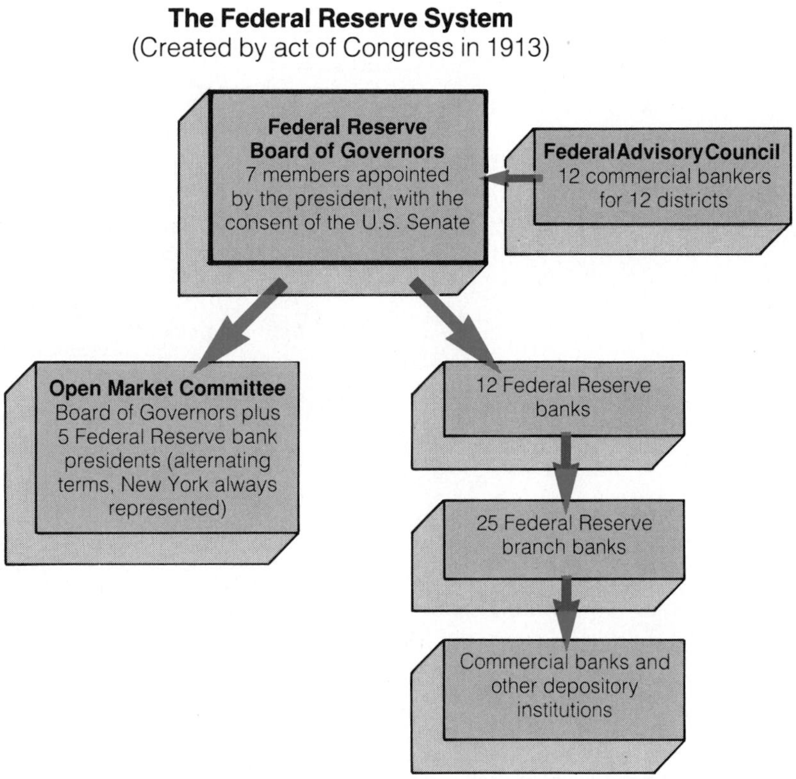

The commercial banking system and other institutions issuing checkable deposits are regulated and controlled by the Federal Reserve System, which is composed of twelve Federal Reserve banks and twenty-five branch banks. Monetary control is exercised through the Board of Governors and the Federal Open Market Committee in Washington, D.C. The seven members of the board, including its chair, are appointed by the president, subject to Senate approval.

The Federal Reserve and Commercial Banking Systems

Federal Open Market Committee (FOMC):
A committee of the Federal Reserve System made up of the seven members of the Board of Governors of the Federal Reserve System and five presidents of Federal Reserve district banks; directs open market operations (buying and selling of securities) for the system.

governors serving staggered fourteen-year terms; the chair of the board serves a four-year term. The board in general and the chair of the board in particular are almost solely responsible for the establishment of national monetary policy.

The **Federal Open Market Committee (FOMC)** consists of the seven members of the board plus five Federal Reserve bank presidents; the president of the New York bank is always on the committee because of the amount of major financial activity that takes place in New York City. Virtually all monetary policy is carried out by the board and the Open Market Committee. The board must approve any changes in regulations that directly affect the supply of money.

In contrast to the centralization of power and action in the hands of the board and the FOMC, the actual structure of the Federal Reserve System is elaborate and decentralized. As Figure 3 shows, the system is organized into twelve districts with one Federal Reserve bank and a varying number of branch

FIGURE 3

The Twelve Districts and Branches in the Federal Reserve System

The Federal Reserve System is geographically decentralized to service banks and other financial institutions throughout the United States. Services include the provision of an elastic currency supply to prevent bank runs, the discounting of paper, and check-clearing facilities. The major purpose of the Federal Reserve System is to help provide full employment, economic growth, and price stability by control of the money supply.

Source: Federal Reserve Bulletin (November 1986).

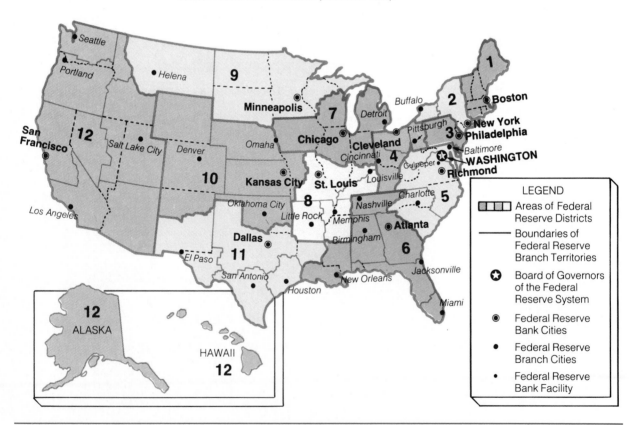

banks for each district. The Federal Reserve bank for the sixth district is in Atlanta, for example, and branch banks for that district are in Miami, Jacksonville, New Orleans, Birmingham, and Nashville. The Federal Reserve banks and their branches are geographically dispersed to service and inspect member banks and other depository institutions in their areas.

Membership. Membership in the Federal Reserve System has fluctuated over the years. Assets and deposits of member banks declined between the mid-1960s and 1980, especially during the late 1970s. The major reason for this decline was the increasing regulatory cost of belonging to the federal system in contrast to looser regulations over banks at the state level. Shifts therefore occurred from national bank charters to state charters. In response, Congress gave the Federal Reserve System sweeping new powers over all banks and over nonbank depository institutions with the passage of the Depository Institutions Deregulation and Monetary Control Act of 1980 (discussed in Chapter 16). The Financial Institutions Reform, Recovery, and Enforcement Act of 1989 gave the Federal Reserve System additional regulatory powers over both banks and nonbanks. Despite declining membership in the Federal Reserve System, the system directly controls all checkable deposits in all U.S. financial institutions, the largest component of the money supply. This control, as we will see in the following chapters, enables the Federal Reserve System to control the overall money supply and greatly influence the course of economic growth.

THE IMPORTANCE OF MONEY: A PREVIEW

Individually, we might take the use of money for granted, for some form of money has always been and always will be part of our lives. However, most economists historically have regarded the control of money as central to sound economic policy. The basis for this belief is the quantity theory of money (discussed briefly in Chapter 8), an idea that is well over two hundred years old and is now the basis for modern monetarist thought. Before turning to the intriguing conflicts over monetary policies, we must more closely investigate how bank money is created, how the Federal Reserve System affects money creation, and how monetarists view the world of aggregate economic activity.

SUMMARY

1. Money was invented to avoid the transaction and information costs of barter, which required a coincidence of wants among traders and imposed limits on the division of labor and specialization.
2. Money serves as a medium of exchange, a unit of account, a standard of deferred payments, and a store of value. Money's most important function is its general acceptability among traders as a means of ex-

change or payment. Virtually anything may serve as a medium of exchange, and there are costs and benefits attached to any item chosen.
3. Fiat money is paper or other low-cost money that is nonconvertible to gold or other commodities. Fiat money is certified by governments, and its general acceptability is fostered by its acceptance by the government as payment for taxes.

4. Money has a number of alternative official definitions, but the one most commonly used by economists is the classification M-1, which consists of all currency and coins in circulation and all checkable deposits at banks and other financial institutions. Currency and checkable deposits are the only two items that are generally acceptable as media of exchange.

5. The major functions of commercial banks are accepting checkable deposits (also called demand deposits) and making loans.

6. The Federal Reserve System was formed in 1913 to regulate and control the banking system. Its functions are to prevent bank collapse and to control the money supply to promote full employment and economic growth and to prevent inflation.

7. The structure of the Federal Reserve System includes twelve geographically dispersed Federal Reserve banks and twenty-five branch banks to serve the commercial banking and financial system. Decision-making power rests with the Board of Governors and the Federal Open Market Committee, both located in Washington, D.C.

KEY TERMS

barter economy	standard of deferred payment	checkable deposits
double coincidence of wants	store of value	fractional reserve banking system
medium of exchange	liquidity	commercial bank
commodity money	money	Federal Reserve System
fiat money	transactions accounts	Federal Open Market Committee (FOMC)
unit of account	demand deposit	

QUESTIONS FOR REVIEW AND DISCUSSION

1. Explain the functions of money. Does inflation rob money of some of its functions?

2. Explain why a money system of exchange is better than a barter system.

3. For money to lower the costs of transactions and to perform its other functions well, it must have some particular physical characteristics. List and explain the desirable physical characteristics and also explain why paper makes better money than M&M's or stamps.

4. Would using gold as a medium of exchange solve the problems of constant changes in the level of prices? Explain your answer.

5. Define money and then discuss why each of the following is not considered money: IRAs, savings accounts, certificates of deposit, and gold.

6. What is the major feature that distinguishes M-1 from M-2, M-3, and L?

7. Essentially, what is a bank and what is the value to society of banks?

8. What is the major purpose of the Federal Reserve System? How does it achieve this purpose?

9. Why might the Federal Reserve be considered a system of decentralized banks rather than one central bank?

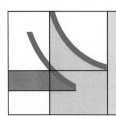

ECONOMICS IN ACTION
The Spontaneous Emergence of Money: The Prisoner of War Camp

Stalag 17, a highly acclaimed play and movie, depicted everyday life in a German prisoner of war camp. Seth, the antihero entrepreneur, ran rat "horse races," sold schnapps fermented in his own distillery, and seemed to be able to obtain almost anything for a price. Money in the form of coins and currency did not exist, but trades were conducted by the prisoners with another form of money—cigarettes. This part of the fictionalized account of prison life has basis in fact, as reported by an economic observer, R. A. Radford, who was a POW in Germany and Italy.[a] Radford's report tells us much about the relation between economic activity and the spontaneous emergence of money.

POWs in Stalag 17 did not do paid work, but they were allotted weekly rations of goods from the Red Cross and other private sources. These rations consisted of such items as tinned milk, jam, butter, biscuits, chocolate, sugar, and cigarettes. Tastes differ among individuals, and with everyone receiving roughly equal amounts of the same commodities, prisoners would barter among themselves for the items they preferred. As time passed, trade expanded and the relative price of one item in terms of others became well known. Trade became increasingly complex, and a generally accepted medium of exchange developed in the form of cigarettes, a commodity in common use. With the camps and their residents becoming semipermanent, prices of items in terms of cigarettes quickly became widely known. An exchange and mart board listing desired trades was set up: a pound of cheese for seven cigarettes, two cigarettes for a drink of schnapps. Unlike the case of Yap money, where stones are not standardized (see Focus, "The Stone Money of Yap," in this chapter), the use of cigarettes as a standardized commodity greatly reduced the transaction and information costs of trade and thus increased the volume of trade.

Additional economic issues were made easier by the new medium of exchange. Price fluctuations from Mondays, when the provisions were handed out, until a new shipment of rations came in on the following Sunday were smoothed out through voluntary exchanges between prisoners that smoothed fluctuations in supplies over time. Speculators would buy on Mondays when the price of toothpaste and food was low. As supplies diminished through the week and prices rose, speculators would sell their hoarded goods for profit. Relative price differences for goods between Mondays and Sundays were thus narrowed.

The POW camp did not avoid the economic problems of inflation and deflation. Periodic injections of higher quantities of cigarettes produced inflation. Scarcity of cigarettes caused the price levels to fall.

As all economists know, prices are also affected by psychological factors. Air raids, good or bad war news, and the

Prisoners of war playing poker for cigarettes at Stalag Luft III, Germany, 1944

weather all affected the prices because these events clearly changed the nonmonetary demand for cigarettes. The prisoners would smoke cigarettes rather than save them. All commodity money standards are influenced by such factors. Altered demand for quetzal feathers as decoration or for gold in dentistry or industry would clearly affect the price level in economies using feathers or gold as money.

The POW camp experience illustrates the naturalness or spontaneity with which money as a medium of exchange emerges. The liberation of prisoners by the U.S. infantry created chaos for the cigarette standard. When commodities are no longer relatively scarce, there is no need for economic organization or activity. The POW economy, as Radford reports, simply collapsed. The lesson to be learned is that scarcity, coupled with the recognition by traders of the costs of barter, will inevitably lead to the use of money.

Question

Money, in order to function efficiently, must be portable, durable, divisible, easily recognized, stable in supply, and relatively scarce. How well do cigarettes conform to these characteristics? Can you think of any other goods likely to be found in a POW camp that would be preferable to cigarettes as money?

[a]R. A. Radford, "The Economic Organization of a P.O.W. Camp," *Economica,* n.s. (November 1945), pp. 189–201.

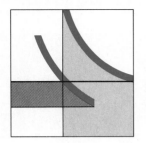

15

Money Creation

Chapter 14 defines *money* as anything that is generally acceptable as a medium of exchange—all currency, coins, and checkable deposits in the hands of the public. The most important part of our generally accepted money is checkbook money, called demand deposits or checkable deposits. In fact, in October 1989, the value of checkable deposits was more than two and a half times the value of dollars and coins in circulation—$560.7 billion in checkable deposits compared to $219.7 billion in currency.

Checkable deposits are money because of our faith that others will accept our checks—our orders to transfer funds—as currency and the faith of others that we will do likewise. This means that when the amounts kept in checkable deposits expand or contract, the economy's money supply also expands or contracts. In this chapter we explore how the process of money creation and destruction works through the commercial banking system. In the next chapter we will look at how the Federal Reserve System regulates the deposits to maintain economic stabilization.

Historically, commercial banks were exclusive issuers of checkbook money, and other nonbank financial institutions, also called thrift institutions—savings and loan institutions, mutual savings banks, credit unions, and the like—limited their services to transferring funds from savers to investors such as home buyers. But nonbank financial institutions are competing strongly for such accounts. The general blurring of the roles of banks and nonbank institutions reflects the dynamic character of the financial side of our economy. For ease of understanding, we discuss money creation from the perspective of commercial banks.

Among the key issues concerning commercial banking you should understand after reading Chapter 15 are

- the important process through which banks create and destroy deposits and money in the banking system.
- the critical role of required reserves—regulated by the Federal Reserve System—in the process of money creation and destruction.
- the impact of currency drains on the money and deposit creation process.
- how banks as privately owned institutions are motivated to make profits and, at the same time, to function in the money creation and destruction process in the interests of society as a whole.

MONEY CREATION BY A SINGLE BANK

The major functions of any commercial bank are to accept deposits and to make loans and investments—the same functions as the early banker-warehousers. We present a simplified balance sheet for a hypothetical individual bank in Table 1 to show how these roles interact. A balance sheet uses the accounting identity, the convention that the sum of all bank assets must equal the sum of all liabilities plus capital or net worth. The assets of the hypothetical bank are listed on the left side and liabilities and net worth on the right side. Double-entry bookkeeping—in which every asset creates an equal liability, and vice versa—guarantees that the balance sheet always balances.

Major bank liabilities are sums that the bank owes to others. These obligations include checkable, or demand, deposits, which depositors can draw on by writing checks, as well as savings, time, and interbank deposits. Liabilities also include the bank's borrowings from other commercial banks and from the Federal Reserve bank. Capital accounts, funds raised from the sale of stocks, are placed on the right side of the balance sheet, along with the liabilities.

The items that balance these figures are all the things the bank owns—cash, notes representing loans to consumers and businesses, securities, bank buildings, equipment, and so on.[1]

Balance sheets give a snapshot of banking activities. To better understand the importance of banks and their role in the expansion and contraction of the money supply, we need to step back for a moment and look at the process of how a bank gets started.

TABLE 1

Simplified Bank Balance Sheet

Capital investments of $2 million permit the formation of the Second Bank of Show Low. The left side of the balance sheet gives the bank's assets—cash, notes representing loans to its customers, securities, and buildings and equipment. This balance sheet shows that the bank's entire initial investment was used to purchase the building and furnishings. The right side of the balance sheet gives the bank's liabilities—all deposits (checkable, time, and savings), its borrowings from other banks, and capital invested in it. Double-entry bookkeeping is used, so every asset creates an equal liability, and vice versa.

Second Bank of Show Low Balance Sheet			
Assets (thousands of dollars)		Liabilities and Capital Accounts (thousands of dollars)	
Cash	0	Deposits	0
Loans	0	Borrowings	0
Securities	0	Capital	2000
Plant and fixtures	2000		
Total assets	2000	Total liabilities and capital	2000

---

[1]Throughout this chapter we will be using the word *cash* to refer to currency and coin held in the bank's vaults or tills plus cash balances held with the Federal Reserve.

How a Bank Gets Started

Suppose that a group of investors organizes and decides that the town of Show Low, Arizona, needs a new bank and that such a bank would be profitable. They apply for and obtain a state charter and pledge $2 million in capital investment. With these funds they purchase a building, elect directors, and christen their bank the Second Bank of Show Low. The balance sheet of the bank after the purchase of the plant and equipment is given in Table 1.

Note that the accounting identity is satisfied in the balance sheet. Total assets are $2 million worth of plant and fixtures (all of the original asset, cash, was converted into the bank building and furnishings). These assets are equal in value to the sum of total liabilities and capital stock because at this point of bank organization, the initial investors have claim against the value of the bank's plant and fixtures. There are no other assets besides the building and no liabilities, but this situation cannot last if investors hope to earn a return on their capital, which they certainly do. The bank must begin to function by accepting deposits.

Assume that an entrepreneur, Josephine Eccentric, is a citizen of Show Low. Josephine has made a fortune as a fast-food restaurant organizer. She deposits $1 million in cash in the Second Bank of Show Low. The bank's new balance sheet appears as Table 2.

The Second Bank has now acquired $1 million in cash and a counterbalancing demand deposit liability. As a result of Josephine's deposit, the total money supply has not changed in amount, but it has changed in composition. Josephine gave up currency for a checking account deposit. The checkable deposit is counted as money, however, so Josephine's deposit simply altered the composition, not the amount, of the money supply. But this act of putting money in the bank as a deposit to be drawn at a later time allows the bank to create more money by means of the fractional reserve banking system.

The Fractional Reserve System

The *fractional reserve banking system*—in which banks keep only a percentage of funds deposited with them available for withdrawals—is a vital aspect of banking behavior regulated by the Federal Reserve System. We will briefly examine how Josephine's cash deposit in the Second Bank becomes part of the money creation process.

TABLE 2	Recording a Deposit on the Balance Sheet

A deposit of $1 million creates liabilities of $1 million for the bank and cash assets of an equal amount. Total assets remain equal to total liabilities plus capital.

Second Bank of Show Low Balance Sheet			
Assets (thousands of dollars)		Liabilities and Capital Accounts (thousands of dollars)	
Cash	1000	Deposits	1000
Loans	0	Borrowings	0
Securities	0	Capital	2000
Plant and fixtures	2000		
Total assets	3000	Total liabilities and capital	3000

Cash reserves:
Commercial banks' and other depository institutions' holdings of vault cash or deposits at the Federal Reserve district banks.

Required reserves:
Reserves against checkable deposits that banks and other depository institutions are required by the Federal Reserve to keep in the form of cash reserves; equal to the required reserve ratio times checkable deposits; also called legal reserves.

Reserve ratio:
The percentage of checkable deposits that banks and other depository institutions hold as reserves.

Excess reserves:
Total reserves minus required reserves.

Cash assets of commercial banks held in their own vaults or at the district Federal Reserve bank are called **cash reserves.** The Federal Reserve specifies that banks and other deposit-issuing institutions must keep a certain percentage of their cash reserves on hand or with a Federal Reserve bank at all times. These **required reserves,** sometimes called legal reserves, can be expressed as a percentage of checkable deposits or as a **reserve ratio:**

$$RR = r \times D,$$

where r is the reserve ratio, D is the amount of demand deposit liabilities, and RR is the amount of required reserves for demand deposits. (Different reserve ratios apply to the various kinds of savings and time deposits.) If, for example, the deposit liabilities at a commercial bank are $1,000,000 and r is 10 percent, or 0.10, required reserves equal $100,000. If r is 5 percent, 0.05, required reserves are $50,000.

Depending on business conditions or expected loan demand, the bank may well decide to hold more than the required percentage of deposits as cash reserves. The total quantity of cash reserves held by a bank or the banking system consists of required reserves and excess reserves. **Excess reserves** are cash reserves over and above those reserves required by the Federal Reserve. If total reserves were $1,000,000, the required reserve ratio were 10 percent, and deposit liabilities were $1,000,000, excess reserves would total $900,000 ($1,000,000 − $100,000 = $900,000). Some of these excess reserves could be desirable for the bank—an extra cushion against the possibility of default, of its being unable to meet its depositors' demands for cash. Some excess, however, may be undesirable, for the bank is holding funds that it could use to earn profits through loans or purchases of securities. Generally, banks try to minimize the amount of excess reserves they keep on hand.

Assume that the bank in Show Low puts all of its cash (Federal Reserve notes) on deposit with the district Federal Reserve bank in San Francisco. Our assumption that the bank keeps none of its deposits in its own vaults is unrealistic, of course, but we are simplifying matters for clarity. The balance sheet of the Second Bank of Show Low now appears as Table 3. The balance

TABLE 3

Depositing a Cash Reserve in a Federal Reserve Bank

The Second Bank of Show Low deposits cash in the amount of $1 million in the San Francisco Federal Reserve bank. These cash deposits are called cash reserves or simply reserves and are recorded as cash reserve assets rather than cash on the balance sheet. Bank cash reserves are sometimes physically held in the bank's own vaults.

Second Bank of Show Low Balance Sheet			
Assets (thousands of dollars)		Liabilities and Capital Accounts (thousands of dollars)	
Cash	0	Deposits (demand)	1000
Cash reserves	1000	Borrowings	0
Loans	0	Capital	2000
Securities	0		
Plant and fixtures	2000		
Total assets	3000	Total liabilities and capital	3000

sheet of the San Francisco Federal Reserve bank appears as Table 4. The composition of the Second Bank's assets has changed—its cash is now listed as cash reserves—but the structure as well as the total amount of liabilities and net worth remain the same as in Table 2. The Second Bank's cash reserves can be instantly converted into cash disbursements as long as the legal reserve requirement is still met. Assuming that the reserve ratio (r) is 10 percent (0.10), legal required reserves against deposits of $1,000,000 are 0.10 × $1,000,000, or $100,000. Excess reserves are $1,000,000 − $100,000, or $900,000.

Table 4 shows the change in the San Francisco Federal Reserve bank's balance sheet after accepting the Show Low bank's cash deposit. In acquiring the cash deposit, the Federal Reserve bank reduces its Federal Reserve note liabilities but incurs equivalent liabilities in the form of claims against the reserves that the Federal Reserve bank holds for the commercial bank.

Advantages and Disadvantages of Fractional Reserve Banking

An alternative to fractional reserve banking would be a system in which banks are required to hold 100 percent of their deposits on reserve. Such a system compares unfavorably to the current fractional reserve system in several respects. To begin with, 100 percent reserve banks would be unable to make loans—their role would consist solely of holding deposits for safekeeping. As a consequence, their only potential source of revenue would be a charge to depositors for the service of protecting deposits. In effect, interest rates on deposits would be negative, since depositors would be charged a fee instead of being paid interest—an unattractive prospect to depositors accustomed to earning substantial interest on deposits.

A second disadvantage of 100 percent reserve banking is that it would increase the costs of coordinating potential lenders and borrowers. Today, fractional reserve banks very ably play the role of intermediary between these two groups—without having to match each desire for a loan of particular size and maturity with a desire to lend that particular sum of money for that time period. Instead, banks gain flexibility with regard to borrowers by pooling the deposits of those with funds to lend.

TABLE 4

The Federal Reserve Bank's Balance Sheet

By accepting the Second Bank's deposit, the San Francisco Federal Reserve bank acquires cash in the amount of $1 million, thereby reducing Federal Reserve note liabilities, and incurs an equal amount of liabilities to the Second Bank in the form of reserves. Reserves are assets to the Second Bank but are liabilities to the Federal Reserve bank.

San Francisco Federal Reserve Bank Balance Sheet		
Assets (thousands of dollars)	Liabilities and Capital Accounts (thousands of dollars)	
	Federal Reserve notes outstanding	−1000
	Claims against reserves (Second Bank of Show Low)	1000

Despite the clear advantages of fractional reserve banking, there is one disadvantage—a lack of overall liquidity. During the normal course of business, an individual bank or all banks as a group can operate with only a small percentage of their deposits on reserve. Each day, customer deposits and withdrawals result in relatively small increases or decreases in the reserves that are available to the bank. However, should all depositors simultaneously choose to withdraw their deposits (perhaps as a consequence of a loss of confidence in the bank), the bank would not have sufficient cash to meet the demands. A single bank might be able to stop a bank run by borrowing reserves from other banks, but a widespread loss of confidence would take away this option; the practice of fractional reserve banking entails some risk of large-scale bank failure. A primary responsibility of the Federal Reserve System is to minimize this risk by making loans to banks when extra reserves are needed to meet deposit demands.

How Checks Clear

What happens within the banking system when a depositor in one bank sends a check to a depositor in another bank? Currency is not trucked from one bank to another; rather, the transaction involves bookkeeping shifts known as check clearance, orchestrated by the Federal Reserve district banks and by other clearing facilities provided by commercial banks.

Suppose Josephine, the initial depositor in the Second Bank of Show Low, plans to expand her restaurant business and requires additional inputs and equipment. She has found bargains at a restaurant supply shop in Needles, California, called Roberto's Restaurant City. A purchase of $400,000 worth of restaurant equipment is arranged, and Josephine writes a check in that amount to Roberto's that is drawn on the Show Low bank.

After Roberto's receives Josephine's check, it deposits the check in the Needles National Bank—a member of the Federal Reserve System with deposits in the Federal Reserve bank in San Francisco. Figure 1 traces the movement of the check. Needles National Bank incurs a new demand deposit liability to Roberto's, but it also acquires a matching asset—cash reserves—after the check is cleared through the San Francisco Federal Reserve bank. When Needles National Bank forwards Josephine's check to the San Francisco bank, the Federal Reserve bank balances its books by increasing its reserve liabilities to Needles National Bank and simultaneously decreasing its reserve liabilities to the Show Low bank. The Federal Reserve bank then "clears" the check by sending it on to the Second Bank of Show Low, which adjusts its own accounts by reducing cash assets by $400,000 and deposit liabilities to Josephine by the same amount. These changes are all summarized in Figure 1.

Check clearance is not a mysterious activity. The simple example of Josephine and Roberto's describes what happens every day for the millions of checks written and cleared. The example actually is one of intradistrict check clearance, where the two banks are in the same Federal Reserve district but in different and distant cities. Check clearinghouse facilities often exist within cities, in which case the services are called intracity clearing. When a check is written to someone who holds an account with the same bank, the check is cleared *intrabank*, or within the bank: Deposit liabilities are simply shifted with a change in the accounting entries on the bank's balance sheet. The principles of clearance are the same whether the writer and the receiver of the

FIGURE 1

Josephine writes a check to Roberto's in the amount of $400,000, and Roberto's deposits the check in the Needles National Bank. Needles National Bank in turn deposits the check in the San Francisco Federal Reserve bank, obtaining reserve assets. The Show Low bank loses reserve assets in the amount of $400,000, as does Josephine's account when the check is cleared and all books are balanced.

Clearing a Check

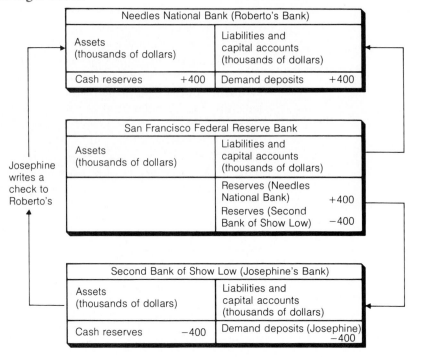

check live in the same city or in separate Federal Reserve districts (interdistrict clearing). In the latter case, all Federal Reserve banks have deposits in other Federal Reserve banks, which permits interdistrict clearing. Bookkeeping entries are adjusted without the necessity for cash to change hands. One bank gains cash reserves, another loses them. Note that the two banks involved both gain and lose reserves and deposits in equal amounts. This point is crucial in describing the process of money creation by a commercial bank or by the banking system as a whole.

Loans and Money Creation

Banking, like any other business, seeks to maximize profits. Banks earn income by investing in various private and government securities, but the most important means of earning income is making loans and earning interest on them. In a fractional reserve banking system, banks are able to make additional loans equal to the amount of their excess reserves. This important principle can be expressed symbolically as

$$L = R - rD,$$

where L is the credit or loan creation potential of a single commercial bank, R is the total reserves of the single bank, r is the legal reserve requirement on demand deposits, and D is total demand deposit liabilities.

New loans, L, cannot exceed the value of excess reserves. Consider the Second Bank of Show Low, whose cash reserves and deposit liabilities have dropped to $600,000 after Josephine's check to Roberto's for $400,000 clears (Table 5). If the Federal Reserve bank's required cash reserve ratio (r) is 10

TABLE 5

Losing Deposits and Reserves on the Balance Sheet

After Josephine's check for $400,000 has cleared, the Second Bank of Show Low loses deposit liabilities in that amount and cash reserves in the same amount.

Second Bank of Show Low Balance Sheet			
Assets (thousands of dollars)		Liabilities and Capital Accounts (thousands of dollars)	
Cash reserves	600	Demand deposits	600
Loans	0	Borrowings	0
Securities	0	Capital	2000
Plant and fixtures	2000		
Total assets	2600	Total liabilities and capital	2600

percent, $60,000 of the cash reserves must be kept on hand, leaving excess reserves of $540,000. Suppose that the Show Low bank lends this $540,000 to one borrower, Madge's Greenhouse, in demand deposits (for simplicity, we assume that no currency is withdrawn). Madge is creditworthy and will pay interest on the loan, providing the bank with returns and, presumably, profits. No one borrows money to let it sit in the bank. Madge promptly writes checks on her demand deposit account for $540,000. These transactions are summarized in Figure 2, beginning with the initial situation of the Second Bank of Show Low.

By lending Madge its excess reserves of $540,000, the bank changes its balance sheet to number 2 in Figure 2, with new loan assets and deposit liabilities. Madge then purchases $540,000 worth of goods and services, so in balance sheet number 3 of Figure 2, $540,000 of the bank's demand deposits and reserves are "checked away" to another bank or banks. In the final accounting, the balance sheet of the Second Bank of Show Low appears as number 4 in Figure 2.

The Second Bank of Show Low has created money in the process of making loans to Madge. It traded a demand deposit, which is money, for a promissory note, Madge's debt, which is not money. The money supply expands by exactly $540,000 (until, of course, the loan is paid off by Madge).

The single bank can lend out only the amount of its excess reserves because it faces the legal reserve requirement as well as the loss of both reserves and deposits. In Figure 2, for example, the Show Low bank is fully committed with loans after Madge's check has cleared (the bottom balance sheet). One more dollar loss in deposits and reserves would force the bank below the legal reserve requirement.

MONEY CREATION IN THE COMMERCIAL BANKING SYSTEM

The single commercial bank can lend only up to the amount of its excess reserves, but what of an entire banking system? How much money can be created by all of the depository institutions under control of a central bank such as the Federal Reserve System? To simplify the answer to this important

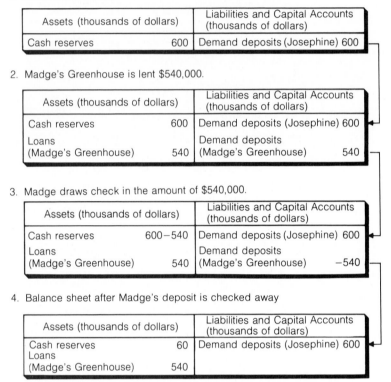

FIGURE 2

The Second Bank of Show Low creates money when it accepts something that is not money—a note pledging future payment from Madge's Greenhouse—and provides something that is—a checkable demand deposit. The bank is fully committed with loans when Madge's deposit, created by the loan, is checked away because $60,000 in reserves is required to support demand deposits of $600,000 when the required reserve ratio is 10 percent.

A Single Bank Making a Loan and Creating Money

Second Bank of Show Low Balance Sheet

1. Initial balance sheet

Assets (thousands of dollars)	Liabilities and Capital Accounts (thousands of dollars)
Cash reserves 600	Demand deposits (Josephine) 600

2. Madge's Greenhouse is lent $540,000.

Assets (thousands of dollars)	Liabilities and Capital Accounts (thousands of dollars)
Cash reserves 600	Demand deposits (Josephine) 600
Loans (Madge's Greenhouse) 540	Demand deposits (Madge's Greenhouse) 540

3. Madge draws check in the amount of $540,000.

Assets (thousands of dollars)	Liabilities and Capital Accounts (thousands of dollars)
Cash reserves 600−540	Demand deposits (Josephine) 600
Loans (Madge's Greenhouse) 540	Demand deposits (Madge's Greenhouse) −540

4. Balance sheet after Madge's deposit is checked away

Assets (thousands of dollars)	Liabilities and Capital Accounts (thousands of dollars)
Cash reserves 60	Demand deposits (Josephine) 600
Loans (Madge's Greenhouse) 540	

question, we initially assume that there is only one bank to service the entire economy—a monopoly bank, in effect. This assumption is farfetched, but it will help us understand the principles of money creation in a multibank context.

Deposit Expansion by a Monopoly Bank

We call our hypothetical monopoly bank the Universal Monopoly Bank. We initially assume that it is under the control of a central bank and that its balance sheet appears as in Table 6. If the reserve requirement imposed by the central bank is 10 percent, then Table 6 indicates that the Universal Monopoly Bank is fully committed with loans. Universal Monopoly Bank holds $150 million in cash reserves against deposit liabilities of $1.5 billion; in other words, cash reserves are exactly 10 percent of total deposits. Universal Monopoly Bank has no excess reserves and therefore no lending capacity.

Suppose that for stabilization purposes, the central bank wishes to buy $50 million of the securities from Universal. (These securities are promises to pay back the principal, or face value, at maturity plus interest over specified time periods.) How does the central bank induce the Universal Monopoly

TABLE 6

Universal Monopoly Bank's Initial Balance Sheet

With deposit liabilities of $1.5 billion and a cash reserve requirement of 10 percent, the Universal Monopoly Bank is fully committed with loans because it holds exactly $150 million in cash reserve assets. The Universal Monopoly Bank does not face the possibility of losing deposits and reserves to other banks, however, because there are no others.

Universal Monopoly Bank Balance Sheet			
Assets (millions of dollars)		Liabilities and Capital Accounts (millions of dollars)	
Cash reserves	150	Deposits	1500
Loans	250	Borrowings	0
Securities	1000	Capital	500
Plant and fixtures	600		
Total assets	2000	Total liabilities and capital	2000

Bank to sell its securities? It goes into the open securities market and increases its demand for securities. The increase in demand raises the price of such securities, provoking a sales response from the monopoly commercial bank, which seeks to earn a capital gain. (For simplicity, the capital gain is omitted in our analysis.) If we assume that Universal Monopoly Bank sells $50 million worth of its previous total of $1 billion in securities, its new balance sheet appears as in Table 7.

In Table 7, securities have been converted into cash reserves, meaning that the monopoly bank now has excess reserves of $50 million. The question now is, What quantity of demand deposit liabilities will this $50 million support?

If the Universal Monopoly Bank lent out all its excess reserves, loans would expand by $50 million, as would deposit liabilities. But what of cash reserves? Since the bank is a monopoly, it cannot lose reserves to other banks in the system via check clearance, for there are no other banks in the system. Cash reserves therefore will remain at the same level—$200 million—after an

TABLE 7

Selling Securities and Creating Excess Reserves

A sale of $50 million worth of securities (such as U.S. Treasury bills) for cash increases Universal Monopoly Bank's reserves by $50 million. These cash reserves of $50 million are excess reserves because they are greater than the amount ($150 million) required against $1.5 billion in deposit liabilities.

Universal Monopoly Bank Balance Sheet			
Assets (millions of dollars)		Liabilities and Capital Accounts (millions of dollars)	
Cash reserves	200	Deposits	1500
Loans	250	Borrowings	0
Securities	950	Capital	500
Plant and fixtures	600		
Total assets	2000	Total liabilities and capital	2000

initial loan and deposit creation of $50 million. Since reserves cannot be checked away, the Universal Monopoly Bank will still hold excess reserves after the loan. Under a 10 percent reserve requirement, deposit liabilities of $1.550 billion require only $155 million in legal cash reserves. The bank still holds excess reserves in the amount of $45 million ($200 − $155 = $45). Suppose it lends that amount. Lending out $45 million in deposits will create still another income-earning asset (loans), and new deposit liabilities will now be $1.595 billion and required reserves will be $159.5 million (10 percent). Excess reserves still remain in the amount of $40.5 million. If the bank continues to lend excess reserves to new borrowers who hold demand deposits (and no currency), the creation of money through **deposit expansion** will be many times the initial amount of excess reserves. Deposit expansion is the total amount of money created above some initial amount of excess reserves.

Deposit expansion:
The total amount of additional money or checkable deposits created by some given amount of excess reserves.

The total amount of deposits that can be supported by cash reserves can be conveniently expressed as

$$D = R\left(\frac{1}{r}\right),$$

where D is the total amount of deposits and demand deposit money created, R is the total amount of cash reserves, and r is the required reserve ratio.[2]

Simple money multiplier:
The reciprocal of the reserve ratio.

The reciprocal of the reserve ratio ($1/r$) is sometimes referred to as the **simple money multiplier**—the number multiplied by reserves to obtain total deposit expansion. In the example of the Universal Monopoly Bank, the money multiplier is 10 (1/0.10 = 10). The lower the required reserve ratio, the larger the money multiplier; the higher the ratio, the smaller the multiplier. For example, a value of r of 20 percent would reduce the value of the multiplier to 5 (1/0.20 = 5).

To see the effects of the money multiplier, consider the final position of the monopoly bank after all excess reserves have been eliminated from the system. The monopoly bank is again fully committed in loans, as shown in Table 8. Reserves of $200 million support $2 billion in deposits (money). This value is calculated from the deposit expansion equation, $D = R(1/r)$, or $2000 = $200(10). The change in deposits and the money supply can be calculated using a slight variation of the earlier expression:

$$\Delta D = \Delta \text{ reserves} \left(\frac{1}{r}\right),$$

or, in the case of the Universal Monopoly Bank,

$$\$500 = \$50 \left(\frac{1}{0.10}\right).$$

---

[2]There is a clear parallel between the investment (or autonomous expenditures) multiplier discussed in Chapter 13 and the money multiplier. Recall that the autonomous expenditures multiplier is equal to the reciprocal of the marginal propensity to save (MPS). It is the multiple by which income changes when autonomous (investment or consumption) spending changes. The money multiplier is calculated in similar fashion, but it is the reciprocal of the required reserve ratio. It is the percentage by which money expands or contracts with increases or decreases in excess cash reserves in the banking system. The MPS is the leakage from the income expansion process, while the required reserve ratio is the leakage from the deposit expansion process.

TABLE 8

Increasing Deposit Liabilities and Loans

Initial excess reserves of $50 million can support an additional $500 million in deposit liabilities in the monopoly bank when the money multiplier is 10. A monopoly bank, unlike a single commercial bank, cannot lose deposits or reserves to other banks.

Universal Monopoly Bank Balance Sheet			
Assets (millions of dollars)		Liabilities and Capital Accounts (millions of dollars)	
Cash reserves	200	Deposits	2000
Loans	750	Borrowings	0
Securities	950	Capital	500
Plant and fixtures	600		
Total assets	2500	Total liabilities and capital	2500

By selling $50 million in securities, the monopoly bank actually increased the money supply by $500 million, the amount of deposits that the cash it receives will legally support.

A crucial principle emerges from this example of the monopoly bank: Single commercial banks, like the Second Bank of Show Low, can lend and create checkbook money only in an amount equal to their excess reserves, whereas a monopoly bank can lend and create money by a multiple $(1/r)$ of its excess reserves. Now we will see how this principle translates into the real world of the U.S. multibank competitive banking system.

Money Expansion in the Multibank System

Just as the monopoly bank cannot lose reserves when deposits are checked away, the banking system as a whole can lose neither reserves nor deposits. **Money expansion** through the loan process is the same for the fractional reserve multibank system used in the United States as for the simple monopoly bank we just described. Once again, we will analyze the process of money creation in the multibank system with the use of balance sheets.

As with the Universal Monopoly Bank case, we must begin with some simplifying assumptions. First, we assume that the entire banking system is initially fully committed with loans. There are initially no excess reserves in the system. Second, all borrowers at all commercial banks are assumed to want their loans in demand deposits rather than in currency. Third, as in the previous balance sheets, savings deposits are assumed not to exist. Fourth, we assume that banks are solely profit maximizers and do not wish to hold any excess cash reserves. In other words, banks do not hold any reserves in excess of legally required reserves. Finally, to simplify matters even further, we assume that in each transaction, the bank granting a loan lends its entire excess reserves to a single borrower who places the loan in another bank, which then does the same thing. We assume that excess reserves work their way through the banking system in this simplified manner.

Initially, we assume that Cut and Shoot National Bank and all other commercial banks are fully committed with loans. Now suppose that Monica, a wealthy miser, deposits $1 million in cash in Cut and Shoot National Bank. The balance sheet change for Cut and Shoot is shown in Table 9a. The bank

Money expansion:
The increase in the money supply created by some given amount of excess reserves.

TABLE 9   Money Creation in the Commercial Banking System

Money is created as loans and demand deposits are created in the banking system. In this example, as before, the reserve requirement is 10 percent. (a) Cut and Shoot National has excess reserves of $900,000, which it lends to Jonathan. (b) When Jonathan checks his new deposit away to Yvonne, a customer of Altoona State Bank, Cut and Shoot loses deposit liabilities and cash reserve assets of $900,000 to Altoona State Bank. (c, d) Altoona State Bank, with excess reserves of $810,000, lends the entire amount to Chris, creating new money in the amount of $810,000 in demand deposits. (e) Chris checks his deposits away to a third bank (not shown), leaving Altoona State Bank fully committed with loans. As excess reserves and deposits move through the financial system, money is created.

(a) Cut and Shoot National Balance Sheet

Cash reserves	+1000	Deposits (Monica)	+1000

(d) Altoona State Bank Balance Sheet

Cash reserves	+900	Deposits (Yvonne)	+900

(b) Cut and Shoot National Balance Sheet

Cash reserves	+1000	Deposits (Monica)	+1000
Loans (Jonathan)	+ 900	Deposits (Jonathan)	+ 900

(e) Altoona State Bank Balance Sheet

Cash reserves	+900	Deposits (Yvonne)	+900
Loans (Chris)	+810	Deposits (Chris)	+810

(c) Cut and Shoot National Balance Sheet

Cash reserves	+ 100	Deposits (Monica)	+1000
Loans (Jonathan)	+ 900		

(f) Altoona State Bank Balance Sheet

Cash reserves	+ 90	Deposits (Yvonne)	+900
Loans (Chris)	+810		

Note: Balance sheet figures in thousands of dollars.

acquires cash reserve assets and demand deposit liabilities (to Monica) of $1 million. Cut and Shoot is now in a position to lend dollar for dollar with its excess reserves. Given the assumptions described and a legal required reserve ratio of 10 percent, excess reserves exist in the amount of $900,000. Total reserves in the bank are $1 million, and required reserves are $100,000. $(R - rD) = \$1,000,000 - (0.10 \times \$1,000,000) = \$900,000$.

Cut and Shoot finds a borrower, Jonathan, for the entire amount of its excess reserves. Table 9b reflects the position of Cut and Shoot after it makes the loan. The asset category Loans is enhanced by $900,000, as are deposits of a like amount. Jonathan, however, does not let his demand deposit lie idle. He has been in debt to Yvonne of Altoona State Bank on a business deal and wishes to pay back $900,000 of the debt. Jonathan writes a check to Yvonne, who deposits it in her bank. When Jonathan's check is cleared through the Federal Reserve System's interdistrict clearinghouse, Cut and Shoot loses cash reserves of $900,000 and Jonathan's deposit liabilities of the same amount. Simultaneously, Altoona State Bank gains cash reserves and deposit liabilities of $900,000. Cut and Shoot is left with an interest-earning asset (the loan to Jonathan), but its cash reserves have been checked away to another bank. At a 10 percent legal reserve ratio, Cut and Shoot is fully committed with loans.

Not so at Altoona State Bank. After Yvonne's deposit, Altoona State Bank has excess reserves in the amount of $810,000 [$900,000 − (0.10 × $900,000)]. These reserves may be lent to provide income for the bank. A borrower, Chris, wants the entire proceeds of the loan in the form of a demand deposit so that he can pay off a debt to Susan, a creditor who lives in Buffalo. Susan accepts Chris's check and deposits it in her bank (Buffalo Bank and Trust, not shown in Table 9). After Chris's deposit is checked away to Buffalo, Altoona State Bank loses deposit liabilities of $810,000 and cash reserves of the same amount. Altoona State Bank is fully committed with loans (Table 9f) when it holds $90,000 in legally required reserves against Yvonne's deposit of $900,000.

Excess reserves make their way through the banking system in the manner described in Table 9. Each individual bank can lend only an amount that is within its excess reserves, but part of these reserves becomes excess to some other bank in the system.

Naturally, the process described in the balance sheets of Table 9 does not end with Altoona State Bank. Reserves are checked away to Buffalo and may stay in Buffalo, be checked away to some other bank, or return to Cut and Shoot. Given our assumptions about the continuous movement of excess reserves through the system, the money creation process stops only when there are no more excess reserves within the commercial banking system. Table 10 summarizes this process.

The initial $1 million deposit of cash creates $9 million worth of new loans and deposits. As the individual commercial banks make loans, they are accepting something from borrowers that is not money—a private note payable to the bank—and are providing the borrower with a demand deposit that is money. Individual banks can lend dollar for dollar with excess reserves only

---

TABLE 10　　　　　**Creating Money as Excess Reserves Work Their Way Through the Banking System**

The money multiplier, the reciprocal of the required reserve ratio, determines the amount by which the money supply can increase. With a required reserve ratio of 10 percent and initial excess reserves of $900,000, demand deposits and the money supply can be increased by $9 million.

Bank	Reserves and Deposits Acquired	Required Reserves	Excess Reserves	Bank Loans	Increase in Demand Deposits	Increase in Money Supply
Cut and Shoot	1000	100	900	900	900	900
Altoona State	900	90	810	810	810	810
Buffalo Bank and Trust	810	81	729	729	729	729
.	.	.	.	.	.	.
.	.	.	.	.	.	.
.	.	.	.	.	.	.
All other banks	7290	729	6561	6561	6561	6561
Totals	10,000	1000	9000	9000	9000	9000

Note: All numbers are in thousands of dollars.

because they face the possibility of losing both cash reserves and deposits, but reserves and deposits cannot be lost to the multibank system as a whole. We may think of this system as closed, just as the monopoly bank could not lose deposits and reserves. In fact, the expression for deposit expansion that applies to the monopoly bank applies to the commercial banking system as well. In both cases, deposit expansion is expressed as

$$\Delta D = \Delta \text{ reserves} \left(\frac{1}{r}\right),$$

or, in this case,

$$\$10,000,000 = \$1,000,000 \left(\frac{1}{0.10}\right).$$

Deposits expand by $10 million when reserves of $1 million are introduced into the system. However, the money supply expands by only $9 million because Monica no longer holds $1 million in cash. Do not forget that the initial cash deposit of $1 million (Monica's deposit) merely altered the form of the money supply from currency outstanding (in Monica's possession before her deposit) to demand deposits. The money supply was not increased by Monica's cash deposit, although Cut and Shoot Bank had to hold a legal cash reserve of $100,000 against it. The money supply increased by $9 million through the process of deposit expansion *after* the initial deposit of $1 million. Thus, the change in the money supply, ΔM, is expressed as

$$\Delta M = \Delta \text{ excess reserves} \left(\frac{1}{r}\right), \text{ or}$$

$$\$9,000,000 = \$900,000 \left(\frac{1}{0.10}\right).$$

Money is expanded on the basis of excess reserves, and money expansion takes place at the same rate as the expansion of loans and deposits. In fact, money expansion is equivalent to demand deposit expansion. The process of money expansion can also work in reverse. Contraction of the money supply is possible within the fractional reserve commercial banking system.

MONEY SUPPLY LEAKAGES

Two important sources of leakage from the money expansion process are cash withdrawals and idle reserves. In the previous section, we eliminated both situations for simplicity. Here we examine how either cash withdrawal or idle reserves can slow or even reverse the process of money expansion.

Currency Drain

In the example described in the previous section, if a depositor had withdrawn cash from his or her account in the Cut and Shoot Bank, a chain of deposit destruction could have been brought about. While the act of currency withdrawal by itself does not initially alter the money supply, the bank's cash reserves—the raw material that it draws on to make loans—would be depleted. Especially if Cut and Shoot Bank fell below its legal reserve requirement, it would be forced to call in or not renew loans. This action would cause reductions in cash reserves in other parts of the commercial banking system. In the limit, deposits could be reduced by

$$\Delta D = \Delta \text{ reserves} \left(\frac{1}{r}\right).$$

Note that the money supply would fall by *less* than deposits fall, since the initial withdrawal of cash from the Cut and Shoot Bank does not alter the money supply. Cash (a part of the money supply) is increased and deposits (also a part of the money supply) are reduced in equal amounts in the initial transaction between bank and depositor.

A normal demand for cash is to be expected, even in a modern system of electronic transfers and at-home computerized bill payment. (For a discussion of the effects of new technology on demand for cash, see Focus, "The Future of Cash.") Currency and coin are still necessary to accommodate day-to-day transactions—coins for a candy bar or soda from a machine or currency to pay for a subway ride or lunch. Economists express this demand for cash through the **currency-deposit ratio,** which is simply the desired ratio of currency holdings to demand deposit holdings, on average and for all money holders. In the United States, the ratio has fluctuated widely through history, from high levels during bank panics and depressions to lower levels with the advent of federally insured and closely regulated commercial banking, as well as with modern computerized credit card payment schemes. In recent years, the ratio has been around $1 in currency desired for every $3 or so in demand deposits.

Let us assume that the currency-deposit ratio approximates 30 percent. What is the significance of a currency-deposit ratio of 30 percent for money expansion in a commercial bank? Any currency drain from the system is a leakage that reduces the ability of the commercial banking system to create deposits and money. If a bank acquires cash reserves of $1 million and lends to the limit with a 10 percent reserve requirement, the bank will lend $900,000. But if the average borrower's desired currency-deposit ratio is 30 percent, the borrower will want 30 percent of the loan, or $270,000, in cash, taking the remainder, $630,000, in demand deposits. (Actually, the person or persons paid by the borrower will hold the cash—a complication we ignore for now.) If this currency leakage continues to circulate and the cash does not find its way back into banks—a likely event—the deposit- and money-creating potential of the banking system is reduced.

Currency withdrawals, then, are a leakage that reduces the ability of the commercial banking system to create deposits and money. They are like required reserves in their ability to restrict deposit and money expansion. A slightly more complicated expression for deposit and money expansion or contraction gives us an idea of the effect of this currency leakage:

$$\Delta M = \Delta \text{excess reserves} \left(\frac{1 + c}{c + r}\right),$$

where c is the currency-deposit ratio, r is the reserve-deposit ratio (the legal

Currency-deposit ratio:
The percentage of total deposits held that people also wish to hold in the form of currency; currency holdings expressed as a decimal fraction of checkable deposit holdings.

FOCUS   The Future of Cash

A generation ago, regulation of the banking industry was much tighter than it is today. Most states strictly limited the hours during which banks could be open for business, and many states prohibited banks from opening branch offices. In addition, banks were legally prohibited from competing by offering higher rates of interest to depositors. Someone once quipped that to succeed in that era, bankers only had to obey the "3-6-3 rule" of banking—pay 3 percent on deposits, charge 6 percent on loans, and close at 3:00 in the afternoon to go golfing. If there was ever any truth in that statement, it certainly doesn't hold for today's bankers; changes both in bank regulation and bank technology have had dramatic effects on the day-to-day operation of commercial banks. One consequence of these changes is that it is now much more convenient for depositors to withdraw cash. In the past, withdrawals could be made only during the regular and quite limited business hours. With limited branch banking, this generally meant arranging a visit to your bank's sole location in the central business district during business hours. Because of the inconvenience of such trips, individuals had an incentive to withdraw relatively large sums on each bank visit. Many customers, therefore, maintained high average cash holdings.

Today, bank hours have been greatly extended, and branch banks have sprung up everywhere—even inside supermarkets. Changes in technology have enabled banks to offer automated teller services. A large bank is likely to have dozens of automated teller machines (ATMs) located throughout its service area, giving customers convenient access to cash twenty-four hours a day. ATMs have also been linked in nationwide networks, making it possible for customers to obtain cash quickly in other cities. Banks are also offering a variety of services by which funds can be transferred electronically from a depositor to a business establishment. Are cash holdings becoming obsolete?

Given the changes we've mentioned and the growing use of credit cards, you might expect the currency-deposit ratio to have decreased dramatically in recent years. However, this has not yet proven to be the case. As Table 11 shows, the currency-deposit ratio in the United States rose fairly steadily from 1960 until 1984. It dropped sharply between 1984 and 1986 and then increased again. The technology for transferring funds electronically already exists, but most retailers and consumers appear reluctant to abandon cash; for one thing, with electronic transfers every transaction is recorded—a departure from cash transactions that, for a variety of reasons, lacks universal appeal.

One factor that undoubtedly has affected the currency-deposit ratio is the growth of the underground economy. Many of the activities in the underground economy are legal, although income often is not reported or is underreported. Waiters and waitresses, bartenders, hairstylists, and cab

TABLE 11
Changes in the Currency-Deposit Ratio, 1960–1989

The ratio of currency to deposits held by the public rose steadily from 1960 to 1984, dipped in 1986, and began to rise again. Growth in the underground economy—for example, in the drug trade—tends to increase the ratio.

Year	Currency-Deposit Ratio
1960	0.257
1962	0.258
1964	0.269
1966	0.284
1968	0.273
1970	0.294
1972	0.293
1974	0.326
1976	0.354
1978	0.371
1980	0.393
1982	0.390
1984	0.400
1986	0.335
1988	0.371
1989	0.386

Source: Council of Economic Advisers, *Economic Report of the President* (Washington, D.C.: U.S. Government Printing Office, 1990), p. 372. Computed from data in Table B-68.

drivers are among those who may not report tips they receive; and, especially among service providers, a certain amount of bartering goes unreported. However, as confirmed by news reports featuring pictures of piles of money recovered in drug arrests, illegal activities play a significant part in the underground economy. Since illegal transactions are almost always conducted with cash, rapid growth in the underground economy will tend to increase the currency-deposit ratio.

It appears that cash is falling into disuse in the traditional economy but that it still plays a major role in the underground economy. The direction of the currency-deposit ratio in the future depends on many factors, one of which is our country's drug policy. Therefore, the Federal Reserve should be alert to any changes in drug policy that might affect cash holdings and, therefore, the money multiplier. If the Fed believes that the "war on drugs" is being waged successfully, it should anticipate a rise in the money multiplier due to a reduction in cash holdings and should be prepared to take offsetting actions to prevent undesired increases in the money supply.

required reserve ratio), and M is money created.[3] If we give a value of 10 percent to r, 30 percent to c, and excess reserves increase to \$900,000 in an otherwise fully committed banking system, how might the money supply expand? The result will be

$$\Delta M = \$900,000\left(\frac{1.30}{0.40}\right), \text{ or } \$2,925,000 = \$900,000(3.25).$$

Deposits and the money stock expand by \$2,925,000, much lower than the \$9 million expansion when no currency drain was considered. The money multiplier in this case is $(1 + c)/(c + r)$, or 3.25, whereas it was $1/r$, or 10, when no currency drain was considered. The existence of a currency drain, therefore, lowers money expansion possibilities in the U.S. fractional reserve banking system because it lowers the money multiplier. It is a leakage in the money creation process.

As Chapter 16 will show, the Federal Reserve System could stem this contraction by supplying supplementary cash reserves to the banking system. Indeed, one of the reasons the Federal Reserve System was created was to stem semihysterical currency drains or bank runs by acting as a lender of last resort. You should be aware nevertheless that the money supply can be shrunk as well as expanded through the banking system.

Idle Reserves

In earlier examples we assumed that banks did not wish to hold idle reserves above those that were required by the central bank. This assumption is clearly not the case, especially during periods of high economic uncertainty. Banks are privately owned, profit-maximizing institutions, but they also tend to be prudent. As we indicated earlier, a bank totally committed with loans will fall below its legal required reserve if so much as \$1 in cash reserves is withdrawn. Banks will not ordinarily let this happen because of the resulting embarrassment and possible repercussions from the Federal Reserve System or from other lenders or clients. Commercial banks therefore usually hold an additional amount in cash reserves. It should be clear that any holding of idle reserves by commercial banks further reduces the possibilities of money and

---

[3]This more complex expression is obtained in the following way. If in addition to demand deposits the public holds cash, then the money stock equals demand deposits plus currency held by the public. Any change in the money supply is equal to the sum of changes in D and C, or $\Delta M = \Delta D + \Delta C$. However, with a currency ratio of c, $C = c(D)$. Any change in the public's currency holdings can be written as $\Delta C = c(\Delta D)$. Substituting into the equation above, $\Delta M = \Delta D + c\Delta D$, so $\Delta M = (1 + c)\Delta D$.

The equation $\Delta D = \Delta$ reserves $(1/r)$ holds only if all new reserves are used to support new deposits. If a portion of the new reserves come to be held as cash, then that equation must be rewritten $\Delta D = (\Delta \text{ reserves} - \Delta C)\,(1/r)$, since ΔC represents the new reserves that cannot support deposits. Rearranging, $r\Delta D = \Delta$ reserves $- \Delta C$, and $\Delta C + r\Delta D = \Delta$ reserves. Substituting $c\Delta D$ for ΔC in this equation yields $c\Delta D + r\Delta D = \Delta$ reserves. Therefore, $\Delta D\,(c + r) = \Delta$ reserves, and $\Delta D = \Delta \text{ reserves}/(c + r)$.

We have seen that $\Delta M = (1 + c)\,\Delta D$. If for ΔD in this equation we substitute Δ reserves/ $(c + r)$, we obtain $\Delta M = (1 + c)\,\Delta \text{ reserves}/(c + r)$. Rearranging, $\Delta M = \Delta$ reserves $\left(\dfrac{1 + c}{c + r}\right)$.

Even this money multiplier is a simplification. For example, if we consider the possibility that financial institutions may hold excess reserves or if we account for noncheckable deposits on which reserves must be held, the money multiplier becomes even more complex. The true multiplier involves approximately forty variables.

deposit expansion. In other words, the holding of idle reserves, like the currency drain, acts as a brake to increases in the money supply as well as a cushion against decreases.

While other, more complex money multipliers involving savings and government deposits could be considered, it is sufficient here simply to understand the major factors affecting money expansion and contraction. By now you may suspect a deeper theme to money creation and destruction than the simple mechanical exercises of this chapter. Another actor in addition to the commercial banks and the public lurks backstage. The Federal Reserve System pulls the strings that control deposit and money expansion within the commercial banking system. We have only indirectly hinted at the tools of the Federal Reserve in manipulating the money stock. The details of this process will be discussed in Chapter 16.

THE BOTTOM LINE: TO MAKE MONEY BY CREATING MONEY

Commercial banks and some other financial institutions are basically no different from firms that sell shoes or hamburgers. (Indeed, banks may take on unusual forms; see Economics in Action, "How Does a Pub Become a Bank? The Modern Case of Ireland," at the end of this chapter.) They are in business to make a profit. Yet they also perform an essential macroeconomic role in that they create money. The proper management of these institutions is crucial to achieve three interrelated goals: (1) pleasing stockholders with adequate—that is, competitive—returns on their investments; (2) keeping the bank solvent and liquid; and (3) reacting to the implementation of ever-changing government (Federal Reserve) regulation over banking activity.

Returns on Investment

Bank management is tricky business. Think about how banks make profits. Banks and other depository institutions sell services such as savings, checking, and money market savings accounts. As any bank customer knows, these services come in a variety of packages. Some checking accounts are interest-bearing, offering limited checking privileges without cost, while others do not bear interest but offer unlimited checking with minimum balances. NOW accounts and super-NOW accounts available at various financial institutions are examples of interest-bearing checking services.

In addition to the costs of supervising many different kinds of accounts, depository institutions must bear the interest costs associated with savings accounts. Interest must be paid on all passbook and other types of savings and time deposits. These institutions have been allowed to pay unlimited interest on money market savings accounts since 1983, with competition for depositors' money leading to higher interest costs to banks and other financial institutions.

Demand deposits and all other deposits form the raw material from which financial institutions can earn income by lending. These institutions make loans for many purposes, but specialization in certain types of loans has occurred. Thrift institutions such as savings and loans and mutual savings banks have traditionally given long-term home and property mortgage loans, while commercial banks have concentrated on short-term consumer and business loans. Many of these institutions also earn interest returns from investments in securities.

The difference between a bank's costs and returns determines the profit to its stockholders. The spread between interest paid and interest received is an indication of the profitability of a bank, but banks incur costs other than interest. Labor costs in the servicing of deposit liabilities are a significant factor, so a spread of 14 percent interest received and 7½ percent interest paid is not necessarily an indication of great profitability. In more specific terms, the profitability of a financial institution depends on management of the bank's portfolios of assets and liabilities. The profit-maximizing structure of the portfolio changes constantly with changing market conditions and Federal Reserve regulations or deregulations.

Solvency and Liquidity

As with any other business, the bank or financial institution must maintain both liquidity, the ability to meet current depositor liabilities in cash, and solvency, the ability of all assets to cover all liabilities. In an attempt to make high returns, an incautious bank manager may develop an unwise or unsafe loan policy, perhaps by lending to speculative or high-risk borrowers. Although longer-term and higher-risk loans typically earn higher interest and income, both liquidity and solvency may be threatened by such loans. To further complicate the problem, variability in deposits and shifts within a bank between types of deposits are not exactly predictable. The possibility of coming up short when depositors demand repayment in cash is always very real for a bank or depository institution. As a result, these institutions have developed sophisticated methods of portfolio management.

Government Regulations

Banks are for-profit, privately owned institutions, but they are also regulated by government. Their major function of creating or destroying money is of the highest importance to economic society. The regulatory umbrella over the entire banking system includes a multiplicity of state and, particularly, federal regulations. The maintenance of legally required reserves is but one of the Federal Reserve System's regulations. Indeed, the U.S. constitutional authority to print and control money is carried out through the Federal Reserve System. The manner in which the Federal Reserve conducts its activities through a privately owned banking and financial system is the subject of Chapter 16.

SUMMARY

1. A bank gets started by accepting capital through selling stock to investors. After purchasing a bank building and equipment, the bank begins to perform the major functions of accepting deposits and making loans.
2. Through double-entry bookkeeping, the deposit of cash by an individual or business means that the bank's cash assets are counterbalanced by a corresponding amount of demand deposit liabilities.
3. The Federal Reserve System requires that all banks and financial institutions accepting checkable deposits must hold a certain percentage, called the required reserve ratio, of cash reserves against deposit liabilities.
4. All reserves above required reserves are called excess reserves. Banks can lend and create demand deposit money on the basis of their excess reserves.
5. An individual commercial bank can lend dollar for dollar with its excess reserves, but a single monopoly bank can lend and create money by a multiple of its excess reserves because its reserves and deposits cannot be checked away to other banks. The commercial banking system, like the monopoly bank, can lend and create money by a multiple of its excess reserves.
6. The multiple of excess reserves by which the banking system can create money is called the money multiplier. The simple money multiplier is the reciprocal of the required reserve ratio ($1/r$). Deposits and the money supply will expand or contract by an amount equal to the multiplier times the change in excess reserves.
7. A currency drain resulting from an increased demand for cash and coin or the maintenance of idle reserves by banks will reduce the value of the money multiplier.
8. Banks create or destroy money in an attempt to make profits. Commercial banks and other financial institutions, though privately owned and motivated to make profits, are nonetheless controlled in the public interest by the Federal Reserve System.

KEY TERMS

cash reserves
required reserves

reserve ratio
excess reserves

deposit expansion
simple money multiplier

money expansion
currency-deposit ratio

QUESTIONS FOR REVIEW AND DISCUSSION

1. Are commercial banks the only creators of money in the market?
2. What are the options for a bank if it finds that its actual reserves have fallen below its required reserves?
3. Explain how checks are cleared within a bank, between two banks in the same Federal Reserve district, and between two banks in different Federal Reserve districts. Look on the backs of some cleared checks. Are there clues as to whether these cleared between banks in the same district or in different districts?
4. By how much can a single bank increase the money supply from a deposit of $1 million of new cash? By how much can the entire banking system increase the money supply from such an injection?
5. If a bank purchases U.S. government securities from the Federal Reserve, does this purchase increase the money supply? Does the money supply change if an individual purchases a government bond from the Federal Reserve?
6. If $2 million were stolen from a bank's vault, would this theft increase or decrease the money supply?
7. What is a currency drain? If the currency drain increases, does it increase the money supply? Why?
8. "Banks do not like to hold excess reserves." Is this statement true? Explain.
9. What is the money multiplier? What does it show?
10. Why would anybody want to own a bank? What is the output of a bank? What is the essential input that banks must purchase to produce this output?

PROBLEM

If the reserve requirement is 15 percent and the currency-deposit ratio is 0, what happens to the money supply if the Federal Reserve injects $150,000 in cash into the banking system? How would this number change with a currency-deposit ratio of 5 percent?

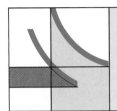

ECONOMICS IN ACTION
How Does a Pub Become a Bank? The Modern Case of Ireland

The proportion of hand-to-hand currency relative to checkbook money is low in most advanced societies. Historically, Americans' use of currency is only one-third the amount of checkable deposits, though the ratio changes over time. Other countries have even lower ratios of currency to demand deposits. Ireland's ratio, for example, was 18 percent in 1966, 15 percent in 1970, and 14 percent in 1976. But Ireland is unique in that its banks close frequently and for longer periods of time than banks of any other relatively advanced nation in the world. In fact, Irish banks closed for varying periods during 1966, 1970, and 1976 because of industrial disputes. For almost seven months (May 1–November 17) during 1970, citizens of the Republic of Ireland were deprived of the services of the Associated Banks, their branches, and their clearing facilities, which controlled virtually all of Ireland's demand deposits. Without 85 percent of its money supply, could Irish society function? Did the Irish resort to barter and to the reduced economic activity associated with barter? In 1979, Antoin E. Murphy of Trinity College, Dublin, presented some intriguing evidence on all of the bank closures, especially the long 1970 closure.[a]

Money did not totally disappear after the bank closures. Irish currency and coin continued to circulate, and some major companies were provided with account facilities and clearing services by North American and non-Associated banks. The Central Bank of Ireland transferred currency to government departments at the beginning of the closure to pay wages and salaries of government employees and to continue welfare payments, but at the end of the closure there was only a net addition of £4 million to the currency supply.

The increased demand for currency was partially offset by the summer tourist trade. Currency freely circulates in Ireland, and from April to November currency in circulation grew from £5 million to about £40 million. The North American and non-Associated banks provided some demand deposit transactions with means of alternative payment, but the aid was very limited because these banks had no branch facilities and were physically incapable of handling the volume of new business. By the end of May most of these banks refused to handle new accounts. In November 1970, according to Murphy's estimate, there was a total of £52 million in new demand deposits to facilitate consumers' money demands. This was less than one-twelfth of the closed Associated Banks' demand deposit accounts! How, then, did the Irish manage to transact?

People simply continued writing checks against pre-closure deposits and against checks received from other parties. During the bank closure, checks were written not against known accounts, but against the value of other uncleared checks along with the check receiver's assessment of the writer's creditworthiness. In such circumstances, default risk increased. Further, there was uncertainty about when the banks would reopen. Credit was therefore undated.

In this situation a personalized transaction system substituted for an institutionalized one. The nature of the Irish economy helped. A high degree of personal contact exists in the Irish population of about 3 million. Where personal information was lacking, credit information often existed at the 12,000 retail shops and at the more than 11,000 pubs in the Republic. One pub exists in Ireland for every 190 citizens over eighteen years of age. A pub keeper does not serve ale to a customer for years, as Murphy put it, "without discovering something of his liquid resources." Thus, pubs and shops provided goods, services, and currency for their customers against undated checks. They in fact formed the nexus of a substitute banking system.

Economic activity actually grew over the period at a somewhat reduced rate. There were no significant differences in retail sales and no significant deflationary trends. The important point is that information was the key to the emergence of a substitute medium of exchange. The Irish economy did not collapse or even cease growing when deprived of over 80 percent of its money. It simply and naturally fell back on or invented new and alternative forms of transacting.

Question

Suppose all banks closed in the United States. Who would experience more difficulty in finding bank substitutes—city dwellers or citizens of small towns? Who would most likely assume the role of banker—your local power company or your local hairstylist?

[a] Antoin E. Murphy, "Money in an Economy Without Banks: The Case of Ireland," *Manchester School of Economics and Social Studies* 46–47 (1978–1979), pp. 41–50.

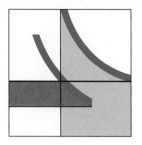

16

Money Regulation by the Federal Reserve System

The economic power of the Federal Reserve Board is awesome. Changes in Federal Reserve policy or even general comments on the health of the economy by the chairman of the Federal Reserve Board frequently send the stock market plunging or soaring. Fed-watching—anticipating the Federal Reserve's next change in policy—is so important to investors that some major investment banking houses pay experts more than $200,000 a year, three times the salary of the Federal Reserve Board chairman, to monitor Federal Reserve activity.

Until 1980, the Federal Reserve System had extensive regulatory control only over banks that were members of the Federal Reserve. The Fed had less authority over nonmember banks or over financial institutions such as credit unions and savings and loans. Federal Reserve controls over nonmember banks did include some regulation of the sorts of liabilities they could issue and the kinds of businesses that could be owned by bank holding companies. However, the Fed could not determine reserve requirements or monitor and control the risk-taking behavior of nonmember banks. As a consequence of two separate developments during the 1970s, this lack of control by the Fed came to be viewed with alarm. The first development was the entry of nonbanks into the checking market—previously, the exclusive domain of banks. The second development was a large-scale withdrawal of banks from the Federal Reserve System. By 1980, then, a large portion of all checkable accounts was held in financial institutions outside the control of the Federal Reserve. Concern was expressed by Federal Reserve chairman Paul Volcker and others over the Fed's growing inability to control the money supply. This concern led to passage of the Depository Institutions Deregulation and Monetary Control Act of 1980, which required all financial institutions to comply with the required reserve ratio established by the Fed. This effectively gave the Fed regulatory control over the entire financial market. Due to large-scale failures of savings and loans (for a discussion of those failures, see the Economics in Action at the end of this chapter), the Financial Institution Reform, Recovery, and Enforcement Act of 1989 was passed, and this legislation further increased the Fed's regulatory powers.

In Chapter 14, we examined the institutional structure of the Federal Reserve. Recall that the Federal Reserve System is made up of twelve Federal branch banks operating in all regions of the country. Overseeing the activities of these banks is the Federal Reserve Board of Governors, appointed by the president and based in Washington, D.C.; the board's role is to establish and oversee the nation's monetary policy. In this chapter we will see how Federal Reserve policy is carried out to control the size of the money supply. After reading Chapter 16 you should understand

- the nature of the tools that the Federal Reserve uses to control the money supply and, indirectly, interest rates in the economy.
- the central nature of one such tool—open market operations—in accomplishing the Federal Reserve's economic objectives.
- how the Federal Reserve influences the monetary base to achieve money supply or interest rate changes.
- how the monetary base and the real-world money multiplier interact to produce a money supply in the economy.
- some of the issues surrounding the debate over how "independent" the Federal Reserve System should be in our economy.

THE FEDERAL RESERVE SYSTEM'S BALANCE SHEET

The Federal Reserve System's basic activities in the banking system are concisely illustrated in its balance sheet, shown in Table 1. Its assets and liabilities are reported in the monthly *Federal Reserve Bulletin,* which compiles statistics on the activities of the central bank and on the financial system in general. The following is a brief description of the major assets and liabilities of the Federal Reserve System, each of which totaled $280 billion in February 1989.

The Federal Reserve's Assets

The first asset listed in Table 1 is gold certificates. The Federal Reserve System no longer holds gold, and since 1968 all ties between gold and Federal Reserve notes (dollars or currency) and other deposit liabilities have been abandoned.

TABLE 1   **Basic Setup of the Federal Reserve System Balance Sheet**

Generally, increases in the Federal Reserve's assets will increase member commercial bank reserves, while increases in its liabilities—except for the reserves deposited with the Federal Reserve by banks themselves—will decrease member bank reserves. Changes in bank reserves have important effects on the overall money supply.

Assets	Liabilities and Capital Accounts
Gold certificates	Federal Reserve notes (outstanding)
Loans and securities (earning assets)	Total deposits
	All other liabilities
Bank premises	
All other assets	Capital accounts

Before 1968, the U.S. Treasury issued and sold gold certificates to the Federal Reserve, which was required by law to hold a percentage of these certificates against currency and other liabilities. Some of these gold certificates remain on the Federal Reserve books as assets.

The next and largest group of items, loans and securities (earning assets), is the most important for understanding the Federal Reserve System's role in regulating bank reserves and the money supply in general. These assets consist of loans to banks and other depository institutions and securities, including federal agency obligations (various kinds of bills and notes) and U.S. government bonds. The Federal Reserve, as we will see, may purchase these securities from banks or from the nonbank public. Lumped together, loans and securities assets (along with other smaller items) are sometimes called **reserve bank credit** because increases and decreases in these assets affect member institutions' reserves—the raw material of money creation. We will explain this process later in the chapter.

Reserve bank credit: The total value of loans and securities owned or held by the Federal Reserve System. Changes in Reserve bank credit affect member institutions' reserves.

The Federal Reserve's Liabilities

Table 1 shows two major liabilities of the Federal Reserve System. One is Federal Reserve notes (currency or dollars) held outside Federal Reserve banks. The dollar bills in circulation are part of this liability because they represent claims against the assets of the Federal Reserve. Cash issued by the Federal Reserve and kept on hand is neither an asset nor a liability: It is paper.

The liabilities also include deposits, such as member institutions' reserves—the required reserves of banks and other depository institutions discussed in Chapter 15 as well as other commercial bank funds deposited at the Federal Reserve. As liabilities to the Federal Reserve, they are assets to the commercial banks, and any excess reserves may be instantly converted by the banks into cash. Recall that money can be created within the fractional reserve system on the basis of such excess reserves.

Other deposits listed as liabilities in Table 1 include checking account privileges to the U.S. Treasury and to foreign countries and their residents. The capital accounts include several liabilities, notably the stock deposits of financial institutions that are members of the Federal Reserve System.

THE MONETARY BASE: RAW MATERIAL OF MONEY CREATION

Our enumeration of the Federal Reserve's major assets and liabilities is more than an accounting exercise. The Federal Reserve balance sheet illustrates how it controls the money supply.

Basically, the Federal Reserve achieves control over the money supply by manipulating member institutions' reserves. Recall from Chapter 15 that banks can lend by a multiple of their excess reserves, thereby expanding or contracting the money supply. By increasing assets, either through new loans to member institutions or by purchasing securities from members, the Federal Reserve makes additional reserve funds available to member banks.

While increases in Federal Reserve assets increase bank reserves, increases in its liabilities other than commercial bank reserves reduce the banks' reserves. Increases in the Federal Reserve's stock of securities would increase bank reserves, for example, while decreases in loans to banks would decrease reserves. The difference between the value of the factors increasing bank reserves and those decreasing reserves is called reserve bank credit outstanding. This statistic is deemed so important that it is reported on a weekly basis in the *Federal Reserve Bulletin*. Changes are often viewed as an indicator of whether the Federal Reserve is increasing bank reserves (and therefore increasing the money supply) or limiting bank reserves (and therefore decreasing the money supply).

Monetary base:
The sum of depository institutions' reserves plus currency held by the public.

The Federal Reserve attempts to control the money supply by controlling the **monetary base,** the sum of banks' reserves (including the reserve in their own vaults as well as the reserves deposited with the Federal Reserve) and currency in the hands of the public. Controlling the monetary base is the object of Federal Reserve control because of the direct relation between the monetary base and M-1, the money supply. Naturally, the public decides how much currency it wishes to hold relative to demand deposits. To control the money supply, then, the Federal Reserve must control bank reserves—the stuff of demand deposit money creation—and adjust for the changes in currency holdings of the public, which also affect the ability of banks to create money.

We know from Chapter 15 that currency withdrawals limit the amount of money that commercial banks can create. Sharp increases or decreases in the public's currency demands could have far-reaching effects on the total quantity of bank reserves in the system and thus on the ability of such reserves to support a certain total money supply. Factors such as currency withdrawals are said to be outside the system's control, which does not mean, however, that the Federal Reserve cannot estimate and predict them. It does mean that overall Federal Reserve control of reserves and the money supply is a complicated business.

METHODS OF FEDERAL RESERVE CONTROL

The Federal Reserve can control the money supply in a number of ways. Some methods, such as open market operations (discussed below), affect the monetary base directly. Others, such as changes in the reserve requirement, affect the ability of depository institutions to lend and affect the monetary base indirectly. The major tools of the Federal Reserve, sometimes called **credit controls,** are the following:

Credit controls:
The method or tools that the Federal Reserve System uses in efforts to control the monetary base and the money supply, including reserve requirements, open market operations, the discount rate, and other selective credit controls.

1. Open market purchases and sales of securities;
2. Changes in the discount rate;
3. Alterations in the reserve requirement;
4. Changes in the margin requirement and, on occasion, imposition of consumer credit controls.

The Federal Reserve can also exercise warnings, generally verbal, to banks—an option called moral suasion, discussed later in this chapter.

Open Market Operations

Open market operations:
The purchase or sale of securities by the Federal Reserve System in order to affect the monetary base and the money supply; the major tool of monetary policy.

The most important and flexible tool available to the Federal Reserve in its attempt to control the monetary base is the **open market operation**—the buying and selling of securities on the open market. The Federal Reserve uses this tool daily to directly affect member banks' reserves. Again, when the Federal Reserve increases its securities holdings by purchasing government-issued bonds, the reserves of banks are increased, meaning that banks have greater capacity to lend money, thus increasing the money supply. When the Federal Reserve sells its securities, the reserves of banks are decreased and the money supply contracts. Open market operations are used to correct short-run, predictable fluctuations in the money supply or to expand or contract the money supply over longer periods. If, for example, the Federal Reserve purchases government securities directly from the portfolio of commercial banks, the bank acquires reserve assets and loses securities assets in an equal amount. The bank will want to turn these reserves into interest-earning assets (loans), a process that creates deposits and expands the money supply. If the Federal Reserve purchases securities from nonbank individuals, the result is essentially the same. Individuals receive the proceeds of the sale in a check, deposit the check in commercial banks, thereby providing the banking system new reserves on which to lend.

Some alterations in the monetary base take place owing to seasonal currency drains, such as the withdrawal of cash in December for Christmas purchases. These drains predictably increase the demands of the public for checkable deposit money. The Federal Reserve intervenes to compensate for these predictable drains. Other currency drains are less predictable and would contract the money supply were it not for the Federal Reserve's attempts to compensate by purchasing securities. When currency needs have passed, the Federal Reserve again compensates by selling securities, depending on business conditions. It may also purchase or sell securities in a concerted effort to expand or contract the money supply, to alleviate recession and unemployment, or to control inflation.

The Role of the Federal Open Market Committee (FOMC). The Federal Open Market Committee, introduced in Chapter 14, is the principal operating arm of the Federal Reserve System. It is responsible for Federal Reserve Board decisions to buy or sell securities. This committee ordinarily meets every three or four weeks to set trading policies, which are kept secret to avoid upsetting the plans of buyers and sellers. In these sensitive, closed-door sessions, the FOMC considers such factors as the inflation rate, the economy's growth or real income (GNP), the unemployment picture, the size of excess reserves and borrowings from the Federal Reserve, probable currency drains, and the international balance of payments. It then decides on a monetary base, or reserve target, and a federal funds rate target to shoot for.

Federal funds rate:
A market-determined interest rate on loans and borrowings of bank reserves among commercial banks and other depository institutions.

The **federal funds rate** is the interest rate commercial banks charge on overnight and short-run loans to other banks. Banks often lend excess reserves overnight and short term in order to earn interest returns; the rate is basically determined by the supply of and demand for these reserves. The key point here, however, is that the Federal Reserve attempts to influence this rate by altering the supply and demand for reserves through open market operations.

When the Federal Reserve targets changes in the federal funds rate, it is attempting, in effect, to change all interest rates, such as the prime interest rate and mortgage rates.

After the FOMC decides how it would like to alter reserves, the money supply, and the federal funds rate, the decision is transmitted to the open market account manager, an officer of the Federal Reserve Bank of New York. This individual, who controls the open market desk at the New York Federal Reserve and deals directly with commercial securities and investment houses on Wall Street, then implements the intentions of the FOMC. According to 1979 rule changes, the account manager has only narrow latitude in affecting monetary aggregates (such as bank reserves, the monetary base, and the money supply), but the account manager is still given a specific target for the federal funds rate.

As of February 1989, the Federal Reserve System held almost $225 billion worth of securities on its balance sheet. In January 1989, it acquired $94 billion, and it also sold $94 billion. Let us see how these open market transactions affect the condition of the banking system, expanding or contracting the money supply. There are two open market channels through which the Federal Reserve can affect bank reserves and the money supply: It can deal directly with banks or with the nonbank public.

Purchase of Securities from Banks.   First consider a Federal Reserve purchase of securities (bonds, notes, or bills) from commercial banks. The effects of a $5 billion purchase are summarized in Table 2, which shows only changes in accounts. The Federal Reserve acquires $5 billion in assets (+ securities) but creates a new reserve liability to the banks to pay for the securities in exactly the same amount (+ reserves). On the other hand, the commercial banks lose a securities asset on the asset side of their balance sheet but gain an asset— reserves—of equivalent amount. The crucial point is that the monetary base rises as excess reserves—those above required reserves—are created in the banking system. Banks cannot lend on the basis of securities, but they can lend on the basis of excess reserves. After the Federal Reserve's purchase of securities, these excess reserves are ready to be lent. Given a specific reserve

---

TABLE 2

Purchase of Securities from Banks

When the Federal Reserve purchases securities from commercial banks or other depository institutions, it provides them with reserves on which the banks may make new loans, increasing the money supply. The Federal Reserve's purchase of $5 billion in securities from commercial banks changes those assets from a securities entry to a reserves entry in the commercial banks' aggregate balance sheet.

Federal Reserve System		Commercial Banks	
Assets (billions of dollars)	Liabilities and Capital Accounts (billions of dollars)	Assets (billions of dollars)	Liabilities and Capital Accounts (billions of dollars)
+ Securities 5	+ Reserves 5	− Securities 5 + Reserves 5	

requirement, the banking system's desired reserve holdings, and a desired ratio of currency to deposits on the part of the public, money creation may proceed apace. In theory, as the Federal Reserve buys securities and as the banks begin supplying new loan funds, interest rates tend to fall initially, encouraging consumers and investors to borrow. (A securities sale would have the opposite effect.) In reality, the monetary expansion also depends on general business conditions and expectations for the future.

Purchase of Securities from the Public. Another method by which the Federal Reserve conducts open market operations pumps demand deposits in or out of the monetary system directly. Suppose that instead of purchasing $5 billion worth of securities from commercial banks, the Federal Reserve buys them directly from the nonbank public. The results of such a purchase are summarized in the balance sheets of Table 3.

When the Federal Reserve buys securities from the public and pays for them with, in effect, checks written on itself, the public gains demand deposit assets and loses securities assets in equal amounts. Note that the commercial banks gain new reserve assets and new deposit liabilities of $5 billion if the public deposits all of its proceeds from the sale into banks. In such a case, the money supply is increased directly by $5 billion by the very act of the public sale. Monetary expansion will depend on banks' desired idle reserves, the legal reserve ratio, the public's desired currency holdings, and, more broadly, general economic conditions. The extent of monetary expansion due to a securities purchase does not depend on the seller of securities to the Federal Reserve—commercial banks or the public.

TABLE 3 **Purchase of Securities from the Public**

When the Federal Reserve buys securities from the public and the public deposits the proceeds in banks, the public gains demand deposit money and commercial banks acquire new reserves. Banks may then lend additional money on the basis of their excess reserves.

Federal Reserve System Balance Sheet		
Assets (billions of dollars)	Liabilities and Capital Accounts (billions of dollars)	
+ Securities 5	+ Reserves	5

Public Balance Sheet		
Assets (billions of dollars)	Liabilities and Capital Accounts (billions of dollars)	
− Securities 5		
+ Demand deposits 5		

Commercial Banks' Balance Sheet		
Assets (billions of dollars)	Liabilities and Capital Accounts (billions of dollars)	
+ Reserves 5	+ Demand deposits	5

These open market operations take place daily and are the most flexible and efficient tool in the Federal Reserve's arsenal. But how can the Federal Reserve be sure that banks or the public will be willing to sell or buy securities on demand? Simple supply and demand analysis provides the answer. When the Federal Reserve sells securities, it increases the supply of securities on the open market in quantities large enough to affect the interest rate. When the Federal Reserve buys securities, demand for them is increased. An increase in supply lowers the price and increases the interest return on securities, making security holdings an attractive investment for banks or the public. Likewise, when the Federal Reserve places an order to buy on the open market, the demand increase causes security prices to rise and the interest return from holding them to fall. Selling securities to the Federal Reserve then becomes attractive to banks and the public because of the possible capital gains from selling and because of the reduced yield from holding the securities. Supply and demand conditions thus assure the Federal Reserve that there will be a response to its actions in the open market.

Who gets the interest return on the large quantity of securities held by the Federal Reserve? The Federal Reserve itself does. Congress permits the Federal Reserve to use this income to finance its operations. Historically, the Federal Reserve has been able to pay its own way out of its earning assets. Excess income is turned over to the U.S. Treasury. Remember, however, that the Federal Reserve is not supposed to be in business to make profits but to control the money supply for purposes of economic stabilization. The same is true of the other earning assets on the Federal Reserve balance sheet such as loans to depository institutions. Like securities, these assets are used to affect monetary policy and are not for profit. (See Focus, "The Quasi-Independence of the Federal Reserve System," for a discussion of the Fed's relationship with the U.S. Congress.)

Loans to Banks: The Discount Rate

Discount rate:
The interest rate charged by the Federal Reserve to depository institutions on loans of reserves from the Federal Reserve.

The process of lending to banks at some interest rate, called a **discount rate,** is the oldest function of a central bank. The discount rate is an interest rate (expressed as a percentage) charged by the Federal Reserve to depository institutions for loans backed up by some form of collateral—securities, notes, or commercial paper. This loan process was originally related to the status of a central bank as a lender of last resort—an institution that provided liquidity and currency to the banking system in times of sudden currency demands. Many of these bank crises or panics took place in the United States prior to the establishment of the Federal Reserve System in 1913. Yet modern banks are not immune to crises. In 1984, the massive Continental Illinois National Bank and Trust Company of Chicago, the nation's largest business and industrial lender, narrowly avoided closing its doors. The Federal Deposit Insurance Corporation (FDIC) and the Federal Reserve came to the rescue, the latter through loans and through the discounting of notes for the bank.

Initially, the discount rate was perceived to be the Federal Reserve System's major tool to avert crises. In modern times, loans to member banks and other financial institutions have performed another function as well—to control expansions and reductions in money and credit. Several discount rates are charged by the Federal Reserve depending on the kind of collateral put up by the banks and the purpose and duration of the loans. The rate for short-run

FOCUS   The Quasi-Independence of the Federal Reserve System

The Federal Reserve System is unique among government regulatory agencies in one important respect: The Federal Reserve enjoys relative freedom from the oversight of Congress or the executive branch. This unique status is called quasi-independence and has been a source of much conflict among politicians, economists, and the investment community.

The Federal Reserve System was created by Congress in 1913 to administer and manage the money supply as directed in the Constitution. As an agency of Congress, the Federal Reserve Board represents or is an extension of Congress, but Congress set up the Federal Reserve to be quasi-independent—that is, at some distance from the control of the president and from direct congressional involvement. For example, Federal Reserve Board members other than the chair are appointed for fourteen-year terms by the president, which means that they can remain on the job regardless of which party controls the White House. The chair is also appointed as a member of the Board for a fourteen-year term. The appointment as chair lasts four years but may be renewed. Independence is also reflected in the fact that the Federal Reserve is not dependent on congressional and administrative budget appropriations. The Federal Reserve finances all of its own operations, mainly through interest earned on government bonds. This independence from congressional appropriations and from the typical auditing procedures applied to all other U.S. regulatory agencies has gone far in placing the Federal Reserve out of the grasp of Congress or the president.

Is the Federal Reserve too independent? Should it be brought under closer scrutiny of Congress or the president, or is its current position appropriate to its intended function? Critics argue that the loose connection between the president and the Federal Reserve System creates discoordination between fiscal and monetary policy. Monetary policy, in this view, should be under the direct control of the executive branch of government so that it is tied closely to the democratic wishes of voters. Such criticism is especially vocal during periods of high interest rates and tight money.

Defenders of quasi-independence claim that there are very good reasons for the special status of the Federal Reserve. In this view, monetary policy is far too important to the well-being of society to be left to self-interested politicians; control of the money supply and other aspects of monetary policy should be insulated from politics. Defenders of the Fed argue that quasi-independence permits monetary policy-makers to have a longer-run perspective, to be able to see beyond the next election. They point out that the Federal Reserve is a creation of Congress and that it can be abolished at any time by an act of Congress. (During the 1980s, when many members of Congress actively opposed the Fed's tight monetary policy, Congress amended the Federal Reserve Act and limited the Fed's ability to change reserve requirements—an action widely interpreted as a symbolic gesture to remind the Fed that too much independence would not be tolerated.)

The Federal Reserve Board chair is required to present periodic reports to Congress, some in person, relating to the management of M-1 and interest rates. To go beyond this level of accountability, some say, might tempt politicians into inflating the money supply to cover budget deficits, unwise government spending, or political ambition. It may be that, despite the periodic criticisms and threats, both the president and Congress have an incentive to keep the Fed relatively independent: The Federal Reserve gives them a place to pass along blame when economic troubles develop.

---

or seasonal credit is lower than that for extended credit to institutions whose loans extend beyond 150 days. These differential rates reflect the Federal Reserve's policy toward banks' motivations for borrowing. A commercial bank may borrow because of seasonal cash drains, to cover very short-run deficiencies in legal reserves, or because it sees the Federal Reserve discount loans as a source of profit. If there is a wide spread between the discount rate paid for borrowing excess reserves at the Federal Reserve and the interest rate banks receive on lending out these excess reserves, banks may seek to borrow from the Federal Reserve to enhance their profits. The Federal Reserve discourages borrowing for this reason by charging higher rates for longer-run credit. In fact, the Federal Reserve may stop this sort of borrowing entirely.

Whatever the reason for borrowing, lending by the Federal Reserve swells the quantity of reserves at the disposal of the banking system. Table 4, for example, shows the Federal Reserve balance sheet and that of a single com-

TABLE 4

Lending to the First Bank of Nome

When the Federal Reserve lends at interest to a commercial bank, the commercial bank acquires reserves as a new asset and a new liability to the Federal Reserve. The bank may now create new demand deposit liabilities along with new loan assets, thereby expanding the money supply.

Federal Reserve System		First Bank of Nome	
Assets (billions of dollars)	Liabilities and Capital Accounts (billions of dollars)	Assets (billions of dollars)	Liabilities and Capital Accounts (billions of dollars)
+ Loans (First Bank of Nome) 2	+ Reserves 2	+ Reserves 2	+ Due Federal Reserve 2

mercial bank, the First Bank of Nome. This process of discounting a note for $2 million from the Bank of Nome has the clear effect of increasing the bank's stock of reserves. If any or all of these new reserves are in excess of the required reserves, money creation may proceed in multiple fashion, again depending on banks' required and desired excess reserves, currency drains, and general economic conditions.

The Federal Reserve has several ways of encouraging or discouraging borrowing: (1) it alters the rate or rates charged; (2) it changes the form of collateral required; and (3) it always retains the option to lend or not to lend. Loans to depository institutions and acceptances (another form of short-run lending with different collateral required) make up a relatively small percentage of the Federal Reserve's financial transactions compared to open market operations. But the ultimate importance of the discount rate hinges not so much on the quantity of loans as on the information the rate conveys concerning the intentions of the Federal Reserve. Commercial and consumer interest rates, such as the prime rate (the rate that banks charge to their lowest-risk commercial borrowers), tend to follow the discount rate. Along with the Federal Reserve's changing monetary base targets, the discount rate is seen by the banking and business community as one indicator of whether the Federal Reserve is following an expansionary or contractionary monetary policy. A higher rate indicates a tightening of credit and a contractionary policy. A lower rate indicates the reverse. The stock market, for one, is apt to react sharply to changes in the Federal Reserve discount rate. Thus, while the discount rate is not the major mechanism of Federal Reserve control over the monetary base, it is often considered the principal messenger of the Federal Reserve's policy intentions.

Changing the Reserve Requirement

Changing the legal reserve requirement is potentially the most powerful tool at the disposal of the Federal Reserve, but it is seldom used. To understand this seeming contradiction, remember that an alteration in the legal reserve ratio affects the ability of any given amount of excess reserves to support new money, and it increases or decreases the amount of excess reserves held by depository institutions. A simple example, utilizing the simple money multiplier without a currency drain, illustrates the importance of the legal reserve requirement for the money supply. If we assume that excess reserves in the banking system are $5 billion and that the legal reserve requirement is 15 percent, the potential expansion in the money supply, neglecting currency drains and other factors, is

$$\Delta M = \Delta D = \text{excess reserves} \left(\frac{1}{r}\right),$$

or

$$\Delta M = \Delta D = \$5 \left(\frac{1}{0.15}\right) = \$33.3.$$

The increase in the money supply M equals the increase in deposit expansion, $33.3 billion. The money multiplier $1/r$ is equal to 1/0.15, or 6.66. As indicated in Chapter 15, the money multiplier is the number by which excess reserves are multiplied to determine potential change in the money supply. It is the reciprocal of the reserve requirement.

A reduction in the reserve requirement from 15 percent to 10 percent would have dramatic effects on the money supply. Suppose that the banking system initially had $500 billion in deposits and $80 billion in reserves. With a reserve requirement of 15 percent, the banks would initially have $5 billion in excess reserves. If the reserve requirement were then lowered to 10 percent, banks would be required to hold only $50 billion as reserves, so their excess reserves would amount to $30 billion. The potential increase in money and demand deposits would be $300 billion.

$$\Delta M = \Delta D = \$30 \left(\frac{1}{0.10}\right) = \$300 \text{ billion}$$

Small changes in the required reserve ratio can bring about large increases or decreases in the money supply.

Actually, banks must observe several reserve requirements, depending on the size of their deposit liabilities. Table 5 provides a summary of reserve requirements in force in May 1989. After implementation of the Monetary Control Act of 1980, reserve requirements apply uniformly to all depository institutions according to the size of checkable, savings, and time deposit liabilities. As Table 5 shows, transactions accounts—all checkable accounts—less than $41.5 million at depository institutions carry a reserve requirement

TABLE 5	Contemporary Reserve Requirements of Depository Institutions

Reserve requirements have been made uniform for all institutions issuing demand, savings, or time deposits. The total amount of reserves required for an individual bank or savings and loan, for example, depends on the type and amount of deposits issued by the institution.

Net Transaction Accounts	Nonpersonal Time Deposits
3% up to $41.5 million 12% over $41.5 million	3% on less than 1½ years maturity 0% on more than 1½ years maturity

Source: Federal Reserve Bulletin (March 1987).

of 3 percent, while 12 percent must be held on deposits over $41.5 million. Some large ($100,000 or more) nonpersonal time deposits, such as certificates of deposit, and savings deposits (less than one and one-half years maturity) now carry a requirement of 3 percent. All in all, these reserve requirements are more uniform and lower than in the past.

Reserve requirements limit the profitability of banking and depository institutions and so are regarded as a necessary evil by the financial system. Changes in the requirements (especially increases) can cause massive disruptions and large-scale adjustments in the portfolios of member banks and other institutions required to hold legal reserves. Even small changes might create financial crises for some institutions, depending on their profitability. When banks are fully committed with loans—that is, have low amounts of excess reserves—an increase of only one-quarter or one-half percent in the legal reserve could reduce lending and money creation by billions of dollars, creating tight money and possibly bank failures. The Federal Reserve is therefore reluctant to make sudden large changes in the reserve requirement. Open market operations are far more flexible in operation and predictable in effect. The reserve requirement will always be a part of monetary control, but it will likely be used sparingly.

The Margin Requirement and Other Selective Credit Controls

Other tools sometimes available to the Federal Reserve through congressional action are selective credit controls, which include credit restrictions on stock market purchases and consumer borrowing for durable goods and home purchases. At present, the Federal Reserve controls only the **stock margin requirement,** which is the percentage of the total price of a stock that must be paid in cash. A margin requirement of 40 percent means that only 60 percent of the purchase price of stock can be borrowed; 40 percent must be paid in cash. The Federal Reserve acquired the power to demand a margin requirement through the Securities and Exchange Act of 1934, allegedly to stem the rampant stock speculation that was thought to have contributed to the stock market crash of 1929 and the ensuing Depression. The purpose of the margin requirement is thus to provide a brake in what is regarded as unwise stock speculation. Alterations in the required margin selectively affect credit for stock market purchases and, therefore, also affect the volume of such purchases. Since 1968, the rate has varied between 80 percent and 50 percent, the latter rate being in force since 1974.

Finally, during periods of potential and real economic crisis, Congress has in the past given the Federal Reserve powers over the terms of home mortgages and consumer credit for the purpose of buying durables. The rationale for restrictions on the amount of down payment and the period of repayment is simple: During periods of all-out war, resources must flow into military spending. Simultaneously, however, the overfull employment that accompanies a war effort means high nominal incomes, which create huge demands for consumer durables and new housing. Consumer credit controls tend to suppress these demands, having the dual effect of releasing real resources to the war effort and keeping a temporary lid on domestic price inflation. Between 1941 and 1947 and again during the Korean War, Congress

Stock margin requirement: The percentage of the price of a stock purchase that must be paid in cash rather than borrowed.

authorized the Federal Reserve to impose restrictions on consumer credit. The Federal Reserve does not especially like the discriminatory impact of these controls because they affect only particular markets, such as home building and automobile manufacturing. At present and for the foreseeable future, the only selective control maintained by the Federal Reserve is the stock margin requirement. Under the Credit Control Act passed by Congress in 1969, the president was given the power to institute consumer credit controls, administered through the Federal Reserve System. With one minor exception, these controls have been unused, probably for some of the reasons given above. The act was not renewed by Congress in 1980.

Moral Suasion

Moral suasion:
The use of advice and suggestion, rather than concrete policy actions, by the Federal Reserve to induce depository institutions to follow a certain course of action.

Another tool of the Federal Reserve—alluded to earlier—is **moral suasion,** the ability to persuade banks that some course of action is desirable or undesirable. For example, during a period of rapid credit and money expansion—deemed undesirable by the Federal Reserve—banks may be warned subtly or not so subtly that continued expansionary behavior will result in implementation of policies that will force banks to cut back on money expansion. As we have seen, these threatened actions could be a raising of the discount rate, the selling of securities, or possibly increases in reserve requirements. To the extent that such suasion achieves the desired results, it could be a tool of the Federal Reserve. Sometimes, however, admonitions do not work, and the threatened action becomes necessary. Thus, the effects of moral suasion, while real, are not exactly predictable.

The Federal Reserve is always on sounder ground if it can affect the nature of banks' portfolios directly. Table 6 summarizes the Federal Reserve's major tools for money control and their likely effects.

TABLE 6   Major Federal Reserve Controls and Their Probable Effects

Alterations in any one of the three major credit controls of the Federal Reserve will affect the monetary base of the financial system, bank reserves, and the money supply.

Federal Reserve System Tools	Effects					
	Bank Reserves	Money Supply	Monetary Base	Excess Reserves	Money Multiplier	Currency
Open market operations:						
Federal Reserve buys bonds	Increase	Increases	Increases	Increase	Remains same	Increases
Federal Reserve sells bonds	Decrease	Decreases	Decreases	Decrease	Remains same	Decreases
Discount rate:						
Raise rate	Decrease	Decreases	Decreases	Decrease	Remains same	Decreases
Lower rate	Increase	Increases	Increases	Increase	Remains same	Increases
Reserve requirement:						
Raise requirement	Decrease	Decreases	Remains same	Decrease	Decreases	Decreases
Lower requirement	Increase	Increases	Remains same	Increase	Increases	Increases

MONETARY CONTROL: RESERVES, THE MONETARY BASE, AND THE MONEY SUPPLY

We have seen that the Federal Reserve has numerous means of altering the stock of reserves and the monetary base. It remains to be shown how the monetary base—the sum of bank-held reserves and currency in circulation— is related to the money supply. In October 1989, for example, the monetary base was $278 billion, while the M-1 measure of the money supply was $787 billion. These figures indicate a money supply on the order of 2.83 times the value of the monetary base. The **M-1 money multiplier** is the number by which the monetary base is multiplied to obtain the M-1 measure of the money supply. This number can change over both short-run and long-run periods. We must understand why and how it changes because the very ability of the Federal Reserve to control the money supply through the monetary base depends on the predictability of the money multiplier.

M-1 money multiplier: The multiple by which the money supply will change given a change in the monetary base.

The Exact Relation Between the Money Stock and the Monetary Base

To understand the forces determining the money stock, M-1, we must come to a more exact formulation of the money multiplier. In simplified terms the money stock may be expressed as

$$\text{M-1} = \text{monetary base} \times \text{M-1 money multiplier}.$$

We have already seen that the Federal Reserve controls the monetary base by pumping reserves into or withdrawing them out of the banking system through its credit control powers. But recall that bank reserves are only one part of the monetary base. Currency in public circulation is the other part of the monetary base, and currency holdings by the public are determined by the desires of the public. An individual may, at his or her discretion, convert demand deposits into cash by writing a check at the bank or some other place that cashes checks. The individual's decision to hold cash has an impact on the banking system's ability to expand the money supply. It would reduce the money-expanding capabilities of the system if an individual made a permanent decision to hold more cash than checkbook money.

The money multiplier discussed earlier in this chapter is actually a simplification, as shown in Chapter 15. The simple multiplier is the reciprocal of the reserve requirement. While we will not account for every factor contributing to the multiplier, a more realistic way of determining the money multiplier must take into account the desires of the public to hold currency in relation to demand deposits. The components of a more realistic money multiplier can be defined as follows:

c = Desired currency holdings of the public relative to demand deposits;
r = Holdings of reserves required by the Federal Reserve and desired by depository institutions relative to demand deposits.

If, on average, people wish to hold 35 cents in cash or coin for each dollar in demand deposits, the value of c is 0.35. If the sum of required and desired (or idle) reserves in the banking system is 15 cents for every dollar of demand deposits issued, the value of r is 0.15. For obvious reasons, c is sometimes called the currency-deposit ratio, and r is called the reserve-deposit ratio.

A slightly more complicated expression for the money multiplier, then, is

$$\text{Money multiplier} = \left(\frac{1 + c}{c + r}\right).$$

This equation differs from the simple money multiplier in its inclusion of the currency-deposit ratio in both the numerator and the denominator. In practical terms, the addition of c reduces the value of the simple multiplier. Using only the reserve-deposit ratio of 0.15 produces a money multiplier of $1/r = 1/0.15$, or 6.66. Use of a multiplier that includes the impact of the public's desire to hold currency gives a money multiplier of 1.35/0.50, or 2.7.

We are immediately able to understand the actual relation mentioned above for October 1989 between an M-1 of $787 billion and a monetary base of $278 billion.

$$\$787 \text{ billion} = \$278 \text{ billion } (2.83)$$

The monetary base of $278 billion is only one factor in explaining the money supply. The composition of the money multiplier, equal to $(1 + c)/(c + r)$, or 2.83 in our real-world example, is the other factor influencing Federal Reserve monetary control.

Federal Reserve Controls

In practice, it is often difficult to tell what the Federal Reserve is attempting to control—the money supply or interest rates. Although the Board of Governors of the Federal Reserve has at various times in the past stated clear objectives concerning the size of the money supply or the level of interest rates, the board has often failed to hit its targets. These failures have raised the question of whether the Fed is able to control the money supply or—through controlling the money supply—interest rates.

Any change in the money supply is caused by either a change in the monetary base or in the money multiplier; if these remain the same, the money supply in the preceding example will remain at a level of $787 billion.

Can the Fed control the size of the monetary base? The answer to this question is yes, though with some difficulty. As we saw earlier (see Table 6), the monetary base changes when the Fed engages in open market operations or when banks borrow additional reserves from the Fed or repay loans previously taken from the Fed. Since the Fed is in total control of open market operations, it can regulate any changes in the monetary base that originate from this source. However, the Fed has only indirect control over bank borrowing at the discount window. For example, the Fed may lower the discount rate to discourage banks from reducing their borrowed reserves, but the Fed cannot prohibit banks from repaying these loans, thereby reducing the monetary base. While this complicates the Fed's control over the monetary base, it does not make control impossible. If banks insist on repaying a certain amount (say $2 billion) in borrowed reserves, the Fed can counter this by purchasing exactly $2 billion in bonds on the open market. In this manner, the Fed can control the overall size of the monetary base regardless of independent action by banks.

If we consider changes in the money supply caused by changes in the money multiplier, we find that the money multiplier can, with difficulty, be controlled by the Fed. Since the money multiplier equals $(1 + c)/(c + r)$, a change in either the currency-deposit ratio or the required reserve ratio will change the size of the money multiplier. The Fed has control over r, but not over c. Should the public elect to reduce the currency-deposit ratio, the money multiplier will rise. To offset this change in c, however, the Fed can increase r by the amount necessary to return the money multiplier to its initial level.

Independent actions by banks or by the public can cause the money supply to change—perhaps in a way not desired by the Fed. However, by making appropriate changes in the required reserve ratio, the discount rate, or in open market operations, the Fed can offset these undesired changes in the money supply—which is another way of saying that the Fed does exercise some control over the money supply.

Real-World Multipliers, the Monetary Base, and the Money Stock

The actual M-1 money multiplier, calculated since 1959, has tended to decline except for a minor upturn from the late 1970s to the mid-1980s. As shown in Figure 1, the real-world multiplier has fluctuated widely since 1960. A brief analysis of variations in the multiplier gives us some valuable information on trends in our banking system.

In general, both the banks' desired holdings of idle reserves and the required reserve ratio set by the Federal Reserve have declined over the period, helping to explain the decline through the late 1970s. The Federal Reserve has very gradually lowered the reserve requirements and has, at the same time, applied them more uniformly to all financial institutions accepting deposits.

FIGURE 1

The actual M-1 money multiplier has, in general, declined over the past three decades in the United States. Reductions in the required reserve ratio (r) over the period would have increased the multiplier, but increases in the currency-deposit ratio have been the primary cause of the overall decline shown in the figure.

Source: Federal Reserve Bulletin, various issues.

The Real-World Money Multiplier, 1960–1989

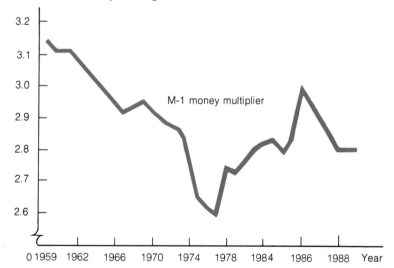

Other things being equal, the reduction in the r ratio would have increased the money multiplier rather than reducing it. But other factors have not remained equal. Since 1960, the ratio of the public's desired holdings of currency to its demand deposits has steadily risen, causing a reduction in the money multiplier. The increase in the public's desired holdings of currency relative to checkable deposits has been accompanied by a shift to money substitutes, notably to the numerous forms of savings and time deposits, many of them new. The Federal Reserve, of course, has been aware of this overall decline and has attempted to adjust the monetary base to fit its money supply policy intentions.

Since deregulation of the financial system, beginning in 1980, holdings of checkable deposits have become more attractive relative to currency. The availability and attractiveness of these deposits has caused a long-term decline in the currency-deposit ratio. The increased holding of large quantities of checkable deposits relative to currency was a major cause of the decrease in the money multiplier over the 1980s.

Month-to-month and week-to-week changes in the money multiplier render Federal Reserve control of the money stock through changes in the monetary base more difficult. Constantly changing market rates of interest on time, savings, and checkable deposits, as noted earlier, are a devilish factor in the Federal Reserve's calculations. But since 1979, the Federal Reserve has made a concerted effort to control the money supply by controlling a monetary aggregate—the monetary base and bank reserves. Before 1979, an interest rate target—the federal funds rate—was the principal means used by the Federal Reserve to direct money and credit conditions. Despite short-run alterations in the money multiplier, the Federal Reserve is perfectly able to control the money supply within fairly narrow bounds by following monetary aggregate targets. The question that concerns macroeconomists is whether any discretionary control over the money stock would be adequate medicine for the macroeconomic ills of inflation, unemployment, and lagging growth in GNP.

SUMMARY

1. Major activities of the Federal Reserve System are summarized in its balance sheet. On the asset side, the Federal Reserve holds a portfolio of earning assets such as loans and securities. Increases in these earning assets indicate an increase in the commercial banking system's reserves, the monetary base, and the nation's money supply.
2. Liabilities of the Federal Reserve System include Federal Reserve notes (currency) in the hands of commercial banks and domestic and foreign governments. An increase in any liability item, except bank reserves themselves, will reduce the monetary base and the nation's money supply.
3. Reserve bank credit outstanding is an important statistic in that it shows the difference between factors increasing reserves and factors decreasing reserves of the commercial banking system.
4. The monetary base is the sum of banking system reserves and currency in the hands of the public. The Federal Reserve attempts to control the monetary base, which is the basis of expansions and contractions in the M-1 money supply.
5. The monetary base is controlled by the Federal Reserve's use of major credit controls: open market operations, loans or discounts to commercial banks, and changes in the required reserve ratio.
6. Purchases of securities from commercial banks or the public, lowering of the discount rate, and lowering of the required reserve ratio all have the effect of increasing bank reserves. Sales of securities, raising of the interest or discount rate charged to banks for loans, and increases in the required reserve ratio decrease bank reserves and the monetary base.

7. Less important controls over bank reserves and lending are sometimes used by the Federal Reserve. Selective credit controls include special powers over consumer credit, mortgage loans, and stock margin requirements. Moral suasion, attempts to alter bank behavior through nonformal nonbinding means, may also be used by the Federal Reserve.

8. Federal Reserve control over the money supply is made trickier by changes in the money multiplier, $(1 + c)/(c + r)$. A change in the money multiplier may be caused, in both the short run and the long run, by changing desires on the part of the public to hold currency relative to demand deposits.

KEY TERMS

reserve bank credit	open market operation	stock margin requirement
monetary base	federal funds rate	moral suasion
credit controls	discount rate	M-1 money multiplier

QUESTIONS FOR REVIEW AND DISCUSSION

1. How does the Federal Reserve System control the money supply through the banking industry? What tools does the Federal Reserve use? How does it control the money supply without using the banking system?
2. What is the monetary base? Is this the same thing as the money supply?
3. "The Federal Reserve can control the minimum amount of reserves that the banking system holds but not the maximum amount." Is this statement true or false? Explain.
4. If the statement in question 3 is true, does it mean that the Federal Reserve can limit increases in the money supply but cannot stop the money supply from falling?
5. What are the things that determine the "powerfulness" of the monetary base?

6. "If the Federal Reserve purchases securities from the nonbank public rather than the banking system, it has a different effect on the money supply." True or false? Explain.
7. Why would a bank want to borrow money from the Federal Reserve and pay the discount rate rather than just accept demand deposits and pay no interest?
8. Is moral suasion an effective monetary tool of the Federal Reserve?
9. Does the reserve-deposit ratio or the currency-deposit ratio have anything to do with the monetary base?
10. "The Federal Reserve is just a big cartel that is operated by the government to make greater profits for the banking industry." Give some arguments that may support this view and some that may refute it.

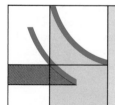

ECONOMICS IN ACTION
Federal Reserve Policy and the Savings and Loan Crisis

By early 1989, the full extent of the problems faced by the U.S. savings and loan industry became clear to the American public; although estimates differ, taxpayer subsidies of at least $100 billion and perhaps as much as $500 billion will be required to bail out insolvent S&Ls. The cost of this bailout may amount to $1400 for each American. However, it is still

a mystery to most Americans how the situation could have developed into a crisis; how could so many loan institutions have gotten so far into debt?

Prior to 1980, the savings and loan industry was subject to extensive government regulations. In particular, S&Ls were prohibited from offering checking services, they were

"AS A MATTER OF FACT, I'D LIKE TO SEE SOME IDENTIFICATION FROM YOU, TOO."

not permitted to pay interest rates of more than 5.5 percent to depositors, and they were precluded from making speculative loans (such as loans to real estate developers). In addition, nearly all the S&Ls in the country were members of the Federal Savings and Loan Insurance Corporation (FSLIC), a governmental agency that insured deposits at member S&Ls. Member savings and loans were charged an insurance fee equal to one-twelfth of one percent of their deposits for insurance coverage protecting all depositors against loss on accounts containing up to $40,000.

In the early 1980s, regulations on maximum interest rates for S&Ls were gradually phased out. As a consequence, S&Ls began offering higher interest rates to attract depositors. At the same time, other regulations that enabled S&Ls to make loans for a variety of risky ventures from which they previously had been excluded were lifted. In addition, insurance coverage by the FSLIC was expanded to cover deposits of up to $100,000.

As a consequence of these regulatory changes, managers of S&Ls found themselves operating in an environment totally different from the one to which they had grown accustomed. Aggressive institutions pursued new deposits by offering higher interest rates, which forced even conservative S&Ls to match the rates or risk losing business. In paying higher interest on deposits, the S&Ls put themselves in the position of having to generate higher interest rates on their loans in order to turn a profit. As a consequence, they turned increasingly to loans to high-risk ventures and to investors willing to borrow at high interest rates. Soon the S&Ls found that their loan portfolios, previously comprised primarily of loans to local customers for the purpose of financing homes and autos, now contained billions of dollars in loans to high-risk ventures in real estate, energy, and farming. Inexperience in making these kinds of loans was one of the factors that eventually led to insolvency.

The ability of S&Ls to attract deposits was greatly enhanced by the existence of federal deposit insurance. Had deposits not been insured, depositors would have become alarmed at the particularly risky loans S&Ls were taking on and would have protected themselves against loss by diverting deposits elsewhere. Because deposits were insured, however, depositors were indifferent about the financial status of the neighborhood S&L. S&Ls on the brink of financial disaster had no trouble attracting additional deposits—right up to the day they were finally shut down by FSLIC examiners. This enabled the S&Ls to run up debts of unprecedented magnitude.

The ongoing financial difficulties of the S&Ls greatly complicate things for the Fed. The survival of many S&Ls depends on repayment of their delinquent loans. If economic growth can be sustained, the default rate on these loans may turn out to be surprisingly low, and relatively few additional S&Ls will fail. This means that the Fed is under unusually great pressure to carry on a monetary policy that leads to continued economic growth. On the other hand, the survival of S&Ls also depends on future interest rates. Many of the loans held by insolvent S&Ls are long-term loans at fixed interest rates; if interest rates rose rapidly, S&Ls would find themselves paying more on their deposits than they receive from their loans, and failure would be inevitable. Whether the Fed will be able to perform this balancing act remains to be seen.

Question

If the Federal Reserve's monetary policy brought interest rates down by 2 to 3 percentage points in the next two years, would you expect the number of savings and loan failures to increase or decrease? Explain.

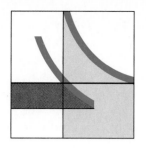

17

Money and Inflation

Money clearly matters. The Federal Reserve Board announces weekly changes in M-1, the nation's basic money supply, and that announcement—which can suggest the possibility of loose or tight credit in the future—creates optimism or pessimism along Wall Street. Investors react by buying or selling stock. Buyers and sellers of home mortgages and all other financial instruments also anxiously observe the weekly changes in M-1 in an attempt to predict changes in interest rates and the future profitability of their financial investments.

The main reason for all of the attention paid to M-1 is the relationship—understood by most Americans—between M-1 and price inflation. Inflation has been perhaps most aptly described as "too much money chasing too few goods," and although economists have constructed elaborate theories to explain inflation, it is still best understood in these simple terms. When the production of real output (bananas or personal computers or hair stylings) does not grow as fast as the M-1 medium of exchange, inflation sooner or later is the result. And most people readily understand that when their nominal money income does not grow at the same rate that prices increase, they are worse off.

In the preceding three chapters we investigated the nature of money, how it is created in the commercial banking system, and how the supply of money is regulated by the Federal Reserve System. In this chapter we take a brief look at monetary theories, specifically at the relation between the money supply—M-1—and the price level. When you finish reading Chapter 17, you should understand

- the three components of the demand for money and their importance for monetary theory and policy.
- how classical, Keynesian, and modern monetarist writers interpret the relation between money, prices, and the real output of goods and services in the economy.
- who wins and who loses from inflation.
- some of the causes of and cures for inflation.

THE DEMAND FOR MONEY

How do economists explain the relation between M-1 and inflation? Economists argue that, like the value of other goods, the value of money—the price level of all output—depends on its demand and supply. However, when discussing how money supply and demand interact to determine the price level, we need to be particularly careful with the terms we use. When economists talk about the demand for money, they are implicitly talking about **real money demand.** Real money demand is a demand to hold or own purchasing power in the form of money (cash and checkable deposits), not just the demand to hold pieces of paper. Thus, real money demand should always be interpreted as a purchasing-power concept. (The purchasing power of a dollar changes with alterations in the price level.) The money supply, though, is a nominal variable unrelated to purchasing power. When economists speak of the supply of money, they simply mean the total current number of dollars that the amount of cash plus checkable deposits in the economy add up to. Throughout the remainder of this chapter, we will use these meanings for money demand and supply.

We have seen that the Federal Reserve controls the nominal money supply, but the Federal Reserve does not control real money demand. People in their roles as money holders determine what real money demand is and what specific quantity of real money they wish to hold. Economists have singled out three reasons or motives for holding purchasing power in the form of money—in other words, for the existence of real money demand. These motives, which may exist simultaneously, are described as the transactions, precautionary, and speculative demands for money.

Real money demand:
Demand on the part of individuals and businesses to hold purchasing power in the form of cash and checkable deposits.

Transactions Demand

People hold or demand money, the medium of exchange, as a simple means of carrying out transactions—to buy chewing gum, dinner at a fancy restaurant, or a personal computer. Businesses demand money to pay for labor, materials, and other inputs. The amount of real money holdings that accommodates transactions of businesses and consumers is referred to as the **transactions demand** for money.

The transactions demand for money is related to the real income of consumers and businesses. As real incomes rise, the demand for more and more money to carry out transactions also rises. For example, a family with an income of $30,000 will have a greater transactions demand for money than a family with an income of only $15,000. This general relation is true of the economy as a whole as well. As real income rises throughout the economy, the transactions demand for money will also increase.

Transactions demand:
Money demand that arises from the desire of businesses and consumers to facilitate exchange with the use of money.

Precautionary Demand

A second reason for holding money is the "rainy day" motive. People usually want to keep some money readily available to meet unforeseen emergencies such as illness or car repair. Likewise, firms generally exercise caution in how much money they hold.

Precautionary demand:
Money demand that arises from the desire of businesses and consumers to hold money in order to facilitate unexpected purchases.

The **precautionary demand** for money is simply the amount of money that households and firms want to hold to meet unforeseen events. Ordinarily, the amount of money that people wish to hold against unforeseen contingencies rises with income. Precautionary demands may therefore be included with transactions demands as being directly related to income.

Speculative Demand

Speculative motive or demand:
Money demand arising from uncertainty of future interest rates and the fact that people can substitute between holding money and holding bonds.

A final explanation for money demand is the **speculative motive or demand.** Like precautionary demand, the speculative motive for holding money is based on uncertainty: Some individuals will want to hold money to speculate in the markets for bonds or other liquid assets whose price and interest return vary. These speculators have to choose between holding money and holding interest-bearing bonds. To make the choice, they consider the present interest rate and the degree of uncertainty about future conditions.

To money holders, the nominal interest rate is the opportunity cost of holding money. It is the return we give up by holding money and not investing it in some other asset (a savings account, a share of a firm's stock, or a bond) that would yield interest. Holding money means keeping or owning some quantity of cash and/or checkable deposits over a period of time. Economists theorize that high interest rates make people want to hold bonds. The price of a bond and its interest yield are inversely related, so high interest rates mean that bond prices are relatively low. Under these conditions, bonds are a good deal for two reasons. One obvious reason is the high interest return; in addition, if the price of bonds rises in the future, bond holders would experience a capital gain. A capital gain occurs when bond buyers purchase bonds at a low price and then bond prices increase. In the event of rising bond prices—which occurs with falling interest rates—selling bonds becomes more attractive. With high bond prices and low interest rates, people generally prefer to hold more money and fewer bonds. Conversely, low bond prices and high interest rates mean that people will hold less money and more bonds.

The speculative motive for holding money means that real money demand is inversely related to the interest rate. As the interest rate rises, bonds are a more attractive asset, and the real quantity of money demanded declines. As the interest rate falls, bonds are less attractive and money is more attractive.

Figure 1 graphically expresses the preceding ideas. The curve labeled L_S is the speculative demand for money (L is demand for money, or "liquidity"). At any time, money holders have formed some expectations about what interest rates and therefore bond prices will be in the future. Given expectations about future bond prices and interest rates, a present interest rate of r_0 means that the real quantity of money demanded for speculative purchases is L_{S_0}. A lower interest rate, such as r_1, means that actual bond prices rise and, as discussed above, the amount of money that individuals will want to hold for speculative reasons will rise. In Figure 1, the real quantity of speculative balances demanded rises to L_{S_1}.

Liquidity preference theory:
A theory stating that the interest rate is determined by the interaction of real money demand and supply, and that interest rate changes due to real money demand or supply changes produce changes in real economic activity.

The speculative demand for money is concerned with *liquidity preference*—how liquid people want to be. The speculative motive for holding money also forms the basis of the **liquidity preference theory,** which states that the rate of interest is determined by overall money demand and supply. As we will see later in this chapter, this theory implies that economic activity, including price changes, flows from changes in the rate of interest.

FIGURE 1

Individuals hold money for speculative purposes—that is, to take advantage of good deals in the bond market. A low interest rate, r_1, means relatively high bond prices and increased real money holdings, L_{S_1}, means relatively high bond prices and increased real money holdings, L_{S_1}. A higher interest rate, r_0, indicates higher bond holdings and lower holdings of money for speculative purposes, L_{S_0}.

The Speculative Demand for Money

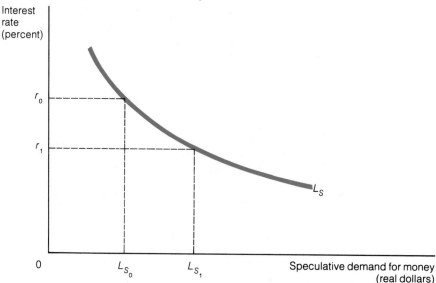

Money Demand: Summary

We now summarize the three influences on the demand for money. Table 1 lists the three types of money demand with the chief factors affecting them and the effects of a change in the factors on the quantity of money demanded. As Table 1 indicates, the total real demand for money is related to income and the rate of interest. As income rises or falls, the transactions and precautionary demand for money rises or falls. If income is held constant, a rise in the interest rate reduces money holdings for speculative purposes. Conversely, a fall in the interest rate produces a rise in the holdings of speculative money.

TABLE 1

The Three Motives for Demanding Money

Both the level of real income and the rate of interest determine the total demand for money. The real quantity of money demanded by all consumers and businesses varies directly with income and inversely with the actual rate of interest, given some level of expectations about future bond prices.

Type of Money Demand	Factor Affecting Demand	Effects on the Quantity of Money Demanded
Transactions To buy and sell goods and services	Rising real income	Higher money demand
	Lowering real income	Lower money demand
Precautionary To save money for unforeseen circumstances	Rising real income	Higher money demand
	Lowering real income	Lower money demand
Speculative To invest in money instruments	Rising interest rates	Lower money demand
	Falling interest rates	Higher money demand

But this information is only half the story. Just as the price of potatoes is the product of both supply and demand, the price level is a product of both money supply and real money demand. On this fact all economists agree. But there are two different theories about how money demand and supply interact to produce a given price level, inflation or deflation, and employment and real income. One theory, the quantity theory of money, places primary emphasis on transactions demand; the other, the liquidity preference theory, highlights the influence of the speculative demand for money.

THE QUANTITY THEORY OF MONEY

Quantity theory of money:
A hypothesis suggesting a predictable positive relationship between the money supply and the price level; specifically, that money supply changes cause price level changes.

Equation of exchange:
An identity used to derive the quantity theory of money; $MV \equiv PQ$.

One of the essential ingredients of classical economic theory and policy, developed toward the end of the eighteenth century, was the **quantity theory of money.** This theory maintains that there is a direct and predictable relation between the money supply, M-1, and prices, given a constant transactions demand for money. If the number of real dollars demanded to carry out everyday transactions (referred to by the classical economists as the income velocity) remains constant, then an increase in the nominal money supply will increase prices.

The quantity theory is derived from an identity (an equation that must be true) called the **equation of exchange.** In economic shorthand, the equation of exchange is written

$$MV \equiv PQ,$$

where M = the nominal money supply, M-1, consisting of currency in the hands of the public and checkable deposits;

V = the income velocity, or the average number of times dollars (the medium of exchange expressed in M-1) are used per year (or week or month) to finance the final purchase of goods and services;

P = the price level of all goods and services; and

Q = the final real output of all goods and services produced and sold in the economy over some period (a year, a month, a week).

Income velocity:
The average number of times that a unit of money (a dollar) is used, or changes hands, in purchasing nominal GNP.

The concept of **income velocity** is crucial to our understanding of the quantity theory of money. M-1 in 1989 was approximately $788 billion. In that same year, GNP, which is expressed as the price level P times final output Q, was $5233 billion. For $788 billion to pay for $5233 billion worth of output, the average dollar must finance at least $6.64 worth of goods ($5233 ÷ $788 = $6.64). We say that the average dollar turned over at least 6.64 times in the course of the year, or that the income velocity of one dollar in 1989 was 6.64. If we know the value of GNP and the quantity of money (M-1) at some point in time, velocity is easily calculated from the equation of exchange as

$$V \equiv \frac{PQ}{(\text{M-1})} \equiv \frac{\text{nominal GNP}}{(\text{M-1})}.$$

While the equation of exchange is useful in some respects, it does not help the economist predict how M-1 is related to P and therefore to inflation. Economists need a theory to do that. To make the equation of exchange a theory, we must specify something about $V, Q, P,$ or M in advance. That is, we must make something in the expression variable and then predict cause and effect on the basis of some hypothetical value of the variable or variables. This is exactly what the classical and neoclassical economists did in converting the equation of exchange into a quantity theory of money.

The Simple Quantity Theory

The simple quantity theory is expressed in exactly the same fashion as the equation of exchange except that the equivalence sign is not given as ≡, which means "must be equal," but as = , which means "is predicted to be equal." The simple quantity theory

$$MV = PQ$$

is stated so that it possibly can be falsified—shown to be untrue—and is therefore a theory.

One of the oldest commonsense macroeconomic propositions is that inflation is "too much money chasing too few goods." The quantity theory explains why that is true. First note that, in general, V and Q were assumed to be constant and predictable. Income velocity—the turnover of money—was thought to be relatively constant over the short run and predictable over the long run. Although the velocity of money, or its average turnover time, for money holders varied from individual to individual, its average remained constant and stable for all money holders taken together.

Why didn't early quantity theorists worry about the level of Q, the final output of real goods and services? They simply assumed that real output was at a maximum. In fairness to these early theorists, we should point out that theirs was a long-run view. Economic disasters created by financial panics, wars, famines, supply shocks, or other disruptions were certainly as much a part of their world as ours, as were beneficial economic events such as inventions and improvements in technology and labor productivity. These events obviously caused reductions or increases in real output. Early monetary theorists such as Adam Smith, David Ricardo, Alfred Marshall, and Irving Fisher neither were unattuned to real-world events nor were they fools. They knew that there would always be short-run fluctuations in output and in the employment of resources—what economists call business cycles. Adjustments were always taking place. The classical economists assumed that output and therefore income were at a maximum because they believed there is a persistent tendency to have economy-wide full employment of resources, implying maximum Q.

As we saw in Chapter 8, the classical and neoclassical economists were believers in Say's law, a principle given expression by Jean Baptiste Say, an early French follower of Adam Smith. Briefly, Say's law states that supply creates its own demand. In other words, the act of producing and supplying goods creates the wherewithal to purchase these goods from the market. Gluts of goods or shortages of goods would not ordinarily take place, but if they did, prices of final goods and services and of labor and other inputs would quickly adjust. This classical assumption of price and wage flexibility meant that adjustment time to full employment would be brief. Should prices and wages fail to be flexible, interest rates would adjust to save the day, according to the classical economists.

The significance of assuming V and Q to be constant or predictable is that the quantity theory of money becomes a theory of cause and effect. Money supply is the cause; prices are the effect. In a modern context, if income velocity and real income are constant, increases in M-1 will increase prices; decreases in M-1 will decrease prices. But by how much do prices increase with increases in M-1? And, more pointedly, how exactly do "too many dollars" end up "chasing too few goods"? A feature of the relation between money and prices assumed by many early economists answers both questions.

Money and Relative Prices

Neutrality of money:
A proposition stating that in the long run the relative prices of goods and services are not affected by changes in the money supply.

Early economists advanced a proposition called the **neutrality of money,** which means that the relative prices of all goods and services (how many computer games trade for rock concert tickets, for example) are independent of the overall price level.

The neutrality of money can be easily understood with a simple example. Suppose that, starting from some stable equilibrium money supply that produces an equilibrium price level—that is, where money demand equals money supply—the money supply is suddenly doubled. That is, we wake one morning to find that the banks will redeem every $1 bill with $2 and will double the value of all of our checkable deposits. The quantity theory predicts what will happen:

$$MV = PQ,$$

so

$$2MV = 2PQ.$$

If consumers' tastes remain the same, the price level will exactly double in the long run when the excess balances created by a doubling of the money supply are spent, but relative prices of goods and services will not change.

What does this mean in practical terms? At first, individuals perceive the increase in their money holdings to be a bonanza. Their new real money holdings exceed their real demand for money. What do these individuals do to restore a balance between money demand and supply? They spend their excess money holdings in the attempt to acquire more goods. If their tastes do not change, their relative expenditures on shoes, candy, and gasoline do not change. But—and here is a major point—there are no more goods to be had. The economy is already at a full-employment level of real output. The only effect of these increased money expenditures is to drive all prices up. The price level doubles, but relative prices remain unchanged if money is neutral. Once the price level has doubled in response to the doubling of the nominal money supply, people find themselves with the same real holdings of money. Their attempts to spend excess real money stop because there no longer is excess real money. The process ends with the price level exactly doubled but no change in relative prices.

We will investigate this process with a numerical example. Consider a simple, three-good world where quantities of beer, pretzels, and pizzas are produced at certain base prices. Table 2 gives data showing the final output of the three goods and an initial set of prices, indicated as P_0. GNP in this simple world is measured by price multiplied by the quantities of goods produced, an initial sum of $80. Now suppose that the money stock doubles

TABLE 2

Effect of Doubling the Nominal Money Stock in a Three-Good World

If money is neutral—that is, if it does not affect relative prices—a doubling of the nominal money stock doubles the price level from P_0 to P_1, though relative prices and output do not change. The price of beer per case in terms of pretzels is the same before and after the price increase.

Good	Final Output Produced (Q)	Initial Price (P_0)	$P_0 \times Q$	P_1	$P_1 \times Q$
Beer	2 cases	$10 per case	$20	$20	$ 40
Pretzels	10 bags	$1 per bag	$10	$ 2	$ 20
Pizzas	5 large	$10 each	$50	$20	$100
Nominal GNP			$80		$160

and that the new nominal GNP equals $160. If money is neutral, the price of each good produced before the money stock increase must exactly double. This means that relative prices of all the goods traded both before and after doubling of the money stock must remain the same. And, in the example of Table 2, they do. One case of beer still trades for ten bags of pretzels and for one large pizza.

Thus, if money is neutral, relative prices are independent of the price level and of the nominal prices of all goods and services traded in the economy. Neutrality means that money is the oil of trade, not the wheel of trade.

The Simple Quantity Theory: Transmission Mechanism

We summarize the cause-and-effect relation between money and prices in Figure 2. Increases in M-1 initially create excess amounts of real money in the hands of consumers and businesses. Their demand for money is unchanged as a proportion of income, but they now actually hold larger real quantities of money. Their spending attempts are met with frustration since real output is already at a maximum. The effects of this attempt to acquire more goods and services simply drive the money price of goods and services upward. The process ends only when prices have risen to the point where money demanders are again holding real balances equal to their real demands for money.

The classical mechanism relating changes in the money supply to aggregate demand—the classical transmission mechanism—is shown graphically in Figure 3. The line from the origin in Figure 3a shows points of equilibrium between MV and PQ—points where the quantity of money (depicted on the vertical axis), given a constant velocity (V) and a constant *real* full-employment level of output and income (Q_f), produces some *nominal* level of income (P times Q), or GNP (depicted on the horizontal axis). The slope of the line from the origin in Figure 3a is given by a constant, k, which is the reciprocal of velocity, or $1/V$. As velocity rises, k falls, and vice versa. Given some value for M, say M_0, a unique value of nominal income, P_0Q_f is produced, since real output and velocity are assumed constant. If the money supply (M-1) is

FIGURE 2   The Simple Quantity Theory of Money

Increases in the nominal money stock initially create excess amounts of real money balances, causing consumers and businesses to attempt additional purchases of goods and services. Assuming a constant output and full employment of resources, price level increases result.

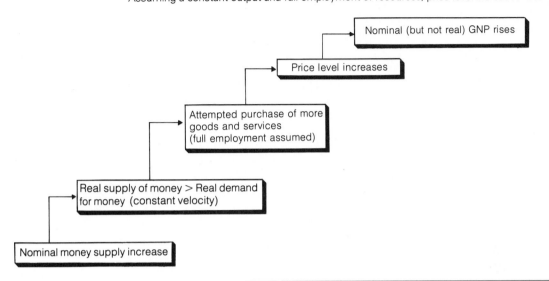

increased to M_1, a new level of *nominal* income, P_1Q_f, is produced. But what happens to the real output of goods and services in the economy?

In Figure 3b, the aggregate supply curve is vertical at full employment. If we now designate Y as real output of goods and services, Y_f represents the full employment of all resources. An increase in the money supply from M_0 to M_1 has the effect of shifting the aggregate demand curve rightward from AD_0 to AD_1. In the classical view of the macroeconomy, an increase in the money supply (assuming full employment at Y_f) has *no* effect on real output; for a time, the real supply of money is greater than the demand for it. People attempt to purchase more goods and services, but these attempts are thwarted by the fact that full employment exists. The result is a rise in the price level, as shown in Figure 3b, from P_0 to P_1. At the new point of equilibrium—E_1 in Figures 3a and 3b—money demanders are again holding actual balances equal to their desired balances. In the classical transmission mechanism, the only impact of a change in the money supply in the long run is to cause an increase in the price level.

SPECULATIVE MONEY DEMAND AND PRICES: KEYNES'S PERSPECTIVE

We now consider a second important theory about the relation between money supply and prices. The classical economists, as we have seen, emphasized the transactions and precautionary motives for holding money and related money demand solely to real income. John Maynard Keynes emphasized a third motivation for holding money—to speculate in bond and other asset markets

FIGURE 3
The Classical Transmission from Money to Prices

An increase in the money supply has no effect on any "real" variables in the economic system such as real output or income. In the long run, prices rise as aggregate demand shifts upward from AD_0 to AD_1.

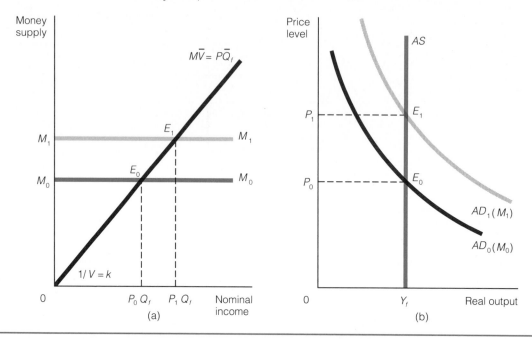

where price and interest rates vary. Recall also that this speculative demand for money varies inversely with interest rates: When interest rates rise, the quantity of money demanded for speculative purposes declines, and vice versa.

The Importance of Speculative Demand

In the Keynesian view of macroeconomics, speculative demand plays a special and important role. Assuming that transactions and precautionary demands are satisfied, the rate of interest is the product of the demand for speculative balances and their supply. This is called the liquidity preference theory of money and interest. More important, *economic activity is determined by changes in the rate of interest*.

The importance of the speculative demand for money becomes apparent when we examine the effects of increases in the money supply on the rate of interest and of changes in the rate of interest on economic activity. Figure 4a shows that the rate of interest is a product of the interplay of speculative balances demanded, L_S (reproduced from Figure 1) and the supply of money devoted to speculation, M_S. (Transactions and precautionary money demands are assumed to be satisfied.) The interplay of speculative demand and supply produces an equilibrium interest rate r_0 when supply is M_{S_0}. As Figure 4a shows, an increase in the supply of money available for speculative purposes—in this case, to M_{S_1}—drives interest rates down. The higher bond prices that result from lower interest rates cause asset holders to opt for fewer bonds and more speculative money balances. In other words, lower interest rates create a preference for the liquid asset, money, over the less-liquid asset, bonds.

FIGURE 4   Money Supply, Interest Rates, and Investment Spending

In the Keynesian framework, an increase in the money supply for speculative balances *may* succeed in lowering the interest rate (a), which *may* increase investment spending in the economy (b). Keynes thought these events unlikely in a depression economy, however.

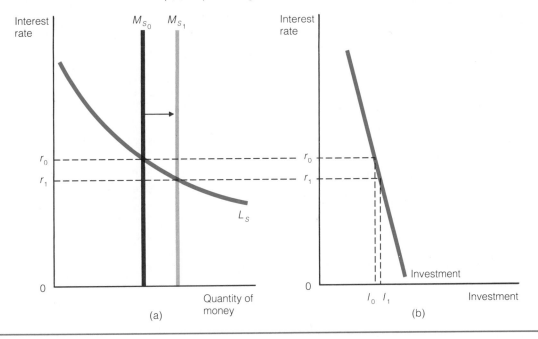

The key to understanding the importance of speculative demand is to observe that investment and consumption might be affected by changes in the interest rate, as the classical economists had suggested. As discussed in Chapter 8, a rise in the interest rate reduces desired investment and increases desired saving, whereas a fall in the interest rate has the effect of increasing both investment and consumption. In the classical approach, lower interest rates ordinarily mean higher spending, higher output, and higher employment. In the event of unemployed resources, monetary policy—altering the quantity of money—could be used to lower interest rates, to increase consumption and investment spending, and to help bring the economy back to full-employment equilibrium if it ever veered from that level.

Keynes rejected the classical assessment. He did not believe that interest rate reductions would necessarily have much impact on investment and consumption. In his view, consumption and investment were largely insensitive to interest rate changes, being autonomous or more responsive to change in income. In Figure 4b, increases in the speculative component of the money supply from M_{S_0} to M_{S_1} produce a small reduction in the rate of interest from r_0 to r_1. These reductions in the interest rate *may* have an impact on investment, but this effect depends on the responsiveness of investment to changes in the interest rate. Keynes believed that individuals would be hesitant to invest in bonds (or in durable consumption goods—big-ticket items) in periods of economic distress. Uncertainty about economic conditions would cause people to hold money even though bond prices were falling (making bonds "a good deal"). Likewise, businesses would exercise extreme caution about investments in new capital in the midst of recessions or depressions. In short, investment would not be very responsive to reductions in the interest rate. Figures 4a and 4b show that interest rate reductions would increase investment only slightly, from I_0 to I_1. Monetary policy, in Keynes's view, would not be a very effective way to nudge the economy toward full employment.

Money and Prices: The Keynesian Transmission Mechanism

What does Keynes's view mean for the short-run relation between the money supply and prices? The addition of speculative demand to the transactions and precautionary demand for money short-circuits the cause-and-effect relation between the money supply and prices. Increases in the money supply may have little or no effect on the price level if the spending generated by an interest rate decrease is small or nonexistent.

Figure 5 illustrates Keynes's scenario. An increase in M-1 creates an excess supply of money. The resulting reductions in interest rates (and concurrent increases in bond prices) cause increased holdings of idle money. Consumption and investment spending increase little, meaning that aggregate demand increases only slightly. Even if resources are fully employed, prices cannot be much affected. If there is widespread unemployment, prices are not affected. The liquidity preference theory, based on the speculative demand for money, therefore implies an uncertain and unpredictable relation between the money supply and prices.

Keynes's view of the transmission from money to prices is depicted in Figure 6. *If* increases in M-1 actually do cause interest rates to fall and *if* the

FIGURE 5   Money and Prices: Liquidity Preference View

According to Keynes, an increase in M-1 has an uncertain effect on the price level. A declining interest rate, for instance, may not encourage additional total demand. Even if demand increases, prices may not increase if the economy is experiencing widespread unemployment.

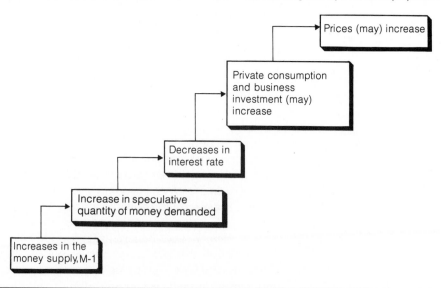

FIGURE 6

Keynes did not have much faith that monetary expansion could increase real output and employment during recessions or depressions. As the money supply increases, investors (and consumers) *might* increase spending *if* the interest rate actually falls. Aggregate demand increases, however, would likely be insignificant.

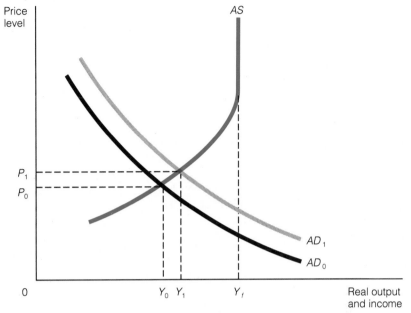

The Keynesian Transmission Mechanism

fall in interest rates causes investment and consumption to increase, total expenditures would increase and aggregate demand would shift rightward. As we have seen, Keynes believed that in the presence of uncertainty about economic conditions money holders, consumers, and investors would hold on to speculative money balances and postpone purchases of consumer and investment goods. We show these effects with a minimal increase in aggregate demand and small increases in real output in the economy in Figure 6. Clearly, the Keynesian prescription for economic recovery had to rely on other factors affecting total spending and aggregate demand—namely, increases in government spending and/or reductions in taxes.

MONETARISM: A MODERN APPROACH TO MONEY AND PRICES

The quantity theory of money predicts a positive long-run relation between the money supply and the price level, whereas the liquidity preference approach explains a possible link between money and prices in the short run through the effects of money supply changes on interest rates. A widely accepted contemporary explanation of inflation and deflation—**monetarism**—combines elements of both views along with a new perspective on the inflation process.

    Monetarists are concerned with both short-run and long-run adjustments of the economy to different rates of change in the money supply. The monetarist view of inflation emphasizes the uncertainty people feel about what inflation rates will be in the future and the effects this uncertainty will

Monetarism:
A theory that centers on money supply growth, real money demand, nominal and real interest rates, and inflationary expectations in explaining the process of inflation or deflation.

have on present behavior. These expectations have a short-run impact on employment and real income, as well as on prices. We focus here on a simple monetarist explanation of the inflation process, which contains three basic elements: a monetarist explanation of the demand for money, a distinction between the market or nominal interest rate and the real interest rate, and the impact of people's expectations concerning future prices and the inflation process.

Money Demand

One of the foundations of modern monetarism is the formulation of a short-run demand for money. Milton Friedman developed a short-run money demand model in the mid-1950s as a direct extension of both the simple quantity theory and the liquidity preference or speculative money demand approach. Earlier economists argued that people hold money for transactions, precautionary, and speculative purposes. Friedman makes no such distinctions, simply accepting the fact that money is held in response to several independent variables. The most important of these variables are real income and the nominal interest rate.

Like the quantity theorists and Keynes, Friedman argues that some money holdings for transactions depend partly on income.[1] Also in the manner of Keynes, the monetarists find that the nominal interest rate affects real money holdings. While other variables affect money demand in the monetarist model, we neglect them in the following discussion of the monetarist view of inflation and concentrate only on y, current real income, and i, the nominal interest rate, as the factors influencing money demand. A shorthand version of money demand can thus be expressed as

$$L_d = L_d(y, i).$$

In this expression the real demand for money is determined only by current income and the nominal interest rate.

The Nominal Interest Rate and Price Expectations

Real interest rate:
The nominal interest rate minus the expected rate of inflation.

Market, or nominal, interest rate:
The interest rate computed from the money values of a borrowing or lending arrangement, such as a savings account; the interest rate unadjusted for expected inflation.

The classical economists had written extensively about the determinants of the real rate of interest. The **real interest rate**—the nominal rate minus the expected rate of inflation—is determined by the real and fundamental forces of thrift (saving) and productivity (investment) in the economy. But this fundamental rate is generally not the rate of interest that one would pay to borrow money at a bank. The **market,** or **nominal, interest rate**—the rate actually paid at banks and lending institutions—has two components: the real rate of interest and a dynamic element based on price expectations. Consider why the market rate includes both elements.

If you decide on January 1 to borrow $100 from a bank for one year, how will the interest rate be determined? Put another way, on what basis will banks decide to make loans? If the real rate of interest, reflecting basic forces of

---

[1]Friedman's assumption rested on permanent income—the income expected over a lifetime—rather than current income. In our simple discussion of inflation, however, we retain current income as a determinant of money demand, neglecting Friedman's more complex measure of permanent income.

saving and investment, is 4 percent, the bank will certainly charge at least 4 percent. But will the bank charge more? If the rate of inflation expected over the year is 8 percent, the bank would lose real income on a 4 percent loan. It would be lending at a return of 4 percent, but the value of the money returned at the end of the year will have also lost 8 percent of its purchasing power. Thus, after the fact, the bank would have made a bad bargain at any loan rate below 12 percent.

The nominal interest rate is thus influenced by the **expected inflation rate** as well as the real interest rate. When inflationary expectations rise, the nominal interest rate also rises. When the inflation rate is expected to fall, nominal rates tend to fall. When actual, realized rates of inflation are different from those expected, borrowers and lenders adjust in the following period. The effect of inflationary expectations on market rates of interest is a stock-in-trade of modern monetarist thought. Through inflation rate expectations, a dynamic period-to-period element is brought into modern interpretations of the quantity theory of money.

How do we form expectations about future prices? A well-known and currently used theory about this matter is the **adaptive expectations theory,** which states that present price expectations about the future are adapted to the public's most recent experience with prices. The basic premise of adaptive expectations is that it takes time for individuals to adjust to changed circumstances. Expectations about occurrences in the future hinge primarily on present knowledge and present experiences. Consistent experiences in the present ("the sun rose in the east every day this week") tend to create the same expectations about future events ("the sun will rise in the east tomorrow"). The adaptive expectations theory simply asserts that our expectations about future price conditions are formed on the basis of actual past price experience, with the most recent experience having the greatest influence. There are other theories about the formation of expectations (some of which will be explored in the following chapters), but the simple adaptive expectations idea goes far in explaining the modern monetarist connection between monetary expansion and the inflation rate.

Expected inflation rate:
The rate of inflation that consumers and businesses expect to exist over a relevant future period, such as the coming year.

Adaptive expectations theory:
A proposition suggesting that consumers and businesses form expectations of future inflation on the basis of actual inflation from the recent past.

MODERN MONETARISM AND INFLATION

The simple tools of the old quantity theorists combined with a modern version of the demand for money and the adaptive expectations theory provide a monetarist explanation for the process of inflation. Before turning to this concept, it is important to recall exactly what inflation is. Inflation is a rate of increase in prices, not a simple rise in the price level. In a static framework, it is sometimes convenient to say, as we did using the simple quantity theory, that a doubling of M produces a doubling of P and to identify this once-and-for-all change as inflation. In a dynamic real-world setting, however, the money supply is constantly being increased or decreased by the Federal Reserve Board at some rate per week, month, or year. Likewise, prices are rising or falling at some rate. Real income is also changing, by values typically expressed in terms of growth rates such as 3½ percent per year, although in the present simple discussion of the inflation process we assume a constant income growth rate. To arrive at the modern conception of inflation, therefore, we must adapt the static quantity theory to a dynamic setting.

The Process of Inflation

The simple process of inflation is best understood by starting from a dynamic equilibrium position in the economy. In this initial position, the economy is characterized by the following conditions.

Rate of monetary expansion:
The annual percent by which the nominal money supply is changing.

1. A constant **rate of monetary expansion** (whether 3 percent or 50 percent growth in the money stock, M-1, per year—the actual percentage is not important as long as it is constant).
2. Expected and actual inflation rates are equal, and further, market participants will expect the inflation rate to be exactly what it has been in the present and recent past.
3. The nominal rate of interest equals the real rate of interest plus the constant inflation rate. Since the inflation rate has been assumed constant in the most recent past experience, according to the adaptive expectations theory the inflation rate (and therefore the nominal rate of interest) is expected to be the same in the future.
4. People are actually holding real cash balances equivalent to their desired holdings of money balances. The quantity demanded of money is equal to the quantity supplied of money in real terms.
5. Real income or real GNP is growing at a constant rate.

If we numerically express the percentage rates of change of the items in the quantity theory, we can calculate a rate of change in prices. If, for example, the monetary expansion rate, which we now designate with a dot on top of M, or $\dot{M}$, is 12 percent, and the constant growth rate in real income, $\dot{Q}$, is 4 percent, and velocity V is constant ($\dot{V}$ is thus zero), the inflation rate $\dot{P}$ is easily calculated. The dynamic quantity theory becomes

$$\dot{M} + \dot{V} = \dot{P} + \dot{Q},$$

or, given the hypothetical numbers,

$$12\% + 0\% = \dot{P} + 4\%,$$

$$\dot{P} = 12\% - 4\% = 8\% \text{ inflation rate.}$$

The inflation rate is thus calculated as 8 percent.

The exercise of casting the quantity theory into rates of change might seem mechanical so far, but it is invaluable in providing a simple understanding of inflation as a process. To initiate the inflation process we need simply to suppose that the Federal Reserve, through its powers over the monetary base, suddenly increases the rate of monetary expansion from 12 percent to 15 percent. Further, the Federal Reserve maintains the rate of monetary expansion at 15 percent from that point forward and forever.

Figure 7 illustrates what happens. The new, higher growth rate in the money supply initially creates disequilibrium among money holders. After the expansion, but before prices begin rising faster, money demanders find themselves holding more real money balances than they want to hold, given the previous state of equilibrium. Consumers and businesses will attempt to rid themselves of these excess balances by spending more on all goods and services.

What, however, is the long-term impact of the increased spending on real income and employment? The answer in real terms is "nothing." Since output and employment were already growing at a constant full-employment

FIGURE 7

The process of inflation begins with an increased rate of M-1 expansion by the Federal Reserve. Excess money holdings are spent, creating higher actual inflation and higher expected inflation. Higher expected inflation causes higher market interest rates, further increasing spending and inflation. The process continues until the Federal Reserve stabilizes the rate of growth in M-1.

How the Fire of Inflation Gets Fanned

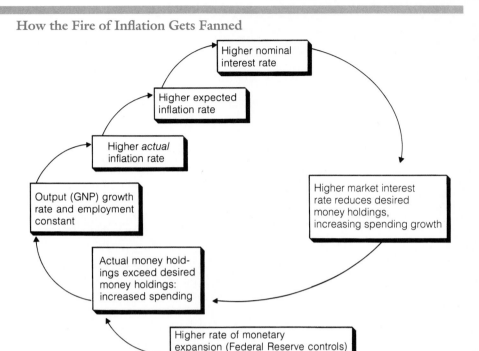

rate, the attempt to purchase more goods will only drive up prices and money income more rapidly. Thus the actual inflation rate begins to rise. Since it takes time for higher actual inflation rates to be translated into expectations of higher inflation—that is, for the adaptive expectations theory to come into play—higher expected inflation rates will lag behind the actual rate.

It is easy to predict what will happen next. Since the nominal interest rate equals the real interest rate (which we assume to remain constant) plus the expected inflation rate, nominal rates begin to climb. This rise in the nominal rate affects the desired real holdings of money. Since the real demand of money is partially a function of the nominal interest rate (the opportunity cost of holding money), the higher interest rate generated by higher inflation expectations leads to lower desired money holdings. This effect reinforces the attempt of money holders to rid themselves of cash balances. That is, the higher nominal rate further fans the rise in the inflation rate.

When does the process stop? When is a dynamic equilibrium reattained? The process will stop only if the Federal Reserve sticks to a constant rate of monetary expansion (15 percent in our example). The process of increasing inflation rates will continue only if the Federal Reserve continues to increase the rate of money creation. If the Federal Reserve holds the rate to 15 percent, for example, equilibrium will be reattained at a new constant inflation rate, a new nominal interest rate, and a new rate of price expectations equal to the actual inflation rate. In the numerical terms of our example, equilibrium will take place when

$$\dot{M} + \dot{V} = \dot{P} + \dot{Q},$$
$$15\% + 0\% = 11\% + 4\%.$$

Prices must rise, in other words, so that *actual* real money holdings are equivalent to *desired* real money holdings. Spending and the inflation rate will rise until real money demand equals money supply.

Some Preliminary Lessons About Inflation

The monetarist view of inflation contains certain explicit and implicit lessons. First and foremost, monetarists argue that inflation is always a monetary phenomenon. Milton Friedman and Anna Schwartz[2] have supported this proposition with massive hundred-year empirical studies of the quantity theory in the United States and England. As we note in Figure 3, the villain in the monetarists' inflation scenario is expansionist policies of the monetary authority that controls the money stock. For a discussion of alternative monetary policies and the rate of inflation in Europe, see Focus, "European Inflation Under a Common Currency Agreement."

In the monetarist version of events, for example, high interest rates do not *cause* inflation; rather, they are the *result* of inflation. What we did not mention in our simplified treatment is that one short-lived initial effect of the Federal Reserve's monetary expansion is a temporary decline in market interest rates. Of course, the market rates begin to rise as expectations of higher inflation take hold of borrowers and lenders. Observers and politicians often make the mistake of arguing that the money stock growth rate should be expanded to lower the interest rates. As we have seen, however, the monetarists show that such a shortsighted policy will have the opposite effect: Increasing the rate of expansion of the money supply will soon raise nominal interest rates. Higher interest rates follow higher inflation rates, but higher monetary expansion is necessary for both events to occur.

Many people also think that inflation is self-generating. Higher nominal interest rates do affect desired money balances and spending. But in the monetarist view, this process must come to an end if the central bank holds the money expansion to a constant rate. It may, of course, take time for inflationary expectations to adjust between consumers and producers, borrowers and lenders, and employers and employees, but when the market adjusts, a dynamic equilibrium will be attained.

It is very important to note that an increased rate of monetary expansion *will* have some short-run effects on the economy. Specifically, the Federal Reserve can temporarily lower both the nominal and the real rates of interest, thereby creating a *temporary* surge in total spending. This might have short-term effects on output and employment as well if employment is not growing at a full-employment rate (or if overfull employment is a temporary possibility). If the economy is at or near full employment, however, the inevitable result in the monetarist view is a higher rate of inflation. A contemporary school of macroeconomics called *rational expectations theory* goes one step further than monetarism on the matter of even the short-run possibility of monetary policy having any real effects on the economy. In an extreme view of this theory, monetary policy can have *no* effects on real output or employment because all of the effects of policy are fully anticipated. We will turn to these considerations in Chapters 18 and 19 after looking at some of the problems caused by inflation.

---

[2]Milton Friedman and Anna J. Schwartz, *A Monetary History of the United States* (Princeton, N.J.: Princeton University Press, 1963).

One of the stated goals of the European Community is to establish a common currency in 1992. On the surface, this proposal appears to have several advantages without any serious disadvantages. Nonetheless, the proposal has become quite controversial.

The major advantage of adopting common currency is reducing transaction costs and thereby increasing the opportunity for trade between the various European countries. It is easier for British firms to do business with firms in France if both countries use a common currency than if the British use the pound and the French use the franc.

However, in agreeing to a common currency system, the European nations are also agreeing to a unified monetary policy. Some type of European central bank (which could be modeled after the U.S. Federal Reserve System, with branch banks in each member country) would be created with the authority to conduct open market operations and set discount rates, among other things. Depending on the policies pursued by the central bank, the money supply within the European Community would rise at some particular rate. However, it would not be possible for member nations to independently control monetary growth within their borders.

If each of the member countries were in agreement over appropriate monetary policy, this would not present a serious problem. However, such a consensus does not exist. Currently, most of the European countries have linked their respective currencies to the deutsche mark (the currency of Germany), but some of the countries, particularly France and Italy, are unhappy with the anti-inflation policies previously pursued by the West German government. The Germans' experience with hyperinflation in 1923 sensitized them to inflation. The German central bank has responded to this sensitivity by pursuing policies to keep inflation rates down. French and Italian objections to a common currency amount to a dispute over control of the central bank. Should France and Italy gain control, there is reason to expect that the rate of inflation in Europe would rise more rapidly than under German control.

Although Germany has publicly supported the proposal for a unified currency, there are signs that the Germans are hesitant to trust their monetary fate to others. Even Switzerland, which is not a member of the European Community, has announced that it would not participate in a common currency agreement because of fears that it would lead to a policy of inflation.

Margaret Thatcher has similarly been reluctant to commit Britain to the monetary union. Instead, she has proposed a system of competing currencies, with all Europeans free to choose the currency they want to use. Prime Minister Thatcher believes that such a system would lead to dominance by the least inflationary currency and would thus discipline the various central banks to vigorously pursue anti-inflationary policies.

Since the various members of the European Community differ with regard both to economic priorities and to economic philosophies, it is difficult to predict what monetary policies would be pursued by a unified European central bank. This uncertainty will prove to be a major obstacle in obtaining participation by the member countries.

INFLATION

Several measures of inflation are used in the real world to guide policymaking. As we mentioned in Chapter 7, a consumer price index and a producer price index are calculated by the Bureau of Labor Statistics. A third major index is the implicit price deflator, a means of converting nominal GNP values into real GNP values. No matter what measure is used, the presence of higher indexes over time indicates a rising price level. Actual U.S. inflation rates are shown in Table 3.

The Effects of Inflation

The statistical presence of inflation in the economy tells us little about the costs and other distortions it inflicts there. Runaway inflation of 80 or 2000 percent per month or per year, such as that sometimes experienced in war-torn or developing countries with low or severely restricted stocks of goods

TABLE 3

Two Measures of Inflation, 1960–1989

Two popular measures of inflation used in the United States are the implicit price deflator, a means for converting nominal GNP into real values, and the consumer price index, which bases the inflation rate on price changes in some hypothetical market basket of consumer goods. The numbers given for both indexes are annual rates.

| Year | Inflation Rate, as Measured by | | Year | Inflation Rate, as Measured by | |
	Implicit Price Deflator	Consumer Price Index		Implicit Price Deflator	Consumer Price Index
1960	1.6	1.6	1975	9.8	9.1
1961	1.0	1.0	1976	6.4	5.9
1962	2.2	1.1	1977	6.7	6.5
1963	1.6	1.2	1978	7.3	7.7
1964	1.5	1.3	1979	8.9	11.3
1965	2.7	1.7	1980	9.0	13.5
1966	3.6	2.9	1981	9.7	10.4
1967	2.6	2.9	1982	6.4	6.1
1968	5.0	4.2	1983	3.9	3.2
1969	5.6	5.4	1984	3.7	4.3
1970	5.5	5.9	1985	3.0	3.6
1971	5.7	4.3	1986	2.6	1.9
1972	4.7	3.3	1987	3.2	3.6
1973	6.5	6.2	1988	3.3	4.1
1974	9.1	11.0	1989	4.1	4.8

Source: Council of Economic Advisers, *Economic Report of the President* (Washington, D.C.: U.S. Government Printing Office, 1990), pp. 301, 363.

and services, can reduce an economy to barter or cause it to collapse altogether. Milder inflation—3 to 15 percent per year—also creates economic costs in any advanced economy. The full effects of increases in inflation rates may take some time to be fully realized, so inflation has both short- and long-run effects.

Inflation, Fixed Incomes, and Assets. The most publicized effect of inflation is the redistributive impact it has between specific groups in society. Inflation affects those who can least afford to pay for it—the sick, the poor, and especially the elderly and others on fixed incomes—through erosions of purchasing power. Congress, in recent years of inflation, indexed or "tied" Social Security and other welfare benefits to a price level index, thereby alleviating some of the problems inflation causes for the retired or the aged. Nevertheless, inflation is a constant threat to the most economically vulnerable groups in society.

Inflation also adversely affects holders of assets denominated in nominal, or money, terms as opposed to real terms. Suppose you purchase a house—a real asset—and hold it for five years, over which time the price level doubles because of inflation. What happens to the nominal value of your investment? Excluding the real factors of natural appreciation and depreciation that might take place over the five years (resulting from the location, deterioration of property, and so on), the money value of your house should closely follow the inflation rate over the period, doubling at the end of the five years.

While the value of real assets tends to follow inflation, the value of money-denominated assets may not. Suppose that you lend a friend $10,000, to be paid at the end of a five-year period, and that your friend issues you a promissory note attesting to the loan. Again suppose that the price level doubles over the five-year span because of inflation. Aside from any interest paid by your friend, what has happened to the real value of your asset? Although the nominal value of the note remains at $10,000, the real value is only half of what it was at the beginning of the five-year period. You will now be able to purchase only half the goods and services that you could have bought before you made the loan. Capital gains or losses—changes in real value—are always associated with holding any kind of asset in the face of unanticipated inflation. Real assets generally gain in value, whereas money assets—those expressed in fixed money terms—generally lose value.

Asset holders also experience transaction and information costs as they move into and out of inflation-prone assets. It is costly, in other words, to find out which real assets will best follow the price level—a Picasso or a Jackson Pollock, a house or IBM stock.

Disruptive Expectations. A second major effect of inflation is that it distorts expectations of inflation, wage rates, and interest rates. When the inflation rate is not perfectly anticipated, workers and employers, buyers and sellers of goods and services, and borrowers and lenders will be uncertain of future real values. Since these transactors will generally make mistakes in forecasting the effects of inflation in specific markets, there will be continuous and unanticipated transfers of wealth among workers and employers, buyers and sellers, borrowers and lenders.

Escalator clause:
Provision of a labor contract that ties changes in nominal wages to changes in some price index.

Market participants try to protect themselves, of course. Workers belonging to labor unions often bargain for **escalator clauses** in their contracts, provisions that tie future wages to some index of the price level as a hedge against inflation.

Inflation and expectations of the rate of inflation also affect nominal interest rates. When the inflation rate fluctuates, so do expectations of inflation as well as nominal and real interest rates. These changes can have severe effects on the economic well-being of various groups and individuals in the economy by altering the real value of indebtedness. In the late 1970s, for example, unexpected inflation worked to the benefit of many homeowners by substantially reducing the real value of their mortgage payments, the real value of the indebtedness incurred when they borrowed money to buy houses. Of course, there is the other side of this coin. Lenders were being paid back, in real terms, much less from homeowners than they had originally agreed to. The presence of volatile inflation and interest rates not only transfers wealth among groups in society, but also will serve to make credit markets function less efficiently. (See Focus, "The Winners and Losers from Unexpected Inflation.")

Pure inflation tax:
The reduction in purchasing power of an individual's nominal money holdings due to inflation.

Inflation as a Tax. Inflation also levies two different kinds of "taxes" on people, taxes that are not directly imposed through the traditional democratic process of taxation by legislation. The first of these is the **pure inflation tax.** No one fills out an inflation tax form and writes a check, but the pure inflation tax is nonetheless very real. The taxpayers are those individuals and businesses who hold money. Anyone who holds money over, say, a month will see the purchasing power of that money decline due to inflation. The amount by which the purchasing power of an individual's money holdings declines is the pure inflation tax.

FOCUS   The Winners and Losers from Unexpected Inflation

Just as price changes for a particular commodity can benefit one group and simultaneously harm another, the financial positions of debtors and creditors also can be modified by unexpected changes in the inflation rate. Expectations of the future inflation rate are built into nominal or money rates of interest. The nominal rate of interest at the time money is borrowed or lent not only reflects the real interest rate, but also the inflation rate that the borrower and lender expect will persist over the term of the loan. If, after the loan is made, the rate of inflation that actually occurs turns out to be different from that expected, the purchasing power of the interest and principal repayments turns out to be different from what both parties to the loan expected it to be. The result is an unexpected wealth transfer between the debtor and the creditor. The direction of the transfer depends on whether inflation was "overanticipated" or "underanticipated."

Consider the more familiar case of underanticipated inflation first. This occurs when the rate of inflation that actually exists turns out to be higher than the rate the debtor and creditor expected when the loan was made. For simplicity, assume that a student wishes to borrow $3000 from a rich aunt for one year to finance college expenditures. Both agree that the real interest rate on this family loan will be 0 percent. Suppose that both expect no inflation—an inflation rate of 0 percent—over the year. The student then promises (a loan contract) to repay $3000 at the end of the year. Since both parties to this agreement expect no inflation over the course of the year, both parties expect the $3000 repayment to have the same purchasing power at the end of the year that the $3000 loan had at the beginning of the year. The promise (or the loan contract) is to repay 3000 nominal dollars. The expectation implicit in the loan agreement is that the 3000 nominal dollars will purchase the same amount of goods and services at the end of the year that they were able to purchase at the beginning of the year.

At the end of the year, suppose that the price level had doubled; that is, suppose that the inflation rate had been 100 percent. The student would be obligated to pay back $3000, but each dollar would purchase only one-half as much as it did at the beginning of the year. In essence, the student would pay back only 1500 constant-purchasing-power dollars. The inflation rate was actually 100 percent, but the debtor and creditor expected 0 percent. Hence, inflation was underanticipated, and as a result, a wealth transfer of 1500 constant-purchasing-power dollars from the creditor (the rich aunt) to the debtor (the student) has taken place.

No matter what the levels of the actual and expected inflation rate, if inflation is underanticipated, debtors win and creditors lose from inflation. The people who borrowed to buy homes in the 1950s and 1960s benefited from the high and underanticipated inflation rates of the 1970s. Their real mortgage payments turned out to be much lower than either they or the lenders thought they would be due to underanticipated inflation. The lenders of mortgage funds, on the other hand, were financially hurt, as was evidenced by the bankruptcy of a number of savings and loan associations during this period. The federal government, as well as state and local governments, probably also benefited from underanticipated inflation. With much debt outstanding that was issued under fairly low expected rates of inflation, the real interest and principal repayments ended up lower than expected. Of course, the holders of these bonds—individuals and businesses who lent funds by buying bonds—saw their real wealth drop as a result of underanticipated inflation. Whenever inflation is underanticipated, debtors win and creditors lose.

The direction of the wealth transfer is not always from creditors to debtors, however. It is quite possible for it to be in just the opposite direction. Consider the fictitious student loan discussed above. Suppose, though, that both parties expect a 100 percent inflation rate over the year. The student will be agreeable to paying back $6000 at the end of the year because it is expected that each dollar paid back will be worth half as much as each dollar borrowed. A constant-purchasing-power payback of 3000 beginning-of-the-year dollars is expected. If the actual inflation rate during the year turns out to be 0 percent, who wins? The rich aunt expected a purchasing-power repayment of $3000 ($6000, but at a doubled level of prices). But with zero inflation, she will receive 6000 nominal dollars that have a purchasing power of 6000 beginning-of-the-year dollars. The wealth transfer here goes from the student (debtor) to the rich aunt (creditor) because both overanticipated inflation when the loan was made.

A second way in which inflation acts as a tax is more direct. In many countries, including the United States, a progressive income tax exists. Higher tax rates are applied to higher incomes. However, when the tax rate that a person is subject to depends on the person's nominal income, inflation has the effect of pushing people into higher tax brackets even though their real incomes have not changed or have even fallen. The individual ends up paying a larger fraction of income in income taxes solely because of inflation, not because of any increase in real income or any direct change in the tax laws.

This phenomenon, sometimes called "bracket creep," became prevalent in the United States during the inflationary years of the 1970s. In 1981, however, the Congress voted to include **tax indexation** as a feature of the federal income tax code. Beginning in 1985, tax indexation eliminated bracket creep due to inflation by adjusting the income tax brackets yearly to account for any inflation that has occurred during the year. This actually makes the U.S. income tax a tax on real, rather than nominal or money, income.

Tax indexation:
Periodic adjustment of the tax brackets of a progressive income tax so as to base taxes on real, not nominal, income; eliminates bracket creep and increased income taxes due solely to inflation.

THEORIES OF INFLATION

Theories about the cause of inflation can be broadly divided into two categories: cost-push and demand-pull. In brief, **cost-push inflation** results from monopoly or union power pushing prices up. Either unions may respond to rising monopoly output prices by demanding higher wages or output monopolists may respond to union demands for higher wages by raising prices. A variant of the cost-push explanation is the supply shock theory of inflation, which explains inflation as the result of a sudden increase in production costs caused by some resource scarcity, such as that created by OPEC or by crop failure.

Cost-push inflation:
Increases in the price level caused by monopoly and/or union power or by shocks to the economy that reduce aggregate supply.

Demand-pull inflation is a rise in prices owing to increases in expenditures on goods and services. When actual holdings of cash balances exceed consumers' and investors' desired holdings, they begin to spend. Such spending drives prices upward until they rise enough to reduce actual real money holdings to desired real holdings. In other words, increases in demand pull prices up.

Demand-pull inflation:
Increases in the price level caused by increases in aggregate demand.

Monetarists adhere to the demand-pull explanation of inflation. In their view, long-run inflation is the result of the Federal Reserve's pumping the money supply above the level necessary to keep its growth in line with the growth in the public's desired real holdings of money. Most Keynesians view inflation as a combined result of demand-side and supply-side forces in the economy.

Cost-Push Theories of Inflation

Cost-push explanations place the blame for inflation on pressures from monopolies or unions or from sudden shortages of natural resources. The corresponding theories of how these factors can cause inflation are called the monopoly power/wage-price spiral argument and the supply, or resource, shock explanation.

The Monopoly Power/Wage-Price Spiral Theory. Some economists argue that one cause of inflation is that the prices of goods and services are pushed up by monopoly power. There are two variants of this argument, depending on the source of monopoly power—output monopolies in product markets or input monopolies, such as labor unions, in resource markets.

Concentration of monopoly power in input or output markets causes rigid constraints on the ability of prices and wages to move downward in response to falling aggregate demand. Output monopolies are able to resist cutting prices by controlling output—by supplying lower quantities in an effort to maintain their revenues. Rather than accept lower wages, input monopolies such as giant labor unions curtail labor's supply in an effort to counteract falling demand for labor. The rigidities imposed by output and input monopolies mean that prices and wages are not freely adaptive to changes in demand. When aggregate demand falls, the result is lower output and employment rather than falling prices and wages.

Further increases in the degree of monopolization or of union membership will create new price and wage rigidities in the economy and, with them, reductions in output and employment. These increases will have the effect of shifting the aggregate supply curve leftward over time. The rate of output and employment will decline and prices will rise.

Wage-price spiral:
The process whereby increased prices of final goods cause increased wage rates and other resource prices, which in turn result in still-higher prices of final goods; for the spiral to continue, the money supply must continually increase or real output must continually fall.

Another version of this argument is that, at any point in time, the price demands of monopolies or the wage demands of unions will create a **wage-price spiral** of inflation. If monopolies can set prices and make higher prices stick, the wage demands of unions will escalate; erosions of real purchasing power will cause union members to demand higher nominal wages. Either increased monopoly price demands or union wage demands will reduce the short-run aggregate supply of output because both market activities have the short-run effect of temporarily reducing the hiring of labor.

The process may also be viewed from a different perspective. Union demands may create cost increases for business. These cost increases, where output markets are monopolized, are passed on to the buying public by monopolies in the form of price increases. A wage-price spiral may develop, and the result is the same whether the original cause is unions or monopolies.

Some economists discount the wage-price spiral explanation of inflation based on monopoly and union power. In the first place, the argument *assumes* the existence of monopoly and union influence on the price level. In the automobile industry, however, industry and union forces often counteract each other's influence, settling on wage bargains and prices that are roughly competitive. Union wage increases cannot automatically be passed on to consumers; sellers, even monopoly sellers, still face a demand curve of a certain elasticity.

Accommodation of cost-push inflation:
Increases in the money supply designed to offset a decrease in aggregate supply caused by monopoly or union action or by an aggregate supply shock; increased aggregate demand results, preventing decreases in real output.

More important, any wage-price spiral must ultimately be **accommodated** by the Federal Reserve. Unless the Federal Reserve validates price and wage increases by increasing M-1, unemployment and reduced output will occur. Pressured by unions and monopolies, discretionary monetary and fiscal authorities may stand their ground, forcing unions and monopolies to endure unemployment until prices and wages fall and the economy is brought back to equilibrium at full employment. Or the Fed may accommodate cost-push pressures by increasing the money stock, thereby validating inflation. At most, argue critics of the wage-price spiral, unions and monopolies can force a once-and-for-all increase in nominal wages and prices—unless the Federal Reserve accommodates these pressures in the economy. The rise in prices will not be continuous—that is, inflationary—unless the Federal Reserve permits it to be so.

The Supply Shock Theory of Inflation.   Another cost-push explanation of inflation is related to **supply shocks**—natural or artificial reductions in the supply of vital natural resources. The Iraqi invasion of Kuwait in August 1990, which gave Iraq control over nearly 20 percent of the world's oil reserves, constitutes such a supply shock. A worldwide embargo of Iraqi oil and Iraqi-held Kuwaiti oil effectively removed four million barrels of oil from the market each day, instantly pushing up the costs of producing and transporting final goods everywhere. (For an account of how the global economy absorbed this latest oil shock, see Focus, "Economic Repercussions of Iraq's Invasion of Kuwait.")

> **Supply shock inflation:**
> Price level increases stemming from a decrease in aggregate supply; decreased aggregate supply usually occurs because of sudden increased scarcity of essential resources.

The United States has experienced oil price shocks before. In the 1970s, the OPEC nations progressively monopolized the oil export industry and raised prices. Since oil-based energy was an important input in U.S. manufacturing and other uses, some observers argued that increases in costs were passed on to consumers in the form of higher prices. OPEC's price demands were seen as ushering in a higher rate of inflation. (Between 1974 and 1980, the average inflation rate was approximately 9 percent.)

While it is certainly correct that oil and energy-related prices rose during the 1970s and, further, that the period witnessed high rates of inflation, it is by no means clear that OPEC *caused* inflation, viewed as a continuous rate of price increase. OPEC lost much of its cartel power in the 1980s, an event that coincides with moderate inflation. Does this mean that OPEC's partial dissolution *caused* the reduction in inflation?

For the supply shock to inflict a continuous increase in prices, other forces must be at work in the economy. For instance, in the 1970s the Federal Reserve Board steadily increased the growth in the money supply, partly in response to the rising prices of oil-related goods brought about by OPEC. By increasing money supply growth, the Federal Reserve not only accommodated OPEC's higher prices but fueled inflation for all other goods as well. As a trading partner with the United States, OPEC nations soon faced higher prices for their imports and responded by increasing the price for their oil. This sequence—higher costs leading to higher prices leading to higher costs, and so on—is a **cost-price spiral,** a variant of a wage-price spiral. Naturally, other forces contributed to the pressure on prices; monopoly and union rigidities complement the effect of a supply shock.

> **Cost-price spiral:**
> The process whereby increased production costs lead to increased final goods prices, which lead to further increases in resource prices and production costs; for the spiral to continue, the money supply must continually increase or real output must continually fall.

In determining who was to blame for the inflation of the 1970s, then, some economists might begin with the oil sheiks. Others believe that the supply shock scenario just described would have been impossible without the cooperation of the Federal Reserve's expansionary monetary policy. Not every OPEC-dependent country suffered the same inflationary consequences. Switzerland, for example, whose central bank followed a much more conservative policy, seemed to suffer least from the OPEC supply shock.

Demand-Pull Theories of Inflation

The theories we have discussed so far—monopoly power, wage-price, and supply shock—focus on the supply side of inflation. These theories predict inflation on the basis of shifts in the aggregate supply curve.

Inflation, of course, also has roots in the demand side of the economy. Any rightward shift in the aggregate demand curve, given an upward-sloping supply curve, will create or increase inflationary pressures. Monetary expansion on the part of the Federal Reserve will shift the aggregate demand curve

FOCUS   Economic Repercussions of Iraq's Invasion of Kuwait

Iraq's August 1990 invasion of Kuwait sent shockwaves through the U.S. economy, many of which seemed to arrive simultaneously with news of the invasion. Less than a day after Saddam Hussein's forces poured over the border into neighboring Kuwait, service stations across the United States were posting higher gasoline prices, prompting concern about an already shaky economy and recollections of the 1974 and 1979 oil shocks. In the days and weeks following the invasion, oil prices were up sharply, despite occasional retreats. The effect at the pump: By Labor Day 1990, U.S. consumers were spending nearly twenty-five cents per gallon more for a fillup.

The United Nations embargo of oil from Iraq and Iraqi-held Kuwait took four million barrels off the world market every day. A majority of OPEC oil ministers eventually voted to allow cartel members to expand production, which reduced the shortfall to between 500,000 and one million barrels a day. Even so, as oil industry experts pointed out, the additional production was not of the same quality as the previously available crude; in other words, the additional crude would yield less gasoline when refined. This, coupled with the loss of 600,000 barrels a day of refining capacity in Kuwait, placed upward pressure on gasoline prices. There were calls for tapping the 586 million barrels of oil in the United States' Strategic Petroleum Reserve to soften the supply shock, but higher prices would have persisted even if President Bush had immediately authorized dipping into the reserves—at least in the short run. U.S. reserves consist entirely of crude, crude that would have had to be refined by facilities that were barely able to meet demand for high-quality refined products before the crisis.

As higher oil prices worked their way through the economy, the inflation rate was expected to jump between 1 and 2 percentage points. The oil shock was also certain to lop at least half a percent off the rate of economic growth, which stood at an anemic 0.4 percent in the second quarter of 1990. Immediately following the invasion, many economists thought the economy would escape recession, but consumers weren't so sure: Both leading measures of consumer confidence declined in August. Since consumer spending makes up two-thirds of GNP, this lack of confidence in the economy loomed large; the ranks of economists who predicted a recession-free 1990 had thinned considerably by September.

Had events in the Middle East not complicated matters, the Federal Reserve might have eased monetary policy in response to generally depressed business conditions and rising unemployment in the fall of 1990. Even after the level of the U.S. military commitment had become clear and hopes had faded for a decline in gasoline prices as dramatic as their rise, some observers urged the Fed to increase the

Supply shock: Consumers were faced with almost daily increases in the price of gasoline in the days and weeks following Iraq's August 1990 invasion of Kuwait.

money supply in the belief that the sluggish economy would put the brakes on inflation. Unwilling to risk setting off a 1970s-style inflationary spiral, however, and fearful of further upsetting an inflation-wary bond market, the Fed did not immediately ease.

The 1990 oil shock jolted the U.S. economy, but the United States and other industrialized nations benefited from having experienced this kind of shock before. Brazil, Chile, Thailand, and South Korea were less prepared, having developed successful but oil-dependent economies mostly since the earlier shocks. The economies-in-transition of Eastern Europe, which had been shielded from the 1970s shocks by a now-defunct barter arrangement whereby the Soviet Union would supply all the oil they wanted at subsidized prices, watched helplessly as higher oil prices forced double-digit inflation rates still higher.

Sources: David E. Rosenbaum, "Economic Uncertainties Are Intensified for U.S. Policy Makers," *New York Times* (August 4, 1990), p. 6; Allana Sullivan, "Renewed Jitters Boost Prices of Oil, Products," *Wall Street Journal* (August 31, 1990), p. A3.

Macroeconomics: Key Trends

In this section, we present graphs of real data to highlight several important macroeconomic trends. Students of economics, economists, and economic observers benefit from this kind of presentation, which can show at a glance, for example, that in the 1980s high federal deficits seem to have pushed up interest rates and prevented their decline. Indeed, it is the task of economists to present, explain, and interpret data in a meaningful and useful way.

Labor Productivity and Investment

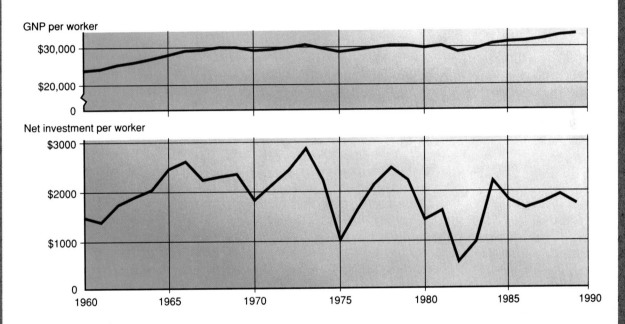

Source: Council of Economic Advisers, *Economic Report of the President* (Washington, D.C.: U.S. Government Printing Office, 1990), calculated from Tables C-2 and C-32.

One measure of labor productivity is output per worker, which is real gross national product divided by the number of persons in the labor force. GNP per worker in the labor force in 1989 was $33,443. Considerable productivity gains in the 1960s gave way to a fifteen-year period of stagnant growth. Since 1985, the productivity picture has improved somewhat, but what accounted for its earlier, persistent flatness? One factor, certainly, was the increased participation of women in the labor force over the period. Another factor was an erratic, generally low level of investment per worker in the United States.

Workers using newer equipment will be more productive than workers using older equipment. You can think of net investment per worker as the amount of new tools or equipment available to each worker. Net investment per worker is found by subtracting the amount of depreciation of existing capital from gross private domestic investment in new capital equipment and then dividing by the number of persons in the labor force. In 1989, net investment per worker was $1745. High interest rates throughout the decade and the 1980 and 1982 recessions are cited as reasons for the low rates of investment per worker in the 1980s.

Real Interest Rates and the Deficit

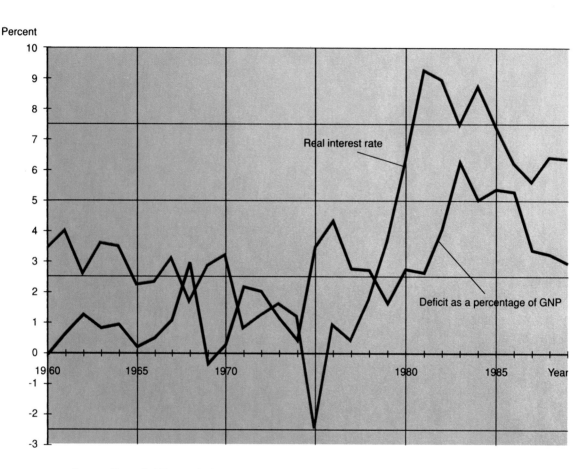

Source: Council of Economic Advisers, *Economic Report of the President* (Washington, D.C.: U.S. Government Printing Office, 1990), Tables C-7 and C-76.

Some economists believe that the enormous deficits run by the federal government in the 1980s pushed up interest rates and kept them high, effectively blocking business borrowing for investment purposes. Federal deficits are financed primarily through the sale of bonds to individuals and commercial banks. Increases in the supply of bonds push bond prices down and simultaneously drive interest rates up; in this way, government borrowing to finance deficits is said to crowd out business investment.

Is there proof of a relation between federal deficits and interest rates? Real interest rates—prime interest rates (the rates banks charge their business customers for loans to purchase new capital equipment) minus the rate of inflation—were relatively stable during the 1960s, volatile in the 1970s, and sharply higher in the 1980s. Since 1960, federal budget deficits—the amount by which government expenditures exceed tax revenues in a given year—have occurred in every year except 1960 and 1969; although deficits have generally risen as a percentage of GNP over the period, the biggest increases came during the 1980s. As the graph shows, the picture prior to 1980 is muddy, but real interest rates did seem to follow federal deficits as a percentage of GNP throughout the last decade.

Gross National Product and Its Components

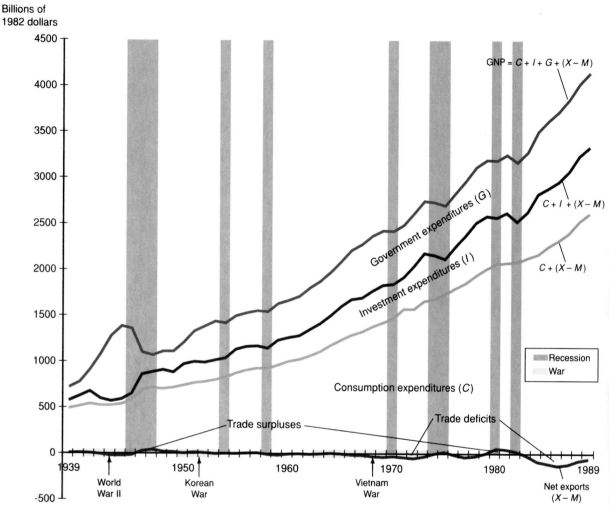

Billions of
1982 dollars

GNP = C + I + G + (X − M)

C + I + (X − M)

Government expenditures (G)

Investment expenditures (I)

C + (X − M)

Recession
War

Consumption expenditures (C)

Trade surpluses
Trade deficits

1939   1950   1960   1970   1980   1989

World
War II

Korean
War

Vietnam
War

Net exports
(X − M)

Source: Council of Economic Advisers, *Economic Report of the President* (Washington, D.C.:
U.S. Government Printing Office, 1990), Table C-2.

Gross national product (GNP) is the dollar value of all final goods and services produced in an economy in
one year. GNP is made up of four components: consumption expenditures, investment expenditures,
government expenditures, and net exports (exports minus imports). Consumption expenditures are by far
the largest component of GNP in the United States, accounting for 64.4 percent in 1989. In that same
year, government expenditures accounted for 19.5 percent, investment expenditures for 17.4 percent, and
net exports for −1.3 percent.

Here, we track GNP in the United States over a fifty-year period, 1939–1989. The top line represents the
level of GNP in 1982 dollars over the period. The graph also breaks down GNP into its component parts.
As you can see, GNP has increased dramatically since 1939, though not without interruption. Declines in
GNP, called *recessions,* occurred—at least one per decade—in four of the five decades shown.

The Emergence of the European Community

European Community
Iceland
United Kingdom
Denmark
Netherlands
Belgium
Germany
France
Luxembourg
Portugal
Spain
Greece
Italy

United States
Population:
    248 million
GDP:
    $4.8 trillion
GNP per capita:
    $19,600

European Community
Population: 325 million
GDP: $4.5 trillion
GNP per capita: $13,770

U.S. Exports to the European Community	
Machinery and Transport	49.1%
Manufactured Goods	6.2%
Chemicals	11.3%
Mineral Fuels	3.2%
Crude Material	8.8%
Beverages and Tobacco	2.1%
Food and Live Animals	5.2%
Others	14.1%

Source: U.S. Department of Commerce, International Trade Administration, *Industrial Outlook,* p. 31.

The European Community, comprised of Belgium, Denmark, France, Germany, Greece, Iceland, Italy, Luxembourg, the Netherlands, Portugal, Spain, and the United Kingdom, is a coalition of nations working toward full economic and monetary union by 1993. The European Community treaty will remove all remaining trade barriers and restrictions on mobility of labor and capital between member nations, creating the largest market in the world. National borders will be no greater a barrier to trade than state borders are in the United States. Plans also call for the designation of a single currency, the European Currency Unit (ECU), within the twelve-nation bloc and the establishment of a central bank, a "EuroFed," to administer monetary policy. The latter goal may materialize first; the European central bank is scheduled to begin operating January 1, 1993, but the United Kingdom has proposed retaining the various national currencies for a time, believing that competition with these currencies will make the ECU stronger.

What effects will the creation of this unified market have on the U.S. economy? American exporters are understandably anxious about the potential for enormous changes in international trade patterns in the coming years. Such a dramatic reorganization of the world market likely will alter at least the composition of U.S. exports. The EC treaty represents a threat to domestic producers because free trade among EC nations will open new markets for member nations. Should the EC collectively pursue protectionist policies, U.S. exporters could find themselves shut out of previously dependable markets. However, the treaty also represents potential opportunities. Given access to the new market, U.S. exporters would benefit from following a coordinated set of trade regulations, and demand for U.S. goods (for *all* goods) is likely to rise in the wake of the community's expected spurt in economic growth.

and drive the price level up. (The effects of demand shifts depend on the shape of the aggregate supply curve.) Other factors that can shift the aggregate demand curve include increased government spending, investment spending, and consumer demand.

Money-Supply Growth and Inflation. Monetarists and other economists believe there is a direct relation between expansionary monetary policy on the part of the Federal Reserve and inflation. In other words, inflation—a continuously rising price level—cannot take place without a continuously rising money supply.

This demand-pull theory of inflation is based on an updated version of the quantity theory of money. Briefly stated, the monetarist demand-pull model assumes that monetary expansion on the part of the Federal Reserve will merely increase the cash holdings of individuals without affecting output. If individuals rid themselves of excess money holdings by spending, but output is constant, then prices will go up. Price increases will fuel expectations of higher prices as well as higher nominal interest rates. Higher interest rates will increase pressure on the Federal Reserve to increase the money supply, and so on.

Monetarists believe that this cycle of inflation can be halted only when the Federal Reserve maintains a steady growth rate in the money supply. Such a policy will stabilize money demand, price expectations, and interest rates and permit steady growth in output.

The Relation Between M-1 and Inflation. Does the monetarist demand-pull theory correspond with actual inflation rates? Milton Friedman, the leading proponent of the monetarist position, argues that M-1 growth rates and inflation should be tracked for a number of years. The relation is fairly consistent: Inflation generally follows an increase in M-1 growth, with about a two-year lag between the change in M-1 and the change in prices. In the early 1980s, M-1 grew at a fairly steady rate of about 8 percent annually. This brought inflation rates down sharply—from above 12 percent in 1980 to less than 2 percent in 1986. Between 1985 and 1986, however, the growth rate in M-1 increased to about 17 percent per year, and the inflation rate increased to over 4 percent annually from 1987 to 1989. Since 1986, the growth rate in M-1 has decreased sharply, which monetarist theory predicts will curtail future inflation.

Inflation and the Deficit. Politicians are fond of blaming high inflation on growing government deficits. Economists, however, are quite unsure of the effects of deficits on the inflation rate. For one thing, deficits are not always caused by increasing government expenditures. They may also result from decreasing revenues. Therefore, the deficit may be increasing at a time when the economy is in a recession and prices are not under inflationary pressure. Deficits can affect inflation, however, if the government finances them in certain ways. When the government borrows money from the Federal Reserve System, it spurs growth in the money supply, setting off the inflationary spiral. Reserves and deposits are added to the banking system with no withdrawals, which would have occurred with taxation. When the government borrows from private sources, it contributes to higher interest rates, another source of inflationary pressure. The relation between federal deficits and inflation is further discussed in Economics in Action at the end of this chapter.

CURES FOR INFLATION

Solutions to inflation—policies that might bring about price stability—are always being hotly debated. Just as there is no single agreed-upon cause for inflation, there is no single accepted cure. When policy-makers attempt to resolve the inflation problem, moreover, they may bring about other, perhaps worse, consequences. Many blame the Federal Reserve's anti-inflationary policy of 1979–1980 for the severe recession that followed almost immediately.

Strategies to combat inflation can be placed in two broad categories: nondiscretionary policies and discretionary policies.

Nondiscretionary Cures

Those who believe that inflation is directly attributable to monetary expansion urge restraint on the Federal Reserve. This restraint may take several forms. Monetarists urge that the Federal Reserve avoid policies that disrupt the price expectations of the public. Sudden expansions or contractions of the money supply, for example, usher in cycles of rising and falling prices. Such changes affect future prices and interest rates and require future discretionary actions. The roller-coaster path of high inflation followed by debilitating recessions is not caused by a destabilized economy but by a destabilizing stop-and-go policy on the part of the Federal Reserve. Monetarists urge that the Federal Reserve adopt a money supply growth rule. Such a rule, they believe, can allow the economy to reach a proper, long-run equilibrium rate of GNP growth with stable prices.

Discretionary Cures

Discretionary policies to combat inflation are varied. The first step in proper policymaking is accurate diagnosis: Is the inflation a supply-side or demand-side phenomenon? If the inflation is caused by excessive demand, the proper fiscal cures involve budget cuts or higher taxes to dampen the growth in expenditures. Such policies are obviously not very popular with politicians or voters, so inflation-fighting measures are often left to the Federal Reserve. The Federal Reserve's proper monetary policies include reductions in M-1 growth rates and higher interest rates. Both actions tend to choke off consumption spending and investment, reducing the pressure on prices (and meanwhile risking a recession).

Policies to combat inflation caused by supply factors such as monopoly or union pressures and the wage-price spiral are also varied. We briefly look at two such policies: price and wage controls and tax-induced policies.

Price and Wage Controls: Gain Without Pain? Under price and wage controls, price and wage increases are forbidden by Congress, with penalties for non-compliance. Direct price and wage controls are a familiar, staple policy of governments. From the Roman emperor Diocletian (and probably earlier) through the Nixon years, governments have tried to put a ceiling on price levels by legal means or by the use of price and wage "guidelines," with means of enforcement ranging from fines to death by firing squad. Two basic beliefs underlie the modern advocacy of price and wage controls: (1) Structural rigidities—monopolies and unions—are the cause of inflation, and (2) fiscal and monetary policies are at times insufficient for dealing with the inflation problem.

Price and wage controls usually fail because they cannot be enforced or because they are too costly to enforce. Black markets develop in both output and input markets where there is excess demand for goods or input services (see Chapter 4). Rationing output through coupons and other devices usually fails to overcome these problems. After the OPEC oil crisis, the Carter administration initiated plans for an emergency rationing program for gasoline. The program sparked much controversy and was eventually dropped.

Relaxation of controls opens the floodgates to price increases. After the price and wage controls accompanying World War II were lifted, for example, huge levels of pent-up demand for consumer goods and services—especially durable goods such as autos—were unleashed on insufficient quantities of these goods. The same effects were felt in 1973 after the Nixon price and wage controls were lifted.

Presidential guidelines are another "voluntary" form of price and wage controls. Congressional arm-twisting of businesses and unions to back off from price or wage demands has the same purpose as legally imposed price and wage controls, but with less strict and even unannounced penalties.

Most economists are opposed to price and wage controls because they distort production and economic relations between transactors in the market. If the government is successful as an enforcer of controls, which is itself a costly and difficult job, short-run price expectations may be somewhat stabilized, helping to contain inflationary pressures. Most often, however, a simultaneous and politically popular increase in monetary expansion takes place along with the price and wage controls, turning expectations in the other direction and creating more difficulties. Many economists believe that announced and concrete action on the part of government to control money and fiscal growth has proved to be of greater benefit in containing and stabilizing expectations and, therefore, inflation. Most economists believe that wage and price controls attack the symptoms of inflation but not the cause.

Tax-Induced Policies. Tax-induced policies for fighting inflation are a recent variant of direct price controls. They were first proposed in the United States in the late 1970s. Institution of tax-induced policies would mean the establishment of price guidelines for businesses and labor. These guidelines would not be legally enforced but would carry penalties for violation in the form of higher taxes. Lower taxes would be applied to price or wage changes that did not exceed the guidelines.

The major advantage in using tax-induced policies is that nonprice rationing, such as long waiting lines that discourage consumers, is eliminated. Those willing to pay higher prices or higher wages get the goods or the resources. The disadvantage of tax-induced policies is also a potential disadvantage of price and wage controls. If inflation is not caused by monopoly-union pressures, but rather by increases in the rate of money expansion, imposition of tax-induced policies will not stop inflation.

SUMMARY

1. There are three basic demands for money: transactions demands, precautionary demands, and speculative demands in the bond or securities market.

2. Transactions and precautionary demands are directly related to income. An increase in income, for example, would cause an individual to hold a proportionately greater amount of money for transactions and precautionary purposes.

3. The public also holds money to speculate on the bond market. Expectations of higher bond prices (lower interest returns) would mean that individuals would choose to hold money rather than bonds, whereas low bond prices (higher interest returns) would mean that individuals would prefer to hold bonds rather than money. Speculative money demands are therefore inversely related to the interest rate.

4. The simple quantity theory of money is a macroeconomic theory of how the price level is formed. When transactions demands are considered proportional to income, velocity is assumed constant. Since real output and income are also assumed to be at a maximum, increases in money supply, M-1, cause proportionate increases in the price level.

5. The modern monetarist theory of inflation integrates the transactions, precautionary, and speculative demands for money into a dynamic view of the inflation process. In the monetarist conception, money demands depend in part on the nominal interest rate, which in turn depends on both the real rate of interest and inflationary expectations.

6. The monetarists view inflation as a dynamic process originating with higher rates of M-1 expansion by the Federal Reserve System. Increased spending leads to higher actual and expected inflation rates (real GNP being constant) and therefore to higher nominal interest rates. Higher nominal interest rates lead to lower money demand, more spending, and more inflation.

7. In the monetarist explanation of inflation, the inflationary process does not end until the Federal Reserve stabilizes growth of the money supply.

8. Inflation is a process of price increases. Inflation redistributes income in society away from those on fixed incomes and those holding dollar-denominated assets. Inflation also disrupts expectations and amounts to a tax that is imposed without having been voted on.

9. Nonmonetary theories of inflation feature structural problems in the economy such as the existence of or increases in monopoly and union power. In this view, unreasonable demands can create a wage-price spiral that can be stopped only through government intervention or through price and wage controls.

10. Monetarists argue that the ultimate cause of inflation is monetary expansion in excess of the economy's ability to produce goods and services. They feel that only rules pertaining to the conduct of both fiscal and monetary policy can create stability in the macroeconomy.

KEY TERMS

real money demand
transactions demand
precautionary demand
speculative motive or demand
liquidity preference theory
quantity theory of money
equation of exchange
income velocity

neutrality of money
monetarism
real interest rate
market, or nominal, interest rate
expected inflation rate
adaptive expectations theory
rate of monetary expansion
escalator clause

pure inflation tax
tax indexation
cost-push inflation
demand-pull inflation
wage-price spiral
accommodation of cost-push inflation
supply shock inflation
cost-price spiral

QUESTIONS FOR REVIEW AND DISCUSSION

1. Why do people hold money? What effect does the level of income have on the amount of money people hold?

2. What is the cost of holding money? If bond prices fall, does the cost of holding money rise or fall?

3. What is the difference between the quantity theory of money and the equation of exchange? When does the quantity theory of money hold true and when does the equation of exchange hold true?

4. What is the income velocity of money, V? How does V relate to the transactions demand for money?

5. If the rate of growth of the money supply is equal to 10 percent, the velocity of money is constant, and real output is falling by 2 percent, what will be the rate of inflation according to monetarist theory?

6. What effect does an increase in the rate of monetary expansion have on the total level of spending? The actual rate of inflation? The expected rate of inflation?

7. According to monetarists, what causes inflation? How is inflation stopped?

8. How does inflation decrease individuals' wealth? How can people protect themselves from inflation?

9. In what sense is inflation a tax? Do government tax revenues increase when inflation occurs?

10. How might monopolies or unions cause inflation? Can monopolies cause inflation without the assistance of monetary expansion?

11. Why do wage and price controls fail to stop inflation when monetary expansion continues?

PROBLEM

Suppose that the rate of monetary expansion is 10 percent per year, the growth rate in real income is 3 percent, and velocity is constant. Calculate the inflation rate through the "dynamic" quantity theory. Now suppose that the rate of monetary expansion rises to 15 percent per year, all else remaining the same. What is the rate of inflation? Clearly explain the process by which the increase in monetary expansion changes the inflation rate.

ECONOMICS IN ACTION
The Impact of Budget Deficits on Inflation

The effects of federal budget deficits on inflation are complex and controversial. As noted in the text, increasing deficits may result from declining tax revenue during periods of recession and falling prices. In the view of many economists, however, deficits may also be associated with inflation.

Take a look at budget deficits and surpluses throughout U.S. history[a] (see Figure 8). Between the establishment of the U.S. Treasury in 1789 and the year 1990, there have been 199 budgets, of which 96 have been in deficit and 103 in surplus. Between 1789 and 1930, the budget was in deficit 32 percent of the time, but between 1931 and 1990 the government ran deficits more than 86 percent of the time. The White House deficit projection for 1991 was $232 billion, which included the cost of the savings and loan bailout but did not take into account the costs of the enormous military buildup in response to Iraq's invasion of Kuwait. With the addition of defense costs and the costs associated with a slowdown in the U.S. economy, the deficit for 1991 appeared likely to soar to between $250 billion and $300 billion.

Since the deficit is simply the difference between what the government spends and what it takes in as taxes, the difference must be made up somewhere. Roughly, the government has two alternatives to finance the deficit: (1) having the Treasury sell bonds to the Federal Reserve System, which in effect means "to print more money," and (2) selling government bonds on the open market, thus competing with businesses for private savers' funds. Though it is difficult to determine the extent to which the money supply increases as a result of deficit financing, most economists (and most citizen-taxpayers) view such financing as inflationary.

If the government finances deficits by selling newly printed bonds in the private markets, interest rates will rise, causing private investment to decline. The rise in interest rates caused by the price-lowering effects of the government's bond sale will also reduce consumption spending. In this view, deficits will crowd out private investment and consumption expenditures, reducing the production and consumption of private goods and services and permitting an increase in the production of public goods and services. Either method of financing deficits forces resources from the private sector into production in the public sector.

Critics of this position on the economic effects of deficits point out that there is no clear correlation between deficits and the money supply. The Federal Reserve, after all, is not required to purchase bonds from the U.S. Treasury. Indeed, the Federal Reserve may attempt to neutralize the impact of deficit financing on M-1 through compensating open mar-

[a]An excellent survey on the effects of deficits is "The Deficit Puzzle: Fitting the Pieces Together," *Economic Review,* Federal Reserve Bank of Atlanta Special Issue (August 1982).

FIGURE 8

Federal Budget Surplus or Deficit as a Percentage of GNP, 1790–1990

Sources: James R. Barth and Stephen O. Morrell, "A Primer on Budget Deficits." *Economic Review,* Federal Reserve Bank of Atlanta Special Issue (August 1982), pp. 10–11; Council of Economic Advisers, *Economic Report of the President* (Washington, D.C.: U.S. Government Printing Office, 1990), pp. 294, 384, 385.
Note: 1990 is estimated.

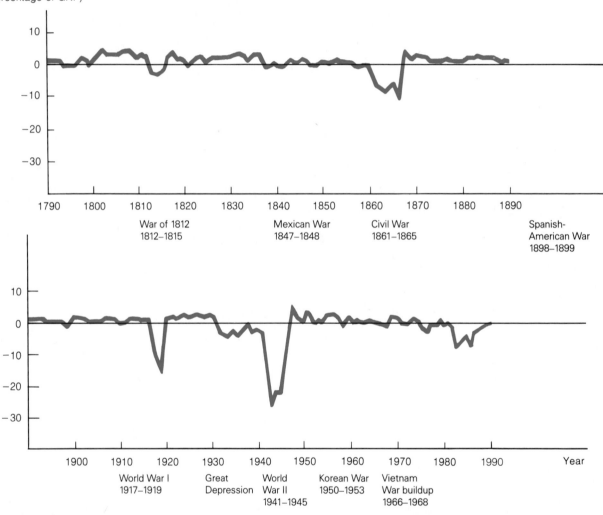

ket operations or with the use of its other monetary policy tools. Still other economists believe that deficits have no long-run effects if they are financed through the sale of bonds in private markets. Why? Because government bonds are "wealth" to those who buy them, but they are an equivalent and corresponding liability to future taxpayers who must pay taxes to finance the principal and interest on the original issue. In the main, however, most economists and citizens believe that deficits are inflationary and that they crowd out private expenditures.

Question

In what ways do budget deficits inhibit long-run economic expansion? Does the existence of a huge deficit affect expectations of how high interest rates or inflation rates will be?

Milton Friedman

James Tobin

Milton Friedman and James Tobin: How Important Is the Money Supply?

Mᴵʟᴛᴏɴ Fʀᴵᴇᴅᴍᴀɴ (b. 1912) is best known for his strong and eloquent defense of capitalism and the free market, for his support of monetarism, and for his arguments against government intervention in the economy.

Born in Brooklyn, New York, Friedman was the son of immigrant parents. His mother was a seamstress; his father, the owner of a small retail dry goods store. When his father died, fifteen-year-old Friedman and his mother were left with very little money. The teenager showed great aptitude in mathematics in high school and won a scholarship to Rutgers University in 1929. While a student at Rutgers, Friedman waited tables to support himself, passed exams to become an accountant, and then became increasingly interested in economics. His professor, Arthur Burns, who later became chairman of the Federal Reserve Board, taught him the importance of empirical research in economics, and another professor, Homer Jones, encouraged Friedman to apply for a scholarship to graduate school at the University of Chicago. Friedman went on to receive his M.A. from Chicago and, in 1946, a Ph.D. from Columbia University. During the 1930s he worked as a statistician for the National Bureau of Economic Research, and in 1938 he married economist Rose Director, a fellow graduate student at the University of Chicago.

Friedman taught economics at Chicago until his retirement in 1977, when he moved his scholarly base to the Hoover Institute at Stanford University. Winner of the Nobel Memorial Prize in Economics in 1976, Friedman has authored many highly acclaimed books, in addition to contributing a regular column to *Newsweek*. In *Capitalism and Freedom* (1962), Friedman argues that market forces are sufficient in both individual and aggregate markets to direct resources and to establish steady growth in the economy. Government fiscal policies, Friedman believes, often bring about results contrary to those that policy-makers intend and disrupt planned expenditures in the private sector. In his classic work, *A Monetary History of the United States* (1963), coauthored by Anna Schwartz, Friedman claims that money velocity—related to the demand for money—is stable enough to make the money supply an excellent barometer of inflation, output, and economic growth. His views provided the basis for modern monetarist theory.

Jᴀᴍᴇs Tᴏʙᴵɴ (b. 1918), winner of the 1981 Nobel Memorial Prize in Economics, grew up during the Depression with an awareness that many of the world's problems were economic in origin. He made the decision to become an economist while taking an introductory economics course during his sophomore year at Harvard University in 1936. One of his major influences at that time was his teacher, Spencer Pollard, who suggested he read Keynes's *General Theory*, which had just been published. According to Tobin, *The General Theory* "was a difficult book, but when you are 19 you don't know what's difficult and what's not. You just plow into it."

Describing himself as a "very, very, shy, noncompetitive individual" during his undergraduate years, Tobin went on to obtain his Ph.D. from Harvard in 1947 and was appointed Sterling Professor of Economics at Yale University in 1957. He faithfully carried Keynesian principles into the public policy arena when he was appointed to President John F.

Kennedy's Council of Economic Advisers in 1961. He was one of the architects of the Kennedy-Johnson tax cut of 1964 and has consistently advocated a loose reign on the money supply. He has also played a key role in the recent effort to join Keynesian macroeconomics and neoclassical microeconomics.

Tobin received the Nobel Prize primarily for his analysis of portfolio selection and financial markets. He was president of the American Economic Association in 1971 and continues to support modern activist economic policies.

KEEPING WATCH OVER THE MONEY SUPPLY

Friedman and Tobin certainly represent different views on monetary and fiscal policies. For Friedman, control of the money supply is the main determinant of economic stability. For his part, Tobin emphasizes the effects of government spending, taxation, and stable interest rates on economic performance. Juxtaposed, the views of each man illustrate the difference between monetarist and Keynesian approaches to the economy.

Are money supply fluctuations a cause or effect of changes in real income? This question may be impossible to answer definitely, but Milton Friedman has consistently argued that money supply growth is the best barometer we have of economic expansion and contraction. Friedman cites a variety of statistics to back his claim. For example, since the turn of the century, fluctuations in rates of growth in real GNP have strongly coincided with annual growth rates in the nation's money supply. Prior to recession and depression, the money supply growth rate has fallen dramatically; prior to expansions and a booming inflationary economy, the money supply growth rate has shown marked increases.

To explain this statistical marriage of money supply and economic activity, Friedman argues that money velocity is a stable variable. Therefore, interest rates, which may vary up or down in response to government spending, do not contribute to economic fluctuations as many economists believe. They are merely a sideshow to the growth patterns in the money supply.

If Friedman's premise is correct, then the government's attempts to fine-tune the economy through spending and taxation policies are largely misdirected. For the sake of stability, Friedman argues, government should concern itself with a stable growth rate in the money supply. By doing so, he believes, the roller-coaster ride of business cycles, of temporary boom followed by temporary bust, can be leveled out and the economy can achieve consistent, measured growth for the future.

There are many complicated issues surrounding Friedman's proposal. For instance, can government officials afford to sit idly by in times of high unemployment, believing that over the long run a stable monetary policy will rescue the economy? Experience in the 1960s and 1970s suggests that Friedman's proposal is perhaps politically unfeasible. A second issue involves the definition of money supply. For Friedman, the only significant money supply definition is M-1—currency plus demand deposits. Recently, however, changes in the banking system have created uncertainties over what exactly constitutes money in the traditional sense of M-1. If the Federal Reserve policy-makers cannot rely on a firm definition of the money supply, efforts to control its growth may be frustrating or even futile. Friedman strongly believes that the concept of M-1, for all its apparent weaknesses, is the Federal Reserve's best measure of money supply. Larger aggregates, such as M-2 or M-3, are far beyond the control of the Federal Reserve System.

FISCAL ACTIVISM AND STABLE INTEREST RATES

For James Tobin, the issue of what determines ups and downs in the economy is not nearly so straightforward. In essence, Tobin believes that consumption and investment activity are the true determinants of economic performance. Controlling or directing such activity, however, is much more complicated than simply monitoring the money supply. On the one hand, it involves spending and taxation policies to counterbalance the rise and fall of aggregate demand. On the other hand, it involves monetary policies to keep interest rates at acceptable levels.

Unlike Friedman, Tobin believes that the velocity of money is unstable. If this assumption is correct, then interest rates are much more important in economic policy than M-1 growth rates because interest rates determine the shifting demand between different kinds of money assets, leading to greater or lesser consumption and investment activity. Tobin argues that the "strict monetarist regime" he believes to have been in effect at the Federal Reserve between 1979 and 1982 was a failure. He blames the recession and high unemployment between 1981 and 1983 on the Fed's attempt to place limits on M-1 growth.[a] Rather than target M-1 or the money base, Tobin believes the Fed should target broader economic aggregates such as the growth rate in nominal GNP and adjust its monetary policy according to its best estimate of where the economy is headed. (Friedman disputes the idea that monetarism has ever been tried by the Federal Reserve System.)

Tobin's position not only admits the need for politicians to do something in times of high unemployment, but it argues for such action. His activist stance, however, can be a two-edged sword. Spending policies can adversely affect interest rates, and therefore fiscal and monetary policies can conflict with one another. The current debate over high government deficits reflects this conflict, for many economists argue that growing deficits drive up interest rates.

[a]For details on Tobin's position see his "Monetarism: An Ebbing Tide?" *The Economist* (April 27, 1985), pp. 23–25.

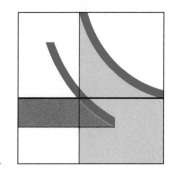

PART FOUR

Monetary and

Macroeconomic

Problems and

Policy

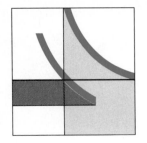

18

Macroeconomic Theory and Policy

As we have seen in previous chapters, economists find it hard to agree on where the economy is heading and what should be done about it. How many times have you heard different predictions of future macroeconomic events by government economic advisers, academics, and business economists? Economists often are equally at odds over the proper policy to correct or sustain economic forces. These differences over policy often arise from differences in theory, particularly whether the economy is seen as inherently stable or unstable. Earlier we discussed how specific theories of the economy, such as early classical theory and Keynesian theory, have led to quite different policy prescriptions. In the view of most economists, these older theories have not fully explained events or predicted accurately.

Over the past two decades new theories have arisen that build upon older ideas and that are currently being tested. In this sense, macroeconomic theory is in a state of flux and in search of new ideas, which might include combinations of older theories. Two major schools of modern thought may be labeled new Keynesian and new classical theories of the macroeconomy, both of which build upon some of the ideas we have already encountered. The reader must be warned, however: Divisions and categories of theories in this chapter by no means encompass every economic view. Many contemporary Keynesians share one or more of the monetarists' views, for instance. As a road map to policy debates, however, the distinctions drawn here are useful. When you complete Chapter 18 you should understand

- how macroeconomic policy prescriptions designed to alleviate inflationary or unemployment situations depend on theories about how the economy functions.
- how new Keynesians and new classical writers—those who lean toward monetarist or "rational expectationist" theories—view fiscal and monetary policy.
- some of the elements in the debate between macroeconomists on the issues of discretionary versus nondiscretionary policies.

POLICY ALTERNATIVES

The purpose of macroeconomic policy is to ensure economic stability—full employment, price stability, and steady growth. There are, of course, various interpretations of exactly what full employment, price stability, and steady growth mean in percentage terms, but most economists and policy-makers would agree, for instance, that persistent unemployment rates of 12 or 14 percent or inflation rates of 15 or 20 percent are unacceptable. Likewise, most economists and observers would agree that unemployment rates of $5\frac{1}{2}$ to $7\frac{1}{2}$ percent, inflation rates of 2 to 4 percent, and real GNP growth rates of 3 percent are "in the ballpark" as acceptable macroeconomic policy goals. These ballpark figures are about the right percentages for a well-functioning economy.

In previous chapters on macroeconomic and monetary theory, we saw that there are a number of interacting monetary and nonmonetary factors that affect prices, real income, and employment. Figure 1 summarizes these various forces. As the figure shows, the nonmonetary factors are consumption, investment, real interest rates, and net foreign trade expenditures on the private

---

FIGURE 1

Both monetary and nonmonetary variables determine whether the goals of economic policy are achieved. Of these determinants only government spending, taxation, and the money supply may be directly altered in discretionary fashion (also see Figure 2).

Determinants of Price Stability, Full Employment, and Economic Growth

Goals of Macroeconomic Policy:

Price stability

Full employment

Economic growth

Statistics to Watch:

Prices

Income

Employment

Private and Public Variables That Determine Goals

Nonmonetary variables	Monetary variables
Consumption expenditures	Money demand
Investment expenditures	Money supply
Real interest rates	
Government spending and taxation	
Net foreign trade	

side and government spending and taxation on the public side. The monetary factors are money supply and money demand.

A subset of these variables can be manipulated through discretionary government policy. Fiscal policy—manipulation of government spending or taxation by Congress and the president—is one means of ensuring overall stability. One organization used by Congress to develop fiscal policy is discussed in Focus, "Fiscal Policy in Action: The Congressional Budget Office." Monetary policy—actions of the Federal Reserve Board to alter the money supply or interest rates—is another means of achieving macroeconomic goals. Table 1 summarizes these two types of policy.

Fiscal and monetary policies differ according to the amount of time each takes to implement, the magnitude of their effects, and the direction of their effects. For example, by using one of its specific tools the Federal Reserve can act quickly to alter the money supply when there is a perceived employment downturn or inflation upsurge, but Congress usually requires a bit more time to enact fiscal correctives. Fiscal policies, moreover, may have more immediate effects on the economy, but the effects of monetary policies may be longer lasting. In the following sections, we consider different views of these possible effects.

NEW KEYNESIAN THEORY AND POLICY

Early Keynesian economics, developed in the 1930s and 1940s, was a product of the era in which it was born: It was primarily oriented toward the problems of depression and unemployment. New Keynesians retain a belief that the economy, left to itself, is unable to adjust to falling aggregate demand and restore the equilibrium level of income and full employment. In this view, fundamental instabilities pervade the economic system. In the broadest sense, the role of policy is to overcome the forces of instability in the economy.

TABLE 1   Types of Macroeconomic Policies

Fiscal policy is controlled by the president and Congress. Monetary policy is directed by the Federal Reserve Board.

Type of Policy	Scope	Tools
Fiscal policy	Changes in government taxation, spending	Alterations in income tax rate or other tax rates
		Changes in government spending on goods and services or for transfer payments
Monetary policy	Changes in money supply, interest rates	Open market operations
		Changes in discount rates
		Changes in reserve requirements

FOCUS   Fiscal Policy in Action: The Congressional Budget Office

In the give-and-take of politics, Congress has a major role in setting fiscal policy. Individual members, who are often greatly affected back home by spending and taxing decisions, find the job of keeping track of the megabillion-dollar federal budget almost impossible. Few if any members know, or could know, what is going on at all levels of fiscal policy and implementation. The difficulty of congressional monitoring of a growing federal budget led, in 1921, to the establishment of a Budget Bureau under President Warren Harding. The Budget Bureau has evolved into the administration-directed Office of Management and Budget. OMB and the president limit items in the budget through limits on procedures of federal agencies and, of course, the veto power. Congress, however, retains fundamental control over the establishment of all revenue (taxation) measures and expenditures associated with the budget. Clearly, Congress as a whole, as well as individual members of Congress, must be able to track the budget as a tool of overall fiscal policy and for the impact that it might have on constituents.

An agency has evolved to assist Congress in these matters. The Congressional Budget Office (CBO) was the creation of the Congressional Budget and Impoundment Control Act of 1974 (which itself was the product of disputes over the president's and OMB's power to "impound" the funds of federal agencies, possibly thwarting the intentions of Congress). The CBO was created along with House and Senate budget committees, and its role is to work with these committees. It is administered by a director, who is appointed for a four-year term by the Speaker of the House and the President Pro Tempore of the Senate, in consultation with the chairpersons of the House and Senate budget committees. CBO makes staff and resources available to *all* congressional committees, with priority given to the budget committees.

CBO is designed to keep both congressional committees dealing with budget matters and individual members of Congress abreast of all matters related to the budget. Specific responsibilities include economic forecasting and fiscal policy analysis; cost projections; annual reports on the budget; and special studies, such as those projecting the economic impact of actual or proposed budget changes on the economies of specific congressional districts or on states.

Importantly, CBO gives Congress the experts and the computer assistance to understand and analyze the president's budget. Indeed, under former CBO director Alice Rivlin, the organization took a more activist stance in working for the entire Congress. Part of this role has included the submission of an alternative budget to the one submitted by the president and OMB. In its budget projections, CBO uses its own economic models and forecasts, which often are at variance with the administration's. (The OMB and the CBO budgets reflect administration and congressional priorities, respectively.) Fiscal policy is hammered out in the ebb and flow of politics. Personalities and shifting political powers are critical in establishing policies that affect microeconomic well-being for some and the macroeconomic health of the entire nation.

An Unstable Economy

Sharp fluctuations in GNP, unemployment, and inflation can occur for a variety of reasons. Investment spending can initiate cycles of rising and falling business activity. Supply shocks, caused by natural disasters or international upheaval, can disrupt domestic markets. Autonomous consumer spending, magnified by the multiplier, can drive GNP and unemployment up or down. (For the macroeconomic consequences of a sudden shift in our international relations, see Focus, "The Macroeconomic Consequences of Peace.")

Our analysis of aggregate demand shifts in Chapter 11 helps illustrate graphically the effects of such disturbances. Figure 2 shows aggregate demand and aggregate supply of a hypothetical economy. Along curve AD_0, the economy reaches full employment, Y_F. Assume, however, that investment spending, in response to a sudden change in profit expectations, drops. As a result, unemployment increases and real output falls. Figure 2 shows the effect: a shift in aggregate demand from AD_0 to AD_1 and a fall in income from Y_F to Y_1. The gap in employment caused by the shift in aggregate demand is usually

FOCUS   The Macroeconomic Consequences of Peace

The widespread abandonment of Soviet-style socialism in 1989 and 1990 marked the true end of the Cold War. U.S. policy-makers found themselves all at once in a brand-new world; it was a time for discarding established ways of thinking made suddenly obsolete, a time for reordering priorities. When the changes took on an air of permanence, even the staunchest cold warrior could not deny the opportunity for substantial reductions in U.S. defense spending. But what should be done with this windfall, this "peace dividend"?

In the debate over what to do with the potential reduction in defense spending, politics took its usual prominent place. Various political groups expressed greatly differing views concerning both the best use of these dollars and the proper magnitude of the spending reductions. The Bush administration initially proposed defense spending reductions of about $8 billion. Others suggested initial cuts of about $30 billion and future reductions of up to $150 billion. The proposed uses of these dollars also varied. There was some support for applying the reductions in defense to reducing the size of the government's deficit; an opposing view was that taxes should be reduced or that government spending on either investments in infrastructure (roads, bridges, mass transit systems) or on various social programs should be increased. Another proposal earmarked defense savings for foreign aid programs to ease the transition to democracy and free markets.

Many economists argued that defense spending should be allowed to fall with no offsetting increases in government spending or reductions in taxes. Such a deficit-reducing act

would lower interest rates and increase private investment. The subsequent buildup of the nation's capital stock would lead to future increases in production. However, other economists held the view that any reduction in government defense spending would decrease aggregate demand and would surely lead to a recession. Therefore, they argued that the reduction in defense spending should be offset by a roughly equivalent increase in government spending on infrastructure or on various social programs such as housing and day-care. According to these economists, failure to offset reductions in defense spending with increases in other types of government spending would run the risk of leading to high unemployment rates, since so many former military personnel would be entering the labor market. Defense contractors would be hard hit by spending cuts, as would the communities that have come to depend on the companies for jobs and revenues. One proposal attempted to stave off the devastating effects of widespread defense cutbacks by involving defense contractors in environmental cleanup efforts. Still other economists argued that at least a portion of the peace dividend should be used to reduce the tax burden on working Americans.

As we have seen, Washington reacted to the prospect of a peace dividend with a number of proposals. While all of these proposals were rendered premature by the 1990 invasion of Kuwait by Iraq—at least temporarily—the peace dividend may eventually materialize. At that time, the powerful economic consequences of a final decision on allocation of the windfall will prove difficult to ignore.

---

referred to as demand-deficiency unemployment. With resources idle and a gap in demand, policy-makers are left with the questions, Will the economy be able to self-correct the deficiency? and How long will it take to do so? In the long run, as we have noted, theory predicts that prices and wages will fall in response to a shift in aggregate demand. But what about the short run? Can the economy or the unemployed afford to wait for the natural market forces to restore full employment?

Countercyclical Fiscal Policy

In the Keynesian view, time is at the heart of the problem and, to Keynes, the short run could last a long time. While the economy might be self-correcting in the long run, the adjustment would be painful and time-consuming. In the short run, prices and wages would not fall sufficiently to restore full employment. Unnecessary economic disruption—in product and labor markets— would occur if the economy were allowed to establish its own natural rate of

FIGURE 2

A decrease in real expenditures causes aggregate demand curve AD_0 to shift downward to AD_1, also causing a shift from full employment, Y_F, to Y_1. This gap in income caused by a shift in aggregate demand produces demand-deficiency unemployment. Keynesians suggest that this unemployment can be eliminated through the use of fiscal policy, returning aggregate demand, income, and employment to their original levels.

The Keynesian Stand on Demand-Deficiency Unemployment

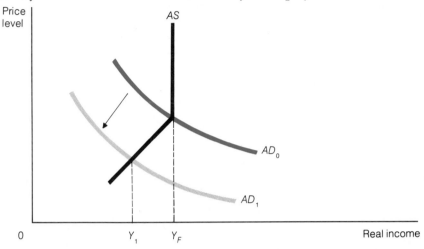

income and employment growth. Keynesians' recommended cure for macroeconomic problems is to apply countercyclical fiscal policy. Proper macroeconomic policy in the event of recession and unemployment is to run budget deficits—that is, to keep government expenditures greater than tax revenues. And, though the advice has seldom been taken, inflation calls for budget surpluses—that is, for tax receipts to exceed government expenditures.

Table 2 simplifies and summarizes the Keynesian position. During recession or depression, Congress, the administration, and state and local governments should increase spending and/or reduce taxes. Inflation calls for the opposite policies.

TABLE 2

Keynesian Prescriptions to Control the Business Cycle

In the fiscal arena, budget deficits should be employed to cure unemployment and lagging economic growth, while inflation should be controlled by budget surpluses. Throughout all phases of the cycle, stable interest rates should be maintained by the Federal Reserve in money markets.

Economic Problem	Keynesian Corrective	
	Fiscal Policy	Monetary Policy
Recession (unemployment and slow income growth)	Budget deficits ($G > T$) (government spending greater than taxation)	Increase M-1 and keep interest rates low and stable
Inflation	Budget surpluses ($G < T$) (taxation greater than government spending)	Reduce M-1

Keynesian Monetary Policy

Note in Table 2 that monetary policy is also included in the Keynesian approach to economic instability. Most Keynesians advocate that the Federal Reserve Board respond to inflationary or recessionary pressures in the economy by keeping order in financial markets. That is, the Federal Reserve should use its discretionary power over the M-1 money supply to stabilize interest rates, which, left unchecked, can rise to levels that discourage or even choke off private spending.

The early 1980s witnessed an application of the Keynesian approach to monetary policy. At that time, the Federal Reserve, in response to severe inflation, initiated dramatic cuts in the M-1 supply. Such cuts, many Keynesians felt, were unwise, since they brought about a sharp rise in interest rates. The economy lurched from high inflation to a costly recession with a high level of unemployment. The Keynesians blamed the recession on the Federal Reserve's failure to maintain low interest rates.

As outlined in the discussion of the liquidity preference curve and the speculative demand for money in Chapter 17, the Federal Reserve might be unable to increase or decrease interest rates at will. Changes in the money supply can affect interest rates, but only if money demanders cooperate. If, for example, money demanders want to hold additional balances for speculative purposes due to dim expectations about bond prices or about the economy in general, an addition to the money supply will not have much effect on interest rates. Alternatively, if the Federal Reserve wanted to increase interest rates by lowering the supply of money, individuals might simply reduce their holdings of money for speculative purposes in roughly equal proportions, which again would result in little or no change in interest rates. Further, any change in interest rates—large or small—might not translate into changes in consumption or investment spending if expectations are that future investment profitability and economic conditions will not be good.

The use of an interest rate target, therefore, is an unpredictable method of changing total spending because the Federal Reserve is constrained by the liquidity preference curve. Since speculative demands for money are based on expectations, liquidity preference is likely to change without much notice. The role of the Federal Reserve, therefore, is to attempt to maintain order in financial markets and, if possible, to keep interest rates low to encourage consumption and investment spending.

Direct Versus Indirect Policy. Given recurring short-run instabilities in the economy, Keynesians consider fiscal policy a more direct and more immediately effective tool to manage aggregate demand than monetary policy. In the Keynesian model, there is no solid link between changes in M-1 and changes in aggregate demand. If M-1 increases, the larger holdings of money by individuals and businesses might not all be spent on more goods and services; some of these funds will be channeled into speculative holdings.

Problems with M-1. In addition, the money supply is less suited to discretionary policy. The Federal Reserve is sometimes unable to keep interest rates within specified targets by manipulating M-1. One reason for this problem is the recent emergence of close money substitutes such as money market mutual funds (a type of checkable deposit not included in M-1), which have tended to blur the definition of M-1 money. Without a reliable measure of the money supply, the Federal Reserve is potentially unsure of the effects of its M-1 policy.

For these reasons and others, Keynesians believe that tax and spending policies can give policy-makers greater discretionary control over the business cycle than can monetary policies. The effects of monetary adjustments, especially on interest rates, are a second, unpredictable line of defense to ensure economic stability.

More important, perhaps, than the issue of whether fiscal or monetary policy is the preferred tool of policy-makers is the issue of whether such policy does what it is supposed to do—correct the instabilities caused by shifts in aggregate demand. Keynesians obviously believe that ignoring such instabilities in the short run would inflict greater potential harm on the economy. As we will see, however, not all economists believe that countercyclical discretionary policy is the best way to ensure stability.

NEW CLASSICAL ECONOMICS: MONETARIST THEORY AND POLICY

New classical economics (NCE) is an alternative view of the macroeconomy that predicts that, in the extreme, monetary policy will have *no* effect on real magnitudes of output and employment and that fiscal policy will not have the effects on output and employment that Keynes had predicted. It combines elements of a number of older theories—classical, supply-side, monetarist—to produce a theory of market behavior based on perceptions and learning by market participants. Much of new classical economics is based on the assumption of rational expectations—the assumption that rational market participants (investors, consumers, taxpayers) learn to anticipate the effects of monetary and fiscal policy changes and act to neutralize them. Because new classical economics takes monetarism one step further, let us again consider the monetarist policy position, aspects of which were treated in Chapter 17. The monetarist, like the classical economist but unlike the Keynesian, views the economy as inherently stable.

A Self-Stabilizing Economy

Figure 3 analyzes demand-deficiency unemployment from the monetarist perspective. Assume there is a reduction in autonomous consumption or investment, shifting the original aggregate demand curve from AD_0 to AD_1. The reduction in autonomous spending is accompanied by an increase in consumers' and businesses' holdings of real money balances. Initially, the economy is in equilibrium at point E_0. The price level is P_0, and the full-employment level of output, Y_F, is being produced. The rate of unemployment in the economy is the natural rate of unemployment that will exist when Y_F is produced. The drop in aggregate demand moves the economy to a new equilibrium at point E_1 in the short run where the level of real income produced is Y_1, less than the full-employment level of income. The rate of unemployment is higher than the natural rate of unemployment, or, what is the same thing, the level of employment is less than full employment. Then the economy self-adjusts to a

FIGURE 3

The economy will self-adjust to the natural rate of unemployment, Y_F, in the event of a decline in aggregate demand. Price and nominal wage reductions occur when aggregate demand declines from AD_0 to AD_1, creating increased real balances, which in turn increase consumption and investment spending. Such price reductions also create, through adaptive expectations, rightward shifts in short-run aggregate supply from $SRAS_0$ to $SRAS_1$. The economy finally readjusts to the full-employment level of output, Y_F, at equilibrium E_2 with lower price level P_1.

Monetarist Policy on Demand-Deficiency Unemployment

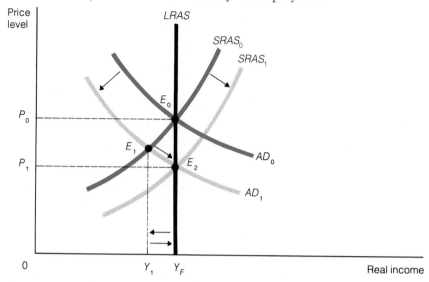

new long-run equilibrium at E_2. Real income rises back to Y_F. The level of employment returns to the full-employment level, and of course, the rate of unemployment falls back to the natural rate of unemployment.

Errors in Real Wage Perceptions: Friedman's View

How might we explain the important process of movement from E_0 to E_1 and then from E_1 to E_2? When aggregate demand falls from AD_0 to AD_1, the level of prices and, to a lesser degree, nominal wages also fall. Employers correctly perceive an increase in real wages and respond by reducing the amount of labor employed. Although the price level has fallen somewhat, workers' price expectations have yet to adjust downward. They still perceive the price level as being P_0. This means that workers believe their real wage has fallen. They will consequently reduce their work effort.[1] The economy will move along the short-run aggregate supply $SRAS_0$ to point E_1, and real income falls to Y_1. Temporarily, unemployment exists in the economy equal to the level of employment associated with real output level Y_F minus that associated with output level Y_1. This unemployment is demand-deficiency unemployment.

From the monetarist perspective, the demand-deficiency unemployment that occurs when the economy produces Y_1 cannot exist permanently. In the monetarist view of the macroeconomy, dynamic forces are at work assuring a return to the full employment of resources at some new equilibrium, E_2. If we assume that no fiscal or monetary actions are undertaken by Congress or the Federal Reserve to deal with unemployment, two sets of automatic changes will dominate. First, falling prices will affect the aggregate demand for goods

---

[1]The expectations-adjusted aggregate supply curve is related to unemployment and inflation in Chapter 19.

and services through the real balance effect. As described in Chapter 11, a decline in the price level will increase real holdings of money, leading to increased consumption and, through lower interest rates brought about by the increased real money supply, to increased investment.

A second effect will act on the short-run aggregate supply curve. When workers' expectations adapt to the lower price levels, their perceptions of the real wage they receive will change. Specifically, they will adapt their expectations to falling actual prices, which signal an increase rather than a decrease in real wages. Time is required, in short, for workers to perceive the actual decline in prices. They will begin to supply more, not less, labor at every wage level. This adaptation in expectations has the effect of shifting the short-run aggregate supply curve rightward from $SRAS_0$ to $SRAS_1$.

Given pressures on prices, where will equilibrium finally reemerge? Downward pressure on nominal wages and prices will exist as long as there is unemployment in the system. As price expectations adjust to lower price levels, the $SRAS$ curve shifts rightward because of unemployed workers' desires to regain work even at lower nominal wages. After effects from the drop in prices have taken place and after expectations have finally adjusted to the lower prices, equilibrium will reemerge at E_2. The economy moves along aggregate demand curve AD_1 and the relevant short-run supply function will be $SRAS_1$. Due to the initial decrease in consumption and investment spending, prices will fall to P_1, a level to which both employers and workers will again adjust.

In the monetarist view, the interplay between price changes and aggregate demand and between price-wage changes and short-run aggregate supply is sufficient to return the economy to full employment at E_2. However, the monetarist result hinges crucially on the *absence* of interventions by Congress or the Federal Reserve. In the monetarist view, such interventions interfere with the adjustment of price level expectations. As a result, they complicate and prolong the adjustment process.

Destabilizing Effects of Fiscal and Monetary Policies

Monetarists adhere to the belief that the market economy will stabilize at full employment. But we observe alternating swings in recession and inflation, as we did over the 1980s. How, then, do monetarists explain the facts of instability?

Like Keynesians, monetarists admit that shifts in aggregate demand can cause waves, or cycles, of unemployment and inflation. Monetarists, however, believe that the primary cause of aggregate demand shifts is not the movement of investment or consumption spending but the actions of government fiscal and monetary policy-makers. According to monetarists, the destabilizing element in the macroeconomy is the shifting expectations of market participants—laborers, businesspeople, consumers, and producers—created by erratic alterations in government expenditures, taxation, and the money supply.

The Effects of Financing Government Expenditures. In the monetarist view, increases in government expenditures—one of the primary tools of fiscal policy—come at the expense of private expenditures. If government spending is financed through taxation, private consumption and investment spending are reduced by the amount of the tax. If government spending is financed through borrowing in private markets, its demand for loanable funds will likely raise real interest rates, and higher interest rates will tend to choke off investment, depending on the responsiveness of investors to the increase. This competition for private funds is termed the crowding-out effect. If government spending is financed through the selling of Treasury bonds to the Federal Reserve, the result is potentially inflationary (Chapters 16 and 17 explain why this is so). In sum, the effects of financing government expenditures may offset any gain those expenditures offer a demand-deficient economy. In addition, such policies may create destabilizing effects.

Lags in Fiscal Policy. Another problem with fiscal policy often cited by monetarists concerns legislative frailties. Given the nature of public policy and the competing demands of political interest, fiscal policy-makers are often slow to recognize and act on economic distress signals. **Recognition lags** are the time it takes the president and Congress to identify impending or existing economic conditions. Predicting economic events is both a science and an art. There are often compelling interpretations offered by both sides to a debate over policy.

In addition to the difficulties of recognizing a problem, there are administrative lags with fiscal policy. **Administrative lags** are the length of time between politicians' recognition of a business cycle problem and their enactment of legislation to correct the problem. (The lag is even more properly called a *decision lag*—the time it takes to decide what to do.) We cite two examples of such lags. The Kennedy-Johnson tax cut of 1964 to stimulate economic growth was proposed as early as 1961 and 1962; its not being enacted until 1964 indicates an administrative lag. Likewise, a jobs bill passed in 1982 to deal with unemployment was debated for months and, when finally passed, was scheduled to go into effect more than a year later. Monetarists emphasize that economic conditions may change before the effects of these legislative acts take place. This would mean that fiscal policy could be procyclical rather than countercyclical in effect, buttressing inflation or recession as the case may be.

Once fiscal policy is enacted, it also takes time for its full impact to be realized—an impact lag, if you will. Estimates vary, but it is thought that tax or spending changes may take from one to two years to have their full impact on income and employment. Recognition and administrative lags make monetarists dubious about the effectiveness of fiscal policy. The unpredictability of how long it may take even well-intentioned fiscal policy to have an effect means that market participants' expectations about prices and future incomes are thrown into uncertainty in the meantime.

Effects of Monetary Policy. Discretionary monetary policy has its own problems in the monetarist view. Like fiscal policy, the attempt to control the money supply in countercyclical fashion is also subject to recognition and administrative lags. In the case of monetary policy, it is the quasi-independent Federal Reserve Board and its Federal Open Market Committee, not politicians, who must recognize macroeconomic problems and then enact and administer a change in policies affecting interest rates or the money supply. While problems of recognizing signs of recession or anticipating unemployment or assessing inflationary pressures may be as great as with fiscal policy, they are

Recognition lag:
The amount of time it takes policy-makers to realize that a destabilizing economic event has occurred.

Administrative lag:
The amount of time between recognition of a destabilizing economic event and the implementation of a policy designed to correct it.

somewhat easier to handle because of the small number of Federal Reserve Board or Open Market Committee members. Concerted discretionary recognition and action is probably quicker than with the larger numbers of participants in the fiscal setting.

Despite the quicker response, the time between enactment of monetary policy and when it takes effect is as unpredictable as the time related to fiscal manipulations. Some economists believe that the lag between growth in the money supply and the rate of inflation is at least two years long. These same economists view the effects of monetary growth on income and employment as somewhat more immediate. Other studies appear to show that most of the effects of monetary growth on prices, income, and employment take place rapidly, perhaps within six months. A third body of evidence seems to indicate that changes in aggregate demand induced by monetary growth will first have an impact on employment and income and will affect prices later, when expectations catch up. Such competing evidence illustrates the present uncertainty over the effects of discretionary monetary policy. The short run, in other words, may be shorter than the lag time between the money supply and policy variables.

The monetarist conclusion is that, on balance, discretionary fiscal and monetary policy will not be able to control swings of the business cycle. Indeed, in some regard, business cycle alterations are *caused* by destabilizing attempts to control cycles of inflation and unemployment. Stop-and-go policies that accelerate, decelerate, or otherwise interfere with private saving and spending are seen as the primary causes of aggregate demand instability, leading to prolonged recession and unemployment. The solution to the problems created by discretionary political or quasi-political attempts to control the business cycle is to establish rules through which fiscal and monetary policy is carried out.

Monetary Rules, Government Restraints, and Market Deregulation

In general, monetarists advocate that both fiscal and monetary policy be taken out of the hands of discretionary authorities—Congress and the Federal Reserve Board. On the fiscal side, government's budget should be balanced at all levels—local, state, and federal—through fiscal restraint or through a balanced budget amendment. Along with balanced budgets, the monetarists and other economists urge that government regulations supporting monopoly should be eliminated or modified. Deregulation in some industries and some occupations would create greater price and wage flexibility. Greater price and wage flexibility would in turn encourage a faster adjustment to both demand-deficiency unemployment and to inflation when the economy is disturbed.

Monetary rule:
A monetary policy consisting of a fixed rate of growth of the money supply.

Monetarists, led by Milton Friedman, also advocate the use of a **monetary rule** over the money supply growth rate.[2] In a study of the effects of monetary growth, Friedman and Anna Schwartz argue that depressions in the United States and other nations have always been preceded and accompanied by severe reductions in the money stock and that all inflations have been precipitated

---

[2]Milton Friedman, *A Program for Monetary Stability* (New York: Fordham University Press, 1960).

by sharp increases in the money stock.[3] With regard to the Great Depression of the 1930s, which was accompanied by a one-third drop in the money stock, Friedman and Schwartz conclude:

> The Great Depression in the United States, far from being a sign of the inherent instability of the private enterprise system, is a testament to how much harm can be done by mistakes on the part of a few men when they wield vast power over the monetary system of a country.[4]

Stop-and-go policies of the Federal Reserve Board—raising the monetary growth rate 16 percent one month and lowering it to a negative 6 percent the next—create uncertainty among market participants. The monetarists' solution: Take discretionary policy out of the hands of the Federal Reserve and institute an announced and constant growth rate in the money stock of 3 to 5 percent per year. Why 3 to 5 percent? Because the average rate of growth in the American economy through increases in labor productivity and technology has been on the order of 3 percent per year for more than a hundred years. In the monetarists' view, a growth rate in the money supply of 3 to 5 percent is consistent with a stable price level and a healthy rate of economic development. Moreover, a monetary rule would create much-needed stability and correspondence between expectations and actual price experience.

Critics of the new classical monetarist notion that there should be a rule for monetary policy point out that such a conclusion rests heavily on the short-run and long-run stability of velocity—the inverse of the demand for money, a process described in Chapter 17. Further, critics argue that adherence to monetary rules would result in unstable interest rates. Dissenters also criticize both Friedman's test methods and his results. The outcome of this debate is far from clear. The monetarists' tracking of inflation to changes in M-1 (with a two-year lag) has nevertheless persuaded a number of macroeconomists that the dog (money supply growth or declines) wags the tail (faster or slower inflation rates).

NEW CLASSICAL ECONOMICS: RATIONAL EXPECTATIONS

Some of the new classical economists are concerned with the ability of the economy to adjust to the policy actions of Congress or the Federal Reserve. In the opinion of traditional classical writers such as A. C. Pigou, market participants (buyers, sellers, consumers, investors) could not be consistently manipulated by government. Their "rationality" was based on an assumption of perfect information, although classical models did not formally take ration-

---

[3]Milton Friedman and Anna Schwartz, *A Monetary History of the United States, 1867–1960* (Princeton, N.J.: Princeton University Press, 1963).

[4]Critics of the Friedman-Schwartz analysis of the Depression (and of monetary policy generally) argue that they have simply shown a *relation* between money and prices but that they have not proved that changes in the rate of money stock expansion or reduction *cause* inflation or deflation. See Peter Temin, *Did Monetary Forces Cause the Great Depression?* (New York: Norton, 1976).

ality into account. This strand of thought is evident even in the earliest classical literature. Consider the following quotation from Adam Smith's *Theory of Moral Sentiments,* published in 1759.

> [The economic planner] seems to imagine that he can arrange the different members of society with as much ease as the hand arranges the different pieces upon a chessboard; he does not consider that the different pieces upon the chessboard have no other principle of motion besides that which the hand impresses upon them; but that, in the great chessboard of human society, every single piece has a principle of motion of its own, altogether different from that which the legislator might choose to impress upon it.[5]

Smith's view conforms well to the new classical belief that expectations occupy a central role in the economic system. We have seen, however, that "adaptive" expectations are central to the monetarist view of the effects of policy. What is the difference between the monetarist conception and the newer theory of rational expectations?

In Chapter 17 we presented the adaptive expectations theory, which holds that market participants form expectations about the future course of the inflation rate by tracking past rates of inflation. To use a simple example, suppose that people expect inflation this year to be what it was last year. If it was 10 percent last year, people expect it to be 10 percent this year, but if the inflation rate turns out to be 5 percent this year, people adapt and expect it to be 5 percent next year. At each period the public adjusts its expectations according to the differences between the actual inflation rate and the predicted inflation rate. It takes time and many readjustments of expectations for people to become convinced that any inflation rate (be it 6 percent or 106 percent) is permanent.

The Rational Expectations Hypothesis

Rational expectations theory:
A theory of behavior that assumes that people make efficient use of all past and present relevant information in forming expectations; implies that people's reactions to policy may neutralize the intended effects of the policy.

Over the past two decades, a group of new classical economists has developed a new theory of expectations to challenge and amend the adaptive expectations hypothesis. It was founded on a pioneering contribution by economist John Muth in 1961.[6] Although much of this work—called **rational expectations theory**—is extremely technical, the major thrust of the idea is simple, straightforward, and intuitively appealing. According to the rational expectations view, people are rational in the sense that they make use of both past and present relevant information in forming expectations of the future. Here, information includes not only the current values of important policy variables such as government expenditure and money growth; it also includes knowledge of the structure of the relationships among variables such as that between

[5]Adam Smith, *The Theory of Moral Sentiments* (1759; reprint, Indianapolis: Liberty Classics, 1976), p. 325.

[6]See John Muth, "Rational Expectations and the Theory of Price Movements," *Econometrica* (July 1961), pp. 315–35. Other innovators in this area include macroeconomists Thomas J. Sargent, Neil Wallace, and Robert E. Lucas; see Thomas J. Sargent, "Rational Expectations, the Real Rate of Interest, and the Natural Rate of Unemployment," *Brookings Papers in Economic Activity* 2 (1973), pp. 429–72; Thomas J. Sargent and Neil Wallace, "Rational Expectations and the Theory of Economic Policy," *Journal of Monetary Economics* (April 1976), pp. 169–84; and R. E. Lucas, "An Equilibrium Model of the Business Cycle," *Journal of Political Economy* (December 1975), pp. 1113–44.

the inflation rate and the nominal interest rates. It suggests that, after some learning, individuals begin to understand some of the fundamental workings of the economy. For example, they will learn through experience that increases in the rate of monetary expansion by the Federal Reserve are generally followed by increases in the inflation rate, which are then followed by higher nominal interest rates. Knowing something of the basic structure of the economy as well as the current values of key policy variables, individuals will be able to form expectations of likely future outcomes in the economy.

Does this mean that market participants will always be correct in their anticipations? In a world filled with uncertainty, outcomes will depend on an enormous number of random occurrences. Individuals will not always be right in their expectations about future economic events, but they will be correct on average.

If people can anticipate discretionary policy and its effects, they are in a position to neutralize the purpose of the policy. For example, if the Federal Reserve Board increases M-1 to increase employment but workers and firms perfectly anticipate the resulting increase in prices, then workers will instantly demand a proportionately higher nominal wage. Firms, anticipating higher nominal revenues, would be willing to pay the higher nominal wage, thus leaving the real wage and the level of unemployment unaffected. In this contest, policy-makers are pitted against market participants, and policy-makers will not win continuously and certainly will not win over time. Policy-makers may attempt to surprise the public, but they cannot do so forever. People catch on to, say, the effects of federal deficits on inflation, anticipate the change, and neutralize or counteract the effects of the change. In the long run, when a model of macroeconomic behavior is learned and actions are correctly anticipated, fiscal or monetary policy is totally ineffective in producing intended alterations on the demand side of the economy. Paradoxically, to have any purposeful effect fiscal and monetary policy would have to be random. If it is not—if policy-makers act in any systematic manner—learned behavior over time will neutralize the policy.

Rational Expectations and Monetary Policy

As with Keynesians and monetarists, time is an important factor in rational expectations. Short-run and long-run effects of rational expectations will depend on whether monetary policy—or any event affecting the macroeconomy—is anticipated.

Anticipated Monetary Policy. We can imagine the (non)effects of rational expectations as a result of the increases or decreases in monetary expansion with the aid of Figure 4. Note that with *adaptive* expectations, an increase in monetary expansion shifting the aggregate demand curve rightward to AD_1 from AD_0 would increase income above the full-employment level, Y_F, because it would take time for the price expectations and perceptions of workers and employers to adjust to the full effects of monetary expansion. In other words, there would be an upward-sloping short-run aggregate supply curve through E_0 in Figure 4, as there is in Figure 3.

But this is not the case under an assumption of rational expectations of anticipated policy. Figure 4 shows no short-run expectations-adjusted aggregate supply curve because all effects are perfectly anticipated by all market

FIGURE 4

According to the rational expectations approach, wages, interest rates, and prices adjust in anticipation of changes in aggregate demand caused by upward or downward adjustment of the money supply. For this reason there is no short-run aggregate supply curve. The economy simply moves along the long-run aggregate supply curve *LRAS*, with prices rising as the money supply is increased, shifting the demand curve from AD_0 to AD_1, or falling as the money supply is decreased, shifting aggregate demand to AD_2.

Rational Expectations and Monetary Policy

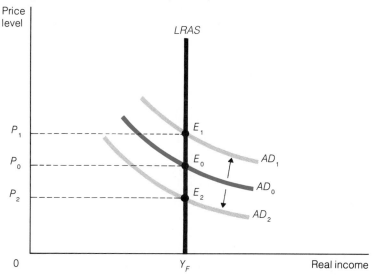

transactors. An increase in aggregate demand from AD_0 to AD_1 caused by a preannounced increased rate of monetary expansion (or a decrease from AD_0 to AD_2 caused by reduction in monetary expansion) simply creates a new equilibrium at E_1 (or at E_2) with all adjustments perfectly worked out instantaneously. In this case, the inflation or deflation is perfectly accounted for by all market transactors, and the full-employment level of income, Y_F, is left undisturbed by policy changes. Only prices change. This principle also applies when, for example, employment falls below the natural rate, due perhaps to some reduction in private autonomous expenditures that reduces aggregate demand. Any attempt on the part of monetary authorities to remedy the situation will be met with counteracting reactions on the part of market participants, leaving the unemployment rate unchanged.

Unanticipated Monetary Policy and Random Shocks. The preceding conclusions apply as long as policy changes aimed at correcting aggregate demand are fully anticipated and expected. When the expectations of market participants about aggregate demand management are fully realized, no change in real income or employment can occur. But the rational expectationist argument also allows for surprises or random events in the short run. If, for example, the Federal Reserve Board changes the M-1 growth rate erratically or if it alters its target, short-run changes in income and employment will occur until all market participants catch on and acknowledge the new policy. Unless Federal Reserve policy is continuously random, expectations will adjust in the long run.

Surprises such as crop failures caused by climatic changes or timber losses caused by a volcanic eruption will also disrupt production and market plans in the short run. The rational expectations theory predicts, however, that all market participants will adapt and adjust behavior to the new conditions in the long run. In sum, the rational expectations idea does not preclude short-run fluctuations in output and employment due to policy or natural surprises. It does predict that policy changes will be neutralized in the long run unless policy is implemented in a random manner.

Rational Expectations and Fiscal Policy

When fiscal policy encounters rational expectations, it may not leave the supply side of the macroeconomy unchanged, especially in the long run. Consider Figure 5, for example, and assume that the economy is initially in equilibrium at full-employment level of income Y_{F_0}. Further assume that Congress enacts increases in government expenditures financed by increases in taxes or by borrowing in private markets.

In the classical, monetarist, or rational expectationist view of the economy, the increase in government expenditures is closely matched by reductions in private consumption, investment, or imports. Such a reduction would leave the aggregate demand curve of Figure 5 stationary. With no further effects, it would appear that equilibrium would remain at E_0, and the level of income as well as employment would remain constant at Y_{F_0}. However, rational expectations theorists assert that fiscal policy would likely have effects on aggregate supply as well as on the public versus private composition of aggregate demand.

Changes in tax rates will affect work incentives. Any reduction in work incentives may reduce the total equilibrium labor input, shifting the aggregate supply curve leftward. Moreover, increased taxes on business investment could adversely affect the demand for labor. Both of these possible effects would reduce the natural level of employment, increasing the natural rate of unemployment. This means that the rate of employment consistent with equilibrium, given all factors (such as taxes) that affect hiring and labor-supply conditions, is lower than before. In Figure 5, the aggregate supply curve shifts

---

FIGURE 5   Rational Expectations and Fiscal Policy

If rational expectations exist in the long run, fiscal policy has no effect on aggregate demand. Furthermore, fiscal policy can cause reductions in labor input or business investment, causing the long-run aggregate supply curve to shift to the left.

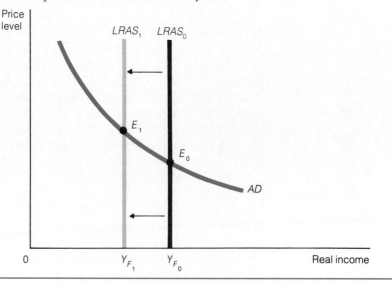

(or drifts) leftward, reducing equilibrium income with a tendency toward higher prices. Fiscal policy therefore may have effects on aggregate supply as well as on aggregate demand.

At base, the theory of rational expectations reinforces the classical-monetarist position: The private economy, while not perfect in providing full employment and maximum income at all times, is superior to fiscal and monetary authorities in providing a relatively stable economy. But rational expectations theory goes further and proposes that over time the effects of fiscal and monetary manipulations can be fully anticipated and therefore neutralized. Policies related to aggregate demand will either have no effect or in the longer run will actually produce reductions in aggregate supply. In short, there is little or no room for discretionary macroeconomic policy. Robert Lucas, a leading proponent of the rational expectations hypothesis, has therefore offered this advice: "The Administration and Congress should stop thrashing around pretending to know better than the economy how much can be produced. And the Federal Reserve should move as quickly as possible to a 4 percent monetary growth."[7]

NEW KEYNESIAN CRITICISMS OF NEW CLASSICAL ECONOMICS

The rational expectations approach, or, more accurately, nonapproach, to policy has generated an enormous amount of interest. Much of the contemporary research has been devoted to the question of whether or not and under what conditions the policy-neutral implications of new classical economics hold. A good deal of sophisticated econometric testing has left open the answer to the question, Does discretionary policy work? Much of the evidence does not support the major positions of the rational expectationists.[8] Until testing yields consistent results, the matter of policy neutrality and the theoretical foundations of the new classical economics will form a lively debate between the rational expectationists and those championing the efficacy of discretionary policy and those with differing theoretical perspectives. Chief among the critics of new classical economics are the new Keynesians.[9]

While many new Keynesians see value in more sophisticated theories of expectations, they retain a belief in the efficacy of discretionary government action in the economy. Policy, to the new Keynesians, is nonneutral and necessary in an economy that is inherently and endogenously unstable over nontrivial clock-time periods. The basic dispute is over the form of the

---

[7]Robert E. Lucas, quoted in "The New Economists," *Newsweek* (June 26, 1978), p. 60. Copyright 1978 by Newsweek, Inc. All rights reserved. Reprinted by permission. For a nontechnical explanation of the rational expectations idea, see "The Rational Expectations Model," *Wall Street Journal* (April 2, 1979).

[8]See, for example, Michael C. Lovell, "Tests of the Rational Expectations Hypothesis," *American Economic Review* (March 1986), pp. 110–24.

[9]For two critical evaluations of the new classical economics, see Robert J. Gordon, "Recent Developments in the Theory of Inflation and Unemployment," *Journal of Monetary Economics* (April 1976), pp. 185–220; and James Tobin, "Are New Classical Models Plausible Enough to Guide Policy?" *Journal of Money, Credit and Banking* (November 1980), pp. 788–99.

expectational assumptions of the rational expectationists and over the related issue of the efficiency of market functioning.

New Keynesians (and others) object that the new classical economics requires market participants to be more sophisticated than they really are in their abilities to predict. How might we expect buyers of VCRs and sellers of rental properties to utilize intricate and sophisticated theories of economic functioning in order to accurately predict prices, outputs, interest rates, or any other economic variable into the future and to quickly and accurately act on the prediction in the present?

Rational expectationists counter with the point that market participants are correct, *but only on average* and only after a "learning" period. If, in other words, policy itself is not random (which would be a peculiar manner of conducting it), those who consistently come up with inaccurate predictions would be severely punished in the market through losses on exchanges. In their own self-interest market participants would attempt to learn the probable effects of policy. Armies of economists in the "think tank" or "prediction service" business are hired by market participants to help them learn or to give them rational information about the future. It would be strange, indeed, for markets not to react in this manner.

Importantly, new Keynesians argue that rational expectations theory fails to explain prolonged periods of unemployment and depression. New Keynesians regard the economy as inherently unstable (especially with regard to investment spending) and characterized by institutionalized sticky prices and wages (from monopolies and other imperfections in both product and labor markets). Rational expectationists do *not* believe, as the old classical writers did, that full production and employment *always* characterize the economic system. Unanticipated policy and price surprises cause real variables such as employment and income to diverge from their natural rates. Once market participants discover the "true" nature of the policy change, expectations catch up with actual economic magnitudes (such as prices) and the economy returns to the rational expectations equilibrium. An important question is, How long does this take?

New Keynesians point to events such as the Great Depression of the 1930s, with its prolonged periods of unemployment and reduced growth rates in real GNP, as proof that market participants do not react in the manner described by the rational expectationists. To restate the question, even if expectations are "rational" and even if they eventually return the economy to the natural or full-employment level of output and employment, aren't the sacrifices unacceptable? (Note the modern version of the "all dead in the long run" precept of early Keynesian economics.)

The question is, of course, a good one. The actual situation of the 1930s economy has proved difficult to gauge. New Keynesians believe that factors such as reduced aggregate demand and sticky nominal wages and prices due to effective rigidities in both product and labor markets are the essential explanation for the prolonged depression of the 1930s. Rational expectationists counter by arguing that that depression was prolonged, if not fostered, by wrongheaded government policies. Price changes failed to clear product and labor markets due to the *continuous* and *persistent* policy and institutional changes by the government. Discouragement of business investment and unanticipated policy "surprises" were the result of the government's increased participation in the private market system. Blame for the origins and length of the Great Depression is also placed at the door of the Federal Reserve System, which failed to perceive and correct for the precipitous decline in the real stock of money.

The debate between the new Keynesian and the rational expectationist views of the proper role of policy will, of course, continue. Whether discretionary policy or "rules" give the best results will not be decided by theory or opinion, but by facts, illuminated by econometric testing.

THE MAJOR POLICY POSITIONS: A SUMMARY

We have now evaluated three major policy positions based on three theories of the functioning of the aggregate economy. Some theoretical or policy views are contrasting and some are complementary, as Table 3 reveals.

New Keynesians hold that the private economy is inherently unstable and unable to correct itself during periods of inflation and unemployment. In their view, government should take a primary role in managing fiscal and monetary policy for economic stabilization. Of the two major arms of policy, new Keynesians advocate discretionary fiscal policy as the primary weapon in controlling unemployment and inflation. Fiscal policies, they believe, have

TABLE 3　　　　　　　　　Alternative Positions on Macroeconomic and Monetary Policy

A simplified menu of economic policy choices includes various recommended roles for fiscal and monetary policy. The new Keynesian position places primary emphasis on fiscal policy, while the monetarist defends a rule for monetary policy and balance in the budget. The rational expectations theory predicts that, over the long run, neither fiscal nor monetary policy will have a positive effect on the aggregate economy.

Policy Position	Role of Monetary Policy	Predicted Effects of Monetary Policy	Role of Fiscal Policy	Predicted Effects of Fiscal Policy
New Keynesian	Maintain orderly and low interest rates through discretionary adjustments in money supply	Possible destabilizing effects on interest rates if Federal Reserve only attempts to control money supply	Primary tool of macroeconomic stabilization; discretionary changes in government spending and taxation	Discretionary fiscal policy capable of ensuring full employment
Monetarist	Maintain a 3% to 5% growth rate in M-1	Discretionary policy will destabilize decision making in private markets; monetary rule will stabilize expectations	Provide stable environment for private economy through balanced budgets	Discretionary policy will bring erratic effects on income, employment, and prices; such policy creates an unstable economy
Rational expectations theory	Same as monetarist	In the long run, rational expectations will neutralize discretionary policy	Same as monetarist	Possible adverse long-run aggregate supply effects

" . . . First I was a Keynesian . . . Next I was a monetarist . . . Then a
supply-sider . . . Now I'm a bum . . . "

© Bill Schorr, 1982 *Los Angeles Herald Examiner*

direct effects on spending in the private economy, whereas monetary policy
(control of the money stock) has only indirect results. Monetary policy should
maintain the order or stability of interest rates, keeping them low or moderate.

Monetarists and rational expectationists view the economy as essentially
stable and self-correcting. Both views envision the private decisions of laborers, employers, money demanders, and consumer-savers and investors as producing a natural equilibrium constituting some natural rate of output and
employment (or unemployment). In the monetarist view of this process, discretionary policy of any sort produces instabilities in private markets that
distort, exaggerate, or accentuate any natural changes. In the monetarist view,
discretionary fiscal or monetary policy contributes to instability in the private
economy. That is, discretionary policy (consciously taken direct government
action) either creates inflation and unemployment of itself or it has erratic
effects on the private economy's ability to establish economic stability. The
solution: Conduct monetary and fiscal policy so as to minimize disturbances
of private market participants' expectations and decisions. In the monetarist's
policy views, such stability can be achieved by invoking a monetary rule, such
as fixing the money supply growth rate, with balanced government budgets.

In the rational expectations variant of macroeconomic theory, the recommended role of fiscal and monetary policy is identical to that espoused by
monetarists. Differences between these two positions lie rather in the rational
expectationists' view of the probable effects of monetary and fiscal policy. As
market participants gain sufficient information about the effects of economic
policy through time, policy can have no effects on the private economy. Participants learn the effects of anticipated policy and act more and more quickly
to counteract them. The rational expectations approach might be regarded as
an extreme view within the monetarist position.

The important point is that *macroeconomists have not reached a consensus on exactly how the macroeconomy works*. Under such circumstances we expect to see a variety of policy views, as Table 3 shows. One of the problems with establishing a consensus among macroeconomists is the difficulty of proving one view with a statistical test that all would accept. The economist, like the meteorologist, is faced with a kaleidoscope of ever-changing conditions; hard-and-fast answers are difficult to come by.

SUMMARY

1. Macroeconomic policies—those prescribed to solve macroeconomic problems such as inflation and unemployment—rest on alternative versions of macroeconomic theory.

2. The tools of policy-makers include changes in taxes, government spending, and the money supply to effect changes in total spending.

3. The new Keynesians argue that fiscal policies—government spending and taxation policies—have direct and predictable effects on the private economy. Discretionary fiscal policies should be used to cure economic problems such as demand-deficiency unemployment and inflation. Money supply changes may affect spending indirectly through their impact on interest rates.

4. Monetarists advocate a stable, nondiscretionary fiscal and monetary approach to economic stabilization. Monetarists assert that lags in the recognition of economic problems on the part of both fiscal and monetary authorities, as well as lags between policy implementation and the effects of policies, are potentially disruptive in controlling the macroeconomy. Monetarists advocate a balanced budget on the fiscal side and a rule fixing money supply growth for the Federal Reserve's conduct of monetary policy.

5. Rational expectations theorists argue that, rather than ignore useful information, market participants use all learned information to predict the outcome of policy-makers' discretionary decisions. Decision-makers with rational expectations are not always right, but they learn through time and are able to predict outcomes over the long run. The result is that when the discretionary decisions of policy-makers are perfectly anticipated, monetary and fiscal policy will have no effect on aggregate demand. Unanticipated policy or events will have short-run effects, which are eventually overcome through natural adjustments. Fiscal demand-side policies, moreover, may result in long-run adverse shifts in aggregate supply.

KEY TERMS

recognition lag
administrative lag

monetary rule
rational expectations theory

QUESTIONS FOR REVIEW AND DISCUSSION

1. Explain how fiscal and monetary policies differ with respect to the amount of time necessary to implement them and the amount of time required for their full force to be realized.

2. Under what conditions is Keynesian fiscal policy most effective? What fiscal policies are called for during times of recession? During inflation?

3. What role do the monetary authorities play in Keynesian policies? In the monetarists' view, what is the proper role of the monetary authorities?

4. According to monetarists, what variables adjust to maintain full employment? What effect do discretionary demand management policies have on the economy?

5. According to monetarists, what effect does increased government spending have on aggregate demand? What effect do recognition and administrative lags have on the cycles of inflation and unemployment?

6. Why do monetarists suggest that monetary rules be followed rather than discretionary policies?

7. What is the difference between rational expectations and adaptive expectations? If individuals have rational expectations rather than adaptive expectations, would discretionary monetary policy be more effective in diminishing swings in the economy?

8. According to the rational expectations view, what are the probable effects of discretionary monetary and fiscal policies?

9. What theoretical conditions would have to exist before discretionary fiscal or monetary policies could completely eliminate the cyclical swings in inflation and unemployment?

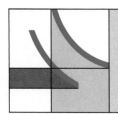

ECONOMICS IN ACTION
Economists in Control of Economic Policy? The Role of the Council of Economic Advisers

President Harry S. Truman is reputed to have once remarked that he would have been willing to pay a princely sum for a one-handed economist. After the Council of Economic Advisers gave their economic policy recommendations, Truman bemoaned, his economists would always end up saying, "But on the other hand. . . . "

What is the Council of Economic Advisers, and what exactly does it do? The Council of Economic Advisers (CEA) was established as an office in the executive branch of the federal government by the Employment Act of 1946. The CEA's basic duties are to supply the president with economic analysis and advice in order to assist in the development and implementation of national economic policy. Outstanding economists such as James Tobin, a Nobel laureate (1981) appointed by President John F. Kennedy, have served as members of the CEA.

The CEA consists of three members who are appointed by the president, with approval of the Senate, one of whom serves as chair of the CEA. The professional staff of the CEA is made up of eleven senior and six junior economists, as well as a statistician. The staff economists specialize in fields of expertise such as macroeconomics, international finance, labor, public finance, taxation, monetary policy, regulation, and agriculture. In most cases, the senior staff economists are on leave of absence from major universities, research institutions, or other government agencies.

By far, the CEA's most important duties are to provide the president with sound economic analysis concerning areas where policy decisions, either legislative or regulatory, are to be made. These areas include, of course, the broad area of national macroeconomic policy. The CEA not only assists the president in formulating macroeconomic policy, but also assists in designing the necessary programs through which such policy is carried out. Forecasts and projections of critical macroeconomic variables such as the deficit, inflation, real GNP growth, and foreign exchange rates are all prepared by the CEA. In addition, the CEA has prepared economic analyses of such microeconomic issues as farm credit, airline and trucking deregulation, banking deregulation, space shuttle pricing, immigration, and antitrust legislation.

At the end of each January, the CEA submits an annual report to the president. This report, together with the president's own report, is then transmitted to Congress. These are then published yearly as the *Economic Report of the President.* The *Report* is not only an informative analysis of recent economic events and current problems, but it is also one of the better sources of economic statistics. Data on everything from budget deficits to farm income to unemployment are reported here, some going as far back as 1929. The CEA also is responsible for data contained in a more up-to-date monthly publication called *Economic Indicators.*

The Council of Economic Advisers, in short, does not decide economic policy. This is the duty of the president and Congress. However, the CEA is in a position to strongly influence economic policy. The CEA chair and members are usually chosen on the basis of shared philosophy with the president, as shown by President George Bush's selection of Stanford University economist Michael Boskin, a moderate, to head his CEA. Like other administration officials dealing with economic questions and problems—the Secretary of the Treasury, the head of the Office of Management and the Budget—CEA members influence decision-making by force of personality, reputation, and personal relationship with the president.

Question

If you were a faculty member at your university, what *economic* factors would enter your decision to accept or turn down a position offered to you on the CEA? Remember that the salary of a CEA member is generally less than what the appointee could earn at a university.

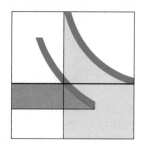

19

Unemployment and Business Cycles

The real GNP of any economy fluctuates up and down over time. Such fluctuations were defined in Chapter 6 as business cycles. In previous chapters we have examined classical, Keynesian, and monetarist theories of the economy to gain insight into why these periodic expansions and contractions take place. In this chapter we will consider business cycles in more detail. We will examine how business cycles are measured, consider some of the costs associated with business cycles, and present various theories of the causes of business cycles. We will also consider some of the tools used by economic forecasters to predict changes in the business cycle and reexamine economic policies designed to prevent or moderate business cycles.

Some critics of capitalism base their criticism on the notion that business cycles are an inherent, undesirable consequence of the operation of a market system. In fact, advocates of central economic planning often contend that government intervention is necessary to prevent frequent and extreme economic downturns. However, evidence from centrally planned economies such as China and the Soviet Union indicates that business cycles are also an economic fact of life in centrally planned economies. Serious recessions in the Soviet Union, East Germany, and in Poland hastened disenchantment with central planning and led to adoption of free-market policies and alternative political systems. After you complete Chapter 19 you should understand

- the fundamental nature of business cycles.
- how economists attempt to predict or forecast cycles on the basis of fundamental economic indicators.
- the role of expectations and labor market adjustments in providing one explanation for short-run cycles of unemployment and inflation.
- how politics might be related to business cycles.

DEFINING AND PREDICTING BUSINESS CYCLES

Over any period of time, economic capacity to produce goods and services tends to increase because of factors such as technological change, growth in labor supply (population), and discovery and development of natural resources. Within the overall trend of long-run growth, economies fluctuate in aggregate output and employment (see Figure 1).

A **business cycle** is a downward or upward fluctuation in the real GNP of an economy that repeats itself over time. Three points should be kept in mind about this definition. First, business cycles recur over time, but not necessarily in a predictable pattern. Recurrent and predictable seasonal variations in business activity—such as the purchase of more firewood in winter than in summer—are not business cycles. For example, everyone is aware of the upsurge in the purchase of goods and services every December as Christmas approaches. This seasonal change in business activity is a short, predictable fluctuation that is fully accounted for and therefore is not a business cycle.

Business cycle:
A recurrent pattern of fluctuations in the level of economic activity as measured by the growth rate of real GNP; or the variation through time of the level of real GNP around its long-term trend.

FIGURE 1

Annual U.S. GNP Growth Rates, 1929–1989

The percentage change in a country's real GNP tends to fall and rise over time; economists refer to these fluctuations as business cycles. Cycles of expansion and recession have characterized the U.S. economy throughout most of its history. Despite these fluctuations, between 1929 and 1989 the average growth rate has been about 3 percent per year.

Sources: Council of Economic Advisers, *Economic Report of the President* (Washington, D.C.: U.S. Government Printing Office, 1966, 1987, 1990); *Federal Reserve Bulletin* (September 1984).

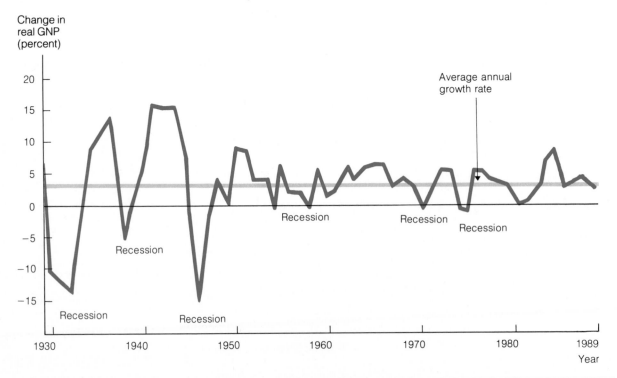

Second, the term *business cycle* normally refers to overall business activity as measured by real GNP. There can also be cycles in the component parts of GNP. Spending on consumer durables, such as refrigerators and cars, exhibits cyclical behavior over time, whereas consumer spending on nondurable items, such as food, does not. Cyclical patterns are also observed in retail sales, business profits, business incorporations, interest rates, residential construction, and many other reported statistics. For our purposes, however, we take business cycles to refer only to the movement of real GNP.

Third, there can be different types of business cycles, depending on the length of time over which a given business cycle runs. Short cycles last less than two years; intermediate cycles extend five years or more; and long-run cycles run over ten years. Indeed, some students of the business cycle have identified cycles that extend over several decades or even centuries.

The Language of Business Cycles

A business cycle includes expansions and contractions of business activity. An expansion is a cumulative increase in real GNP, while a contraction is a cumulative decrease. Contractions are often called recessions or depressions. A **recession** is a decline in real GNP that lasts for six months or more. **Depression** is a more ambiguous term, but it generally refers to a serious and persistent decline in economic activity lasting several years, accompanied by an unemployment rate of 15 percent or more. Depressions are preceded by recessions, but not all recessions are followed by depressions.

Recession:
A contraction in overall economic activity, usually defined as a decrease in real GNP over a period of at least six months.

Depression:
A severe, persistent recession that may last several years.

The period, or length, of a business cycle can be measured in two ways: from peak to peak or trough to trough. Figure 2 illustrates the alternative measurements. Peaks are upper turning points in a cycle where an expansion finally peters out. Troughs are the opposite of peaks; they are the lower turning points of a cycle where contractions bottom out. The length of a business cycle differs depending on whether it is measured from peak to peak or trough to trough.

The trend line in Figure 2 measures a hypothetical long-run growth path of the economy. The extent of deviations from the trend line, at either a peak or a trough, indicates the intensity of a business cycle. Business cycles have no set patterns. They recur over time, but each one is slightly different. Each business cycle varies in length and intensity.

Business Cycles in the United States

Using statistical analysis, researchers have identified numerous business cycles in U.S. economic history. Table 1 presents some data on business cycle activity in the United States since the turn of the century. The statistics show that business cycles are recurrent but have different lengths. Nineteen cycles were identified from 1900 to 1981. Measured peak to peak, the average duration of these cycles was approximately 51 months, or a little over four years. The shortest business cycle (January 1980–July 1981) lasted 18 months. The longest (April 1960–December 1969) lasted 116 months.

Moreover, the business cycles exhibited varying degrees of intensity. In the two-year expansion from April 1958 to April 1960, real GNP rose by 8 percent. By contrast, in the expansion from July 1980 to July 1981, real GNP rose by only about 2 percent. Each business cycle and its phases possess a

FIGURE 2

Hypothetical Business Cycle

The curve represents the phases of a hypothetical business cycle. One phase is contraction or recession, when aggregate output and employment fall. The trough occurs when this part of the cycle bottoms out. The expansion or recovery phase occurs when the economy exhibits expanding output and employment. The peak occurs when general business activity and employment stop rising. When the next recession begins, the economy starts another business cycle. The period of the cycle is measured from peak to peak or trough to trough. This cycle has a period of $t_1 t_2$, measured peak to peak. The intensity of the cycle is given by the deviation of the peak or trough from the trend line of long-run growth.

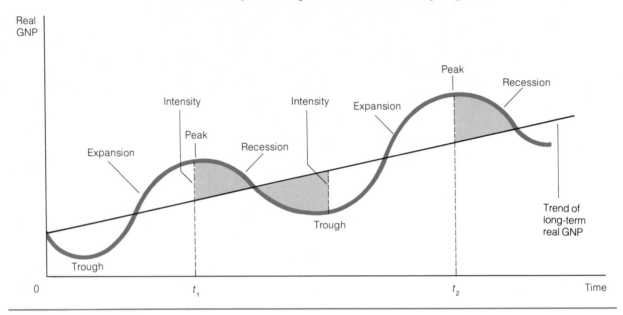

unique character. Since 1982, the business cycle pattern has diverged somewhat from its traditional look in that it has not shown a traditional fluctuating pattern.

Forecasting Business Cycles

Some economists specialize in forecasting business conditions. These individuals are often called econometricians because they are highly trained in the use of statistics, called **econometrics,** to predict events in the economy. Some well-known economic forecasters are Lawrence Klein of the University of Pennsylvania, who won the Nobel Prize in economics in 1980; Michael Evans, who has his own forecasting firm; and Alan Greenspan, who was chairman of the Council of Economic Advisers under President Ford and who was appointed chairman of the Federal Reserve Board in 1987.

Forecasting is both a science and an art. The science of forecasting involves the construction of statistical models of the operation of the economy and of economic indicators that predict the future level of such variables as GNP. The art of forecasting is the use of past experience and commonsense judgment about what types of variables are important in predicting how the economy will behave, since no two business cycles are precisely alike.

Who are some of the users of economic forecasts? Business decision-makers and government policy-makers need reliable data on the future course

Econometrics:
The combined use of economic theory and formal statistical techniques to analyze, explain, and predict economic phenomena.

TABLE 1   U.S. Business Cycles, 1900–1990

Trough	Peak	Length of Cycle (peak to peak in months)
December 1900	September 1902	39
August 1904	May 1907	56
June 1908	January 1910	32
January 1912	January 1913	36
December 1914	August 1918	67
March 1919	January 1920	17
July 1921	May 1923	40
July 1924	October 1926	41
November 1927	August 1929	34
March 1933	May 1937	93
June 1938	February 1945	93
October 1945	November 1948	45
October 1949	July 1953	56
May 1954	August 1957	49
April 1958	April 1960	32
February 1961	December 1969	116
November 1970	November 1973	47
March 1975	January 1980	74
July 1980	July 1981	18
November 1982	. . .[a]	. . .

Source: Department of Commerce, Bureau of Economic Analysis, *Business Conditions Digest* (July 1986), p. 104; U.S. Bureau of the Census, *Statistical Abstract of the United States* 1989, p. 534.

[a]In September 1990, many observers felt that this expansion would end with a recession in the fourth quarter of 1990.

of GNP to plan their activities. When business executives make decisions about investments in plant and equipment that will lead to increased output in the future, they need to have some idea of what the state of the economy will be when this output comes on the market. Overall tax revenues will usually depend on the level of national income and consumer spending in the future. To plan government spending, policy-makers need estimates of future tax revenues.

To produce a forecast, the forecaster seeks information about what changes in the economy today are a good indication of what the state of the economy will be tomorrow. For this purpose economic forecasters have developed **economic indicators,** key economic statistics that provide clues about the state of the future economy.

Economic indicators come in three basic varieties. Leading economic indicators anticipate a business cycle. They tend to turn down before a general economic downturn and up before an expansion. A coincident indicator runs in step with a business cycle, and a lagging indicator follows changes in the business cycle. Of these three sets of indicators, the most attention is paid to leading indicators because they give decision-makers clues about the future course of the business cycle.

The commonly used leading indicators are listed in Table 2. Data on these statistics are published quarterly by the Department of Commerce, and the trend of leading indicators is usually reported in the press. The leading indicators tend to change together over time, and a particularly useful sum-

Economic indicators: Important data, or statistics, such as the money supply, investment spending, unemployment, and inventories that are used to help forecast economic activity and business cycles; these indicators are classified as leading, lagging, and coincident indicators.

TABLE 2   Leading Economic Indicators

Indicator
New business orders
Unfilled orders
Construction approvals and starts
New company formation and vacancies
Average hours worked
Average profits
Inventory change and level
Production bottlenecks
Stock prices
Changes in raw materials prices
Tendency surveys of expected production

Source: Department of Commerce, Survey of Current Business (August 1989), p. 24.

mary statistic is the composite or combined index of leading indicators. The behavior of this index since 1948 is shown in Figure 3.

How reliable is the composite index of leading economic indicators in predicting downturns? Compare the path of this index to the occurrence of recessions, represented by the shaded areas in Figure 2. Prior to each recession, the index of leading indicators dropped. Sometimes, however, it dropped more than a year before a recession started (as in the 1957–1958 recession), and at other times it dropped just months prior to a recession (as in the 1953–1954 recession). Moreover, the index dropped several times during the 1960s and no recession ensued. Economist Paul Samuelson once quipped that economic indicators "have correctly predicted nine of the last five recessions."

No predictive model of the future is perfect, but the fact that the leading indicators are widely used by economists, government officials, and business-people is a testimony to their usefulness as inputs to economic forecasts.

THE COSTS OF BUSINESS CYCLES

Business cycles have received much attention from economists and politicians because they entail genuine economic costs. When the economy goes into a recession or depression, the production of goods and services falls, causing living standards to fall. It may seem that these reductions in living standards are only temporary and that rapid increases in production during the recovery stage of the business cycle will counteract them. However, much of the lost production can never be regained. An economic downturn results in unemployment of economic resources of all types. Plants are closed down, farmland may lie idle, and workers with all types of labor skills remain out of work. Although all of the idle resources may become employed when the economy recovers, the lost production cannot be regained; a worker unemployed for a year cannot make up for lost production during the ensuing year. Production that is lost due to idle resources is production that is lost forever.

FIGURE 3

A Comparison of Business Cycles with the Composite Index of Leading Economic Indicators, 1948–1988

The shaded areas represent business downturns or recessions. The composite index of leading economic indicators dropped before each recession. However, the lag between the drop and the subsequent recession varied. In addition, the index sometimes forecast a recession that did not materialize.

Source: Department of Commerce, *Business Conditions Digest* (various issues).

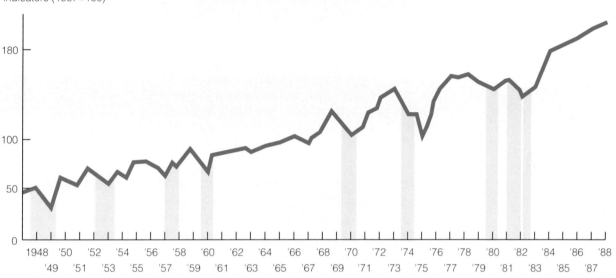

The second way in which business cycles reduce living standards is by depleting the capital stock. At any point in time, a society's ability to produce goods and services depends crucially on the size of its capital stock. As we saw in Chapter 2, a society's production possibilities curve is shifted rightward when capital accumulates and leftward when the capital stock declines. During an economic recession or depression, existing capital continues to depreciate, which lowers the capital stock. In a normal business environment, business firms have an incentive to replace and even add to depreciating plant and equipment; in a recession, firms are less likely to replace depreciating capital. Sales are so low that existing firms have idle capital and little incentive to replace equipment that becomes worn out. As a consequence, business downturns tend to erode the stock of productive capital and to reduce future production ability.

Similar choices by individuals also lead to a decline in the stock of another kind of capital—human capital in education and on-the-job training. In a recession, individuals have less incentive to invest in human capital: Why study to become a welder if there are no jobs for welders? This is precisely what happened in the United States and elsewhere during the Great Depression of the 1930s. Some of the anti-depression policies implemented by the Roosevelt administration were designed to prevent the nation's stock of both human and nonhuman capital from declining. Programs such as the PWA and the WPA hired unemployed workers to construct bridges, highways, and public buildings. In doing so, they provided job skills for workers (human capital) and improved the nation's infrastructure. Despite these programs, the United States entered World War II with a greatly reduced stock of capital goods, which hampered U.S. military mobilization at the outset of the war.

Who Pays for Business Downturns?

In the preceding section we saw that business downturns are costly, since downturns lower living standards both in the short run and in the long run. This does not mean that the burden is borne evenly by all citizens in terms of uniformly lower real incomes. Since U.S. firms tend to respond to downturns in business by laying off a portion of their labor force instead of reducing the hours of all workers (a practice common in Japan), the experiences of workers will vary. Workers who are laid off experience huge reductions in incomes, while other workers are barely affected. Table 3 indicates that the overall unemployment rate has risen on average by more than two percentage points during each of the eight recessions since World War II. In a typical recession, the unemployment rate has risen from about 4 percent to just over 6 percent.

| TABLE 3 | **Changes in Unemployment Rates During Recessions** |

During the eight recessions that have occurred in the United States since World War II, the overall unemployment rate increased by an average of over two percentage points. However, increases in the unemployment rates for teenage workers and for black workers were substantially higher over the recession periods.

Recession Year	Unemployment Rate			
	All Workers	Females	Blacks	Teenagers
1947	3.8%	4.1%	5.9%	9.2%
1948	5.9	6.0	8.9	13.4
1952	2.9	3.6	5.4	8.5
1954	5.4	6.0	9.9	12.6
1957	4.2	4.7	7.9	11.6
1958	6.6	6.8	12.6	15.9
1960	5.4	5.9	10.2	14.7
1961	6.5	7.2	12.4	16.8
1969	3.4	4.7	6.4	12.2
1971	5.8	6.9	9.9	16.9
1973	4.8	6.0	9.0	14.5
1975	8.3	9.3	13.8	19.9
1979	5.8	6.8	11.3	16.1
1980	7.0	7.4	13.1	17.8
1981	7.5	7.9	14.2	19.6
1982	9.5	9.4	17.3	23.2

Source: Council of Economic Advisers, *Economic Report of the President* (Washington, D.C.: U.S. Government Printing Office, 1989), p. 353.

While the unemployment rate for most types of workers rises during a business downturn, it rises much more for some types of workers than for others. The data in Table 3 indicate that, during recessions, unemployment rates for teenage workers and for black workers tend to rise about 60 percent more than the overall unemployment rate. However, the unemployment rate for female workers generally rises a little less than the overall rate. Statistics for workers in different industries or in different parts of the country also reflect the uneven burden of unemployment among workers. During recessions, sales of consumer durables like new homes and cars generally fall sharply, causing extremely high unemployment for workers in building trades and in the auto industry. Since the auto industry and its suppliers are concentrated in certain parts of the United States, some states—Michigan, in particular—are hit harder by economic downturns. The unemployment costs of recessions therefore tend to be borne disproportionately by workers in such states.

Inflation and the Business Cycle

The economic disadvantages of business cycles are not necessarily limited to the costs associated with high unemployment. There is also evidence that business cycles are a cause of inflation. During economic "booms," when demand for goods and services grows rapidly, bottlenecks in the production process are likely to arise. Rapid economic growth often frustrates the economy's ability to quickly match unemployed workers with job openings; the newly created jobs may arise in geographic areas or in industries with relatively few unemployed workers. The consequence of production bottlenecks is that wages and prices are bid up, causing inflation. (Such bouts of inflation are examples of the demand-pull theories of inflation discussed in Chapter 17.) Consider the economic experience of the United States since World War II. The average postwar inflation rate is about 5 percent per year. Inflation rates of over 6 percent correspond to upturns in the business cycle; the figure for downturns is less than 3 percent.

INFLATION AND UNEMPLOYMENT: IS THERE A TRADE-OFF?

Most vexing for policy-makers is the possibility that there may be a trade-off between inflation and unemployment. If so, achievement of price stability would require unemployment, or full employment would require inflation.

British economist A. W. Phillips published an important paper related to inflation and unemployment in 1958,[1] in which he used actual data to show that there may be a long-run trade-off between inflation and unemployment.[2]

[1]See A. W. Phillips, "Relation Between Unemployment and the Rate of Change of Money Wage Rates in the United Kingdom, 1861–1957," *Economica* 25 (November 1958), pp. 283–99.

[2]Actually, neoclassical economist Irving Fisher was the first to notice the inverse relation between inflation rates and unemployment rates. See Irving Fisher, "A Statistical Relation Between Unemployment and Price Changes," *International Labor Review* (June 1926), pp. 785–92. Reprinted posthumously as "I Discovered the Phillips Curve," *Journal of Political Economy* (March–April 1973), pp. 496–502.

Phillips's data are based on money wage rates; since they follow the inflation rate, money wage changes may serve as a proxy for inflation. Phillips's data showed an almost hundred-year (long-run) inverse relation between inflation and unemployment for the United Kingdom. The data also indicated that the cost of less unemployment is higher inflation rates or, conversely, that the cost of lowering the inflation rate is a higher unemployment rate.

Phillips's study caused a great stir among macroeconomists because an inverse relation between unemployment rates and inflation rates means that the long-run aggregate supply curve is positively sloped, not a vertical line. In other words, higher levels of output and employment are invariably associated with higher price levels. (Alternatively, a long-run curve relating unemployment rates with inflation rates would be negatively sloped.) This means that long-run income and employment growth must come at the expense of inflation. If Phillips is right, the promise of achieving one economic goal (price stability or full employment) means that the other economic problem cannot be solved simultaneously. The policy-maker must choose between problems in a no-win trade-off.

Phillips Curves: Hypothetical and Actual

Phillips curve:
A graph showing the relation between the rate of inflation and the unemployment rate.

Before analyzing American experience with inflation rates and unemployment, examine a hypothetical **Phillips curve** and what it means. Figure 4 depicts a hypothetical relation between the unemployment rate and the inflation rate that Phillips's long-run data suggested. Note that in place of the level of income or employment, the unemployment rate appears on the horizontal axis. When these data are displayed against the inflation rate, a curve of negative slope results.

Phillips's basic argument is straightforward: A reduction in unemployment comes at the expense of higher inflation. The degree of the inverse relation, however, depends on the initial rate of inflation. At higher rates of inflation, the trade-off is less severe. For instance, as Figure 4 shows, a reduction of 2 percent in inflation from an initial rate of 16 percent causes unemployment to rise by only 1 percent (from 4 to 5 percent), whereas a similar reduction at a lower inflation level (from 10 to 8 percent) may force unemployment to rise by a full 3½ percent (from 8 percent to 11½ percent).

In the analysis of the Phillips curve, inflation is a necessary evil. Resource scarcities are such that higher and higher inflation rates are required to coax the resources into use. Likewise, lower and lower rates of inflation are insufficient to put large quantities of labor resources to work. The economy requires inflation to achieve high rates of employment and real income growth. Alternatively, the cost of price stability at low rates of inflation is high unemployment, low income, and lower growth rates.

Neither new Keynesian nor new classical economists believe that there is a *long-term* trade-off between inflation and unemployment, but what is the evidence for a short-run Phillips curve for the United States? Figure 5 relates the inflation rate to the unemployment rate for the years 1960–1989, using the GNP price deflator as the measure of inflation. From looking at the raw data of Figure 5, it appears that trade-offs are indeed a fact! Note, for example, that a reduction in the unemployment rate between 1967 and 1969 was accompanied by a rise in the inflation rate.

FIGURE 4

According to A. W. Phillips, there is an inverse relation between the inflation rate and the rate of unemployment. At an inflation rate of 16 percent, the unemployment rate is 4 percent. If the inflation rate falls to 14 percent, unemployment rises to 5 percent. At zero inflation, unemployment is very high.

A Hypothetical Phillips Curve Relating Inflation and Unemployment

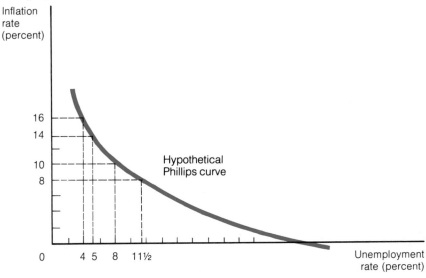

As we get closer to the present, the trade-off still appears to hold for some time periods. Look at the movements between 1972 and 1973, between 1976 and 1979, and between 1981 and 1982. In the latter case, a reduction in the inflation rate from 9.4 to 6.0 percent was accompanied by an increase in the unemployment rate from 7.6 to 9.7 percent, a dramatic increase with all sorts of economic and political consequences. The inverse relation appeared as recently as 1986–1989, with gradual increases in the inflation rate (from 2.6 to 4.1 percent) contrasted with a gradual reduction in the aggregate unemployment rate (from 7.0 to 5.3 percent).

Consider, however, the relation between the unemployment rate and the inflation rate for other recent time periods. Between 1969 and 1970, 1971 and 1972, 1973 and 1974, 1975 and 1976, 1979 and 1981, and 1982 and 1986, it appears that a positive rather than inverse relation existed between the unemployment rate and the inflation rate. Does this positive relation mean that Phillips's theory is wrong, or does it mean that the sometimes positive relation indicates a movement of the trade-off to higher and higher rates of unemployment and inflation? The answer given by some economists—mostly new classical and new Keynesian—is that the Phillips relation must be viewed from both short-run and long-run perspectives and that expectations play a major role in explaining cycles of inflation and unemployment.

A Phillips Curve Adjusted for Expectations

When the Phillips relation is analyzed both from short- and long-run views, the expectations of consumers and producers regarding the inflation rate become important. Suppose that the inflation rate is zero, the unemployment

FIGURE 5

Combined Unemployment and Inflation Rates, 1960–1989

The Phillips relation—the theory that increases in inflation rates are associated with decreases in unemployment rates, and vice versa—appears to hold over selected years in the United States. Shaded areas represent possible Phillips trade-offs between inflation and unemployment.

Source: Council of Economic Advisers, *Economic Report of the President* (Washington, D.C.: U.S. Government Printing Office, 1990), pp. 299, 338.
Note: Inflation data based on GNP price deflator; unemployment rates apply to civilian workers.

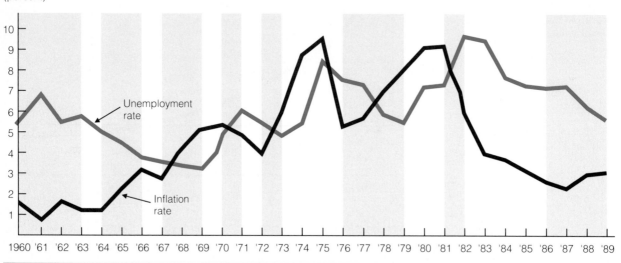

Short-run Phillips curve:
A downward-sloping curve indicating an inverse relation between the rate of inflation and the unemployment rate, holding constant the inflation expectations of workers.

rate is at the natural rate U_N, and that people do not anticipate any inflation. In terms of Figure 6, the initial state of the economy is depicted by point *a* on the **short-run Phillips curve** ($SRPC_0$). Now suppose that a sudden increase in aggregate demand causes some shortages to develop and drives the inflation rate up to 3 percent. The economy will move to point *b* on $SRPC_0$, and the unemployment rate will temporarily fall to U_1. The reason for this temporary decrease in unemployment is that workers who anticipate zero inflation remain willing to work for the initial nominal wage, since they do not anticipate inflation. Employers who correctly perceive that inflation reduces the real wage are then willing to employ more workers.[3]

Once workers adjust their expectations to the new inflation rate of 3 percent, the unemployment rate will again rise to the natural rate U_N. Workers will no longer be willing to work for the old nominal wage but will remain willing to work only at a new nominal wage, which is 3 percent higher. Employers will then have no incentive to retain the additional workers. In terms of Figure 6, the Phillips curve will have shifted upward from $SRPC_0$ to

---

[3]The so-called "fooling model" of expectations adjustment was developed in large part by Milton Friedman in "The Role of Monetary Policy," *American Economic Review* (March 1968), pp. 1–17.

FIGURE 6   **Short-Run and Long-Run Phillips Curves**

Each short-run Phillips curve shows the trade-off between the inflation rate and the unemployment rate when expectations are fixed. If people expect zero inflation and the inflation rate rises to 3 percent, the unemployment rate will fall to U_1. Once expectations adjust to an inflation rate of 3 percent, the short-run Phillips curve shifts upward, from $SRPC_0$ to $SRPC_3$, and the unemployment rate rises back to U_N. The long-run Phillips curve, LRPC, assumes fully anticipated inflation. It indicates that the natural rate of unemployment will exist in the long run no matter what rate of inflation occurs—as long as the rate of inflation is anticipated.

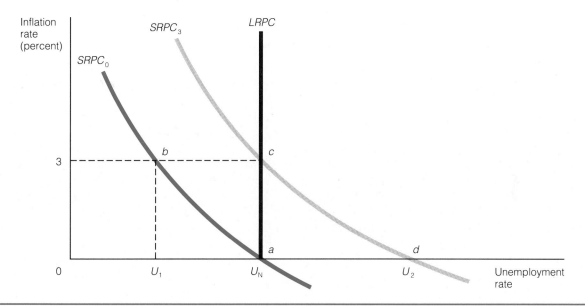

$SRPC_3$. This upward shift will equal the 3 percent increase in the anticipated rate of inflation. In Figure 6, the economy will move from point *a* to point *c* by way of point *b*. When the actual inflation rate exceeds the expected inflation rate, unemployment will temporarily drop below the natural rate. Then, when workers' expectations of inflation rise to the new inflation rate, the unemployment rate will rise from U_1 to U_N.

By similar logic, we can see that an unanticipated decrease in the inflation rate will temporarily lead to an increase in unemployment. Suppose that after workers adjust their expectations to the new inflation rate of 3 percent, a decrease in aggregate demand causes the inflation rate to fall to zero percent. Workers who fail to realize that inflation has ceased will continue to demand 3 percent annual increases in their nominal wages; they view these increases as necessary to keep their real wages from falling. With constant prices, real wages will rise, causing employers to reduce the number of workers they employ. The economy will temporarily move to point *d* in Figure 6. The unemployment rate will remain above the natural rate until workers adjust their inflation expectations downward to the actual level of inflation. This will shift the Phillips curve downward from $SRPC_3$ to $SRPC_0$.

This suggests that whenever the actual inflation rate differs from the anticipated rate, the unemployment rate will move away from the natural rate. Higher-than-anticipated inflation will cause unemployment to fall temporarily below the natural rate. A lower-than-anticipated rate of inflation will push unemployment above the natural rate.

If we make the assumption that workers eventually come to anticipate existing inflation rates, we see that *in the long run,* there is no trade-off between unemployment and inflation. As the economy moves from a low inflation rate to a higher rate, unemployment falls but then returns to the natural rate. In the long run, unemployment will be unaffected by changes in the inflation rate, as illustrated in Figure 6 by the vertical **long-run Phillips curve** (*LRPC*).

Long-run Phillips curve: A vertical line at the natural rate of unemployment; indicates that if there is enough time for workers' expectations to adjust to the actual rate of inflation, then changes in the inflation rate produce no change in the rate of unemployment.

Prices, Wages, and Employment Adjustment: A Keynesian Perspective

Some economists, notably new Keynesians, argue that misconceptions or "fooling" of laborers is not necessary to explain the slow adjustment of nominal wages to changed aggregate demand conditions over the short run. Price level changes, such as inflation, are felt immediately at the grocery store or at the gas pump—and confirmed, certainly, in countless media reports. Workers, in short, catch on quickly.[4]

Although workers may be temporarily fooled into supplying more or less labor due to misconceptions about real wages, other reasons may be stressed for the slowness of nominal wages to adjust to changed demand conditions. Certain forces work on firms and on workers to avoid frequent or unnecessary job changes. Employers typically spend considerable time and money for on-the-job training specific to their needs. These trained workers are paid a premium (over untrained workers), a premium that workers might lose by moving to another job or occupation. For this reason, during periods of rising demand and lagging nominal wages, workers will hold out and actually work harder in anticipation of future nominal wages adjustments to an increased price level.

Additionally, a large number of industrial workers are covered by union contracts—often lasting up to three years—that also contribute to sticky wages. These union contracts are designed to avoid strikes and costly and frequent negotiations with workers. They remain in force whether aggregate demand rises or falls. Though these contracts often contain escalator or cost-of-living clauses that provide for nominal wage increases over the contract period (often through some tie with an index of prices), they seldom provide for a full increase. Individual firms will not ordinarily agree to tie fully the wages paid their laborers to a price index, since the increase in aggregate demand that precipitated the higher price level may not materialize for their own product. A computer firm that made such an agreement, for example, might find itself with higher wage costs and no increase in the nominal demand for computers.

Wage contracts are not tied to aggregate demand conditions, and nominal wages are only partially adjusted to changing demand and price conditions. Aspects of the employer-worker relationship and long-run wage contracting, in addition to short-run misconceptions of workers, help explain the stickiness of nominal wages over short-run periods. Just as expectations catch up with actual price behavior, workers will also request that nominal

---

[4]A fuller discussion of these issues may be found in Robert J. Gordon, *Macroeconomics,* 5th ed. (Glenview, IL: Scott, Foresman, 1990), pp. 195–99.

wage increases match price level increases when union and other bargaining contracts come up for renegotiation, especially during expansionary or boom periods of high output and employment. Workers will also be convinced to negotiate nominal wage cuts during periods of recession and low employment. Ultimately, real wages readjust to equilibrium levels of employment and output.

CAUSES OF BUSINESS CYCLES

Eighty years ago, the primary goal of some economists was to gain an understanding of the business cycle and its causes. Although many economists at the time believed that economic science would one day arrive at a single explanation for business cycles, this has not yet proven to be the case. Instead, we now have many competing theories of business cycles. The first set of theories can be described as investment theories because they suggest that the causes of the business cycle can be traced to variations in the level of private investment spending. Recall that Keynesians emphasize destabilizing tendencies in the economy, especially the uncertainty of profit expectations on the part of business investors.

The second group of theories examines a wide variety of causal factors, all of them external to the private economy. For instance, monetary theorists emphasize the unpredictability of the money supply process and its impact on the economy. Theories of a political business cycle emphasize the effects of political institutions on the general economy. We devote the remainder of this chapter to an examination of the various theories of the causes of business cycles.

Investment Theories

The central proposition of the various investment theories of the business cycle is that any change in the level of private investment spending will have a significant impact on the level of GNP. Investment theories include many of the ideas of Keynes and his followers, particularly the concept of the investment multiplier (see Chapter 10). In a simple Keynesian model of the economy, the investment multiplier is expressed as the reciprocal of the marginal propensity to save.

$$k_I = \frac{1}{1 - MPC} = \frac{1}{MPS},$$

where k_I is the investment multiplier, MPC is the marginal propensity to consume, and MPS is the marginal propensity to save. The investment multiplier enables statisticians and economic forecasters to determine how much a given change in autonomous investment spending, I, will affect an overall change in GNP, Y.

$$\Delta Y = k_I \Delta I = \frac{1}{MPS} \Delta I.$$

What does this mean in practical terms? Suppose that the economy is initially in equilibrium at an output level of $500 billion when business investors' expectations about future profits suddenly change for the worse and businesses reduce investment spending by $10 billion. By how much will GNP fall from its initial equilibrium level of $500 billion? By $10 billion or by more than $10 billion?

In Chapter 10, we saw that a reduction in investment spending causes an initial decline in income, which in turn reduces both consumption and saving. The reduction in consumption spending reduces income, which further reduces consumption and saving, and so on until a new, lower level of GNP is reached. The amount of the reduction in GNP depends on the values of the *MPC* and the *MPS*. As seen above, the multiplier is equal to the reciprocal of the *MPS*. For example, if the *MPS* is one-fourth, or 0.25, the reduction in GNP will be the multiplier ($1 \div 0.25 = 4$) multiplied by the initial reduction in autonomous spending, $10 billion. The initial GNP of $500 billion will fall to $460 billion, a new equilibrium level.

Combining the notion of the investment multiplier with the possibility of volatile investment spending results in a potential explanation of business cycles. A group of economists associated with Keynes argued that business firms typically adjust their capital stock in response to changes in sales. In an industry experiencing rising sales, business firms respond by increasing investment. The increases in investment then, through the multiplier process, lead to increases in sales, which bring about additional increases in business investment and national income. This view of the world suggests that even a minor increase in aggregate demand can lead to a major economic upswing, as can a minor business downturn lead to recession. In the case of a business downturn, these economists argued that business firms would respond to decreased sales by canceling orders for new plant and equipment, a decline in investment spending that would then lead to a larger decrease in national income.

Today, relatively few economists view the relationship between business sales and business investment in such rigid terms. Nonetheless, many economists still attribute business cycles to changes in business investment. The following sections discuss various causes of business investment fluctuation.

Business Expectations. Many economists have concluded that the level of investment spending in the economy depends largely on expectations of future economic conditions. Will the economy grow or stagnate? Will interest rates go up or down? Will inflation increase or decrease? All of these questions weigh heavily on business decision-makers. In Chapter 17, we mentioned the concepts of adaptive expectations and rational expectations. Both concepts have been used to explain the investment behavior that leads to business cycles. Pessimistic forecasts naturally lead to less and less investment spending, while optimism about the future leads to more investment. Keynes even spoke of "animal spirits"—unexplained changes in business investors' decisions leading to large overall changes in spending.

Supply Shocks. Sudden changes in the supply of certain resources owing to natural disasters or international conflicts may also initiate business cycles. In addition to their effect on the costs of production, these supply shocks may drastically alter business expectations. The OPEC supply shock in the 1970s is a case in point. The sudden cutback in the availability of oil drove up prices for gasoline and all other petroleum products and affected output around the world. The OPEC crisis also shook investor confidence, contributing to the recessionary conditions that plagued many economies for several years afterward. (A more recent oil shock is discussed on page 400.)

Creative Destruction. Another theory focuses on the role of the entrepreneur, the person whose new ideas and new products offer expanding opportunities for profit. According to Joseph Schumpeter, the contributions of entrepreneurship to the economic process—the new commodity, the new technology, the new source of supply, the new type of organization—spur economic growth by "destroying" old ways of doing things.[5] Innovators who succeed at cutting costs or fulfilling previously unmet demands earn economic profits, and these profits attract entry by new firms that rush to emulate the discovery. In the scramble to obtain a share of the profits, however, overinvestment by new entrants occurs, and the market becomes saturated. Some of the firms go bankrupt, and a period of reversal follows, precipitating a downturn in economic activity. In microcosm, the recent upheaval in the computer industry in which a temporary boom has been followed by lagging profits and a rash of bankruptcies illustrates the sequence. The cycle finally turns up again as new ideas and new profit opportunities arise. To Schumpeter, the business cycle—a cycle of creation and destruction of profit opportunities—is a necessary accompaniment to capitalist development. This point of view has been called the **creative destruction theory.**

Creative destruction theory:
A business cycle theory that emphasizes the role of the entrepreneur as an innovator supplying new products and services, thereby creating new profit opportunities and destroying old ones; competitors follow the innovator's lead, which creates business cycles.

Monetary Theories

Monetary theories of the business cycle are based on the idea that business cycles arise from attempts by government to fine-tune the macroeconomy. In the case of monetary policy, decisions by the monetary authority (the Federal Reserve) made in the presence of implementation lags, in error, or in a conscious attempt to influence political outcomes destabilize the economy in one direction. A period follows during which the Federal Reserve takes necessary corrective action. The business cycle is thus thought to be generated by a stop-and-go monetary policy cycle.

To see how monetary policy might generate a business cycle, we return to the concept of a Phillips curve. The short- and long-run Phillips relations are depicted in Figure 7. In the short run there is a trade-off between inflation and unemployment, and in both Figure 7a and Figure 7b this trade-off is represented by a family of negatively sloped Phillips curves, each corresponding to a different expected rate of inflation.

Recall that the long-run Phillips curve is a vertical line at the natural rate of unemployment, U_N. When the expected rate of inflation is equal to the actual rate, the economy will be in long-run equilibrium with an unemployment rate equal to U_N. In other words, there is no trade-off between inflation and unemployment in the long run, and many possible inflation rates are consistent with long-run equilibrium.

Consider now the effects of an unforeseen increase in the rate of monetary expansion. In Figure 7a, the economy was initially in equilibrium at E_1

---

[5]Joseph A. Schumpeter, *Capitalism, Socialism, and Democracy,* 3rd ed. (New York: Harper & Row, 1950), esp. pp. 81–86.

FIGURE 7   Monetary Policy and the Business Cycle

The economy's long-run Phillips curve is *LRPC*, and several short-run Phillips curves (*SRPC*) are also shown. (a) An unexpected increase in money supply causes the unemployment rate to fall for a while from U_N to U_1, but ultimately its impact is to increase the rate of inflation that is consistent with the natural rate of unemployment. (b) An unexpected decrease in the money supply causes the opposite process of adjustment. Through these processes, uneven performance by money supply authorities can lead to cyclical behavior in the economy.

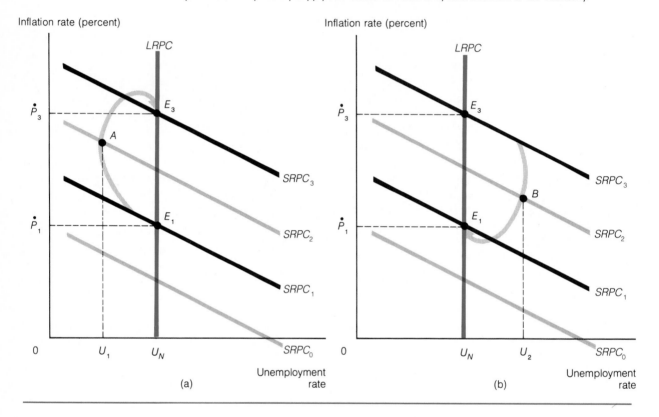

on the short-run Phillips curve $SRPC_1$, with unemployment at the natural rate and an inflation rate of $\dot{P}_1$. If individuals form their expectations about inflation adaptively, they will continue to expect an inflation rate of P_1 for a time. Because unexpected monetary expansion pushes the actual inflation rate higher than $\dot{P}_1$, however, some workers will believe that their real wage has risen, while employers will begin hiring additional workers in the mistaken belief that the demand for their products has increased. As a result, individuals will accept jobs for which the real wage will eventually turn out to be too low. Unemployment nevertheless falls, and the economy moves leftward along $SRPC_1$.

As workers and employers begin to recognize the more rapidly rising price level, they revise their expectations about inflation, and as a result, the short-run Phillips curve begins shifting to the right to $SRPC_2$. At some point, say A on $SRPC_2$, the unemployment rate reaches its lowest level at U_1 but then begins to rise again as individuals' expectations about inflation begin to catch up. A new equilibrium is eventually reached at E_3, when the expected rate of inflation is equal to the higher actual rate, $\dot{P}_3$. The unemployment rate returns to the natural rate. In the long run, the expansionary monetary policy did nothing more than raise the inflation rate from $\dot{P_1}$ to $\dot{P_3}$. In the short run, however, what looks like the expansionary phase of a business cycle was generated.

Suppose that the inflation rate $\dot{P_3}$ is viewed as too high, inducing the Federal Reserve to take corrective measures. In particular, suppose that the Federal Reserve adopts a policy of reducing the rate of growth in the money supply. The adjustment process now operates in reverse. Beginning from E_3 in Figure 7b, the inflation rate starts to fall, but workers and employers continue to expect inflation rate $\dot{P_3}$. Some workers will be fooled into thinking their real wage has fallen as employers begin laying off workers in response to a mistaken belief that demand has fallen. Individuals will refuse job offers for which the real wage will eventually turn out to have been acceptable. Unemployment rises, and the economy moves rightward along $SRPC_3$.

Downward revisions in the expected inflation rate shift the short-run Phillips curve downward and to the left. The unemployment rate reaches its highest level, U_2, at B on $SRPC_2$ and then falls again until a new equilibrium is attained at E_1, when inflationary expectations catch up. When that occurs, the unemployment rate is again at the natural rate, U_N, and the expected and actual inflation rates have fallen from $\dot{P_3}$ to $\dot{P_1}$. The short-run adjustment process looks like the contractionary phase of a business cycle. Using historical data, monetarists have argued that mistaken money supply adjustments by the Federal Reserve have been responsible for business cycle swings, including the Great Depression, as described in Focus, "The Monetary Explanation of the Great Depression."

It is important to keep in mind that some degree of surprise is required for monetary policy changes to generate a business cycle. As discussed in Chapter 18, if individuals form their expectations about the effects of monetary policy rationally rather than adaptively, then monetary policy will have a milder impact on the levels of the real variables in the economy. Consumers, workers, savers, and investors will adjust if expectations are rational, but cycles of unemployment and income may be generated until expectations are fully adjusted to new conditions.

POLITICAL BUSINESS CYCLES

Political business cycle:
A business cycle that results from the manipulation of policy tools by incumbent politicians hoping to stimulate the economy prior to an election and thereby improve their reelection chances.

Some economists have suggested that there is a **political business cycle.**[6] Incumbent politicians pursue economic policies that promote their reelection, and as a consequence the economy goes through a business cycle every four years. In an attempt to enhance their reelection prospects, incumbent politicians promote expansionary policies prior to election day—tax cuts, increased government spending, and greater money supply growth. These policies have politically popular consequences in the short run: lower unemployment and interest rates, along with increased real income (output). Immediately after the election, the politicians often reverse course. To limit the higher inflation rates that the reelection strategy fosters, they raise taxes and cut spending, and money supply growth is reduced. The result of these political moves is a business cycle whose length is roughly equal to the interval between elections.

---

[6]The political business cycle idea is usually attributed to William Nordhaus, "The Political Business Cycle," *Review of Economics and Statistics* 42 (April 1975), pp. 169–90.

FOCUS The Monetary Explanation of the Great Depression

The Great Depression, occurring over the decade of the 1930s in the United States and abroad, was a period of record low levels of employment, industrial production, and real income.

Monetarists Milton Friedman and Anna Schwartz lay the blame for the Great Depression on a series of blunders by the Federal Reserve Board.[a] Between August 1929 and March 1933, the Federal Reserve allowed the money supply to decrease by 35 percent. In defense of the Fed, the monetary base did grow during that period, but rapid decreases in the money multiplier led to a decrease in the money supply. Some historians have argued that the Fed thought that its policies during that critical period were expansionary. However, other Fed decisions during the period seemed to be designed to prolong the economic crisis. For example, the board allowed the New York Federal Reserve Bank to lower the discount rate—a proper countercyclical policy—only if the district bank ceased its purchases of securities on the open market, a decision that prevented the New York Federal Reserve Bank from using its primary tool for increasing the money supply. Moreover, the Board of Governors voted in early 1933 to reduce the monetary base by $125 million, and twice in 1937 the board raised the reserve requirements it imposed on member banks. The latter action was sufficient to choke off an economic recovery that had begun in late 1934. Friedman and Schwartz cite additional evidence to support their main point that the actions of the

[a]Milton Friedman and Anna Schwartz, *A Monetary History of the United States, 1867–1960* (Princeton: Princeton University Press, 1963). For some different perspectives on the cause of the Great Depression, see Karl Brunner, ed., *The Great Depression Revisited* (Boston: Kluwer-Nijhoff, 1981).

monetary authority during the 1930s helped prolong and deepen the worst economic contraction in U.S. history.

Other, less technical reasons might be offered for the passivity of the Federal Reserve System during the banking panics of the early 1930s. One possible reason is that the Federal Reserve Board did not understand the critical impact that bank failures might have on the money supply and economic activity. Bank failures feed on themselves by lowering confidence in all banks. The rush to acquire "safe" currency on the part of money holders will increase the currency-deposit ratio (see Chapter 16) and further reduce the ability of the entire banking system to expand loans and the money supply. The effect is to strongly discourage business activity and consumer spending. The Federal Reserve System chalked up small bank failures to "bad management," not realizing that such failures put big-city banks in jeopardy. Another reason offered for the apparent failure of the Federal Reserve System to soften the jolt of the Great Depression was internal jealousy between the Board of Governors in Washington, D.C., and the Federal Reserve Bank of New York. Until 1928, the New York Bank was the dominant political force within the System. The New York Bank strongly argued for large open market purchases of securities to stave off bank panics (a policy that might have been effective), but to no avail. The Board of Governors, in a fight to obtain control of the monetary system, resisted the policy.

Citing such poor historical performance by the Federal Reserve, Friedman has argued that a rule governing the rate of growth of the money supply over time would be superior to the present system of discretionary monetary management. Friedman's policy proposal for a monetary rule is discussed in Chapters 17 and 18.

Do Political Business Cycles Exist?

Three main arguments have been raised against the concept of political business cycles. First, the model is said to be naive because it assumes that voters in a presidential election care only about inflation and unemployment. The critics note, correctly, that election results turn on a variety of issues, including foreign relations, the distribution of income, and the personalities of the candidates. A second criticism raises the question of timing. Monetarists in particular argue that monetary policy lags are long and unpredictable. Since the repercussions of a change in the rate of monetary expansion are not felt immediately but occur over a period of perhaps two years, it may be difficult for incumbents to chart an economic course that ensures their political support within the confines of a four-year election cycle.

The most important question, of course, is whether voters can be systematically fooled. If individuals are in fact shortsighted, then the political business cycle hypothesis would seem to be plausible. Under the rational expectations thesis, however, no such policy cycles can be manufactured because voters will foresee the consequences of reelection macroeconomic manipulation. Individuals would quickly revise upward their expectations about inflation when confronted with a higher rate of monetary expansion, thus deflating the political gain the incumbent had hoped for.

A number of attempts have been made to test various aspects of the political business cycle theory. Most of the direct tests consist of searches for patterns in unemployment rates or other macroeconomic variables during the periods surrounding congressional or presidential elections. The studies concerning the existence of a political business cycle have so far been inconclusive. This is not really surprising given the relatively few opportunities for observation and the ambiguous effects of election years in which different parties control the White House and Congress. Nonetheless, there is evidence on both sides of this issue, and the idea continues to intrigue economists. In this regard, Economics in Action, "Can Economics Help You Predict the Next Presidential Election?" at the end of this chapter offers a unique perspective on the Federal Reserve's possible involvement in the political business cycle.

The Austrian Theory of the Political Business Cycle

Economists who work in the tradition of the Austrian economic theorists of the late 1800s (Menger, Von Weiser, Böhm-Bawerk) are referred to as the neo-Austrian school of economics. These modern Austrians or neo-Austrians include Friedrich A. von Hayek, who won the Nobel Prize in economics in 1972.[7]

Neo-Austrian political business cycle:
A business cycle that results from political action to influence specific markets and industries rather than broad macroeconomic variables; microeconomic manipulation distorts industry-specific investment decisions and leads to a business cycle.

Following the lead of Hayek, the modern Austrians have presented a special theory of the political business cycle. The **neo-Austrian political business cycle** theory stresses two basic points. First, the inspiration for a political business cycle is microeconomic, not macroeconomic. Politicians do not manipulate aggregate economic variables such as the unemployment rate; rather, they seek to influence specific markets and industries, a process that in turn has aggregate economic consequences. To take just one small example, a subsidy to the domestic steel industry benefits steelworkers directly by providing jobs. It also represents a large expenditure on the part of government. If such legislation is carried out for many industries or for many separate economic groups, the government will incur huge costs, leading to a large deficit and subsequent macroeconomic problems.

The second neo-Austrian point is that real economic distortions and reductions in income result from politically inspired monetary expansions and contractions. In essence, the Austrians argue that politically inspired expansions and contractions in the money supply upset production plans by changing the nominal rate of interest. The process works in the following way: An unexpected and politically motivated expansion in the money supply creates

---

[7]Friedrich A. von Hayek, *Monetary Theory and the Trade Cycle* (New York: Harcourt Brace, 1932).

an artificially low rate of interest. In the division of labor between production for present and future consumption, the interest rate, which reflects the forces of real saving and investment, is the price that coordinates production plans efficiently. A low interest rate leads to an overinvestment in capital goods in the economy. In effect, the lower interest rate misleads investors; it provides them with a signal that is not compatible with the real plans of consumers and savers in the economy. The overinvestment in capital goods leads to huge losses on the part of investors and then to an economy-wide reduction in income and employment, or to what we normally call a recession. The recession will not end until the plans of producers of capital goods and producers of consumer goods are coordinated again—that is, until they plan according to the same relative price and interest rate data. The cycle bottoms out when the excess capital equipment caused by the overinvestment is depreciated and the accompanying economic losses cease.

The essential problem that the Austrian theory of the business cycle addresses is the distortion in relative prices and the loss of economic efficiency that results from a political manipulation of the money supply. The aggregate economic effects of this manipulation, such as inflation, are merely incidental to its impact on relative prices.

Moreover, the Austrian theory of the political business cycle focuses on groups of voters, not on voters in the aggregate. The question is not whether voters in general will respond positively or negatively to the inflation rate; it is how certain groups in the electorate will react to specific changes in public policies.

It is safe to say that there is no single theory of the business cycle. None of the hypotheses we have reviewed in this chapter provides a completely satisfactory explanation for the recurrent fluctuations in the general level of economic activity. At most, economists have developed a rich statistical and factual knowledge of business cycles. It remains to find a generally acceptable theory to explain these facts.

The Role of Government in Regulating the Business Cycle

In this chapter we have pointed out many of the costs associated with business cycles and discussed alternative theories about the cause of business cycles. One topic of ongoing debate among economists is the proper role of government in moderating business cycles. Essentially, there are two schools of thought. One group of economists advocates an active interventionist role by the government. Activists consider stabilization to be the primary economic role of government. Furthermore, they feel that economic policy should be modified frequently to take account of the latest changes in economic conditions. They advocate continuous fine-tuning of taxes, government spending, and interest rates to offset destabilizing changes that arise in the private sector. These activists feel that only the proper use of discretionary economic policy will assure a reasonably stable economy.

In contrast, many other economists feel that frequently changed government policy ends up having a destabilizing impact on the economy. Nonactivists advocate steady and predictable long-term policies by the government. For example, they would prefer that the central bank pursue a policy of steady monetary growth instead of making constant adjustments. Although there are several differences between the two groups, one essential difference is the confidence the groups place in economic forecasts.

Earlier in the chapter we discussed leading economic indicators. We saw that economic forecasters have had mixed success using these measures to predict upturns and downturns in the economy. Those who believe that future changes in the economy can be accurately predicted tend to advocate a more activist role for the government. They feel that it is irresponsible for the government to sit idly by when economic difficulties are apparent. In contrast, economists who are skeptical about the ability to make accurate forecasts tend to be less inclined to advocate government intervention. The fear is that forecasting errors will compromise any activist policy, as likely leading to destabilization as to stabilization.

SUMMARY

1. A business cycle is a recurrent but not predictable fluctuation in GNP. No two business cycles are exactly alike.

2. The four phases of a business cycle are expansion, peak, recession, and trough. The length of a cycle can be measured from peak to peak or from trough to trough. The intensity of an upturn or downturn in business activity is measured by the degree to which a peak or trough deviates from the long-run growth path of real GNP in the economy.

3. Economic forecasters try to predict economic upturns and downturns. Economic indicators are an integral part of the forecaster's tools. Leading economic indicators, economic variables that tend to turn up or down before a general business upturn or downturn, are key statistics for forecasters.

4. Investment theories of the business cycle stress the instability of private investment spending as a primary cause of economic fluctuations.

5. Other investment theories of the business cycle are the creative destruction theory of Joseph Schumpeter and those relating to business expectations. The expectations of businesspeople are also emphasized as an important determinant of investment spending in Keynesian theories of the business cycle.

6. The monetary theory of the business cycle sees the uneven and unpredictable management of the money supply by the Federal Reserve Board as the basic cause of economic fluctuations. Concern over Federal Reserve behavior has led some monetarists, such as Milton Friedman, to propose that discretionary authority over the money supply of the Federal Reserve be replaced with a rule to govern the growth of the money supply.

7. Some economists have identified the possibility that business cycles are politically inspired. Given short-sighted voters, incumbent politicians win reelection by inflating the economy prior to an election, driving down unemployment, and then allowing unemployment to rise and inflation to recede after the election. Each four years, the cycle is repeated, and so we say that there is a political business cycle. The evidence for this type of manipulation of the economy by politicians is inconclusive.

8. The modern Austrian theory of the political business cycle is that politicians intervene in specific markets and industries to affect specific groups of voters. Relative prices and interest rates in the economy are thus distorted, leading to an overinvestment in capital goods industries. This overinvestment must subsequently be wrenched out of the economy. These cyclical effects are caused by political manipulation of the money supply.

9. Economics has developed a rich factual understanding of business cycles, but no single plausible theory of the cycle has yet emerged.

KEY TERMS

business cycle	econometrics	short-run Phillips curve	political business cycle
recession	economic indicators	long-run Phillips curve	neo-Austrian political business cycle
depression	Phillips curve	creative destruction theory	

QUESTIONS FOR REVIEW AND DISCUSSION

1. Why do we say that business cycles are recurrent but not predictable?
2. To which theory of the business cycle would you attribute cycles caused by the following events?
   a. The Federal Reserve Board increases the money supply dramatically.
   b. Sales in the garment industry fall.
   c. The French suddenly change governments and close their doors to American goods.
   d. Major new oil reserves are discovered in Alaska.
3. An increase in the unemployment rate can be caused either by an increase in the number of persons who become unemployed during a year or by an increase in the average duration of unemployment. Which of these two factors do you think best explains rising unemployment rates during recessions?
4. How can the Federal Reserve Board cause a business cycle?
5. In a modern economy, information about the motives and activities of politicians is relatively easy to obtain, much easier than it was years ago. Does the availability of information mean that a political business cycle is presently more or less likely than in the past?
6. Do changes in leading economic indicators actually cause the changes in GNP?
7. What would macroeconomic policy-makers need to know in order to eliminate the business cycle?

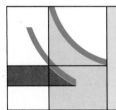

ECONOMICS IN ACTION
Can Economics Help You Predict the Next Presidential Election?

Political pollsters, TV commentators, special-interest groups, and especially political candidates would like to know what it takes to win a presidential election. Many believe that presidential elections are won through political organization, TV advertising, good luck, and charisma. Others are more likely to view economic variables such as personal income and inflation as critical variables. Some have tried to determine which economic variables are the most reliable indicators of success or failure for an incumbent candidate.

Ray Fair concluded that both the inflation rate and growth in real GNP are concerns to voters in presidential elections.[a] It is the *change* in these variables prior to the presidential election that matters, not their level. Incumbents who can boast of strong growth rates in GNP and low inflation rates usually remain in office; those who cannot, are voted out.

However, another predictor of election outcomes may be the Federal Reserve's handling of the money supply, M-1,

before the election. Although the Federal Reserve was designed as a semi-autonomous branch of government, some economists and political observers believe that the Federal Reserve behaves politically to protect its own interests and those of the party in power. David Meiselman has presented evidence that monetary expansions and contractions are possibly politically inspired. Figure 8 shows the rate of growth in M-1 prior to the last eight presidential elections. The vertical axis in each graph shows the six-month rate of change in M-1. The rates shown are annual percentages.

In four of the eight cases, money supply growth rapidly accelerated for six to twelve months prior to the election and contracted soon after.[b] In 1960, when Vice-President Richard Nixon lost to John Kennedy, and in 1976, when incumbent Gerald Ford lost to Jimmy Carter, money supply growth did not accelerate very rapidly in the year before the election. Interestingly enough, in the year prior to Ronald Reagan's landslide victory over Walter Mondale, money growth declined significantly. The rate declined six months prior to George Bush's election in 1988 and fell dramatically after the election. These elections emphasize the critics' contention that money growth prior to an election is not the only factor influencing election results.

Tracking economic variables such as the growth rate in per capita GNP and the rate of M-1 growth may not always

[a]See Ray C. Fair, "On Controlling the Economy to Win Elections," Cowles Foundation Discussion Paper No. 397, 1975; and "The Effect of Economic Events on Votes for President," *Review of Economics and Statistics* 60 (May 1978), pp. 159–73. For an excellent survey of the evidence, see Friedrich Schneider and Bruno S. Frey, "Politico-Economic Models of Macroeconomic Policy: A Review of the Empirical Evidence," in Thomas D. Willett, ed., *Political Business Cycles* (Durham, N.C.: Duke University Press, 1988), pp. 239–75.

[b]David I. Meiselman, "The Political Monetary Cycle," *Wall Street Journal* (January 10, 1984), p. 32.

FIGURE 8

These graphs show the relation of the growth rate of the money supply, M-1, to presidential elections between 1960 and 1988. Notice that in most cases, the money supply increased sharply before the election. This finding suggests that there may be a link between monetary policy and elections.

Sources: David I. Meiselman, "The Political Monetary Cycle," *Wall Street Journal* (January 10, 1984), p. 32; and *Federal Reserve Bulletin,* various issues.

Money Supply and Presidential Elections

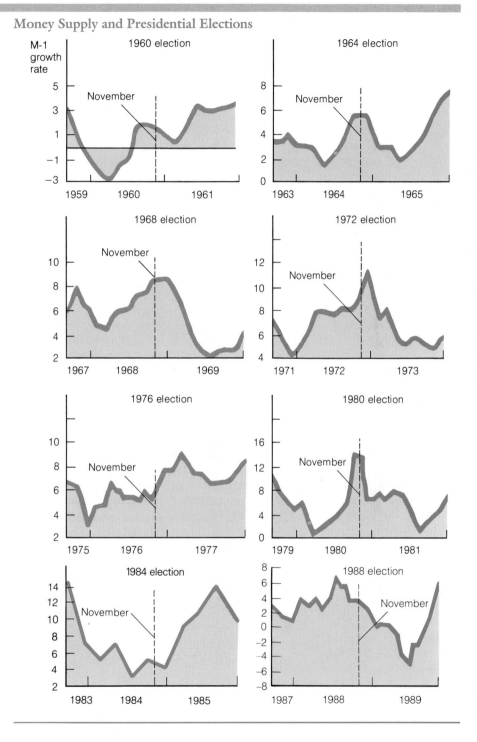

allow for accurate predictions of presidential election outcomes. However, such an analysis does provide interesting evidence of how closely our economic health is related to the four-year cycle of presidential elections.

Question

How might the unemployment rate be a predictor of election outcomes? Would it likely be more important in congressional contests or in presidential elections?

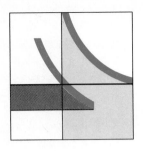

20

Economic Growth and Productivity

A full-employment economy without inflation is the major goal of macro-economic policy. But achievement of this goal does not necessarily mean that an economy is growing over the long run. Full employment and price stability surely affect long-run economic growth prospects, but factors such as population, natural resources, capital growth, and improvements in technology also determine the economy's future.

Long-run growth has been the key to the United States' prosperity. The **standard of living,** usually defined as the quantity of real goods and services that the average citizen is able to consume per year, has risen by an average of 2 to 3 percent per year for more than 150 years in America. Other nations have not experienced such good fortune. Many developing nations in Asia, Africa, and Latin America, for example, are stymied in their growth prospects because of a lack of productive labor or capital equipment or because population is growing as fast as or faster than output of real goods and services.

Unfortunately, there is some evidence of a slowdown in long-run growth rates in the United States. Is this slowdown temporary or is it a permanent state of affairs owing to the fixed or dwindling supplies of some of our natural resources? Will future generations of Americans suffer the effects of a shrinking economy, or are there economic policies that might ensure steady prosperity? This chapter attempts to provide insight into such questions. After reading Chapter 20 you should understand

- how economic growth is defined and some of the factors that lead to growth.
- the insights of the classical economists into the growth process.
- how aggregate demand and labor productivity are key elements in explaining economic growth.
- some of the features of U.S. economic growth, past and present.

Standard of living:
The real value of the quantity of goods and services consumed by the average member of the economy.

THE MEANING OF ECONOMIC GROWTH

Economic growth:
Increases in real GNP or real per capita GNP over time.

Real per capita GNP:
Real GNP divided by the population size; real output per person in the economy.

Economic growth actually has two definitions. It may simply refer to increases in real GNP, the value of the annual output of final goods and services in the economy adjusted for inflation. While this measure certainly tells us whether overall economic performance has improved, it does not tell us much about whether the average citizen is better or worse off than at some previous time.

An increase in **real per capita GNP** is a more accurate measure of economic growth. If real GNP increases by 4 percent over some period and population increases by 2 percent, real economic growth per capita has taken place. By contrast, a population increase of 6 percent with 4 percent growth in real output means that the average citizen is worse off, that economic decline has occurred in per capita terms.

Both measures are useful for understanding growth processes. For example, a statement that Mexico's real GNP grew at a rate of 3 percent last year tells us that some of the prerequisites for growth exist in Mexico. Likewise, to say that per capita GNP grew at only 1½ percent last year indicates that Mexico may be having population problems, since per capita income growth depends on population growth. Both measures, however, are merely statistical concepts; economists generally recognize that neither measure, no matter how useful for comparison purposes, can tell us definitively about the quality of life or the distribution of wealth in a society.

The Causes of Growth

The causes of economic growth are complex. We have already pinpointed some of the important short-run requirements of economic growth: Adequate employment of productive resources, price stability, efficient allocation of resources, and other such conditions generally ensure a rising standard of living.

To sustain long-run growth in real GNP, however, an economy must enjoy steady growth in population, natural resources, productivity of labor and resources, capital formation, human capital, and technological improvement, encouraged by a free-market environment and free-trade policies.

Population. Population may be detrimental to growth in real per capita GNP in many modern nations, but under certain conditions, an expanding population may be essential to growth. During the industrialization of the United States in the nineteenth century, rapid population growth, much of it achieved by immigration, fueled a phenomenal economic growth rate. On the supply side, growth in population and labor supply led to increased efficiency in production through higher productivity in the use of machinery and natural resources. Mass production such as assembly-line techniques greatly improved the productivity of labor through increased specialization. On the demand side, higher population led to increased demand for all goods and services, making possible mass production and greater consumption. Population growth is therefore an ingredient in growth, but increases in population by themselves are insufficient for sustained economic growth. As we will see later in this chapter, rampant or unrestrained population increases may retard, halt, or even reverse any progress in per capita GNP.

Natural Resources. Every society is endowed with some quantity of land and natural resources such as fresh water, forests, and minerals. The United States, the Soviet Union, and many developing countries have large quantities of both. Possession of land and natural resources may make growth easier, but it will not guarantee growth; nor will lack of natural resources prevent growth. Japan has a small quantity of land and natural resources, yet Japan's post–World War II growth rate has been greater than that of most other countries.

By themselves, natural resources are valueless. They must be developed by labor and capital. Improvements in technology, moreover, may make resources more productive—as in fertilizing land—or even contribute to the development and invention of new resources. Aluminum, for example, is an invented alloy. It is a common misconception that the quantity of certain natural resources is absolutely fixed in supply. For example, as technology develops, it becomes possible to tap oil reserves at previously unreachable depths. New technology also may create opportunities to profitably extract oil from shale. Should the supply of oil ever begin to run short, new technology would likely bring alternative fuel sources to the market. Technological change continuously alters the relative scarcity of natural resources.

Productivity of labor:
Output per worker over any given period of time.

Productivity of Labor. Economic growth is very closely tied to the **productivity of labor**—how much output per hour, week, and so on, results from labor input. Labor's productivity depends on a number of factors, including the quantity (population size) and quality (degree of education and skill) of the labor supply, the stock of capital and other resources each laborer has to work with, and the technology available for production. Educational development and on-the-job training of laborers—growth in human capital—is a rather obvious requirement for productivity increases, but productivity increases are also closely linked to capital formation and technology.

Capital Formation and Infrastructure. A fourth ingredient of economic growth is growth in the size and quality of the capital stock—productive assets like buildings, machinery, and equipment used in production and the infrastructure, the roads, bridges, and communications systems used in moving goods and disseminating information. (For a discussion of the importance of infrastructure as a determinant of economic growth, see Economics in Action, "Infrastructure and Economic Growth," at the end of this chapter.) Labor productivity—output per worker—is enhanced when the stock of capital available grows faster than the labor supply. When capital is growing faster than the labor supply, capital is said to be deepening. **Capital deepening** has occurred throughout most of the economic history of the United States. In contrast, many countries experience rapid population growth and little capital accumulation, which causes labor productivity to fall and adversely affects the growth potential of these countries.

Capital deepening:
Increases in the total stock of capital in conjunction with increases in the ratio of the capital stock to the labor force; occurs when the capital stock grows at a faster rate than the labor force.

Increases in capital stock are costly, however. Resources, including time, must be sacrificed to produce capital goods that are not directly consumable, so capital growth requires saving or abstention from current consumption. For new investments in machinery, buildings, and equipment to grow, society's ability to save must grow. The reward for saving is greater future growth in either consumable goods or in more capital stock. In the latter sense, economic growth is cumulative: It feeds on itself by using capital to produce more capital.

Improvements in Technology. Technological growth and invention—improvements in the methods by which goods and services are produced and sold—is another key to economic growth. The Industrial Revolution of the eighteenth and nineteenth centuries in Europe and the United States ushered in the age of mechanization, increasing the productivity of labor and natural resources. The result has been the highest standards of living for the greatest numbers of people in the recorded history of humanity. Such living standards would be unthinkable without the invention of items such as the steam engine, the spinning jenny, assembly-line production, and indoor plumbing. Who could have imagined twenty or thirty years ago, for example, that a high-speed digital computer no larger than a breadbox would be within the reach of the average American to calculate income taxes, store recipes, or play games on? Technology and invention have been responsible for nothing less than the modern world.

The Market Environment. Most Western economists believe that the market environment surrounding the growth in, among other things, natural resources, labor productivity, and capital formation is a large contributing factor to economic growth. A competitive market system, many believe, encourages invention and rapid innovation. Those holding this view generally argue that free-trade policies also enhance a country's ability to grow economically; such policies enable the country to specialize in the production of the goods and services at which it is most efficient. However, Japan's experience shows that growth can also occur in a restrictive environment; despite the Japanese government's elaborate system of barriers to internal and external trade, the country has achieved a remarkable record of economic growth since 1950.

The Production Possibilities Frontier Revisited

All the fundamental elements of long-run economic growth may be summarized in terms of a production possibilities frontier. A production possibilities frontier, introduced in Chapter 2, shows the choices available to society in producing two goods given a fixed quantity of resources—labor, capital, and natural resources—and assuming a given state of technology. If society is positioned on the production frontier, it is fully employing and efficiently allocating all resources and utilizing technology to its best advantage. However, most societies, even highly efficient ones, are at times positioned inside the frontier because of unemployment or underemployment of resources. Societies cannot advance beyond the frontier because of absolute limits at any given time in the quantity and quality of resources.

Figure 1 shows production possibilities frontiers for two economic societies—country X and country Y, respectively—both of which must choose production levels for consumption goods and capital goods. Each country is assumed to possess a similar resource base and the same technology. Country X's initial choice between capital goods and consumer goods is labeled A in Figure 1a; country Y's choice in Figure 1b is labeled B. Country X has devoted a higher proportion of its resources to capital goods production in year 1 than has country Y. The net result—and the key to understanding the principles underlying economic growth—is that country X's choice results in a higher production possibilities frontier in some future year, say year 2. In year 2, societies X and Y will again choose some capital–consumer goods combina-

FIGURE 1   Economic Growth and the Production Possibilities Frontier

Growth is assumed to result from increases in the stock of capital goods. (a) If an economy forgoes a relatively large amount of consumption goods to obtain more capital goods, then the production possibilities frontier will shift outward by a larger amount than the economy that does not make the sacrifice. (b) Country Y's preference for consumer goods in year 1 results in significantly less growth by year 2.

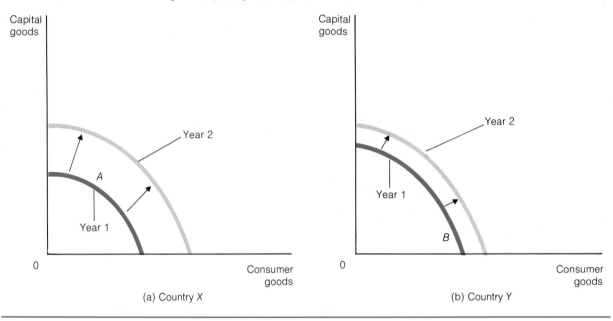

tion on a new frontier, but if both countries remain fully employed, country X's economy will have grown to a higher level of output and presumably to a higher level of real GNP per capita.

Economic growth, in other words, is determined by society's choice of future goods over present goods. This fact does not mean that the capital stock is the only element in growth. Capital combines with labor and natural resources to increase society's growth possibilities, even with a constant state of technology.

Different forms of resource growth would have similar effects on the production possibilities frontier. Consider Figure 2, which shows an economy based on two products—computer hardware and food. An equal growth rate in all resources, or in all nonspecialized resources, would shift the curve uniformly out, as in Figure 2a, whereas faster growth rates in resources specialized in computer hardware or in food production would enhance the production possibilities of either computers or food, as in Figure 2b.

The Law of Diminishing Marginal Returns

As always, the law of diminishing marginal returns (or of increasing marginal cost) applies. The law states that as more and more units of any variable resource are combined with some fixed amount of another resource or resources, successive applications of the variable input will increase total output by smaller amounts. Consider the farmer who has planted a field of corn. If

FIGURE 2

Technological Change and the Production Possibilities Frontier

The hypothetical economy is based on just two products—computer hardware and food. An improvement in technology shifts the production possibilities frontier to the right. (a) A change in technology that affects both products equally causes an increase in output of both products. (b) A change that affects either one product or the other but not both equally increases the output of one but not the other.

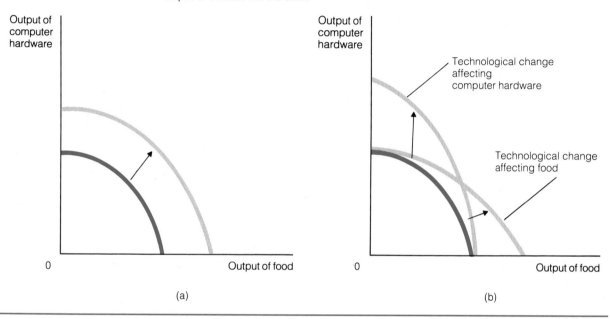

(a)   (b)

the farmer could spend only one day during the growing season tending the field, his efforts during that day would be devoted to the activities that yield the greatest return. It is likely that production in the field with one day's labor would exceed production in an untended field by a substantial amount. Should the farmer apply an additional day tending his field, output would again rise, but by a smaller amount; the activities available to the farmer on the second day would be less imperative than those of the first day. Similarly, additional days of labor would raise production by successively smaller amounts. The law of diminishing marginal returns explains the shape of short-run production and cost curves to any firm producing any sort of goods or services. The law also explains some macroeconomic aspects of growth.

As we know from experience, resources, talents, and training are not all alike and are not perfectly adaptable to alternative uses. Given any state of technology and level of knowledge, one good cannot be transformed with equal facility into another good. As we learned in Chapter 2, orange groves cannot be converted into peanut farms at constant opportunity costs. The same applies to any two goods or classes of goods: The most adaptable resources are transformed first. As less adaptable resources are transformed, total additions to output get smaller and smaller. This fact explains the concave shape of the typical production possibilities curve.

The law of diminishing marginal returns also applies to growth in the following way: In the event that any factor affecting growth is fixed or grows at slower rates than the others, output possibilities will increase, but at slower rates. Successive incremental applications of expanding resources to fixed production factors will result in smaller and smaller additions to output. If labor supply is fixed, for example, progressive increases in all other resources, excluding technology, will increase output potential, but at slower and slower rates. Technological change may enhance possible increases in output by "economizing" on the necessity to use labor. The gain would only be temporary, however. Given any state of technology, the point of diminishing marginal returns will be reached in time.

Comparative Growth Rates

Countries' economies are growing at different rates, for various reasons. Diminishing marginal returns when one or more resources is fixed or growing slowly is a major feature of theories featuring limits to growth. For instance, bottlenecks may be predicted when all arable land and freshwater resources in a country are already being used intensively for food production. Regardless of whether there are absolute or relative limits to long-run economic growth, it is clear that growth is an extremely complex matter. Further, it is clearly the case that even small differences in growth rates matter a great deal over time.

Table 1 presents actual average growth rates in real GNP between 1984 and 1989 in seven industrialized nations. The growth rates vary from 4.58 percent in Japan to 1.93 percent in the Soviet Union. These growth rates are then applied to a hypothetical $500 billion GNP in each of the countries in 1990 to project real GNP in each of the countries in future years. With these differences in growth rates, the Japanese GNP will grow to a level almost twice that of the Soviet Union by 2010. Relatively small differences in the growth rate will produce huge differences in real income in the not-too-distant future.

A warning about the determinants of growth in different nations: Many cultural and institutional factors heavily influence actual growth rates. Significantly different growth rates even in highly developed nations may ultimately be explained only in terms of a particular society's cultural, government, and institutional structures, areas where the economist may not be able to analyze key differences. Why, for example, has the Japanese economy grown recently at a faster rate than that of most other industrialized nations of the world?

Economists are accustomed to focusing on measurable factors such as the saving rate or the level of net investment—hard data. Trying to get at the reasons for Japan's success puts economists on less familiar ground; contributing factors mentioned include the rigorous Japanese work ethic and the practice of providing employees with what amounts to guaranteed life employment. While workers in other cultures might be inclined to exploit job security by shirking and reducing productivity, company loyalty and peer pressure seem to be a powerful motivating force in the Japanese workplace—especially compared with the United States. The tremendous loyalty that workers in Japan display to their employers is one factor that has enabled the Japanese to reach such high quality standards in the production of many goods. Attempts to apply Japanese techniques to production in the United States have been made, but economists have no special insight into how to successfully transplant these techniques to an alien culture—or even into whether such a transplant is possible.

TABLE 1   Cumulative Effects of GNP Growth

Different growth rates applied to the same hypothetical GNP in 1990 will produce dramatic changes in real GNP in the future. GNP will double in twenty years with an approximate growth rate of 3.5 percent per year.

Country	Actual Growth Rate of Real GNP, 1984–1989 (annual percent change)	Hypothetical Real GNP, 1990 (billions of dollars)	Projected Real GNP, 1995 (billions of dollars)	Projected Real GNP, 2000 (billions of dollars)	Projected Real GNP, 2005 (billions of dollars)	Projected Real GNP, 2010 (billions of dollars)
United States	4.00	500	610	740	900	1095
Canada	4.43	500	620	770	960	1190
Japan	4.58	500	625	780	980	1225
France	2.37	500	560	630	710	800
Italy	3.05	500	580	675	785	910
United Kingdom	3.42	500	590	700	830	980
Soviet Union	1.93	500	550	605	665	735

Source: Council of Economic Advisers, *Economic Report of the President* (Washington, D.C.: U.S. Government Printing Office, 1990), p. 419.

To understand the economic development of any nation, we must look to cultural and institutional factors, as well as the quantifiable features of growth.

THE CLASSICAL DYNAMICS OF GROWTH

More than any other economists before or since, the classical writers of the period 1776–1848 were interested in why economies grow, stagnate, or decline. Of the classical writers, David Ricardo (1772–1823) and Thomas Robert Malthus (1766–1834) were notable for their predictions about growth. Both Ricardo and Malthus predicted that society would reach some stationary state because of diminishing marginal returns in agriculture and severe population pressures.

Diminishing Marginal Returns and the Malthusian Population Principle

Malthus and Ricardo wrote about a hypothetical, purely agrarian economy with fixed quantities of land and natural resources and only one output, food. They also assumed that technology was fixed. They reasoned that as more and more capital and labor were applied to land of any given quality, marginal output of food would decline, for two reasons: (1) diminishing marginal returns—as more capital and labor were applied to any given quantity of land, marginal output would decline; and (2) scarcity of fertile land—as capital and labor were applied to agriculture, lower and lower grades of land would be used, yielding smaller quantities of food per acre.

At the same time that the marginal productivity of land was falling, society's demand for more and more food to feed a growing population would

Malthusian population principle:

The notion that the population has the capability to grow geometrically while the food supply can only grow arithmetically; leads to the concept of the subsistence wage.

Subsistence wage:

A real wage rate that is only high enough to allow for a zero rate of population growth.

be rising. The **Malthusian population principle,** developed by Malthus in 1798 in his book *On Population,* states that population tends to increase geometrically over successive generations (1, 2, 4, 8, 16, 32, . . .), while the food supply is capable of increasing only at an arithmetic rate through the generations (2, 4, 6, 8, 10, 12, . . .).

Related to the population principle is another Malthusian idea—that real wages are always tending toward the subsistence level. A **subsistence wage** was defined by classical economists as a wage sufficient for a husband and wife to reproduce themselves—to bring two children to adulthood. A wage above the subsistence level would lead to larger families. This would shift the labor supply to the right and eventually depress wages to the subsistence level.

The population–subsistence wage mechanism is presented in simple terms in Figure 3, which shows labor supply and demand curves and an initial equilibrium at E_0. We assume that the population, as well as the input of labor, is at level N_0 and receives a subsistence wage W_S. If the demand for labor increases from D_1 to D_2, a new equilibrium is established along the labor supply curve S_1 at E_1, and a new wage rate W_0 is established that is higher than subsistence. This shift occurs slowly—it may take a generation or more to reach the higher wage rate. If, as Malthus assumed, individuals react to a higher-than-subsistence wage rate by increasing family size and population to N_1, the supply curve of labor will shift rightward, bringing society back to the subsistence wage. If the increased economic well-being of workers ($W_0 - W_S$) is squandered in increased population, there is little hope for the progress of society. According the Malthus's theory, the subsistence wage will always

---

FIGURE 3   The Classical Population–Subsistence Wage Mechanism

Malthus's analysis starts from equilibrium E_0, where the quantity of labor N_0 calls for the subsistence wage W_S. An increase in the demand for labor increases the wage to W_0, a level above the subsistence wage, and equilibrium is established at E_1. This surplus for workers, however, is eventually squandered through increased population. As the population increases from N_0 to N_1, the labor supply increases, and in the long run the wage returns to the subsistence level, at E_2.

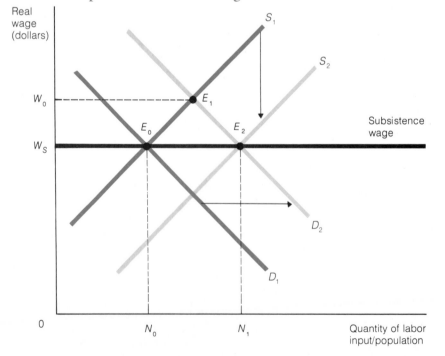

tend to prevail over the long run. If unrestrained, population will grow from N_0 to N_1, returning the per capita income of workers to subsistence.

Malthus also considered a worse possibility. If population and labor supply overreacted to the high wage rate W_0 and increased beyond S_2, wages would temporarily fall below the subsistence wage. Starvation would result for some, and Malthus predicted all sorts of dire consequences, including famine, plague, wars, and urban crowding. In Malthus's view, abstinence was the only "moral" way in which population could be restrained.

Deficiencies in Classical Growth Theory

While this classical theory is a marvelous simplification of the growth process, it suffers from several oversimplifications. The first is the Malthusian population theory. Does the population mechanism operate as Malthus described it? Do individuals squander increases in real income by increasing population growth rates? Evidence since the days of Malthus does not give a great deal of support to his idea, especially in industrialized countries. Massive growth in real GNP per capita has been made possible largely because increases in real income did not create an urge to procreate. Growth rates in the U.S. population have remained at relatively low levels since 1940 and, as indicated in Table 2, have actually declined since the early 1960s. Some developing nations have had population problems, however. Indeed, Malthus's model may be more applicable to countries with rapidly expanding populations, such as India or Ethiopia.

TABLE 2

Population Growth in the United States, 1961–1990

The U.S. growth rate has shown a dramatic decline since the 1950s baby boom, when population growth averaged between 1.7 and 1.8 percent per year.

Year	Population (millions)	Percent Change	Year	Population (millions)	Percent Change
1961	183.7	1.7	1976	218.0	1.0
1962	186.6	1.5	1977	220.2	1.0
1963	189.2	1.4	1978	222.6	1.1
1964	191.9	1.4	1979	225.1	1.1
1965	194.3	1.3	1980	227.7	1.2
1966	196.6	1.2	1981	230.1	1.0
1967	198.7	1.1	1982	232.5	1.0
1968	200.7	1.0	1983	234.8	1.0
1969	202.7	1.0	1984	237.0	1.0
1970	205.1	1.2	1985	239.3	1.0
1971	207.7	1.3	1986	241.6	1.0
1972	209.9	1.1	1987	243.9	1.0
1973	211.9	1.0	1988	246.1	1.0
1974	213.9	0.9	1989	248.6	1.0
1975	216.0	1.0	1990	251.1	1.0

Source: U.S. Bureau of the Census, *Statistical Abstract of the United States,* 1989 (Washington, D.C.: U.S. Government Printing Office, 1989), p. 7.

Note: Years 1989 and 1990 are authors' estimates.

A second major deficiency in the classical theory of economic growth is the classical theorists' mistaken belief that technology, especially related to food production, was a relatively constant factor in growth. In the early nineteenth century, one farm worker could feed only three or four nonfarm workers. Today, one farm worker in the United States is able to feed more than eighty people. While it is true that agriculture today is more mechanized—farm workers have more capital with which to work—a portion of the increase in productivity can be explained by technological advances. For example, farmers planting disease-resistant hybrid seeds can expect dramatically larger yields than farmers of just a generation ago. The tremendous increase in technology and invention in the nineteenth and twentieth centuries has been the mainspring of real per capita GNP growth, and it has accrued on an unprecedented scale. The steam engine in transportation, highly sophisticated mass production processes, modern electronics, and a host of other technological breakthroughs have all helped forestall what Malthus perceived to be an inevitable decline in growth.

GROWTH AND MODERN MACROECONOMIC THEORY

Modern economic theory has much to say on the issue of growth. Foremost in current analysis is the importance of capital formation and improvements in technology. According to modern analysis, growth potential also depends on the ability of an economy to absorb growth.

The Demand Side of Growth

Growth absorption:
Increases in total spending sufficient to purchase additional output generated by increases in productive capacity.

Growth absorption means keeping up with the expanding productive capacity of the economy through increasing total expenditures. Recall that aggregate demand must always be sufficient to create full employment at any point in time. The same must hold true to create full employment and maximum economic growth over time.

Figure 4 shows total expenditures on the vertical axis and the output capacity of the economy over time on the horizontal axis. Along the 45-degree line, total expenditures equal the total output capacity of the economy. A central requirement for sustainable economic growth is that total expenditures, private and public, must keep the economy on or near this 45-degree line through time; otherwise, unemployment and slower growth will result. If output capacity is Y_0 in 1970, total expenditures must be at the level of TE_0 to achieve maximum income and income growth. A given level of net investment and capital formation in 1970 creates a larger output capacity in 1980, Y_1, which in turn requires a rise in total expenditures in 1980 to realize the growth potential of the 1980 economy.

Ensuring adequate aggregate demand for maximum growth is one of the goals of short-run macroeconomic theory. New Keynesians argue that the economy should be managed in discretionary countercyclical fashion to keep aggregate demand at full-employment levels. Monetarists and new classical economists argue that adequate growth in aggregate demand can be achieved only through stable rules for Congress and for the Federal Reserve System.

FIGURE 4

Growth in Total Expenditures Required for Economic Growth

In this simple model, increases in total expenditures must keep up with expanding resources and population to bring about maximum economic growth. If the economy grows from an output capacity of Y_0 in 1970 to Y_1 in 1980, the aggregate demand curve must shift from TE_0 to TE_1 by 1980 to keep resources fully employed. Total output equals total expenditures along the 45-degree line.

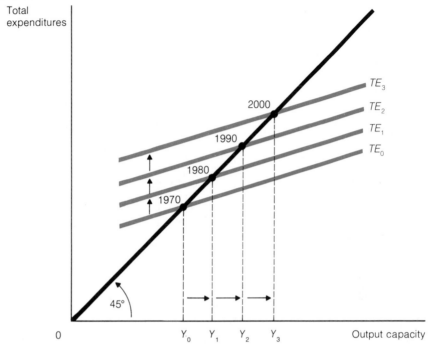

However one looks at the matter, policies to ensure adequate aggregate demand are essential in maintaining a sustained high rate of economic growth.

The Supply Side of Growth

The other facet of economic growth involves the factors that enhance or enlarge the productive capacities of the economy. All the factors—capital growth, technological improvements, growth in natural resources—discussed earlier in this chapter create growth in supply. We call these supply-side factors because they have the effect of shifting the aggregate supply curve of real output to the right.

In Figure 5, we assume that the economy's demand for goods and services will be sufficient to absorb the increased output of goods and services made possible by growth. The question we ask instead is, What factor or factors underlie rightward shifts in the aggregate supply curve? The long-run supply of goods and services is influenced by certain variables—capital accumulation, the productivity of labor, taxation, and so on. For purposes of discussion, however, there are two major economic factors to watch in predicting the growth rate in the productive capacities of any economy:

1. Growth in private saving and investment, which leads to capital formation; and
2. Growth in the numbers of laborers, in laborers' participation in the work force, and in labor's productivity.

FIGURE 5

Over time, the level of technology or the supply of resources may increase, shifting the long-run aggregate supply curve to the right and increasing full-employment income.

Economic Growth and Rightward Shifts in Long-Run Aggregate Supply

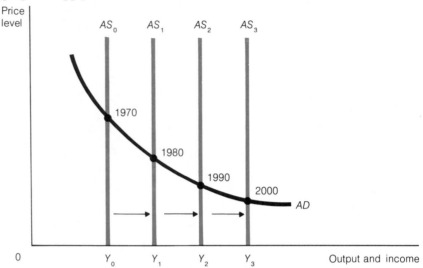

Any variable, policy, or institutional factor that affects these two factors will affect economic growth through its effect on the long-run aggregate supply curve. Consider some recent trends in the United States of these components of economic growth.

RECENT U.S. ECONOMIC GROWTH AND PRODUCTIVITY

The various growth rates in real GNP and per capita GNP in industrialized nations reported in Table 1 have numerous causes. Short-run economic stabilization—the ability of an economy to provide full employment of resources—will naturally affect long-run growth prospects. But the supply-side features of economic growth are of greatest importance in explaining U.S. growth trends.

Capital Formation

Capital formation:
The process whereby the stock of capital in an economy increases.

A useful measure of **capital formation** is net investment as a percent of GNP. This shows the proportion of total output being put into new plant and equipment—an indicator of future productivity. As Table 3 shows, net investment fell to $64 billion in 1982, barely 2 percent of GNP. Since then, the investment rate has risen sharply—to levels more in line with historical norms.

Saving

Personal savings are the primary source of new investment and capital formation in the United States. However, corporations also engage in saving, as do governments when they run government surpluses. In recent years, foreign

TABLE 3

Net Private Domestic Investment, 1970–1987

Net investment as a percentage of GNP remained fairly steady between 1970 and 1987, though there were dips in 1982 and 1983.

Year	Net Private Domestic Investment	Percentage of GNP
1970	60.0	5.91
1975	57.8	3.62
1980	133.1	4.87
1981	167.7	5.49
1982	64.1	2.02
1983	105.7	3.10
1984	249.4	6.61
1985	205.9	5.13
1986	210.0	4.95
1987	233.0	5.15

Source: U.S. Bureau of the Census, *Statistical Abstract of the United States,* 1989 (Washington, D.C.: U.S. Government Printing Office, 1989), pp. 421, 533.

capital has flowed into the United States, providing an additional source of savings. Figure 6 shows that while, historically, Americans have saved about 7 percent of their disposable income, the rate in the late 1970s and for most of the 1980s was lower—at times, significantly so.

The dip in personal savings coincided with an era of enormous government deficits. To finance these deficits, the government has been forced to

FIGURE 6

Personal Saving Rate in the 1980s

The personal saving rate moved up to 5.5 percent in 1989, rebounding from an average 1987 low of 3.2 percent of disposable income but still considerably lower than the 7.2 percent average for the period 1950–1979.

Source: Council of Economic Advisers, *Economic Report of the President* (Washington, D.C.: U.S. Government Printing Office, 1990), p. 41.

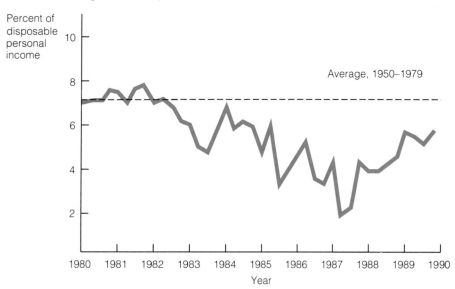

compete with private investors. Accumulated savings drained to finance government deficits greatly reduce the funds that are available for private capital formation.

Productivity

The declines in net investment and saving combined to reduce U.S. productivity in the early 1980s (see Table 4). After 1982, total output and output per hour rose dramatically; the 8.3 percent rate of output growth in 1984 was the highest since 1950. Since 1984, the growth rate has moderated somewhat, and while the rate remains much higher than it was in the late 1970s and early 1980s, productivity growth remains low compared with what it has been throughout most of U.S. history.

Small differences in productivity growth rates and in the rates of investment and capital formation that cause them may seem inconsequential. Over the long run, however, they are critical to growth. As the Council of Economic Advisers pointed out in 1983,

> The consequences of reduced productivity growth for our standard of living over the long run are greater than those of any other current economic problem. In 1981 the American economy produced approximately $12,780 worth of output per capita. Had productivity growth continued at the 1948–67 rate during the 14 years subsequent to 1967, output per capita would have reached $16,128 in 1981, 26 percent higher than the actual value.[1]

Small changes in growth rates in productivity, investment, and capital formation can have a major impact on economic growth. Increasing the annual productivity growth rate by only 2 percentage points, for example, would more than double the standard of living in terms of goods and services by the year 2020.

TABLE 4   **Output and Productivity Growth Rates in Nonfarm Business Sector, 1980–1989**

The output growth rate fluctuated throughout the 1980s, with growth in productivity (output per hour) lagging stubbornly behind.

	Growth Rates (percent)										1980–1989 (average)
	1980	1981	1982	1983	1984	1985	1986	1987	1988	1989	
Output per hour	−0.4	1.1	−0.9	3.0	2.1	1.3	2.0	1.1	2.0	0.8	1.2
Output	−1.2	1.7	−3.3	5.0	8.3	3.9	3.0	4.4	5.4	3.0	3.0

Source: Council of Economic Advisers, *Economic Report of the President* (Washington, D.C.: U.S. Government Printing Office, 1990).

Note: Figures for 1989 are averages of the first three quarters of 1989.

---

[1]Council of Economic Advisers, *Economic Report of the President* (Washington, D.C.: U.S. Government Printing Office, 1983), p. 83.

DENISON'S STUDIES

The somewhat disappointing picture of growth in the U.S. economy over the last fifteen years has many interrelated causes. Unfortunately, economists cannot pinpoint the exact causes of the slowdown. More important, once the causes of the slowdown in productivity are identified, are policies available to reverse the trend?

The slowdown in labor productivity has been attributed to, among other things, lower research and development expenditures; a transition to a high-technology economy; higher energy prices; swings in the business cycle; increased regulation affecting saving, investment, and labor markets; changing composition of the labor force; and changing attitudes of workers. Some experts place responsibility for the decline of labor productivity on the reduction in capital formation.[2] Discrimination against private capital formation has taken a number of forms, including tax policies, destabilizing inflation created by expansionist monetary policies, and the competition for investment funds by the federal government through government budget deficits. Public policies of the Reagan administration, for example, were aimed at countering some of these trends in hopes of increasing capital formation and thus promoting growth. Increases in both saving and investment beginning in 1984 are encouraging, although the large federal deficit could choke the recovery.

A more comprehensive accounting for productivity declines and for slower overall growth must be found in the identification of the sources of economic growth itself. Since the early 1960s, economist Edward F. Denison has sought to account for the relative importance of all of the major ingredients of economic growth by using index numbers. Denison has converted trends in total output (national income) and in various factor inputs (labor, capital, legal and human environment, and so on) for the period 1929–1982 into index numbers (see Figure 7).

According to Denison's estimates, U.S. national income rose at an average annual rate of 2.9 percent per year over the period 1929–1982. Of the factors contributing to this rise, increases in factor inputs—labor and capital combined—were most significant. Increase in the labor supply consisted partly of increased education and partly of an increased rate of employment. Recall that new net capital growth is the result of growth in savings and in net investment. The remaining major factors contributing to growth, in order of importance, are advances in technology (knowledge), economies of scale, and improvements in resource allocation.

Note that changes in the legal and human environment actually reduced economic growth. The latter statistic makes sense because investments in environmental protection, for example, do not increase the quantity of the output of goods and services but do increase the quality. To the extent that quality is important in assessing economic growth and well-being, output per worker is understated because capital investments in environmental and pollution production do not ordinarily result in more real salable output but

---

[2]See, for example, John A. Tatom, "The 'Problem' of Procyclical Real Wages and Productivity," *Journal of Political Economy* 88 (February 1980), pp. 385–94.

FIGURE 7   **Denison's Estimates of U.S. Growth Factors, 1929–1982**

In addition to the growth in factor inputs themselves, Denison estimated that advances in technology or in knowledge accounted for the largest contribution to economic growth. Environmental restrictions reduced the output rate by 0.03 percent, but the quality of output may have increased.

Source: Edward F. Denison, *Trends in American Economic Growth* (Washington, D.C.: Brookings Institution, 1985), p. 30. Reprinted by permission.

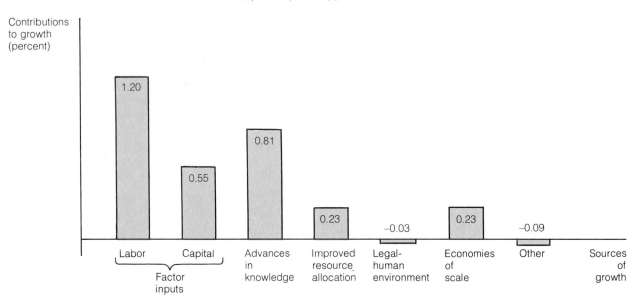

simply in output with fewer by-products. Naturally, a number of interrelated factors contribute to growth. Focus, "The Rise and Fall of Nations: Growth and the Age of Economies," discusses a new and provocative thesis relating economic growth to an economy's age.

LOOKING AHEAD

Denison's careful studies of the sources of growth point out the complexities of trying to identify causes of growth and then trying to stimulate them. Factor growth and, with it, technological change—the importance of which was downplayed in classical economics—are the two essential causes of growth. The long-run benefits and the possible short-run costs of rapid technological change have received a great deal of attention from politicians, economists, and the media in recent years, creating a rather muddy picture.

It is clear that the United States is experiencing a transformation from traditional smokestack industries (coal, steel, heavy machinery) toward high-technology industries (computers, communications). This transformation was clearly evident in the 1982 recession, when there were 25,346 business bankruptcies but 566,942 new companies opened. There were massive worker layoffs in the automobile, steel, and shipbuilding industries and in most heavy industries, while engineers and computer scientists were able to choose between high-paying jobs.

FOCUS   The Rise and Fall of Nations: Growth and the Age of Economies

An interesting and controversial theory of economic growth, developed by economist Mancur Olson, relates the relative economic growth of societies and regions to their age and the respective levels of bureaucratic controls created within their governmental processes.[a] In this view, industry, business, and labor unions (or any other organization) will lobby for legislation or rulings that will allow them to act monopolistically to influence prices or wages to benefit themselves. While success is often difficult to predict, ordinarily the smaller the group, the greater the success of collective action. Large groups, such as taxpayers, consumers, the poor, and the unemployed, are most often not in a position to combine in order to achieve group objectives.

Comprehensive organization of all common interest groups will not be possible in any society, but those who are successful tend to persist. As time goes on, some of these organizations will persist and new ones will emerge if the conditions for monopolization are favorable. Organizations receiving special rewards (higher prices or wages) through collective action have no incentives to disband. Their elimination would spread benefits across the society, but the benefits would be small to group members, smaller than those they can receive from cartelization and collective group action.

The straightforward implication of Olson's thesis is that "new" societies or "younger" societies are at an advantage because they carry less "excess baggage" in the form of efficiency-reducing organizations. Older societies, such as England or France, have had slower growth rates over the past two hundred years, or in the past twenty-five, than the United States. Some societies are destroyed through war, revolution, or totalitarianism and thus may be considered "new." This fact may help explain the experience of high post–World War II growth rates in Germany and Japan relative to other developed nations.

Other testable implications of the theory relate to the economic development of regions. Olson argues that his theory helps explain the relatively high economic development rates in the South and the more recently settled and more westerly states than in the Northeast and the older midwestern states of the United States.[b] Long-settled areas have had more time to accumulate special-interest organizations, and Olson points to the relative lack of labor organizations and to other factors as contributing to an explanation of higher relative economic growth rates in other regions since World War II. Naturally, the factors influencing economic growth are as numerous as they are complex. Olson's thesis provides an interesting possible explanation for economic growth.

[a]Mancur Olson, *The Rise and Decline of Nations: Economic Growth, Stagflation, and Social Rigidities* (New Haven: Yale University Press, 1982).

[b]Mancur Olson, "The South Will Fall Again: The South as Leader and Laggard in Economic Growth," *Southern Economic Journal* 49 (April 1983), pp. 917–32.

The political blame for much of this economic change has been placed on foreign competition. The United States is no longer a self-sufficient economy; it imports more than twice as many goods now as in 1970. For example, the United States now imports 28 percent of its autos, 18 percent of its steel, 55 percent of its consumer electronic products, and 27 percent of its machine tools.

The two major reasons for heightened foreign competition are the lower wage rates and the swift spread of technology to foreign countries. Labor costs in South Korea and Taiwan are about one-fifth those in the United States. Japan, relying greatly on automation, uses approximately six times as many industrial robots as the United States. Some economists and business leaders fear that more automation in the United States will lead to higher unemployment, while other economists feel there will be a shift into other jobs.[3]

According to projections, new jobs are being created in the service industries. The Labor Department has predicted employment in 1995 of 28.5 million people in **service industries**—those offering teaching, health care, and

Service industries:
Those industries whose major, or sole, output is a consumer service, such as banking, entertainment, and health care.

[3]See, for example, "The New Economy," *Time* (May 30, 1983), pp. 62–70, from which the discussion in this section is developed.

food service, for example, rather than manufactured goods—compared to 27 million in 1989. There has been a 53 percent increase in the number of service industry workers since the mid-1970s. By contrast, the number of employees in manufacturing has dropped 2.7 percent since 1973, and predictions are that only 22 million workers will be employed in manufacturing industries in 1995, considerably fewer than the 28.5 million service workers. An example of the increase in service industries compared to heavy industries is the fact that McDonald's now employs more workers than USX (formerly U.S. Steel).

The United States is not alone in its transition from heavy industry to high-technology and service industries. European industrial nations are also having difficulty with changing economies. Even Japan is experiencing some decline in heavy industry, but Japan, unlike Western countries, encourages changes in the economy. Japanese companies diversify greatly in areas of production. One company produces products ranging from foodstuffs to nuclear power plants. This diversity allows workers whose jobs become unnecessary to move into other branches of production within the same company. The setup requires large-scale retraining programs within the companies.

Rather than following the Japanese model, politicians, businesspeople, and workers in the United States have demanded protection for the old smokestack industries against foreign competition. During the late 1970s and through the mid-1980s, the United States experienced its worst outbreak of protectionism (the establishment of legal artificial trade barriers and restrictions such as tariffs and import quotas) since the 1930s. The United States has tried to reduce imports and place quotas on autos, steel, and many other products, as we will see in Chapter 21. However, trade restrictions could well do more harm than good to the United States. The United States now exports more than twice the quantity of products it exported ten years ago, and retaliation (in the form of trade restrictions on U.S. goods set in place by foreign governments) by other nations in response to U.S. restrictions is always a possibility. Such reactions inevitably reduce economic growth and well-being among all traders.

It is not likely that the United States will meet the challenge of economic growth by increasing restrictions and regulations on competition or on capital formation but rather by adapting to new technology through competition and human capital development. The management of change in a complex economy is a difficult matter. It often amounts to a balancing of the present interests of workers and other resource suppliers against the overall interests of consumers and economic growth. American prosperity is clearly the result of earlier technological challenges that were met head-on within the context of vigorous and open competition, with due regard for the temporary distortions that new trade and technology might create.

SUMMARY

1. Economic growth is defined as growth in real GNP or in real GNP per capita.
2. The sources of economic growth are complex, but they certainly include growth in population, labor productivity, capital accumulation, and technology.

3. The classical writers envisioned an economy progressing to a stationary (no-growth) state. A Malthusian population mechanism with a long-run tendency to a subsistence wage was a cause of the stationary state, as was a diminishing return to food production.

4. The classical economists also viewed technology as being constant, but modern economists have pointed to growing technology as the mainspring of the economic growth of the Western world.
5. Economic growth requires increases not only in the productive capacity in the economy but also in aggregate demand, which must keep pace with increases in potential output.
6. An essential feature of slower U.S. economic growth in the 1980s was the decline in the growth rate of the productivity of labor—in output per worker. Though numerous factors caused the decline, the major factor appears to be a reduction in capital formation.
7. A lower saving rate, which has led to a lower growth rate in investment expenditures, is a major factor in explaining the lower rate of capital formation.
8. The United States is faced with a high-technology challenge to economic growth—a movement away from heavy industries such as steel, automobiles, and shipbuilding to industries based on electronics and other advanced technologies and to service industries. America's response to this challenge will determine growth prospects for many decades to come.

KEY TERMS

standard of living
economic growth
real per capita GNP
productivity of labor

capital deepening
Malthusian population principle
subsistence wage
growth absorption

capital formation
service industries

QUESTIONS FOR REVIEW AND DISCUSSION

1. What is the difference between growth in real GNP and growth in real GNP per capita? Would it be accurate to suggest that the percent change in real GNP per capita is equal to the percent change in real GNP minus the percent change in the population?
2. Do increases in population cause increases in real GNP per capita? Would an increase in the labor force participation rate (the percentage of the population that is in the labor force) increase real GNP per capita?
3. Would it be accurate to suggest that a developing country with an abundance of natural resources has the potential for a high growth rate? What must occur in such countries before a high rate of growth can occur?
4. What is the cost of capital? What happens to real GNP per capita when the number of machines increases?
5. What changes occurred during the Industrial Revolution that resulted in large increases in real GNP per capita? Are similar changes necessary to obtain growth in developing countries?
6. Explain what economic growth means in terms of production possibilities curves. What causes this

growth? Is this identical to increases in aggregate supply?
7. Suppose that 1000 tractors were added to a nation's stock of capital every year. Would total farm output rise by the same amount every year? Why or why not?
8. What did Malthus predict about the real GNP per capita? Explain why this prediction has not occurred in the United States. Does his theory appear accurate for some countries?
9. If growth causes an increase in aggregate supply, what must happen to the price level to achieve the higher level of output? Does this suggest that increases in aggregate demand must accompany increases in aggregate supply to maintain price level stability and full employment?
10. What has happened to the rate of growth in real GNP per capita in the United States since the late 1960s? What has caused or accompanied this trend?
11. If you had to choose between price and employment stability and sustained growth in real GNP per capita, which would you choose?

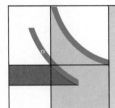

ECONOMICS IN ACTION
Infrastructure and Economic Growth

Discussions of economic growth typically focus on the impact of private investment and capital formation, but the size and condition of government's capital stock is also critical to growth. What is the society's capital stock? In the United States, society's share of the capital stock is approximately one-quarter of the total and is composed of highways, schools, streets, bridges, sewers, and other public goods. The bulk of the nonmilitary government capital—or infrastructure—is owned by state and local governments, although some of the original investments were federally provided. Often, as in the case of highways, maintenance and upkeep expenditures are shared by federal and the other government entities.

The value of infrastructure in economic growth tends to be undervalued and underappreciated in the United States; government investment in goods such as highways, schools, and airports is not generally subject to a market test of profitability, as are investments in the private sector. The value of an investment in computer chip production or in building new privately provided student apartments soon becomes apparent as investors make or lose returns on the difference between revenues taken in and costs incurred. Such measures of profitability are difficult or impossible to apply to new investments in public university buildings or city streets. It would be a mistake, however, to take the absence of a market test for these kinds of goods to mean that infrastructure is not critical to private sector productivity and economic growth.

That this nation's infrastructure is deteriorating is undeniable. Water main breaks are an almost daily occurrence in New York City, and bridge closures (or, worse, collapses) are common everywhere. Over the past two decades, according to the President's Council of Economic Advisers, there has been a dramatic decline in the growth in state and local infrastructure investments.[a] Growth in infrastructure investments at state and local levels fell from an average rate of 4.9 percent per year in the 1950s and 1960s to 2.2 percent in the 1970s and to only 0.9 percent in the 1980s. Completion of the interstate highway system and a decline in the size of the school-age population (the petering out of the post–World War II baby boom) explains some of the decline in infrastructure investment, but certainly not all of it. To many observers, failing local government services, underinvestment in real education plant and equipment, outmoded air-port facilities, and overcrowded streets and poor or failing rapid transit systems suggest that there is an infrastructure crisis in America and that investments are far from adequate. Critics also point out that rapidly growing countries such as Japan and Taiwan are devoting huge amounts of resources to infrastructure to complement increased productivity in the private sector.

As usual, the issue of infrastructure provision comes down to this: Who pays? In general, the federal government has shifted the financial burden for infrastructure provision to state and local governments under the Reagan and Bush administrations. State and local governments complain that access to new taxes for infrastructure items is limited and that the federal government is acting irresponsibly by refusing to shoulder more of the tab for maintaining and expanding facilities. The void left by slashes in federal funding has largely been filled with a controversial mix of privatization schemes and user fees.

For their part, economists concur that "taking advantage of productive opportunities to maintain and improve the infrastructure is an important part of federal, state, and local government policies to raise economic growth."[b] Economists warn, however, that maintenance priorities as well as new projects must be carefully weighed according to costs and benefits. Since governmentally provided infrastructure does not have to meet a market test, detailed estimates of the net benefits of any project (new or continuing) are critical if waste is not to be incurred. There are some classic cases of government miscalculation. Anxious to encourage movement of its population westward from coastal urban cities such as Rio de Janeiro, Brazil built a new inland capital—Brasília. The problem has been that few people want to live there; billions of dollars' worth of infrastructure and facilities lies grossly underutilized and deteriorating. While these kinds of costly miscalculations are possible in infrastructure provision or in maintenance priorities wherever market signals cannot be used, maintenance and expansion of the nation's capital stock is indisputably a necessary condition for increased productivity in any nation that aspires to higher economic growth.

Question

Can the investment returns on the privately financed construction of a new movie theater and the publicly financed construction of a new school building be compared? Why or why not?

[a]Council of Economic Advisers, *Economic Report of the President* (Washington, D.C.: U.S. Government Printing Office, 1990), pp. 122–23.

[b]*Economic Report of the President* (1990), p. 123.

Paul Samuelson

Robert E. Lucas, Jr.

Paul Samuelson and Robert Lucas: Do We Need Discretion or Discipline in Policy?

Paul Samuelson (b. 1915) "... has done more than any other contemporary economist to raise the level of scientific analysis in economic theory." So announced the Swedish Academy of Sciences in 1970, when Samuelson became the first American recipient of the Nobel Memorial Prize in economics. Although he has been called on frequently by presidents and Congress for his advice on economic matters, Samuelson has never held an official policy role in any administration. He has worked principally in the service of his profession: as a professor of economics at M.I.T., as president of the American Economic Association, and as a frequent contributor to journals and magazines. Born in Gary, Indiana, Samuelson received his Ph.D. in economics from Harvard in 1941. His doctoral dissertation, titled *Foundations of Economic Analysis,* was published in 1947 and became one of the definitive technical treatises on neoclassical economics. Today, Samuelson is one of the most widely respected Keynesian economists. He is known as a policy activist, one who recommends the use of fiscal and monetary policy to counter recessionary and inflationary cycles of economic activity.

ROBERT E. LUCAS, JR. (b. 1937), credited with introducing rational expectations theory into macroeconomics, has helped change the way economists view the role of macroeconomic policy. Born in Yakima, Washington, Lucas received his Ph.D. in economics in 1964 from the University of Chicago, where he gained a firm background in Keynesian economics. One of the texts he found particularly influential at that time was Paul Samuelson's *Foundations of Economic Analysis,* which he believes is "a great book for first-year graduate students."

After graduate training, Lucas became increasingly disillusioned with Keynesian interpretations of the macroeconomy. His article "Econometric Testing of the Natural Rate Hypothesis," published in 1972, is one of many that discuss the implications of rational expectations theory. This theory assumes that people will make rational and intelligent economic decisions based on their knowledge of economic policy, their past experiences, and their expectations of future events. In theory, such rational behavior can distort or even neutralize the effects of well-publicized fiscal and monetary policies. According to Lucas, he and his early followers were initially regarded as "very far out" by colleagues for their nontraditional views. However, appreciation of rational expectations theory has grown so that Nobel Prize–winner George Stigler has suggested that Lucas himself may soon share the award. Lucas has held academic posts at Carnegie-Mellon University, the Ford Foundation, and the University of Chicago, where he currently teaches.

THE CASE FOR ACTIVISM

In 1964, the unemployment rate stood at 5.2 percent and GNP was $638 billion. The economy was near the end of a bitter recessionary period. Government policy advisers, following Keynesian theory, called for direct intervention in the form of a massive tax cut. Congress responded by passing the 1964 Revenue Act, which slashed personal income taxes by almost 20 percent and corporate taxes by almost 8 percent.

The tax cut, aided by a strong surge in the money supply, ushered in several boom years. Over the next four years, GNP grew over 11 percent and unemployment dropped to 3.8 percent. Policy activists such as Paul Samuelson cite the 1964 tax cut as good evidence of the usefulness of well-planned fiscal and monetary actions. Although the evidence since the 1960s has been somewhat less clear-cut, the case for activism rests on the assumption that the economy cannot easily readjust to full employment without some form of countercyclical policy, whether in the form of monetary growth, monetary restraint, fiscal cutbacks, or fiscal spending. The fiscal actions are generally preferred by activists because they can exert a direct impact on the flow of expenditures. Monetary policy works somewhat more slowly and less directly on expenditures, through the mechanism of interest rates.

Defending the need for activism, Samuelson and other economists focus on the terrible social costs of economic downturns and sudden shocks to the system. Left to correct itself, a shrinking economy could inflict insufferable damage on millions of people before prices and aggregate demand readjust to full-employment levels.

The record of policy activism gives some support for this view. For the past thirty years, the United States has suffered several recessions, but depressions seem to be a thing of the past. "Another depression on the order of the 1930s just doesn't seem possible," says Samuelson. The government nowadays "will do what it has to do" to avert economic disorder. "There's no longer the sense that we must somehow sweat these things out."[a]

Although activist policy has eased the severity of business cycles, it has not found a means to avoid them altogether. Indeed, there are many who argue that the economy's boom-and-recession pattern since World War II has been more the effect of discretionary policy than the cause. Also, there are many economists who point to the accelerating inflation suffered over these years and the failure of government to apply the appropriate countercyclical fiscal medicine: budget surpluses.

THE CASE AGAINST ACTIVISM

For Robert Lucas, the attempts on the part of policy-makers to unbend the business cycle through discretionary, countercyclical policy are based on some unexamined assumptions. For such a policy to work, individuals and firms must respond cooperatively; when the government tries to close a recessionary gap, they must respond as though such actions will have no effect on prices.

Lucas believes that expectations about prices will always direct behavior, whether one is speaking in microeconomic or macroeconomic terms. If individuals and firms believe that government policy will drive up prices, they will act to protect themselves: Wage earners will demand higher wages, investors will seek higher interest rates, and so on. When such expectations are considered, Lucas deems most countercyclical policy to be futile and counterproductive. For instance, if policy-makers try to reduce unemployment through deficit spending, wage earners who have experienced the effects of such spending in the past will anticipate higher inflation. They will naturally try to keep the wages they have and to increase them. In the face of such demands, employers will find it more and more difficult to hire additional labor, and unemployment will remain despite the increase in aggregate demand. Rather than bend the recessionary cycle, the policy-makers will have managed to foster inflationary pressures, perhaps ushering in high unemployment and high inflation, or what is known as stagflation.

The checkered performance of macroeconomic policy in the early 1980s provided Lucas plenty of ammunition to blame discretionary policy for a variety of economic ills. To Lucas, appropriate macroeconomic policy would try neither to fool nor to ignore the expectations of individuals and firms. Instead, Lucas calls for some fixed limits for policy that recognize the long-run patterns of growth in the economy, which have been in the range of 3 to 4 percent for GNP over the past one hundred years. He also advocates a monetary rule proposed by Milton Friedman that would keep the growth rate of the money supply to approximately 3 percent.

Economists who accept the rational expectations hypothesis have begun the large task of accumulating evidence in its behalf. In the meantime, many find the rational expectations model extreme in its assumptions. How is it, they ask, that citizens can adopt an accurate set of expectations about the effects of policy when even competent observers of the economy are often misjudging the rate or even direction of economic change? Moreover, what happens when fiscal or monetary policies are overwhelmed by a supply shock? Will government then be required to overcome the instability? Questions such as these have brought lively debate over the future course of policy. The issue of activism versus nonactivism in policy is certain to occupy economists for years to come.

[a]Quoted in "Economists Don't See Threats to Economy Portending Depression," *Wall Street Journal* (October 12, 1984), p. 1.

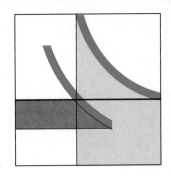

PART FIVE

International

Trade and

Economic

Development

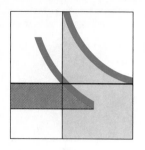

21

International Trade

We do not often stop to ponder all the ways in which imported goods enrich our lives and improve the material well-being of all nations of the world. On a typical day, for example, an American student's consumption patterns are clearly global. She awakes on sheets made in England and prepares breakfast on a hot plate made in Taiwan. Donning a cotton dress made in India and shoes made in Mexico, she catches the morning news on a TV with components manufactured in Japan. She drives to campus in a Japanese-made Honda Civic.

The desirability of a diverse array of available goods and services and the interrelation of the U.S. economy with the economies of other nations present us with issues and problems we have left unexamined until now. The issue of the competitiveness of U.S. firms in world markets may have directly affected you or your family. The large foreign trade deficit that arose in the 1980s spawned much debate in business, labor, and government circles on the desirability of a new U.S. trade policy with countries such as Japan and Canada. Large swings in the value of the U.S. dollar overseas can alter not only vacation plans but consumption patterns and employment as well.

To this point, we have simplified our analyses of the national economy by treating it as closed—as isolated and with no international interchange. In the next three chapters, we focus exclusively on international trade, finance, and development, with special attention to U.S. involvement.

Today's revolutions in technology are enabling nations to become more and more economically interdependent. In a sense, the whole world is now an economic system. International economics is the study of this world economy with the tools of economic theory. The concepts of supply and demand and production possibilities are quite useful in discussing worldwide trade, the international finance system, and the problems facing the developing economies of the world. These chapters examine the organization and functioning of national economies such as those of the Soviet Union and Eastern Europe that are replacing organized central planning by government with systems in which private property and markets play larger roles.

International economics is composed of both microeconomic and macroeconomic elements. This chapter focuses essentially on the microeconomics of trade. After reading Chapter 21 you should understand

- the reasons for and the advantages of specialization and trade.
- the factors that determine actual amounts and directions of trade between countries.
- how artificial interferences with trade, such as tariffs and quotas, affect the prices and quantities of goods and services sold in importing countries.
- how historical and contemporary trade policies and international integration, such as that contemplated by Western European nations, affect world trade.

THE IMPORTANCE OF INTERNATIONAL TRADE

Specialization:
An economic entity's (an individual's or a nation's) producing only one good or service, or the performance of a single task in a production process by an individual.

All nations have particular talents and resources; like individuals, whole nations can specialize in one or many activities. For example, the islands of the Caribbean have abundant sunshine and good weather year round, and so these islands specialize in tourism. **Specialization** enables nations to emphasize the activities at which they are most efficient and at the same time gain certain advantages through trade.

Examples of international specialization and trade abound. France has a favorable climate and specialized land for wine growing, so it exports wine to Colombia and the United States and imports Colombian coffee and U.S. machinery. Likewise, both Colombia and the United States specialize and trade products that best utilize their qualities and quantities of resources.

Trade and specialization take place within a given economy as well as among economies. The former type of trade is called intranational or interregional trade; the latter is called international trade. In principle, the two types of trade are the same. As we saw in Chapter 2, Canada may specialize in lumber production and Mexico may specialize in silver production. Each meets its wants for the commodity it does not produce through international trade. Likewise, Texans import potatoes from Idaho, while residents of Idaho import beef produced in Texas. Such intranational or interregional trade is common—so common in fact that most of us do not even think of it as interregional trade. This process is not fundamentally different from the trade of U.S. wheat for Japanese television sets.

In practice, important differences exist between interregional and international trade. Resources—climate, fertile land, and work forces with specialized skills—cannot easily be moved between countries or regions. What distinguishes international trade from interregional trade is *lower* factor mobility between nations than within countries. A nation generally trades with the products and services of its resources, not with the resources themselves. Beyond this basic point, countries have different currencies and political systems and values. (See Focus, "1992: Dawn of the European Community.") For such reasons, international trade is different from interregional trade and therefore merits special study by economists.

FOCUS   1992: Dawn of the European Community

The goal of eliminating economic barriers and creating new levels of integration in Western Europe is set for 1992. The European Community (EC)—forged largely from the European Economic Community, or Common Market—will become a unified market of twelve member nations, making trade within Europe almost as easy as trade between states in the United States. (The twelve countries are the United Kingdom, France, Denmark, Belgium, Greece, Italy, Luxembourg, The Netherlands, Portugal, Ireland, Spain, and a recently reunified Germany.) In economic terms, this means that all tariff and nontariff trade barriers will eventually fall to zero, making the EC market the largest and most populous in the world.

The economic advantages of the union to the well-being and progress of the countries involved are outlined in the theory presented in this chapter. Specifically, the free flow of goods and services and the unrestricted migration of labor and capital will be the central forces propelling economic growth in the whole region. The advantages of specialization and trade by comparative advantage *with no artificial impediments to trade* will be enormous. Just as Texas trades oil and gas for Idaho potatoes without barriers, so Ireland will be able to freely trade finished textiles for Italian shoes. EC countries have begun the process of eliminating barriers in telecommunications, life insurance, and auto production (the EC's biggest employer). Deregulation and free trade in many of these areas will mean (sometimes) painful relocations of production.

European union also raises many larger questions.[a] How, and in what sense, will the EC evolve in terms of monetary and political union? There is much debate (and some dissension) among member nations about these two issues. An elected European Parliament and Council of member country representatives meet in Strasbourg to discuss and approve decisions about future policies of the EC, but the real power is based in Brussels with the European Commission and with the European Court. These permanent (and unelected) bureaucracies make binding rules on the member countries to further integration.

[a]See Peter Brimelow, "The Dark Side of 1992," *Forbes* (January 22, 1990), pp. 85–89, upon which some of this discussion is based.

Just how far political and monetary integration will go is debatable. For example, a European central bank and a common currency might evolve over time, but enforced central banking with a common currency is unlikely to be accepted by all member nations at the outset. Countries that have typically taken a hard line on inflation, such as West Germany, are unwilling to relinquish control over their respective monetary units. Likewise, common policies such as uniform welfare subsidies to citizens of all EC countries could actually reduce the comparative advantage of some regions. This would occur if specialization were based upon low-priced labor or real wage differences. Of even more fundamental difficulty in achieving full integration are the different political traditions and legal systems within EC countries. Great Britain, for example, has a long history of independence and self-government, while some Continental nations have traditionally embraced centrist or Catholic socialist traditions—France and Italy, respectively. The actual outcome of EC integration is, for these reasons and others, most unclear.

The benefits and costs of European integration in 1992 is of great concern to EC trading partners. Will full economic integration of these twelve nations restrict or shut out American, Canadian, or Japanese exporters of goods such as beef and automobiles? In other words, will the EC become a giant protectionist monster with new monopoly powers to restrict U.S. and world trade? While the United States has been an ardent supporter of European union in the past, its motivations have been chiefly military, not economic. The remarkable "decentralization" in the Soviet Union and Eastern Europe that began in 1989 and the reduced threat of armed aggression has caused the United States to rethink a united Europe. On the one hand, protectionism by the EC would reduce world trade and welfare. On the other hand, an *external* policy of free trade by EC nations along with similar policies from other major trading nations could expand world specialization and economic well-being. Open access to the EC consumers (along with reciprocal access to American consumers) could provide an enormous and revitalized world market for America's goods and services and significant economic growth. Only time will tell.

National Involvement in International Trade

The overall magnitude of international trade and countries' shares in this trade can be measured in a variety of ways. The value of goods in international trade is given in Table 1 by major areas of the world. In 1988, world trade totaled almost $3 trillion, measured in exports or imports.

TABLE 1

World Trade: Exports and Imports, 1987–1988

Area	Exports (billions of dollars)	Imports (billions of dollars)
Industrial countries	1988.1	2067.7
Developing countries	699.8	701.6

Source: International Financial Statistics (Washington, D.C.: International Monetary Fund, 1990).

Table 2 lists the foreign trade of eleven nations as a percentage of gross national product for 1988; the percentages vary widely. Exports accounted for over 30 percent of West Germany's total output but less than 10 percent of Brazil's or the United States's output. Imports were about one-fourth to one-third of the real consumption of such countries as South Africa, West Germany, Sweden, and Switzerland.

Percentage figures do not tell the whole story, of course. In absolute terms the United States was the world's largest trader in both exports and imports in 1988. The value of merchandise exports totaled $319.3 billion and the value of merchandise imports was over $446.5 billion. The United States trades with virtually every nation of the world, the primary sources of imports being Canada (19 percent in 1988) and Japan (20 percent). The main destinations of U.S. exports in 1988 were Canada (23 percent), Japan (12 percent), and Western Europe (27 percent). In terms of products, the three main U.S. imports are crude oil, motor vehicles, and food, and the three main exports are machinery, motor vehicles, and grain.

Why Trade Is Important: Comparative Advantage

The reason for all this trading is that all nations benefit from some degree of specialization and trade. Suppose two nations produce computer components and food with an equal expenditure of time and resources. Trade between the two countries will likely emerge because each can specialize at what it does

TABLE 2

Exports and Imports as a Percentage of GNP in 1988

Country	Exports as a Percentage of GNP	Imports as a Percentage of GNP
United States	8.8	11.0
United Kingdom	23.0	26.8
Switzerland	34.5	34.2
Sweden	33.0	30.9
Japan	13.0	10.1
Italy	18.2	18.4
West Germany	32.4	26.7
Canada	27.0	26.5
Brazil	9.5	6.2
South Africa	29.8	24.4
Venezuela	22.5	28.2

Source: International Financial Statistics (Washington, D.C.: International Monetary Fund, 1990).

better—emphasizing the production at which it is more efficient—and trade with the other country for the other good. As we will see, both countries will be better off because specialization and trade lead to increases in production and therefore to increases in the attainable consumption levels of both goods in both countries.

According to the principle of **comparative advantage,** countries will specialize in producing those goods and services in which they have relatively lower opportunity costs than their trading partners. For example, a hilly, rocky country will not be able to raise as many sheep per acre as a country with fertile grasslands, but the rocky land cannot support any production other than sheep raising, whereas the grassland will support more lucrative cattle production. Even though the grassland is absolutely more productive at raising both sheep and cattle, the rocky land has a comparative advantage in sheep growing because the opportunities forgone are very small. The rocky country will therefore tend to specialize in sheep, the grassy country in cattle.

Consider the simplicity and power of the idea that each country produces those products that it can produce with relatively greater efficiency—at a lower relative opportunity cost. Countries that have relatively lower opportunity costs of producing certain goods and services have a strong incentive to produce those goods and services. Production across the world will thus come to reflect the principle of comparative advantage at work. The large amounts of fertile U.S. farmland combined with advanced farm technology have made the American farmer the most productive in the world. America has a clear comparative advantage in certain farm products and raw materials. America's skilled labor force and high rate of technological advance through huge investments in private and public research and development have helped make the United States relatively efficient in producing highly sophisticated machinery and equipment. Trading partners of the United States, especially Japan, have specialized in routinized productions such as automobiles and steel. Energy regulations and increased demand have forced the United States to import immense quantities of petroleum. The pattern of United States imports and exports therefore shows the process of economic specialization and comparative advantage at work.

Production Possibilities Before Specialization. To demonstrate more precisely how all trading partners benefit by exercising their comparative advantages, we must look at what happens in each country before and after specialization and trade. Suppose that both the United States and Japan, in isolation, produce just two goods: computer components and food. Further assume that the production possibilities schedules facing the United States and Japan are depicted in Table 3, which gives the alternative combinations of food and computer components that could be produced in the United States and Japan if resources are fully employed. The United States, for example, may choose to produce 60 units of food and no computer components, 40 units of food and 10 units of computer components, 20 units of each, or 30 units of computer components and no food. With fully employed resources, Japan may choose between 45 units of computer components and no food at one end of the production spectrum and no computer components with 30 units of food at the other, or combinations between these extremes, as shown in Table 3.

Comparative advantage:
An economic entity's (an individual's or a nation's) ability to produce a good at a lower marginal opportunity cost than some other entity.

TABLE 3

U.S. and Japanese Production Possibilities Schedules for Food and Computer Components

Within the United States 2 units of food cost 1 unit of computer components. Within Japan, $\frac{2}{3}$ unit of food costs 1 unit of computer components. The relative opportunity cost of food production is lower in the United States, and the relative opportunity cost of computer component production is lower in Japan.

	Production Possibilities (at full employment)			
	1	2	3	4
United States				
Food	0	20	40	60
Computer components	30	20	10	0
Japan				
Food	0	10	20	30
Computer components	45	30	15	0

These production alternatives are merely the trade-offs that are implicit in the countries' production possibilities curves. For the United States, the extreme choice is between producing 60 units of food (F) or 30 units of computer components (CC). That is, if the U.S. produces 60F, it will have to forgo 30CC. Within the United States, then, the opportunity cost of producing 1F will be ½ a unit of CC. Alternatively, the cost to the United States of producing 30CC is 60F, or 1CC costs 2F. In summary, within the United States,

60F costs 30CC to produce, or
1F costs ½CC to produce, or
1CC costs 2F to produce.

These costs measure how many units of food must be given up to obtain a unit of computer components, or how many units of computer components must be given up to get an additional unit of food. In either case, what is being measured is the relative opportunity cost of producing food or computer components in the United States—that is, what must be given up to increase the production of food or computer components.

Exactly the same analysis can be applied to Japan. For Japan, the production possibilities schedule indicates that, in the extreme, either 45 units of computer components and no food or 30 units of food and no computer components can be produced. The opportunity cost of producing 1F in Japan is then 1½CC. Likewise, 1CC costs ⅔ a unit of F. In Japan, the opportunity cost of production is summarized as

30F costs 45CC to produce, or
1F costs 1½CC to produce, or
1CC costs ⅔ F to produce.

Gains from Specialization and Trade. The concepts of production possibilities and opportunity costs provide a perspective for understanding the benefits of trade. Continuing our example of trade between the United States and Japan, first look at the U.S. and Japanese production possibilities curves in Figure 1. Notice that these production possibilities curves are straight lines. In practical terms, this means that resources can be transformed from food production to computer component production at constant opportunity cost, that resources are perfectly adaptable to one production process or the other in both economies. The simplicity of this assumption does not compromise the argument for specialization and trade.

The important part of the argument for gains from specialization turns on the pretrade opportunity costs of producing the two goods that face Japan and the United States. Before trade, consumers in the United States must sacrifice 2 units of food to produce 1 unit of computer components, while Japanese consumers must sacrifice only ⅔ unit of food to produce the same amount of computer components. On the other side of the coin, American consumers must sacrifice only ½ unit of computer components to obtain 1 unit of food, while their Japanese counterparts must give up 1½ units of computer components to get 1 unit of food.

Both countries can gain from trade. Since the United States produces food at an opportunity cost of ½CC and Japan produces computer components at an opportunity cost of ⅔F, we know that the Americans would gain if trade gave them more than ½CC for 1 unit of food, and the Japanese would gain from ⅔F for a single unit of computer components. These differences in relative opportunity costs of producing food and computer components yield a basis for specialization and trade between the two countries.

FIGURE 1 Prespecialization Production Possibilities Curves

The straight-line production possibilities curves for the United States and Japan indicate that resources can be transferred from computer component production into food production at constant opportunity cost. The different slopes of the two curves indicate that different opportunity costs provide the basis for both countries to benefit from specialization and trade. The United States has a comparative advantage in food production, whereas Japan is relatively more efficient at producing computer components.

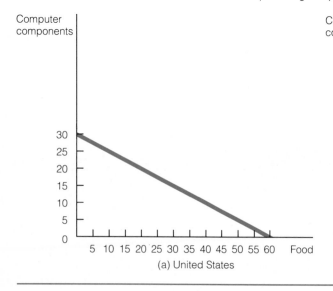

(a) United States

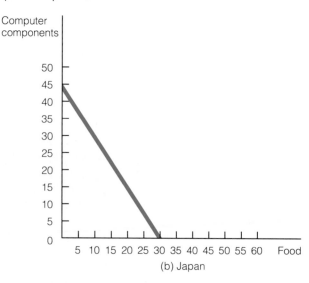

(b) Japan

Terms of trade:
The number of units of one good that exchange in the market for one unit of some other good; a relative price.

Consumption possibilities curve:
All the possible combinations of two goods that could be consumed by first specializing according to comparative advantage and then trading at the terms of trade.

At what price will trade take place? The **terms of trade**—the ratio at which two goods can be traded for each other—will settle somewhere between the relative opportunity cost ratios for each country. For example, terms acceptable to both Japan and the United States will fall between ⅔F = 1CC (Japan) and 2F = 1CC (United States). We might say that the two countries bargain to set the terms of trade, and the bargaining range is determined by each country's internal opportunity cost trade-off. For simplicity, let us assume that the terms of trade settles at 1 unit of food for 1 unit of computer components, or 1F = 1CC.

Figure 2 illustrates the potential outcomes of this agreement in terms of the production possibilities curves and each country's posttrade **consumption possibilities curve.** If the countries choose to specialize totally according to comparative advantage, the United States produces 60 units of food and Japan produces 45 units of computer components. Each country can now trade for the product it no longer produces; each country is no longer restricted to consuming a combination of goods on its production possibilities curve. Without trade, a country is restricted to consuming whatever it produces. In

---

FIGURE 2   **Production and Consumption Possibilities Curves**

The production possibilities curves for the United States and Japan are the dark straight lines. The United States specializes in food, producing 60 units; Japan specializes in computer components, producing 45 units. Once trade can take place at the terms of trade of 1F for 1CC, the consumption possibilities curves become relevant. The United States exports 25F and imports 25CC, increasing its consumption (over the pretrade situation) of food by 15 units and computer components by 5 units. Japan exports 25CC and imports 25F, increasing its consumption (over the pretrade situation) of food by 5 units and computer components by 5 units.

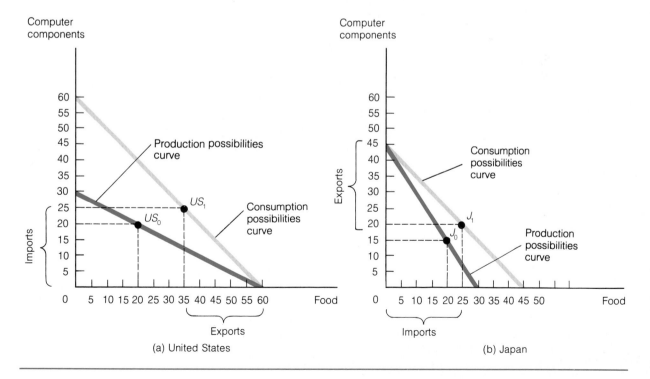

(a) United States

(b) Japan

the absence of trade, its production possibilities curve and its consumption possibilities curve would be one and the same.

With trade, however, each country's consumption opportunities are determined by how much of its specialized output is produced and the terms of trade. A country's consumption possibilities curve shows all the possible combinations of the two goods that could be consumed if production were specialized (according to comparative advantage) and trade could take place at the given terms of trade. Of course, only one combination can actually be consumed, so the consumption possibilities curve should be viewed as a menu of alternatives open to the country. The consumption possibilities curve with trade will always lie beyond the production possibilities curve, indicating that specialization and trade will leave the country economically better off. Remember, without trade the country's consumption opportunities are identical to its production opportunities.

Given that each country specializes and can now trade (at a price or terms of trade of 1F = 1CC) for the product it no longer produces, the consumption possibilities curves in Figure 2 become relevant. In contrast to a domestic opportunity cost of 60F for 30CC, the United States now enjoys a situation in which production of 60F could be traded for 60CC. Japan enjoys a similar expansion of consumption opportunities with specialization and trade. By specializing and trading, both countries are made economically better off. Each has the ability, with trade, to consume a bundle of goods beyond its production possibilities curve. This would be impossible, given each country's resources and technology, without trade. Specialization does not even have to be complete for the two countries to gain from trade. We have used the example of complete specialization here for simplicity.

If we assume that U.S. consumers originally consumed the bundle of food and computer components labeled US_0 in Figure 2a, we can note the improvement in their well-being by considering a new, posttrade consumption bundle, US_1, on their consumption possibilities curve. More of both goods are consumed after specialization and trade. A similar conclusion arises for Japan if we compare hypothetical pre- and postspecialization and trade consumption bundles, J_0 and J_1, respectively. Specialization and trade enlarge the consumption possibilities of the trading nations so that both countries can consume more of both goods after trade occurs.

Note that trade between the United States and Japan in this example takes place according to the principle of comparative advantage. Figure 3 shows the explicit pattern of trade. The United States exports food (25 units) because it has a comparative advantage over Japan in food production. This is so because 1F costs the United States only ½CC to produce, whereas 1F would cost Japan 1½CC to produce. Japan exports computer components for the same reason. It has a comparative advantage in producing them over the United States. Each country imports the good for which it is at a comparative *dis*advantage—that is, the good for which its trading partner possesses a comparative advantage. Gains from trade accrue to producers and consumers. In this example, American consumers of computer components benefit from the lower prices made available by imports, while American food producers benefit by obtaining a price for the food they export higher than the price they could obtain by selling it in the United States—which is not to suggest that no one is harmed by free trade. U.S. food consumers must pay higher food prices as a result of the decision to export some U.S. production. Similarly, U.S. pro-

FIGURE 3

Japan has a comparative advantage in computer component production; the United States, in food production. This means that Japan will export computer components and import food, whereas the United States will export food and import computer components. The terms of trade, 1F for 1CC in this example, must be between the two countries' opportunity costs of production.

The Pattern of U.S.-Japan Trade

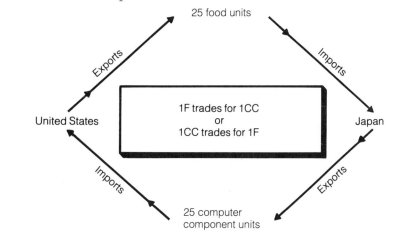

ducers of computer components are harmed when Japanese supplies enter the market and cause prices to fall. On balance, however, gains from free trade exceed losses; free trade leads to improved standards of living.

Our discussion has been based on a simple example of how the principle of comparative advantage works. In discussing two-good trade between Japan and the United States, we assumed that each country was absolutely more efficient than the other at producing one of the two goods. What if one country is absolutely more efficient in producing both goods? Suppose that productivity in the United States tripled—production of computer components increasing to 90 units and production of food increasing to 180 units. U.S. production capacity in this case would outpace Japan two to one in computer components and six to one in food. Nonetheless, the opportunity cost to the United States of producing each computer component would still be 2 units of food, which is higher than Japan's opportunity cost. It would still be mutually advantageous for the United States to specialize in food and to obtain computer components from Japan through trade. Remember, the argument for free trade is based on the principle of *comparative* advantage. Trade between two countries is mutually beneficial whenever the countries bear different opportunity costs of producing goods. This is true even if one of the countries is absolutely more productive at both goods.

Tariffs and Quotas

Despite the advantages of specialization and trade, certain barriers to trade exist in the real world. Some are natural costs of exchanges, such as negotiating and transportation costs, and cannot be avoided. Other barriers to trade are artificial, contrivances of governments designed to raise revenues or protect domestic producers from foreign competition. The major examples of artificial trade barriers are tariffs and quotas. A **tariff,** or import duty, is simply a tax levied on particular imported goods. For example, the United States imposes a tariff on imported shoes and steel. A **quota** is a partial or absolute limitation on the quantity of a particular good that can be imported. For example, until

Tariff:
A tax or levy on imported goods.

Quota:
A restriction or limit on the quantity of an imported good.

1972 the United States imposed a quota on the importation of foreign oil and permitted oil refiners to import only the allowed amount of oil. Both tariffs and quotas reduce the extent of specialization and trade and, therefore, the gains that consumers obtain from free trade. Both raise the prices of imported and domestically produced goods and restrict imports. In these respects, tariffs and quotas are similar. For an analysis of the similarities and differences of quotas and tariffs that concentrates on the quotas the Reagan administration imposed on Japanese automobiles in 1981, see Economics in Action, "Voluntary Export Restraints: A Quota Is a Quota Is a Tariff," at the end of this chapter.

THE EFFECTS OF ARTIFICIAL TRADE BARRIERS

Though tariffs and quotas presumably are adopted by governments out of national self-interest, they usually do not benefit most citizens in the long run. Tariff duties on imports were an essential source of U.S. government revenues from the Revolution until the late nineteenth century, and the use of tariffs to protect domestic industries is still being promoted. The effects of tariffs and quotas have long been debated. Adam Smith made the definitive economic statement on the matter in his *Wealth of Nations* in 1776.

> To give the monopoly of the home-market to the produce of domestic industry, in any particular art of manufacture, is in some measure to direct private people in what manner they ought to employ their capitals, and must, in almost all cases, be either a useless or a hurtful regulation. If the produce of domestic industry can be bought there as cheap as that of foreign industry, the regulation is evidently useless. If it cannot, it must generally be hurtful.[1]

Smith knew that individual traders, such as tailors and shoemakers, could gain from specialization and trade. But he went further and argued that the principle applied no less to nations.

> What is prudence in the conduct of every private family, can scarce be folly in that of a great kingdom. If a foreign country can supply us with a commodity cheaper than we ourselves can make it, better buy it of them with some part of the produce of our own industry, employed in a way in which we have some advantage. The general industry of the country, being always in proportion to the capital which employs it, will not thereby be diminished.[2]

Free trade:
The exchange of goods between countries without the presence of artificial trade barriers such as tariffs and quotas.

With very few exceptions (to be discussed later in the chapter), **free trade**—trade without artificial barriers—leads to maximum economic welfare among nations. Free trade and specialization expand consumption possibilities and deliver goods to consumers at the lowest possible costs. Yet given all

---

[1]Adam Smith, *An Inquiry into the Nature and Causes of the Wealth of Nations,* ed. Edwin Cannan (1776; reprint, New York: Modern Library, 1937), pp. 423–24.

[2]Smith, *Wealth of Nations,* p. 424.

the benefits of free trade, the world does not often seem to allow it to work, at least not completely. The reason is that some parties are harmed by free trade. Pressures are brought to bear on governments by producer groups for protection from foreign competition. Sometimes these groups win political favors, such as tariffs or quotas, to reduce the competitive threat. In this section we use economic theory to show how these interferences with free trade reduce the overall economic welfare of a country.

Trade and Tariffs: Who Gains? Who Loses?

To understand who really gains and loses from a tariff, consider Figure 4. It shows two possible prices facing domestic suppliers of automobiles: the free-market world price of autos, P_w, and the free-market world price plus some per unit tariff on autos imported to the United States, P_{w+t}.

Imposition of a tariff on imported autos clearly benefits domestic automobile manufacturers. Since imported cars are now more expensive, domestic suppliers can raise their prices, without any increase in costs. The higher price P_{w+t} encourages domestic auto producers to increase output from quantity Q_0 to quantity Q_1, increasing domestic suppliers' profits by the shaded area $P_{w+t}E_1E_0P_w$. This increase in profits is often described as an increase in producer surplus. Naturally, because the tariff increases domestic production, it also increases domestic employment in the industry producing the tariffed good. We must be careful, though, not to generalize that a tariff on a specific good or set of goods will increase the overall level of employment in a country. The tariff is likely to have economic repercussions that are felt in the markets for other goods and services and that tend to reduce employment in those markets.

What if the auto tariff were reduced? A reduction in the tariff would reduce producers' profits (their *producer surplus*) as well as domestic em-

FIGURE 4

Imposition of an import tariff on imported automobiles allows U.S. producers to raise the prices of their automobiles from the free-market world price, P_w, to P_{w+t}. The higher prices encourage them to increase the quantity of automobiles they produce from Q_0 to Q_1. Their profits are therefore increased by the shaded area $P_{w+t}E_1E_0P_w$. This increase in profits is also referred to as an increase in producer surplus. Employment of domestic resources increases because domestic production rises from Q_0 to Q_1.

Domestic Producers' Supply Schedule for Automobiles

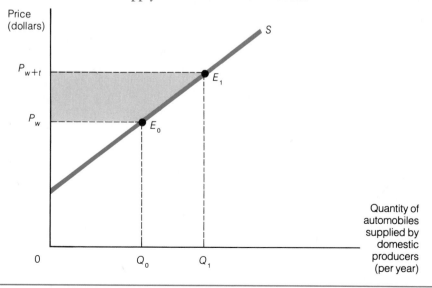

ployment in the auto industry. But before we can present an economic assessment of tariffs, we must investigate their effects on consumers.

The effects of a tariff on consumers are shown in Figure 5. The figure shows an initial price, P_w, and an initial quantity of autos, Q_0, purchased by consumers. Imposition of a tariff on imported cars increases the price to P_{w+t} and reduces consumption of autos from Q_0 to Q_1. A reduction in benefits to consumers accompanies the increase in price. (These benefits are known as *consumer surplus.*) The shaded area $P_{w+t}E_1E_0P_w$ in Figure 5 represents the reduction in consumer surplus caused by the tariff on automobiles. This concept will be elaborated in the following sections.

The Benefits of Free Trade

Using the concepts of consumer and producer surplus, we can now see the benefits of free trade. We will first examine an industry in which the United States is an importer—the automobile industry. Then we will look at the effects of free international trade on an industry in which the United States is an exporter—the wheat industry.

Consider Figure 6, which shows the U.S. domestic supply curve for automobiles, S_{US}, the curve S_F, which shows the supply of cars to the U.S. market by foreign producers, and the American demand curve, D. The domestic supply curve and the foreign supply curve for automobiles are added together horizontally to produce S_T, a curve showing the total supply of cars to the U.S. market by domestic and foreign producers.

If no cars were allowed to be imported, the domestic price of cars would be P_D, and the quantity bought and sold would be Q_D. However, if cars were imported without restriction, the market would clear at E_1, where the price is P_T and the quantity is Q_T—the point at which domestic demand for cars

---

FIGURE 5

A tariff on imported automobiles causes the price to increase from P_w to P_{w+t}, which in turn causes a reduction in the quantity of automobiles demanded by consumers from Q_0 to Q_1. Benefits to consumers are reduced by the amount represented by the shaded area $P_{w+t}E_1E_0P_w$. This loss is referred to as a reduction in consumer surplus.

Effects of Tariff on Consumer Demand

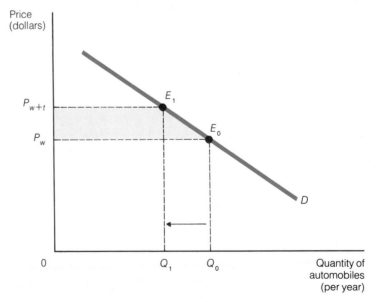

FIGURE 6

The total supply curve S_T is the horizontal summation of domestic (S_{US}) and foreign (S_F) supplies of automobiles. In the pretrade situation, when consumers purchase only domestic automobiles, equilibrium E_0 is established at price P_D and quantity produced Q_D. Under free trade, imports lower prices from P_D to P_T and increase quantity consumed in the domestic market from Q_D to Q_T, with equilibrium established at E_1. Consumers benefit from free trade in the amount represented by $P_D E_0 E_1 P_T$.

The Benefits of Importing Freely

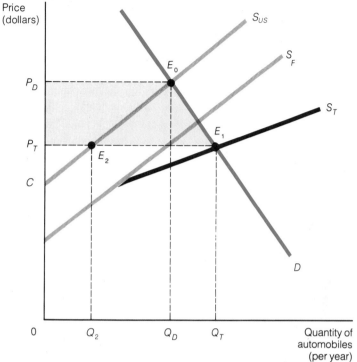

equals total supply of cars. If we compare the equilibrium under free trade with the equilibrium under no trade, we see that the consumer surplus is larger by an amount $P_D E_0 E_1 P_T$. However, under free trade and a price of P_T, domestic producers produce only Q_2 cars and receive a producer surplus that is smaller by the amount $P_D E_0 E_2 P_T$ than the surplus they previously received. In other words, domestic car producers are harmed by free trade, since they sell fewer cars (Q_2 instead of Q_D) at a price of P_T. However, the gain that consumers receive by moving to free trade, $P_D E_0 E_1 P_T$, is larger than the cost of free trade to U.S. producers by an amount equal to $E_0 E_1 E_2$.

Figure 7 shows the effects of free trade in an industry like the wheat industry in which the United States is an exporter. In Figure 7, D_{US} and S_{US} show domestic demand and supply of wheat, respectively. D_F shows foreign demand for U.S. wheat, and D_T shows the horizontal total of U.S. and foreign demand for wheat. If wheat is not permitted to be sold abroad, the wheat market in the United States will clear at E_1, with a price of P_D and with Q_D units bought by U.S. consumers from U.S. producers. However, if the United States allows free trade, the market will clear at E_2. The equilibrium price of wheat will rise to P_T and the equilibrium quantity will rise to Q_T. Of the Q_T units sold by domestic producers, Q' will be sold to domestic consumers, and the remainder ($Q_T - Q'$) will be exported. As a consequence of free trade, U.S. producers will experience an increase in producer surplus of $P_T E_2 E_1 P_D$. U.S. consumers will find that their surplus has fallen by $P_T E_3 E_1 P_D$. The gain to producers exceeds the loss to consumers by $E_3 E_2 E_1$.

FIGURE 7

The total demand curve, D_T, is the horizontal sum of domestic demand (D_{US}) and foreign demand for U.S. wheat (D_F). In the pretrade situation, the equilibrium is at E_1. If exports are permitted, the price rises from P_D to P_T. Domestic producers increase sales from Q_D to Q_T, but domestic consumers reduce purchases from Q_D to Q'. As a consequence, the increase in the producer surplus of domestic producers is larger than the decrease in the consumer surplus.

The Benefits of Exporting Freely

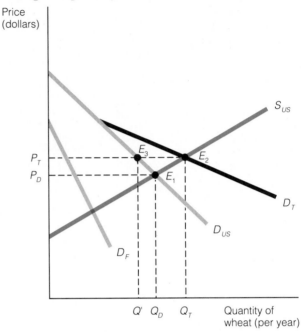

We see that, as a group, consumers and producers benefit from free trade. Although some parties are harmed, the gains by others more than offset these losses. There are net gains from trade both for an import industry and an export industry.

Welfare Loss from Tariffs

We have now seen how trade creates net benefits to domestic consumers and producers. Let us now look at the effects of a protective tariff on the society as a whole, using a hypothetical market for television sets.

Figure 8 represents the domestic market for TV sets, including the domestic supply of the product and the U.S. demand. Prior to the imposition of a tariff, American consumers buy Q_4 units at the world price P_w. Of this quantity purchased, Q_1 are sold by domestic manufacturers and $Q_1 Q_4$ are imported from abroad.

Assume that a tariff is imposed in the amount t, causing the price of TVs to American consumers to rise to P_{w+t}. (For clarity, we have assumed that the foreign TV supply curve is horizontal. This totally elastic supply curve could arise from TV production in the world being a constant-cost industry or from the idea that the United States buys such a small share of total world TV output that it is a price-taker country.) American TV producers gain additional profits in the amount represented by $P_{w+t}E_2E_1P_w$ because of the increased domestic output permitted by the higher price. Imports are reduced to $Q_2 Q_3$, and the total number of sets sold decreases to Q_3. Consumers lose total benefits in the amount of $P_{w+t}E_3E_4P_w$. At the same time, the tariff on

FIGURE 8

The Effects of a Tariff

Gains in producer profits and government revenue do not equal consumer losses from tariff imposition. Net consumer losses are shown in the shaded triangles in the figure. Before a tariff on TV sets, consumers purchase Q_4 units at price P_w. The tariff causes the price to rise to P_{w+t}, imports to decrease from Q_1Q_4 to Q_2Q_3, and the total number of TVs sold to decrease to Q_3. Consumers' total loss is represented by $P_{w+t}E_3E_4P_w$, but producers gain $P_{w+t}E_2E_1P_w$, and government tariff revenues are E_2E_3AB. The net loss to society is therefore the sum of the areas E_2BE_1 and E_3E_4A.

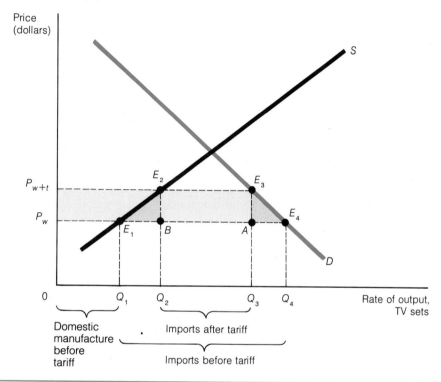

imported TV sets creates government revenues. These revenues are composed of the per unit amount of the tariff multiplied by the units of TV sets imported after the tariff is imposed (area E_2E_3AB in Figure 8).

Economists typically assume that the government revenue is used in a manner that produces benefits equivalent to those lost by consumers of TV sets. However, the tariff causes a net loss in benefits to society, of which TV consumers are a part, represented by the sum of the two areas E_2BE_1 and E_3E_4A. The sum of these triangles represents a loss that is not counterbalanced by the sum of producers' gains and government revenue resulting from the tariff. Economists call this loss a **welfare loss to society.**

Welfare loss to society:
The *net* loss to an economy resulting from the imposition of an artificial trade barrier; government revenues plus producer gains minus consumer losses.

Why Are Tariffs Imposed?

If tariffs create a welfare loss to society, why are they imposed? Certainly tariff revenue to the federal government is minuscule when compared to other sources of government revenue. More than two hundred years ago, Adam Smith identified the real cause of protective tariffs:

Merchants and manufacturers are the people who derive the greatest advantage from this monopoly of the home-market. . . . Manufactures, those of the finer kind especially, are more easily transported from one country to another than corn or cattle. It is in the fetching and carrying manufacturers, accordingly, that foreign trade is chiefly employed. In manufactures, a very small advantage will enable foreigners to undersell our own workmen, even in the home market. . . . They [merchants and manufacturers] accordingly seem to have been the original inventors of those restraints upon the importation of foreign goods, which secure to them the monopoly of the home-market.[3]

The source of tariff protection is to be found in the urgings of "merchants and manufacturers" as well as from labor in domestic import-competing industries, today as it was in Smith's day. Consumers of TV sets and of any goods that actually bear a tariff could conceivably convince both producers and the government not to impose tariffs because, as we have shown, consumers lose more than producers and government gain from tariffs. Practically, however, the world does not work this way. Consumers, the gainers from free trade, are widely dispersed and costly to organize in any fight for free trade. Interest in fighting a tariff or quota is also apt to be low among consumers because their pro rata share of losses from artificial barriers to trade is generally small. To an individual consumer, for example, the tariff is a small proportion of the total price of an automobile. The incentive to organize and fight protective tariffs is therefore small.

Not so for producers. The pro rata, or proportionate, share of the effects of tariff protection is much higher among manufacturers, for they are far fewer in number than consumers. Manufacturers thus have stronger incentives than consumers to form an interest group, and, being fewer in number, their costs of organizing are lower. For such reasons, the consumer interest in free trade is often thwarted.

Nontariff Barriers to Trade

Nontariff trade barriers:
Alternative (to tariffs and quotas) means of restricting trade; examples include domestic content legislation and health and safety regulations.

Historically, tariffs and quotas have been the most important types of artificial trade restrictions. In recent years, other types of restrictive practices, which are generally called **nontariff trade barriers** (NTBs), have taken on increased importance. Examples of nontariff trade barriers include domestic content legislation (laws that require a certain portion of goods sold in a country to be produced there) as well as safety or health regulations designed to discriminate against foreign products. NTBs have grown rapidly in recent years because many countries have enacted trade legislation that forbids tariffs or quotas; NTBs represent an alternative form of protectionism. The use of NTBs varies greatly among countries. In the United States, NTBs exist for about 25 percent of imported goods. The corresponding percentage for Japan is about 12 percent. Within the European community, percentages vary but average about 20 percent.

Although it is difficult to determine the specific effects of nontariff trade barriers, the general effects are quite similar to those of tariffs. Figure 8 shows how a tariff artificially raises the price of imported goods and causes the

---

[3]Smith, *Wealth of Nations,* pp. 426, 429.

quantity of imports to fall. NTBs have similar effects. If, for example, the United States were to enact legislation requiring that cars sold in this country have a 50 percent domestic content, the Japanese could continue exporting cars to the United States only if at least half of the parts and the assembly were American. The cost of compliance would be higher production costs to the Japanese, but it would be very difficult to determine how much costs would rise. The effect therefore would be identical to the imposition of some specific tariff. Without knowing by how much this legislation would increase production costs, it would be impossible to determine what an equivalent tariff would be.

Nontariff trade barriers have become a major issue in the United States, particularly with regard to the economic unification of the European community. There is some concern that a unified Europe will implement technical standards that discriminate against foreign firms. Some observers have suggested that U.S. exports to Europe would fall sharply as a result of any such barriers. Although it is impossible to predict what economic policies the unified European community will pursue, the economic unification of Europe is sure to present certain advantages to U.S. exporters. For one thing, U.S. firms will no longer have to contend with different NTBs in each of the European countries nor have to meet different standards by producing a different product for each country.

THE CASE FOR PROTECTION

Throughout history numerous arguments have emerged in defense of protection from free trade. Some arguments are well constructed; others are but thin veils for producers' interests. All the arguments—both the well-constructed and the questionable ones—deserve careful scrutiny.

National Interest Arguments for Protection

The two oldest and best-formed arguments in defense of protection and against free trade are the national defense argument and the "infant industries" argument. Both arguments contain a grain of truth, but each should be closely scrutinized before serving as a base for protectionist policies.

National Defense. The oldest argument for protection—and the one with superficially the best justification—is that such restrictions are necessary for national defense. As military technology has changed, steel, gunpowder, manganese, uranium, and a host of other inputs have all been commodities essential to making war at various times, and they have been the subject of tariffs and quotas to keep domestic production of these commodities strong.

The logic of protection for defense is clear: Since the ultimate function of government is national defense, any possible threat to national defense, such as the unavailability of some resource during a crisis, must be avoided. A loss in consumers' benefits from protection is thus justified for a greater benefit—the availability of essential materials to be prepared for war. Artificial barriers to trade in these materials are used to protect domestic industries considered essential for national defense.

The national defense argument is plausible for some industries and some products, but consider that cheese, fruit, and watch manufacturers and other, non-defense-related industries have all resorted to the argument. History seems to prove that patriotism is the last and best refuge of a producer seeking protection from foreign competition. The national defense argument has seen double duty as an argument for maintaining unprofitable routes on railroads and protecting truck, air, and railroad companies by setting legalized cartel rates. The telephone industry was long protected on similar grounds.

Other ways can be devised to handle the national defense issue besides imposing tariffs and quotas. A tariff is nothing but a hidden subsidy or cash grant to domestic producers. Thus, if an industry is to be protected for national defense reasons, an explicit subsidy may be more straightforward than tariff protection. That way the national defense issue is made clear, and voters know how much defense actually costs them. If, for example, it is deemed vital to national security that the United States have a certain capacity to produce iron and steel, an alternative public policy would be to subsidize domestic iron and steel producers rather than to protect them against foreign competition with a tariff or quota.

Protection of Infant Industries. Possibly the most frequently heard argument for protection, especially in developing nations, is the so-called **infant industries** argument. Discussed by Adam Smith and supported by Americans such as Alexander Hamilton, the infant industries argument reached its highest expression in the mid-nineteenth-century writing of German nationalist Friedrich List (1789–1846). List sought to unify and develop the German states against the incursions of British imports. He argued that protective tariffs were necessary in the transition from an agricultural-manufacturing to an agricultural-manufacturing-commercial stage of development. His reasoning was clear: Specific tariffs were necessary to maintain fledgling industries until they could compete with foreign imports on their own. After the "infancy" period of industrial development was over, protective tariffs would be lifted, forcing the businesses to meet the rigors of competition.

The infant industries argument is related to the idea of economies of scale. Economies of scale exist when, as plant size increases up to a point, long-run unit costs decline. This occurs because individual workers become more proficient at narrowly defined tasks, and machines are more closely tailored to individual processes. Scale economies may also occur because both workers and managers "learn by doing" and acquire more experience as output grows. Often, moreover, production of certain manufactured goods results in an enormous initial setup cost. As firm and industry output grow larger, these setup costs are spread over larger and larger numbers of units produced. A number of developing nations use this economies of scale or infant industries argument today in their quest for unilateral tariff protection. One-crop economies, whose foreign earnings are heavily dependent on a single export, seek to use an umbrella of protectionist policies to buy time for diversification.

As much as one might be concerned for the economic plight of poor nations, great care must be exercised in applying the infant industry argument to them. At best, the argument is one for allowing domestic industry to gain a foothold in international competition. Protection for any reason, as we have seen, means lost benefits for consumers. Obviously, any gains from ultimate

Infant industry:
A new or developing domestic industry whose unit production costs are higher than those of established firms in the same industry in other countries.

independence must be balanced against the costs of lost consumer benefits over the period of protection.

A final question that should be applied to the infant industries argument concerns the vagueness of the goal of removing protection "when the industry grows up." It is hardly legitimate to apply the infant industries argument to the present-day steel industry in the United States and Western Europe, but the argument is still being used. Entrenched protectionist interests will always attempt to prolong the "infancy" of any industry. The dangers of giving protectionists a general legal foothold negate any merit the argument might have in limited and specific cases.

Industry Arguments for Protection

A number of other arguments for protection crop up from time to time, usually put forward by domestic firms and industries seeking protection for protection's sake. We characterize these arguments as wrong because they are assaults on the very principle that gains may be realized from trade. They are all variations on the theme that special-interest groups deserve protection from international competition.

The "Cheap Foreign Labor" Argument. A common argument for tariff or quota protection is that labor or some other resource is cheaper abroad, enabling foreign manufacturers to sell goods at lower prices than U.S. manufacturers. The defenders of this argument are often producers or workers displaced by imports and foreign competition. During the early 1980s, for instance, U.S. producers and workers bitterly complained through their union representatives that imports were creating unemployment.

While the argument may be correct—foreign producers may be more efficient combiners of resources—this truth in no way denies the benefits to free trade. The *absolute* level of wages in any other country does not matter. As we have seen, gains from trade derive from *comparative* advantage. Indeed, the request for protection from cheap labor turns the gains from trade position on its head: The reason *for* trade becomes a reason to limit or restrict trade. Open trade is beneficial precisely because resources may be cheaper or combined more efficiently elsewhere. The opening or extension of trade creates a temporary disruption of markets, including the unemployment of resources. To impose tariffs or quotas on the grounds that some groups of U.S. laborers are temporarily thrown out of work or that some U.S. stockholders are losing wealth is to subsidize special interests at a greater cost to all U.S. consumers of the subsidized product or service. Moreover, the domestic economy may actually gain from the movement of domestic resources into new fields of comparative advantage. For example, resources released from domestic steel production may be reallocated to computer production.

Side issues arise in the cheap foreign labor argument. One common complaint is that foreign governments subsidize the production of exported goods to shore up their domestic industries and prevent unemployment. This complaint is used as a plea for protection from cheaper imports. But to argue for tariffs on these grounds is to look a gift horse in the mouth. The benefits from trade are independent of the reasons that imports are cheaper. If governments choose to subsidize their exports, they in effect tax their own citizens to benefit foreign consumers.

Dumping, selling goods abroad at a lower price than in the home market, is also related to the cheap foreign labor argument for protection. The practice means that foreign buyers gain greater benefits from consuming the commodity or service than domestic consumers. In practice, it is often difficult to determine whether goods are being dumped. As defined by U.S. trade policies, dumping occurs when a foreign producer sells in the American market either below costs or at a price below that charged to the foreign producer's domestic customers. In real-world cases, then, a producer could be selling to his or her own customers at monopoly rates and be prohibited from selling to American consumers at lower rates (even though they more than cover costs). Such restrictions, if enforced by trade authorities, could work against American consumers.

Special interests in the favored country often complain that dumping constitutes "unfair competition," but the argument for free trade remains intact nonetheless. Consumers in the favored nations are able to purchase goods at lower prices, and overall welfare in the consuming country is enhanced.

It should not matter why foreign prices are low, as long as the foreign supplier who is dumping goods in U.S. markets has no monopoly power. If the producers of Japanese television sets undersell U.S. producers with an eye to putting them out of business and subsequently raising their price to a monopoly level, dumping does pose an issue for public concern. This is not usually the case, however. More often, alleged dumping by foreign producers is simply a reflection of their lower costs of production and puts competitive pressure on U.S. producers.

The "Buy American" Argument. The "buy American" argument, a call to patriotism, means to keep money at home. More specifically, "buy American" means that imports should be restricted so that high costs or inefficient producers and their employees may be protected from foreign competition.

This well-known argument is fallacious on several counts. First, it asks consumers to pay higher prices for goods and services than are available to them through trade, thereby negating the potential expansion of trade benefits. Second, when money is kept at home, foreign consumers are unable to purchase domestic exports, reducing the welfare of domestic export producers and their workers and other input suppliers.

"Terms of Trade" Advantage. A final argument applies to countries that have monopoly or monopsony power in international markets. It suggests that a country employ its power to increase its share of the gains from international trade. Thus, if the United States is the world's largest supplier of computers, putting restrictions on computer exports will drive up the price of computers in the international market. Although the United States will then sell fewer computers, it will get a higher price per computer and possibly higher computer sales revenues. In effect, by restricting computer exports, the United States would alter the terms of trade in international transactions in its favor.

The **terms of trade argument** suggests that countries exercise monopoly and monopsony power where possible. Doing so is a means for a country to increase its revenues from international trade. The argument founders, however, on a simple point: the possibility of retaliation by other countries. If all countries seek terms of trade advantages, the trading nations of the world *collectively* may be made worse off. The exercise of monopoly or monopsony power to improve the terms of trade for all countries could mean a shrinking of total world production for exports. This negates the gains possible from comparative advantage and from the division of labor and reduces specialization within nations.

Perhaps the greatest flaw in all arguments for protection lies in the implicit assumption that other nations will lose export markets and will not retaliate. It is improbable that a country could win permanent terms of trade advantages on a unilateral basis while its trading partners sit idly by. U.S. history is peppered with examples of tariff wars. One of the fiercest tariff wars in history took place in the midst of the Great Depression of the 1930s, discussed in the next section. Tariffs or other forms of trade barrier retaliation can only create a reduction in worldwide economic welfare and massive and inefficient allocations of resources. Whatever the initial reasons for protective tariffs, consumers ultimately suffer the costs.

U.S. TARIFF POLICY

U.S. tariff history has been punctuated by cycles of free trade and of protectionism, with a move toward free trade in the past fifty years that may be more apparent than real. The average tariff rates for the years between 1821 (the year of the first good statistics) and 1989 are shown in Figure 9, along with some highlights of our tariff history. Import duties as a percentage of the value of all imports subject to duty ranged from almost 60 percent in the early 1930s to a mere 3.5 percent in 1989.

Why has the average tariff fluctuated so widely during U.S. history? Before turning to a specific analysis of changing conditions, one broad issue will help us answer the question. With the minor exception of tariffs imposed for revenues to fight wars or to apply foreign policy pressures, the average tariff has varied with business conditions, falling in periods of prosperity and rising during prolonged recessions or depressions. During periods of rising prosperity, manufacturers and workers displaced by free trade find little political support for the imposition of tariffs. When general business conditions turn downward, creating reduced demand for products and increased unemployment, the cry for protection grows louder in the political arena.

Early Tariff Policy

Tariffs were a major source of revenue for our republic in its early years, as they are for some developing countries today. Post-1820 tariffs tended to vary with business conditions, rising during recessions and falling during more prosperous periods of business activity. On the eve of the Civil War, tariff revenues stood at about 19 percent of the value of imports, the lowest level in American history up to that time. In 1861, the Morrill tariff passed Congress under the pretext of generating much-needed revenue for the Union treasury. Whatever the initial intention, the Morrill tariff set off a wave of protectionism

FIGURE 9

Level of Tariffs

The United States today has lower tariffs, as measured by the ratio of tariff fees collected to the value of imports, than at any time in its history. Since the establishment of the General Agreement on Tariffs and Trade (GATT) in 1947, tariffs have followed a downward trend.

Sources: U.S. Bureau of the Census, *Historical Statistics of the U.S.,* 1976; *Statistical Abstract of the United States,* 1985, p. 823; Tax Foundation, *Facts and Figures on Government Finance* (Baltimore: Johns Hopkins University Press, 1990), p. 91.

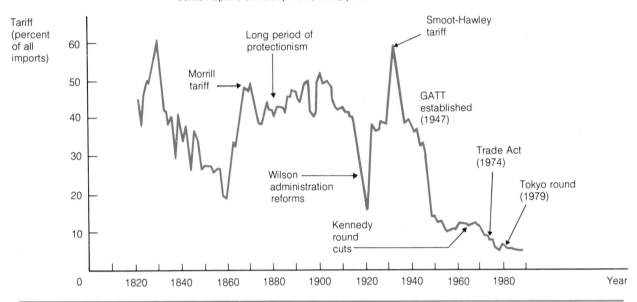

in U.S. policy that lasted until the second decade of the twentieth century. Tariffs declined dramatically during the Wilson administration, standing at only 16 percent in 1920.

The dramatic downturn in the economy beginning in the late 1920s had a stark and lingering effect on protectionism in the United States. Manufacturing and commercial interests, coinciding with a willing political climate, produced the Smoot-Hawley Act of 1930, which legislated the highest peacetime tariff in U.S. history. Average tariff levels were raised to almost 60 percent of the value of imports, setting off a frenzy of protectionist retaliations in other nations. The result of what was perceived as American self-interest was falling real incomes, sharply reduced consumer welfare, and a deepened and prolonged worldwide depression in the major world-trading countries.

Modern Tariff Policy

Contemporary tariff policy may be viewed as an attempt to overcome the disastrous effects of protectionism embodied in the Smoot-Hawley Act. The first Roosevelt administration, under the aegis of Secretary of State Cordell Hull, acted swiftly to counteract the protectionism of the Smoot-Hawley tariff. In 1934, the Reciprocal Trade Agreements Act was passed, giving the president power to negotiate bilateral tariff reductions of up to 50 percent with other countries. This act was the important first step in establishing the character of modern U.S. tariff policy. It established a framework within which free trade is envisioned as a goal of policy, and to a large extent it stripped Congress of its tariff-making power (but not the power to set nontariff barriers). While Congress could legally remove the tariff-setting powers of the president, these powers have been renewed and strengthened a number of times since 1934.

In the post–World War II era, the powers of the president have been expanded to include multilateral negotiations for tariff reductions—that is, negotiations with all nations simultaneously. A manifestation of America's multilateral policy was its support of the multinational organization called GATT (General Agreement on Tariffs and Trade) in 1947. Originally a twenty-two-member body, GATT now includes more than eighty world nations representing about 80 percent of world trade. GATT sets rules and conditions for tariff reductions and oversees bargaining with all participating nations simultaneously.

Modern U.S. trade policies evolve through GATT, and tremendous gains and expansion of world trade have occurred since the formation of this multinational body. Moreover, Congress has expressed some willingness to move toward free trade. In 1962, a Trade Expansion Act was passed, permitting the president to negotiate tariff reductions on all commodities simultaneously rather than commodity by commodity. This act led to the so-called Kennedy round of tariff reductions (1964–1967), which produced huge concessions on manufactured and industrial products, with special concessions for poor or developing countries.

Where Does the United States Stand in the Battle for Free Trade?

Given the rhetoric of the Reagan and Bush administrations and recent changes in U.S. tariff policy, one can be forgiven for concluding that the U.S. unabashedly supports free trade. Beyond a doubt, there has been movement toward free trade in recent years. The United States has forcefully worked toward lowering tariffs worldwide in a series of GATT negotiations and, through these same channels, has actively supported measures to free up trade in agricultural products. In addition, the United States and its largest trading partner, Canada, removed all trade barriers between the two countries in 1989. Efforts to reduce trade restrictions between the United States and Mexico have been made. Finally, the disintegration of the Soviet bloc made long-standing trade and finance restrictions against Eastern European countries obsolete—virtually overnight.

The United States is a long way from having completely free trade, however. With two exceptions—Canada and Israel—no country escapes having certain of its imports taxed by the United States. For Cuba, South Africa, and China, the current policy essentially prohibits trade. The U.S. tariff policy for the European Community after 1992 is indeterminate, but creation of a free trade zone with the member countries appears unlikely. In fact, many observers foresee trade restrictions on the European Community greater than those used against members of the European Common Market.

In terms of nontariff barriers, the United States has been moving away from a policy of free trade. Since the authority to enforce laws against dumping was transferred to the Department of Commerce in 1980, the number of dumping cases has risen sharply. In the last ten years, the United States initiated about 30 percent of all the antidumping cases worldwide—a percentage exceeded only by Australia. The United States has applied pressure on other countries to enter into "voluntary" agreements to limit exports of various products to the United States. In addition to the well-known agreement with Japan to limit the number of cars sold in the United States, voluntary export agreements have been negotiated with other countries to limit the amounts of textiles, steel, and various agricultural products that enter the United States. In short, the United States is actively protectionist in its use of nontariff barriers to trade.

SUMMARY

1. All individuals possess talents that give them advantages in trade. Nations, like individuals, benefit from specialization and trade. Nations trade not resources but rather the products and services created with resources. Differing resource endowments are the basis for trade in products because products are ordinarily more mobile than the resources that produce them.

2. Specialization and trade may take place between countries of vastly differing degrees of economic development. The reason is the law of comparative advantage, which states that trade is possible when the relative opportunity cost of producing two goods differs between two countries.

3. Specialization according to the law of comparative advantage permits the production possibilities and hence the rate of sustainable consumption of nations to expand. That is, the parties to trade may obtain more of both traded goods after specialization and trade.

4. There are both natural and artificial barriers to trade. Natural barriers are all exchange costs, including transportation costs of moving goods from one country to another. Artificial barriers include taxes on imports of goods, or tariffs, and limitations or prohibitions on imported items, or quotas.

5. Tariffs on imports increase the profits of domestic producers and the revenue of government, but consumers lose more than producers and governments gain. This net welfare loss is the reason most economists oppose protectionist policies.

6. Though tariffs carry a net loss to society, they are imposed whenever domestic producer-competitors are strong enough to supply gains to politicians. Consumer groups may oppose tariffs but are seldom well enough organized or vocal enough to oppose them successfully.

7. Two substantive arguments are made for protection: the national defense and infant industries arguments. Most economists, however, question the adequacy of these arguments in actual operation. Other arguments—such as "cheap foreign labor" or "buy American"—are regarded by most economists as only thinly veiled protectionist fallacies.

8. U.S. trade policies have historically waxed and waned with prosperity and depression, becoming more protectionist during economic downturns. Although import tariffs have been reduced dramatically in the past fifty years, freer trade has not necessarily resulted. Protectionism lives on in the form of quotas and nontariff trade barriers.

KEY TERMS

specialization
comparative advantage
terms of trade
consumption possibilities
  curve
tariff

quota
free trade
welfare loss to society
nontariff trade
  barriers
infant industry

dumping
terms of trade argument

QUESTIONS FOR REVIEW AND DISCUSSION

1. Evaluate and discuss the following statement: "Trade across international boundaries is essentially the same as trade across interstate boundaries."
2. How can two countries simultaneously gain from trade? Under what circumstances can two countries not gain from trade?
3. What is the difference between natural barriers and artificial barriers to trade? Was the development of the Panama Canal an artificial encouragement of trade?
4. What does a tariff do to the terms of trade? Are consumers in both countries hurt by a tariff?

5. What are the differences and similarities between tariffs and quotas? Would consumers prefer one of these barriers to the other?
6. Who is hurt by a tariff? Who is helped? Who encourages government to impose tariffs?
7. What is the purpose of protective tariffs? Who or what is protected?
8. Evaluate the following statement: "Tariffs discourage the movement of goods between countries; therefore, they encourage the movement of resources such as capital and labor between countries."

PROBLEMS

Nations Alpha and Beta have the following production possibilities for goods X and Y.

Alpha	X	0	3	6	9
	Y	12	8	4	0
Beta	X	0	4	8	12
	Y	15	10	5	0

1. Draw the production possibilities curves for both countries. What does 1 X cost in Alpha before trade? What does 1 Y cost in Beta? If these countries traded, which would export X and which would export Y?
2. If some country Omega can produce 100 units of X with all its resources or 60 units of Y, how much does 1 unit of Y cost? If another country, Gamma, can produce 60 X or 40 Y, what does 1 unit of X cost in Gamma? Which country has a comparative advantage in the production of X?

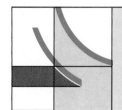

ECONOMICS IN ACTION
Voluntary Export Restraints: A Quota Is a Quota Is a Tariff

Voluntary export restraints (VERs)—quota agreements between two countries to voluntarily limit exports from one country to the other—have become a popular alternative to tariff controls. In 1990, for example, President Bush used the device to restrict imported steel through 1992, but a precedent for this had been established during the Reagan administration with VERs on automobiles. On April 1, 1981, an international trade agreement between the governments of Japan and the United States was put into effect. Under the VERs, the government of Japan would prevent Japa-

nese automakers from exporting as many cars as they would like to the U.S. market. Japanese car manufacturers were restricted to shipping only 1.68 million cars to the U.S. market per year from 1981 to 1984. What was the economic effect of the VERs on U.S. automobile producers and consumers?

In order to answer this question, we must first recognize that this "voluntary" restraint was nothing more than a quota of 1.68 million cars. The U.S. government effectively restricted imports from Japan to a level of 1.68 million cars.

The next question to answer is, What effect has the imposition of an import quota had on the domestic (United States) market for automobiles?

Figure 10 will help answer this question. In Figure 10, P_W is the price of a car in the United States before the quota. Domestic producers sell Q_1 cars, and imports equal Q_4 minus Q_1 autos. Once the quota, equal to Q_3 minus Q_2, is imposed, how does the domestic market move to a new equilibrium? Recall that an equilibrium price is one at which quantity demanded equals quantity supplied. Part of quantity supplied is supplied by foreign producers, the amount of the quota in this case. To find what equilibrium price will be under the quota, we need only find a price at which the horizontal distance between the demand and supply curves equals the quota. At price P_{W+Q} domestic output, Q_2, plus the quota, Q_3 minus Q_2, equals total quantity demanded, Q_3. Thus, at price P_{W+Q} quantity demanded equals total quantity supplied. P_{W+Q} will then be the domestic price of a car if a quota of Q_3 minus Q_2 is imposed.

Figures 8 and 10 are similar in many respects because tariffs and quotas are similar in many respects. They both raise domestic price and reduce imports, but the tariff works initially by affecting price and letting quantity adjust, whereas the quota directly affects quantity with the result that prices adjust. Whichever method is used to restrict trade, higher domestic prices and fewer imports result.

Economist Robert Crandall of the Brookings Institution in Washington, D.C., has studied the Reagan administration's VERs in an attempt to gauge the economic effects on consumers and producers of automobiles.[a] He estimated that in 1984 the price of a Japanese car sold in the United States was about $2500 more than it would have been without the VERs. Additionally, the higher prices of Japanese imports allowed U.S. automakers to charge about $1000 more per car than they would have been able to in the absence of quotas. The stockholders of U.S. auto companies and the employees of these companies clearly benefited from the VERs. Crandall also estimates that American auto consumers paid approximately $16 *billion* more for cars in 1984–1985 than they would have in the absence of the quotas.

Although Figures 8 and 10 suggest that tariffs and quotas yield identical results in the domestic market, there can be

[a]Robert W. Crandall, "Detroit Rode Quotas to Prosperity," *Wall Street Journal* (January 29, 1986), p. 30.

FIGURE 10   The Effect of a Quota on the Domestic Market

When the quota is imposed, it is still necessary for quantity demanded to equal quantity supplied for the domestic market to be in equilibrium. Only at price P_{W+Q} will total quantity demanded, Q_3, equal total quantity supplied. Total quantity supplied equals quantity supplied domestically, Q_2, plus imports, Q_3 minus Q_2. The quota raises price, increases domestic producers' profits, and produces welfare losses—just as a tariff does.

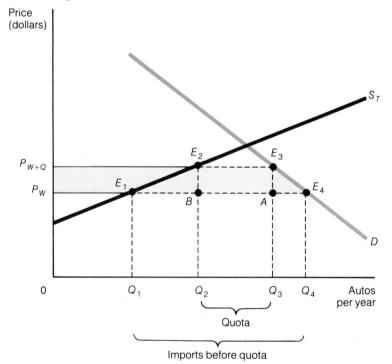

differences. In Figure 10, if a tariff had driven domestic price up to P_{w+Q}, the U.S. government would have collected tariff revenue in the amount of area E_2E_3AB. However, under the VERs, no tariff revenue was collected from Japanese automakers. In fact, the United States government merely allowed the Japanese government and Japanese automakers to decide for themselves which companies would fill the quota of 1.68 million units. With the import rights left specifically unassigned (and not charged for) by the U.S. government, the area E_2E_3AB became revenue to Japanese producers (and their U.S. dealers) rather than tariff revenue for the United States. Crandall estimates this area to have been on the order of $10 billion over the 1984–1985 period. This is one of the wealth transfers, from American consumers to Japanese producers, of a quota designed in this fashion.

An interesting alternative study expands on the effects of U.S.-Japanese VERs on autos by calculating the impact of third parties on American consumers. Producers in Germany, Sweden, and France, though *not included* in the VER arrangement, were very much affected by it. These European auto exporters also were able to increase prices—by about one-third over the pre-VER level, according to economists Elias Dinopoulos and Mordechai Kreinin.[b] This price hike, which is a direct transfer from U.S. consumers to European producers, added considerably to the total welfare loss in the United States. Dinopoulos and Kreinin reveal a threefold welfare loss: "the loss to Japan (estimated at $2.3 billions in 1982 and $2.4 billions in 1984); the loss to Europe (estimated at $1.5 billions in 1982 and $3.4 billions in 1984); and a small social loss within the United States, over and above the pure internal transfer from consumers to producers ($208 millions in 1982)."[c] Further, they put the total cost of the auto VER in 1982 at $4 billion. The automobile VER may have saved 22,358 auto-related jobs in 1982, but American consumers had to pay $181,000 for each of those jobs, many times each autoworker's average annual compensation. The Bush administration appears determined to maintain and extend such VERs as a basis for trade policy.[d] In 1991, for instance, VERs on steel will be set at 20.14 percent of the total U.S. steel market—meaning, on balance, more losses to American consumers.

Question

If you had designed the voluntary export restraints, how could you have designed them so as to eliminate the $10 billion wealth transfer from American consumers to Japanese producers?

---

[b]Elias Dinopoulos and Mordechai E. Kreinin, "Effects of the U.S.-Japan Auto VER on European Prices and on U.S. Welfare," *Review of Economics and Statistics* 70 (August 1988), pp. 484–91.

[c]Dinopoulos and Kreinin, p. 491.

[d]See Peter Truell, "U.S. Agrees to Quotas on Steel Imports with EC and 16 Other Major Suppliers," *Wall Street Journal* (December 13, 1989), p. A2.

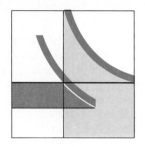

22

The International Monetary System

When a car dealer in Virginia buys cars from a Detroit manufacturer to sell in Virginia, both use the same medium of exchange—U.S. dollars. Suppose, however, that the dealer buys cars from Japanese or German manufacturers to sell in Virginia. The Japanese firm will likely want payment in yen; the German firm, in marks. The car dealer thus confronts an international monetary problem. Are the prices stated in yen and marks fair? This question brings up others. How are dollars converted into yen and marks? Is there a fixed rate for currency exchange or does it vary? How would changes in exchange rates affect import prices in the United States? How do fluctuating exchange rates influence foreign investors seeking to buy real estate or stocks and bonds in the United States? U.S. exporters face the same questions from a different perspective. They sell to citizens in foreign countries and seek payment for their goods and services in U.S. dollars. They must be careful, therefore, to pay attention to exchange rates because these rates can determine the prices and profits of their foreign sales.

The monetary, or financial, side of international trade concerns the ways in which countries pay for the goods and services they exchange. In this chapter we examine many aspects of the relations among the currencies of the world, relations that reflect a kaleidoscope of changing conditions in each country, from interest rates and inflation rates to exports and imports of goods and capital. When you finish Chapter 22 you should understand

- how international trade takes place when transactions must be made in terms of other countries' currencies.
- how currency transactions are determined when governments fix their respective currencies' value and when the market determines the relative value of currencies.
- how macroeconomic fiscal and monetary policies both affect and are affected by foreign trade and international exchange rates.
- the meaning of the balance of payments, its relation to exchange rates, and its importance for economic growth.

THE FOREIGN EXCHANGE MARKET

Foreign exchange:
The monies of countries that are used to facilitate international trade in goods, services, and financial assets.

International sellers and buyers usually prefer to deal in the currency of their own country. American sellers prefer U.S. dollars for their products, and Japanese sellers prefer yen. The currency of another country that is required to make payment in an international transaction is called **foreign exchange.** Foreign exchange is bought and sold in **foreign exchange markets**—typically, large brokers and banks scattered about the globe.

Foreign exchange markets:
The interaction of the suppliers and demanders of foreign exchange, through which exchange rates are determined in a flexible exchange rate system.

Sometimes consumers demand foreign exchange; for example, when travelers land in a foreign airport, they often exchange dollars for the local currency. Large firms dealing in international transactions simply keep bank deposits in foreign currencies to cover their foreign transactions. An American importer of French wine will likely pay for it by writing checks on an American bank that holds an account in a French bank. The American bank will use the importer's dollars to purchase the francs needed for payment.

The demand for foreign exchange arises because a country's residents want to buy foreign goods. Conversely, the supply of foreign exchange arises because foreign customers want to buy U.S. goods. For example, we have a demand for francs by the U.S. importer who wishes to purchase French wine and a supply of francs by French customers who wish to purchase U.S. personal computers.

Exchange Rates

Exchange rate:
The (relative) price of one national currency in terms of another national currency.

An **exchange rate** is the price of one country's money in terms of some other country's money. It is a relative price, much the same as the relative price concept discussed in Chapter 4, except that it is the relative price of one national currency expressed in terms of another national currency. Like the relative prices of goods, exchange rates can be expressed in one of two equivalent ways. We can talk about one U2 concert ticket "costing" five pizzas, or we can say that one pizza costs one-fifth of a concert ticket. Either way, the relative price of one good in terms of another good (one concert ticket in terms of pizzas or one pizza in terms of concert tickets) is expressed. Which expression we choose is simply a matter of choice or convenience.

So it is with exchange rates. Because they are relative prices of one money in terms of another money, the way we choose to express the exchange rate is a matter of choice and convenience. For example, in 1989, one U.S. dollar traded on the foreign exchange market for about six French francs (ff), the national currency of France. (The actual rate was 6.3802 to one dollar.) One U.S. dollar cost six French francs to buy, or one U.S. dollar sold for six French francs. This exchange rate is the relative price of the U.S. dollar in terms of French francs. Alternatively, it would be just as accurate to say that one French franc cost, or would buy, sixteen and two-thirds cents. This would be the relative price of the French franc in terms of the U.S. dollar. One is nothing more than the inverse or reciprocal of the other.

Exchange rates are often expressed both ways. An American in France must use French francs to make purchases. Starting out the vacation, the traveler may have a budget, say $500, that she wishes to spend on meals. By using the U.S. dollar in terms of French francs exchange rate (6 per dollar), she can calculate that she will have 3000 ff (6 ff per dollar × $500) to spend on meals in France. Once in France, if our tourist pays 100 ff for a lunch, she may wish to know how many dollars the lunch cost. A quick calculation using the French franc in terms of the U.S. dollar exchange rate will give the answer ($0.1667 per ff × 100 ff = $16.67).

Of equal importance are changes in exchange rates, for such changes can alter the prices of imports and exports. Suppose that a bottle of French wine sells for 100 ff. Ignoring transportation costs and any tariffs, with a dollar-franc exchange rate of $0.1667 per French franc, the wine will cost $16.67 in the United States. But suppose the exchange rate were to change to $0.20 per French franc? The same bottle of wine would still cost 100 ff in France, but its cost in the United States would rise to $20. Changes in exchange rate can alter the prices of foreign goods in home markets, as well as the prices of domestic goods in foreign markets.

Just as tourists must pay attention to exchange rates in order to make plans and informed decisions, so must businesses and governments. International trade, like interpersonal trade, requires the use of money. The prices of these monies relative to one another are important economic variables. A sudden change in an exchange rate can alter the actual values of any business transaction, making it more or less profitable than at first thought. Such changes influence business decisions and can alter the volume of international trade. At issue, then, is what determines exchange rates. Why, in 1989, did a dollar buy (cost) six French francs and not about four or ten French francs? What has caused the U.S. dollar price of French francs, or for that matter German marks, Japanese yen, Mexican pesos, or any other country's money, to change from day to day and year to year?

Exchange Rate Systems

Exchange rates, like any other price, are determined in markets by the forces of supply and demand. However, exactly who suppliers and demanders are, and under what constraints the market operates, determines the type of system within which the exchange rate will be determined. One type, the **flexible,** or **floating, exchange rate system,** is a system whereby the exchange rate is determined solely by the interaction of private demanders and suppliers of foreign exchange. This is the type of system most major trading countries employ today to determine the world market value of their respective currencies. Of course, government fiscal and monetary policies can help determine the exchange rate under such a system by influencing the behavior of private market participants. But government policies usually are not specifically designed to directly influence the exchange rate.

A second system of exchange rate determination is called a **fixed exchange rate system.** A fixed exchange rate system was in existence from the late 1940s until 1971. A few countries today still fix the value of their currencies on world markets in terms of U.S. dollars. Under a fixed exchange rate system, government intervenes directly in the foreign exchange market, either as a buyer or as a seller, in order to fix the exchange rate at some level. Some European countries combine elements of both the fixed- and flexible-rate systems. The values of these European currencies are fixed relative to one another, but all float against the U.S. dollar.

Flexible, or floating, exchange rate system: An international monetary arrangement in which exchange rates are determined by private suppliers and demanders without government intervention.

Fixed exchange rate system: An international monetary arrangement in which exchange rates are set by the government, which then must intervene in the foreign exchange market in order to maintain the pegged exchange rate.

Since 1973, the exchange rate system determining the relative prices of national currencies has been a blend of these two systems. By and large, the flexible-rate system is in use for the currencies of the United States and other major industrial countries. No country, however, allows its exchange rate to float freely all the time. Wide swings in the exchange rate are controlled by government intervention in the foreign exchange market. For this reason, the present international monetary system is called a **managed flexible-rate system.** In the next two sections we analyze how floating exchange rates and fixed exchange rates work.

Managed flexible-rate system:
Primarily a flexible exchange rate system, but with occasional government purchases or sales of foreign exchanges intended to influence the exchange rate.

FLEXIBLE EXCHANGE RATES

As we pointed out earlier, U.S. demand for foreign currency arises because U.S. citizens wish to buy foreign products, travel in foreign countries, invest in foreign companies, and carry on other international activities. The supply of foreign currencies to the United States arises because foreigners want to buy U.S. goods, travel in the United States, send their children to school in the United States, invest in this country, and so on. All of these forces of supply and demand affect the exchange rate between the U.S. dollar and other currencies. In effect, they form the basis of the supply and demand schedules in the foreign exchange markets.

Exchange Rates Between Two Countries

We begin our analysis with a simple model of the determination of floating, or flexible, exchange rates. For simplicity, we assume that international trade takes place only between two countries, the United States and Switzerland. The U.S. demand for foreign exchange is thus a demand for Swiss francs; the supply of foreign exchange is a supply of Swiss francs.

Supply, Demand, and the Market for Foreign Exchange. Before beginning our analysis of the factors that determine, and change, exchange rates, some preliminaries are in order. The exchange rate is determined in the foreign exchange market. It is the relative price of one money in terms of another. As we have indicated, the actions of both the Americans and the Swiss are manifested in this market. But any action on the part of residents of one country is mirrored in the actions of residents of the other. For example, Swiss exports are American imports, and vice versa. This means that technically we would want to look at both the supply and demand of dollars and the supply and demand of Swiss francs to the foreign exchange market in order to examine exchange rate determination. But because the dollar-franc exchange rate is just the inverse of the franc-dollar exchange rate (so that changes in one are mirrored by changes in the other), and because Swiss imports are American exports, we can simplify matters. We need only examine the supply and demand for either francs or dollars on the foreign exchange market in order to be able to discuss exchange rate determination. We will look at the supply and demand for Swiss francs, the foreign exchange in our discussion.

Figure 1 depicts the supply and demand for foreign exchange, Swiss francs. What establishes the supply and demand for francs on the foreign exchange market? Consider the demand for franc foreign exchange first. American importers of Swiss goods must pay Swiss producers with francs. Thus, American imports from Switzerland are the basis of foreign exchange demand. The demand for foreign exchange slopes downward because, other things constant, a higher exchange rate (more dollars per franc) implies higher import prices, fewer imports, and a smaller quantity demanded (by Americans) of foreign exchange.

The supply of foreign exchange arises from Swiss import activity and, therefore, American export activity. Swiss importers must pay for goods produced in the United States (American exports) with dollars. In order to obtain dollars, they must buy them with francs in the foreign exchange market. The supply of foreign exchange originates with Swiss imports or, what is the same thing, American exports. It is upward-sloping because, other factors considered, a rise in the dollar price of the franc (the exchange rate measured on the vertical axis) means that one franc now buys more dollars, making American goods cheaper to the Swiss. This implies an increase in the desire of the Swiss to import from the United States. They will then offer more francs for sale at the higher exchange rate to obtain additional dollars. The additional dollars are then used to purchase the larger quantity of imports.

The equilibrium exchange rate, like any other price, is one that equates quantity demanded with quantity supplied. In Figure 1, this equilibrium exchange rate is $0.50 per Swiss franc. Suppose, for some reason, the exchange rate were below equilibrium, at $0.20 per franc. The quantity demanded of foreign exchange would then exceed the quantity supplied of foreign exchange.

FIGURE 1

The exchange rate—in this case, the dollar price of one Swiss franc—is measured on the vertical axis. The quantity of francs is measured on the horizontal axis. The equilibrium exchange rate is $0.50 per Swiss franc because this is the only exchange rate that equates quantity demanded with quantity supplied. At the exchange rate of $0.75 per franc, there exists a surplus of francs, and the exchange rate will fall. At the $0.20 exchange rate, a shortage of francs on the foreign exchange market exists, which will drive the exchange rate back to $0.50.

A Two-Country Foreign Exchange Market

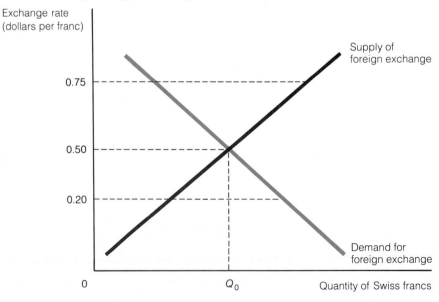

There would be a shortage of francs on the foreign exchange market. As in any other market, a shortage in the foreign exchange market will tend to drive price back toward equilibrium.

Given the fundamental economic factors determining exports and imports in both countries, an exchange rate below the equilibrium exchange rate ($0.20 per franc in Figure 1) creates a situation in which Americans wish to import much more from Switzerland than the Swiss wish to sell. At this exchange rate, Swiss goods are "too cheap" to Americans because the dollar price of the franc is "too low." On the other side of the coin, American goods are "too expensive" to the Swiss. Swiss imports are too low, and thus the quantity supplied of foreign exchange is also too low. To stimulate the quantity of Swiss imports and increase the quantity supplied of foreign exchange, as well as to reduce the quantity of U.S. imports and reduce the quantity demanded of foreign exchange, an increase in the exchange rate is necessary. The movement to equilibrium from $0.20 to $0.50 results from the bidding up of the dollar price of francs by American consumers eager to obtain Swiss goods. (Americans demand Swiss francs and *simultaneously* supply U.S. dollars.) The actions of American consumers tend to elevate the price of Swiss francs in terms of dollars, returning the dollar-franc market to equilibrium. Naturally, the rise in the dollar price of francs reduces the quantity demanded of Swiss goods and services by Americans as equilibrium is approached. (The Swiss are willing to supply the additional francs because of the higher price of their currency expressed in dollars.)

Likewise, the exchange rate of $0.75 per franc is too high for equilibrium, creating a surplus of foreign exchange. At $0.75 per franc, Swiss products are very expensive for Americans and American products are relatively inexpensive to the Swiss. As the Swiss demand dollars to get American goods, the price of dollars in terms of francs rises and the price of francs in terms of dollars falls. Simultaneously, with Americans wanting to import less than the Swiss wish to export to the United States, a surplus of franc foreign exchange exists. A fall in the dollar price of the franc will increase American imports and the quantity demanded of foreign exchange. This same fall will also make American goods more expensive in Switzerland, reduce imports, and thus reduce the quantity supplied of francs to the foreign exchange market. Equilibrium is restored, as shown in Figure 1, when the dollar price of francs returns to $0.50.

Changes in Flexible Exchange Rates

The foreign exchange market is much like any other market studied in economics. Supply and demand determine price, whereas surpluses and shortages of foreign exchange will move the exchange rate toward its equilibrium value. We now examine why the supply of or demand for foreign exchange might change, producing a change in the equilibrium exchange rate in a flexible exchange rate system.

Appreciation and Depreciation. The dollar price of the Swiss franc, or any other currency, fluctuates from day to day and even minute to minute. Trying to explain every small fluctuation in the exchange rate would be a fruitless exercise. However, broad and significant changes in exchange rates have occurred since the collapse of the fixed-rate system and subsequent inception of

Depreciation:
A decrease in the equilibrium exchange market value of a country's currency in a flexible-rate system; an increase in the number of units of a country's money required to purchase one unit of a foreign country's money.

Appreciation:
An increase in the equilibrium exchange market value of a country's currency in a flexible-rate system; a decrease in the number of units of a country's money required to purchase one unit of a foreign country's money.

the managed flexible-rate system in 1973. The late 1970s was a period of dollar **depreciation.** A depreciation of a country's currency on world markets means that the equilibrium exchange rate has changed such that it requires more of the currency to purchase other money. An increase in the equilibrium dollar price of the Swiss franc from $0.50 to $0.70 constitutes a depreciation of the dollar. It takes more dollars to buy a franc than previously, or equivalently, one dollar buys fewer francs. Another term used frequently by the financial press to describe a depreciation is a "weakening" of the currency on the foreign exchange market. The early 1980s was a period of dollar **appreciation.** An appreciation is the opposite of a depreciation; less of the money is required to buy other monies on the foreign exchange market. A fall in the equilibrium exchange rate from $0.50 to $0.30 per franc signifies a dollar appreciation (and a franc depreciation). A currency that has appreciated is said to have "strengthened" on world currency markets or is a "strong" currency. The basic reasons and fundamental causes of currency appreciations and depreciations are addressed in the following sections.

Price Levels, Money Supplies, and Inflation Rates. One factor that can cause the exchange rate to change is a change in the price level of either country. Suppose that the price level in the United States were to increase by 20 percent while the general level of prices in Switzerland was stable. Figure 2a depicts the effects this would have on the foreign exchange market and the exchange rate. Other things equal, higher U.S. prices would reduce Swiss import demand for American goods. This would, in turn, cause a decrease in the supply of foreign exchange, shown as a shift of the supply curve of francs from S to S_1. The rise in the prices of U.S. goods also would make Swiss goods relatively more attractive to Americans. American import demand would increase, and the demand for foreign exchange also would then increase. In Figure 2a, the demand for foreign exchange shifts from D to D_1.

The effect is to increase the dollar price of the franc. The equilibrium exchange rate rises from e_0 to e_1, or the dollar depreciates on the foreign exchange market. Of course, one could also say that the franc has appreciated. Had the price level in Switzerland risen by 20 percent with the price level in the United States constant, just the opposite would have occurred. Swiss goods would have become more expensive to Americans, reducing American import demand and the demand for foreign exchange from D to D_2 in Figure 2b. Swiss import demand would increase as American goods become cheaper in Switzerland, causing the supply of foreign exchange to increase from S to S_2. The equilibrium exchange rate would fall from e_0 to e_2, and a dollar appreciation (franc depreciation) would have taken place.

If in our first example the dollar had depreciated by 20 percent in response to the U.S. price level increasing by 20 percent, our model of exchange rate determination would reflect the **purchasing power parity (PPP) theory** of exchange rates. Formulated by Gustav Cassel around 1917, PPP is an intuitively appealing notion. Basically, PPP theory implies that if a dollar can buy a certain basket of goods in the United States, then converting that dollar into francs at the market exchange rate should yield enough francs to buy the same basket of goods in Switzerland.

If in Figure 2a the change in the exchange rate from e_0 to e_1 is a 20 percent change, then PPP holds. The dollar has lost purchasing power at home

Purchasing power parity (PPP) theory:
A theory that predicts that the equilibrium exchange rate will adjust so as to equate the purchasing power of a unit of each country's money.

FIGURE 2   Price Level Changes in the Flexible Exchange Rate System

S and D are the initial foreign supply and demand curves. In Figure 2a, an increase in the U.S. price level, holding the Swiss price level constant, causes the supply of foreign exchange to shift to S_1, while the demand for foreign exchange shifts to D_1. This causes the Swiss franc to appreciate from e_0 to e_1. This can also be described as a depreciation of the dollar. If the Swiss price level increased while the price level in the United States remained unchanged, the supply and demand curves would shift to S_2 and D_2 in Figure 2b. This would cause the exchange rate to fall from e_0 to e_2.

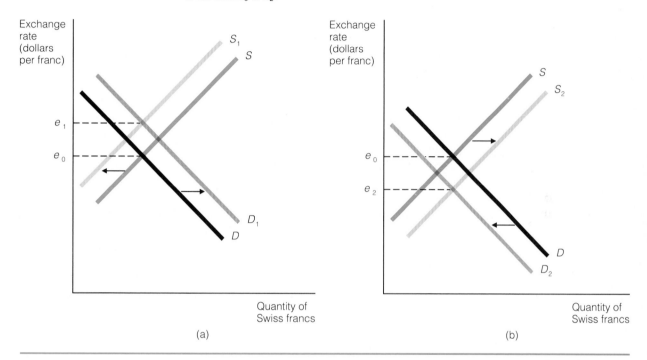

(a)   (b)

to the tune of 20 percent. It buys 20 percent fewer goods and services in the United States. A depreciation on the foreign exchange market of 20 percent guarantees that one dollar will buy 20 percent fewer Swiss goods also and that the franc's purchasing power over United States goods is maintained. According to PPP theory, the exchange rate adjusts to reflect changes in the purchasing power of currencies. While the PPP theory seems to do a fair job of describing long-term movements in exchange rates (given other determinants), it has not proved a very powerful explanation of short-term exchange rate fluctuations during the recent floating-rate period.

Note that in the long run, given other factors, if the Federal Reserve had increased the money supply, the price level in the United States would have risen. Because price level increases in the United States will depreciate the dollar on the foreign exchange market, and because money supply increases can cause the price level to rise, increases in the U.S. money supply can cause the dollar to depreciate on the foreign exchange market. In fact, some economists believe that money supply changes are one of the prime sources of exchange rate changes. Of course, an increase in the foreign money supply, *ceteris paribus,* will cause the dollar to appreciate.

Consider the possibility that both countries experience continuous increases in their price levels or positive, but constant, inflation rates. Assume that the rate of inflation differs between the United States and Switzerland. In such a scenario, the supply and demand for foreign exchange would be constantly changing, causing the equilibrium exchange rate to change continuously. We can make a statement about the direction of the change in the exchange rate if we know something about the relationship between the two inflation rates. Suppose that the rate of inflation in Switzerland is greater than the rate of inflation in the United States. Under these circumstances, the Swiss price level is rising faster than the U.S. price level. We would then see the dollar price per franc continuously falling on the world market. The dollar would be appreciating. If the U.S. inflation rate were larger than that of Switzerland, just the opposite would happen. The dollar would then continuously depreciate on the foreign exchange market.

Real Income, Exports, and Imports.   Other factors also can cause a currency to appreciate or depreciate on world currency markets. Consider the effect of an expansion in the Swiss economy that results in an increase in Swiss real income. As Swiss real income increases, the demand for imports from the United States also increases. More francs are supplied to the foreign exchange market at any given exchange rate, and the supply of foreign exchange increases. In Figure 3, the foreign exchange supply curve shifts from S to S_1 and the equilibrium exchange rate falls from e_0 to e_1. The increase in Swiss real income has caused the dollar to appreciate on the foreign exchange market or, equivalently, the franc to depreciate.

Should real income in the United States rise, the dollar would depreciate on the foreign exchange market. Larger U.S. real income would cause a desire

FIGURE 3

An increase in real income in Switzerland has the effect of shifting the supply of foreign exchange from S to S_1. This appreciates the dollar in the foreign exchange market, causing the exchange rate to fall from e_0 to e_1. Should U.S. real income rise, the effect will be to increase the demand for foreign exchange to D_1 and depreciate the dollar, moving the exchange rate from e_0 to e_2.

Real Income Changes and the Exchange Rate

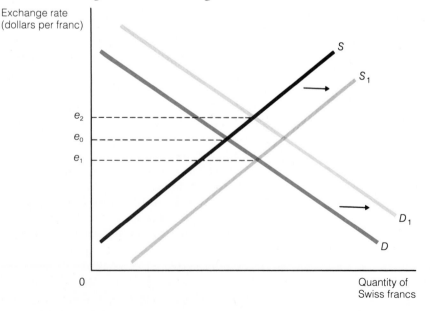

for greater imports from Switzerland. The demand for francs would increase in Figure 3 from D to D_1. Given the initial supply of foreign exchange, S, the rise in U.S. real income causes a depreciation of the dollar (appreciation of the franc) on the foreign exchange market. In this case, the exchange rate rises from e_0 to e_2.[1]

Changes in factors that directly affect exports and imports can also cause changes in exchange rates. Should consumer tastes in the United States change in favor of goods produced at home, for example, the demand for foreign exchange would decrease, causing an appreciation of the dollar. Government policies aimed at restricting imports or encouraging exports tend to reduce the demand for foreign exchange and appreciate the country's currency on world markets.

Interest Rates. So far, we have discussed the supply of foreign exchange as arising from the desires of foreigners to buy goods and services produced in the United States. But foreigners purchase real estate and financial assets in the United States as well; for instance, Rockefeller Center in New York was purchased by Japanese investors. Stocks and bonds of U.S. businesses and governments (state, local, and federal) are other, less-publicized examples of such purchases by foreign businesspeople. Both such examples are foreign investments in the United States. Just as the purchase of U.S. goods by foreigners creates a supply of foreign exchange, so does the purchase of financial assets or real assets such as automobile or computer assembly plants. Likewise, U.S. citizens purchase the financial assets of other countries, adding to the demand for foreign exchange. Our next task is to determine how changes in the purchases of financial or real assets may affect the exchange rate.

An increased desire on the part of the Swiss to invest in the United States, to buy more U.S. financial or real assets, signals an increased supply of foreign exchange. More francs are supplied to the foreign exchange market to purchase the dollars necessary to buy U.S. assets. In Figure 4, the supply of foreign exchange increases from S to S_1 and the exchange rate falls from e_0 to e_1. What would cause this to happen?

Investors everywhere look at many different variables in deciding how to allocate their investment funds among particular firms, industries, or countries. Such factors as risk, liquidity, and the degree of political stability are all important. However, a primary factor that goes into any investment decision is the real rate of interest those funds earn.

The real interest rate, recall, is the rate of interest earned adjusted for inflation. Suppose that the real interest rate in the United States rose. That would make U.S. financial assets more attractive to own and would increase the demand by foreigners to purchase U.S. financial assets. This increase in the U.S. real interest rate would have caused the increase in the supply of francs to the foreign exchange market depicted in Figure 4. The effect of a rise in the real interest rate in the United States is dollar appreciation, a decline in the dollar price of the Swiss franc on the foreign exchange market from e_0 to e_1.

Alternatively, should the real interest rate increase in Switzerland, the demand for francs on the part of Americans would increase, from D to D_1 in

---

[1] We are assuming that as real income rises, the money supply increases enough to accommodate the extra demand for money.

FIGURE 4

When the U.S. real interest rate rises, the Swiss wish to invest more in the United States, to buy more financial assets. The supply of foreign exchange increases to S_1, and the exchange rate falls to e_1. Higher U.S. real interest rates cause dollar appreciation. When the real interest rate in Switzerland rises, Americans wish to buy more Swiss securities and the demand for foreign exchange increases. The exchange rate moves from e_0 to e_2, and the dollar depreciates.

Real Interest Rate Effects on the Exchange Rate

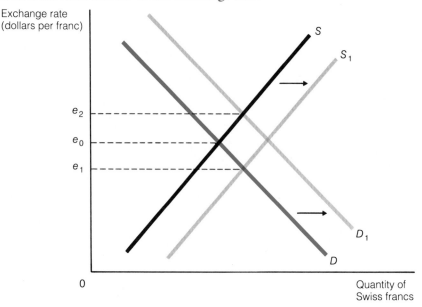

Figure 4. Given the supply of franc foreign exchange of S, the exchange rate would rise to e_2. An increased Swiss real interest rate causes the dollar to depreciate, or the franc to appreciate, on the foreign exchange market.

FIXED EXCHANGE RATES

As we have seen, a system of flexible exchange rates allows the foreign exchange market to determine the prices at which currency will change hands. By contrast, a fixed exchange rate system does not allow exchange rates to float in a free market. Government intervenes in the foreign exchange market to fix the international price of its currency. Once fixed exchange rates are established, governments stand ready to protect the rates through intervention in the foreign exchange market.

The Operation of a Fixed Exchange Rate System

Undervalued:
A term describing the foreign exchange market value of a country's money; occurs when the number of units of a country's money that purchases one unit of a foreign currency is *greater* than the equilibrium exchange rate.

Although the United States and Switzerland no longer trade on the basis of a fixed exchange rate, imagine what would happen if they did. Figure 5 illustrates what happens when a fixed exchange rate between francs and dollars does not happen to correspond to ever-shifting market conditions. If the current market equilibrium rate is e_0, but the U.S. government seeks to maintain an exchange rate of e_1, the official or fixed rate is above the equilibrium rate. In this case, the dollar is said to be undervalued relative to the Swiss franc. The dollar is **undervalued** because at exchange rate e_1 each dollar will buy fewer francs than it would at the lower equilibrium exchange rate, e_0. Of course, if the

FIGURE 5

If the government sets an exchange rate below equilibrium, such as e_2, a shortage of foreign exchange develops, and the central bank must continuously sell foreign exchange from its exchange reserves to keep the rate at e_2. If the rate is set at e_1, a surplus of foreign exchange is created, and the central bank must continuously buy foreign exchange, adding to its exchange reserves, in order to maintain the fixed rate.

Fixed Exchange Rates Above and Below Equilibrium

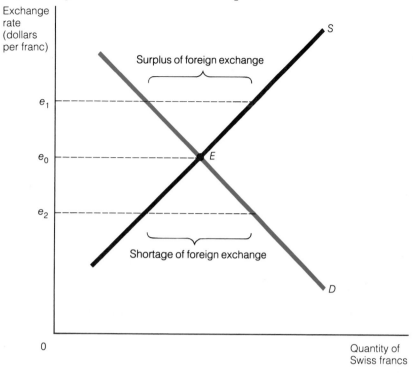

Overvalued:
A term describing the foreign exchange market value of a country's money; occurs when the number of units of a country's money that purchases one unit of a foreign currency is *less* than the equilibrium exchange rate.

Foreign exchange market intervention:
Purchases or sales of foreign exchange by government, usually a central bank, with the goal of maintaining a fixed exchange rate or influencing the exchange rate in a flexible-rate system.

Foreign exchange reserves:
The stock of a foreign exchange held by a central bank that is available for use in exchange market intervention.

dollar is undervalued, then the franc is overvalued. Similarly, if the government were to fix the exchange rate at e_2, each dollar would purchase more francs than it would at the equilibrium exchange rate, e_0. In this case, the dollar (franc) would be **overvalued** (undervalued).

Suppose that the government decides to fix the price of its currency in the foreign exchange market at e_1. In order to do so, the government must not merely decree that all currency trades take place at an exchange rate equal to e_1. The government, usually the central bank, must instead become a big enough player in the market to make the exchange rate e_1. To do this, the central bank must continuously engage in **foreign exchange market intervention.**

When the government fixes the exchange rate at e_1 even though fundamental foreign exchange market forces dictate an equilibrium exchange rate of e_0, a surplus of francs on the foreign exchange market is created. At the high dollar price of the franc, quantity supplied of francs will exceed quantity demanded. Without exchange market intervention, as described earlier, the exchange rate would fall back to its equilibrium value, e_0. The central bank can prevent this fall, and maintain exchange rate e_1 only if it intervenes in the exchange market by buying up the franc surplus. The buying of francs, in this case, by the central bank builds up the central bank's **foreign exchange reserves,** its holding of foreign currencies. Such an intervention is not a one-time affair. Each month or year that the exchange rate is fixed above its equilibrium value, the central bank must purchase the surplus of francs in order to maintain the fixed rate. Fixing the rate above equilibrium tends to make a country's exports cheaper and its imports more expensive. Hence, such a policy may be used by governments in an attempt to reduce imports and encourage exports.

Sometimes central banks fix the exchange rate below the market equilibrium exchange rate, such as rate e_2 in Figure 5. This creates a shortage of foreign exchange, since quantity demanded at exchange rate e_2 is greater than quantity supplied. Again, without continuous exchange market intervention, the exchange rate would move back toward its equilibrium level, e_0. In this case, foreign exchange market intervention takes the form of sales of foreign currency (Swiss francs) from the central bank's foreign currency reserves. Setting such an exchange rate, one that deliberately overvalues the country's currency in world markets, is not a policy that most countries could pursue indefinitely. Sooner or later the central bank would run out of reserves and be unable to support the fixed exchange rate. Fixing the exchange rate below equilibrium tends to encourage imports and discourage exports.

Fixed Exchange Rates

The fixed exchange rate set by government can stray significantly from the equilibrium exchange rate. A country will therefore experience persistent problems in international trade; namely, it will confront persistent surpluses or deficits in its foreign trade. In the balance of trade between exports and imports, a country whose exports have greater value than its imports is said to have a **balance of trade surplus;** one whose imports' value exceeds its exports' value has a **balance of trade deficit.** What are the options under a fixed-rate system for alleviating such situations?

Changes in Domestic Macroeconomic Policy. Consider first the example of Figure 5, where the dollar price of the franc is maintained at e_1 while the equilibrium price is e_0. The dollar is undervalued, and the United States experiences a balance of trade surplus, while Switzerland runs a persistent deficit, importing more than it exports. The Swiss will demand that something be done.

One option is to change domestic macroeconomic policies in the two countries. Suppose the United States allows its money supply to rise and Switzerland lets its money supply fall. In the United States the increase in money supply will lead to higher prices and costs. In Switzerland the opposite effects will occur: There will be lower prices and costs. Thus, U.S. exports will fall because they are now relatively more expensive on world markets, and U.S. imports will rise because foreign goods are now cheaper and income is higher. In Switzerland exports will rise because Swiss goods are now relatively cheaper, and imports will decline because U.S. goods are more expensive and Swiss GNP has fallen. The basic tendency in both countries, then, is toward adjustments that erase the surplus of exports over imports in the United States and the corresponding deficit in Switzerland.

An important point emerges from this discussion. In a fixed exchange rate system, where the government chooses to defend the fixed rate at all costs, imbalances in foreign trade must be resolved through macroeconomic adjustment of entire domestic economies. To keep one price—the foreign exchange rate—fixed, the United States and Switzerland manipulate the level of all the

Balance of trade surplus: Occurs when the value of a nation's exports exceeds the value of a nation's imports; also called a trade surplus.

Balance of trade deficit: Occurs when the value of a nation's exports is less than the value of a nation's imports; also called a trade deficit.

other prices in their economies. A flexible-rate system, by contrast, changes one price—the foreign exchange rate—to resolve balance of trade problems.

Devaluation and Revaluation. The second option facing two fixed-rate countries with a trade imbalance is to change the official exchange rate. In this way, the two governments can avoid costly manipulation of their domestic economies to restore foreign trade equilibrium. There are two possible changes in this regard.

Devaluation:
An official change in a country's exchange rate in a fixed-rate system; the number of units of a country's money that purchases one unit of another country's currency is *increased* by the government.

One is **devaluation** of one country's currency. When the dollar is overvalued (e_2 per franc in Figure 5), the United States suffers a trade deficit and Switzerland a trade surplus. With Switzerland's agreement, the United States can lower the official exchange value of its currency. In this case, we say that a devaluation has occurred. In Figure 5 this means that the dollar price of francs is moved upward, closer to its equilibrium value. This change in the exchange rate changes the relative prices of each country's imports and exports so as to help erase the U.S. deficit and the Swiss surplus without each country's having to resort to costly deflation and inflation of its domestic economy.

Where the official rate is above the equilibrium rate (such as e_1 per franc in Figure 5), the opposite process can be applied. In this case, the United States has a trade surplus and Switzerland a deficit. The two countries can support this exchange rate if the United States buys francs or if Switzerland sells dollars or some combination of both. However, to avoid inflation in the United States and deflation in Switzerland to correct the balance of trade situation, the two countries might agree to revalue the dollar. A **revaluation** occurs when the official price of a currency is raised. This means that the dollar price of francs would move downward in Figure 5, closer to its equilibrium value. The value of the dollar is thus raised, or revalued, and the corresponding value of the franc is lowered, or devalued.

Revaluation:
An official change in a country's exchange rate in a fixed-rate system; the number of units of a country's money that purchases one unit of another country's currency is *decreased* by the government.

Adjustments in official exchange rates seem less costly than the manipulation of whole economies. However, as we will see later, such adjustments are not always easy to accomplish. The Swiss may reap advantages from a balance of trade surplus and may resist efforts to devalue the dollar or to implement a domestic economic policy that chips away at their surplus. Complex international negotiations are inherent in a fixed-rate system.

Changes in Trade Policy. A third option for resolving balance of trade difficulties under a fixed-rate system is for a deficit country to erect barriers to international trade. Tariffs, quotas, and other barriers to the free movement of people and goods across international borders can be established to try to solve a trade problem. This is not an option that would find much favor among economists, however. As detailed in Chapter 21, such impediments to international trade cost the worldwide economy economic efficiency and gains from specialization.

Instead of erecting trade barriers, another policy is pressuring trading partners to abolish current import restrictions. This strategy has been advocated as a means of reducing the persistent trade deficit between the United States and Japan.

Both floating and fixed exchange rate systems have been used in the past. The most economically powerful countries presently operate essentially on a floating system and have done so since early 1973. Before that, starting shortly after World War II, a fixed exchange rate system governed international monetary relations. For an analysis of the balance of trade problems as they persist in the 1990s, see Economics in Action, "Trade Deficits, Flexible Exchange Rates, and the Competitiveness of the U.S. Economy," at the end of this chapter. We will discuss the historical evolution of the international monetary system later in the chapter.

MACROECONOMIC POLICY, EXCHANGE RATES, AND TRADE BALANCE

Foreign trade can have dramatic effects on a government's macroeconomic policy. We consider briefly how monetary policy and fiscal policy are affected by foreign trade.

Monetary Policy

The link between the foreign exchange market and monetary policy depends on whether trade takes place under a system of fixed or floating exchange rates. In the former case, the central bank fixes the exchange rate and allows the money supply to be determined by the economic system; in the latter case, the central bank lets the exchange rate be determined in the market for foreign exchange and manipulates the domestic supply of money.

The Case of Fixed Exchange Rates. To support a fixed exchange rate, the central bank must be prepared to buy and sell whatever foreign exchange is necessary to keep the exchange rate at the fixed level. Suppose there is a surplus in the balance of trade: At the current exchange rate, the quantity of foreign exchange supplied by exporters exceeds the amount of foreign exchange demanded by importers. In this case, the central bank must purchase foreign exchange by an amount equal to the excess supply to eliminate the tendency for the exchange rate to fall. The central bank purchases foreign exchange by printing more domestic currency, and this increase in the supply of money sets forces in motion that tend to restore equilibrium. Other things being equal, domestic prices rise with a larger money supply, and these higher prices will discourage exports and encourage imports, thus diminishing the trade surplus. In the case of a trade deficit, the central bank will be selling foreign exchange (in effect decreasing domestic currency) to keep the exchange rate from rising. This action will lower the domestic money supply, and the accompanying lower domestic prices will tend to discourage imports and encourage exports. The important point is that to fix one price—the exchange rate—the central bank must give up other money supply controls and allow all other prices to adjust.

The Case of Flexible Exchange Rates. If the government instead is using a flexible exchange rate system, the central bank can use its domestic monetary policy tools, allowing the exchange rate to be determined by the market. Starting from equilibrium, an increase in the domestic money supply tends to raise prices, and these higher prices tend to encourage imports and discourage exports. Thus, there is a trade deficit (an excess demand for foreign exchange) at the old exchange rate. For individuals to be willing to supply the extra foreign exchange to finance these trade movements, the exchange rate must rise by whatever amount is necessary to eliminate the excess demand. The result of an increase in the domestic money supply is therefore a rise in the exchange rate by exactly the same proportion.

Fiscal Policy

The effects of a government's fiscal policy initiatives on exchange rates depend largely on how the changes in government spending are financed. If we assume, for simplicity, that all increases in government expenditures are financed by borrowing, then expansionary fiscal policies stimulate aggregate demand, including the demand for imports on the one hand, and raise government borrowing on the other. The increased demand puts upward pressure on the exchange rate because of the additional foreign currencies required to finance the increased imports. But the increased government borrowing tends to raise interest rates, attracting foreign capital and placing downward pressure on the exchange rate. The net change in the exchange rate owing to the expansionary policy depends on which of the two effects dominates.

Similarly, contractionary fiscal policies may raise or lower the exchange rate. A lower level of government spending will reduce aggregate demand, reduce the demand for imports, and, at the same time, lower government borrowing. The lower import demand will tend to lower the exchange rate by fostering an excess supply of foreign currencies. But with less government borrowing, interest rates tend to fall. Capital outflows increase, putting upward pressure on exchange rates. Again, the net change of the exchange rate depends on which event—the fall-off in imports or the decline in interest rates—has greater effect.

THE GOLD STANDARD

Gold standard:
An international monetary system in which currencies are redeemable in gold at fixed rates or prices.

The **gold standard** is a type of fixed exchange rate system with a long history in international trade. David Hume (1711–1776), a Scottish philosopher and friend of Adam Smith, was the first person to analyze the workings of an international gold standard. The world economy functioned on a gold standard as recently as World War I. Many observers today wistfully call for a return to the gold standard.

Under a gold standard, all trading nations are willing to redeem their currencies for gold. With each currency linked to gold, the precious metal becomes, in effect, a world currency.

Price-specie flow mechanism:
The channels by which gold inflows or outflows would cause price level increases or decreases in a country on the gold standard, thereby eliminating trade surpluses and deficits.

A key element of the gold standard is that each country links its money supply to its holdings of gold. Both foreign and domestic citizens are allowed to redeem currency for gold in a country at a fixed rate. This action creates a natural equilibrating mechanism (Hume called it the **price-specie flow mechanism**), which keeps the imports and exports of countries in balance. Suppose that while operating on a gold standard, the United States imports more than it exports over a given period of time. This differential of purchases has to be paid in gold. Since money supplies are tied to gold, the gold payment causes the money supply of the United States to fall and the money supplies of trade surplus countries to rise. Prices and costs in the United States would thus fall, and prices and costs in the trade surplus countries would rise. Deflation in the trade deficit countries such as the United States would stimulate exports and dampen imports, and inflation in trade surplus countries would dampen exports and stimulate imports. Balance of trade equilibrium is thus restored in both types of countries under a gold standard.

The gold standard is very much like the fixed exchange rate system. However, a gold-based standard is not necessary to operate a fixed exchange rate system. What is required is that countries act as if they are on the gold standard. When a country runs a trade surplus, it increases its money supply, and its domestic prices and costs rise; ultimately, exports decrease and imports increase. When a country has a trade deficit, it decreases its money supply, prices and costs fall, and thus exports increase and imports decrease. In both cases, a country is required to manipulate its whole economy to maintain equilibrium in its balance of trade with a fixed exchange rate.

The crucial difference between the gold standard and modern fixed-rate systems managed by government intervention in the foreign exchange market is that under a gold standard the domestic authorities do not have a choice about changing the money supply, thereby inflating or deflating currency. No international negotiations are required; the system works automatically. A modern fixed-rate system requires that countries agree to follow the appropriate domestic monetary and fiscal policies or to devalue or revalue the official rates when disequilibrium exchange rates lead to persistent deficits and surpluses. To reach such agreements requires complex and costly international negotiations. Modern fixed-rate systems are thus at the mercy of individual action by each country. Countries may or may not follow the rules of the game. The gold standard left no such discretion to political authorities. (Focus, "Should We Return to a Gold Standard?" details the advantages and disadvantages of the gold standard.)

THE BALANCE OF PAYMENTS

Balance of payments:
An official accounting record of all the foreign transactions of a nation's residents, businesses, and governments.

Countries keep track of the flow of international trade and periodically publish a report of their transactions, called the **balance of payments.** The balance of payments is essentially an accounting record of a nation's foreign business. It contains valuable information about the level of exports, imports, foreign investment, and the transactions of government such as purchases and sales of foreign currencies.

The balance of payments, as an accounting statement, is kept according to the principles of double-entry bookkeeping. The concept of double-entry bookkeeping is simple: Each entry on the credit side of the ledger implies an equal entry on the debit side. Thus, each international transaction creates both a debit (−) and a credit (+) item in the balance of payments ledger.

There is a simple rule to follow in classifying debits and credits: Any foreign transaction that leads to a demand for foreign currencies (or a supply

FOCUS Should We Return to a Gold Standard?

The relatively high inflation rates experienced by the United States during the late 1970s and early 1980s led to a variety of proposals for a return to a gold standard. Proponents of the gold standard argued that linking the nominal money supply to gold would prevent large increases and decreases in the money supply that lead to inflations and deflations. Congress established a U.S. Gold Commission to study the question, and the members not only debated the desirability of again tying the dollar to gold but also considered how to implement a new gold standard.

Proponents of a return to the gold standard argue that the Federal Reserve has neither the willingness nor the ability to follow monetary policies that promote price stability and that some constraint on excessive monetary expansionism is necessary. What are the advantages and disadvantages of gold-backed dollars?

Under a gold standard, currency is freely convertible into gold at some fixed rate, such as $35 per ounce, which was for many years the official U.S. price of gold. Thus, a nation's currency supply is directly related to its supply of gold. The supply of currency can be expanded relative to the supply of gold only by devaluing the dollar in terms of gold—that is, by raising gold's dollar price. A gold standard therefore enforces monetary discipline. In the absence of devaluation, the currency supply can be increased only at a rate equal to the increase in the output of gold, an expansion that has occurred historically at about 1.5 to 2 percent annually. Such a monetary policy would foster price stability with little or no inflation in the economy.

There are several major drawbacks to a gold standard. Real resources are tied up in money production—gold must be mined, stored, and transported. Also, the supply of gold is relatively inelastic. Expansion in the demand for money as economic growth occurs will generate downward pressure on the general price level. If the supply of gold rises more slowly than the demand, a gold standard will bring about persist deflation. Discovery of new gold sources or improvements in the technology used to extract gold from existing mines would likely bring about rapid inflation.

Even though the dollar price of gold is fixed, a variety of demand-side factors can cause the market price of gold to diverge from its official price. Indeed, it would be the sheerest coincidence for the two prices to be equal. Cooperation among nations is required to maintain the official price in such circumstances. For instance, during the late 1960s, a two-tier system evolved in which a world price of $35 per ounce was supported through sales among Western central banks and by an agreement between governments not to buy or sell gold in the open market. Prior to that time, a group of countries had formed a gold pool for the purpose of using their gold reserves to intervene periodically to stabilize the open market price at the official price.

Finally, incentives to engage in monetary expansionism are not completely eliminated by a gold standard. Increases in the stock of currency can be purchased for a time by a willingness to suffer a drain on gold reserves. That is, domestic inflation tends to create a trade deficit, which under a gold standard is balanced by shipments of gold to trade surplus nations. However, the inflating country's currency becomes overvalued, and pressures to devalue gradually become irresistible. In fact, persistent monetary expansion by the United States ultimately led to the collapse of the earlier world gold standard.

---

of dollars) is treated as a debit, or a minus, item. The act of importing is a debit entry in the balance of payments. Any foreign transaction that leads to a demand for dollars (or a supply of foreign currency) is entered as a credit, or a plus, item. The act of exporting is a credit entry in the balance of payments.

Suppose a U.S. firm exports computers to France, and the French importer of the computers pays for the purchase with an IOU. The French IOU is entered on the credit side in U.S. balance of payments bookkeeping because the French importer must ultimately demand dollars to pay off its IOU to the U.S. firm. The sale of computers is entered on the debit side as the offsetting part of the transaction. The U.S. firm must give up a computer in return for the French importer's payment. Since each transaction implies an equal debit and credit, the balance of payments must always balance. In this respect, the balance of payment is like any other accounting balance sheet.

Of course, although the total balance of payments of a country must always balance (debits minus credits equal zero), its component parts need not balance. For example, the imports and exports of specific merchandise such as automobiles do not have to balance. But overall, surpluses in one part of the balance of payments must be canceled out by deficits in other parts. This is not to say, of course, that countries do not experience balance of payments problems. Problems arise, as we will see, from persistent surpluses or deficits in the component parts of the balance of payments. (See Focus, "Debtor Nations in the 1990s," for a discussion of the consequences of persistent deficits.)

Exports and Imports: The Balance of Trade

Table 1 presents the data on the U.S. balance of payments for 1988. Items 1 and 2 represent exports and imports of goods and services. The difference between the sums of these aspects of the balance of payments—exports contrasted with imports—is the balance of trade. Note that trade in merchandise is only one facet of this balance. Merchandise trade figures are the result of a country's international trade in physical goods, such as books, cars, planes, and computers—the visible exports and imports. The data in Table 1 show that in 1988 merchandise exports (1a) were less than merchandise imports (2a) by $127.2 billion. This figure is sometimes called the merchandise trade balance and is equal to merchandise exports minus merchandise imports. If the figure is positive, there is a merchandise trade surplus. It was negative in 1988, so there was a merchandise trade deficit.

Many imports and exports are invisible. U.S. citizens and firms supply various services to foreigners, such as transportation, insurance, and telecommunications. Payments are received for these services just as in the case of visible exports. Items 1b and 2b represent invisible exports and imports in the balance of payments. When both visible and invisible exports and imports are considered in Table 1, U.S. exports were still substantially less than U.S. imports, yielding a trade deficit of $111.8 billion.

Net Transfers Abroad

Net unilateral transfers abroad are one-way money payments from the United States to foreigners or United States citizens living abroad. Included in this category are such items as foreign aid and pension checks to retired U.S. citizens living abroad. Nothing tangible comes back to the United States for these transfers, but they do give rise to a demand for foreign exchange. They thus are entered as a debit item in the balance of payments. In 1988, the United States made $14.7 billion worth of such transfers.

Current Account Balance

The balance on current account is equal to exports of goods and services minus imports of goods and services minus net unilateral transfers abroad. The United States had a deficit on current account in 1988 of $126.6 billion.

TABLE 1

U.S. Balance of Payments, 1988

U.S. exports enter the balance of payments with plus signs because buyers of these exports must pay U.S. firms with dollars. Dollars thus flow into the United States and are recorded as a plus, or credit, in the balance of payments. U.S. imports receive a minus sign, indicating that to pay for foreign goods U.S. buyers must supply dollars to foreign countries. Dollars thus flow out of the United States, and imports are then treated as a minus, or a debit, in the balance of payments. Similarly, outflows of U.S. capital and inflows of foreign capital are treated as debits and credits, respectively. To classify an item as a debit or a credit, think of whether dollars are leaving or entering the country. If they are leaving, the item is a debit; if they are entering, the item is a credit.

Item		Amount (billions of dollars)
1. Exports of goods & services		+529.8
a. Merchandise, excluding military	+319.3	
b. Other goods & services	+210.5	
2. Imports of goods & services		−641.7
a. Merchandise, excluding military	−446.5	
b. Other goods & services	−195.2	
3. U.S. government grants		− 10.4
4. Remittances, pensions, and other transfers		− 4.3
5. U.S. assets abroad, net (capital outflow)		− 82.1
a. U.S. official reserve assets, net	− 3.6	
b. Other U.S. government assets, net	+ 3.0	
c. U.S. private assets, net	− 81.5	
6. Foreign assets in the U.S., net (capital inflow)		+219.3
a. Foreign official assets, net	+ 38.9	
b. Other foreign assets, net	+180.4	
7. Statistical discrepancy		− 10.6
8. Total		0

Source: U.S. Department of Commerce, *Survey of Current Business* (December 1989), p. 22.

Note: Total does not add to zero due to rounding.

Net Capital Movements

When U.S. residents purchase foreign stocks and bonds, they obtain a claim to foreign capital (buildings, factories, future foreign government payments, and so forth). Funds that would otherwise be invested in the United States are exported, or, to put it another way, capital is exported. When foreign citizens purchase the stocks and bonds of U.S. businesses and governments, foreign capital is imported into the United States. In 1988, capital outflows were $82.1 billion, whereas capital inflows were $219.3 billion.

Note what happens in bookkeeping terms when capital flows into and out of a country. Capital outflows are treated as a debit item in the balance of payments because they constitute a payment; they give rise to a demand for foreign exchange with which to make foreign investment. Capital inflows are a credit item because they consist of receipts by U.S. residents from foreigners; they generate a supply of foreign exchange necessary to obtain dollars with which to purchase U.S. financial assets.

FOCUS   Debtor Nations in the 1990s

In recent years, much concern has been expressed concerning international indebtedness. To take but one example, Mexico alone owed U.S. banks more than $20 billion in 1988. In this discussion, there is a tendency to view international debt as an economic evil. Those who hold this view advocate any policy designed to eliminate such indebtedness. However, a more careful examination of the issue shows that debt is not the result of sinister forces but of choices made by individuals and business firms within a country. Further, the acquisition of debt often is a sensible way for a country to undertake economic growth.

In examining this issue, it is useful to draw an analogy between countries that become indebted and individuals or families who do the same. Many college students elect to go into debt. Fully capable of entering the labor force and being self-sufficient, many high school graduates opt instead for more education, taking out student loans and incurring significant debts. This choice will not necessarily prove to be profitable for every student; some will choose majors of questionable value in the job market and these same majors may not even yield any personal satisfaction. Still, most students find borrowing to pay for a college education worthwhile. Enhanced earning power in the future will enable the college student both to pay off student loans and to have a better standard of living.

Of course, paying for tuition and room and board is not the only way to go into debt. Perhaps you have borrowed money to buy a car or run up your credit cards to pay for clothes and vacations. Again, however, your indebtedness is the consequence of your own choices. In most cases, the decision to borrow will prove to be a wise one; it is usually "worth it" to have less in the future in order to have more now. Only when the repayment of debts involves great future sacrifices can the decision to borrow be considered positively unwise.

The reasons students incur debts and the reasons countries incur debts are of a kind. In many cases, poor countries with growth potential obtain loans from abroad to build plants, office buildings, highway systems. Often, these turn out to be wise investments, much like most educational loans and for a similar reason: The future productivity of the country is enhanced, which enables the debt to be easily repaid. Sometimes, countries borrow huge sums but fail to use them in a way that enhances future productivity. During the past two decades, Argentina, Peru, Mexico, and Chile have all incurred huge debts but have failed to achieve much in the way of economic growth. Hence, the loans now represent a real burden to the countries, as repayment will require marked decreases in living standards. Debt forgiveness for these countries is possible—most likely in exchange for lower tariffs and elimination of other trade barriers against U.S. goods.

As a consequence of large trade deficits since 1982, the United States has also become a debtor nation. This position is a manifestation of the choice to consume foreign goods far in excess of any willingness on the part of other nations to buy American goods—not the consequence of any sinister forces. This choice has enabled Americans to enjoy a higher standard of living during this period than would have been possible otherwise. The consequence will be a somewhat lower living standard in future years than would have been the case without so much borrowing. This does not mean that it is a mistake for the United States to have gone into debt. The United States resembles a well-to-do family with large credit card bills—bills easily paid in the future.

Transactions in Official Reserves

Items 5a and 6a in Table 1 reflect the activities of government in the foreign exchange market. The official reserve assets of a country are its holdings of gold and foreign exchange. Also included in reserve assets are special drawing rights (SDRs) with the International Monetary Fund, an international central bank located in Washington, D.C. SDRs are supplementary reserves of purchasing power that a country can draw on to pay international debts. SDRs are simply bookkeeping entries that member countries may draw against to settle an international payments deficit. They are not money in any physical sense, but SDRs may be used as a means of payment. Suppose that Mexico experiences a balance of payments deficit and is without dollars to repay Canada for its purchases of capital goods. Mexico, as a member of the IMF, may opt to settle the debt by transferring some of its special drawing rights credit to Canada. In this way international reserves and liquidity are increased without any actual transfer of funds. After the transfer, Canada may utilize the increased credit to settle some international obligations.

A government can finance an excess of imports over exports by drawing down its holdings of official reserves. Countries experiencing surpluses may want to add to their official reserves. During the 1947–1973 period of fixed exchange rates, these reserve accounts were quite important because countries used the reserves to stabilize their exchange rates. Deficit countries used reserves to defend the value of their currency, and surplus countries accumulated valuable international reserves.

Item 5a is U.S. holdings of official reserve assets. In 1988, these holdings increased by $3.6 billion. This item enters the balance of payments as a debit because an increase in official reserve holdings means an increase in the demand for foreign exchange. Item 5a is thus treated like a merchandise import.

Item 6a is net investments of official agencies of foreign countries, such as the OPEC countries, in the United States. Since these investments represent demand for dollars, they are treated as a credit item in the balance of payments.

In 1988, the United States increased its net position in international reserves by $35.3 billion, the sum of items 5a and 6a.

Statistical Discrepancy

Item 7 in Table 1 is called statistical discrepancy, an accounting fudge factor. When all the data were collected and debits and credits computed, the credits outweighed the debits by 10.6 billion. The negative statistical discrepancy is added to make the balance of payments balance by compensating for imperfections in data gathering. Some debits have apparently gone unrecorded in computing the balance of payments. These could include hidden imports or unrecorded capital outflows. Most experts think that the former is the source of most of the discrepancy, which is clearly quite large.

The Balance of Payments and the Value of the Dollar

The last entry in Table 1 is zero, indicating that the balance of payments must balance. This is the way any double-entry accounting system works.

The balance of payments, however, is an aggregate record of a country's international payments for one year. Behind this record are the myriad transactions of U.S. citizens and firms with foreign citizens and firms. These transactions determine how the U.S. dollar fares in the foreign exchange market. If, over time, the value of the dollar rises against other currencies, we say that the dollar is strong. This is precisely what happened over the period 1982–1985, although the dollar generally depreciated in the latter half of the 1980s. The dollar appreciated in the range of 10 to 15 percent against most major foreign currencies between 1982 and 1985. Most observers feel that this appreciation of the dollar reflected high U.S. interest rates that attracted an inflow of foreign capital into the United States.

This capital inflow led to a higher demand for the dollar and thus to its appreciation. There are obviously costs and benefits associated with large inflows of foreign capital into a country. Foreigners thereby own more U.S. assets and firms, but the United States has an expanded supply of capital as a consequence. The important point is that the dollar appreciated in currency markets during the early 1980s, and though this fact is not directly reflected in the balance of payments, it indicates that the U.S. foreign economic position might loosely be described as a surplus. That is, the impact of all our foreign transactions over time has been to cause the dollar to rise in value. Since 1986, the dollar has been on a path of depreciation vis-à-vis most major foreign currencies. While dollar depreciation can be expected to turn our loosely described balance of payments surplus around, such reactions are usually relatively slow in occurring. It is still too early to gauge the impact of this latest dollar depreciation on the overall balance of payments, although the trade deficit decreased between 1986 and 1988.

THE EVOLUTION OF INTERNATIONAL MONETARY INSTITUTIONS

Major world trading nations today rely on floating exchange rates. These governments will occasionally intervene in the foreign exchange market when exchange rate changes are significant, but generally currency prices are free to adjust according to the forces of supply and demand. We briefly review the developments over the past hundred years that led the major trading nations to adopt floating exchange rates in 1973.

The Decline of the Gold Standard

In the period before World War I, dating back to the 1870s, most currencies in the world economy were tied to gold. This means that each country was prepared to redeem its currency at a fixed price in gold to both its own citizens and foreigners. The United States, for example, stood ready to exchange an ounce of gold for $20.67 over this period. In addition, countries on the gold standard linked their money supplies to their holdings of gold bullion.

The gold standard worked reasonably well in eliminating balance of trade surpluses and deficits over the period 1870–1914. Nonetheless, for a variety of reasons the gold standard broke down after World War I. There were attempts to return to the gold standard in the 1920s, but the shock to the international economy caused by the Great Depression in the 1930s brought the gold system down once and for all.

Bretton Woods and the Postwar System

Bretton Woods system:
The fixed exchange rate system established among Western countries after World War II.

International Monetary Fund:
An international organization, established along with the Bretton Woods system, designed to assist in the efficient functioning of the Bretton Woods fixed exchange rate system.

Not until after World War II were the problems of the international monetary system addressed in a concerted way. Negotiators for the free-world countries met in Bretton Woods, New Hampshire, in 1944 to develop a new international monetary order. The **Bretton Woods system,** which lasted almost thirty years, consisted of a system of fixed exchange rates and an international central bank, called the **International Monetary Fund** (IMF), to oversee the new system.

We have already discussed the economics of fixed exchange rates. The basic idea of the Bretton Woods system was that, over time, countries would obtain or pay for their imports with their exports. However, there might be temporary periods over which a country might wish to run a trade deficit to obtain more imports than its current level of exports allowed it to obtain. Under the Bretton Woods system the country could do so by borrowing international reserves from the IMF. Over time, the country was expected to return to a trade surplus, out of which the earlier loan of reserves could be repaid.

The IMF was the bank that held the reserves that allowed the system to operate in this way. When the IMF was formed, each member country was required to contribute reserves of its currency to the bank. The bank thus accumulated substantial holdings of dollars, marks, francs, pesos, and so on, and when member nations ran into balance of trade deficits, the bank would lend them reserves. Each time a loan was made, the debtor nation was encouraged to reform its economic policies to avoid future deficits. Sound economic management might also lead to a trade surplus and a source of funds to repay the IMF loan.

The Bretton Woods system sounds fine in principle, and indeed it functioned tolerably well for a number of years. However, as we saw earlier, fixing the price of a currency is like fixing the price of any other good or service—it is very likely to cause surpluses and shortages in the currency market. As the conditions affecting imports and exports across countries change, the demand and supply of currencies will shift. Countries can find themselves with overvalued fixed exchange rates, which means that they will face persistent balance of trade deficits. Under the IMF system the deficit country could draw on its IMF reserves to settle the deficits, but it could not do this forever because it would exhaust its reserves. Chronic deficit countries with overvalued exchange rates were thus said to be in fundamental disequilibrium.

In our discussion of the theory of fixed exchange rates, we reviewed the various courses of action that a country in fundamental disequilibrium could take. First, it could devalue its currency as a step toward restoring equilibrium in its balance of trade. Once its currency was devalued, the exchange rate would again be fixed and defended. Second, the country could attempt to improve its trade balance by imposing tariff and quota barriers to imports and perhaps by subsidizing exports. In other words, the country could move away from free trade to balance its imports and exports. Third, the country could behave as if it were on the gold standard. This would mean adopting restrictive monetary and fiscal policies designed to promote domestic deflation and high interest rates in the hope that such changes would restore the balance of trade to equilibrium. This, of course, is a problematic course of action for any country. For example, if the country's unemployment rate were already high, it is hard to believe that the nation's leaders would be sufficiently disciplined to undertake a deflationary course of action.

Speculation by buyers and sellers of currencies also undermines a fixed exchange rate system. Suppose Great Britain is running chronic trade deficits, and everyone, including speculators, expects that the pound will be devalued (even though British central bankers will deny such rumors vehemently). In effect, speculators are in a no-lose position. Will they continue to hold pounds? Clearly, they will not; pounds are about to become less valuable relative to other currencies. Speculators will sell their pounds for other currencies, increasing the supply of pounds to the foreign exchange market and putting additional downward pressure on the pound. By selling the weak

Speculation:
The buying and selling of currencies on the foreign exchange market with the intent of profiting from possible devaluation or revaluations in a fixed-rate system or from possible future movements in the exchange rate in a flexible-rate system.

currency and buying a strong currency, speculators make it more difficult for authorities to find a new fixed value for the pound. This is why speculation in a fixed exchange rate system is often termed destabilizing.

In the early period of the Bretton Woods system, the United States ran a large trade deficit, and this deficit provided a means of supplying dollar reserves to the rest of the world. It was thought that this deficit was a temporary problem that would soon be replaced by a U.S. trade surplus. This was the premise of the Bretton Woods system. Yet the dollar was overvalued, and the U.S. deficits continued and grew larger into the 1950s and 1960s. The United States was in a difficult position. It was hard for it to devalue the dollar because the dollar was held by virtually every nation as an international reserve asset. A U.S. devaluation would have decreased the wealth of all those countries holding dollars. Several times, the United States tried to impose a restrictive macroeconomic policy to correct its balance of trade. However, when unemployment rose as a consequence, such policies were rapidly abandoned, as political pressures were brought to bear on policy-makers. U.S. deficits continued to grow, and foreign holdings of dollars rose.

Speculators entered again. Many holders of dollars became concerned about what the United States was going to do. There were various runs on the U.S. gold stock, as dollars were traded in by foreigners. In 1950, the United States had 509 million ounces of gold; by 1968, this stock had fallen to 296 million ounces. Confidence in the dollar fell further, and the stage was set for a drastic change in the international monetary system.

The Current International Monetary System

The present international monetary system was born in 1971. In the face of continuing large trade deficits and mounting speculation against the dollar, President Nixon broke the link between the dollar and gold in August 1971. No longer would the United States stand ready to exchange gold for dollars at $35 an ounce. In effect, the dollar was set free to fluctuate and seek its own level in the foreign exchange market. As a result, the overvalued dollar depreciated substantially against other major currencies. There were interim attempts to fix the price of the dollar again, but they failed. By early 1973, all the major currencies were floating.

The international monetary system that has been in effect since 1973 is a managed flexible-rate system. Exchange rates are allowed to seek their free-market values, as long as fluctuations are within an acceptable range. If fluctuations fall outside this range, governments may intervene with their reserve holdings to dampen the fluctuations in their currencies. Thus, exchange rates are not completely free; government intervention in the foreign exchange market will be forthcoming if a country's currency falls dramatically in value. In 1978, for example, the dollar fell sharply, and the Carter administration intervened to restrict this decline with international reserves and loans from West Germany and Japan. The central banks of major trading countries also have stepped up intervention activity since September of 1985. It should be remembered, though, that under the managed flexible-rate system, the ranges within which governments consider exchange rate fluctuations acceptable are not well defined as a matter of policy. As a result, it is difficult to tell how far a nation's currency would have to appreciate or depreciate before central bank interventions would occur.

Although the new system abandoned fixed exchange rates, it did not abandon the IMF, which still exists as an international monetary organization. The role of the IMF under the managed flexible-rate system is still evolving, and to this point it has consisted of helping countries that have persistent balance of payments problems by giving them loans and policy advice about how to conduct domestic macroeconomic policy to overcome these problems. The World Bank, which is part of the IMF system set up by the Bretton Woods agreement, has also played an increasing role in the new system. This sister institution of the IMF makes long-run development loans to poor countries.

Advantages of the Current System. The consensus view seems to be that the new system has worked very well under difficult circumstances. The following are the major advantages of the flexible-rate system.

1. It allows countries to pursue independent monetary policies. If a country wants to inflate its economy, it can do so by letting its exchange rate depreciate, thereby maintaining its position in international markets without sacrificing its preferred monetary policy.
2. Under the fixed-rate system, a country sometimes had to deflate its economy to solve a balance of trade deficit. With floating rates it only has to let its exchange rate depreciate. Clearly, it is easier to change one price than to change all prices to resolve balance of trade difficulties.
3. The current exchange rate system has proven capable of handling large economic disturbances. When the OPEC countries dramatically raised the price of oil in 1973–1974, the world economy experienced a tremendous shock. The greatest achievement of the flexible-rate system is the way it handled this shock. Oil-importing countries developed large trade deficits; huge trade surpluses built up in OPEC countries. These deficits and surpluses were accommodated by floating rates. Moreover, the huge oil revenues of the OPEC countries were recycled into Western investments. Though exchange rates changed significantly over the period, the new system weathered the storm and got the job done.

Disadvantages of the Current System. The flexible-rate system is not, however, without its critics.

1. Some observers point out that flexible rates can be very volatile, and this volatility creates considerable uncertainty for international trade. Thus, exchange rate flexibility leads to conditions that can retard the amount of international trade and therefore the degree of specialization in the world economy. Table 2 lists the exchange rates for several major currencies from 1973 to 1989. It is clear that some rates have changed significantly—the Swiss franc and the yen appreciated strongly, while the value of the French franc dropped considerably. The strength of the dollar against all these currencies is evident from 1982 through 1984. Since 1985, as noted earlier, the general trend has been one of dollar depreciation against the major world currencies shown. Do these changes impede international trade? Several studies suggest that they have not. They have found basically that the volume of a country's trade is not very sensitive to fluctuations in its exchange rate.[2]

---

[2]See Leland B. Yeager, *International Monetary Relations* (New York: Harper & Row, 1976), chapter 13.

TABLE 2

Foreign Exchange Rates, 1973–1989 (currency units per U.S. dollar)

Year	French Franc	German Mark	Japanese Yen	British Pound	Swiss Franc
1973	4.4534	2.6714	271.30	0.408	3.1687
1974	4.8106	2.5867	291.84	0.427	2.9804
1975	4.2876	2.4613	296.78	0.450	2.5839
1976	4.7824	2.5184	296.45	0.554	2.5001
1977	4.9160	2.3236	268.62	0.573	2.4064
1978	4.5090	2.0096	210.38	0.521	1.7906
1979	4.2567	1.8342	219.02	0.471	1.6643
1980	4.2250	1.8175	226.63	0.439	1.6772
1981	5.4396	2.2631	220.63	0.494	1.9674
1982	6.5793	2.4280	249.06	0.572	2.0327
1983	7.6203	2.5539	237.55	0.660	2.1006
1984	8.7355	2.8454	237.45	0.748	2.3500
1985	8.9799	2.9419	238.47	0.771	2.4551
1986	6.9257	2.1705	168.35	0.681	1.7979
1987	6.0122	1.7981	144.60	0.610	1.4918
1988	5.9595	1.7570	128.17	0.561	1.4643
1989	6.3802	1.8808	138.07	0.610	1.6369

Source: Council of Economic Advisers, *Economic Report of the President* (Washington, D.C.: U.S. Government Printing Office, 1990), p. 418.

2. A second criticism of floating rates is that they promote increased world inflation rates. Under a fixed-rate system, countries experience a balance of trade deficit if they inflate their respective economies. This link is severed under a flexible-rate system. Hence, domestic political authorities can more easily give in to those interests who benefit from inflation. Some proponents of the gold standard argue for its return to guard against domestic inflation.

3. Some countries that have relied primarily on adjustments in exchange rates to resolve trade imbalance problems have found that the solution has been a long time in coming. For example, despite depreciation of the dollar, the U.S. deficit with Japan has persisted for years, causing some observers to conclude that it never will solve the problem. Indeed, in certain cases, depreciation of the dollar will not improve the U.S. trade deficit. When the dollar depreciates against the yen, Japanese goods become more expensive to Americans, so Americans buy less from Japan. However, this does not necessarily mean that Americans will spend fewer dollars overall. If the price of a Japanese car rises by 10 percent and U.S. consumers reduce the quantity of Japanese cars purchased by less than 10 percent—if our demand for Japanese cars is inelastic—then Americans end up spending more dollars on Japanese cars, which tends to make the U.S. deficit worse. As more time is allowed to pass and our demand increases in elasticity, the devaluation is more likely to work. However, those interested primarily in an exchange system's ability to quickly eliminate trade deficits have become disillusioned with the current system.

4. Some regard the present system of various international monies as an anachronism. These critics argue that it would be more beneficial for the world to adopt a single currency and to become a unified currency area.

Such a system would allow various benefits to the world economy and would do away with the need to convert one currency to another in international trade. Although monetary unification has been tried on a modest scale in some areas of the world—notably, the recent monetary cooperation of the European countries in seeking to establish a European currency unit—a single global currency seems to be some distance in the future. After all, the forces of national autonomy are still strong, and virtually no government would lightly give up its power to control its money supply.

In sum, there are pros and cons with respect to the present international monetary system, but in general the system seems to have worked well over a difficult period in the international economy. Growing problems in the international payments system, however, call for the prospect of still further reform of the system.

SUMMARY

1. Foreign exchange is the currency of another country that is needed to make payment in an international transaction.
2. Foreign exchange can be obtained in the worldwide foreign exchange market. The demand for foreign exchange arises from the desire to buy foreign goods. The supply of foreign exchange arises from the desire of citizens of one country to buy the goods of another country.
3. A foreign exchange rate is the price of one currency in terms of another. A currency's value appreciates when its purchasing power in terms of other currencies rises. It depreciates when its purchasing power falls.
4. The demand for foreign currency in one country depends largely on income and relative price levels in the two countries.
5. Under a floating, or flexible, exchange rate system, a country allows its exchange rate to be set by the forces of supply and demand in the foreign exchange market. Flexible exchange rates change in response to changes in countries' money supplies, price levels, inflation rates, real interest rates, and fundamental factors such as technology, consumer rates, and government export and import policies. Under a flexible-rate system, exchange rate movements act to alleviate balance of trade surpluses and deficits.
6. Under a fixed exchange rate system, governments intervene in the foreign exchange market to set and defend the value of their currency. When a country's currency is overvalued relative to the equilibrium rate, the country will run a balance of trade deficit. It can seek to cure this deficit by deflating the domestic economy, establishing trade barriers, or devaluing its currency to a new, lower, fixed rate of exchange. When the fixed exchange rate is below its equilibrium value, a country will experience a balance of trade surplus and will sometimes revalue its currency upward.
7. Under a gold standard, a historical form of a fixed exchange rate system, each country makes its currency redeemable in gold and ties its money supply to its stock of gold. When a surplus of imports over exports appears, gold is shipped to foreigners to settle the balance of trade deficit, causing deflation in the domestic money supply of the deficit country and inflation in the surplus country, restoring equilibrium.
8. An important difference between floating- and fixed-rate systems is that the former changes one price to maintain equilibrium in the balance of trade, while the latter changes all prices in the economy to maintain a fixed exchange rate.
9. The balance of payments is a record of the international transactions of a country's economy. It follows the principles of double-entry bookkeeping and must therefore always balance in an accounting sense. Transactions that give rise to a demand for foreign exchange are entered as debits; transactions that give rise to a supply of foreign exchange are treated as credits.
10. The modern history of the international monetary system began with the gold standard, followed by a system of fixed exchange rates managed by the International Monetary Fund. The present international monetary system is a managed floating-rate system. Exchange rates are set by supply and demand, but governments can and have intervened if exchange rate movements are too large.

KEY TERMS

foreign exchange	purchasing power parity (PPP) theory	revaluation
foreign exchange markets	undervalued	gold standard
exchange rate	overvalued	price-specie flow mechanism
flexible, or floating, exchange rate system	foreign exchange market intervention	balance of payments
fixed exchange rate system	foreign exchange reserves	Bretton Woods system
managed flexible-rate system	balance of trade surplus	International Monetary
depreciation	balance of trade deficit	Fund
appreciation	devaluation	speculation

QUESTIONS FOR REVIEW AND DISCUSSION

1. Suppose that the British pound is worth $1.50, and that $1 is worth about 6.5 Swedish kronor. How much would a Jaguar automobile cost in U.S. dollars if the British price is 20,000 pounds? How much would a Volvo cost in U.S. dollars if the Swedish price is 84,000 kronor?

2. The following exchange rates came from a newspaper report for February 1, 1987.

	U.S. Dollar per Currency Unit	
	Wednesday	Tuesday
Swiss franc	0.6656	0.6696
Italian lira	0.0007849	0.0007874

	Currency per U.S. Dollar	
	Wednesday	Tuesday
Swiss franc	1.5025	1.4935
Italian lira	1274	1270

  a. Did the Swiss franc rise or fall from Tuesday to Wednesday?
  b. What about the Italian lira?
  c. What happened to the dollar value of the franc?
  d. What about the dollar value of the lira?

3. Suppose the United States and Sweden are on a floating exchange rate system. Explain whether the following events would cause the Swedish krona to appreciate or depreciate.
  a. U.S. interest rates rise above Swedish interest rates.
  b. American tourism to Sweden increases.
  c. Americans fall in love with a newly designed Volvo, and Volvo sales in the United States skyrocket.
  d. The U.S. government puts a quota on Volvo imports.
  e. The Swedish inflation rate rises relative to the U.S. rate.
  f. The United States closes a military installation in Sweden at the urging of the Swedish government.

4. What happens to the floating exchange rate of a country that has a higher inflation rate than other countries? Show your answer graphically.

5. How would you treat the following items in the balance of payments? In other words, would you enter them as debits or credits?
  a. An American travels to Canada.
  b. A U.S. wine importer buys wine from Italy.
  c. A California wine grower sells wine to England.
  d. An Austrian corporation pays dividends to American stockholders.
  e. General Motors pays dividends to French investors.
  f. Several Japanese visit Hawaii on an American cruise ship.
  g. A Swedish citizen invests in a U.S. company based in Houston.

6. Explain why capital inflows are a credit entry in the balance of payments and capital outflows are a debit entry.

7. When we say that the gold standard required that all prices but one be changed to overcome a balance of trade deficit, what do we mean?

8. What are the primary advantages and disadvantages of the present international monetary system?

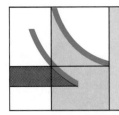

ECONOMICS IN ACTION
Trade Deficits, Flexible Exchange Rates, and the Competitiveness of the U.S. Economy

Two of the concepts explored in this chapter cropped up again and again in the financial news during the 1980s. The value of the dollar abroad during the flexible exchange rate period has fluctuated significantly. Depreciation was the order of the day during the late 1970s, whereas the early 1980s saw a record strengthening of the dollar. (In general, the dollar has depreciated since 1985, although there was some appreciation between 1988 and 1989.) The United States has not only seen merchandise trade deficits every year since 1976, but this deficit was at an all-time high of approximately $150 billion in 1987. These events have provoked much debate concerning the worldwide competitiveness of U.S. producers, the desirability of new tariffs and quotas to stem the deficit, and suggestions to return to a fixed exchange rate system. A clearer focus on the concepts involved in the debate, as well as a review of their behavior in the 1970s and 1980s, can lead to a better understanding of the current problem.

The merchandise trade balance is, for most people, the most familiar international economic statistic. This is the number that we usually hear or read in the media as representing the trade deficit. As pointed out in this chapter, however, the merchandise trade deficit only measures the amount by which the value of imported goods exceeds that of goods exported.

A truer measure of trade flows and imbalances includes trade in services along with trade in goods. Both goods and services are traded among nations, and trade in both goods and services is subject to the same fundamental economic forces. In discussing trade, there is little reason to exclude trade in such services as travel and telecommunications, just as there would be little reason to exclude the value of services consumed by an individual from a measure of the individual's economic well-being.

Figure 6a shows both measures of the trade balance since 1971. While the balance on merchandise trade has been in deficit since 1976, once trade in services is included (military transactions have been excluded) serious balance of trade deficits did not appear until 1983. In fact, as Figure 6a shows, the balance on goods and services was in surplus for most of the flexible exchange rate period.

Since 1983, however, even the surpluses on the services trade account have not prevented large deficits in the overall trade balance. What has caused such large deficits, however measured, in the last few years? Unfortunately, no simple answer exists, much less a cure. Economists have focused attention on a number of possible causes and have offered suggestions for possible cures.

One explanation for trade balance movements is the exchange rate. Figure 6b depicts the movement of an index of the average dollar price of the currencies of ten of the major trading partners of the United States. As Figure 6b indicates, the period of the middle to late 1970s was a period of dollar depreciation on foreign currency markets. The dollar price of foreign exchange rose by approximately 17 percent from 1976 to 1980. While the merchandise trade balance remained fairly level in this interval, the balance on goods and services went from deficit to surplus. Notice, however, that the goods and services balance responded a year or so after the beginning of the exchange rate movement.

From 1980 through 1985, the dollar appreciated significantly vis-à-vis other major currencies. As the average dollar price of foreign currency fell, imports became less costly to Americans, while the prices of American-produced goods and services abroad rose. This strengthening of the dollar in the early 1980s, some economists believe, was a major factor in explaining the burgeoning trade deficit. Again, the balance on goods and services responded to dollar appreciation with a lag of about one year.

As the trade deficit ballooned, the issue of American "competitiveness" in international markets arose. Merchandise exports of the United States actually decreased from 1981 to 1986, while imports climbed steadily. A popular explanation was that American industry could no longer compete with more efficient foreign manufacturers, resulting in high prices of U.S.-made goods. Opponents of this argument noted that between 1980 and 1985, unit labor costs rose by 11 percent in the United States but by 16 percent in other major countries.

Thus, it does not appear that U.S. firms lack the ability to compete on world markets. Smaller increases in unit labor costs imply production efficiency gains. However, the reduction in the world relative prices of U.S. exports that would have occurred from these relative productivity gains were more than wiped out by appreciation of the dollar. As a result, the prices of U.S. exports on world markets rose, while the prices of foreign goods in the United States fell or did not rise as much. American firms did not lose their ability to compete; they were instead the victims of exchange rate appreciation.

Large government budget deficits undoubtedly contributed to the continued strength of the U.S. dollar on world

FIGURE 6 **Trade Balances and Exchange Rates, 1971–1988**

(a) Both the balance of merchandise (goods) trade and goods and services trade are shown. While the balance of merchandise trade was in deficit throughout most of the period, the goods and services balance did not go into significant deficit until 1983. The difference between the two lines is the surplus in services trade. Both measures exclude military purchases. (b) The index of exchange rates is an average of the dollar prices of ten major U.S. trading partners' currencies. Increases in the index signal general dollar depreciation and rising import (falling export) prices. Decreases in the index indicate dollar appreciation and falling import (rising export) prices for Americans.

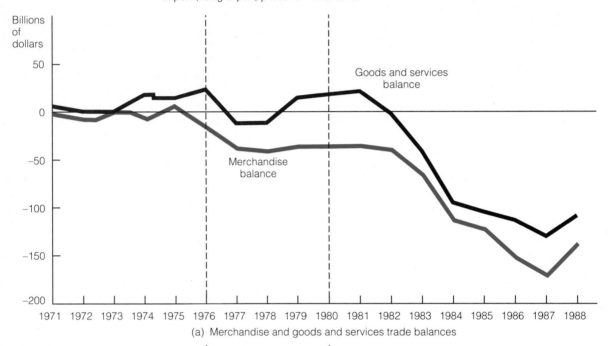

(a) Merchandise and goods and services trade balances

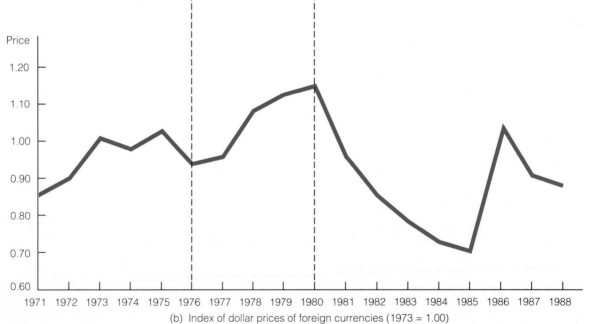

(b) Index of dollar prices of foreign currencies (1973 = 1.00)

markets during the 1980s. In 1982, the budget deficit rose to over $100 billion, and it remained there through the end of the decade. Actions by the U.S. Treasury to finance these deficits kept real interest rates high in the United States compared to other countries. As we saw in this chapter, a rise in the real interest rate in a country will lead to an appreciation of the currency of that country on world markets. Therefore, we can see that there is a link between the "twin deficits"—the trade deficit and budget deficit. The large budget deficit brought about high interest rates, which led to an appreciation of the dollar. With the dollar remaining strong, American business firms found it difficult to compete in world markets, so the large U.S. trade deficit persisted.

In 1990, real interest rates in West Germany and Japan began to rise relative to those in the United States. If the trend continues, reductions in the U.S. trade deficit may not be far behind. As Figure 6 suggests, the generally lowered price of foreign exchange between 1986 and 1988 has been associated with a gradual improvement in both the merchandise and goods and services balances.

Question

With trade deficits come foreign capital inflows into the United States—that is, investment in U.S. plant and equipment by foreigners. In the long run, is this good or bad, economically, for the United States?

Sources: Council of Economic Advisers, *Economic Report of the President* (Washington, D.C.: U.S. Government Printing Office, 1987), pp. 358, 365; U.S. Department of Commerce, *Survey of Current Business* (December, 1986), p. 28.

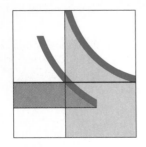

23

Economic Systems and Economic Development

Comparative economics:
The study of the differences in economic systems; particularly, the differences between capitalist and socialist economic systems.

$\mathbf{P}$ast chapters have focused on the operation of a mixed capitalist economy, in which a private market sector plays the primary role in the production and distribution of goods and services. The study of **comparative economics** analyzes the differences between capitalist systems and other types of economic systems, particularly socialist economies. Under socialism, the state (the public sector) plays a primary economic role in the economy. The state controls most of the nonhuman productive resources in the economy and makes decisions about the allocation of these resources. The overall distribution and variety of goods and services available to final consumers are essentially determined by the state. Historically, socialism has taken many forms. In this chapter, we focus on what used to be called Soviet-style socialism—an extreme form of socialism that has fallen out of favor. Increasingly, existing socialist systems are mixed, with differing degrees of reliance on central planning and markets to determine production and allocation of goods and services. A number of historically socialist economies are experimenting with democracy and greater economic freedom. "Soviet-style" socialism no longer means what it once did. What role will economics and the implementation of market systems play as these countries search for economic efficiency and prosperity?

This chapter also introduces the study of economic development and the economic challenges facing the poorer economies of the world. For example, per capita income in 1990 in India and Burma was less than $300. Why are these countries so poor? How can they be made richer? What is the proper role of richer countries, such as the United States, in helping poor countries reach higher standards of living? While a complex array of cultural, political, and institutional factors affect economic development, economic systems and the incentives they create are key to understanding the varying levels of growth in these countries. When you complete Chapter 23 you should understand

- some of the underlying differences between socialist and market economic systems in generating economic efficiency.
- the historical role of central planning in the Soviet Union and other socialist nations.

- how the Soviet Union's and Eastern Europe's recent attempts to transform some of the basics of their economic systems from planning to market orientations have fared.
- some of the economic aspects of development and growth in developing countries.

COMPARATIVE ECONOMIC SYSTEMS

What do we mean by an economic system? The economic system of a given country is based on institutions of ownership, incentives, and decision making, which underlie all economic activity.

Recall the device we used in Chapter 3 to compare economic systems— the spectrum that ranges from pure capitalism to pure communism. Again, a society organized along the lines of **pure capitalism** is one in which most resources are privately owned and in which government economic control is minimal. In such a society, government's role is limited to protecting and enforcing private property rights and to providing pure public goods such as national defense. An economic system characterized by common ownership of productive resources, both human and nonhuman is **pure communism.** In between is **socialism,** in which the state owns some nonhuman productive resources and makes production decisions by planning the economy's output. The real world is complex, however; there simply are no pure economic systems (although there are some that come close).

Although there are many complex differences between any two economies, we can focus on two basic types of systems. To a varying degree, the economies of the United States, the United Kingdom, and France, for example, share the characteristics of **mixed capitalism.** In such a system, the state is an important participant in the economy, but by and large the bulk of productive activity is undertaken by private firms and individuals.

In a decreasing number of countries the dominant economic institutions are fundamentally different from those in capitalist societies. For many years, China and the Soviet Union headed lists of such countries—communist countries. As we will see, even these two models have attempted, to varying degrees, to mix market or capitalist elements and socialist planning in recent years. Under extreme socialism (that which is termed *communism* in the real world but which falls short of the pure communism on our spectrum), resource allocation is determined by central planning rather than by market forces. At least in theory, resources are allocated and utilized according to a centrally determined and administered overall economic plan. The quantity and composition of output, the relative proportions of consumption and investment, the use of resources in production, and the allocation of final output are all decided by the central authorities. The central plan is also likely to include detailed decisions on quantities of raw materials and inputs, techniques of production, prices, wages, location of plants and industries, and the pattern of employment of the labor force. The objectives of the central plan reflect the goals and preferences of the central planners. Consumers themselves have no direct input into the planning process; central planning effectively replaces the consumer sovereignty of capitalism.

Pure capitalism:
An economic system in which most resources are owned, and most relevant decisions are made, by private individuals.

Pure communism:
An economic system in which most productive resources, both human and nonhuman, are publicly owned.

Socialism:
An economic system in which most nonhuman productive resources are owned by the state.

Mixed capitalism:
An economic system in which most economic decisions are made by the private sector but in which government also plays a substantial economic and regulatory role.

Under Mikhail Gorbachev's stewardship as leader of the Soviet Union, numerous economic reforms have been proposed. Included in these reforms are attempts to streamline the bureaucracy of central planning, to build more economic incentives into production decisions, and to liberalize the Soviet economy's international trading relations.

In part heeding Gorbachev's example, in part reading into it a more tolerant mood in Moscow, most of Eastern Europe—namely, Poland, Romania, East Germany, Czechoslovakia, Hungary, and Bulgaria—minimized or eliminated the influence of socialist planning in their own economies. In 1989 and 1990, all of these nations, along with the Soviet Union, restructured, in varying degrees, their political systems to permit freer elections and "democratization." In other words, there has been a great deal of movement away from the pure communism end of our pure capitalism–pure communism spectrum. However, in the belief that it is impossible to understand where these countries are today without knowing where they have been, we present in this chapter a somewhat stylized comparison of capitalist and socialist systems.

THE GENERALITY OF ECONOMIC ANALYSIS

The basic economic problem of scarcity confronts all economic systems. Scarcity means that choices have to be made. To have more of one thing means having less of another. If a socialist economy wants to have a larger army, the resources for the army must come from alternative uses in the economy, such as agricultural labor. The fact that an economy is socialist does not make such trade-offs go away. Scarcity pervades economic organization; it is not something that confronts capitalism but not socialism.

Scarcity is not the only economic concept that applies generally to all economies. We consider the relevance of the following economic principles to the study of comparative economic systems: the law of demand, opportunity cost, diminishing marginal returns, and self-interest.

The Law of Demand

The law of demand is a general proposition about human behavior, not simply an economic law that applies to capitalism and private markets. The law of demand says that, other things being equal, price and quantity demanded will vary inversely. That is, the lower the price, given quality, the greater the quantity demanded, and vice versa. If socialist planners want to encourage the use of public transit and discourage the purchase of private cars, they will set relatively low prices on transit tickets and relatively high prices on cars. Consumers will respond according to the law of demand. If meat is scarce, its price will be set high to reflect its relative scarcity, and consumers will reduce their purchases of meat in state stores. If the socialist planners set zero prices on basic services such as medical care, quantity demanded will be so great that queues will develop and forms of nonprice rationing will emerge to determine who receives medical care.

Opportunity Cost

There is no such thing as a free lunch—in any economic system. It may well be that a socialist republic offers "free" medical care at zero price to recipients. But in no sense are the resources allocated to medical care free. They do not come out of thin air; they are directed away from alternative uses in the economy. The best alternative uses of these resources are a measure of their opportunity cost. If a socialist government wishes to increase its spending on space research, the resources must be reallocated from some other sector of the economy. The opportunity cost of a larger space program might be resources otherwise available for producing consumer goods.

Diminishing Marginal Returns

The law of diminishing marginal returns states that the increased application of a resource will ultimately lead to smaller and smaller increments of output, other things being equal. This phenomenon can be found in all economic systems. Worldwide, agriculture exhibits the law of diminishing returns. Generally, the stock of land in an economy is fixed, and the increased application of capital, such as tractors or fertilizer, to the fixed stock of land will lead to diminishing marginal returns. Soviet agriculture as well as American agriculture is subject to diminishing marginal returns. The only way that societies overcome the law of diminishing marginal returns over time is by investing in capital goods production and technological change. That is, as societies expand their resource base and technical capabilities, they are able to produce more output.

Self-Interest

Economic analysis is based on the idea that individuals weigh the costs and benefits of economic choices and normally respond according to their individual self-interest. Self-interest does not mean that individuals are totally

Drawing by Koren; © 1984 The New Yorker Magazine, Inc.

selfish. Individuals can demand or want anything, including a better life for others. Economics simply says that the amount of things individuals actually choose is determined by the costs and benefits of having those things.

Some socialist scholars have argued that self-interested behavior will disappear under socialism and that individuals will come to work for the common good instead. This is perhaps an appealing thought, but it does not seem to be true. The structure of personal incentives helps determine the actions of individuals in both capitalist and socialist economies. For example, in the Soviet Union managers of oil prospecting teams were once rewarded in a piece-rate fashion according to the number of meters they drilled. But drilling goes harder and slower as one drills deeper, with a greater chance that the pipe and drill bits will crack or break. With meters drilled rather than oil discovered as the indicator of success, drillers quickly concluded that they should drill only shallow holes, and lots of them, significantly retarding the discovery of new oil reserves. As this one example indicates, even socialist producers and consumers weigh costs and benefits in terms of self-interest. Ignoring such tendencies often results in poor economic performance.

THE EXPERIENCE OF CENTRAL PLANNING

With the understanding that the economic realities of the law of demand, opportunity cost, diminishing marginal returns, and self-interested behavior prevail in all economic systems, we turn now to an examination of how socialist states—in particular, the Soviet Union—have determined what gets produced, how, and for whom. One thing is certain, whatever economic systems the Soviet Union and its neighbors ultimately settle on: These new systems will be colored by decades of a much purer form of socialism.

In 1917, the Bolsheviks, a group of revolutionary socialists, came into political power in Russia and formed a new state, the Soviet Union. The Bolsheviks, influenced by the writings of Karl Marx and Friedrich Engels and the leadership of Vladimir Ilyich Lenin, sought to implement pure socialism— an economy in which all the means of production were owned and operated by the state and in which all economic activity would be centrally planned and controlled by the central government. Although Lenin, the revolutionary leader, did not live to see these goals accomplished, Joseph Stalin, his successor, was responsible for implementing them to a very great extent in the 1930s. In 1928, Stalin embarked on an ambitious mission to institute central planning in the Soviet economy, focusing his efforts on agriculture. The First Five-Year Plan emphasized heavy industry and established collective farms. Almost immediately, factory workers were needed—not farmers. Implementation of the plan, therefore, required the displacement of millions of peasants. The defiant were murdered; the rest had no choice but to move to the cities, where living conditions were dreadful.

Subsequent plans were less socially disruptive, and a sense of permanence—if not, eventually, correctness—settled over the notion of economic planning. The repeated failure of central planning to provide levels of real

Perestroika:
Economic reformation of the Soviet Union's command economy.

income even half those of Western (capitalist) nations led to reforms in the Soviet system in the 1980s, however. Mikhail Gorbachev's policy of *perestroika,* or restructuring, actually has meant a dismantling of many of the principles of planning. However, until markets guide most production, distribution, and consumption decisions in the Soviet Union as they do in capitalist nations, we will do better to approach the Soviet economy from the perspective of long-standing differences between their planned economy and the U.S. market economy. The Soviet economy entered the 1990s on the verge of collapse, yet resistance within the entrenched bureaucracy to drastic changes ensured the survival of certain elements of the command economy.

A Command Economy

Command economy:
An extreme form of socialist economy characterized by less private economic decision making than exists in a socialist economy.

The Soviet economy is sometimes loosely described as a **command economy.** Under authoritarian control, its economy is directed by a central planning system that oversees the production and distribution of most of its resources. The managers of individual state-owned enterprises follow orders imposed by the central plan that tell them what to produce, how to produce, and how to organize production. In effect, socialist managers are more like floor supervisors than the chief executive officers of capitalist firms; they have little independent authority.

The Soviet government basically owns and operates all industry, including the capital goods sector, transportation, communication, banking and financial institutions, and even the entire wholesale and retail network. In one sense, the Soviet economy is like a giant vertically and horizontally integrated firm. However, the analogy should not be taken too far. As we will see, the socialist state is not like a giant corporation, and its citizens are not its shareholders. Whereas corporate decisions are implemented by voluntary contractual agreements, the decisions of the central planning board are coercive.

In the case of the Soviet Union, the Communist party has historically played an important role in the management of the planned economy. This has been true of many other planned economies based on the Soviet model, such as those of Poland, East Germany, and China, although many of the economies of Eastern Europe as well as that of China have instituted market and democratic reforms in the 1980s. The Communist party is responsible for the selection of enterprise managers; it monitors the performance of both labor and management for the central planning board. This party monitoring is carried out through the various ministries of industry, which administer the central plan in individual enterprises.

Central Planning

Although the details of the actual operation of a large economy with millions of participants are extremely complex, the basic pattern of operations of a centrally planned economy is briefly summarized in Figure 1.

The state central planning agency (called Gosplan in the Soviet Union) drafts an economic plan for the entire economy. This plan includes a long-range five-year plan as well as an annual plan. These plans have the force of law. The basic economic plan is directed to the more than 200,000 different Soviet enterprises, setting production targets and allocating inputs to each

FIGURE 1

Basic Macroeconomic Sectors in an Idealized Command Economy

This is a highly simplified model of the command economy. Households supply labor inputs to enterprises in exchange for money. Labor inputs are assigned to firms by the planning process and not by a labor market. Money earned by labor is in turn exchanged for consumer goods and services produced by the enterprises. Exchange takes place in terms of money, although prices are fixed by the central planning board and remain fixed for long periods. In this simplified model, production takes place entirely within the state production establishment. Composition of output is determined not by consumers but by the central planning board.

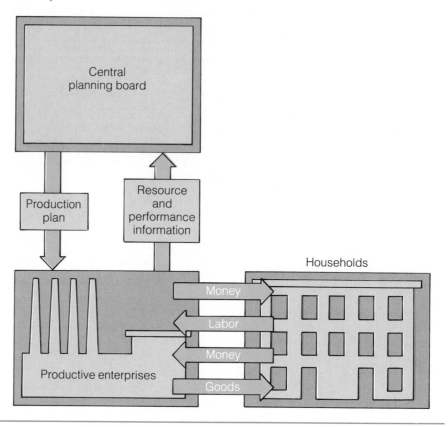

enterprise for all resources, including labor. Virtually all Soviet production is organized in the form of enterprises, which include everything from huge steel mills to small local baking plants. The manager of each enterprise is responsible for taking the resource inputs that have been allotted and using them to accomplish the goal assigned to the enterprise by the central plan. These targets are used to judge the performance of the firm over particular periods and to reward or penalize the responsible manager accordingly. For example, the plan might call for a steel mill to increase its production of rolled steel 5 percent over its previous year's output and reward the manager with a bonus for meeting the assigned quota (and a greater bonus for exceeding the quota).

Essentially, the central planning board attempts to ration raw materials throughout the entire economy without having to resort to the price system used in capitalist economies. It performs this task by the method of **materials balancing**—the maintaining of a balance sheet of all available supplies in the economy and of all sources of demand. In other words, the central planning board attempts to keep a comprehensive inventory of all raw materials and factor inputs—minerals, timber, labor, and so on—as well as a similar listing of the demand for these inputs by all the production units, given their assigned production goals. The method of materials balancing works out a consistent pattern of resource allocation throughout the economy that is compatible

Materials balancing: A method of central planning entailing the monitoring of the quantity and availability of resources so as to allocate these resources among state enterprises to produce final output; a substitute for the price system method of allocating resources.

with the established planning priorities—that is, allocating necessary inputs perhaps first to military production, then to agricultural development, and so on.

In contrast to a capitalist economy, the socialist economy's central planners exercise essentially full control over production in the economy and can direct resources to whatever ends they choose. Production in the economic system is not directed by the final demand of consumers, who instead play a passive role. This is a fundamental difference in the two economies. In a capitalist economy the mix of goods provided reflects the demands of consumers. But in a centrally planned economy, the mix of goods provided reflects the decisions of the central planners. For example, if the Soviet government estimates that military spending should be 15 percent of GNP, it can reallocate resources accordingly to achieve this goal, without having to convince consumers or voters to rearrange their priorities.

The Problems of Central Planning

Central planning has never been without problems. Yet not until the 1980s did these problems become acute. The major problem of central planning is this: The central planning board must coordinate millions of different inputs and potential output—an enormous, perhaps impossible, task. Computer technology makes a coordinated overall plan feasible in principle, but the system must be constantly revised to accommodate unplanned circumstances; droughts and other climatic events may cause crop failures, for example, creating a need to revise agricultural plans. In recent years, the planning system in the Soviet Union has consistently failed to adjust to changed circumstances rapidly enough to prevent food shortages and reductions in overall GNP growth. Consumer unrest has been the result.

Other types of unforeseen events also can severely disrupt the central plan. In 1986, the nuclear reactor at Chernobyl underwent a disastrous meltdown. This reactor supplied electrical power to a large area of the Soviet Union's Ukraine region. Not only has power had to be diverted from other areas (thus creating shortages in those areas) in order to make up for lost power in the Chernobyl area, but a significant amount of both residential and farm land in the Soviet Union as well as in neighboring countries may have been contaminated and made unusable.

Planning, some arbitrary set of production goals and prices, robs the economy of flexibility. Planning eliminates the price system's ability to provide accurate information about relative scarcities and surpluses. Production bottlenecks arise when prices are inhibited from performing their rationing and information-signaling functions. When prices do not reflect actual resource scarcities, a supplier could unexpectedly fail to deliver a critical input. The customer, who may in turn be some other enterprise's supplier, is not free to place an order with some other supplier of the necessary input. Enterprises have assigned suppliers, and securing official permission for shifting suppliers can be difficult and extremely time-consuming. Enterprise managers may be confronted with the choice of cutting corners where they can—perhaps radically reducing the quality of the goods they produce—or missing an assigned quota (or even failing to produce any output at all). An alternative is to make unofficial and basically illegal private arrangements with other enterprise managers to overcome bottlenecks by switching suppliers. But such arrangements, however necessary, amount to cheating on the central planning process and to a partial introduction of the market process.

The Soviet planners must constantly monitor managerial performance to detect such cheating. To do so, the central planning board depends on information supplied by the managers themselves, whereas a capitalist economy would rely on a firm's success or failure in marketing its output. The incentives thus created can encourage managers to fabricate reports of available resources to avoid blame or to satisfy output quotas. Soviet planners have long been aware of these and many other problems with planning and—with great fanfare—have periodically undertaken programs to overcome them. While Gorbachev's *perestroika* is the latest attempt at "reforming" the economic system, previous attempts have not succeeded.

The Legal and Extralegal Private Sectors in the Soviet Economy

Although it seems inconsistent with the rhetoric of social planning, a legal private sector has always existed in the Soviet Union and in most other centrally planned economies. *Glasnost,* a new openness, and *perestroika* have provided the atmosphere for an expanded private sector. Private economic activity, while not entirely prohibited by Soviet law, is restricted in two major respects. First, a private individual cannot act as a middleman; second, no employee can be hired for the purpose of making a profit. These two restrictions obviously greatly limit the extent to which legally sanctioned private enterprise may operate. Effectively, the only areas in which private enterprise is permitted are personal services and farming. Professionals such as doctors and teachers and craft laborers like carpenters and shoemakers are free to sell their services to consumers. And peasants working on state-owned farms are permitted to grow crops on small assigned plots and are free to sell whatever they produce. In both cases, production of personal services or of goods for private sale can legally take place only after the completion of the day's labor in the individual's state-sector job. In effect, only moonlighting is legally permissible in the private sector.

Despite these restrictions, activities in the legal private sector realize a considerably higher rate of productivity than do comparable activities in the state sector. The primary evidence for this productivity differential is the output record of the privately cultivated agricultural plots. These private plots, which constitute only slightly more that 1 percent of land under cultivation in the Soviet Union, account for approximately 25 percent of the nation's total agricultural output, in spite of the fact that the private plots are typically far below the optimum size for efficient production of the crops grown on them.

The productivity of private plots is strong evidence for the crucial role of incentives in determining rates of output. The private plot owners gain the full value of any increase in the efficiency of resource use on their own plots. In marked contrast, the collectivized state agricultural sector is plagued by poor efficiency and poor productivity. It is true that relatively more land-intensive agricultural products—such as cotton and wheat—are grown on collective farms, partially accounting for the disparity in productivity because the value per acre of these crops tends to be relatively low. But this fact only explains a small portion of the difference. Incentives clearly play a large role in the productivity of private Soviet agriculture.

Although evidence concerning the relative performance of the privately provided personal services industry is scarce, the productivity advantages there are similar. Quality seems higher, too. Although in theory medical treatment is provided free to all Soviet citizens, the quality of such care often tends to be low. Some surgeons are able to command private fees of over 1000 rubles (about $1350) for major operations from individual patients concerned with the quality of their care.

In addition to the legally sanctioned private sector in the Soviet Union, there has been a booming underground or extralegal private economy, somewhat like the underground economy in the United States. The private sector continues to be much larger than that permitted by Soviet law. An underground sector characterized by black market activity will likely continue to flourish as long as the Soviet economy continues as an essentially planned economy.

Some underground activity involves theft of state-owned resources, but a large part of it involves what might be termed "capitalist acts between consenting adults." John Lennon records, blue jeans, and moonshine have been objects of trade, but the underground economy does not function solely to shift consumer goods to the highest bidder. The extralegal private sector helps ease shortages and reduce inefficiency in the planned sectors of the economy, as well. Managers of collective farms admit that often the only way to meet production targets is to buy supplies on the black market. In the Soviet economy and in other planned economies as well, production has always depended on extensive bribery to function; Russian enterprise managers have employed professional expeditors, who bribe suppliers to provide necessary inputs.

In general, bribery (both actual payments and favors) has performed a vital role in greasing the wheels of the planned economy. The underground private sector provides coordinating services that increase the efficiency of the planned sector.

Comparative Performance

Despite the problems of centrally planned socialist economies, their performance relative to capitalist economies is worth noting. See Table 1 for a comparison of U.S. and Soviet production. In general, the Soviets have concentrated, through the force of central planning, on capital goods infrastructure—especially that related to defense—rather than on consumer goods and services.

The total output of the U.S. economy is roughly twice that of the Soviet Union, although the Soviet Union has both a larger land area and a larger population. More food per person is produced in the United States by fewer agricultural workers; the United States also produces many more automobiles. However, the Soviet Union produces more oil and steel than the United States.

The Soviet Union has emphasized investment over consumption to a much greater extent than the United States. The Soviet growth rate in investment lagged to 3.2 percent between 1980 and 1985 but rose to an average of 5 percent during the Twelfth Five-Year Plan, 1986–1990. Centralized planning

TABLE 1   A Comparison of U.S. and Soviet Production
Characteristics, 1985–1986

Production patterns in the United States and the Soviet Union for 1985–1986 reflect basic differences in the two economies and the natural resources abundant in each country.

	United States	Soviet Union
Total output (trillions of dollars per year)	4.0	2.2
Per capita GNP (dollars per year)	16,492	7,736
Steel (million metric tons)	80.1	154.7
Oil (million metric tons)	428.2	615.0
Electricity (billions of kwh)	2,583	1,598.9
Coal (million metric tons)	738.9	512.9
Wheat (million metric tons)	50.8	92.3
Corn (million metric tons)	209.6	12.5
Meat (million metric tons)	17.9	14.0
Population (millions)	244	284
Land area (million square miles)	3.6	8.6

Source: U.S. Bureau of the Census, Statistical Abstract of the United States, 1989 (Washington, D.C.: U.S. Government Printing Office, 1989).

allows planners to stress industrial development and capital accumulation. In the United States, both investment and capital accumulation are dependent on the savings and investment decisions of individuals and, in the long run, on the decisions of consumers.

While the investment rate in the Soviet Union has been relatively high, the efficiency of investment has remained generally low. Productivity of both labor and capital lags appreciably behind that of Western economies. For example, while Soviet investment in agriculture has increased fivefold since World War II, the growth in Soviet agricultural output has been low, and negative per capita growth rates in annual grain production are common. (Other problems have arisen in the Soviet economy; see Focus, "Soviets Plagued by Budget Deficits and Inflation.")

In the early 1970s, the growth rate of the Soviet economy appeared to be relatively high. Table 2 presents data on the growth of real gross national product during the period 1984–1989 for a variety of countries, including the United States and the Soviet Union. Over the entire period, the Soviet growth rate was 1.9 percent. The U.S. growth rate was higher, 4.0 percent. China's unusually high growth rate over the period in large part reflects the market-oriented economic reforms that have been underway there since the late 1970s.

At times, Soviet GNP growth has been quite high, however. The rate of economic growth in 1961–1965 averaged 5 percent. This figure encompassed a high of 7.6 percent in 1964 and a low of 2.2 percent in 1963—which suggests something important about Soviet growth rates: They have tended to be erratic (see Figure 2). Analysts suggest that Soviet GNP growth is gradually declining because of the increasing cost of raw materials as more accessible sources dry up. The Soviet Union is extraordinarily rich in raw materials, holding a large proportion of the world reserves of most economically important minerals, as well as oil and natural gas. But reserves of these resources

FOCUS   Soviets Plagued by Budget Deficits and Inflation

Budget deficits and inflation are apparently not limited to market economies such as the United States. In late 1988, in the wake of Gorbachev's economic reforms, the Supreme Soviet adopted a 1989 budget of $795 billion, with a projected budget deficit of over $55 billion at the official exchange rate. The projected Soviet deficit for 1989 was about 4 percent of domestic production; the corresponding figure for the United States was 3 percent. Deficits may be as severe in the Soviet Union as they have been in recent U.S. experience, but probably for different reasons.[a]

In the Soviet Union, a bureaucracy has for years set prices and production quotas in state-run enterprises without regard to supply and demand and virtually without any system of accounting to show profit and loss. When prices are determined by a planning bureau without reference to opportunity costs, accounting values cannot accurately reflect the real cost of producing goods and services. For many decades, the Soviets have geared production to provide low-priced necessities, resulting in incredible prices for items that are deemed luxuries. When prices are robbed of their signaling power, shortages, surpluses and noneconomic, inefficient production develops. Consumers either do not get what they want or do not get goods and services in the quantities they desire. The absence of market-determined interest rates has also meant that capital investment is used inefficiently; modern capital equipment sits unused and unfinished construction projects dot the urban landscape. Soviet finance authorities acknowledge that huge numbers of bankrupt businesses and budget deficits have resulted from their attempts to sidestep the price system, since revenues from goods production have not covered actual costs.

These same finance authorities, keen to introduce the reforms suggested by Gorbachev, are introducing a West-ern-style accounting system into Soviet production. Soviet legislators are attempting to increase production of consumer goods, so several hundred factories are being retooled. This move will tend to reduce the deficit if additional revenues are produced. (Critical to the success of these programs to introduce more consumer goods, however, is allowing supply and demand to decide what goods will be produced and sold.) For the present, massive production misallocations are occurring under price controls, and these are contributing to inflation.

Inflation—often thought to be a major curse of capitalism—is an actual and much-feared problem in the Soviet Union. While Soviet economists officially estimated inflation at 1.5 percent in 1988, some concede that the rate was actually over 7 percent, which is closer to the calculations of Western observers. In addition to massive dislocations in production, inflation also results from the overuse of the Soviet printing press. Wage pressures are also building up the threat of a Western-style wage-price spiral (fueled and validated by printing more money). If, as promised, Gorbachev lifts price and wage controls in the consumer goods system and decontrols the prices factories pay for fuel, tools, and raw materials in 1990, some experts predict a short-term rise in the inflation rate of from 10 to 20 percent.

Deficits and inflation, well known in capitalist societies, are certainly not new to the Soviet Union. The secrecy of central planning and the lack of any accurate accounting system merely kept them hidden for many decades.

[a]For an interesting account of Soviet deficit and inflation problems, see Bill Keller, "Deficits in Soviet Budgets Are Disclosed by Kremlin: Wasteful Subsidies Blamed," *New York Times* (October 28, 1988), pp. A1, A11.

are increasingly located in more remote areas, making exploitation more costly.

Finally, comparisons of Soviet and Western GNP do not take into account the qualitative aspects of the goods produced. The quality of Soviet consumer goods is generally recognized to be quite poor relative to similar Western goods. As the planned economy does not function on the basis of consumer sovereignty, a considerable proportion of production represents low-quality goods—indeed, goods that consumers do not want at all.

Income Distribution in a Command Economy

One of the stated goals of socialist economies is to reduce income inequality among members of society. What can be said about the performance of socialist economies in this regard?

TABLE 2

Average Annual Rate of Growth in Real GNP for Various Economies, 1984–1989

Real GNP growth rates differed significantly over the period 1984–1989 across various national economies. Japan led Western-style democracies in terms of percentage growth, while China led less-developed nations.

Country	Rate of Growth, GNP
United States	4.0%
Canada	4.4
West Germany	2.9
United Kingdom	3.4
USSR	1.9
China	9.3
Eastern Europe	1.5
Japan	4.6

Source: Council of Economic Advisers, *Economic Report of the President* (Washington, D.C.: U.S. Government Printing Office, 1990), p. 419.

Data issued by the Soviet government are fragmentary, but they allow a rough comparison of income distribution in the Soviet Union with that in Western countries. One such comparison, involving the Soviet Union, the United States, and Sweden (a socialist democracy), is presented in Table 3. Interestingly, differences in the degree of inequality in the respective income distributions appear to be comparatively minor. The percentage of low-income individuals is about the same in the three economies, as is the percentage of individuals earning the highest incomes.

But this comparison may understate the degree of inequality in the Soviet economy. Real transfer payments such as health care or subsidized food would indicate a greater degree of equality in Soviet (and Swedish) income distributions. Conversely, special privileges are available to an enormous extent to Communist party members and bureaucrats, especially at the upper levels. For example, automobiles can usually be quickly purchased by members of the elite. An ordinary citizen, however, may have to place an order and wait for a year or more or attempt to purchase a used car on the black market at an inflated price. Soviet party officials and specially favored

TABLE 3

Estimated Shares of Personal Income, by Quintile

Estimates of income quintiles in the United States, Sweden, and the Soviet Union show surprisingly small differences in income distribution.

Income Quintile	Share of Income (percent)		
	United States	Sweden	Soviet Union
Lowest	6.9	7.7	7.5
Second through fourth	52.5	56.5	55.0
Highest	40.6	35.9	37.5
Top 5 percent	15.9	12.9	14.0

Source: Lowell Gallaway, "The Folklore of Unemployment and Poverty," in S. Pejovich, *Governmental Controls and the Free Market* (College Station: Texas A&M University Press, 1976), pp. 41–72.

FIGURE 2

Soviet economic growth was erratic between 1975 and 1989 and has generally declined over time.

Sources: Hearings Before the Joint Economic Committee of the Congress of the United States, *Allocation of Resources in the Soviet Union and China, 1982,* 97th Cong., 2nd sess. (Washington, D.C.: U.S. Government Printing Office, 1981), p. 4; Council of Economic Advisers, *Economic Report of the President* (Washington, D.C.: U.S. Government Printing Office, 1990), p. 419.

Growth of Soviet GNP

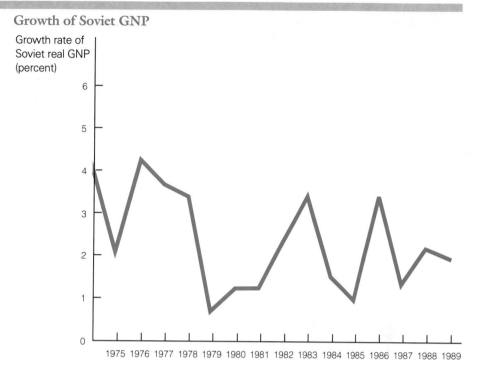

groups are permitted to shop in special stores stocked with foreign goods unavailable to ordinary citizens. Thus, the elite are often protected from the problems of shortages, waiting in long lines, and poor-quality goods that plague ordinary citizens. These special privileges mean that the effective degree of inequality in Soviet society is much higher than published figures suggest. Focus, "Soviet Economists on Living Standards and Wealth Distribution in the USSR," suggests that when wealth rather than income is considered, the Soviet Union has a very small middle class.

The Gorbachev Reform Proposals

The lackluster performance of the Soviet economy under central planning has led, under the leadership of Communist party chairman and General Secretary Mikhail Gorbachev, to a policy of *glasnost,* or "openness." The policy brings a new openness into Soviet society, especially in the realm of human rights and greater social freedom, as well as in the functioning of the Soviet economy. As you know, *perestroika* seeks to reform central planning to include a greater role for the price system in allocating and distributing resources, and the devotion of more resources to consumer goods production. Gorbachev has tacitly admitted that planning schemes of the past did not motivate people to produce at high-efficiency levels, and he has proposed new profit incentives for the purpose of achieving greater economic growth.

Perestroika is an admission that technology and investment cannot be fully imposed from above. In the past, the growth potential inherent in new investment or new technology was completely determined by the uses to which it was put by bureaucratic industry and firm managers. With little or no

FOCUS   Soviet Economists on Living Standards and Wealth Distribution in the USSR

As the "liberalization" of the Soviet economic system proceeds under *glasnost* and *perestroika,* Soviet economists have taken a hard look at their system. For example, Table 3 in this chapter shows a very similar income distribution between the Soviet Union and the United States (unadjusted for factors such as medical care and other welfare transfers). According to recent research by two Russian economists, such figures wildly overstate the well-being of the average Soviet citizen.[a] The true measure of equality, according to Soviet economists Andrei Kuteinikov and Alexander Zaichenko, is not *income* but *wealth* in the Soviet Union. Zaichenko utilizes consumer goods as a proxy for wealth (since Soviet citizens may own no liquid private property such as stocks or bonds) and finds a radical disparity between rich and poor. According to his estimates, originally published in the Soviet weekly *Argumenti i Fakti,* the "super-rich elite" comprise 2.3 percent of the population, while the poor make up the vast majority—86.5 percent. Within this social pyramid, the middle class, those who own an apartment or home, a car, and (perhaps) a summer house, comprise only 11.2 percent of the population. In Western countries the middle class represents 50 to 70 percent of the population. Even in Hungary, East Germany, and Czechoslovakia, 40 to 50 percent of the population would be considered middle class, using wealth as a standard.

According to Kuteinikov, official Soviet statistics bear out Zaichenko's estimates. Welfare expenditures account for only about 20 percent of Soviet GNP, compared to 28.5 percent in the United States. Kuteinikov also argues that disproportionate welfare benefits (such as health care, recreation facilities, and education) go to the Soviet elite. Old-age pensions are likewise disproportionately channeled to "personal pensioners"—retired members of the elite—who receive 500 rubles per month rather than the 84 rubles per month received by everyone else. (At black market rates, 84 rubles equals $12.50.)

Who are the elite? According to Zaichenko, the elite (estimated at about 400,000 individuals) come from the spheres of politics, science, sports, art, and diplomacy. Also included are cooperative managers, black marketeers, and service sector workers (who have access to desirable goods and who can facilitate black market sales). All of this points up potential problems for reform in the Soviet Union. A weak middle class means less stability in society. Furthermore, cooperation for system reforms from those in control of wealth will be difficult to obtain. Although economic reform was initiated by the Soviet leadership, Soviet citizens eventually began pressuring their leaders for more rapid implementation of new policies. The system seems to be responding. In March of 1990, the Soviet Union passed a law permitting private citizens and companies to buy land, buildings, and factories—for the first time in seventy years.[b] Further, foreign investment and joint ventures with outside investors are being encouraged by the government. Gains in output and welfare will be costly, but an ultimately more equitable distribution of wealth may well be the result.

[a]Andrei Kuteinikov, "Soviet Society—Much More Unequal Than U.S.," *Wall Street Journal* (January 26, 1989), p. A14.

[b]Kevin Maney, "U.S.S.R. Permits Private Ownership," *USA Today* (March 7, 1990), p. 1B.

---

incentive to manage resources and technology efficiently, managers were complacent and inefficient. (This outcome was predicted by Ludwig von Mises; see Economics in Action, "The Socialist Calculation Debate and the Transition from Planning to Markets.")

Gorbachev initially proposed that productive energies at all levels be guided by the partial use of profits and prices, (partially) replacing poor production incentives that have become institutionalized within the Soviet economic system. But the inadequacy of any half measure to fix the Soviet economy soon became evident. Faced with political pressure from new Russian Republic president Boris Yeltsin and rising discontent with a still-deteriorating economy, Gorbachev unveiled a more radical reform plan in autumn 1990. This plan would put up to 70 percent of the Soviet Union's factories, stores, and service enterprises up for sale—effectively ending government subsidies and necessitating sharp cutbacks in the central planning system. Some skeptics wonder whether Gorbachev will be able to push truly dramatic reforms past party conservatives and entrenched bureaucrats—or whether, if implemented, even these changes are enough.

Soviet leader Mikhail Gorbachev

Eastern Europe in the Early 1990s: No Gain Without Pain?

The opening of the Berlin Wall in 1989 (followed by the monetary and political union of East and West Germany in 1990), the election of democratic-minded leaders in Poland and Czechoslovakia, and outright declarations of independence from the Soviet Union by the Baltic states—Estonia, Lithuania, and Latvia—are all manifestations of political change left in the wake of *glasnost*. By 1990, most of the East European nations had withdrawn from exclusive international trade within the Soviet bloc, opening the way for bilateral trade negotiations with countries throughout the world. Table 4 provides data on population, per capita GNP, and hard currency debt—debt measured in dollars—for six Eastern European countries.

TABLE 4

GNP, Population, and Debt in Six Eastern European Countries

Comparative statistics show that East Germany had the highest per capita (adjusted) gross domestic product in Eastern Europe for the year shown, while Romania had the lowest. As these countries struggle to raise growth rates and economic performance, they will be faced with hard currency debt to other countries.

Country	Population (1989, in millions)	Adjusted GDP per capita (1986, in U.S. dollars)	Hard currency debt (1988, in billions of dollars)
Poland	38.2	$3250	$38.5
Romania	23.2	2770	2.2
East Germany	16.6	5660	19.5
Czechoslovakia	15.6	4910	6.1
Hungary	10.6	3890	18.0
Bulgaria	9.0	3540	7.1

Sources: New York Times (January 7, 1990), p. E3; Central Intelligence Agency; Population Reference Bureau; Jan S. Hogendorn, *Economic Development* (New York: Harper & Row, 1987).

While events in Eastern Europe were greeted with amazement and encouragement in the West, difficult periods of adjustment clearly await these economies. The transitions from central planning (of one form or another) to markets will be painful. Poland was the first country to plunge into market reforms in the face of a deteriorating economy.[1] As such, it is a model for the formerly planned nations of Eastern Europe and elsewhere.

In the late 1980s, the Polish economy experienced an inflation rate of several thousand percent annually, along with nearly bare shelves, thriving black markets, and consumer-goods smuggling. With the financial backing of the United States, West Germany, and other industrialized democracies, Poland launched an effort to stabilize its currency in 1990. (Both Poland and Czechoslovakia sharply devalued their currencies against the U.S. dollar in 1990.) The government—headed by officials of the formerly outlawed Solidarity union—began by reducing subsidies on housing, food, and fuel, and, as expected, the artificially low prices on these items rose. Almost immediately, bread prices rose 38 percent; coal prices rose 600 percent. As gasoline and automobile insurance prices soared out of reach, thousands of Poles turned in their license plates. These very painful steps were necessary to create a market mechanism in which supply, demand, prices, and the value of money are rationally interrelated. The choice between artificially low prices for low-quality goods in short supply and higher-priced, higher-quality goods of more dependable supply is a very real one for citizens of Eastern Europe and the Soviet Union.

The link between politics and economics is evident as these countries struggle for reforms that lead to prosperity and political freedom. In the context of economic systems, moreover, it is unclear whether these "democratic" changes will translate into economic reforms for freer markets. Entrenched interests can be expected to fight reforms, unless they can be convinced that change would create new benefits for them. For instance, workers long guaranteed a job might be reluctant to test their fortunes on free and open markets. The same goes for bureaucratic managers, planning directors, and other vested interests who enjoyed privileges in these economies for years. While private property was introduced in a limited way in both Poland and Czechoslovakia, the Czechs have been reluctant to privatize manufacturing in order to modernize technology. Politicians who want to be reelected do not want reputations for lowering living standards, although this is necessary as a short-run measure to achieve long-term prosperity. High levels of international debt also plague the economies of Eastern Europe (see Table 4). A great deal of international cooperation is needed to help Eastern Europe handle its external debt problem.

The ultimate outcome of the transition of Eastern European nations from centrally planned to wholly or partially democratic societies fueled by market systems is unpredictable. The mix of planning and market functioning that will result in a particular country cannot now be predicted, especially given the differing cultures and institutions. Most economists believe that expanded international trade holds great promise, but many wonder how far the price and profit system could be allowed to go without a fundamental restructuring of the goals of socialism. Capitalism, even modified capitalism,

---

[1]See Craig R. Whitney, "East Europe Joins the Market and Gets a Preview of the Pain," *New York Times* (January 7, 1990), p. E3, from which some of this section is derived.

may be incompatible with the goals of a socialist society. Whatever else is accomplished in the stirrings of the Soviet Union and the Eastern bloc toward democracy and market orientation, economists now have an unparalleled opportunity to compare the results of central planning and markets.

THE PROBLEM OF ECONOMIC DEVELOPMENT

We turn now from comparisons of socialist and capitalist economic systems to a consideration of the disturbing differences between developed and developing countries.

In economic terms, development is not quite the same as growth. Economic growth usually refers to the increase in per capita GNP in an economy; **economic development** is the process of capital formation, entrepreneurial and labor skills improvement, and the growth in economic productivity that causes rates of economic growth to rise. The history of the U.S. economy provides a model of successful economic development, leading to high and sustained rates of economic growth combined with a growing population. The U.S. economy in 1776 was in many respects an underdeveloped economy. The transition from a low to a high state of development occurred rapidly during the nineteenth century.

In the modern world, the developed nations are the relatively rich economies, and the developing nations are the relatively poor economies. Many, though not all, developing countries are relatively stagnant economically. While population in these countries is often growing rapidly, per capita income grows slowly, if at all. As we will see, the form of economic institutions plays an important role in determining the extent to which economies develop.

Economic development: The process through which an economy achieves long-run economic growth; involves capital formation, the development of markets, productivity growth, and the improvement of entrepreneurial ability and labor skills.

The Characteristics of Less-Developed Countries

Most countries of the world, including the most populous, China, are defined as developing, or **less-developed, countries;** three-quarters of the world's population lives in less-developed countries. But there is an amazing amount of diversity among these countries; the only thing they have in common is their less-developed status. Economically, what characteristics are associated with the low development rates of less-developed countries?

In describing less-developed countries, there is general agreement that four features stand out: low per capita income, a dominant agricultural-household sector, relatively low saving rates, and rapid population growth.

A less-developed country is a poor country in the sense that its per capita GNP is low. Compared with poverty in developed countries, poverty in less-developed countries is more severe. In many of the countries, the plight of the lowest income group has not changed dramatically in hundreds of years. The second defining characteristic of less-developed countries is a dominant agricultural-household sector. In a way, this is merely another way of saying that less-developed countries are poor—a large proportion of their population is engaged in subsistence agriculture. Nearly two-thirds of the labor force of the low-income countries of Asia, Africa, and South America are employed in agriculture. In contrast, only 2 percent of the U.S. labor force is employed in agriculture. The size of the household (or nonmarket) sector in less-developed

Less-developed countries: Countries with relatively low levels of per capita real GNP; generally characterized by a large subsistence agriculture sector, low saving rates, and high population growth.

countries is generally much larger than in developed nations. Most households in less-developed countries are engaged in subsistence production in the sense that they raise their own food, make their own clothes, and construct their own homes. The degree of specialization in production in these economies is limited, compared to the more-developed economies. With the degree of specialization limited and a large amount of time devoted to subsistence production, the opportunities for welfare-enhancing exchange and trade with others in the society becomes relatively limited also. (Greater household production in less-developed countries does mean that real income levels in these countries are not as low, by comparison with developed countries, as suggested by measured income levels.)

The other two characteristic features found in most less-developed countries (although there are exceptions) are low saving rates and high rates of population growth. Many poor economies have low saving rates because saving is very difficult (or even impossible) when income is at or near the subsistence level. Low saving rates mean that very little income is set aside each year for investment in capital goods for increased production. This inability to save, in turn, contributes to continuing low rates of development. The term sometimes used for this problem is the **vicious circle of poverty.**

Rapid population growth is another condition commonly associated with less-developed countries. The population of the poor countries of Asia, Africa, and South America has been expanding at an average rate of about 2.5 percent per year. At this rate, the populations of these nations double every twenty-five or thirty years. In contrast, the populations of developed nations grow less than 1 percent per year on average. The difference is often taken to mean that rapid population growth is a major contributor to low rates of development because such growth imposes an increasing burden on the limited resources of less-developed countries. The more people, the greater the need to provide education, health care, and other basic services—which require resources that would otherwise be available for capital investment. To the extent that rapid population growth represents more mouths to feed, per capita income will decline as population grows, other things being equal.

Vicious circle of poverty: An attempt to explain why some countries remain less developed that centers on low savings and investment causing low real incomes, which in turn lead to low saving and investment rates.

THE ECONOMIC GAP BETWEEN DEVELOPED AND LESS-DEVELOPED COUNTRIES

Like wealth and poverty, development and underdevelopment are relative concepts. In 1750, England was probably the richest and most-developed country in the world, but by modern standards mid-eighteenth-century England was relatively poor and undeveloped. Moreover, we cannot judge reliably whether any given country should be counted as a developed or less-developed economy on the basis of secondary characteristics—such things as the rate of population growth, degree of literacy, or degree of industrialization. There are, for example, some developed countries that have high rates of population growth and a lesser degree of industrialization than do some less-developed countries. A more reliable way to distinguish quantitatively between the developed and less-developed countries is by per capita income—that is, the level of a country's GNP divided by its population.

Comparing per capita income across countries is problematic, however. Per capita income measures the availability of goods and services to individuals, but we cannot draw meaningful comparisons between incomes in Mexico, China, and Australia when GNP in each case is calculated in terms of a different national currency—pesos, yuan, and pounds, respectively. The simplest means of overcoming this problem is to use the exchange rate between national currencies to convert the GNP of each nation into a common currency. Most international income comparisons follow this technique, with U.S. dollars usually constituting the common currency. The term for this technique is the **exchange rate conversion method.**

Unfortunately, even international income comparisons based on the exchange rate conversion method can be misleading. When international comparisons are made, the intention is to measure the differences in standards of living between different countries. Exchange rate conversion may reflect these differences poorly. While the exchange rate generally reflects differences in the purchasing power of currencies for goods that are traded across international markets, it may be a poor indicator of differences in the purchasing power of currencies with respect to goods and services that are not exchanged across international markets. For example, if 1 U.S. dollar will purchase 1½ Chinese yuan in the foreign exchange market, this exchange rate does not mean that the dollar will purchase exactly 1½ yuan of housing, dental care, or education in the United States (as 1½ yuan would in China). Differences in climate, culture, and tastes must be taken into account.

A technique for greatly improving international income comparisons involves expressing the conversion ratio between currencies in terms of their ability to purchase a typical bundle of goods and services in the countries where they are issued.[2] For example, the bundle of goods for the United Kingdom might include relatively expensive housing, heating, and food products, and the bundle for Thailand relatively cheap housing, heating, and food products. The United Nations International Comparison Project, a study begun in 1968 by the U.N. Statistical Office, has devised a workable purchasing power index for several currencies. In this **purchasing power parity method,** each category in the bundle of typical goods and services is weighted according to its contribution to GNP. The dollar cost of purchasing the typical bundle is then compared to the dollar cost of purchasing a similar bundle in the United States. After the purchasing power of the nation's currency is determined in terms of the typical bundle, this information is used to convert the GNP of the country in question to a common currency unit, the U.S. dollar.

The size of the gap in per capita income between the developed and the less-developed countries has been calculated by the World Bank using both methods. The results are shown in Table 5. Using the exchange rate conversion method, per capita income in the industrial market economies in 1987 was estimated to be $14,324, while that in less-developed countries was estimated to be $1160. By this method of comparison, the industrial market economies appeared to have a per capita income twelve times greater than that of the less-developed countries. However, the relative figures calculated in terms of the

Exchange rate conversion method:
The comparison of real GNP across countries by converting all nations' GNPs to a common currency denomination through the use of exchange rates.

Purchasing power parity method:
The comparison of real GNP across countries by converting GNPs to a common currency through use of the comparative cost of purchasing a typical assortment of goods and services in each country.

---

[2]Dan Usher, *The Price Mechanism and the Meaning of National Income Statistics* (Oxford: Clarendon Press, 1968).

TABLE 5   Measuring the Economic Gap Between Developed and Less-Developed Countries: Per Capita GNP, 1987

Per capita GNP in industrial market economies was more than twelve and one-half times that in less-developed countries in 1987. Per capita purchasing power (in U.S. dollars) in the developed world was more than five times greater than that of developing nations.

Country Group	Exchange Rate Conversion Method (dollars)	Purchasing Power Parity Method (dollars)
Less-developed countries	1,160	2,454
Industrial market economies	14,324	12,047

Source: World Bank, *World Bank Development Report 1981* (New York: Oxford University Press, 1981), p. 17, and authors' calculations.

purchasing power parity method indicate that the more-developed countries' per capita GNP is only five times greater than that of the less-developed countries.

Purchasing power parity estimates of per capita income are a more accurate indicator of relative international performance. The problem is that they are more difficult to construct. However, even in purchasing power parity terms, there is still a very significant gap between the incomes of developed nations and less-developed nations.

UNDERDEVELOPMENT: CAUSES AND CURES

Looking at the economic policies of underdeveloped countries that have succeeded in achieving substantial rates of economic growth and at the policies of countries that have failed to develop, it becomes clear that there is no single secret to economic development. Policies that appear to work in one country often fail when applied elsewhere. Nonetheless, we can talk confidently about certain keys to achieving economic growth: (1) an economic system that relies on a price system to efficiently allocate resources; (2) growth in the foreign sector based on the principle of comparative advantage; (3) acquisition of human capital; (4) increased savings and investment to acquire technology; and (5) efficient agricultural techniques. This is not to suggest that a country that takes these five steps will necessarily be a success or that economic development is impossible in countries that fail to pursue these five objectives.

Even if the government of an underdeveloped country implements a market system and pursues free-trade policies, the goal of economic development often proves to be elusive; success may be thwarted by an unmotivated or unconvinced populace. The acquisition of human capital requires that some family members undertake training or schooling when, instead, they could be earning income in the work force or producing goods at home. This is a luxury families on the verge of starvation cannot afford. Similarly, when the vast majority of families are poverty-stricken, encouraging saving and investment may be futile. A high percentage of output goes for consumption in many poor countries; very little is left for saving and investment. Because attaining agricultural efficiency hinges on use of capital equipment, it may be that many poor countries can do nothing but fail—they are trapped in the vicious circle of poverty.

Population Growth and Economic Development

One of the characteristics shared by most developing countries is rapid population growth. The population of poor countries in Africa, Asia, and South America has been expanding in recent years at an annual rate of about 2.5 percent. By contrast, the population of the developed countries of Europe, Japan, and North America has been growing at a rate of about 1 percent per year. A cause-and-effect relation between rapid population growth and retarded economic growth of less-developed countries has often been claimed. Surely, the argument goes, rapid population growth must impose substantial costs on less-developed countries, insofar as education and health care—as well as elemental necessities like food and clothing—must be provided from limited available resources. While this line of reasoning is plausible on the surface, there are reasons to believe that blaming underdevelopment on rapid population growth is an oversimplification; in economic terms, both costs and benefits may be associated with population growth.

First, the high rate of population growth in less-developed countries is fostered not by increasing birth rates but by stable birth rates combined with a sharp decline in mortality, or death, rates. Mortality rates in the less-developed world have fallen by 50 percent in the last thirty years because of advances in disease control. Although infant mortality remains relatively high, life expectancy at birth in the less-developed world increased from about thirty-five years in 1950 to about fifty-eight years in 1990. Life expectancy at birth is an important measure of economic development. Hence, the population explosion in less-developed countries evidences, paradoxically, economic advance.

High rates of fertility in less-developed countries—that is, a high demand for children—are also cited as a cause of underdevelopment. Both modern and traditional methods of birth control are generally available in less-developed countries, but this has not slackened demand for large families. High rates of fertility, other things being equal, do imply reduced per capita income. But the costs of having children that families in less-developed countries must face are lower than the costs faced by families in Western countries. In less-developed countries, children frequently represent valuable capital assets. It is common for quite young children—four or five years of age—to enter the labor force, especially in the agricultural sector. Only very young children are usually dependent in the sense that the marginal product of their labor does not substantially offset the cost to their families of clothing and feeding them. This usefulness of the young is reflected in the high labor force participation rates for many less-developed countries compared with developed countries. In short, children in less-developed countries apparently make a more substantial contribution to aggregate output than children in developed countries.

International Wealth Distribution and Economic Development

Is economic exploitation by richer countries a cause of underdevelopment? If so, will financial help from more-developed countries solve the problem? In 1974, the U.N. General Assembly adopted a Declaration on the Establishment of a New International Economic Order (NIEO), in which it asserted that only large-scale redistribution of wealth from rich to poor countries can accelerate the latter's agonizingly slow development process.

Two ideas lie behind the NIEO: the vicious circle of poverty and the responsibility of developed countries for the underdevelopment of poor countries. In the minds of NIEO advocates, presently developed countries are colonial powers who developed their own economies largely through a redistribution of resources taken from less-developed countries. Today, the less-developed countries' circle of poverty is unbreakable unless the redistribution of wealth is reversed through trade preferences for less-developed countries, commodity agreements (in effect, long-run contracts for various agricultural and other goods), and, most important, cancellation of some of the enormous foreign debts owed by less-developed countries to foreign banks. An important clause of the declaration states that discrimination (that is, any restrictions on the use of funds) should not be involved in grants of aid to governments of less-developed countries. What those governments choose to do with the aid should be entirely left to them.

The claims of the advocates of the NIEO are understandable. Many presently developed nations long colonized many of the presently less-developed nations. International trade has continued among developed and less-developed countries on a large scale, yet the less-developed countries have not yet been brought to high stages of development. Finally, common sense would seem to suggest that additional aid could only help matters.

The NIEO proposal, however, has many opponents, who refute the claim that past and present commercial contact between the developed countries and the less-developed countries is a source of the less-developed countries' persistent poverty. Opponents point out that the list of the least-developed countries consists almost entirely of those that have had little or no involvement with international trade, such as Burundi, Chad, Rwanda, and Bhutan. Those with a record of the most extensive contacts with developed countries, including Mexico, Singapore, and Brazil, are among the most advanced poorer countries.

Opponents of NIEO also challenge the notion that trade between the developed nations and the less-developed nations has been a one-way street. They stress that there were and are gains to the less-developed countries from this trade. Opponents also disagree with NIEO's proposal to abolish economic discrimination against the less-developed countries, which would effectively allow them to follow any sort of economic policy. Opponents cite economic policies of the less-developed countries that have severely retarded their own economic development, including persecution and expulsion of productive minority groups (Asians in East Africa, Chinese in Southeast Asia, and many others), enforced collectivization of farming, the establishment of state export monopolies, and the confiscation of the property of productive groups for political purposes.

Thus, the economic policies pursued by governments in less-developed countries seem to play a crucial role in their own economic development.

Many government policies seem to inhibit economic growth and reduce the performance of the economy. In this context, critics question unrestricted aid to less-developed countries. The same governments that promulgate policies detrimental to economic development are unlikely to invest foreign aid in an economically efficient manner. To opponents of the NIEO proposals, the theory of exploitation from without underestimates the importance of internal institutions and economic policies in the development process. These critics argue that development is not determined by the greed or generosity of already developed nations but, to a large degree, by economic policies in the less-developed countries themselves.

Property Rights Arrangements and Economic Development

Can differences in economic institutions be pinpointed as a major cause of underdevelopment? It is often argued that economists are not able to bring societies into the laboratory and use the experimental method to test their theories. While this is certainly true, economists are able to make careful observations of how different economic institutions affect economic performance. There are contemporary examples of different economic systems that have a common basic cultural setting, a similar climate, and a common ethnic-religious origin but that have taken radically different routes to economic development (recall Economics in Action, "Contrasts in Economic Institutions: The Two Koreas," in Chapter 3). Comparison of such countries helps shed some light on the causes of underdevelopment.

Mainland China, Hong Kong, and Taiwan.   The People's Republic of (Mainland) China is the world's most populous economy, with an estimated population in 1988 of over a billion (1,088,169,000). Unlike some other communist countries, until recently China apparently did not have a legally sanctioned private sector in its economy; economic activity was even more tightly controlled by the state than in the Soviet Union. Unlike the case of the Soviet economy, there has been little evidence in China of an underground economy, which in the Soviet Union restores some degree of flexibility to the centrally planned system.

Since 1959, China has not issued economic statistics, so evaluation of the country's economic performance is based on outside estimates. But there is general agreement that despite promising reserves of oil, gas, coal, iron ore and other natural resources, China is still one of the world's poorest countries. In 1985, the (estimated) GNP per capita was $318. However, even this low figure tends to overstate the standard of living in China, where quality consumer goods remain in scarce supply. Relative to average wages, goods tend in general to be more expensive than similar goods in the West. A worker can reasonably hope to save enough to buy a bicycle, but definitely not a car. In the past decade, the Chinese leadership has begun relaxing the reliance on central planning by encouraging greater initiative on the part of enterprise management and encouraging private economic ventures to a limited extent.

In 1978, China introduced a contract responsibility system for some of its 800 million peasant farmers. The system allowed these farmers to sell their crops on the open market after they had turned over a certain percentage of their yield to the government. The response of China's farmers to these economic reforms, which basically vested farmers with partial property rights over their production, was phenomenal. Between 1981 and 1985, wheat production in China rose by 43 percent, the production of cotton increased by 40 percent, and meat production rose by 39 percent. It is unlikely that such dramatic production increases were due solely to technological advancement or to favorable climatic conditions. In 1984, China extended this free-market experiment to urban workers. In the past, urban workers had little incentive to produce; each job was guaranteed for a worker's lifetime, and both industrious and laggard workers were equally rewarded. Now, state-run plants are able to keep whatever profits they earn in excess of state taxes and distribute these profits to workers in the form of wage incentives. Managers are able to hire and fire workers and to set different wages for different jobs.

The most significant change in China's economy has been its adoption of a modified price system. The government has slowly relaxed its controls over prices, and the costs of many basic consumer items now fluctuate in response to supply and demand.

Although many Chinese are enjoying greater prosperity because of these changes, the overall success of China's attempt to bring market principles into a command economy will depend on many factors, including the stability of the country's leadership. Eventually, the world's most populous nation may become a powerful economic force in international trade.

Although the people of Taiwan and Hong Kong are ethnically identical to the Chinese people, Taiwan and Hong Kong are market economies, with relatively small public sectors. In fact, in both countries government regulation of the economy is considerably more limited than it is in the United States. Of the two, Taiwan has the greater endowment of natural resources. Hong Kong is very poor in natural resources; it has little level land for agriculture and must import both food and water from the mainland. Yet each of these economies has enjoyed successful economic development. Estimated 1985 GNP per capita for Taiwan was $3109; for Hong Kong, $6330. The standard of living in each economy is high and visibly improving. Largely unrestricted by government, individual entrepreneurship thrives. Whether Hong Kong's rapid economic growth will continue after it is returned to mainland China in 1999 is uncertain. The Chinese have assured Hong Kong businesspeople of some freedom of action after the switch in regimes.

CONCLUSION: EXPLAINING ECONOMIC DEVELOPMENT

Why have economies developed at different rates? More specifically, why do less-developed countries seem to have such difficulty matching the levels of development typical of Europe, Japan, and North America? This question is the object of much controversy; we have already discussed some of the major issues in the debate, such as the vicious circle of poverty. It appears that neither the vicious circle of poverty nor large populations have prevented development of economies such as Hong Kong, Taiwan, and South Korea, which have developed rapidly by attracting foreign investment, rather than relying primarily on foreign aid.

Likewise, the level of technology in most less-developed countries tends to be low. But this is an effect, not a cause, of low levels of development. Poor countries are unable to afford equipment and techniques common in rich countries. The technology itself—inventions, new processes and techniques—is widely available to less-developed countries. The knowledge necessary to improve productivity is not lacking, but the economic development making that technical knowledge worthwhile is. Less-developed countries often have untapped reserves of entrepreneurial ability, a problem that countries such as China are only beginning to address.

In terms of economic growth, economists are generally satisfied that economic incentives matter. Property rights arrangements and institutions that reward economic efficiency and permit consumers to choose freely the kinds and amounts of goods and services produced tend to promote development. Consider Japan. Despite its dense population and sparse resource base, Japan has risen rapidly from a poor agricultural country to a model for what a capitalist-style market structure and incentives to savings and investment can accomplish.

SUMMARY

1. The study of comparative economic systems focuses on the alternative institutional arrangements of different economies—such as who owns productive resources and who makes economic decisions—and the impact of these arrangements on economic performance.

2. Capitalism is an economic system in which a large proportion of economic activity is conducted by private individuals and firms. The private ownership of resources and the freedom to employ resources as the owner sees fit are a hallmark of capitalist economic systems. By contrast, socialism is an economic system in which the state owns most nonhuman productive resources. Resource allocation under socialism is determined in the main by central planning rather than by private initiative.

3. The basic economic concepts introduced in the earlier chapters of this book have general applicability to all economic systems. The law of demand, opportunity cost, diminishing marginal returns, and self-interest, for example, apply equally to capitalist and socialist economies.

4. Historically, the Soviet economy has been a command economy, in which virtually all economic decisions were made through a detailed system of central planning. The recent introduction of *perestroika,* or economic restructuring, is a move toward less central planning and a somewhat greater reliance on markets to provide goods and services.

5. There is a growing legal private sector in the Soviet Union in agriculture and personal services. Until recently, private agricultural plots have occupied a small percentage of cultivated land but have been quite productive. There is also an extensive extralegal private sector in the Soviet Union that eases the bottlenecks caused by central planning.

6. Comparisons of the performance of the Soviet economy and other economies are tricky, especially since the Soviet economy is in transition. Data seem to indicate that the Soviet Union has achieved high but erratic growth rates over recent years. Moreover, when comparisons involving the quality of output are involved, Soviet performance in the consumer goods sector is generally poor.

7. Though an aim of Soviet policy is avowed to be greater equality in income distribution, the available evidence indicates that the effective distribution of income in the Soviet Union is similar to that in the capitalist U.S. economy and the democratic socialist economy of Sweden.

8. Economic development is the study of how countries grow economically.

9. The less-developed countries of the world are characterized by low per capita income, large and growing populations, and low saving and investment rates.

10. Comparisons of per capita income between the industrial countries and the less-developed countries can be made by the exchange rate conversion method or the purchasing power parity method. However the computation is handled, the economic gap between the developed and the less-developed countries is large.

11. The vicious circle of poverty refers to the fact that there is little saving in a poor economy and, therefore, little chance for future development. Economies are thus said to be poor tomorrow because they are poor today. This idea has some merit in explaining underdevelopment, but it must be applied carefully.

12. Population growth is a serious obstacle to economic development. However, much of the recent popula-

tion growth in less-developed countries is due to a declining death rate and to the need for young children to augment the labor supply in the agricultural sector, so the phenomenon of population growth in the less-developed countries must be interpreted cautiously.

13. There have been various responses to the New International Economic Order (NIEO) adopted by the United Nations in 1974. Under the NIEO, the rich countries of the world would transfer wealth to the poor countries. This and similar proposals are pred-icated on the idea that the poverty of the poor countries is due to the policies of the rich countries and not to policies and institutions that prevail in the poor countries.

14. Comparative economic development suggests that property rights, incentives, personal freedom, and other similar institutions are important in sparking economic growth. The examples of Hong Kong, Taiwan, and Japan support the validity of this approach to development.

KEY TERMS

comparative economics
pure capitalism
pure communism
socialism
mixed capitalism

command economy
materials balancing
perestroika
economic development
less-developed countries

vicious circle of poverty
exchange rate conversion method
purchasing power parity method

QUESTIONS FOR REVIEW AND DISCUSSION

1. Would you expect the illegal private sector to be larger in the United States or in the Soviet Union? Why?

2. A socialist economy does not recognize private property rights. The state "owns" all resources. Name three consequences of this lack of private property rights.

3. Is income distribution in the Soviet Union fundamentally different from that in Western economies? Why or why not?

4. Give three examples not discussed in the text of how basic economic principles apply to a command economy.

5. What are the primary characteristics of a less-developed economy?

6. The vicious circle of poverty asserts that the less-developed countries are poor today because they were poor yesterday. Do you agree? Explain.

7. Evaluate this statement: "To achieve economic growth, an economy requires lots of resources, including land, and a low rate of population growth."

8. Explain why you agree or disagree with the following statement: "A major difference between a planned economy and a market economy is that the supply of any particular good in a planned economy is perfectly inelastic while in a free market it is elastic."

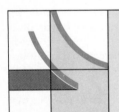

ECONOMICS IN ACTION
The Socialist Calculation Debate and the Transition from Planning to Markets

The astonishing turn of events in the Soviet Union in the 1980s gave way to events in Eastern Europe that were characterized as "unthinkable." While the news media and others may have been caught by surprise, economists were somewhat better prepared—having for years debated whether socialism could exist as envisioned by Marx and Lenin, and then whether socialism could survive.

The debate originated with Austrian economist Ludwig von Mises (1881–1973) and a paper he published in 1922 entitled "Economic Calculation in the Socialist Commonwealth." Mises attacked the position taken by contemporary socialist theorists that after a socialist state abolished money, the price system, and markets, it would be able to plan and direct all production. He argued that money prices determined across markets were necessary for rational economic calculation. The price system allowed resources to flow to their most highly valued uses in society. For example, although it would be technically feasible to build subway rails out of platinum, this would be an economically inefficient allocation if less expensive substitutes were available for the rails. But only the price system, representing the competing bids of all potential users of platinum, allows for such judgments to be made. Without it, Mises argued, resources could not be allocated efficiently, and the economy could function only at a primitive level at best. A modern, technologically advanced, and complex economy would be impossible to achieve under socialism.

Socialists took Mises's challenge very seriously, and some prominent writers (Oskar Lange and Abba Lerner, in particular) acknowledged that Mises had identified a very important weakness in the socialist position. Lange even half-seriously proposed that in the future socialist commonwealth, a statue be erected in Mises's honor so that no one would forget that prices and markets would be essential under socialism, too. In effect, the socialist counterattack partially retreated from the original socialist position. Lange claimed that socialism might still work if central planning were abandoned in favor of a system wherein the state would set prices for goods and factors of production. Managers of state-owned firms would then produce until the marginal cost of their output equaled the assigned price of the good. These managers would simply requisition the inputs necessary to produce according to this rule: The state would adjust the prices it assigned in response to any shortages or surpluses of the factors of production.

While this plan seemed clever, Mises and his student, Friedrich von Hayek, countered that these "market socialist" schemes failed to solve the real problem of socialism. Although the socialist state could establish an arbitrary set of prices, it would not perform the function of a market price system unless these "prices" were able to convey an equal amount of information regarding the true opportunity costs associated with resource use. For the socialist state's prices to serve this purpose, they would have to reflect an enormous amount of information regarding the availability of resources, updated continually. If this task were possible at all, it would require high transaction costs. Furthermore, for such a system to approximate the efficiency of a market

economy, incentives would have to be structured to ensure that individuals within the system would use information and resources efficiently. But this could be possible only where factors of production were privately owned, while the market socialists insisted that all resources be owned by the state.

The seven-decade-long record of central planning bears out many points Mises made. As predicted, centrally planned economies, including those in Eastern Europe, failed to achieve the early goals of Marx and Lenin due to an inability to use prices as information. These early socialist theorists and later practitioners also underestimated the drag placed on the system by the inevitable bureaucracies.[a]

When Mises first voiced doubts about the practicality of socialism, socialism and central planning were just theories. We now know that a socialist system founded on central planning can exist; planning was the hallmark of Soviet bloc countries for many years, and growth did occur. Mises's primary point, however, was that no economy could approach high levels of efficiency and development without a price system and free markets to guide resources into their most highly valued uses. On this point, there is substantial empirical evidence that planning does not maximize the welfare of consumers or economic efficiency in society.

The socialist calculation debate, even with the recent shifts from planning to greater reliance on markets, cannot tell us what the future of formerly planned economies will be. Some people believe there is a third way, a middle ground between communism and capitalism where the excesses of the two systems can be reconciled in some form of social democracy or mixed economy. Mises and Hayek argued that all forms of social democracy are inherently unstable and will—owing to costs and inefficiencies generated by planning of any form—evolve into freedom and market capitalism or into socialist planning and totalitarianism. Where the recent steps taken by the countries of the Soviet bloc will lead only time will tell.

Question
Does Mises's indictment of central planning mean that planning is impossible or, rather, that, due to some ever-present characteristics of human nature and institutions, planning can seldom if ever guarantee that the goals of planners are reached? Explain. Does Mises's insight have any contemporary relevance for Western societies?

[a]Ludwig von Mises, *Bureaucracy* (New Haven, Conn.: Yale University Press, 1944).

P. T. Bauer

Gunnar Myrdal

P. T. Bauer and Gunnar Myrdal: Third World Development and Trade

PETER TAMAS BAUER (b. 1915) is the most distinguished critic of development theory. Bauer's studies of the rubber industry and the West African trade paved the way for his works on development—*Dissent on Development* (1972) and *Reality and Rhetoric: Studies in the Economics of Development* (1984). Bauer struck his central theme concerning economic development in earlier works: Economic growth, Bauer argued, is the product of voluntary responses and efficient domestic and international markets—not of state intervention or central planning by governments.

Born in Hungary in 1915, Bauer was a fellow of Gonville and Caius College at Cambridge (England) between 1946 and 1960 and again from 1968 and 1984. He was also professor of economics in the University of London at the London School of Economics from 1960 until his retirement in 1983. While in these academic posts, Bauer launched attacks on the conventional wisdom regarding economic development, including theories relating to the widening gap of income differences within and between countries, the vicious circle of poverty, the operation of marketing boards and commodity agreements in developing countries, and the operation of foreign aid. Principally, Bauer targeted the economic development theories of Gunnar Myrdal.

GUNNAR MYRDAL (1898–1987), sociologist and economist, was a joint recipient of the Nobel Memorial Prize in economics with Friedrich A. von Hayek in 1974. Myrdal is best known for his work on racial discrimination and social problems. His most famous work, *An American Dilemma:*

The Negro Problem and Modern Democracy, began as a study commissioned by the Carnegie Corporation in 1938 and had an enormous impact on American attitudes toward integration. His later works explored trade and economic development: *The Political Element in the Development of Economic Theory* (1935) focused on the philosophical foundations of classical free-trade doctrine, and *Rich Lands and Poor: The Road to World Prosperity* (1957) discussed the application of the free-trade doctrine to the problems of economic development.

Myrdal was born in the Gustaf parish of Sweden. He studied law as an undergraduate at the University of Stockholm and received his PhD in law from the university in 1927. In 1924, he married Alva Reimer, with whom he researched and wrote a study of Sweden's decreasing population, which was published in 1934. After graduation, Myrdal taught economics, traveled abroad, and served the government of Sweden both as a representative of the Social Democratic party and as cabinet minister. In 1947, he was appointed executive secretary of the United Nations Economic Commission for Europe, a position he retained for the next ten years. In 1960, he became a professor of international economics at the University of Stockholm.

WHAT IS THE PROBLEM?

Both Bauer and Myrdal pursued answers to timeless questions regarding the economic development of Third World nations. Does free trade promote or impede economic development in poor nations? Which is more conducive to economic growth and progress in developing nations—central planning or free markets? What is the nature and what are the effects of economic aid from industrialized nations to poor and developing nations of the world?

Bauer and Myrdal occupy opposite ends of the philosophical spectrum; they could not agree on what the problem of economic development is, much less any solution. Myrdal, for example, would center the investigation around the causes of poverty, while Bauer would have economists investigate the causes of prosperity and development. In other words, the burden of any theory of development is either to explain how certain nations and people got rich (Bauer) or why certain nations remained poor (Myrdal).

Not only are Myrdal and Bauer worlds apart on the definition of the problem of development, they stand apart on the philosophical nature of equality and power. Of great importance here is the concept of "equality," which both economists support, but in vastly different forms. As an important modern commentator on their views has remarked, "Whether Myrdal or Bauer is more in favor of equality depends entirely on whether equality is conceived as equality of economic results or equality of political process. Myrdal clearly believes more in equality of economic results—and Bauer equally clearly prefers equality of social processes."[a] In other words, the goal of economic development, in Myrdal's view, is to promote economic equality—similar levels of development and equitable income distributions—between rich and poor nations. Economic power exemplified by concentrations of monopoly power, Myrdal believed, is the root cause of inequalities. Bauer, on the other hand, believes that economic development requires that social processes and *access* to economic activity be open to all and be free and unfettered. In Bauer's view, power restricts the choices of others, most often exemplified by government planning and regulation. The rich, according to Bauer, most often get that way by expanding the choices and opportunities of others.

TRADE, CENTRAL PLANNING, AND ECONOMIC AID

Not surprisingly, the philosophical differences between Bauer and Myrdal show very different views of key elements in economic development. Here we consider only three of these key elements.

TRADE

In Myrdal's view, the principle of comparative advantage and free trade works in favor of rich nations and keeps poor nations locked within a vicious cycle of poverty. The low saving rates of poor countries mean low investment, which means low economic growth, which means low savings, and so on. To Myrdal, trade with other countries does not unlock this vicious cycle. In *Rich Lands and Poor: The Road to World Prosperity,* he writes, "The forces in the market tend to increase, rather than to decrease, the inequalities between regions." Myrdal points to the so-called banana republics, underdeveloped nations that specialize in one product. In Myrdal's view, such overspecialization leaves a country

vulnerable to changes in demand and its economy in continuous peril. He suggests that tariffs and subsidies would provide the impetus for developing nations to diversify production and to reduce dependence on one or a few exports.

In Bauer's analysis of trade, these views are wrongheaded and counterproductive. In the first place, Bauer denies that there is a vicious cycle of poverty in underdeveloped countries. Saving and investment take place even where people are poor and illiterate. In his classic study of the rubber industry, Bauer showed that very rapid growth was possible as a consequence of voluntary responses by peasants to expanded opportunities and contacts of developed countries in the West.[b] Further, Bauer argued that trade restrictions and attempts to substitute domestic production for goods that can be obtained more cheaply abroad were a certain path to welfare reductions and to lower growth and development. Development could be maximized only with free interaction between *all* trading nations.

CENTRAL PLANNING AND AID

Myrdal urged central planning as an extension of his belief that unequal distribution of power and property was the principal obstacle to equitable economic growth. Institutional planning, production goals, and price planning are all parts of the system that Myrdal urged on developing nations as prerequisites to growth and changing attitudes. He had faith that, with enough information and competent managers, planning would be superior to any other method of achieving growth and human development. Further, he believed the role of industrialized countries was to provide aid to poor nations.

Sentiments expressed by Bauer twenty years ago have a very contemporary feel. Bauer pointed out then that planning, if it works at all, does not maximize an economy's opportunities. All investment undertaken for political motives is wasted. Bauer likewise criticized foreign aid as intergovernmental grants of taxpayers' money. While such aid augments resources in recipient countries, Bauer believes there is no reason to expect that, in the hands of politicians, bureaucrats, and administrators, it will be put to productive uses. With few exceptions, foreign aid promotes centralized and closely controlled economies (factors that choke growth), and it sometimes generates resentment and suspicion toward the donor.[c] Of far greater effect is aid provided on a commercial basis, direct foreign investment in developing nations, and—of ultimate importance in Bauer's view—free and open trade between rich nations and poor.

[a]Thomas Sowell, *A Conflict of Visions* (New York: William Morrow and Company, 1987), p. 159.

[b]A. A. Walters, "Peter Tamas Bauer," in *The New Palgrave: A Dictionary of Economics,* edited by John Eatwell, Murray Milgate, and Peter Newman (London: The Macmillan Press Limited, 1987), vol. I, p. 207. For further information on Myrdal, see Paul Streeten, "Gunnar Myrdal," *The New Palgrave,* vol. III, pp. 581–83.

[c]For more on economic aid, see P. T. Bauer, *Dissent on Development: Studies and Debates in Development Economics* (Cambridge: Harvard University Press, 1972), p. 114–35.

GLOSSARY

Numbers in parentheses indicate pages on which key terms are discussed.

Ability-to-pay principle: A method of determining individuals' tax burdens on the basis of those most capable of paying taxes. (297)

Absolute advantage: The ability of an economic entity to specialize and produce a greater amount of some good than another entity can. (51)

Accommodation of cost-push inflation: Increases in the money supply designed to offset a decrease in aggregate supply caused by monopoly or union action or by an aggregate supply shock; increased aggregate demand results, preventing decreases in real output. (398)

Accounting costs: Actual money expenditures associated with any activity; out-of-pocket costs. (9)

Adaptive expectations theory: A proposition suggesting that consumers and businesses form expectations of future inflation on the basis of actual inflation from the recent past. (389)

Administrative lag: The amount of time between recognition of a destabilizing economic event and the implementation of a policy designed to correct for it. (420)

Aggregate demand: The total spending that occurs in an economy at various price levels during a specified period of time. (160)

Aggregate demand curve: Graphical relation showing the different levels of national income that exist at different price levels. (261)

Aggregate supply: The total output that will be produced by an economy at various price levels during a specified period of time. (160)

Aggregate supply curve: A graph showing the different levels of aggregate output produced at different price levels. (266)

Appreciation: An increase in the equilibrium exchange market value of a country's currency in a flexible-rate system; a decrease in the number of units of a country's money required to purchase one unit of a foreign country's money. (516)

Arc elasticity: A measure of the average elasticity between two points on the demand curve. (125)

Artificial barriers to trade: Restrictions created by the government that inhibit or prevent trade; includes import quotas and tariffs. (53)

Automatic stabilizers: Taxes and government expenditures whose levels do not depend on decisions by policy-makers for change but instead change countercyclically in response to changes in the level of economic activity. (290)

Autonomous consumption: Consumption expenditures that are independent of the level of income. (214)

Autonomous consumption multiplier: The multiple by which equilibrium income will change given a change in autonomous consumption expenditure: $1/MPS$. (237)

Autonomous government expenditures: Government expenditures that are independent of the level of income. (243)

Autonomous investment: Investment expenditures that are independent of the level of income. (221)

Average propensity to consume (*APC*): The percent of a particular level of income that is spent on consumption; total consumption divided by total income. (213)

Average propensity to save (*APS*): The percent of total income that is saved; total saving during any given period divided by total income in the same period. (213)

Balance of payments: An official accounting record of all the foreign transactions of a nation's residents, businesses, and governments. (526)

Balance of trade deficit: Occurs when the value of a nation's exports is less than the value of a nation's imports; also called a trade deficit. (522)

Balance of trade surplus: Occurs when the value of a nation's exports exceeds the value of a nation's imports; also called a trade surplus. (522)

Barter: Direct exchange of one good or service for another without the use of money. (14, 63)

Barter economy: An economy in which money is not used to facilitate exchange between individuals and firms; goods trade directly for other goods. (314)

Benefit principle: A method of determining individuals' tax burdens on the basis of the beneficiaries of the expenditures that are financed by taxes; an example is a gasoline tax. (297)

Bonds: Financial instruments that create future obligations on the part of the issuers to make principal repayments and, in most cases, interest payments. (296)

Bretton Woods system: The fixed exchange rate system established among Western countries after World War II. (532)

Budget deficit: The amount by which government's expenditures exceed government's tax revenues in a year. (291)

Budget surplus: The amount by which government's tax revenues exceed government's expenditures in a year (291)

Business cycles: Recurrent, systematic fluctuations in the level of business activity; usually measured by changes in the level, or rate of growth, of real GNP over time; or the variation through time of the level of real GNP around its long-term trend. (158, 434)

Capital deepening: Increases in the total stock of capital in conjunction with increases in the ratio of the capital stock to the labor force; occurs when the capital stock grows at a faster rate than the labor force. (460)

Capital formation: The process whereby the stock of capital in an economy increases. (470)

Capital stock: The amount of nonhuman resources available in the economy. These include tools, land, machinery, equipment, and so on. (39)

Cash reserves: Commercial banks' and other depository institutions' holdings of vault cash or deposits at the Federal Reserve district banks. (337)

Ceteris paribus: The Latin phrase for "all other things held constant." (88)

Change in demand: A shift of the entire demand curve to the right or left. (89)

Change in quantity demanded: A change in the amount of a good a consumer is willing and able to purchase that is caused by a change in the price of the good or service. (89)

Change in quantity supplied: A change in the amount of a good a producer is willing and able to produce and sell that is caused by a change in the price of the good or service. (96)

Change in supply: A shift of the entire supply curve to the right or left. (96)

Checkable deposits: Demand deposits plus other types of transaction accounts that pay interest but that may carry some restrictions on use, including minimum balance and limits on the number of checks that can be written per month. (320)

Choices at the margin: Decisions based on the additional benefits and costs of small changes in a particular activity. (35)

Circular flow of income: The movement of real goods and services, payments, and receipts between households and business firms. (63)

Classical long-run equilibrium: The hypothetical adjustment of an economy to full employment given an actual supply of resources, population, technology, and degree of specialization. (192)

Classical macroeconomic theory: A view of the macroeconomy as being self-adjusting and capable of generating full employment and maximum output in the long run without government intervention; dominant from the late eighteenth through the early twentieth century. (190)

Classical process of economic growth: A process based on the division of labor but also involving increases in saving, investment, capital accumulation, and, ultimately, growth in real GNP. (190)

Classical range: A vertical segment of the aggregate supply curve; indicates that attempts to increase aggregate output will result only in a higher price level since resources are fully employed. (267)

Classical self-adjustment mechanism: The theory that, through Say's law, full employment will be reached given interest rate flexibility and price-wage flexibility. (201)

Command economy: An extreme form of socialist economy characterized by less private economic decision making than exists in a socialist economy. (547)

Commercial bank: Chartered financial institution that accepts deposits of various types, especially demand deposits, and that makes commercial and consumer loans. (325)

Commodity money: An item that serves as a medium of exchange and that is also a good itself. (315)

Comparative advantage: An economic entity's (an individual's or a nation's) ability to produce a good at a lower marginal opportunity cost than some other entity. (45, 486)

Comparative economics: The study of the differences in economic systems; particularly, the differences between capitalist and socialist economic systems. (542)

Competition: A market situation satisfying two conditions—a large number of buyers and sellers and freedom to enter and exit the market—and resulting in prices equal to the costs of production plus a normal profit for sellers. (67)

Complements: Products that are related such that an increase in the price of one will decrease the demand for the other or a decrease in the price of one will increase the demand for the other; two goods whose cross elasticity of demand is negative: $\epsilon_c < 0$. (91, 134)

Consumer price index (CPI): A price index that uses the prices of goods and services consumers generally buy to calculate the price level and the rate of inflation. (182)

Consumption function: The positive relationship between levels of consumption expenditures and levels of income, holding all other relevant factors that determine consumption constant. (214)

Consumption possibilities curve: All the possible combinations of two goods that could be consumed by first specializing according to comparative advantage and then trading at the terms of trade. (489)

Contractionary gap: The amount by which total planned expenditures at the level of full-employment income fall short of the level required to generate full-employment income; also called a recessionary gap. (240)

Costs: An implication of scarcity; the necessary sacrifices associated with making any choice. (4)

Cost-price spiral: The process whereby increased production costs lead to increased final goods prices, which lead to further increases in resource prices and production costs; for the spiral to continue, the money supply must continually increase or real output must continually fall. (399)

Cost-push inflation: Increases in the price level caused by monopoly and/or union power or by shocks to the economy that reduce aggregate supply. (397)

Countercyclical fiscal policy: Changes in government expenditures or taxes that are designed to reverse changes in private expenditures or savings that produce unemployment or inflation. (248)

Creative destruction theory: A business cycle theory that emphasizes the role of the entrepreneur as an innovator supplying new products and services, thereby creating new profit opportunities and destroying old ones; competitors follow the innovator's lead, which creates business cycles. (449)

Credit controls: The method or tools that the Federal Reserve System uses in efforts to control the monetary base and the money supply, including reserve requirements, open market operations, the discount rate, and other selective credit controls. (359)

Cross elasticity of demand: Measures buyers' relative responsiveness to a change in the price of one good in terms of the change in the quantity demanded of another good. The percentage change in the quantity demanded of one good divided by the percentage change in the price of another good. (133)

Crowding out: The competitive pressure exerted on private investment by government expenditures. (302)

Currency-deposit ratio: The percentage of total deposits held that people also wish to hold in the form of currency; currency holdings expressed as a decimal fraction of checkable deposit holdings. (349)

Curve: Any curved or straight line showing the relation between two variables on a graph. (26)

Cyclically balanced budget: A long-term view of the budget, in which surpluses generated during expansions match deficits created during recessions over a period of years. (291)

Deflation: Sustained decreases in the average level of prices. (154)

Demand curve: A graphic representation of the quantities of a product that people are willing and able to purchase at all possible prices. (87)

Demand deficiency unemployment: A short-run situation in which the level of employment is less than if the full-employment level of output were produced; arises when aggregate demand is insufficient to purchase the full-employment output given the price level. (276)

Demand deposit: A type of transaction account with virtually no restrictions as to the size, timing, or number of checks that can be written on the account. (320)

Demand elasticity coefficient: The numerical representation of the price elasticity of demand: $\epsilon_d = (\Delta Q/Q) \div (\Delta P/P)$. (119)

Demand-pull inflation: Increases in the price level caused by increases in aggregate demand. (397)

Demand-side policy: Fiscal or monetary policy intended to alter the overall level of spending, or aggregate demand. (163)

Deposit expansion: The total amount of additional money or checkable deposits created by some given amount of excess reserves. (344)

Depreciation: A decrease in the equilibrium exchange market value of a country's currency in a flexible-rate system; an increase in the number of units of a country's money required to purchase one unit of a foreign country's money. (516)

Depression: A severe, persistent recession that may last several years. (435)

Devaluation: An official change in a country's exchange rate in a fixed-rate system; the number of units of a country's money that purchases one unit of another country's currency is *increased* by the government. (523)

Direct government purchases: Real goods and services, such as equipment, buildings, and consulting services, purchased by all levels of government. (74)

Discount rate: The interest rate charged by the Federal Reserve to depository institutions on loans of reserves from the Federal Reserve. (363)

Discretionary fiscal policies: Government policy actions that attempt to influence aggregate demand. (265)

Discretionary policy: A policy or change in policy that is determined by choices or decisions of policymakers. (162)

Disposable personal income: Personal income minus taxes; income available to spend. (179)

Dissaving: Occurs when consumption is greater than income; the use of previous years' savings or borrowing to finance consumption expenditures that are greater than income. (214)

Double coincidence of wants: A situation in trading in which each party to the trade has what the other wants and wants what the other has. (315)

Dumping: The selling of goods in foreign markets at prices lower than those charged in domestic markets. (502)

Econometrics: The combined use of both economic theory and formal statistical techniques to analyze, explain, and predict economic phenomena. (436)

Economic development: The process through which an economy achieves long-run economic growth; involves capital formation, the development of markets, productivity growth, and the improvement of entrepreneurial ability and labor skills. (559)

Economic goods and services: Goods and services that are scarce. (4)

Economic growth: A sustained increase in the productive capacity of an economy over time; increases in real GNP or real per capita GNP over time. (40, 156, 459)

Economic indicators: Important data, or statistics, such as the money supply, investment spending, unemployment, and inventories that are used to help forecast economic activity and business cycles; these indicators are classified as leading, lagging, and coincident indicators. (437)

Economic stabilization: The goal of governments' attempts to prevent adverse swings of inflation rates, interest rates, unemployment rates, and economic growth rates over time in the economy; a situation in which the price level and the unemployment rate vary from desired levels only temporarily and by small amounts. (72, 158)

Economic system: The part of the social system determining what, how, and for whom goods and services are produced. (59)

Elastic demand: A situation in which buyers are relatively responsive to price changes; the percentage change in quantity demanded is greater than the percentage change in price: $\epsilon_d < 1$. (119)

Elasticity: A measure of the relative responsiveness of one variable to a change in another variable; the percentage change in a dependent variable divided by the percentage change in the independent variable. (117)

Elasticity of supply: A measure of producers' or workers' relative responsiveness to price or wage changes; the percentage change in quantity supplied divided by the percentage change in the price or wage rate. (134)

Equation of exchange: An identity used to derive the quantity theory of money: $MV \equiv PQ$. (379)

Equilibrium level of national income: In the income-expenditures model, the level of income at which total private expenditures equal total output. (224)

Equilibrium price: The price at which quantity demanded is equal to quantity supplied; other things being equal, there is no tendency for this price to change. (101)

Escalator clause: Provision of a labor contract that ties changes in nominal wages to changes in some price index. (395)

Excess reserves: Total reserves minus required reserves. (337)

Exchange costs: The opportunity costs of the resources used in making trades; includes transaction costs, transportation costs, and artificial barriers to trade. (52)

Exchange rate: The (relative) price of one national currency in terms of another national currency. (511)

Exchange rate conversion method: The comparison of real GNP across countries by converting all nations' GNPs to a common currency denomination through the use of exchange rates. (561)

Expansionary gap: The amount by which total planned expenditures at the level of full-employment income exceed the level required to generate full employment without inflation; also called an inflationary gap. (240)

Expected inflation rate: The rate of inflation that consumers and businesses expect to exist over a relevant future period, such as the coming year. (389)

Explicit costs: Accounting costs. (9)

Exports (X): Total spending by foreigners on domestically produced goods and services. (175, 247)

Externally held debt: The amount of a country's total federal debt that is owned by foreign governments, businesses, and individuals. (304)

Factors affecting demand: Anything other than price, such as consumer income and preferences, that determines the amount of a product or service that consumers are willing and able to purchase. (88)

Factors affecting supply: Anything other than price, such as technology or input costs, that determines the amount of a product or service that sellers are willing and able to produce and offer for sale. (97)

Fallacy of composition: Incorrectly generalizing that what is true for a part is also true for the whole. (18)

Federal debt: The total value of federal government bonds outstanding; arises from both current and past budget deficits. (291)

Federal funds rate: A market-determined interest rate on loans and borrowings of bank reserves among commercial banks and other depository institutions. (360)

Federal Open Market Committee (FOMC): A committee of the Federal Reserve System made up of the seven members of the Board of Governors of the Federal Reserve System and five presidents of Federal Reserve district banks; directs open market operations (buying and selling of securities) for the system. (330)

Federal Reserve System: The central bank of the United States; regulates financial institutions and establishes and conducts monetary policy. (326)

Fiat money: Money, usually paper, that is made acceptable in exchange by law; usually not backed by any commodity such as gold. (316)

Final goods: Goods sold to the final consumers of the goods. (169)

Fiscal policy: The use of government spending and taxation to effect changes in aggregate economic variables. (162)

Fixed exchange rate system: An international monetary arrangement in which exchange rates are set by the government, which then must intervene in the foreign exchange market in order to maintain the pegged exchange rate. (512)

Flexible, or floating, exchange rate system: An international monetary arrangement in which exchange rates are determined by private suppliers and demanders without government intervention. (512)

Flow of earnings: Total income received by resource suppliers during any given time period. (171)

Flow of expenditures: Total spending of consumers, businesses, and government on final goods and services during any given time period. (171)

Foreign exchange: The monies of countries that are used to facilitate international trade in goods, services, and financial assets. (511)

Foreign exchange market intervention: Purchases or sales of foreign exchange by government, usually a central bank, with the goal of maintaining a fixed exchange rate or influencing the exchange rate in a flexible-rate system. (521)

Foreign exchange markets: The interaction of the suppliers and demanders of foreign exchange through which exchange rates are determined in a flexible exchange rate system. (511)

Foreign exchange reserves: The stock of a foreign exchange held by a central bank that is available for use in exchange market intervention. (521)

Fractional reserve banking system: A banking system in which banks hold only some percentage of deposits as reserves. (325)

Free enterprise: Economic freedom to produce and sell or purchase and consume goods without government intervention. (66)

Free goods and services: Things that are available in sufficient amounts and provide all that people want at zero cost. (6)

Free trade: The exchange of goods between countries without the presence of artificial trade barriers such as tariffs and quotas. (492)

Full employment: A situation in which unemployment exists only because of normal market adjustments to changing demand or supply or to outmoded skills of workers; also a numerical federal government goal for the unemployment rate; to the classical economist, a situation in which all workers willing and able to work at the current market real wage rate are employed. (150, 281)

Full price: The total opportunity cost to an individual of obtaining a good; includes money price and all other costs such as transportation costs or waiting time costs. (112)

Gold standard: An international monetary system in which currencies are redeemable in gold at fixed rates or prices. (525)

Goods: All tangible things that satisfy people's wants and desires. (2)

Government purchases (G): Total spending by federal, state, and local governments on final goods and services. (175)

Government transfer payments: Money transferred by government through taxes from one group to another, either directly or indirectly; also called income security transfers. (74)

Gross domestic product (GDP): A measure of the final goods and services produced by a country with resources located within that country. (79)

Gross national product (GNP): The dollar value measured at market prices of all final goods and services produced in an economy over a given period of time, usually a year. (79, 156, 166)

Gross private domestic investment (I): Total spending by private businesses on final goods, including capital goods and inventories. (174)

Growth absorption: Increases in total spending sufficient to purchase additional output generated by increases in productive capacity. (466)

Human resources: All forms of labor and skill used to produce goods and services. (6)

Implicit costs: Nonpecuniary costs associated with the consumption of a good or service. (9)

Implicit price deflator: A price index that uses the most comprehensive set of prices to calculate the level of prices and the rate of inflation facing households, businesses, and government; also called the GNP deflator. (182)

Imports (M): Total spending by domestic residents on foreign-produced goods and services. (175, 247)

Income elasticity of demand: A measure of consumers' relative responsiveness to income changes; the percentage change in quantity demanded divided by the percentage change in income, holding price constant. (132)

Income-expenditures model: A theory suggesting that private expenditures are basically determined by the level of national income and that these expenditures in turn determine the levels of output and employment in the economy. (210)

Income velocity: The average number of times that a unit of money (a dollar) is used, or changes hands, in purchasing nominal GNP. (379)

Industry regulation: Government rules to control the behavior of firms, particularly regarding prices and production techniques. (71)

Inelastic demand: A situation in which buyers are relatively unresponsive to price changes; the percentage change in quantity demanded is less than the percentage change in price: $\epsilon_d<1$. (120)

Infant industry: A new or developing domestic industry whose unit production costs are higher than those of established firms in the same industry in other countries. (500)

Inferior good: A good that a consumer chooses to purchase in smaller quantities as income rises, or in larger amounts as income falls. (90)

Inflation: A sustained increase in the general level of prices; inflation reduces the purchasing power of money. (14, 142)

Information: A scarce and important element in the process of economic exchange and growth. (7)

Institutions: The sum total of the traditions, mores, laws, and governmental structures of an economy. (8)

Interest rate effect: The effect on investment spending that results from a change in the interest rate produced by a change in the price level. (261)

Intermediate goods: Goods used as inputs in the production of final goods. (169)

Intermediate range: A positively sloped segment of the aggregate supply curve; indicates that aggregate output and the price level will both change in the same direction. (267)

Internally held debt: The amount of a country's total federal debt that is owned by the country's various governments, businesses, and individuals. (304)

International Monetary Fund: An international organization, established along with the Bretton Woods system, designed to assist in the efficient functioning of the Bretton Woods fixed exchange rate system. (532)

Investment function: In the income-expenditures model, all investment is autonomous, or independent of the level of income. The investment function is horizontal when plotted against income. (221)

Investment multiplier: The multiple by which equilibrium income will change given a change in autonomous investment expenditure: $1/MPS$. (235)

Investment spending: Expenditures made by businesses on capital goods plus any change (positive or negative) in business inventories. (220)

Investment tax credit: A percentage or amount of new investment expenditure that is directly subtracted from the investor's tax bill in calculating total taxes. (299)

Keynesian range: A horizontal segment of the aggregate supply curve; shows that output can increase with no change in the price level because of some unemployment of resources. (267)

Laissez-faire economy: A market economy that is allowed to operate according to competitive forces with minimal government intervention. (67)

Law of demand: The price of a product or service and the amount purchased are inversely related. If price rises, then quantity demanded falls; if price falls, quantity demanded increases, all other things held constant. (86)

Law of increasing costs: As more scarce resources are used to produce additional units of one good, production of the other good falls by larger and larger amounts. (38)

Law of one price: In perfect markets, the market forces of supply and demand produce a single, equilibrium price for a good or service. (99)

Law of supply: The price of a product or service and the amount that producers are willing and able to offer for sale are positively related. If price rises, then quantity supplied rises; if price decreases, quantity supplied decreases. (95)

Less-developed countries: Countries with relatively low levels of per capita real GNP; generally characterized by a large subsistence agriculture sector, low saving rates, and high population growth. (559)

Linear relation: One variable changes by a constant rate, and the other variable also changes by a constant rate. (27)

Liquidity: The ease with which any asset or commodity can be converted into money with little or no risk of loss to the holder. (320)

Liquidity preference theory: A theory stating that the interest rate is determined by the interaction of real money demand and supply, and that interest rate changes due to real money demand or supply changes produce changes in real economic activity. (377)

Long-run Phillips curve: A vertical line at the natural rate of unemployment; indicates that if there is enough time for workers' expectations to adjust to the actual rate of inflation, then changes in the inflation rate produce no change in the rate of unemployment. (446)

Lump-sum tax: A fixed level of total taxes; total taxes do not change as the level of income changes. (245)

M-1 money multiplier: The multiple by which the money supply will change given a change in the monetary base. (369)

Macroeconomics: Analysis of the behavior of an economy as a whole. (19)

Malthusian population principle: The notion that the population has the capability to grow geometrically while the food supply can only grow arithmetically; leads to the concept of the subsistence wage. (466)

Managed flexible-rate system: Primarily a flexible exchange rate system, but with occasional government purchases or sales of foreign exchange intended to influence the exchange rate. (513)

Margin: The difference between costs or benefits in an existing situation and after a proposed change. (12)

Marginal analysis: Looking at changes in the costs and benefits of a change from the status quo to a proposed new situation. These marginal changes in costs and benefits are the basis for rational economic choice. (12)

Marginal opportunity cost: The extra cost associated with the production of an additional unit of a product; this cost consists of the unproduced amounts of some alternative product. (94)

Marginal opportunity production cost: The number of units of one good that do not get produced when one additional unit of another good is produced. (45)

Marginal propensity to consume (*MPC*): The percent of an additional dollar of income that is spent on consumption; change in consumption divided by change in income. (212)

Marginal propensity to save (*MPS*): The percent of an additional dollar of income that is saved; change in saving divided by change in income. (213)

Marginal tax rate: The tax rate, in percentage terms, that applies to additional taxable income; additional taxes divided by the additional income taxed. (291)

Market: The interaction of buyers and sellers producing and buying goods and services. Prices tend toward equality through the continuous exchange between suppliers and demanders. (13, 99)

Market demand: The total amount consumers are willing and able to purchase of a product at all possible prices, obtained by summing the quantities demanded at each price over all buyers. (92)

Market, or nominal, interest rate: The interest rate computed from the money values of a borrowing or lending arrangement, such as a savings account; the interest rate unadjusted for expected inflation. (388)

Market society: An economic system in which individuals acting in their own self-interest determine what, how, and for whom goods and services are produced, with little government intervention. (61)

Market supply: The total amount producers are willing and able to offer for sale of a product at all possible prices; obtained by summing the quantities supplied at each price over all producers. (98)

Materials balancing: A method of central planning entailing the monitoring of the quantity and availability of resources so as to allocate these resources among state enterprises to produce final output; a substitute for the price system method of allocating resources. (548)

Measure of economic welfare (*MEW*): A concept of social and economic well-being that accounts for the production of all goods and services, not just those transacted for in markets. (169)

Medium of exchange: An item that is generally acceptable as payment for goods and services. (315)

Microeconomics: Analysis of the behavior of individual decision-making units, including individuals, households, and business firms. (19)

Mixed capitalism: An economic system in which most economic decisions are made by the private sector but in which government also plays a substantial economic and regulatory role. (60, 543)

Model: A simplified abstraction of the real world that approximates reality and makes problems easier to analyze; also called a theory. (17)

Monetarism: A theory that centers on money supply growth, real money demand, nominal and real interest rates, and inflationary expectations in explaining the process of inflation or deflation. (387)

Monetary base: The sum of depository institutions' reserves plus currency held by the public. (359)

Monetary policy: The use of money supply changes to effect changes in aggregate economic variables. (162)

Monetary rule: A monetary policy consisting of a fixed rate of growth of the money supply. (421)

Money: A generally accepted medium of exchange. (14, 320)

Money expansion: The increase in the money supply created by some given amount of excess reserves. (345)

Money price: The dollar price that sellers receive from buyers; a price expressed in terms of money, not in terms of an amount of another good. (112)

Moral suasion: The use of advice and suggestion, rather than concrete policy actions, by the Federal Reserve to induce depository institutions to follow a certain course of action. (368)

National income (NI): Total earnings of resource suppliers during a given period of time. (176)

National income accounting: The process of statistically measuring the nation's aggregate economic performance. (166)

Natural rate of unemployment: A theoretical concept; the unemployment rate that coexists with macroeconomic stability or labor-market equilibrium in the long run; the rate of unemployment due to frictional unemployment plus structural unemployment that will exist when expectations of inflation reflect actual inflationary conditions and all short-run macroeconomic adjustments have been made. (150, 281)

Negative externality: A cost of producing or consuming a good that is not paid entirely by the sellers or buyers but is imposed on a larger segment of society, such as pollution. (69)

Negative, or inverse, relation: The variables change in opposite directions. A negative relation is graphed as a downward-sloping curve. (26)

Neo-Austrian political business cycle: A business cycle that results from political action to influence specific markets and industries rather than broad macroeconomic variables; microeconomic manipulation distorts industry-specific investment decisions and leads to a business cycle. (453)

Net exports (*X − M*): Total spending by foreigners on domestically produced goods and services minus total spending by domestic residents on foreign-produced goods and services. (175)

Net national product (NNP): GNP minus capital consumption allowances (depreciation); the value of total output less the value of the capital used up in producing output. (178)

Neutrality of money: A proposition stating that in the long-run the relative prices of goods and services are not affected by changes in the money supply. (381)

Nominal GNP: The economy's total production of final goods and services measured in dollars unadjusted for changes in the price level. (157)

Nominal income: Income measured in terms of money, not in terms of what the money can buy. (154)

Nonhuman resources: All resources other than human resources, such as machines and land. (6)

Nonlinear relation: One variable changes by a constant rate, and the other variable changes by a rate that is not constant. (27)

Nontariff trade barriers: Alternative (to tariffs and quotas) means of restricting trade; examples include domestic content legislation and health and safety regulation. (498)

Normal good: A good that a consumer chooses to purchase in smaller (larger) amounts as income falls (rises). (90)

Open market operations: The purchase or sale of securities by the Federal Reserve System in order to affect the monetary base and the money supply; the major tool of monetary policy. (360)

Opportunity cost: The highest-valued alternative forgone in making any choice. (9, 33)

Overvalued: A term describing the foreign exchange market value of a country's money; occurs when the number of units of a country's money that purchases one unit of a foreign currency is *less* than the equilibrium exchange rate. (521)

Perestroika: Economic reformation of the Soviet Union's command economy. (547)

Perfect market: A market in which there are enough buyers and sellers that no single buyer or seller can influence price. (99)

Personal consumption expenditures (C): Total spending by households on final goods and services. (174)

Personal income (PI): Total earnings resource suppliers actually receive during a given period of time plus transfer payments. (178)

Personal saving: Disposable personal income less personal consumption expenditures. (179)

Phillips curve: A graph showing the relation between the rate of inflation and the unemployment rate. (442)

Policy trade-off: A situation in which a policy that promotes the attainment of one macroeconomic goal necessarily implies that the attainment of another macroeconomic objective becomes more difficult. (162)

Political business cycle: A business cycle that results from the manipulation of policy tools by incumbent politicians hoping to stimulate the economy prior to an election and thereby improve their reelection chances. (451)

Positive externality: A benefit of producing or consuming a good that does not accrue to the sellers or buyers but can be realized by a larger segment of society, such as vaccinations. (69)

Positive, or direct, relation: Both variables change in the same direction. A positive relation is graphed as an upward-sloping curve. (26)

Post hoc fallacy: The incorrect linking of unrelated events as a cause-and-effect relationship simply because one event happens after the other. (18)

Precautionary demand: Money demand that arises from the desire of businesses and consumers to hold money in order to facilitate unexpected purchases. (377)

Price control: The setting, by government, of a price in a market different from the equilibrium price. (107)

Price elasticity of demand: A measure of buyers' relative responsiveness to a price change; the percentage change in quantity demanded divided by the percentage change in price. (119)

Price floor: A form of regulation in which a minimum legal price is established by government below which exchange between buyers and sellers is illegal. (108)

Price index: A statistic used to calculate the price level and the rate of inflation. (180)

Price level: The average of the prices of all goods and services in the economy; used for calculating the inflation rate and for converting nominal into real values. (180)

Prices: The market-established opportunity costs of goods and services obtained through exchange. (13)

Price-specie flow mechanism: The channels by which gold inflows or outflows would cause price level increases or decreases in a country on the gold standard, thereby eliminating trade surpluses and deficits. (525)

Price stability: A situation of no inflation or deflation in the economy; no change in the overall level of prices of goods, services, and resources. (150)

Price-wage flexibility: An economic principle whereby prices and wages can fluctuate with changing economic conditions; thus the economy will be self-adjusting toward full employment even in response to shocks in supply and demand. (198)

Private sector: All parts of the economy and activities that are not part of the government. (72)

Private-sector equilibrium: A situation of equality between total private expenditures and output. In this equilibrium, there is no unplanned investment and no tendency for the level of output to change. (223)

Producer price index (PPI): A price index that calculates the general level of prices and the rate of inflation of goods businesses purchase. (182)

Product market: The forces created by buyers and sellers that establish the prices and quantities exchanged of goods and services. (84)

Production possibilities frontier: The curve that graphs all the possible combinations of two goods that an economic entity can produce given the available technology, the amount of productive resources available, and the fact that these resources are fully utilized. (37)

Productivity of labor: Output per worker over any given period of time. (460)

Progressive income tax: A tax that is a percentage of income and that varies directly with the level of income. (298)

Property rights: Any legal and/or enforceable rights to the use of resources of any kind. (8)

Proportional income tax: A tax that is a percentage of income and that varies directly with the level of income. (298)

Public assistance programs: Efforts by government to provide a more equitable distribution of income. (70)

Public finance: The study of how governments at the federal, state, and local levels tax and spend. (292)

Public goods: Goods that no one individual can be excluded from consuming once they have been provided to another, such as national defense. (69)

Purchasing power parity method: The comparison of real GNP across countries by converting GNPs to a common currency through use of the comparative cost of purchasing a typical assortment of goods and services in each country. (561)

Purchasing power parity (PPP) theory: A theory that predicts that the equilibrium exchange rate will adjust so as to equate the purchasing power of a unit of each country's money. (516)

Pure capitalism: An economic system in which most resources are owned, and most relevant decisions are made, by private individuals. (60, 543)

Pure communism: An economic system in which most productive resources, both human and nonhuman, are publicly owned. (60, 543)

Pure inflation tax: The reduction in purchasing power of an individual's nominal money holdings due to inflation. (395)

Pure socialism: An economic system in which most nonhuman productive resources are owned by the state. (60)

Quantity demanded: The amount of any good or service consumers are willing and able to purchase at all various prices. (86)

Quantity supplied: The amount of any good or service that producers are willing and able to produce and sell at some specific price. (95)

Quantity theory of money: A theory stating that in the long run with output and velocity fixed, changes in the money supply cause proportional changes in the price level. (199, 377)

Quota: A restriction or limit on the quantity of an imported good. (491)

Rate of inflation: The percentage change in the average level of prices over a period of time; the speed at which prices in general are rising. (152)

Rate of monetary expansion: The annual percent by which the nominal money supply is changing. (390)

Rational expectations theory: A theory of behavior that assumes people make efficient use of all past and present relevant information in forming expectations; implies that people's reactions to policy may neutralize the intended effects of the policy. (423)

Rational self-interest: The view of human behavior espoused by economists. Given circumstances and preferences, people weigh the costs and benefits of choices in order to do the best they can for themselves. (10)

Rationing: The allocation of goods among consumers with the use of prices. The equilibrium price rations the limited amount of a good produced by the most willing and able suppliers, or sellers, to the most willing and able demanders, or buyers. (101)

Real balance effect: The effect on investment and consumption spending of a change in the price level that alters the real value of pecuniary assets. (258)

Real GNP: The total production of final goods and services measured in dollars that have been adjusted for changes in the price level. (157)

Real income: The purchasing power of money income; the quantity of goods and services that money income can buy. (154)

Real interest rate: The nominal interest rate minus the expected rate of inflation. (388)

Real money demand: Demand on the part of individuals and businesses to hold purchasing power in the form of cash and checkable deposits. (376)

Real per capita GNP: Real GNP divided by the population size; real output per person in the economy. (459)

Real rate of interest: The nominal interest rate minus the inflation rate; the interest rate that measures the true incentives and costs that savers and investors face. (196)

Recession: A contraction in overall economic activity, usually defined as a decrease in real GNP over a period of at least six months. (435)

Recognition lag: The amount of time it takes policymakers to realize that a destabilizing economic event has occurred. (420)

Regressive income tax: A tax that is a percentage of income and that varies inversely with the level of income. (298)

Relative price: The price ratio or "trade-off" in consumption between one product (or service) and another product (or service) or between one good and other goods taken as a whole. (86)

Required reserves: Reserves against checkable deposits that banks and other depository institutions are required by the Federal Reserve to keep in the form of cash reserves; equal to the required reserve ratio times checkable deposits; equal to the required reserve ratio times checkable deposits; also called legal reserves. (337)

Reserve bank credit: The total value of loans and securities owned or held by the Federal Reserve System. Changes in Reserve bank credit affect member institutions' reserves. (356)

Reserve ratio: The percentage of checkable deposits that banks and other depository institutions hold as reserves. (337)

Resource market: The forces created by buyers and sellers that establish the prices and quantities exchanged of resources such as land, labor services, and capital. (84)

Resources: Those things used to produce goods and services. These include land, machines, energy, and human labor and ingenuity. Resources are also called factors of production. (3)

Revaluation: An official change in a country's exchange rate in a fixed-rate system; the number of units of a country's money that purchases one unit of another country's currency is *decreased* by the government. (523)

Saving function: The positive relationship between levels of current saving and levels of income, holding constant all other relevant factors that determine saving. (216)

Say's law: A proposition of the classical economists that the production of goods and services will generate incomes sufficiently large that those goods and services will be purchased. (194)

Scarcity: The condition whereby the resources, goods, and services available to individuals and society are limited relative to the wants and desires for them. (4)

Service industries: Those industries whose major, or sole, output is a consumer service, such as banking, entertainment, and health care. (475)

Services: All forms of intangible but useful activities that are valued by people. (2)

Shortage: The amount by which quantity demanded exceeds quantity supplied at a price below the equilibrium price. (100)

Short-run Phillips curve: A downward-sloping curve indicating an inverse relation between the rate of inflation and the unemployment rate, holding constant the inflation expectations of workers. (444)

Simple money multiplier: The reciprocal of the reserve ratio. (344)

Slope: The ratio of the change in (Δ) the y value to the change in (Δ) the x value; Δy divided by Δx. (30)

Socialism: An economic system in which most nonhuman productive resources are owned by the state. (543)

Specialization: An economic entity's (an individual's or a nation's) producing only one good or service, or the performance of a single task in a production process by an individual. (41, 483)

Speculation: The buying and selling of currencies on the foreign exchange market with the intent of profiting from possible devaluation or revaluation in a fixed-rate system or from possible future movements in the exchange rate in a flexible-rate system. (533)

Speculative motive or demand: Money demand arising from uncertainty of future interest rates and the fact that people can substitute between holding money and holding bonds. (377)

Standard of deferred payment: A standard measure for expressing contractual values over time, such as the future payments associated with loans and debts; a function of money. (319)

Standard of living: The real value of the quantity of goods and services consumed by the average member of the economy. (458)

Stock margin requirement: The percentage of the price of a stock purchase that must be paid in cash rather than borrowed. (367)

Store of value: The ability to own wealth in the form of some item, such as money: a function of money. (319)

Subsistence wage: A real wage rate that is only high enough to allow for a zero rate of population growth. (466)

Substitutes: Products that are related such that an increase in the price of one will increase the demand for the other or a decrease in the price of one will decrease the demand for the other; two goods whose cross elasticity of demand is positive: $\epsilon_c > 0$. (91, 133)

Supply curve: A graphic representation of the quantities of a product or service that producers are willing and able to sell at all possible prices. (95)

Supply shock inflation: Price level increases stemming from a decrease in aggregate supply; decreased aggregate supply usually occurs because of sudden increased scarcity of essential resources. (399)

Supply-side economics: Policy designed to stimulate production by altering incentives of producers; policy that has the purpose of shifting the aggregate supply curve to the right. (283)

Supply-side policy: Fiscal or monetary policy intended to directly alter the incentives to produce output; policies designed to shift aggregate supply. (163)

Surplus: The amount by which quantity supplied exceeds quantity demanded at a price above the equilibrium price. (99)

Tariff: A tax or levy on imported goods. (491)

Tax indexation: Periodic adjustment of the tax brackets of a progressive income tax so as to base taxes on real, not nominal, income; eliminates bracket creep and increased income taxes due solely to inflation. (155, 397)

Technology: Knowledge of production methods associated with producing a particular good. (7)

Terms of trade: The number of units of one good that exchange in the market for one unit of some other good. Although not expressed in terms of money, it is a price nonetheless. (49, 489)

Terms of trade argument: Defending the use of artificial trade barriers combined with monopoly or monopsony power in international markets in order to produce an improvement in a country's terms of trade. (502)

Total expenditure: The total amount spent by consumers on a good or service; calculated as equilibrium price times equilibrium quantity. (126)

Total revenue: Total receipts of businesses; always equal to total expenditures by consumers. (126)

Transaction costs: The opportunity costs of the resources directly associated with trade; includes time costs, brokers' fees, and so on. (52)

Transactions accounts: Demand deposits or other checkable accounts that allow the transfer of funds by writing a check. (320)

Transactions demand: Money demand that arises from the desire of businesses and consumers to facilitate exchange with the use of money. (376)

Transportation costs: The value of resources used in the transportation of goods that finalize any trade. (53)

Undervalued: A term describing the foreign exchange market value of a country's money; occurs when the number of units of a country's money that purchases one unit of a foreign currency is *greater* than the equilibrium exchange rate. (520)

Unemployed: A labor-force status characterized by an individual who is actively seeking employment but is not working. (148)

Unemployment rate: The percentage of the labor force without jobs. (148)

Unemployment of resources: A situation in which some human and/or nonhuman resources that can be used in production are not used. (38)

Unit elasticity of demand: A condition where the percentage change in quantity demanded is equal to the percentage change in price: $\epsilon_d = 1$. (120)

Unit of account: A standard measure, such as the dollar, that is used to express the values of goods and services; a function of money. (319)

Value added: The increase in value or market worth of a good associated with each stage of production. (170)

Velocity: The average number of times a unit of money changes hands per year in financing the purchase of GNP. (200)

Vicious circle of poverty: An attempt to explain why some countries remain less developed that centers on low savings and investment causing low real incomes, which in turn lead to low saving and investment rates. (560)

Wage-price spiral: The process whereby increased prices of final goods cause increased wage rates and other resource prices, which in turn result in still-higher prices of final goods; for the spiral to continue, the money supply must continually increase or real output must continually fall. (398)

Wealth: The total value of monetary plus nonmonetary assets in existence at a point in time; a stock variable. (257)

Welfare loss to society: The *net* loss to an economy resulting from the imposition of an artificial trade barrier; government revenues plus producer gains minus consumer losses. (497)

x-axis, y-axis: Perpendicular lines in a coordinate grid system for measuring variables on a two-dimensional graph. The x-axis is the horizontal line; the y-axis is the vertical line. The intersection of the x-axis and the y-axis is the origin. (26)

ACKNOWLEDGMENTS

Photo

Unless otherwise acknowledged, all photos are the property of HarperCollins. Page abbreviations are as follows: (T) top, (C) center, (B) bottom, (L) left, (R) right.

p. 5: Robert E. Murowchick/Photo Researchers; p. 11: Copyrighted, Chicago Tribune Company, all rights reserved; p. 20: © Sam C. Rawls 1984; p. 112: Photo supplied by authors; p. 142L: The Granger Collection, New York; p. 142R: The Granger Collection, New York; p. 153: S. Kogure/Gamma-Liaison; p. 185: UPI/Bettmann Newsphotos; p. 271: SHOEMAKER'S SHOP, Greek 520–510 B.C., B/F amphora. H: .361 m, H. L. Pierce Fund 01.8035, Courtesy, Museum of Fine Arts, Boston; p. 310L: The Bettmann Archive; p. 310R: The Bettmann Archive; p. 317: The University Museum, University of Pennsylvania, Neg. S4-139881; p. 333: Neg. No. A53972, Courtesy The American Red Cross; p. 374: Reprinted with special permission of King Features Syndicate, Inc.; p. 400: NYT Pictures; p. 407L: Courtesy of Milton Friedman; p. 407R: T. Charles Erickson, Yale University Office of Public Information; p. 430: Reprinted by permission, Los Angeles Times Syndicate; p. 479L: Courtesy of Paul Samuelson; p. 479R: Courtesy of Robert Lucas; p. 557: UPI/Bettmann Newsphotos; p. 570L: John Cole/Impact Photos; p. 570R: The Bettmann Archive.

Text

p. 76: Figure 6 data from *Facts and Figures on Government Finance* (Washington, D.C.: Tax Foundation, Inc., 1983); p. 152: Figure 3 from Robert J. Gordon, *Macroeconomics,* 5th ed., p. 14. Copyright © 1990 by Robert J. Gordon. Reprinted by permission of Scott, Foresman and Company—a division of HarperCollins Publishers; p. 427: Robert Lucas's quote from "The New Economists," *Newsweek,* June 26, 1978, p. 60. Copyright © 1978 by Newsweek, Inc. All rights reserved. Reprinted by permission; p. 457: Figure 8 from David I. Meiselman, "The Political Monetary Cycle," *The Wall Street Journal,* January 10, 1984, p. 32. Reprinted by permission of *The Wall Street Journal,* © Dow Jones & Company, Inc. 1984. All rights reserved; p. 474: Figure 7 data from Edward F. Denison, *Trends in American Economic Growth* (Washington D.C.: Brookings Institution, 1985), p. 30. Reprinted by permission; p. 554: Table 3 from Lowell Gallaway, "The Folklore of Unemployment and Poverty," in Svetozar Pejovich, ed., *Governmental Controls and the Free Market: The U.S. Economy in the 1970s* (College Station: Texas A&M University Press, 1976), pp. 41–72. Reprinted by permission of the author; p. 562: Table 5 from World Bank, *World Development Report 1981,* p. 17.

INDEX

Boldface numbers indicate pages on which definitions of key terms appear.

Inflation, *continued*
  money supply and, 401
  process of, 390–92
  rate of, 152–54
  supply shock, **399**
  as tax, 395
  taxes and, 403
  theories of, 397–402
  unemployment and, 441–47
  wage-price spiral and, 397–98
Inflationary gap. *See* Expansionary gap
Information, 7–**8**
Institutions, **8**, 82
Interest, net, 177
Interest rate(s), 519–20
  consumption and, 219
  cost of capital and, 221–22
  credit and, 219
  flexibility of, 195–98
  foreign exchange and, 519–20
  inflation and, 304–305
  and investment, 196–97
  nominal, 388
  real, 196, 388
  stable, 408
Interest rate effect, 259–**61**
Intermediate goods, **169**
Intermediate range, **267**
Internally held debt, **304**
International Monetary Fund (IMF), 530,
  532–33, 535–37
International monetary system, 510–37
  balance of payments, **526**–32
  capital movements, 529
  evolution of, 532–34
  fixed exchange rates, **512**, 520–25
  flexible exchange rates, **512**–20, 539–41
  foreign exchange market, **511**
  gold standard, **525**–27, 532
  managed flexible-rate system, **513**
International trade. *See* Trade
Inverse relationship, 26
Investment
  autonomous, 221
  classical concept of, 197
  gross private domestic, 174
  in Keynesian theory, 221
  long-run factors affecting, 221–22
  return on, 351–53
  and savings, 225–27
Investment function, **221**
Investment multiplier, 235–37
Investment spending, **220**
Investment tax credit, **299**
Investment theories, 238–40, 447–49
Iraq, invasion of Kuwait, 400
Ireland, monetary system of, 355

Japan, 153, 567
Johnson, Lyndon B., 73

Kahn, Richard, 208
Kennedy, John F., 505
Keynes, John Maynard, 72, 163, 202, 208,
  310–11
Keynesian macroeconomic theory, 72, 208–32
  vs. classical theory, 202, 208–10, 427–31
  consumption and saving model in, 213–17
  historical context of, 252
  macroeconomic adjustment and, 446–47
  money and, 209–210, 416–17
  policy and, 72, 274–76, 383–87, 412–17
Keynesian range, **267**
Klein, Lawrence, 441
Kurihara, K. K., 230n

Kuwait, invasion by Iraq, 400
Kuznets, Simon, 166, 167

Labor
  costs of. *See* Wage(s)
  division of, 43, 190
  elasticity of supply for, 135–36
  foreign, 501
  productivity of, 192, 460
  supply of, 42
  See also Employment; Unemployment; Wage(s)
Labor market, aggregate supply and, 281
Labor supply, elasticity of, 135–36
Laissez-faire, 67, 68, 203
Laissez-faire economy, **67**
Lange, Oskar, 569
Law, property rights and, 65
Law of demand, **86**, 91
Law of diminishing marginal returns, 462–65
Law of increasing costs, **38**
Law of one price, **99**
Law of supply, **95**
Leading economic indicators, 438
Lenin, Vladimir Ilyich, 546
Lerner, Abba, 305, 569
Less-developed countries, **559**–65
Liability
  of banks, 328
  of Federal Reserve, 358
Life-cycle hypothesis, 229–30
Linear relation, **27**
Line-standing (service profession), 11
Liquidity, **320**, 353
Liquidity preference theory, 377
Loans, bank, 340–41, 363–65
Long, Robert, 11
Long-run equilibrium, 192
Long-run Phillips curve, **446**
Lovell, Michael C., 427n
Lucas, Robert E., 480
Lump-sum tax, 245–46

M-1, 416
  money multiplier, 369–70
Macroeconomic policy, 410–31
  aggregate demand and, 160–62
  aggregate supply and, 160–62
  alternatives, 411–12
  direct vs. indirect, 416
  discretionary, **162**–63
  foreign exchange rates and, 522–23
  future of, 308–309
  Keynesian theory and, 72, 274–76, 383–87,
    412–17
  monetarist theory and, 417–22
  rational expectations theory and, 423–31
Macroeconomics, **19**, 146
  goals of, 72, 147–57
  issues in, 162–63
Macroeconomic theories. *See* Classical
  macroeconomic theory; Keynesian
  macroeconomic theory
Macroeconomy. *See* Gross national product;
  National income accounting
Malthus, Thomas, 465
Malthusian population principle, **466**
Managed flexible-rate system, **513**
Margin, **12**
  choices at, 12, **35**, 38
Margin requirement, **367**
Marginal analysis, **12**, 23
Marginal cost (*MC*), 12
Marginal opportunity cost, 51, **94**
Marginal opportunity production cost, **45**
Marginal propensity to consume (*MPC*), **212**, 235

Marginal propensity to save (*MPS*), **213**, 235
Marginal returns, diminishing, 462–65
Marginal tax rate, **291**
Market(s), **13**, 99
  economic growth and, 461
  for labor. *See* Labor market
  perfect, **99**
  product, **84**
  resource, **84**
  in United States, 59–65
  See also Monopolistic competition; Monopoly
Market demand, **92**
Market interest rate, **388**
Market society, **61**
  circular flow of income in, 63–65
Market supply, **98**
Marshall, Alfred, 3
Marx, Karl, 142–43
Materials balancing, **548**
Maurice, S. Charles, 42n
Measure of economic welfare (MEW), **169**,
  187–88
Medium of exchange, 315–18
Meiselman, D. J., 456
Menger, Carl, 310
Microeconomics, **19**
Mixed capitalism, **60**, 68, **543**
Mixed economies, 60
Model, **17**, 35
Modigliani, Franco, 230
Monetarism, **387**–92, 417–31
Monetary base, 358–**59**, 369–70
Monetary policy, **162**, 524
  aggregate demand and, 276–78
  anticipated, 424
  effects of, 419–22
  foreign exchange rates and, 524
  Keynesian, 416–17
  monetarism and, 417–21
  rational expectations and, 423–31
  unanticipated, 425
Monetary rule, **421**–22
Monetary theories, 449–52
Money, **14**–15, 63, **320**
  banking system and, 321–31
  commodity, **315**–17
  creation of. *See* Money creation
  definition of, 320–21
  demand for, 376–79, 388
  emergence of, 332–33
  Federal Reserve and, 321
  fiat, **316**–18
  functions of, 314–20
  Keynesian theory on, 209–210
  as medium of exchange, 315
  neutrality of, 381
  precautionary demand for, 377
  prices and, 381–82
  quantity theory of, 379–83
  speculative demand for, 377, 383–87
  as standard of deferred payment, 319
  as store of value, 319–20
  transactions demand for, 376
  as unit of account, 318–19
  See also International monetary system
Money creation, 63
  by banks, 335–41
  in commercial banking system, 341–48
  loans and, 340–41
  philosophy of, 351
Money expansion, **345**–48
Money multiplier, **369**–70
  M-1, 369–70
  simple, 344
Money price, 111–**12**
Money stock classifications, 322–23
Money supply, 408
  economic activity and, 408
  foreign exchange and, 516